GUIDE TO THE MOST COMPETITIVE COLLEGES

Edited by the
College Guide Staff
of
Barron's Educational Series, Inc.

All inquiries should be addressed to:
Barron's Educational Series, Inc.
250 Wireless Boulevard
Hauppauge, NY 11788
http://www.barronseduc.com

Library of Congress Catalog Card No. 98-16763

International Standard Book No. 0-7641-0029-7

Library of Congress Cataloging-in-Publication Data

Barron's guide to the most competitive colleges / edited by the college guide staff of Barron's Educational Series, Inc.
p. cm.
Includes indexes.
ISBN 0-7641-0029-7
1. Universities and colleges—United States—Directories.
2. College choice—United States—Handbooks, manuals, etc.
I. Barron's Educational Series, Inc.
L901.B2656 1998
378.73—dc21 98—16763
CIP
AC

PRINTED IN THE UNITED STATES OF AMERICA

9 8 7 6 5 4 3 2 1

❑ CONTENTS ❑

❑ INTRODUCTION ❑

Of the 1650 four-year colleges included in Barron's *Profiles of American Colleges*, only 53 qualify for consideration as Most Competitive, based on the standards of Barron's Selector Ratings. (One of the Most Competitive institutions declined our invitation to be included in this book.) They have earned this distinction based on their acceptance of only the best and the brightest students.

We have now turned to recent graduates of each of these institutions, and asked them to write an essay on what it's *really* like on campus. We have requested them to comment specifically on those aspects of campus life that would be of most concern to a college-bound student trying to decide which institutions should be sent applications. Two contributors had not graduated at the time they wrote their essays, and some older graduates also contributed. All, though, have close ties to their alma maters, and their essays reflect current circumstances.

Geographic locations of the colleges range from California to Florida and from Maine to Texas. Some are large, others small. Most are private, but state universities are also represented. And all five of the service academies are here.

In addition to the college essays, we have also included some advice that will be helpful to the prospective college applicant—from first applications while still in high school to study habits after enrolling.

The Most Competitive chart beginning on page 725 shows at a glance how each of the fifty-two stack up against one another in areas such as acceptance numbers, test scores, and other comparisons.

Thumbnail sketches of each of the fifty-two colleges that are profiled here are included, as are short bios of the contributors. And finally, for quick geographic locating, the book concludes with an index by state.

It is our hope that these perceptive essays will be helpful in guiding the college-bound reader to intelligent choices in the major decision-making area of college applications.

The College Guide Staff
Barron's Educational Series, Inc.

THE MOST COMPETITIVE COLLEGES

AMHERST COLLEGE

Amherst College Photo

Amherst College
Amherst, MA 01002-5000

(413) 542-2000
Fax: (413) 542-2040

E-mail: admissions@amherst.edu
Web site: http://www.amherst.edu

Enrollment

Full-time ❑ women: 755
❑ men: 852

INTRODUCING AMHERST

The Freshman Quad at Amherst, flanked by plain-faced brick dorms and the clock tower of Johnson Chapel, is the hub of this small college located in the Pioneer Valley. Whether those on its shady lawn are reading, playing Frisbee, strumming guitars, throwing snowballs, walking to class, or trudging from the gym to the dining hall, Amherst students appear to be experiencing the quintessential New England liberal arts education. However, to get a fuller picture of life at "The Fairest College," all visitors have to do is turn to see the churchless Stearns Steeple, the yellow Campus Center, the tile-green string course of the computer center or the view of the Holyoke Range from Memorial Hill (complete with its frequently ignored NO SLEDDING sign) and they'll see that Amherst provides the excellent education it is known for —and then some. An Amherst education is founded on the ideals of a liberal arts curriculum and is layered in diversity of thought, expression, and character.

Amherst has a reputation as one of the country's best colleges academically. But academics alone are not what makes so many people apply or why students who are there like it so much or why alumni still come back every year for Homecoming. It's the balance of academics and the social aspects; it's the people you meet and the conversations you have.

Amherst provides its students with a solid education in all disciplines, but its strength and energy comes from its liberal arts philosophy—an Amherst student learns *how* to listen, think, analyze, and question. An Amherst student learns not only how to formulate ideas, but how to express and defend them. An Amherst education does not end in the classroom; students learn as much from the background and diversity of their classmates as they do from their top-notch professors.

Amherst, with an enrollment of approximately 1,600, is small. Everyone, eventually, knows everyone else. This familiarity truly makes Amherst not just an academic institution, but a community. Not only do students form close friendships with each other, but professors, coaches, administration, and staff take an active interest in students. It is not unusual to see someone from the Dean's Office rooting on the sideline of a field hockey game. It is not uncommon to hear a cafeteria employee inquire about a student's latest all-nighter. It is not strange for a student to drop into the Office of the Dean of Students to chat or to have dinner at a professor's house. Amherst students don't just attend class and head straight for the library; they live, work, and play at Amherst, and it quickly becomes their second home.

Amherst is not perfect. Occasionally, an Amherst student, like anyone else anywhere else, will have a bad day (or two). The college has both formal and informal support systems. The Dean of Students Office, the Counseling Center, peer and disciplinary advocates, and the resident counselors, coaches, professors, and friends form a network to help students in many different ways at many different levels.

Amherst students are aware of the college's imperfections, but the difference between Amherst and other academic institutions is that Amherst students do not just sit and grumble—Amherst students take action and Amherst administrators listen. The college paper sometimes seems entirely made of Op-Ed letters. Students often meet with Dean of Students Ben Lieber or other administrators including President Gerety, and represent student opinion on committees. In the past few years student concerns over the disciplinary system resulted in the formation of the disciplinary advocates, students' observations of first-year housing produced the reorganization of freshman dormitories, and student debate over the role of athletics at Amherst prompted the organization of forums and panels. As in many other instances, these changes and actions were rooted in student opinion and executed by their peers. Amherst is a community, and its students recognize their responsibility toward making it their own.

You first realize it when you go home for vacation that first time. You begin thinking about Amherst differently—it's not just your school, it's your space, it's where you are starting to build your own life. When you first catch a glimpse of the campus on your way back from break, you feel in some way as if you are returning home.

The Amherst experience is different for every individual and every class, but in each case it is a solid education, made rich by its emphasis on thought and expression and made deep by the people who compose the "College on the Hill."

ADMISSIONS REQUIREMENTS

Recently, Amherst received 5,210 applications for roughly 434 spots, making it one of the most competitive liberal arts colleges in America. While academic achievement is the most important factor for admission, it is not the only one. Nor is there any set formula—Amherst staffers do not sit around plugging your test scores, extracurriculars, or class rank into a computer to determine a winning applicant. Instead, they read through each application looking at the whole profile.

Of course there are some general requirements: the SAT I or ACT, three SAT II: Subject tests (preferably the writing test), a high school diploma, or GED. There are also some recommendations: four years of English, math through pre-calculus, three or four years of a foreign language, two years of history and social science, at least two years of natural science (including a laboratory science).

Amherst staffers read each application contextually. Realizing that students bring to the table different backgrounds and experiences, and that each student has been presented with various opportunities that others haven't, Amherst admissions officers look at *how* students made use of where they were and what they were offered. Amherst seeks multifaceted students who will not only give their intellects, energies, and talents to the school, but who will also gain the most from the Amherst education and experience. Many of those who work in the Admissions Office are Amherst grads themselves; they know what being an Amherst student is like, and thus, know what kind of applicant is best suited for the school.

Admissions staffers warn that when filling out your application, elaborate strategizing is a waste of time. Instead, they say, spend the time figuring out if Amherst is the best school for you. If the answer is yes, then use your application to express your many dimensions as a student and as a person.

ACADEMIC LIFE

Amherst has no core curriculum, giving students the freedom to construct their own course of study. Although there are requirements in each major, the only general required course is the First-Year Seminar, an interdisciplinary course taken by all freshmen in their first semester. The lack of a core follows in the true liberal arts philosophy of the school. Students can take classes in a wide range of disciplines: an art history major can take a physics class, a premedical student can major in English, a psychology major double in music. So while the bulk of a student's studies may be in one subject, he or she has the luxury of being able to dabble in another discipline, often stumbling across a passion for art, science, philosophy, or language that they wouldn't have otherwise discovered.

> *Even as a psychology and economics double major, I was able to take a variety of classes from The Social Organization of Law to Autobiographies of Women to The Catastrophe of Cancer and AIDS. It was the lack of core classes that allowed me to experience the true meaning of a liberal arts education.*

Amherst students work hard. Classes are demanding. There are long hours spent in the libraries and computer center. Amherst students are always writing—in every discipline. Yet, for the most part, students are engaged in their work. While not every class and every professor is well loved by every student, there are many that are. Class discussions are not restricted to the classroom, but are carried back to the dorms and dining hall.

Don't get me wrong, I learned a tremendous amount from my classes and my professors, but it was the conversations in the hallways or dorms or around a Valentine lunch table that taught me how to really listen and how to be confident in speaking my own mind.

While Amherst is an extremely competitive environment, it is not cutthroat. Though it varies from department to department, students often work in study groups and are usually willing to help each other. The first few weeks can be intimidating to the freshman who, used to being at the top of the class in high school, realizes that he or she is now with the 400 other top students, but after a while Amherst's collaborative atmosphere dispels these worries.

Professors

Professors, for the most part, are not out to get you. They have office hours and expect students to make use of them whether they are having trouble with the class or not. Classes are small enough so that professors get to know each student personally. The class size very often makes it impossible to hide; students are expected to participate in class discussion.

It's very hard to fail out of Amherst—professors want you to do well and are willing to help point you in the right direction. They expect you to work hard, but they also expect you to speak up when you don't understand something.

Surrounding Colleges

If, after a while, the classes at Amherst don't hold that same thrill, or if you're looking for a change of scene, make use of the surrounding four colleges: Smith's art department, museum, and library draw Amherst students to its Northampton campus. The other all women's school in the valley, Mount Holyoke, also offers various classes not offered at Amherst. Looking for an experience in alternative education? Try taking a class at Hampshire College down the road. Or maybe you'd like to see what a large university has to offer, if so, take a class at UMass. Still looking for something new and different? Almost half the junior class spends a semester or two abroad or takes advantage of the Twelve-College exchange program.

Amherst veterans advise making use of office hours and the Writing Center. And don't be afraid to use the add/drop period at the start of each semester—there's no sense wasting a class on a blah professor or boring subject when Amherst has so many other incredible ones.

The Amherst academic program is a rigorous but rewarding one. At its cornerstone is the exchange of ideas between students and professors of various backgrounds and disciplines.

SOCIAL LIFE AND ACTIVITIES

At Amherst, we work hard and we play hard.

Just as Amherst students dedicate themselves to their studies, they dedicate themselves to their playtime. The biweekly event of Amherst legend and lore, Tap, still takes place on Thursday and Saturday nights. A school-sponsored party, Tap features a DJ or band and keg for those who are over twenty-one in the Taproom. Theme taps have become increasingly popular in recent years: Madonna Tap, Jackson Tap, Prince Tap, to name a few. But for those of you who think that Amherst social life is limited to biweekly theme nights, think again. Parties not sponsored by the school, but by students, often kick off the evening. At Amherst, parties are usually open to everyone and they are usually free. While parties are usually the focus of many an evening, Amherst and its surroundings provide much entertainment.

The recently revamped Social Council has been working hard to plan all campus events. There's bound to be a concert (most likely *a cappella*) or play either on campus or in the surrounding valley. And if you're not watching something, chances are you're helping to run it. Between the publications, singing groups, volunteer organizations, clubs, and athletics, Amherst students are always involved with something.

Publications and Organizations

Stacked in the lobby of the dining hall, floating from round green table to round green table of the Campus Center, or stuck into a backpack, Amherst publications abound. Besides the weekly newspaper, *The Student*, *The Indicator*, *Prism*, and *Capitol Pages* keep the flow of debate and opinion alive. *The Amherst Review*, *Madness This?*, and *A Further Room* round out the literary magazines.

Amherst has been called the "Singing College," and with good reason. Not only does the school have five *a cappella* groups, but men's and women's choruses, as well as many instrumental ensembles. There are also tons of clubs to join including Hillel, the Newman Club, Christian Fellowship, the Hawaii Club, the Debating Club, WAMH Radio, and others, not to mention the many organizations that are active around campus: The Women's Center, Outreach, LBTGA, BSU, La Causa, ASA, ISA, Women in Science.

WHERE TO EAT IN AMHERST

Coffee Shops:
- The Black Sheep, Rao's, Blue Moon Café, Starbucks, Bonducci's

Non-Valentine Cheap Eats:
- Antonio's, Bueno y Sano, Subway, Nancy Jane's

Dining Out:
- Judie's, Bertucci's, Walker's Grill, Pasta E Basta, Panda East

Parents' Weekend:
- Season's, Carmelina's, Pinocchio's

Ordering In:
- Sugar Jones
- DP Dough
- Pinocchio's

Northampton Restaurants:
- Spotelo's
- Eastside Grill
- Mullino's
- Harrell's Ice Cream

Worth the Trip:
- Atkins Farms
- The Whatley Diner
- The Book Mill
- The Yankee Candle Factory

Athletics

Amherst is an athletic college. While not every-body is a member of a varsity team, most Lord and Lady Jeffs take part in some athletic pasttime, whether it be a workout in the gym or a walk through the beautiful bird sanctuary. Amherst may be small, but its teams are mighty, regularly making it to the ECAC, NESCAC, and NCAA tournaments. Not only does Amherst offer a strong varsity program, but it also offers club and intramural teams as well. The women's and men's rugby clubs are among the best in the Northeast. Other club teams are the ski team, men's volleyball, water polo, tai kwan do, and Ultimate Frisbee.

Students also participate in school activities on other levels. Many students serve in the student government, others sit on committees, while others act as liaisons between the administration and students. The peer advocates, disciplinary advocates, and resident counselors play an active role in student life. Indeed, central to the character of Amherst social life is the residential aspect of the school. Students get to know each other well through common classes, interests, and living situations. And often how you know someone will overlap. Your next-door neighbor can be in your chem lab, your teammate can also be a member of your magazine staff, your RC may be in your English class. Amherst students get to know each other on many levels in many environments.

> *Sometimes the stupidest things will bring a floor or building together, like trying to fit an oversized couch through a door or having an impromptu study break or water fight. Then, when we really need to help each other out with the serious stuff, the bonds are already there.*

WHERE TO DRINK IN AMHERST

- Charlie's Tavern
- Rafters
- The Pub
- The Alehouse
- Amherst Brew-Pub
- Walker's Grill

There is always something to do at Amherst, whether it be a keg party or a theme party, a night at a concert or a play, or an evening spent at the movies or in a coffee shop. Amherst students spend time working and playing together, social interactions that help to build friendships that last well past graduation.

FINANCIAL AID

Amherst makes its need-blind admission policy a priority. Indeed, a current campaign aims to raise $35 million toward continuing need-blind admission. Those in the Development Office estimate that Amherst ranks among a dozen or so institutions that admit students without regard to financial need, and, more important, maintain the aid for all four years. Currently, thirty-five percent of students in the freshman class receive financial aid; the average amount offered is $15,511. There are plenty of jobs available on campus even if you aren't in a work–study program. Although many jobs are posted, many are obtained from word of mouth. Students work in Valentine and the library, as well as in the campus center and administrative offices, physical plant, and custodial shop. Not only do students earn spending money, but they are given the chance to get to know the staff of the college as well as the ins and outs of the running of the school.

GRADUATES

I never really understood how strong the ties to Amherst were until I went to my first Homecoming as a graduate. I was surprised and thrilled at how genuinely happy I was to see everyone again. There's always a big turnout for Homecoming, and now I know why—as corny as it sounds, it really is like coming home.

Amherst graduates are an interesting bunch. They can be found in many professions in many parts of the globe. You read their names in newspapers, you randomly run into them in restaurants, you meet them at Homecoming. Amherst grads all seem to have taken their education and run with it, though not in the same direction.

Amherst does have a strong on-campus recruiting program for banking, consulting, and other careers, as well as a strong network in the nonprofit, education, and publishing fields. Amherst grads find what they are looking for—many are gainfully employed, many are in graduate school, many are pursuing fellowships and grants. Whatever they are doing, Amherst grads are not sitting still; they are active and energetic, armed with their Amherst education and their enthusiasm for learning at all levels.

PROMINENT GRADS

- **Henry Ward Beecher, 1834, Preacher, writer, and thinker**
- **Melville Dewey, 1884, Inventor of the Dewey Decimal System**
- **Calvin Coolidge, 1885, President of the United States**
- **Clarence Birdseye, '10, Inventor of Frozen Foods**
- **Burgess Meredith, '31, Actor/Director**
- **Lloyd Conover, '45, Inventor of Tetracycline**
- **Stansfield Turner, '45, Director of CIA**
- **William Webster, '45, Director of FBI**
- **Thomas Eagleton, '50, U.S. Senator**
- **Scott Turow, '70, Author**
- **Albert A. Grimaldi, '81, Prince of Monaco**
- **Archibald MacLeish, Poet**

The Amherst alumni are deeply connected to the school, contributing to its strong professional network as well as in the school's large endowment. About two-thirds of Amherst grads give to the school, the highest percent nationally. And when asked in a recent survey if they'd do it all over again, approximately ninety-two percent said they'd choose Amherst again.

The Amherst experience is one that is taken with you past graduation and built upon; the school, for many, is the bedrock of graduates' professional skills and personal outlooks.

I did not realize how extensive the Amherst network really was until my senior year. Whether it be chatting on the sidelines of a football game or in the corner office of a New York City firm, I was amazed at the amount of time Amherst alums spent answering questions and offering advice to students on future career choices.

SUMMING UP

Amherst, with an enrollment of about 1,600, is a small school. Students, faculty, and staff get to know each other well in many different arenas and in many different capacities, making the school, not just an academic institution, but a community. You'd have to look far and wide to find a school that would match Amherst's academic record, commitment to a liberal arts philosophy, and diversity of students and faculty. It'd be difficult to find a group of more enthusiastic and intellectually curious students, more caring and supportive faculty and administration, and more loyal and generous alumni.

Amherst admission officers do not look for perfect students; instead, they look for those who will gain the most from an Amherst education while at the same time, contributing to the experiences of others. Amherst students learn from this diversity of thought and background just as they learn from their challenging classes. They learn from the shared experience of freshman-year anxieties, from the conversation at the lunch table or during a professor's office hours, from a tough loss on the playing field or from an exhilarating victory. They learn from the common experience of getting a paper back loaded with criticism, or spending the wee hours of the morning in the computer center, or even spending all night at a party. They learn from discussions with graduates, lectures from experts and authorities, talks with the building and grounds crew.

And while all this learning is going on, Amherst students are having fun, taking each opportunity that comes along. Amherst students know when and how to work hard, but they also know when and how to take the time to play.

When Amherst students graduate, they do not graduate as perfect people. They may be better versed in many different disciplines; they may have discovered a passion for art, or a love of economics; they may have questioned and challenged and reenforced their beliefs; they may have found their voices. What they have learned at Amherst will be used everyday—how to communicate, to think, to question. They will be able to contribute their Amherst-honed talents while knowing how to experience all the world has to offer.

❑ *Molly Lyons, B.A.*

BATES COLLEGE

Photo by Phyllis Graber Jensen

Bates College
Lewiston, ME 04240

(207) 786-6000
Fax: (207) 786-6025

E-mail: admissions@bates.edu
Web site: http://www.bates.edu

Enrollment

Full-time ❑ women: 851
❑ men: 760

INTRODUCING BATES

Choosing the right college or university is often thought of as a difficult task. One obvious reason for this perception is that many college applicants are preoccupied with the academic, social, and athletic rigors of their senior year in high school. Deeper examination may reveal that the student is struggling with the important task of discovering exactly who they are. The successful choosing of the right college, in fact, involves a recognition and understanding of the true identity of an individual. It is also a reflection of what he or she wishes to become.

My college selection process was probably very similar to many other prospective students of the small liberal arts colleges in New England. I had interviews at many top schools and had a chance to walk around several campuses with students. My visit to Bates was definitely different than the others. From the beginning, the people at Bates made me feel very welcome and important. After my interview and tour I wandered into the science building to see the biology facilities (I was pretty sure I wanted to be a bio major). Walking down a hall with my family, we happened by an open door where a student was doing research. This student welcomed us into his lab and proceeded to tell us what he was doing and asked if we had any questions about Bates. I remember vividly this student's willingness to help me find the biology labs, but more importantly, what I took away from this conversation was the student's genuine interest and warmth. I also met with the lacrosse coach, and even though I was not a recruit and had just met him, he talked with me and my parents for over an hour, took us to lunch in the dining hall, and even walked us to our car. Of all the top schools I had visited, Bates was the one that felt right. With so many fine academic colleges to choose from, I went with a gut feeling that Bates was the best for me. I applied early and never looked back.

Bates College is a small liberal arts college located in Lewiston, Maine. The school is known for its excellent academics, internationally distinguished debate team, competitive athletics, and its history. The college was founded in 1855, as the college course catalog states, "by people who felt strongly about human freedom and civil rights. Bates is among the oldest coeducational colleges in the nation, and from its beginning the college admitted students without regard to race, religion, national origin or sex."

From its creation, the college has never had fraternities and sororities. College activities are open to all its students. These long-held values of Bates pervade every aspect of the college, and are what makes it unique. Walk on the campus and talk to the students, the faculty, and the staff . . . talk to the people who make up what Bates is today. In these conversations, the values and ideals upon which the school was founded become obvious. There is a warmth in the interaction, a "friendliness" that over the years remains a characteristic of the typical Batesie.

I asked a friend about his college selection process, and his response often echoes what other students say of Bates:

I loved Bates from the first time I set foot on the campus. There is something about the college, the feel of the quad, the people who inhabit this place, that makes Bates so inviting—that makes Bates "friendly." In the summer before my senior year of high school, I visited about fifteen schools in several different regions of the country. In pursuit of a good education, and following my heart, I decided to apply early decision. I liked the obvious reasons for wanting to attend Bates, which were advertised in the viewbook, but I also liked the excellent facilities, the small size that allows one to get to know a lot of different people well, and also gives everyone the opportunity to make a difference. I also liked the cohesiveness of Bates, which can be seen in the absence of fraternities and sororities—thus helping to remove social barriers— and in the committed and accessible faculty.

Bates has much to offer its students. In addition to its human resources of faculty and staff, Bates continues to be committed to providing the latest equipment and finest facilities for its students. A new academic building is under construction and will be finished in 1999. This five-story building will be the new home of the social science departments with classrooms, offices, and an atrium overlooking Lake Andrews or, as the students call it, "the puddle."

The Bates-Morse Mountain Conservation Area is 574 acres of salt marsh and rocky forested terrain adjacent to one of the last undisturbed barrier beaches where Bates students and faculty can study geology, botany, and zoology. In addition, the college owns eighty acres of freshwater habitat just north of the conservation area.

From electron microscopes to the Olin Arts Center, from the Davis Fitness Center to having the entire campus hooked up to a computer network and being Internet ready, Bates provides an environment in which students enjoy the benefits of attending a large university, while getting the personal educational experience of a small college.

ADMISSIONS REQUIREMENTS

Bates continues to be highly selective in its admissions process. Currently listed as one of the nation's Most Competitive colleges by *Barron's Profiles of American Colleges*, and similarly ranked by other major college review publications, the school's reputation for academic excellence draws highly motivated and talented students from all over the country and around the world. One big difference between Bates and most top schools is that, in its admissions process, standardized test scores are not required. Although most students do submit these scores and do very well, Bates recognizes that these tests are not always a true indicator of aptitude and future achievement. Admissions readers are more interested in the entire high school record. In addition to grades, evidence of a student taking challenging courses, the essays that are required with the application, extracurricular activities and interests, and recommendations by teachers and other school officials, are all carefully inspected by admissions personnel.

Bates, throughout its history, has recognized that diversity in its student body is a crucial requirement for an educational environment. Bates was coeducational before being coed was popular. Bates also makes great efforts to attract students from diverse cultures and backgrounds.

Interviews

An on-campus visit and interview are strongly encouraged. If this is not possible, in most cases an alumni interview can be scheduled. An interview is the opportunity for an applicant to link a personality with an application in the mind of an admissions reader. Often, this impression on an interviewer makes a difference in deciding on many applicants who have similar credentials.

Early Decision and Other Admissions Plans

Although not for everyone, the Early Decision admission plan is one way to separate yourself from other applicants. By applying Early Decision, prospective students declare that Bates is their first choice and, if accepted, they will withdraw all other college applications. When looking at it from an admissions point of view, they want students who know that they love Bates and have decided that this is the school that they want to attend. It is this type of applicant who will most likely get involved and improve the educational experience for others. In recent years, as many as thirty percent of the entering class was admitted through Early Decision.

Many applicants are not willing or able to decide early, of course. In addition to the regular admissions process, other possibilities include: Deferred Admission, January Admission, Transfer Admission, and the option to attend Bates as a visiting student.

If you get the chance to drive up the Maine Turnpike and stop into Bates for a visit, you would notice that the academic buildings in which students attend classes are very close to each other around the tree-filled quad. A short walk through some of these buildings, such as Carnegie Science, or Hathorn Hall, would give a visitor a realistic impression of the academia of Bates.

Although Bates is one of the most competitive colleges in admissions, there is an obvious lack of student competition. Students have a collaborative work ethic and competition within themselves. They are self-motivated and, at times, the library becomes more familiar than one's room. Perhaps the best perspective on the academic environment of Bates could be seen in the copy room of the library during the week of final exams. Large groups of students meet and help each other grasp concepts and challenge each other in a process that polishes each participant's understanding of the subject matter. Even in the premed classes, such as Organic Chemistry, students are more supportive than competitive with each other.

Faculty

At Bates, students do not feel a sense of pressure, although throughout the campus one senses their willingness to work very hard. The Bates faculty makes the campus and the student body part of its life. Although time in the classroom makes up the majority of the time in which students interact with their professors, it is certainly not the only time. The Bates faculty is a central part of one's Bates experience inside *and* outside the classroom. Whether it is a departmental barbecue outside one of the residence halls, an all-campus barbecue during the fall or the spring, or even at the President's Gala, the faculty interacts with students and makes connections that enrich the educational experience. All professors have office hours, which allow a student to meet one-on-one, but they will also make appointments with a student outside of these hours, if necessary. Most professors stay well after class to talk with students and explain any difficult material of that day's lecture, and give their home phone numbers out on the first day of class. Although at first this can be an intimidating way to get help, after a short time one comes to realize that members of the Bates faculty are happy to be available. They never leave the "teacher" role in their office; rather, they are teachers who are more than eager to aid a student who shows a willingness to learn.

In one of the first days of my Russian literature class, Tolstoy and Dostoyevsky, I realized that I was the only science major in the class. I found myself frustrated in the first few weeks because the professor turned the class over to the students for discussion of the stories instead of lecturing and telling us what the author meant. As the semester progressed, however, I came to value each student's opinion and realized that the process of thinking about what the passages meant to me, and to others who had read it, was as educational as the memorizing of facts that I was used to.

Courses

The Bates academic year follows a 4-4-1 calendar. Students take four courses (the normal course load) during the fall and winter semesters, and for at least two of the four years take a five-week-long intensive course during the spring. This session, called Short Term, allows professors to have more freedom and creativity in designing each course and in many cases allows the class to leave the campus to study a subject by touching it and seeing it rather than just reading about it. Short Term courses allow geologists to study geologic history from inside a kayak in the intercoastal waterways of Maine; biologists study evolution by learning about the finches of the Galapagos Islands, as Darwin did from the *Beagle*.

Degrees

Bachelor's degrees are fulfilled after completion of thirty-two courses and two Short Term units. A degree can be conferred after three years. This accelerated program requires completion of thirty courses and three Short Term units.

General Education Requirements

To ensure that the graduating student has had exposure to a wide variety of arts and sciences, the college has established several general education requirements. These requirements are what ensures the student a liberal arts education. Students are required to take:

- at least three courses from the curriculum in biology, chemistry, geology, or physics and astronomy

- at least three courses from the curriculum in anthropology, economics, political science, psychology, or sociology
- at least one course or unit in which the understanding and use of quantitative techniques are emphasized
- at least five courses from the curriculum of three of the following fields: art, English, foreign languages and literatures, music, philosophy, religion, theater, rhetoric, and history. Three of the five courses must have a common theme and fit together in what is called a "cluster."

Although some may balk at the sight of such a list, very few of the students at Bates have negative opinions about the courses that these requirements led them to take. They often are remembered as some of the best courses they have taken.

Bates provides an environment that allows a student to achieve. I remember coming into my first year having little confidence about my writing ability. After one of the first writing assignments, my professor suggested that I make an appointment at the writing workshop. That experience was invaluable. We talked about my ideas and how I could change my paper to more clearly convey them. The instructor offered to read a second draft that afternoon. I returned a number of times during all of my four years. The assistance I received not only helped me get better grades in that class, but also gave me the organization and confidence to succeed in writing throughout my college career.

SOCIAL LIFE AND ACTIVITIES

Sports

While students are conscientious about their work, there are very few who don't have several extracurricular activities keeping them busy. Bates supports twenty-eight varsity teams and seventeen club sports teams. For many students, athletics are a very important part of the Bates education. More than half of the current student population participated in varsity and club sports. Bates' athletic teams compete in the New England Small College Athletic Conference (NESCAC). Without a doubt, the most intense rivalries are between Bates and Bowdoin and Colby, referred to as the BBC. One of the goals of every team is to become champs of this "mini-conference" for bragging rights of Maine.

In addition to these intercollegiate programs, Bates students can be found playing intramural sports all year long. Intramural sports are coed and include soccer, ice hockey, basketball, and softball. Intramurals are open to students of all abilities and are a great way to get away from the books for an hour. Although Bates athletics are competitive and successful, student athletes are constantly reminded that they are students first. Participation in athletics provides the student with a classroom in which the subject is character, leadership, tenacity, and teamwork. At Bates, academics and athletics are not separate entities, but are considered to be complementary to one another in a student's education and intellectual growth.

Clubs/Activity Groups

Bates also supports sixty-seven activity groups on campus, including art, chess, choir, dance, drama, gay-lesbian-bisexual alliance, international, jazz band, newspaper, orchestra, political, radio and TV, religious, social, and student government. Students can also start a group if motivated. One example is the Bates Aviators Club, which was recently started by a student who came to Bates already experienced in piloting. Activity groups are entirely student-run and provide students with opportunities to grow in interests outside of the classroom. In all facets of the college, Bates encourages its students to explore different areas and to take on new responsibilities.

One popular group is the Outing Club. Founded in 1920, the second oldest only to that of Dartmouth, the Outing Club sponsors outdoor activities almost every weekend and provides outdoor recreational equipment for students to use. In a recent year the Outing Club celebrated its seventy-fifth anniversary in what was called "Peak Day." In one day, alumni, students, and staff joined to summit forty-five mountains in Maine and New Hampshire, including Mt. Washington and Katahdin.

Social Life

The social life at Bates is definitely "alive." Social activities are primarily on campus due to the fact that ninety-one percent of all students live on campus. Students can take study breaks at the Den or meet with classmates at the Ronj, an entirely student-run coffeehouse where students perform music and read poetry. Some like to play pool or Ping-Pong in Chase Hall. During the weekend, campus-wide parties, film club movies, and dance and theater productions give the students almost too many choices.

Bates activities and social events are open to all students. This is not only an administrative policy, but something that Bates students support and enforce. There are no fraternities or sororities at Bates, and all college-sponsored parties are open to anyone. Student groups sponsor parties every weekend and an occasional Wednesday night, and the college itself sponsors a number of social events. One of the biggest events is the annual President's Gala, to which the entire college community is invited, where big band orchestras and jazz bands perform. The Chase Hall Committee, a student-run activities group, does a great job of getting big-name bands to come and play on campus; past groups include The Mighty Mighty Bosstones, Live, Blues Traveler, Dave Mathews Band, Ani Di Franco, Tribe Called Quest, and The Indigo Girls.

Off-Campus Activities

Being in the metropolitan area of Lewiston-Auburn also provides students with a number of options. Several multi-screen cinemas, shopping malls, and restaurants, accessible by student-run shuttle vans throughout the weekend, give students an off-campus release when needed. Add in the fact that the Maine coastline, Portland's Old Port, and hiking and skiing are all less than an hour away, and one recognizes the opportunities students have to enrich their Bates experience.

Alchohol

The social scene at Bates in many ways revolves around alcohol, as at any other college. Recently, Bates has attempted to ensure that state liquor laws are enforced at college-sponsored parties. On-campus parties that serve alcohol employ outside caterers to effectively reduce underage drinking at Bates. On weekends the Den turns into a pub that serves great food and, for students who are twenty-one, fine beer. This area has become more popular not only for the cold ones, but also for the late night karaoke sessions. Off-campus bars are also a part of upperclass social life, the most popular being The Blue Goose, the Cage, and O'Sheills. The Goose is well loved by Batesies, if not for the low prices and great atmosphere, then for the foosball table. "Burgers and Beers" at the Cage is another senior tradition on Wednesday nights. For O'Sheills, I need only say, "Disco party and karaoke nights."

Short Term

While this five-week session is a unique period of learning, it is also an opportunity for students to enjoy the spring and *socialize.* For seniors, Short Term offers a last chance to live it up before they are forced into the real world. Weekly barbecues on the quad, outdoor parties, intramural softball, picnics at nearby Range Pond or Popham Beach state parks, and the annual Outing Club-sponsored clambakes, give students plenty of opportunities to procrastinate.

FINANCIAL AID

Fortunately, getting into Bates is often harder than getting help to afford it. In recent years, more than half of all first-year and continuing students received some form of financial aid. Although the Financial Aid Office has rules and guidelines to follow, it deals with families individually when putting together an aid package. In addition to aid through scholarships, which are need-based, students can take out loans and have the opportunity to hold part-time jobs on campus. Recently, average first-year packages, which include scholarships, loans, and work-study, totaled almost $18,000. Even if a student does not qualify for need-based aid, student loans and part-time work are available. Half of the student body works. On-campus jobs range from lifeguarding at the pool to driving the shuttle vans to the nearby mall. In my experience, even more students could work if they wanted to; there are always jobs at the student employment office.

Each semester I worked between five to eight hours per week as part of the work-study portion of my financial aid. During my first semester, I took a job cleaning glassware for the biology department and another job monitoring the entrance to one of the athletic facilities. I soon learned that there were some jobs that required less attention than others. While the glassware job was easy and offered a sometimes needed break from the books, the monitoring job demanded much less attention and during those three hours a week I could read or study while getting paid.

Other jobs have slow periods during which students can study. Thus, part-time work covers the weekly expenses during a semester, and rarely encroaches on the time needed for coursework.

Leigh Campbell, Bates class of 1964, and the staff of the Financial Aid Office make it easy for the students to focus on their education rather than its cost. A meeting in the Financial Aid Office reveals not only that they are extremely knowledgeable and helpful, but that with all the worries of applying to Bates, getting financial aid won't be one of them.

GRADUATES

Mention Bates to older alumni, and there is a certain sparkle in their eyes when they talk to you. Bates is a special place with so much proud history and such bright promise. It has a special place in the hearts of its alumni, and being a fellow Batesie connotes a special bond, a bond of values and morals, a bond of shared memories of place and common interests that upon realization is priceless to its graduates.

Talking to Bates alumni about their college experiences reveals that over the years Bates has stayed the same in many ways. Even with the addition of modern dormitories and academic buildings, and of new majors and faculty, the impressions and impacts made on students over the years—more importantly, the values and the character of the students that the institution attracts—are remarkably similar. When fellow Bates alumni meet, there is an obvious passion and loyalty they feel toward the school. Perhaps the best physical example of this feeling is the commitment alumni show in the number of them who come back every fall for the Back to Bates weekend, the number of admissions interviews that alumni conduct, or the number of graduates who stay and make Bates a part of their life as well as a career.

PROMINENT GRADS

- **Bryant Gumbel, '70, Television News Personality**
- **Stacey Kabat, '85, Documentary Filmmaker**
- **David Chokachi, '90, Television Actor**

Bates alumni share a strong bond with one another, and the alumni network is similarly strong. From the regional clubs that keep Bates grads in touch, to the alumni who volunteer their time to help a student or recent grad explore their career, being a Batesie lasts well beyond commencement.

In my fourth year, the lacrosse team went on a winter break trip to North Carolina. After one of the two games that we played, we had a tailgate party with Bates alumni who were living in the area. I remember standing with the recent grads whom I knew and the alumni who brought their children to the game and realizing that, as happy as we were to have the support, they were equally happy to reconnect with Bates and talk to the students whether they were old friends or not.

Perhaps the beauty of the liberal arts degree is the vast possibility that lies ahead of its recipient. Graduates leave Bates on paths that lead all over the world, and use their education in all sorts of careers. Bates students are not "trained" for jobs, but are rather educated in how to think and how to educate themselves. From breakthrough research scientists to professional athletes, government officials to television personalities, musicians to founders of the civil rights movement, Bates grads share a belief in hard work to achieve their goals, and a sense of moral responsibility with which they enter the world.

For many, a Bates education is a motivating step to pursue further education. Bates students learn the liberal arts and gain a moral responsibility, but they also gain a passion for the process of learning. Approximately two-thirds of Bates graduates continue on to graduate school within five years of commencement. This high number reveals the quality of the students that Bates admits, as well as the education and inspiration that the college provides.

SUMMING UP

The college selection process can be difficult, there are many fine institutions. A person trying to make a decision based on academic reputation and "numbers" would be hard-pressed to differentiate between many of the schools in the "Most Competitive" category. Bates distinguishes itself with the characteristics many visitors cite: openness, warmth, inclusiveness, and respect for the members of its community. Throughout its history, Bates has been a role model for its peers in its policies and programs for students. From its beginning, Bates admitted students without regard to race, gender, religion, or nationality. Today, its admissions policies (SAT scores optional), study abroad programs, and service learning program are all examples of Bates' values and leadership.

Bates is an environment in which students can excel. The small size, great facilities, and committed faculty provide students with resources on a par with large universities, yet support that can only be found in a small college. Fellow students at Bates are equally supportive.

While some might say that Bates's location is a drawback, there are many positives in being in Lewiston, Maine. In fact, many Bates students cite Bates's location as a major reason for choosing the school. Although not located in a major metropolitan area, Bates is urban enough so that students can easily get to many activities, stores, and businesses. For many, the absence of a large city is a positive. Maine has much to offer in the areas of outdoor activity and beautiful landscapes. Bates is within an easy drive of Portland, the coastline, and the ski slopes.

Another possible complaint about Bates is its small size. There are positives and drawbacks to both large and small schools that must be considered in the selection process. Even though Bates is considered small, it is very unlikely that a student could get to know everyone at the school and feel limited socially. On the contrary, the familiarity of a small school in many ways allows students to make more friendships than at a larger school. Even so, many Bates students study abroad or at some other college or university in the United States for at least a semester and get to experience the big school scene. The small size at Bates is hardly viewed as a drawback academically. No classes are taught by graduate students, and students find it very easy to build a relationship with their professor in even the largest classes.

So come on up to Bates, and see for yourself. Talk to the students on the Quad and observe a class. After a little while, you might get that gut feeling too, and realize that the academic excellence, warmth, and egalitarian values that can be seen in the Bates community are qualities reflected by you.

❑ *Christopher Byrne, B.S.*

BOSTON COLLEGE

Photo by Gary Gilbert

Boston College
Chestnut Hill, MA 02167

(617) 552-3100, (800) 360-2522
Fax: (617) 552-0798

E-mail: admissions@bc.edu
Web site: http://www.bc.edu

Enrollment

Full-time ❑ women: 4,775
❑ men: 4,183

INTRODUCING BOSTON COLLEGE

The hallmark of Boston College is its Jesuit commitment to a diverse education. Boston College offers exceptional academics and various extracurricular activities; however, the students' participation in community service projects is often the most valuable element of the Boston College education. The college sponsors numerous community assistance programs and encourages all students to become involved in these activities. For example, the course, Pulse, combines classroom academics and volunteer work. Students participating in this program fulfill their requirements in theology and philosophy while also volunteering ten to twelve hours a week in various projects. This program was initiated at BC in 1970 and has continued to gain acceptance among students. Today, more than 300 students per year enroll in this unique course.

The Boston College Campus School for the multiple-handicapped and developmentally disabled (ages preschool to twenty-one) is a popular volunteer program.

My freshman year, I volunteered at the Campus School and worked with severely disabled men and women. I helped students draw pictures, finger paint, and bake desserts. It was a challenging but extremely rewarding experience. All of these students were confined to wheelchairs and could not speak, but they became animated when participating in the day's activities. Often, students' squeals of excitement filled the room.

Although I was a teacher's aide at the school, I often felt I was the student. Specifically, I was reminded to appreciate all that I had ignored around me, such as the vivid colors of a Boston autumn and my campus walks from the dorms to classes. My course at the Campus School was a life lesson that has proved invaluable.

BC's dedication to community service projects is a significant feature of the university. Approximately one-fourth of BC's students volunteer their time to a variety of activities. Providing assistance to others is an integral aspect of the Boston College Jesuit education and a characteristic that distinguishes BC from other universities.

Project Agora

In addition to sponsoring countless community service programs, BC offers significant communication resources that allow students to further educate themselves outside of the classrooms. In 1995 BC initiated Project Agora, a technology project that catapulted Boston College into the information age. Today, the university provides students with Internet access from their residence halls as well as phone service and cable television. Students can access the Internet and their e-mail accounts twenty-four hours a day. Boston

College also enables students to research information in the school's library from their rooms. The convenience of this system is incredible.

Each student also has an individual telephone number that remains constant throughout the student's four years at BC. This eliminates frequent roommate quibbling about the use of the phone and the monthly bill. An individualized voice mail system accompanies the phone service and remains active for six months after the student's graduation. This ensures that the student will get messages from prospective employers who may be trying to get in touch with the student or from friends who might not know where the student has relocated.

Another feature provided by BC is cable television. Students have access to over fifty channels, five of which are designated for BC programming. The BC movie channel is extremely popular. The university chooses a variety of movies that play on this channel each month.

My roommates and I often huddled under blankets on snowy evenings watching the BC movie channel. I specifically remember one evening when we watched Higher Learning, *a movie depicting college students dealing with prejudice and racism on campus. This film had a significant impact on us and we stayed up until four in the morning discussing this and many other issues. I learned a great deal about myself, my friends, and society that night.*

Although Boston College has embraced the modern technology era, the campus maintains its gothic appearance. Four gothic-style buildings, collectively known as the quad, stand in the center of the campus. These buildings house classrooms, a cafeteria, and even an art museum, which displays international collections of artwork. Sprawling grass lawns surround this spectacular architecture and serve as hangouts for students between classes. Anchoring the campus is a reservoir where students can be spotted getting in their daily workout runs.

Location

The location of BC, six miles west of Boston in the suburban town of Newton, is also ideal. Students enjoy the beauty and safety of a suburban campus as well as access to a major city. The green line of the Boston transit system, better known as the "T," is located at the base of the campus and carries students into Boston within twenty minutes.

Size

In addition, BC's medium size of approximately 9,000 undergraduates is advantageous. Boston College has the intimate charm and community aspect of a smaller university while also providing programs such as Division One sports teams often found at larger universities. This aesthetically pleasing campus coupled with a variety of educational opportunities distinguishes BC from other universities around the country.

ADMISSIONS REQUIREMENTS

The admissions process is comprised of two elements: application by the student and evaluation by the college.

Applying

Students must first submit their applications to Boston College. Consistent with the information age, BC accepts applications on diskette, by the Internet, and through the mail. Students must also determine whether to apply to the Early Action plan or regular admissions. BC accepts approximately thirty-five percent of students who apply early. Applications are due October 15 and BC notifies Early Action students of acceptance before December 25. Applying early has its benefits. Students who meet this deadline have completed their task and do not have to worry about racing to submit the application before the final due date. Also the applications of those who are not accepted through this process are deferred and reevaluated during the regular admissions process. In this way, students have a second opportunity to gain acceptance. Applications for the regular admissions process are due January 1 for enrollment in the fall semester, and November 1 for enrollment in the spring semester. BC informs prospective students of acceptance between April 1 and April 15. BC also accepts applications from transfer students. The deadline is May 1 for enrollment in the fall.

Evaluation of Candidates

Once BC has received applications, the Admissions Committee begins evaluating the candidates. The admissions process at Boston College is extremely selective. It accepts just over one-third of the 16,500 applicants. In evaluating the candidates, the Admissions Committee searches for those it believes will actively contribute to the Boston College community; therefore, BC considers a number of factors in the admissions process.

An individual's academic achievements are of considerable importance. BC looks favorably upon those students who have enrolled in honors and advance placement courses. The Admissions Committee also examines SAT I or ACT scores. The majority of BC students in a recent freshman class scored between 1210 and 1340 in combined Verbal and Mathematics on SAT I. Extracurricular activities are another focus of the Admissions Committee's attention. Boston College strives to admit those individuals who have exhibited exceptional leadership skills, possess unique talents, or who have overcome obstacles to be successful. In addition, Boston College requires applicants to submit an essay and complete one SAT II: Subject test in each of the following areas: writing, mathematics, and any third subject.

ACADEMIC LIFE

Faculty

Boston College has an outstanding academic reputation, due, in large part, to its prominent faculty. Ninety-five percent of faculty members have achieved doctorates and all continuously conduct research in their respective areas of interest. Students benefit from this greatly, as professors stimulate and encourage free thinking and class participation. Often, course sessions are devoted to class discussions where students share their own theories, beliefs, and experiences on particular issues. Furthermore, professors are closely attuned to the needs of their students.

In high school my English teacher told me that college professors were not available outside of class to help students who might be having difficulties in a course; therefore, I was pleasantly surprised my freshman year to learn that the opposite was true at BC. My first major assignment in college was a ten-page paper for my history course. The week before the paper was due, my professor maintained daily office hours from eight in the morning to six o'clock at night. She vigorously encouraged all of us to drop by or sign up for a meeting.

I immediately took advantage of her offer. She listened as I proposed the thesis of my paper and aided my brainstorming. Later she read the rough draft of my paper and offered constructive criticism. I worked diligently on this assignment and was ecstatic when I received an A.

This is the typical practice at BC. Professors have an open door policy and actively encourage students having difficulty with the course to seek their assistance. Professors are also available to continue discussions and debates with students outside of the classroom. In addition, students at BC have the opportunity to develop personal relationships with professors.

Sophomore year I enrolled in a core communication course. The extremely talented professor kept the class alive with his wit and humor. Through class participation and office hours, I came to know the professor well. We remained friendly after the completion of the course and my senior year he asked me to be his teaching assistant for the course. Although I was to assist him, this professor became my mentor providing advice on courses and life after graduation, and introducing me to other professors and prominent persons at BC. I was even invited to the communication department's Christmas party. Today, this professor and I remain in touch. He is a tremendous resource and friend.

Class Size

Class size also enhances student/teacher interaction. The average class size in a standard course is thirty, a small size that enables professors to become familiar with students and their individual needs. Students are also less inhibited in more intimate settings such as this, and therefore eagerly participate in class. Approximately one hundred students are enrolled in each lecture course; however, these courses are broken into fifteen-person sections where students meet with the professor weekly to discuss the course materials. Therefore, students in a lecture course also receive individual attention.

Academic Resources

The university supplies numerous academic resources as well. The computer lab provides students with over 200 computers for research and word processing. In addition, the library has research databases and a computerized card catalog. BC also has a learning center and offers tutoring services.

Curriculum

The curriculum at BC is diverse and demanding. There are four broad areas of study: the arts and sciences, business, nursing, and education. All students, regardless of their major, are required to take courses in philosophy, theology, literature, writing, the natural and social sciences, the arts, and cultural diversity. These courses lay a stable foundation for continued coursework in these and other areas.

In addition, Boston College provides special study programs. Students may study abroad, participate in internship programs, and cross-register with certain schools in the Boston area. The college offers an honors program for freshmen and supports twelve national honor societies. Students in various majors may also research and write a thesis paper.

Courses at Boston College are rigorous and students must be prepared to devote much time to academics. Students who do not put an effort into their studies will suffer, but there is much opportunity to do well. Professors conduct interesting classes and are committed to each student's comprehension of the course material.

SOCIAL LIFE AND ACTIVITIES

Boston College students participate in a wide variety of social activities. In addition to community service projects, BC supports 120 on-campus clubs, as well as thirty-three Division One sports teams. Activities range from the pep band and photography club to intramural sports and student government. Each fall there is an activities day where BC clubs and organizations set up booths and distribute information. In this way, students are introduced to a multitude of activities and are presented with the opportunity to become involved in the Boston College community.

Sports

Supporting BC athletics is another opportunity for students to participate in the BC community. During the fall, tailgate parties precede and follow every home football game. In-between the tailgating, students cheer on BC football in Alumni Stadium. When the football team is away, students can watch their team and classmates on television. The major networks often broadcast Boston College games. Students continue to focus their attention on BC sports during the winter, voicing support for the prominent basketball and hockey programs.

My sophomore year was an incredible time for BC sports. We gained a national reputation as "the upset school." BC football ousted Notre Dame from its number one ranking, beating the Irish with a field goal kick in the final seconds of the game. In March, BC basketball qualified for the Elite Eight in the NCAA tournament, upstaging number one ranked North Carolina and beating Bobby Knight's Indiana University. The hockey team raged that season also, bringing home the trophy in the Beanpot tournament. With each win the campus exploded with excitement. Students ran around campus shouting and cheering for our teams. Certainly, several of my most memorable BC experiences are linked to these famous wins.

Off Campus

BC's proximity to Boston presents further social activities. Students may go into downtown Boston to attend a Red Sox game, visit a museum, or soak up the history of the city. The Freedom Trail is a popular tour, taking sightseers to Paul Revere's house and Faneuil Hall where speakers once solicited support for the American Revolutionary War. Students can also go shopping on Newbury Street or grab lunch in one of the city's outdoor cafes. The Boston nightlife is popular as well. Students trek into the city to go to dance clubs, bars, restaurants, and comedy shows.

Parties

For those who do not want to venture into the city, there are always several parties on campus. Senior housing, known as the mods (for "modular townhouses"), are often the site for these parties. The mods are two-level apartments with backyards where students play volleyball, toss footballs, and have barbecues. The BC bus system is also available to take students into Cleveland Circle where there is a movie theater, and bars and restaurants packed with BC students.

Libraries and Dorms

Although the parties and bars are big social scenes, the most popular spots to socialize are the library and residence halls. Certain floors of O'Neill Library have been labeled social hangouts, and students often travel to the library to meet up with friends or conveniently bump into someone they have noticed in class. Students who truly wish to study go to Bapst Library where it is so quiet one can literally hear a pin drop. The residence halls are just as lively as O'Neill Library. Most students keep their doors open and bounce from room to room visiting friends. At one o'clock in the morning the dorms are still hopping.

Boston College offers an abundance of social activities where all types of students can find their niche whether it be participating in club activities, attending Big East conference games or heading into Boston.

FINANCIAL AID

Boston College is a private university and the price tag of the education reflects this status; however, Boston College provides much financial assistance to its students. Approximately $10 million in scholarships is awarded to incoming freshmen and sixty percent of undergraduates receive financial aid. A major portion of this aid is awarded through scholarships and need-based grants, neither of which students have to pay back. In addition, scholarships are awarded to students for academics, sports, and other demonstrated talents. Students also use loans to meet the expenses at BC. Other students participate in work-study programs to fund attendance at Boston College. This requires students to work a few hours a week in on-campus jobs, ranging from research assistantships with faculty to sandwich making in the Eagle Deli.

Upperclass students also have the opportunity to be resident assistants, students assigned to work in the residence halls, whose main task is to maintain order. Resident assistants are responsible for administrative duties such as room inspections and writing up work orders for clogged sinks and toilets. Resident assistants also arrange social gatherings in the dorms and are available to help any student who may need assistance. In exchange for their efforts, BC provides free housing for them. This is quite a perk, and many students apply for these positions. It is a popular way to alleviate the financial burden of college.

The Financial Aid Office at BC is extremely efficient. Those working in financial aid strive to accommodate everyone and are attentive to students' needs. As a result, the process goes ahead smoothly and students are generally pleased with the results.

GRADUATES

Boston College graduates are devoted to their alma mater and are a substantial reason for the college's success. The resources alumni donate for the maintenance and continued growth of the college are tremendous. In the past five years, BC has used alumni donations to build new residence halls, a cafeteria, and a parking garage, as well as to renovate older classroom buildings and the football stadium. Students benefit significantly from these improvements, and therefore are inclined to give back to the college once they too have graduated.

PROMINENT GRADS

- Thomas P. O'Neill, Jr., '36, Late Speaker of the U.S. House of Representatives
- Michael C. Hawley, '60, President and CEO, Gillette Company
- Susan M. Gianinno, '70, CEO, J. Walter Thompson
- Marianne D. Short, '73, Justice, Minnesota Court of Appeals
- Douglas R. Flutie,'85, Heisman Trophy Winner, Canadian Football League
- Chris O'Donnell, '92, Actor

Boston College graduates can be found all over the United States—nurses, teachers, attorneys, stockbrokers, doctors, and business analysts. Many also attend graduate school.

BC graduates have a strong affinity to one another. Alumni in several states have established BC clubs, where graduates occasionally gather to attend BC football and basketball games, dinners, and cocktail parties. These are great opportunities for graduates of all years to share their BC experiences. Furthermore, BC graduates are a networked community eager to assist one another as well as the students at BC. Often, alumni return to the school to recruit graduating seniors for their companies.

The Boston College education prepares students well for future challenges. Evidence of this are the thousands of highly successful graduates who continue to support their alma mater, Boston College.

SUMMING UP

The Jesuits founded Boston College in 1863 with the goal of educating students both academically and spiritually. Today, Boston College continues in that tradition. The academic curriculum at Boston College is nationally recognized as one of the top programs in the country. The foundation for this outstanding academic program is the faculty. Professors at Boston College are exceptional instructors, often designing courses to stimulate class debate. In addition, the faculty is devoted to the students. Unlike the faculty at many schools, the professors at Boston College are readily accessible and eager to assist students.

Spiritual development is another component of the Boston College experience. BC is committed to producing graduates who recognize the needs of the less fortunate and are eager to assist those individuals. Boston College sponsors a multitude of community service projects and hundreds of students become involved in these organizations. The education students receive through these volunteer experiences is invaluable.

In addition to offering a diverse educational experience, BC provides varied social opportunities. Students may participate in a myriad of activities—whatever suits their tastes. Highlights of the social scene at BC are attending Big East conference games and riding the "T" into Boston for a day of sightseeing or shopping. The friendships students develop at BC, however, are probably the most valued social experiences. Students at BC form tight bonds with one another and these friendships persist after graduation.

Alumni remain in close touch with each other, and also continue to actively support Boston College after graduation. BC graduates are like no others, consistently pledging monetary assistance to the college and returning to campus to cheer on the football team. The experiences students have at Boston College are unique and the alumni are extremely faithful to their alma mater.

Overall, an accurate description of Boston College is "extraordinary." This adjective fittingly describes the education, the faculty, the students, the social life, the graduates, the campus, and the location. Students searching for a school that offers diverse opportunities and challenges should visit the BC campus and talk to the people there. It's a great way to experience first-hand the extraordinary spirit of the Boston College community.

❑ *Christen English, B.A.*

BOWDOIN COLLEGE

Photo by Abramson

Bowdoin College
Brunswick, ME 04011

(207) 725-3100
Fax: (207) 725-3101

E-mail: admissions-lit@polar.bowdoin.edu
Web site: http://www.bowdoin.edu

Enrollment

Full-time ❑ women: 799
❑ men: 775

Part-time ❑ women: 3
❑ men: 4

INTRODUCING BOWDOIN

One of the characteristics that distinguishes Bowdoin among the nation's premier liberal arts colleges is its location in coastal Maine. The prestigious history of the 200-year-old college, the opportunities for studying the natural sciences, the nature of the people, and the innovative residential and social life of Bowdoin complement its location in the bustling town of Brunswick, situated on the coast of Maine just twenty miles north of Portland.

It is easy to settle into campus life on the idyllic 110-acre campus. Bowdoin's dining services have been recognized as one of the best in the country. In fact, one of the most popular campus traditions is the annual lobster bake just before classes begin. Upperclassmen have the luxury of choosing from among a wide variety of housing accommodations, including two brick dorms with two-room suites, several houses, a sixteen-story tower of single rooms, and several college-owned on- and off-campus apartment complexes. For most students, this is the first opportunity for independence and self-reliance. First-year students live in the brick dorms, which places them in the middle of all the action on campus and fosters class unity.

Naturally, the academic instruction, faculty, technology and information resources are the world-renowned cornerstones of the college. That said, the common thread that runs throughout all aspects of the college, from admission to course selection to intellectual growth, is freedom of choice; Bowdoin recognizes that there are numerous different styles of learning.

Bowdoin is the ideal college for students who wish to choose their own paths through independent exploration, self-study, intense coursework, and a collaborative social and extracurricular infrastructure. It is a place where students learn to make important choices and decisions—a key tool for success in the professional world.

ADMISSIONS REQUIREMENTS

Admission to Bowdoin is highly competitive. For a recent class, 1,354 out of 3,974 applicants were accepted. The average full class size is about 430. Getting into Bowdoin is now more competitive than ever. One explanation for its rise in popularity is that Bowdoin accepts the common application, making it quicker and easier for prospective students to apply to a larger number of colleges and universities. Also, the submission of SAT I scores has been optional since 1969. About one-fifth of all applicants and accepted students do not submit their scores. The Admission Committee reviews all aspects of each candidate's application, including high school grades, personal and faculty recommendations, honors and awards, a personal essay, and extracurricular activities and accomplishments. Interviews are strongly encouraged but not required, and can be done during a campus visit or in your hometown with an alumni interviewer. Contact the Admission Office to be put in touch with an alumni interviewer. Alumni interviews and on-campus interviews are equally weighted. Alumni interviews are especially useful for students who are unable to visit the campus. Bowdoin also encourages the submission of supplementary materials to the basic application, such as musical tapes, works of art, or anything else that might give a clearer picture of a student's unusual musical, theatrical, or visually artistic talents. As Richard Steele, Dean of Admissions states:

We seek men and women who are not only bright and well prepared academically, but also eager to learn and anxious to explore new academic interests. Bowdoin is a college for people who love to test ideas, develop skills, explore activities, and discover interests.

Early Decision

Bowdoin has two Early Decision programs. The first requires application by November 15, with notification in mid-December. The second requires application by January 1, with notification by mid-February. Both Early Decisions rounds are binding, and applicants are required to sign a form upon applying that says they will enroll at Bowdoin if admitted.

I was accepted to Bowdoin via Early Decision in December. If I had waited until the Regular Decision period, I don't think I would have been accepted. You see, I came from a small high school where I was ranked fourteenth out of 130 classmates. When Regular Decision rolled around, just about every one of the thirteen class members who were ranked above me applied to Bowdoin. Naturally, Bowdoin couldn't accept all of them, so they chose only the top two. Both accepted and attended Bowdoin. If I had waited until Regular Decision, there's no way I would have beat that level of competition.

To get a good look at Bowdoin, it is possible to stay on campus overnight as a guest of a current student in one of the dorms. This provides an insider's view of Bowdoin and a sampling of the food, the classes, the workload, sports, and social outlets. Plus, if you eventually study at Bowdoin, you'll already have a friend or two.

ACADEMIC LIFE

The following statement from the Bowdoin viewbook best articulates Bowdoin's academic mission: "Bowdoin encourages you to plunge in, to take risks, to explore new areas of study—to assume responsibility for the crafting of your own education." In other words, because the course requirements are very broad, you are free to take classes in many different fields outside of your major. It is common for a student to major in two completely unrelated subjects, such as chemistry and English, or biology and French. Furthermore, since the college does not calculate grade point averages (GPAs) or class rank, students can learn at their own pace without feeling that they're competing against their classmates. In fact, until just a few years ago, grades were simply high honors, honors, pass, or fail. Of the thirty-two courses required for graduation, students are permitted to take a total of four "pass/fail" courses, which provides even greater opportunity for academic exploration without the pressure to perform at the level required of courses within the major. That is not to say that learning at Bowdoin is easy!

While first-year students enroll in several small seminars where they learn analytical and study skills, juniors and seniors frequently undertake independent study and honors projects to study in depth a specific topic related to their major.

Because there are just a few core course requirements, students are able to explore a wide variety of academic interests, which allows for the full experience of a true liberal arts education.

Students choose from more than forty majors, including art history, mathematics, and music. The most popular majors are the natural sciences, government and legal studies, and history. The most distinctive majors are neuroscience, classics/archaeology, philosophy, African studies, and visual arts. There are also programs in arctic studies, film studies, Latin American studies, and theater and dance.

In addition, Bowdoin has the prime coastal location and the ideal setting for the study of biology, environmental studies, geology, chemistry, physics, and neuroscience. A state-of-the-art science complex opened in the fall of 1997, and a new science library opened in 1992. Additionally, Bowdoin owns a 118-acre site of forest, wetlands, and fields along the shore just eight miles from campus on Orr's Island. It includes a center for research in marine biology, ornithology, ecology, and geology.

The Writing Project

Students can always count on the advice and guidance of their advisors, professors, and fellow students. The Writing Project is a peer tutoring program in which uniquely qualified students provide educated but nonjudgmental feedback of students' work as they draft, edit, and revise papers. The program is conducted through the Department of Education.

Study Off Campus

Ironically, one of the most exciting opportunities that Bowdoin affords is the opportunity to study away from campus. Each year about 200 students—usually juniors—spend part of the year at another academic institution within the United States or abroad.

> *I spent first semester junior year in Madrid, Spain. Three of my Bowdoin classmates were also on the same program. Since all of my classes were in Spanish, my reading and conversational skills improved dramatically. The Spanish family with whom I lived exposed me to the entire Spanish culture, history, religion, cuisine, and social norms. Living in a family with five daughters, I became fluent in the language. I made long-lasting friendships with my Spanish family and classmates and we have kept in close touch throughout the seven years since I lived with them. Learning to live with another country's advantages and disadvantages, I became more understanding and patient and learned about a whole new world—all of which can only be learned hands on. It was the best experience of my life.*

Students can also study for a year at one of eleven other colleges involved with the Twelve College Exchange: Amherst, Connecticut, Dartmouth, Mount Holyoke, Smith, Trinity, Vassar, Wellesley, Wesleyan, Wheaton, and Williams. Students must be accepted into the specific program.

Independent Study Projects

Upon returning to Bowdoin, with a new-found independence, it is a good time to undertake an independent study project in place of the more traditional classroom course. Students can choose their own topics, set their own goals and time lines, and work one-on-one with particular faculty members. They learn good time management skills, independence, creativity, and perseverance. It's also their best chance to study a topic that otherwise might not be offered in the curriculum, or to explore further a subject area that was touched upon during a particular course.

Students graduate from Bowdoin with superior analytical and critical thinking skills, and a broad base of knowledge in a variety of literary, cultural, historical, and scientific fields. They are treated to a diverse menu of courses taught by a distinguished group of faculty members who are leaders in their fields. It is no wonder that Bowdoin has educated such legendary literary figures as Henry Wadsworth Longfellow and Nathaniel Hawthorne, and prominent political figures of today such as Defense Secretary William Cohen and former Senate Majority Leader George Mitchell.

SOCIAL LIFE AND ACTIVITIES

A myriad of off-campus activities are available within a short distance of the campus. Bowdoin is just steps from downtown Brunswick, where students enjoy a variety of shops, restaurants, concerts, markets, and movies—all within a five-minute walk. The college owns two miles of waterfront property on which a state-of-the-art coastal studies center is being completed. The Outing Club arranges canoe trips, hiking, biking, skiing, and a slew of other outdoor activities. In fact, a large percentage of incoming students participate in preorientation trips for three or four days, at which time new students bond with their classmates through a shared adventure. A long-standing tradition is the midnight outing to L.L. Bean in Freeport, just fifteen minutes down the road, and since all Bowdoin students are permitted to have cars on campus, trips to Bean and other locations are frequent!

The new Smith Union provides much of what students need, including a general store, a café, a three-story pub, an art gallery, the post office, a game room, quiet study space, and a bright and comfortable lounge for socializing and relaxation. This same spot, the hub of campus life, is the location of several concerts and dances throughout the year, and has proven to be a very popular gathering spot on weekend nights. The architectural design of the Union creates a wide-open central space, which is encircled by a ramp taking people past lounges, art exhibits, the campus bookstore, and the game room. Whether you're simply reading a book in one of the living room-type floral chairs, or sipping a latte in the café, it's the perfect place to see and be seen!

Sports

Morrell Gymnasium is home to a brand-new fitness center, two basketball courts, a dance facility, and several squash courts. One would have difficulty finding a Bowdoin student who is not involved with one of Bowdoin's twenty-nine intercollegiate athletic teams, intramural sports teams, or just plain physical fitness. The Farley Field House, which is located in the middle of seventy-five acres of playing fields, has a sixteen-lane swimming pool, which is used for the women's and men's swim team, diving, and water polo. There is also a 200-meter, six-lane track and an aerobics studio. At the root of Bowdoin's athletic pride and showmanship are the hockey games, held "beneath the pines" in Dayton Arena. During the cold winter months when "polar bears" tend to hibernate, the hockey games provide an outlet for students to show their tremendous sense of pride, loyalty, and camaraderie, which is a hallmark of Bowdoin students and alumni well past graduation.

Bowdoin is a very active place, and athletics are extremely popular. Men's varsity hockey is the most popular spectator sport, and Bowdoin has a long tradition of having one of the best Division III teams in the nation. Women's soccer, men's lacrosse, and the swimming and cross-country teams have also enjoyed great success in recent years. One does not have to be a superstar to play on most varsity teams, and determination and enthusiasm are usually the priority.

At a Division III school everyone has the chance to participate in any number of sports. I played lacrosse in ninth and tenth grades, yet I was able to pick it up again at Bowdoin and played varsity for all four years.

Club sports like rugby and crew are also appealing to many, as are the three levels of intramural competition. The crew team regularly competes in the Head of the Charles Regatta in Boston. Bowdoin is not a "jock" school, but there are relatively few idle bodies.

Polar Bears

While first-time visitors to the campus are awed by the natural beauty of the campus, they are even more surprised by the omnipresent polar bears, one of two symbols of Bowdoin's enormous alumni pride. The Bowdoin Sun symbolizes Bowdoin's location in the easternmost state, which is the first to see the rising sun each morning.

The Residential Experience

In recent years Bowdoin has undertaken an intense project of self-study aimed at revitalizing the residential experience of college living, including housing and dining arrangements, social life, and the Greek system. The decades-old coeducational fraternity system is being replaced with a "House System," which will provide to all students many of the benefits of the old fraternity system, such as self-governed houses, friendships with students from all four classes, leadership opportunities, social events, and house competitions, to enhance the extracurricular undergraduate experience. For the most part, students will continue to reside in the traditional dorms and apartments, but will be affiliated with one of the college-owned houses beginning the day they set foot on campus as first-year students.

With the social scene no longer revolving around fraternities, parties continue, but they are now open to the entire campus and often revolve around a theme. On a typical weekend there are plays, concerts, movies, and lectures, some by students and some by celebrities and other off-campus groups and organizations. Each semester speakers and bands such as Carlos Fuentes, Livingston Taylor, Ani DiFranco, Patty Larkin, The Kinks, Ralph Nader, and Mario Cuomo come to campus. Plans are underway to transform a portion of the old president's house into an arts barn for photography, pottery, jewelry making, and other crafts popular with students.

To explore the Maine area, owning a car is a real asset, and is a great way to make friends. Not everyone on campus has a car, but it isn't usually hard to find someone willing to drive. With Bates and Colby colleges nearby, Bowdoin students can take advantage of their events as well.

Having a car on campus opened up a wealth of options. There was the possibility of driving out to the nearby islands for a lobster dinner or heading to Portland (about a thirty-minute drive) for a movie or to visit one of the many restaurants, shops, bars, and galleries in the Old Port. In the winter, I would occasionally drive two hours with a friend or two to some of the best skiing in New England. In the spring, the two-and-a-half hour drive to Boston for a Red Sox game was an annual event.

Publications

The *Bowdoin Orient,* the student newspaper, is the oldest continuously published campus college weekly in the country; the *Bowdoin Forum* just released its first edition in the fall of 1997. Founded by two students, *The Forum* aims to increase the Bowdoin community's awareness of recent international events with a compilation of essays submitted by students, faculty, alumni, and staff. Both publications represent students' desires to implement new ideas.

Performing Groups and Other Organizations

Masque and Gown, the drama club, puts on a variety of plays each semester. WBOR (Bowdoin on Radio), the student-run radio station, is a good college radio station and is equipped with the latest technology. Miscellania, the female *a cappella* singing group, and the Meddiebempsters, their male counterparts, perform regularly on campus and on the road. BOCA, created by students in 1996, is Bowdoin's first coeducational *a cappella* singing group. There are a multitude of other organizations such as African American, Latin American, and Asian student societies, and clubs for students with similar political, religious, and cultural interests. Bowdoin also has a popular student volunteer organization involved with a Big Brother/Big Sister Program, the American Red Cross, a local homeless shelter, and a wide variety of other programs.

There's something to appeal to everybody. I tried to take part in as many activities as possible because this is the only time in one's life when there are so many options at hand. I belonged to the Bowdoin Film Society, the Bowdoin Literary Society, Beta Sigma fraternity, student government, and the varsity lacrosse and soccer teams. Plus, I studied in France for one semester. Even though I had a heavy course load, I always made time to do everything else.

Meals

Bowdoin has always been known for its amazing food. Students can choose from a variety of meal plan options. Meals can be taken at either of the two dining halls, which were both recently renovated and enlarged to create warm, attractive gathering and dining spaces. Students may also dine informally in the Café and at Jack McGee's Grill and Pub, located in the Student Union. Wentworth Hall is attached to the Coles Tower, a residential complex. For Tower residents it is a fantastic luxury on a snowy Sunday morning to just take the elevator downstairs and enjoy brunch in your slippers. For students too busy to dine, bag lunches are available.

Housing

Most first-year students are housed in two-room triples (usually arranged as one bedroom and one living room) in one of six brick dorms. Each of the first-year dorms is affiliated with a college house, mainly newly renovated former fraternities, under the new House System. Each house has its own kitchen and plenty of common space with a television, VCR, and other comforts from home. After the first year, each class has a lottery, with the best numbers going to seniors. The already good quality of living increases each year.

For my freshman year I lived in Winthrop Hall, a brick dorm, with just one roommate. The dorm provided a cozy atmosphere. As it turned out, the people on my freshman floor were my best friends at Bowdoin for all four years and even to this day. I found that to be the case on other floors as well. My second year I lived in Coleman Hall with a friend from my freshman dorm. We weren't lucky enough to get a sophomore apartment, but we had the chance to meet first-year students and make new friends. Plus, since all of my friends had sophomore apartments, I could go there to cook and hang out, but return to the privacy of my room whenever I wanted to. For both junior and senior years I lived in Coles Tower and loved having my own bedroom. Another group of my friends lived in an adjoining suite. I have never heard of another college that has such great living spaces. My friends and I have found that our best college memories are the ones made in our dorms and apartments where we could be at ease watching television, partying, renting movies, playing games, or just talking.

Students can also pursue their own housing arrangements around Brunswick and along the coast. Some live in apartments or houses in town, while others share houses on the ocean with a few friends. Some spectacular locations on the water are available, but a car and a sense of discipline (in order to drag oneself out of bed on a winter morning and drive to class) are essential. Keep in mind that even with all of these extracurricular happenings, studying is a major priority of Bowdoin students, and it requires plenty of time.

FINANCIAL AID

Parents receive billing statements each semester, and may opt to complete payments via one of several payment plans. The college is committed to making a Bowdoin education accessible to students regardless of their financial circumstances. To that end, in a recent year the college awarded $10,237,000 in need-based financial aid to about forty percent of the student body. That is to say that financial aid is not awarded for academic or athletic merit. Aid packages include grants, loans, and student employment.

The amount of aid awarded to an individual student is dependent on the financial situation of the family. Need is determined by an analysis of the statements of financial resources submitted to the Student Aid Office. Decisions are made on a case-by-case basis and are carefully determined by the college's Financial Aid Committee. The awards are continued throughout each of the four years of college as long as the student is in satisfactory academic standing. What is nice is that financial aid can be continued even when students study off campus in the United States or abroad for a semester or year. Additionally, through the generosity of Bowdoin's many benefactors, the college is able to offer a number of scholarships for post-graduate study at other institutions. The college recently offered $255,700 in graduate scholarship assistance to sixty-eight students.

The Student Employment Office and the Career Planning Center assist students in finding jobs both on and off campus. In addition to the financial incentive to work, it is possible to gain hands-on experience which will be useful in students' careers following graduation.

The summer following my junior year, I stayed on campus to work for the Annual Giving Office. I was just doing basic clerical work, but I learned all about fund-raising and what it means to be an alumni volunteer for Bowdoin. After graduation, I became the Class Agent for my class, and then I became a professional fund-raiser! To this very day I use experiences from the Bowdoin Annual Giving Office to make decisions in my professional job.

GRADUATES

About two thirds of graduates go on to graduate or professional school within five years of graduating from Bowdoin. There are classes to prepare students for the GRE, LSAT, and

MCAT. These classes are not sponsored by the college, but are run by outside groups. Graduate school recruiters come to the campus every year to recruit students. Because the average class size is around twenty, students usually get to know their professors really well. This comes in handy when they need references for graduate school or jobs.

Career Planning Assistance

If graduate school isn't your thing, the Career Planning Center has a wealth of resources for job searches. The staff helps students write glowing résumés, and routinely presents workshops on successful interviewing. One-on-one interview training with alumni, which can include critiquing a videotaped practice interview, is also available. The center has information on more than 1,000 internships across the country, as well as full-time, postgraduate employment in any part of the country. There are also workshops to help students make important career decisions. Alumni offer job counseling, informational interviews, and networking. Every year, several dozen corporations visit campus to interview candidates. Secondary schools, eager to recruit new teachers, also visit campus. After graduation, alumni can still use the Career Planning Center resources, which include an extensive alumni network and a newsletter with job postings.

PROMINENT GRADS

- **Nathan Lord, 1809, President of Dartmouth University**
- **Franklin Pierce, 1824, President of the United States**
- **Nathaniel Hawthorne, 1825, Author**
- **Henry Wadsworth Longfellow, 1825, Poet**
- **Major General Oliver Otis Howard, 1850, Founder and President of Howard University**
- **Joshua Lawrence Chamberlain, 1852, Governor of Maine**
- **Admiral Robert E. Peary, 1877, First Man to Reach the North Pole**
- **Harold Burton, '09, Chief Justice of the U.S. Supreme Court**
- **Alfred C. Kinsey, '16, Psychologist, Sexologist**
- **Charles T. Ireland, Jr.,'42, Former President of CBS**
- **William S. Cohen, '62, Secretary of Defense**
- **Joan Benoit Samuelson, '79, Gold Medal Winner in the First Women's Olympic Marathon**

The Office of Career Services has a directory that lists alumni by field and location, and they are more than willing to talk to students. In whatever city you choose, whatever field interests you, chances are there is a Bowdoin alum in the area who will be more than willing to lend you a hand.

Alumni Gifts

Once you matriculate at Bowdoin, you always feel at home there. There is a very strong sense of school pride and Bowdoin alumni have historically been extremely supportive of the college, which is a good measure of alumni satisfaction. In October of 1997, an alumnus pledged $30 million for the endowment to renovate Searles Science Building and to pay for the new science center. This was the fourth largest single gift ever made to an American liberal arts college. This type of support shows that Bowdoin alumni are happy with their Bowdoin educations, are proud to display their loyalty, and want to insure that a Bowdoin education is available for future students to enjoy. Bowdoin is annually among the leaders in terms of giving to the alumni fund, and reunions and Homecoming always draw big crowds back to campus. It gives you a warm feeling to know that you're a part of this vibrant and active alumni association. There are plenty of opportunities to network with each other. The regional alumni clubs have as their mission keeping alumni connected to one another and the college through social gatherings, a career directory, volunteer positions at a local school, breakfasts and luncheons with distinguished speakers, and much more. For most graduates, their affiliation with Bowdoin endures long after graduation day, and usually lasts a lifetime.

SUMMING UP

In every respect, Bowdoin College is positioned to be a world-class educational leader well into the twenty-first century and beyond. After 203 years of educating leaders in business, education, politics, medicine, and law, among other professions, the school has perfected the craft of offering an outstanding liberal arts education to students from diverse backgrounds.

When I describe Bowdoin, all I can say is that Bowdoin does everything perfectly, with a lot of thoughtful consideration. I mean this in regard to the quality of the faculty, the offering of courses, the dedication of the coaches and staff, and the maintenance of the campus. You can always count on Bowdoin to do things first class.

Students who benefit the most from Bowdoin are those who seek out new challenges and opportunities, are willing to take risks, and take pride in achieving goals. This could be in the classroom, on the athletic fields, in intramural sport, or simply among friends, classmates, or residents of the same dorm. Bowdoin students learn to develop and explore previously untapped academic, cultural, political, and artistic interests that are carried throughout their lives. Bowdoin students are exceptionally prepared to succeed academically and professionally, and to obtain the cultural, artistic, and historical knowledge typical of a confident, well-respected, mature adult.

The best part of Bowdoin is the interaction between the most ambitious, experienced, and accomplished students in the country. Everyone who is there has something to share, some accomplishment that will improve the college or fellow students. Because of the caliber of these students and the foresight of the administration and faculty, the college is evolving to present an even greater education to top-notch students.

A person's academic credentials are carried with them throughout their lives, and they determine a person's qualifications for jobs and graduate education. When you graduate from Bowdoin you have a sort of "insurance." You can be proud of graduating from one of the best colleges in the country, you know that there is a network of alumni willing to help you professionally, and you can be assured that the Bowdoin name on your résumé will open up a whole multitude of possibilities. In short, a Bowdoin degree opens the world's doors.

❑ *Nathaniel Bride, A.B.*
❑ *Holly Pompeo, A.B.*

BROWN UNIVERSITY

Photo by John Forasté

Brown University
Providence, RI 02912

(401) 863-2378
Fax: (401) 863-9300

E-mail: admissions@brown.edu
Web site: http://www.brown.edu

Enrollment

Full-time ❑ women: 3,028
❑ men: 2,597

Part-time ❑ women: 186
❑ men: 152

INTRODUCING BROWN

My Brown experience can be summed up in one word: Choice. Life at Brown is a sequence of choices; there is no set path or mandated direction. You, and you alone, decide your own destiny.

Choice is probably the best word to use as an introduction to Brown University. From its lack of core requirements to its varied social life, Brown gives open-minded and self-directed students the opportunity to use the resources of an Ivy League institution to craft their own educations. Students see this chance as Brown's greatest offering and work hard to take advantage of it.

Brown is located in Providence, Rhode Island, a city now in the midst of a renaissance. As the result of a major downtown rebuilding effort now nearing completion, the city center has become a pleasant place to look at and walk around in. Providence should also benefit from the imminent construction of a mall downtown. The university overlooks the city from atop College Hill. This particular part of Providence, also known as the East Side, is a residential area filled with large Victorian houses. The campus itself, a sort of oasis of activity in the quiet of the East Side, is bisected by Thayer Street (essentially Providence's scale model of Harvard Square). Thayer is an energetic street lined with record stores, clothing shops, restaurants, and, above all, coffeehouses.

From this location Brown provides students with access to all of its educational resources. The university has the materials of a top research institution, but it has committed itself to educating undergraduates. Undergrads have access to all of Brown's top professors as teachers and often as advisors as well. The university also gives them full use of the university and departmental library systems. Indeed, Brown pays so much attention to undergrads that graduate students have even complained about feeling neglected by the administration. While neglect is probably too strong a word, Brown does not favor grad students at the expense of its undergrads.

Brown's commitment to academic liberalism draws a politically liberal student body, but politics do not dominate the lives of Brown undergraduates. While a majority of Brown students do have leftward political leanings, the opposite side of the political spectrum is well represented and both sides are not particularly vocal about their views.

While the institution has a reputation for being a very activist school, in recent years the campus political climate has been rather calm. A few student political organizations do lead small-scale protests, but they are most often of the fifteen-angry-people-with-signs variety and play a relatively small part in campus life. If a major issue comes to the fore, many more people might join a protest but this rarely happens. Although Brown certainly encourages free speech and open discourse, the vast majority of students does not choose to use a public forum to express their opinions.

This is not to say that the Brown student body is apathetic. Most students are deeply involved in extracurricular activities and many take time to do community service projects in the Providence area. Their interests can range from participating in singing groups to helping elementary school students learn English, but the majority of Brown students choose to be involved in the world around them.

ADMISSIONS REQUIREMENTS

Brown is highly selective in its admissions process and accepts only a small portion of its applicants every year. In a recent year Brown accepted 2,856 out of 15,012 applicants (about nineteen percent). The academic standards of each admitted Brown class are quite high, with SATs averaging almost 1400 and the majority of students in the top ten percent of their high school class.

Nevertheless, many who are not accepted meet these standards and the Admissions Committee frequently makes its decisions based upon the distinctive, intangible aspects of an application.

I can recall discussing admissions with some of the other residents of my freshman dorm. We had all heard the standard line about finding some activity that would leap out at an Admissions Officer and, as a game, each of us tried to pick out the special quality that we felt had sufficiently distinguished our applications from those of our peers. One person had spent her junior year of high school studying in New Zealand, another was a recruited basketball player, a third had edited and produced a weekly video journal in high school. None of us felt that our lives or even our high school experiences were summed up by these characteristics, but we were amused that they could have such an impact upon the fate of our applications.

Each year the university seeks to assemble a class of students with a diverse range of interests and a unique set of abilities who also have a demonstrated ability to perform academically. The admissions process is the way that Brown creates its university community; consequently, it looks for distinctive students who will add richness to the academic environment. For instance, Brown prizes musicians, writers, and people skilled in the fine arts for the creativeness they bring to the university; athletes are valued for their contributions to Brown's teams; people with unique personal experiences are sought for the liveliness that they bring to the student body. All of these characteristics lend flavor to the campus while also insuring the continuity of existing organizations.

Geographic and Ethnic Diversity

These personal characteristics play a large part in Brown's admissions decisions but the university also places a premium on geographic diversity. For this reason students from underrepresented states or foreign countries are sought. For example, a student from Montana might find it easier to gain acceptance than one from Massachusetts because there is a smaller number of applications from the West. International students are especially prized and often recruited. Such efforts yield a community of students with origins from all over the country and the world.

Brown's commitment to geographic diversity is matched by a similar interest in promoting ethnic variety. Nearly one-third of Brown's admitted class are not Caucasian and students are able to share their cultures with the entire community through strong cultural organizations. Despite the strong sense of community among minority groups and the inevitable tendency for people of the same ethnicity to bond more readily, there is a good deal of mingling between people of different heritages. No campus group can be said to have isolated itself from the rest of the university, and probably would be unable to even if it tried.

Application Process

The application process for Brown is fairly standard. SAT I or ACT and three SAT II: Subject tests are required in addition to a transcript showing achievement in a high school course of study including a number of core courses. The application also requires a personal essay. More than anything else, this statement gives applicants a stage on which to display their personal talents and hint at their potential impact upon the university. Because the essay allows students to convey the intangible aspects of their personality, it can serve to distinguish them from others with similar records.

Applications can be submitted according to two time schedules. Normal applications are due by January 1 and word of the admissions decision is released on April 15.

Early Action Option

In keeping with its commitment to individual choices, Brown also offers a non-binding Early Action option. Unique among Ivy League schools, the Early Action plan allows the applicant to apply early to Brown and hear from the university in mid-December. Depending upon their preferences, accepted students can either accept the offer at that time (most do) or they can continue to submit applications to other schools and decide whether to accept Brown's offer in April. Early Action applications are due on November 1; decisions are sent on December 15.

ACADEMIC LIFE

Requirements

Brown's liberal educational philosophy dominates academic life. The university has no core curriculum, holds no distribution requirements, and does not require that students take any of their classes for a grade. The university only demands that a student pass thirty courses and that he or she complete the requirements for a concentration (as majors are called). Because each concentration has a different set of requirements, the number of requirements Brown students have to meet varies widely within the university. Some degrees demand as few as eight courses while the more strict departments can mandate as many as twenty courses. Brown has so few universal standards because it gives students complete control over their educational plans.

The lack of requirements really frightened me when I got to Brown. I had no idea what I wanted to do in college and so many different classes looked too interesting to pass up. I saw my first year as a smorgasbord and took eight classes in eight different departments. This really helped me to discover my main interests. By exposing myself to the ideas of different disciplines and learning the style of teaching in each department I thought that I could see which subject most interested me. As unlikely as this sounds, this random sampling really helped narrow my interests. When I declared my concentration at the end of my second year, I chose the department that I knew from experience was the field that best suited me.

In essence, the belief that students are able to find their individual academic interests and that they posses the wisdom to pursue them on their own rests at the core of Brown's academic liberalism. Nevertheless, while this educational philosophy gives students the opportunity to complete college without focusing their intellectual interests or ever taking a class for a grade, few take it to that extreme. A combination of driven students and capable advisors helps ensure that Brown students can take advantage of this freedom without abusing it.

I came to Brown knowing that I wanted to concentrate in classics and the curriculum allowed me to load my schedule with the low- and mid-level language and history classes that were required for my concentration. By my third year I had developed such a solid background in classics that I was able to take a sequence of independent study classes. The work I did in these classes became the foundation of a 150-page senior thesis and a published article. If I had been required to devote my first two years to fulfilling requirements, there is no way that I would have gotten so far in my field.

CAP Advisors

The university administration realizes the responsibility the open curriculum gives to students and it makes an effort to provide them with guidance and advice throughout their time at Brown. During the first week of orientation, freshmen meet with their assigned advisors to discuss their academic plans. These professors, the majority of whom are called CAP advisors, are faculty members who have volunteered to provide guidance to a small group of freshmen enrolled in one of their classes. The hope is that the freshmen will enroll in a class whose subject matter interests them, then the CAP experience will provide them with an introduction to the discipline. Nevertheless, CAP advisors generally are a good resource for information about the entire university.

After the first year students have the option of retaining their CAP advisors, selecting another professor as their advisor, or being assigned a new advisor. At this point the students become responsible for seeking out the help that they need. Most students do get help when they need it and, while the system can have its faults, most people are satisfied.

Brown's general academic atmosphere is rather calm. There is little overt competition for grades (except among some premeds) or external pressure to perform. Students prefer to view classes as opportunities to learn together rather than as a competitive forum in which to outperform each other.

Pass/Fail Grades

Despite the lack of a gladiatorial atmosphere, most people at Brown are internally driven to take their studies very seriously. This does not mean, however, that Brown students are averse to taking academic risks; the pass/fail grade option ensures this. Officially called S/NC (for satisfactory/no credit), pass/fail is a scheduling tool much beloved by Brown students who are able to use this option for any class offered on campus. Administrators designed the S/NC option to encourage students to take courses outside of their discipline without fear of having a low grade show up on a transcript.

> *I was a biology major at Brown and I knew early on that I wanted to focus my studies upon the sciences. This attention I paid to the sciences meant that I did not take any humanities classes my first two years. In the first semester of my junior year a friend of mine convinced me to take a class in late antique Christianity offered by his advisor. Although I had not written a paper in two years and was uncomfortable with my writing skills, I decided to take the class anyway. I took it S/NC, and despite my initial fears it ended up being a very thought-provoking class that I enjoyed immensely.*

The S/NC system is open to abuse. There are people who choose to "blow off" their pass/fail classes, and others who wait until the first returned assignment to decided whether to take a class for a grade or not. These people are the exceptions, however, and the pass/fail option really does work to encourage academic experimentation.

Brown's decision not to award Ds or Fs (any grade lower than a C is a failing grade), and its refusal to release failing grades on any external transcript, also encourages students to take a broad range of courses. This again lowers the risks of taking difficult courses or tackling difficult subject matter. Like the pass/fail grade option, the grading policies have generally had the positive effect of freeing people to create very diverse academic plans.

Classes

The actual classes at Brown vary greatly in both size and style of instruction. Most classes are taught by full professors who devote considerable time to undergraduates. Each professor is required to attend office hours, and most are eager to schedule appointments to speak to students outside of office hours. Professors of small classes tend to become very close to their students, often taking the entire class out to lunch or serving them dinner. Most also are very willing to work closely with students on individual projects.

Brown classes are generally small in size, although introductory classes in popular departments such as political science or biology, can have upwards of 200 students. In smaller departments, such as art history or philosophy, there might be thirty-five to fifty students in the introductory classes. The mid- and upper-level classes at Brown do tend to be quite small with less than thirty students the rule. Frequently, the mid-level classes do not have prerequisites and are open to students with the initiative and interest to skip the introductory class. There is no need to be confined to large lecture classes and it is not uncommon for freshmen to have a full schedule of classes with less than thirty people.

Grades

Professors at Brown are not known as brutal graders. Bs are by far the most common grade, with As reserved for high-quality work and Cs indicative of below-average performance. Science professors tend to grade slightly more harshly than humanities professors, but like all generalizations this is by no means true in every case.

PLME

One final aspect of academic life at Brown is the Program in Liberal Medical Education (PLME). This program was designed to produce a more humane and well-rounded crop of doctors by accepting high school seniors into a combined undergraduate/medical program that encourages them to study the liberal arts. Students enter Brown and are assured of a place at Brown's medical school (without taking the MCAT), provided they maintain a minimum GPA. While undergraduates, PLMEs (students in the program) are encouraged to experiment widely with the course offerings of the university and many end up concentrating in the humanities before going on to medical school. Despite being enrolled in the PLME program, these students are not segregated or cut off from campus life; indeed, most people are unaware who is PLME and who is not.

SOCIAL LIFE AND ACTIVITIES

Units

The social experience at Brown really begins when first-year students arrive and meet their freshman unit. The unit, a group of between forty and sixty freshmen who live in the same dorm, is intended to serve as a social base that helps first-year students become accustomed to college life. For the first few months of the year, freshman units are frequently inseparable. It is common to observe entire units—"flocks of first years"—going to dinner together. While this herd mentality often breaks down after a month or so, many Brown students remain close to members of their unit throughout their time on campus and a lot of people count unitmates among their closest friends.

There is also a rumor that ten percent of Brown students marry within their unit, but this is unconfirmed.

Fraternities/Sororities

While the unit provides an initial framework for social life at Brown, people begin finding their own non-unit activities almost immediately. This is not at all difficult because life at Brown is vibrant and alive, no matter what social scene a person feels most comfortable in. The university's diversity means that there is an abundance of things to do at night or on weekends. The Greek scene at Brown exists, but is by no means the dominant influence (approximately ten percent of men are members of fraternities; about two percent of women are involved with sororities). The average weekend sees one or two fraternity and sorority parties; open to all students, these are usually well attended. Fraternity parties are the place to be for people who like drinking beer and dancing in a packed room, but the majority of Brown students prefer smaller, more independent activities on weekends.

Other Social Activities

For many upperclass students, the alternative to the fraternity parties are smaller, more laid-back off-campus parties. Often these consist of a small group of people hanging out together listening to music, or dancing. Less crowded and more low-key than fraternity parties, off-campus parties are common enough that on most weekends people can spend the night hopping from party to party without ever seeing a fraternity. The Underground (the campus pub) is another favorite weekend gathering place. It features live music, the occasional student DJ, and on Thursdays the ever-popular Funk Night (a dance party held outside whenever possible). For seniors and some juniors, the Grad Center Bar is also popular but, because the bartenders are rather strict about checking IDs, underclass students tend to stay away.

While parties tend to dominate any discussion of college social life, there is no real pressure to go out or to drink when one does go out. Like the rest of the Brown experience, an individual's personal choices about what he or she wants to do are generally respected.

My first two years of college I stayed in just about every weekend. I took a very full schedule of classes and, because of this, rarely had the time to do much else. However, the fact that my weekends were booked did not prevent me from seeing my friends or meeting interesting people. Every day I ate lunch with a large group of people and had dinner with another set of acquaintances. I also started something with my roommate called "attractive coffee." Once a week each of us would meet for coffee and bring along a friend the other person had not met. It was sort of an outlandish way to meet new people, but it worked well.

Off Campus

Providence also contributes to the social scene at Brown. Providence has a wealth of superb restaurants (Providence recently beat Boston, a city with twenty times its population, in a restaurant challenge), evocative jazz clubs, and clubs where almost mainstream acts like Ani Di Franco play live. Boston (one hour north) and New York (four hours south) are both places students go for a change of scenery.

Dating

One of the things that people find interesting about social life at Brown is that people do not date. Many relationships on campus grow out of friendships, which makes the dating phase rather unnecessary. They also frequently develop between people who share an extracurricular interest or have a class together. Because relationships often develop informally, there are many single Brown students. Most of the unattached, while vaguely discontented about it, do not have any great problem not being involved with someone and take the opportunity to play the field. In addition, couples at Brown do not tend to remove themselves from their group of friends.

Sports

While they definitely play a role in romantic life at Brown, athletic teams and campus groups also help students get out and meet each other. Brown offers a broad range of varsity sports (thirty-five different teams), and although most varsity sports recruit it is always possible to walk on (some coaches even approach freshmen in orientation lines to pitch their sport). The recent court decision ordering Brown to implement a plan to bring it into compliance with Title IX (a law that, among other things, mandated equal participation numbers for men and women in college athletics) has opened up many opportunities for women athletes and has led the university to expand the rosters of many women's varsity programs. The effect on men' s teams has varied. While some teams have been asked to cut rosters' sizes, the university is committed to the continued strength of men's athletic progams and most have not been adversely affected by the decision.

Athletes, especially those on larger teams like track or football, tend to form very close bonds with teammates and socialize a great deal within their teams. Some of this may come from the (largely untrue) perception that the campus is unfriendly toward them, but mainly athletes congregate together because of the time they spend together and their common interests.

Groups

Besides athletics, Brown students can participate in theater groups, dance performances, write for the various campus publications, or be involved in any of a host of other activities. One of the best-known campus organizations is WBRU. This FM radio station (and its lesser-known and rarely heard AM cousin) is student-run and operated, with all of the managers and DJs coming from the ranks of Brown students. In recent years, *Rolling Stone* magazine has ranked WBRU as a top regional radio station and it is the station most often listened to around campus.

FINANCIAL AID

Brown's need-aware admissions policy is the most important (and most controversial) aspect of financial aid at the university. Need-aware means that for ninety-five percent of admitted students, the applicants were accepted without regard to their financial situations. In the other five percent of accepted students, financial considerations may or may not have played a role. This has been a source of great distress to many students on campus and there have been a number of unsuccessful protests urging Brown to become need-blind.

Even with the need-aware admissions policy, approximately one-third of Brown students receive some sort of financial aid, and in a recent year the average freshman package totaled over $14,000. Because a portion of aid awards are made up of loans, the average indebtedness of a Brown graduate was $12,000 at the time of graduation.

Many Brown students have part-time on-campus jobs, either as part of a work-study program or just to get additional spending money. Food service jobs are the most common forms of campus employment although there are many opportunities to work in academic departments or campus administrative offices. Salaries work on a sliding scale, with the hourly wage of most jobs increasing after a certain period of service is met or a specified number of hours worked. In a recent year the yearly earnings from campus employment was $1,360.

The deadline for submission of financial aid forms for freshman applicants is January 1 and financial aid awards must be renewed every year.

GRADUATES

More than ninety-four percent of freshmen who enter Brown graduate; then they have to find something else to do. While this is a constant source of *angst* to the students who have to determine their future, Brown provides considerable resources to help students with their postgraduation plans. Almost one-quarter of Brown graduates continue right into graduate or professional schools, with many of them entering their field's top institutions. For students looking at graduate school, professors with similar interests are the best resources. Professors are always eager to advise people planning graduate study and help them decide which programs best match their interests.

PROMINENT GRADS

- **John Hay, Personal Secretary to Lincoln**
- **John Heisman, the Trophy's Namesake**
- **Charles Evans Hughes, Chief Justice, Supreme Court**
- **John F. Kennedy, Jr., Publisher**
- **Horace Mann, Educator**
- **Joe Paterno, Football Coach**
- **John D. Rockefeller, Jr., Philanthropist**
- **Ted Turner, Media Mogul**
- **Thomas Watson, Jr., Former IBM Head**

Deans

For preprofessionals, Brown has prelaw and premed deans who meet with students considering legal or medical careers and go over strategy for applications. Although these deans have a reputation for being quite blunt about an applicant's chances for admission to specific schools, the general feeling is that they prepare students extremely well for the application process.

In addition to deans responsible for applicants for professional schools, Brown also has a dean responsible for helping students apply for scholarships and fellowships. Because of the resources it has dedicated to helping its applicants prepare their applications and practice for interviews, Brown has historically done quite well in competitions for postgraduate awards, such as the Rhodes and Marshall scholarships.

Job Hunting

Brown also has extensive resources for students looking for jobs right out of college. The Maddock Alumni network can help students use alumni connections to find out about positions, while the Office of Career Services runs on-campus recruiting and has information about numerous jobs from other sources. Like the rest of Brown life, the university's graduates enter diverse careers. Nevertheless, jobs in the fields of technology and finance seem to be the most popular areas.

Time Off

Many graduates also take some form of the proverbial year off, either by working in a job that they do not plan to hold for a long time or by literally taking the year off. The main scenarios for those who take jobs for a brief time are to try and find suitable positions open on campus, to look for some other kind of opening in Providence, or to go to a major city that would be fun to live in and find something there. Most people who take a year off do find themselves in grad school eventually. As one person who later went back to school said, "The first slushy day in January that you take the 5:30 A.M. train to your job makes you committed to going back to school."

A lot of Brown graduates choose to stay in Providence for a time after leaving school. New York, San Francisco, and Boston also attract many graduates and people who have moved to these cities say that it is easy to stay in contact with other alums in these areas. The ties between alumni are further fostered by the various Brown Clubs and notices in the Brown Alumni Monthly.

SUMMING UP

Brown, both as a university and as a community of students, embraces the idea of personal and intellectual freedom. Of all things on campus, the university curriculum expresses this most visibly. Brown students have complete control over their selection of courses with the only true graduation requirements being that they pass thirty classes and complete a concentration. Brown's pass/fail option enhances this liberty to explore academically by removing the risk from broadening one's schedule.

By devoting considerable time to undergraduates, the faculty of the university makes this process of intellectual discovery much more rewarding. Brown students get to know their professors well, and this teacher-student bonding makes the learning environment comfortable.

In spite of all the attention to academics, life at Brown really does not revolve around the classes and schoolwork. Brown has been known as a laid-back school, and in many respects this is true. While Brown students must work hard to excel, for most students there is a time to work and a time to play. People at Brown do enjoy themselves, and they take the same individualistic approach to their social lives that they bring to their education. Just about every imaginable social scene thrives at the school and there is little pressure to conform. Basically every person is able to do his or her own thing without getting much grief from anyone else.

Brown allows its students to make their own choices and, while this represents the university's greatest virtue, it also means that the people who do not have a great deal of personal initiative tend to feel lost. The university devotes considerable resources to advising students and helping them feel comfortable with the number of options they have, but some still feel overwhelmed. One problem with these resources, though, is that after their first year students have to seek them out to use them. This invariably leads to students who meander through, lacking direction without making any effort to change this.

The same can be true of social life. Besides Spring Weekend and the Campus Dance, there are no real campus-wide social events; people find their own things to do within their own social groups. This can be a problem for those who enjoy a social calendar of large group events, but most Brunonians have no problem with this independence.

Brown caters to individuals with the desire, determination, and drive to make their own choices. It opens its human and material resources to such people and it encourages them to follow their inclinations and explore themselves and their world. Self-directed people can truly thrive in this environment and most relish the chance for an Ivy League education on their own terms that Brown gives them.

❑ *Edward Watts, B.A.*

CALIFORNIA INSTITUTE OF TECHNOLOGY

Photo by Bob Paz

California Institute of Technology
Pasadena, CA 91125

(626) 395-6341, (800) 568-8324
Fax: (626) 683-3026

E-mail: ugadmissions@caltech.edu
Web site: http://www.caltech.edu (general)
http://www.admissions.caltech.edu
(Undergraduate Admissions)

Enrollment

Full-time ❑ women: 226
❑ men: 656

INTRODUCING CALTECH

Caltech is highly directed and small, with approximately 900 undergraduate and 1,000 graduate students, and 280 professional and 284 research faculty members, yet its reputation and accomplishments are disproportionate with its size. Caltech is where science happens—where spacecraft are designed and built, where cold fusion was debunked, where giants of theoretical physics make bets about the makeup of the universe, and where news vans congregate whenever an earthquake rocks the West Coast. Caltech's primary focus is on research, and hundreds of millions of dollars are invested in people and facilities to ensure that both are state-of-the-art. (If something isn't advanced enough, we'll build it, and if there isn't an expert around, we'll make one.)

For the student this translates into learning environments, research opportunities, and laboratory experiences. Caltech professors recognize the students of today as the thinkers and experimentalists of tomorrow and encourage their participation in class and in lab. At Caltech, you don't just learn the answers to questions already solved, you learn to ask questions and to ultimately find the answers yourself. Professors often treat their students more as intellectual peers than as peons and respect student input as much as that of their professorial colleagues. Many undergrads work as research assistants on campus and some even get assistant authorships in major scientific journals. This kind of involvement means that students (with proper authorization) can be given access to any computer, library, or laboratory facility they might need.

Yet in spite of the seriousness and dedication to scientific knowledge and discovery that exists, Caltech has a friendly atmosphere. Students, faculty, and staff interact in both academic and social situations. When you aren't in the lab, Caltech's beautifully landscaped 124-acre campus in Pasadena provides a backdrop for relaxation and fun in the sun, Southern California–style. On any given day, you might find professors and students sharing a table outside the Red Door Cafe and people playing Ultimate Frisbee on the lawn in front of Beckman Auditorium. Graduate and undergraduate students might work together in class or lab in the afternoon and then play basketball or water polo with each other in the evenings. Caltech's size provides boundless opportunities to participate in almost any kind of activity you want, whether it be musical, athletic, social, or academic.

ADMISSIONS REQUIREMENTS

Getting in is not easy. By campus tradition, the target size of the freshman class is always 215—the number of seats in the physics lecture hall. Comparing that number to the 2,395 applications that were recently received for entrance and the 540 letters of admission that subsequently were sent will give you some idea of the competition involved. Additionally, the academic quality of the applicant pool is always high; recently, the middle fifty percentile of SAT I scores ranged from 620–740 Verbal and 700–790 Math, and eighty percent of the applicants were in the top ten percent of their high school class.

Despite those numbers, test scores and GPA play only a supporting role in the admissions decision. Unlike many schools, Caltech has no minimum SAT scores, no minimum GPA, and no formula for automatic admission or rejection. There are no geographic or demographic quotas, and there are no interviews. The Admissions Committee considers each applicant as he or she is portrayed by the application materials to determine whether or not the applicant possesses the three qualities Caltech seeks:

- a strong interest in mathematics, science, or engineering
- high academic ability
- demonstrated initiative with respect to learning

In order to look for those qualities, the Admissions Committee considers carefully the more subjective parts of the application—essays, choice of high school curriculum, activities, and teacher recommendations—and encourages creativity, self-reflection, and self-expression.

As a Caltech alum, I often speak to high school students about admission to Caltech, and they always ask, "How can I be sure that I will get in?" My answer, of course, is that there is no sure way, but there are definitely things that you can do to increase your chances. Take the most challenging courses offered at your high school. Look for ways that you can express your love of science outside of school. Ask for recommendations from teachers who really know you and what makes you tick, and who are willing to write about you in depth. And finally, spend time on your application essays! Your essays speak for you to the admissions committee, and they want to hear what you have to say, not what you think they want to hear.

Serving on the Admissions Committee are faculty from all academic divisions at Caltech, undergraduate student representatives appointed by their fellow students, and admissions officers. All the members of the committee bring to the decision table their personal experiences of Caltech as well as the expectations of their peers, and they work together to discover and admit those students who share the Caltech spirit of dedication to learning and discovery.

Serving on the Freshman Admissions Committee as a student representative was an incredible honor and an awesome responsibility. As I read applications, I was constantly amazed at the quality of the applicants—they were almost all excellent in some way. And yet it was ultimately part of our duty to turn more than three-quarters of them down. Being on the committee really made me think about what it meant to be a Caltech student, and I found that the students we were looking for were the ones that we believed would be the best Caltech students—those who would be able to succeed and be happy here. It was rarely an easy decision.

ACADEMIC LIFE

When I came to Caltech, I had to totally readjust my way of thinking about myself and my abilities. In high school, I was the cream of the crop; everything came easy—classes, activities, awards. At Caltech, I was just another student working hard to get my calculus homework done on time. At first it was very daunting and I feared that I would fail, but by working together my classmates and I pulled through. Graduating from Tech gave me a renewed sense of faith in myself and what I can do, if I just put my mind to it!

The Honor System

The Honor System is one of the most central tenets of the institute. Eschewing long lists of rules prohibiting plagiarism, theft, and the like, Techers instead live by the simple and elegant statement of the Honor Code: "No member of the Caltech community shall take unfair advantage of any other member." Under the Honor System, faculty and students alike are held responsible for their actions, and there is an inherent atmosphere of trust and respect. For example, almost all Caltech quizzes, tests, and exams are unproctored and take-home. The professor will state on the outside of the test the time limit, open- or closed-book, and when the test is due. The student is free to take the test whenever and wherever he or she wants: in his or her room with a favorite album playing, in the quiet study carrels in

Millikan Library, at the beach—you name it! Most buildings on campus, including the computer labs, are accessible twenty-four hours a day (all you need to do is sign out a key). Under the Honor System, which is overseen by student representatives, everyone lives by the principles of truth and integrity that are so important in the realm of science. As one current student puts it:

> *The integrity and consideration that have to be a part of my everyday life have been a great learning experience. Even if ten years down the road I have forgotten all the quantum mechanics I ever learned, I hope that I will always remember the qualities of honesty and integrity that are integral to a Caltech education.*

Transition from High School

To help freshmen make the transition at Caltech, the first two terms of the year (there are three terms per year) are graded pass/fail. In addition, Caltech has a somewhat unique attitude towards learning and homework that helps to make adjusting easier. Collaboration is the norm of study at Caltech. Students are encouraged to work with each other on homework assignments—to share ideas, possible ways of thinking about problems, and encouragement. Although everyone tries to do their best, competition for the best grades is almost nonexistent, and "trolling" (locking yourself up in your room to study by yourself) is discouraged. Caltech's homework collaboration policy not only works (due to the Honor System), but gives students a taste of what it will be like to work with a group in a research laboratory.

Core Curriculum

At the heart of a Caltech education is the core curriculum: a set of classes required of all undergraduate students. The core includes five terms of math, five terms of physics, two terms of chemistry, one term of biology, one term of astronomy or earth and environment, one term of chemistry lab, two other introductory laboratory courses, twelve terms of humanities and social sciences, and three terms of physical education. The core curriculum occupies most of the freshman and sophomore years. Although the names of the core classes may seem simple (Math 1 and 2, Physics 1 and 2, Chemistry 1, etc.), don't be deceived—

the contents of the courses are anything but simple. All Caltech students, whether majoring in physics or literature, study topics including multivariable calculus, analytic geometry, quantum mechanics, thermodynamics, and covalent and organic chemistry. Caltech is not for the faint of heart, but the core curriculum ensures that all students have a firm grasp of the fundamental concepts of science across all of the major fields.

Declaring an Option

When students have reached the end of the freshman year, the time has come to declare an option—Caltech's version of the major. In addition to a wide range of options in the pure science, applied science, and engineering fields, Caltech students can also choose options in the humanities and social sciences, such as history, economics, literature, and science, ethics, and society. The highly motivated student could choose the Independent Studies Program and major in virtually any field of interest; he or she is responsible for designing the curriculum to meet personal goals. Students can choose multiple options and are free to change options if they wish.

Research

Caltech's small size and abundance of top-notch facilities make undergraduate research accessible to almost any Caltech student who wants to learn what it's really like to be part of a major research laboratory, and research is an important part of the academic experience of many Caltech students. How? The three most common ways to become involved in research at Caltech are:

- work as a paid research assistant
- do research for academic credit
- participate in the SURF (Summer Undergraduate Research Fellowship) program. SURF provides grants for students to do independent research projects during the summer in which students write their own proposals, conduct their research, and ultimately present their research at SURF Seminar Day, modeled after professional scientific meetings. Ask a Caltech student on campus in the summer what he or she is doing and the answer is likely to be, "SURFing!"

A Caltech education is more than just the sum of the classes that you take, the books you read, and the homework that you do. It's everything that you do here, including your interactions with your professors and the other students. It's how you learn to take concepts that you know and apply them to problems that you don't know how to solve. Take the annual ME 72 engineering design contest, for example. You are given a bag of stuff—rubber bands, pieces of plastic, screws and bolts, small motors—and you have to build a machine from it, a machine that has to accomplish some kind of task such as climbing a rope or collecting Ping-Pong balls. And you will use your machine to compete against your classmates. That kind of experience—applying skills and knowledge to real-world applications—is an invaluable part of Tech.

SOCIAL LIFE AND ACTIVITIES

When I told my high school friends that I was going to Caltech, they laughed and told me that only nerds and geeks went there and that everyone spent all of their time studying. That is totally not true. Studying is important, but relaxing and having fun with friends is also important. At Tech, I'm surrounded by interesting and intelligent people who are just as likely to be arguing about philosophy or superstring theory as they are to be driving to Hollywood for a chili cheeseburger at 3:00 A.M.!

Houses

Social life is generally not one of the reasons why a high school student would choose Caltech, but freshmen are often surprised at the vast array of activities that are available to them. Social interaction centers around the seven on-campus undergraduate houses: Blacker, Dabney, Fleming, Lloyd, Page, Ricketts, and Ruddock. More than just residence halls, each house has its own traditions and unique personality derived from its members. Each house has its own lounge and dining room, where everyone in the house meets for student-waited dinners every weeknight. Each house also has one or two faculty or graduate student resident associates who live with the students, as well as nonresident faculty associates. The student houses are a place to work, host parties, or just generally hang out.

Athletics

Athletics is another way that students relieve their academic pressures. Students can choose from a variety of physical education classes each term, including some nontraditional offerings such as scuba diving and rock climbing. An often overlooked benefit of Caltech's small student body is that almost everyone can play any sport they want. The coaches rarely turn anyone away who wants to play and is willing to make practices. In fact, almost thirty percent of the student body is involved in intercollegiate athletics at Caltech.

The Arts

The arts also thrive at Caltech, with offerings in music, theater, and the fine arts. Many students and faculty are talented musicians as well as scientists, and they get together to express themselves instrumentally or chorally every week through jazz band, concert band, chamber music, orchestra (with Occidental College), and men's and women's glee clubs. TACIT (Theater Arts at CIT) puts on several productions each year, and if you don't happen to be star material, there is plenty to do backstage. Hands-on art classes are offered every term. Add to this mix the backdrop of the incredible Los Angeles music, theater, and arts scene, and there is more than enough arts for a lifetime.

Everyone has seen Los Angeles and Hollywood on TV and in the movies, and when I decided to come to Caltech I couldn't wait to see what living in Southern California is really like. Well, there is more to do in and around Los Angeles than I could ever hope to do in a lifetime—excellent restaurants, theme parks, great movies, the beaches, shopping, museums, concerts, happening dance clubs—you name it. Pasadena even has its own hip Old Town district with trendy places to shop and eat. If you come here, you really have to try to be bored.

Clubs and Organizations

In addition to athletics and the arts, Caltech is home to over eighty different student clubs, spanning a huge range of student interests. These clubs include ethnic organizations, religious groups, social clubs, hobby and interest groups, and gaming societies.

FINANCIAL AID

I knew that Caltech would be expensive, but the good thing is that Caltech's price tag includes everything: tuition, room and board, student fees, health insurance, money for books, extra meals, and personal expenses, even travel money if you live far away. There aren't any hidden costs.

Caltech's policy with respect to financial aid is simple: If a student is admitted, the institute will make it financially possible for that student to attend. As long as the required forms are turned in, every applicant will receive a financial aid package that will fully meet his or her demonstrated financial need. Applying for financial aid consists of completing the FAFSA (Free Application for Federal Student Aid) and the College Scholarship Service Profile form. These documents enable the Financial Aid Office to determine the amount that the student and his or her family can reasonably be expected to contribute toward a Caltech education. Any difference between that amount and the cost of attending Caltech is considered the student's financial need, and the Financial Aid Office will prepare a student aid package consisting of any combination of scholarships, grants, loans, and work study that will fully meet that need.

Caltech strives to be fair but generous with its financial aid. For example, Caltech's application process is "need blind"—an applicant's financial situation will not influence the decision to admit or deny. If a student receives an outside scholarship, that award will go toward reducing the student's loan or work study, rather than reducing scholarship or grant awards. Additionally, freshmen are not expected to work during the first term. At the same time, however, Caltech does not use financial aid as a bartering tool to attract students. An admitted student who tries to bargain for more financial aid using a full scholarship from another university is bound to be disappointed. However, Caltech is extremely sensitive to actual financial considerations, and will make alterations in financial aid awards based upon unusual or changing financial circumstances.

Work-Study

A number of students take advantage of the fact that there are more jobs for students on campus than there are students and work off a fair portion of their costs through work-study before they graduate. This is made easier by the fact that Caltech offers flexibility with loans and work-study—it is quite easy to switch from one to the other. There are all kinds of jobs for students; some of the most popular include research assistant, teaching assistant, tutor, office assistant, and student waiter. Most of the jobs on campus pay well over seven dollars an hour.

Scholarships

Most of the scholarships awarded by Caltech are need-based; however, each year a limited number of merit-based scholarships are awarded to incoming students. These merit awards are for $10,000 each and are renewable for a second year. There is no separate application for the merit awards; all admitted students will be considered. Sophomores, juniors, and seniors may be awarded other Caltech scholarships based upon academic excellence.

GRADUATES

In mid-June of every year, Caltech confers upon approximately 200 happy seniors the degree of Bachelor of Science. What do Caltech graduates do after they leave Tech? Not unpredictably, about fifty percent of graduates continue on to a Ph.D. degree in graduate school. These students form the backbone of Caltech—those who will dedicate their lives to the study and teaching of scientific knowledge. Yet don't be fooled into thinking that all Caltech grads become professors. The remaining fifty percent use their Caltech education in fields they may never have dreamed of as high school students.

PROMINENT GRADS

- **Frank Capra, '18, Film Director**
- **Linus Pauling, '25, Chemist, Political Activist; Two-time Nobel Prize Winner**
- **Arnold Beckman, '28, Chemist, Entrepreneur, Philanthropist**
- **Moshe Arens, '53, Engineer, Politician, Israel's Defense or Foreign Minister**
- **Gordon Moore, '54, Intel Corporation, Founder and Chairman**
- **David Ho, '74, Biologist, *Time's* Man of the Year**

Thirty percent enter the workforce, where despite the ups and downs of the national economy, Caltech students are highly successful at finding excellent jobs, with average starting salaries five or more percent higher than national averages. Engineers and computer scientists are in high demand, but an increasing number of job offers are coming from the financial sector, as management consulting and other firms become aware of the fact that Caltech grads have the problem-solving skills, technical background, and thinking-around-corners attitude that they want.

A proportion of graduates don't fit into any particular mold. Although Caltech does not currently offer a premedical or prelaw program, a score of graduates are accepted every year into the top medical and law schools in the country. Surprising? How about the students who join the Peace Corps, travel around the world, work or teach abroad, or decide to start their own businesses? Recent Caltech graduates have done all of those things and more. Don't think that just because you get a degree from Tech you are locked into a certain career path. The kind of education that Caltech provides is one that will serve you well, no matter what path you choose to follow.

It's been several years since I graduated from Caltech, and I have to admit that I have forgotten most of the calculus that I learned. But I have found that some of the things that I learned at Caltech serve me better than integrals and derivatives: how to work together with my coworkers, how to approach problems, and how to come up with unexpected and innovative solutions. And Caltech has a very supportive network of alumni, many of whom have helped me throughout my career to find jobs, make business contacts, and generally serve as sources of information and support. Having the California Institute of Technology on my résumé has often been tantamount to the words "open sesame" in my business career. It can really make a difference.

SUMMING UP

Trying to capture the spirit of Caltech in a book is like trying to solve a problem in n-dimensions—it can work on paper, but it's difficult to visualize what it's truly like. Ask any Caltech student or alum what Tech means to him or her, and you will get a different answer.

It's a school that will forever change the way that you think about yourself and the rest of the world. It's a place where you will make friends that you'll struggle with through endless homework sets and maybe keep for the rest of your life. It's a tradition of scientific inquiry that is over 100 years old but is still on the cutting edge. It's a beautiful campus that is home to some of the most advanced equipment and esteemed scientific minds in the world, yet is so casual that you'll often see your professors in shorts and T-shirts. It's the birthplace of an Honor System that proves that students will rise to high standards of behavior when given privilege and responsibility. It's a crazy and amazing four years that will be unlike any you've ever known before.

Caltech is not for everyone. But most Caltech students will agree that their time at Caltech is one of the most exciting periods of their lives. And to any student who attends Caltech, it is an experience they will never forget—once a Techer, always a Techer.

❑ *Debra L. Tuttle, B.A.*

CARNEGIE MELLON UNIVERSITY

Carnegie Mellon University **Pittsburgh, PA 15213-3890** (412) 268-2082 Fax (412) 268-7838 E-mail: undergraduate-admission@andrew.cmu.edu Web site: http://www.cmu.edu/enrollment/admission	**Enrollment** **Full-time** ❑ women: 1,636 ❑ men: 3,148 **Part-time** ❑ women: 25 ❑ men: 67

INTRODUCING CARNEGIE MELLON

The atmosphere at Carnegie Mellon is one of the most eclectic of any school. The name "Carnegie Mellon" is often associated with computers and engineering; others think of it as a school that specializes in art and drama. All of these people are right. And when you add outstanding programs in the sciences, the humanities and business administration, you've got the basic academic view of Carnegie Mellon. The students here are as different from each other as you can get, yet everyone still finds ways to interact. There are students here from halfway around the world; there are students here from two miles away. There are students from all fifty states and over forty foreign countries. Some people are here building complex electronic devices, and some are making beautiful art. The one thing that everyone does have in common is that they're committed to what they're doing, and they work hard.

Carnegie Mellon, located about five miles from downtown Pittsburgh, is surrounded by three culturally active, residential neighborhoods. Pittsburgh is no longer a city full of factories and smokestacks. Today, the city has cultural activity and diversity and there is no shortage of things to do and learn. This serves as the perfect setting for one of the fastest growing universities in the country.

In 1900 Andrew Carnegie, a Pittsburgh industrialist and philanthropist, founded Carnegie Institute of Technology and Margaret Morrison Women's College to educate the sons and daughters of local working class families. In 1967 Carnegie's institutions merged with Mellon Institute, founded by Andrew Mellon, and formed Carnegie Mellon University. In 1968 Margaret Morrison was closed and the College of Humanities and Social Sciences was founded, forming the basic model of Carnegie Mellon that is seen today. There are now six colleges within the university: Carnegie Institute of Technology (engineering) (CIT), Mellon College of Science (MCS), School of Computer Science (SCS), School of Industrial Administration (SIA), College of Humanities and Social Sciences (H&SS), and College of Fine Arts (CFA).

Carnegie Mellon has an incredibly distinctive history and, luckily, many of the traditions live on. Directly inside the doors of Baker Hall is a portrait of the profile of Arthur Hamerschlag, the first president of the university. Legend has it that it's good luck to rub his nose. Although they wouldn't admit it, many students have been caught rubbing the nose during exam time.

One of the rituals that students would not deny taking part in is the painting of the fence. When Carnegie Mellon was still divided between men and women, the two schools were literally separated by a ravine. The one footbridge that connected the two campuses was where all of the men and women met in their free time. Then, when the College of Fine Arts building was built, the builders leveled a hill and filled in the ravine. The students of both schools were so disappointed that the administration built a fence in the bridge's place, but this was not a good idea because the fence really had no point. The night before it was to be torn down, a group of fraternity brothers painted the fence to advertise a party. The party was such a huge success that it became a tradition to paint the fence. Today, anyone can paint the fence. The only rules are that the fence must be painted, with a paintbrush, between 12:00 A.M. and 6:00 A.M., and whoever paints the fence must guard it for twenty-four hours or as long as they want their painting to stay. The fence paintings range from messages from fraternities advertising parties to happy birthday wishes to friends.

Carnegie Mellon is also one of the only universities that uses bagpipes to greet its freshmen on the first day and say farewell to graduates at commencement. Carnegie's Scottish heritage is celebrated even today. The name of our marching band, the Kiltie Band, says it all; every member of the band wears authentic Scottish garb (yes, including kilts). Carnegie Mellon is also the only university in the United States that offers a music degree in bagpiping. If you're not interested in majoring in it, there's also a bagpipe club (no kidding).

I never realized how different my college experience was from that of my friends. I never knew how many different people could live together on one campus. Like a lot of other people that have never really left home, I just figured everybody would be more or less like me. I was so wrong. But I've learned so much from just being here that I wouldn't trade it for anything.

ADMISSIONS REQUIREMENTS

What does it take to get into Carnegie Mellon? The Office of Admission looks at a lot of different elements when choosing who gets in. Basically, the admissions counselors are trying to get a feel of who you are and what you've done. Unlike many people think, it isn't only your transcript that admissions counselors look at. Of course, high school grades are fairly important, but they are definitely not everything. The Office of Admission also looks at your standardized test scores (SATs or ACTs), your essay, activities you've been involved in, personal recommendations, your portfolio, your audition, and your interview. Obviously, depending on your major, you probably won't need to submit all of these things.

There is no set formula for how people get accepted. In some cases, one element (like test scores) may not be as strong as you'd like, but something else (like extracurricular activities) will make up for it. What admissions counselors look at also depends heavily on what your intended major is. For example, if you are applying to be a math major, they will concentrate on your math grades and scores more than on other things.

However, what they *are* looking for is a relatively well-rounded student who will take full advantage of the opportunity to come here. Your best bet is to do your best in everything and, above all, get involved! Most Carnegie Mellon students are involved in much more than just class work—the admissions counselors want to find people who will be willing to take part in other things. This doesn't mean just sports or clubs. Your activities can be interests or hobbies.

There is no grade or score that will get you in or keep you out of Carnegie Mellon. The decision comes from a number of different considerations that the counselors use to decide whether Carnegie Mellon is right for you.

To apply to Carnegie Mellon, you can call or write and request an application for admission. You can also apply on the Web. Once you're on the mailing list, the university will send you all the information you need. When you apply, you must indicate which college within the university you'd like to apply to. If you're still not sure what you want to major in (which college), you can mark as many colleges as you'd like for no additional charge. Keep in mind that it is possible to be admitted to one college and rejected from another.

Requirements for Majors

The classes that you need to have taken in high school depend on what you're planning on majoring in. Each major has slightly different requirements, so be sure to check on that. Every major requires that you take four years of English; beyond that, it depends on the major. Of course, as long as you carry a normal high school course load, you should fulfill all of the requirements. You must submit scores from either the SAT I or the ACT. In most cases, you also need to take at least one SAT II (in most cases you need to take three). If your intended major does require an SAT II, it will be English Composition. Beyond that, you're usually required to take one in math (any level) and another of your choice.

Interviews

Recommendations and interviews are two of the best ways to show the Office of Admission who you really are. Interviews are suggested, but not required. They not only give an admissions counselor an opportunity to learn more about you, but give you an opportunity to learn more about the school. For those students who are too far away to come to campus for an interview, the school also offers hometown interviews. These interviews serve the same purpose as campus interviews (although you won't see the campus). Alumni interviews in your hometown are available as well.

ACADEMIC LIFE

The students of Carnegie Mellon come from a number of different backgrounds. The one thing that everyone has in common is that they have worked hard to get here. Most of the students come from the top of their high school classes. At first, many of them are surprised that they are not necessarily in the same position here; however, they soon realize that they are gaining something even more valuable than a class rank. They are surrounded by people and situations that challenge them and inspire them to work harder.

Nobody ever said that being a student at Carnegie Mellon was easy, but it is certainly not impossible. You may be working hard and studying more than you'd expected, but so is everybody else. People understand what their colleagues are going through and they help each other.

When I was getting ready to come here, I was really worried because I thought I wouldn't be able to handle the work load. All I had heard was how hard it was and how much everybody had to work. Now that I look back on it, I do have a lot of work to do, but it was as if I was eased into it. I'm used to it. Plus, all of my friends have the same amount of work to do, so I don't feel that I'm the only one studying so much.

Although Carnegie Mellon is an extremely competitive school, students learn early that they need to help and support each other to succeed. People are willing to explain a difficult concept or give constructive criticism because they know that at some point they will probably need the same favor.

For every class, there is a study session offered before a test. In many cases, the professor or a teaching assistant will organize a review session to help members of the class. In addition to this, many students take it upon themselves to start their own study groups. In addition to helping and being helped by their peers, many students find this to be a good way to get to know people in their classes.

Classes and Faculty

The faculty/student ratio is nine to one; the average class size is between twenty-five and thirty-five students. This also takes into consideration the larger lectures. The largest lecture hall on campus seats 250, which is relatively small compared to other universities. Most of the classes that have lectures this size are introductory classes that many students are required to take. In classes with lectures this size, there is always a recitation offered with the lecture. The recitation is a smaller group (ten to twenty people) led by a teaching assistant (TA) or graduate student who discusses the concepts and subjects covered in the lecture. In all cases, the TA and professor will always have office hours for people who may need extra help, and, in most cases, they will also give the class members (no matter how many) their office (and sometimes home) telephone number and e-mail address. Some professors even host social gatherings to become better acquainted with their students.

When I was looking at schools, I was intimidated by Carnegie Mellon's reputation. I came for a visit and was really surprised to find that the students were normal people—their rooms were messy and they procrastinated, just like me! Since I've been here, I've found teachers and classmates to be very supportive. It's an intense environment, but I don't feel I'm in it alone.

The course load and the kind of work you do depends on what college you're in and what you're majoring in. Computer science majors will obviously spend a lot of time at their computers, while architecture majors will spend a lot of time in their studios. While one person is working on problem sets every night, another will be writing a long paper. Everyone will say that his or her work is the hardest, but the truth is that everyone is doing the kind of work they enjoy (or they should be). It's impossible to classify the class work here into one category. Every class has its own pattern.

No matter what a person's major is, he or she will have a few classes in other areas. For example, computer science majors are required to take non-computer related electives (such as an English class), people in the humanities are required to take a math class and two science classes, and every freshman needs to take an introductory English class.

Computers

Any student at Carnegie Mellon would tell you that this is a very computer-oriented campus. Almost everything, from communicating with professors to signing up for classes is done over the Internet. One of the first things students are taught when they come here is how to use the campus network, Andrew. Every freshman is required to pass a class called Computer Skills Workshop (CSW), which covers everything from word processing to e-mail. Students with computer experience can test out of the class. Almost everything is announced over the Internet. Most classes and student organizations have their own electronic bulletin boards to make announcements and have discussions.

Students aren't required to have their own computers, but many have them. There are computer clusters in many of the dorms and in every academic building. Every dorm room has ethernet hookups in case the students do have a computer of their own, so they have access to the Internet from their rooms. The need for a computer depends on the major. Some people, who have a lot of work to do on computers, find it convenient to not have to leave their room to get their work done. Others, who don't do a lot of work with computers, don't have any need for them. Your best bet is to wait until you get to school and figure it out then (if you don't already have one).

SOCIAL LIFE AND ACTIVITIES

The Campus

Carnegie Mellon is technically in a city. The campus is self-contained and surprisingly open for a city campus. There's grass and trees and (if you're in the right dorm) you never have to cross the street. The campus is also fairly safe. Pittsburgh's crime rate is relatively low compared to the national average. With relative security and other cultural benefits, Pittsburgh has continually been named one of the country's most livable cities. Because the Carnegie Mellon campus is so self-contained, it's even safer.

The university has about fifty security employees. About half are sworn police officers who have the power to make arrests; the other half are security guards. These guards and officers patrol the campus (on foot and in cars) twenty-four hours a day. If something does happen on campus, the campus police will hang up "crime reports" on all of the bulletin boards and in all of the dorms to keep everybody informed.

In addition to the campus police, there are many student-run safety organizations. There is an escort shuttle bus (driven by students) that runs within two miles of the campus and will bring you home if you don't want to walk off campus alone. If you feel unsafe walking across campus alone, you can call Safewalk and two students will come and walk you wherever you need to go.

Unwinding

Although the academic environment can get fairly intense, Carnegie Mellon students definitely know how to unwind. After a full week of classes and schoolwork, everybody's ready to relax and have some fun. A common stereotype of Carnegie Mellon students is that they can never tear themselves away from their computers. While everybody here has probably had a few weekends when they spent much of it working, it is much more common for students to find other, non-work-related things to do.

When I got here, upperclassmen kept telling me about how they had pulled all-nighters and had gone days without sleep. I got a little scared, and then I got worried because I was *sleeping (I thought maybe I was doing something wrong). Finally I realized that it was said to psyche each other out. I've noticed that people say they haven't slept as a way to brag about how much time they've spent working. I'm a junior now, and I can honestly say that I've never pulled an all-nighter. I've had a few very late nights, but those are spent just as much talking with friends as they are working.*

Off Campus

A lot of students jump at the chance to get off campus on the weekends. The Carnegie Mellon campus is situated in the middle of three major shopping areas: Oakland, Shadyside, and Squirrel Hill. Between these three areas you can find shopping, restaurants, movie theaters, coffeehouses, museums, and nightclubs (and this is all within walking distance). Beyond that, it is easy to catch a city bus going downtown or to a nearby shopping mall. Pittsburgh is full of things to do, from the cultural to the just plain fun. You can go to the symphony one night and then go to a Pittsburgh Penguins game the next. The possibilities are endless.

Athletics

Of course, you don't need to leave campus to find something to do. Carnegie Mellon has nine varsity sports. There are also many more intramural and club sports (these range from very competitive to strictly for fun). Even if you're not interested in participating in one of these sports, you'll probably have at least one friend who does. Around ninety percent of the student body participates in an intramural or club sport at one point or another.

Organizations

Beyond sports, there are over 100 student organizations on campus. The student body of Carnegie Mellon is incredibly diverse, so it is obvious that the list of clubs would be just as diverse. From organizations celebrating ethnic heritage to clubs based on political views to clubs made up of people who like to play chess, there is a club here for everyone. And even if there isn't, all you have to do to start one is find a few people with your common interest and apply to the student senate to be recognized. Student organizations recognized by the senate are open to any student and vary in size from a few people (usually the newer clubs have fewer members) to a lot of people.

I had been involved in drama in high school, but I knew I wouldn't be able to take part in the drama productions here because I wasn't a drama major. I was so excited when I found out about Scotch and Soda, a group of non-drama majors who put on shows throughout the year. I've met some of my best friends through S&S.

Scotch and Soda, an amateur theater group, has a long tradition at Carnegie Mellon. Throughout the year the group produces two full-length shows and several one-act plays. The playwrights of both Godspell and Pippin were not only Carnegie Mellon alumni, but Scotch and Soda members.

Fraternities and Sororities

Throughout the year, the thirteen fraternities and five sororities on campus plan various events open to the entire campus. These events have, in the past, included talent shows, dance marathons, and the annual Mr. Fraternity contest. The Greek system (fraternities and sororities) make up about twenty percent of the campus. Many of those involved in the Greek system enjoy it because it gives members a chance to get to know other students and to take part in large social events (each fraternity and sorority also takes part in several charity events), but the number is low enough to not overwhelm the campus. If a student chooses not to join the Greek system, he or she will still have no problem having a social life. It is also very common for people to interact with many people in an organization without being a member.

Spring Carnival

Each spring, the campus comes together for Carnegie Mellon's annual Spring Carnival. This three-day event includes shows, concerts, and contests. The two biggest elements of Spring Carnival are Booth and Buggy. Each organization has the opportunity to build a booth corresponding to the carnival's theme, and each structure includes a game in which all of the money raised goes to charity. These booths are often quite large and quite elaborate.

These same organizations build buggies, high-tech soapbox derby cars, to race through Schenley Park. The buggies look like torpedoes on wheels and are driven by the smallest student (usually a female) that the organization can find. People push the buggies up the hill and then let them coast through the park (some get up to speeds of thirty-five to forty miles per hour).

Buggy has been one of the highlights of my life at Carnegie Mellon. At first, I wasn't sure about it. Everyone seemed to know exactly what they were doing but I had no clue. However, the first time I pushed, the whole team ran along beside me cheering—after that first push, I felt like a pro. I've also made a lot of friends through Buggy. There's a lot to be said about the friends you can make getting up at 5:00 A.M. on a weekend.

FINANCIAL AID

The total cost of a year at Carnegie Mellon, including tuition, room and board, books, etc.), can run as high as $30,000. With a price tag like this, it's obvious that many students will need some kind of financial aid. Depending on your financial need, your financial aid package might include a combination of grants, loans, and work-study. About seventy percent of the freshmen who entered in a recent year received some sort of financial aid. The average package was about $16,600. Although you are not guaranteed financial assistance, most people who are eligible and in need receive it.

Work-study gives students the opportunity to have on-campus jobs in order to make money to pay some of their college expenses. These jobs include positions in offices, food service, the child-care facility, and the library, to name a few. These jobs usually don't take up more than ten to fifteen hours a week and they allow the student to make extra money that they might need to buy books or for other necessities. Since there are so many jobs available, students may work on campus even if they don't qualify for need-based work-study.

My parents own a small business and don't have a lot of extra money. When I applied to Carnegie Mellon, I was worried that the cost would be too high for them to afford. If it wasn't for the financial aid, there is no chance that I would be here. I've talked to several of my friends about this and many of them are in the same position.

GRADUATES

There are almost 46,000 Carnegie Mellon alumni spread out all over the world. The goals achieved and backgrounds of these alumni are as diverse as when they began their careers at Carnegie Mellon. There is no one category that all graduates fit into. There are Carnegie Mellon alumni who have become great actors, writers, artists, and scientists, over 2,000 alumni are presidents or vice-presidents of corporations, more than 1,400 teach as professors at universities, and thirty are deans.

PROMINENT GRADS:

- **Jack Klugman, '48, Actor**
- **Andy Warhol, '49, Artist**
- **Raymond Smith, '59, Bell Atlantic Chairman and CEO**
- **Paul Allaire, '66, Xerox Chairman and CEO**
- **Iris Ranier Dart, '66, Novelist**
- **Ted Danson, '72, Actor**
- **Holly Hunter, '80, Actress**
- **Rob Marshall, '82, Choreographer**
- **Keith Lockhart, '83, Music Conductor**

Very few of these people graduate and go immediately to the top; however, many of these graduates are used to working hard to achieve their goals. After four years at Carnegie Mellon, these people know how to get the job done. Because of Carnegie Mellon's reputation for preparing students with real-world and practical experience, employers are eager to hire recent Carnegie Mellon graduates. About seventy-five percent of graduates get job offers within six months of graduation, while another twenty-two percent go on to graduate school immediately after commencement.

There is a large network of Carnegie Mellon graduates organized all over the world. This network helps fellow alumni who decide to relocate or need advice concerning a job. It is also an invaluable resource for meeting people in your field. The one thing that all Carnegie Mellon alumni do have in common is the pride and tradition of being part of this network. You could go anywhere in the world and be able to chat with alumni about Spring Carnival or Schenley Park. Although alumni may have complained about their classes or other things while they were here, very few can admit that being a student at Carnegie Mellon did not help them in the long run.

SUMMING UP

Carnegie Mellon has, in a word, everything—there is nothing that you could not find at Carnegie Mellon. Walking across the Cut (the grassy area in the middle of campus), you can see people studying, playing Frisbee, reciting poetry, sleeping . . . the list could go on and on. The people who end up coming to Carnegie Mellon are from all over the world, with different cultures, different beliefs, and different interests. But they all exist together. People say that going away to college is as educational outside of the classroom as it is inside. This has never been more true than it is at Carnegie Mellon.

Being from Pittsburgh originally, I was worried when I came to Carnegie Mellon because I thought that I'd miss out on the experience of going to a college out of state, but I've met so many interesting people, not only from all over the country, but all over the world! Even though I didn't leave Pittsburgh, I feel that I've learned more than I would have if I had gone away to another school.

There is so much here, it can be very intimidating at first. Where do I go? What do I do? How do I make friends? It's impossible to know exactly how to approach it. Fortunately, somebody has already planned this. For the first week that freshmen are on campus they are involved in, as many students would tell you, the best orientation anywhere. Through the entire week, students take part in planned activities, learn how to deal with being away from home, and meet more people than they could ever remember. This orientation is just the beginning of the series of support systems that exist here. No matter what you're doing, there will always be somebody there to help you. There are programs here ranging from peer tutoring to peer counseling. If you have a problem that you don't think a peer can help you with, the professors and other staff are always willing to try to help you. Basically, no matter what's going on, if you look for help, you'll find it.

The students that attend Carnegie Mellon are motivated, driven, and goal-oriented. Everyone here knows that everyone else has worked hard to get here. They're all in the same boat, and this brings everyone closer together. College is about the things you learn and the friends you make in the process. You'll have both at Carnegie Mellon.

There isn't anybody who goes here—or has ever gone here—who won't tell you that everything about this place is intense. People work hard. They have goals and dreams. But they also have friends and fun. Don't ever let anybody tell you that it's too hard.

❑ *Jennifer Demers, Class of 1999*

CLAREMONT MCKENNA COLLEGE

Claremont McKenna College
Claremont, CA 91711

(909) 621-8088

E-mail: admission@mckenna.edu
Web site: http://www.mckenna.edu

Enrollment

Full-time ❑ women: 411
❑ men: 541

INTRODUCING CLAREMONT MCKENNA

At Claremont McKenna College, each student is looked at as an individual. Each education has a significant meaning, as if each student is an investment. Indeed, CMC believes its small liberal arts environment is a training ground for tomorrow's leaders. Boasting alumni who include California State Senator Robert Hurtt and Congressman David Dreier, CMC has proven that a personal education provides its students with much sought-after decision-making abilities.

CMC's strength is leadership, with its curriculum emphasizing economics, government, international relations, and public affairs. From the first day of freshman introductions, students are encouraged to speak up, speak out, and speak clearly. When students are not taking oral exams or giving individual presentations, CMCers are found engaged in debate with their professors and each other. With a 9:1 student-faculty ratio, the "large" classes contain around thirty students. Some classes are as small as six, and it is not unheard of to have a one-on-one course with a professor. There is no getting lost in the throng, nor escaping the probing eyes of a professor who wants to make sure each and every student is comprehending the course material.

My first freshman literature class assignment was to write a 250-word essay on a book I felt was significant to my life. The professor said it wouldn't be graded; he merely wanted to get a feel for who we were and what our writing styles were like. I wanted to choose something that defined me, something that truly stood out. Amidst the essays on Walden, the Grapes of Wrath, *and the* Bible, *I slipped my paper atop the pile—a piece on Dr. Seuss'* Oh, the Places You'll Go!

Our professor brought back a pile of crumpled essays, stained from top to bottom with red ink. We sucked in our breath as he began to pass out the papers. "Weak. Lacking. Drivel." He offered a one word comment for each student, laying each essay face down. When he reached my seat, he paused a moment before laying my marked up essay face-up. "Mediocre."

After momentarily reveling that my paper hadn't been labeled as "Trash," the insult set in. Mediocre? Me, the composition goddess, the mighty ruler of the written word? Believing my book choice to be the cause of the resulting comment, I marched to my professor's office and demanded an explanation.

"The content was lacking, your argument was weak, and the grammatical errors were horrendous," I was told. But before I could hang up my hopes for a tasseled mortarboard, my professor added: "The risk you took was mediocre."

That was the day I found out my perceived status of Queen Ruler—the one my ego had claimed after tallying an endless stream of compliments in high school—had been reduced. Strangely, I didn't mind. My new status was Student. And boy, did I have a lot to learn!

Outside of the classroom, students continue to debate everything from current political issues to whether Collins Dining Hall should serve more ice cream or frozen yogurt. The majority of students participate in student government, whether as a dormitory president, a liaison to the Academic Committee, a party chair, or a community service coordinator. Even socially, CMC teaches students to be the kind of leaders who are responsible decision-makers.

Background and Location

CMC was established in 1946 as the third college in the five—soon to become six—Claremont Colleges cluster. Modeled after England's Oxford University and its tradition of multiple small colleges, The Claremont Colleges offer the best of both worlds. Students can cross-register for any class offered at any of the other Claremont Colleges. CMC students thus have the personal attention a small college offers, along with the diversity of a large campus that the cluster presents with its various academic strengths and social offerings.

Located in a small town thirty-five miles east of downtown Los Angeles, the fifty-acre campus is self-sustaining by necessity. Students are responsible for planning their own entertainment, and there is never a shortage of activities or parties. Whenever a desire for some special interest activity pops up, students quickly jump on the organizational bandwagon.

Why CMC? It's a question I've grown accustomed to hearing, and one that I've never had to stop to ponder an answer.

Attending school in Claremont had been the furthest thing from my mind before I visited CMC. Claremont seemed too close for comfort to my home and family, and I envisioned my college years to be on a large campus in a metropolitan area. But Mom and Dad swore by the excellent reputation of The Claremont Colleges, so I promised at least to consider CMC, if only to humor them.

Was I ever glad my parents twisted my arm! From the first time I visited the campus, I sensed CMC possessed something special. The students seemed truly upbeat here, and I was amazed at how friendly everyone was. As I walked through the quad with my host, every passing student said hello, and many stopped to chat with us—quite a contrast with the sterile environments I had viewed at larger campuses.

Classes were equally amazing. Not only were they smaller than any I'd seen elsewhere, but the professors actually knew every student's full name! That was the deciding factor. I realized the best place for me was here, where I was an individual with a face and an opinion rather than just a name on a roster.

ADMISSION REQUIREMENTS

CMC recruits for potential alumni; if the qualified candidate is the one who admission officers believe will succeed in the classroom and contribute to the campus community, then the ideal candidate is the one who they believe will take that successful education and apply it in their career and in life.

At the first level of the admission process, an applicant's academic achievement is reviewed, with the assumption that past performance will correlate with future performance. A habit of high school activities, such as community service, athletics, student government, or a part-time job, is another important indicator of an ability to manage time wisely. High school involvement also shows the possible ways a student might contribute to the campus community.

"We would like to see a few activities in which the student has maintained long-term depth and commitment over time rather than a long laundry list of things that look like they're just trying to gather brownie points on their application," says CMC Dean of Admission Richard Vos.

Applicants are asked to list the number of years and of hours they participated in each high school activity. The application also asks if the student plans to participate in similar college activities.

At the next level of admission analysis, application readers look for evidence of advanced coursework. The types of courses a student has taken are looked at in the context of what the high school offers, as some secondary schools have honors courses, others Advanced Placement or international baccalaureate, and others college preparatory classes.

A student's transcript is reviewed for the pattern of grades throughout the high school career. CMC admission officers target students with progressive grades and those with outstanding academic performance in the senior year. That last year is crucial, Vos said, because students who carry their grades through to the end will likely be people who see projects through and complete tasks to the best of their ability. Each year, CMC draws a number of National Merit finalists and semifinalists, as well as high school valedictorians.

Standardized Tests

CMC uses the SAT I and the ACT as numerical measures of academic performance. At least one of these two tests is required, though most students opt to submit scores for both. The majority of those admitted in 1997 scored above 600 on the Verbal portion of SAT I (eight-four percent). On SAT I Math, fifty-three percent scored above 600. Scores for the ACT were also high, with ninety percent of applicants garnering above twenty-eight points. The admission committee highly regards those who strive for self-improvement. Don't wait until the last minute to take the tests. Those who make an effort to improve their test scores are looked upon favorably.

Recommendations and Personal Statement

The remainder of the freshman application consists of recommendations from the applicant's school guidance counselor and from a teacher; a personal statement in which the student may discuss personality traits, special achievements, or an unusual experience, any of which may distinguish their application from others; and an essay on an event, occurrence, or issue of local, state, national, or international importance that took place within the last five years. Students tend to write their essays on the hot topic of the moment (many recent essays have dealt with police brutality, cloning, and the media's coverage of the O.J. Simpson case). An interview is recommended, but not required.

Admission Plans

Freshmen are admitted in both the fall and spring. Early Decision, Early Admission, and Deferred Admission plans are available. To apply for Early Decision, applicants must submit all materials by November 15. Regular Admission applications are due January 15 for fall entry and November 1 for spring entry.

In its entirety, the application tells a lot about the personal makeup of each applicant, including behavior, attitude, beliefs, and preferences.

"We're not trying to maximize pure intellectual performance," Vos says. "Certainly, we want to have good grades, test scores, and recommendations, but we balance it a lot more with other considerations."

Adds Professor John Ferling, chairman of the Admission Committee, "What we are looking for are men and women with all-around qualifications. While we are interested very much in the academic part, we do not like 'grade grabbers'—students who study very hard for grades, not necessarily for understanding and learning."

There are no geographical or gender quotas at CMC, and the Admission Committee is gender- and ethnicity-blind in the reading of applications. The school does try to recruit nationally, and is active in encouraging women and minorities to apply.

ACADEMIC LIFE

The faculty at CMC takes an interest in each of their students. With average class sizes ranging from eighteen to twenty-one, the professors address each student by name after only a few class sessions. It is quickly noticed when a student is absent from class, and professors are known to telephone students to find out the reason. CMC professors are easily accessible, and many will accommodate meetings with students outside of their regular office hours. Many professors will have lunch in the dining hall, and spirited debates between groups of students and professors often arise during the meal.

I had assumed my class was going to be canceled. The entirety of my Introduction to Comparative Government course consisted of myself and the professor. Even stranger, my professor wasn't waiting for anyone else to arrive that first day of class. He began promptly at 2:30 P.M. by handing me a syllabus and explaining why each text had been chosen.

I looked around nervously, knowing I needed to take this course this semester in order to get through my required courses. There was no way a professor would teach a course—and an intro course at that—to a single student. We talked for the remainder of the class period, me on the edge of my seat thinking at any minute the professor would say, "It's canceled."

As we reached the end of the hour, my professor smiled and said, "See you next week." And that's how it went for the entire semester. Talk about personal attention!

Majors

CMC offers single majors, double majors, and a specially designed dual major, which rewards students for intense study in two subjects with fewer required courses than a double major. Many students choose this option to allow for a greater number of electives. There are also special majors like politics, philosophy, and economics (PPE), or students may design their own major, subject to approval.

Because of the unique set-up of The Claremont Colleges cluster, students may take courses from a wide spectrum including Dances of Mexico, Literature in the Age of Darwin, Science Fiction and the Alien, Life Course of Women, and Juvenile Delinquency.

Grades

Grades are based on a twelve-point scale, with 12 equaling an A, 11 an A–, and so forth. Attendance, class participation, essays, and tests all mean points, and are thus all pivotal to academic success at CMC. Because students are competing only against themselves, cutthroat practices are unknown here. Making the Dean's List for a semester requires a 10.0 average. Students maintaining 11.0 and above qualify as Distinguished Scholars.

Requirements

At the core of the CMC education are general requirements of three semesters of social science, two each of sciences and humanities, and one each of English, math, a foreign language, and civilization. There is much room to explore through the general requirements, and these can help the undecided major choose a field of study.

Additionally, all CMCers are required to complete a senior thesis, a substantial paper on the subject of the student's choice. Seniors choose a faculty reader and decide whether the work will be a one-semester or two-semester project. A thesis is considered by almost every student to be the greatest challenge of their scholastic career. Students compose between seventy and several hundred pages for this feat, and after dropping off the final submission, many can be seen dancing in the fountain, spraying each other with fine mists of champagne. Indeed, the feeling is that after you've done a CMC thesis, everything else life throws your way will be a piece of cake.

Research and Other Programs

Opportunities to participate in ground-breaking research abound. The school supports no less than eight research institutes, including the Rose Institute of State and Local Government, which was a key resource for government officials during the redistricting of

California. CMC also organizes practicum programs in a variety of subjects for students to have a hands-on experience. Recent programs have included practica on creative cinematography and a simulation of how groups interact when confined in small spaces.

Lectures

Outside of the classroom, students may increase their educational awareness by attending lectures on current topics of debate. International Place, the home of the international program of The Claremont Colleges, offers weekly luncheon speakers on the CMC campus with discussions on the political climate abroad. Most weeknights CMC holds lectures in the Marian Miner Cook Athenaeum. Drawing prominent guest lecturers in politics, psychology, music, art, entertainment, and many other fields, the "Ath" offers a taste of culture along with culinary splendor. Feasting on such delights as gazpacho, couscous, Maine lobster, and petit fours, students have interacted with speakers including authors Ray Bradbury and Ken Kesey (*One Flew Over the Cuckoo's Nest*) and actor Danny Glover. Best of all, every Ath lecture is free to CMC students. With the fine dining and conversation in the plush meeting hall, many students find time to attend Ath lectures several times a month.

SOCIAL LIFE AND ACTIVITIES

It's 8:00 on a Thursday night at CMC. Hamlet *has been read, bio notes for Monday's test reviewed, the Con Law paper due in two weeks has been outlined. Once the studying is done, what on earth does a CMC student do?*

A flyer on the dorm bulletin board says that Claremont musician Matt Nathanson is performing at eleven. There's an action flick playing on the big screen over at the Hub (the student snack bar and lounge) in an hour. Party at Benson Hall. Still have some time before the evening's adventures get started—maybe a buddy will want to grab a cup of frozen yogurt at the nearby 21 Choices.

Choices. That is what social life at CMC is all about. There is so much to do, so many clubs to join, sports to play, causes to espouse. With so many options, the question CMC students find themselves asking is not "What will I do today?" but rather "Which activities am I going to have to sacrifice this semester?"

Around ninety-five percent of CMC students choose to live on campus. CMC offers plenty of high-tech options for entertainment. There's cable television on the Hub's big screen and TVs with satellite dishes in all of the dorm lounges. Each dorm room has its own Internet hook-up, and there are additional hook-ups in the computer lab.

Gender and Ethnic Activities

CMC sponsors a variety of gender and ethnic activities. Some recent events included workshops on how to spot and prevent sexual harassment and a speaking appearance by actor James Earl Jones during Black History Month. An annual International Festival, complete with traditional food, dance, and song from countries around the world, is the best-attended event on campus. CMC has its own Women's Forum, a club focusing on women's issues. It also supports ethnic education centers shared by The Claremont College's cluster, including the Office of Black Student Affairs, the Chicano/Latino Studies Center, and the Asian-American Resource Center.

"The relationship between different ethnic groups on campus is very fruitful," says Anton Winder, '98, an African American. "There are a lot of politically active organizations and a lot of persons who are very concerned with promoting cultural diversity and demonstrating why it's important to value cultural diversity."

Community Service

Community service is a popular activity both groups of students and individuals engage in. CMC students have volunteered at the local House of Ruth shelter for battered women, tutored at area public schools, and assisted with environmental clean-ups at southern California beaches and mountain regions. Recent group efforts included a trip to an orphanage in Tijuana, Mexico, where participants held a volunteer clean-up.

On- and Off-Campus Activities

A thriving nonalcoholic scene is present throughout the week. Events include Coffeehouse, a weekend evening "cafe" at the student center where students can enjoy free coffee, hot chocolate, and tea while listening to live bands. There is also Thursday Night Live, an evening event that has included performances by a hypnotist and comedy routines. The campus Playbill club presents recently released movies on campus for two dollars a showing.

For a truly cultural experience, students can head off campus for a play, museum, or sporting event with the Cultural Affairs Committee, a group that purchases group rate tickets and coordinates transportation for these activities. The committee has held recent trips to Cirque du Soleil and major productions of *Joseph and the Amazing Technicolor Dream Coat* and *Riverdance*.

Just about any weeknight after 9:00 P.M., the Hub's snack bar, dining area, and video game corner are filled with bodies and activity. Right next door, students line up in the Frazee student lounge for games of foosball and pool, or a chance to switch the music on the stereo system.

Parties

There's always a party in progress on at least one of the campuses within the Claremont cluster. CMC throws its share, including a popular seventies-themed "Disco Inferno" party, where students head out to area thrift shops to purchase bell-bottom slacks and platform shoes. The annual Homecoming bash, also known as Monte Carlo, serves up the appropriate gambling atmosphere complete with faux blackjack, craps, and roulette tables.

Dorms

Dormitory spirit runs high at CMC. While the college does not have fraternities or sororities, dorms fiercely compete to be number one at anything and everything. After struggling to create the best-themed party or to collect the most clothing for local shelters, dorms head for the battleground of glory—the local ice rink. There, opposing dorm teams butt heads in games of broomball, a version of ice hockey played with brooms in place of hockey sticks.

The majority of CMCers engage in multiple activities through the entire week. Many are involved in sports, clubs, community service, student government, and campus employment. Among the 185 groups on campus, CMC has booming Republican and Democrat clubs, a forensics team, a literary magazine, two campus newspapers, and an international club with its own facility.

Before breakfast, after class, during my lunch hour, into the wee hours of the morning—whenever I could find a spare moment, I was participating in some club or activity. Like most CMCers, I found time for the evening meetings of a spectrum of clubs: College Republicans, Women's Forum, the Volunteer Student Admission Committee. On Sundays, I was at meetings challenging other dorms to broomball competitions in my capacity as a dormitory president, on Tuesday afternoon I was planning a trip to see a taping of The Jay Leno Show *through the class council, and Wednesday I met with the other members of the Social Affairs Committee to scheme how we could get a local company to donate food and beverage for a campus country western party.*

Mondays were production nights at the student newspaper office. I'd usually take a change of clothes and my books with me to the newspaper, in case it was going to be an all-nighter. And sleep? I don't remember getting any. By graduation, it felt like I had been involved with half the clubs on my campus. I only wished I had another four years to try out more of the others.

FINANCIAL AID

The first time I saw the price tag of a CMC education, my eyes bulged and my heart fell. I handed the information packet back to the admission officer, picked up my bag, and muttered, "There's no way my folks can afford this." With the price tag of many private colleges being what it is, a working class kid like me has to leave it at that, abandoning the dream of attending anything but a community college. But the CMC admission officer reassured me that if I was admitted, the college would make every effort to work with my family on the financial end.

Though I trusted that promise, I still anticipated heartbreak. I didn't even bother to show my dad the numbers. CMC seemed an impossible dream.

The acceptance letter arrived in the same envelope as my financial aid award. Hands trembling, I ripped open the financial aid packet and tallied the numbers. I'd have to take out a reasonable loan, I'd have to work a few hours every week at an on-campus job, and there it was—a completely affordable amount from my family. CMC said it would foot a huge chunk of the bill in the form of a grant that I wouldn't be required to repay. Thank goodness for a fiscally responsible college with strong financial support from its alumni!

Almost seventy-five percent of all CMCers receive some form of financial aid, with more than half receiving need-based aid. The average freshman award is $15,808. Campus jobs abound, with everything from ringing up sales in the student store, to proofreading copy for the school newspaper, to putting the tablecloths on at the Athenaeum lecture hall.

Additionally, CMC invites freshmen to compete for the thirty McKenna Achievement Awards of $3,000 or $5,000 each. The awards are not need-based, though applicants must have the full CMC admission application completed by January 1 to apply. McKenna Scholars are required to maintain a GPA in the upper half of their class and carry a minimum of three courses in a semester in order to remain eligible for the grant.

Another way CMC works to keep the student's cost down is to keep them on the "four-year plan." The college does its best to ensure that everyone is taking all of their required classes by holding one-on-one mandatory meetings between students and the faculty advisor of their choice. Unlike many state colleges, it's relatively easy to enroll in all of one's required courses.

GRADUATES

The CMC education does not stop after graduation. Throughout the year, CMC's active alumni association plans educational seminars, speaker events, and mixers for alums, many of which are free. In recent years, all-day alumni workshops have been held on campus with topics including use and significance of the Internet and building an investment portfolio. Another recent event was a luncheon speaker series held in downtown Los Angeles. Speakers included Republican vice-presidential nominee Jack Kemp and California Senator Dianne Feinstein.

The Alumni Association works hard to keep alums in touch with each other by publishing an updated alumni directory every five years. At any time, both alums and current students can access contact and business information on other alumni. The association also holds a series of career nights where students can speak directly with alums who work in different industries.

PROMINENT GRADS

- **Paul Brickman, Motion Picture Writer/Director**
- **David Dreier, U.S. Congressman**
- **Ray Drummond, Jazz Musician**
- **Robert Nakasone, Toys "R" Us President**
- **Thomas Pritzker, Hyatt Corporation President**
- **Laura Angelica Simón, Documentary Film Producer**

The staff in the career center at CMC had been extremely helpful to me when I was job searching as a student. Still, I was somewhat surprised how supportive—and helpful—the staff was when I returned to campus on a job hunt two years after I graduated. I was working at my second job since graduation, and, dissatisfied, decided it was time for a change. The career counselors provided me with resource books, lists of Internet job sites, alumni contacts, and actual job listings. One lead I was given sounded particularly appealing, and the career staff gave me some good advice on how to woo the prospective employer. I ended up applying for the position and today I'm working in the position of my dreams.

SUMMING UP

At Claremont McKenna College, students are offered the chance to carve out an education—both scholarly and social—that is as unique as the students themselves.

The life skills one learns at CMC take students far beyond the walls of the classroom. Professors emphasize leadership and communication in all courses through classroom debate, oral presentations, and group projects. Students learn to depend on others and trust in themselves.

Debate does not end when the students exit the classroom. Rather, the subjects touched on in class are taken back to the dormitories and into the common areas to be further pondered and debated. CMCers turn things inside and out to reach an understanding of concepts and do not give up on a matter if a solution doesn't readily present itself. Students here know that the questions are as important as the answers.

Each student is treated as an individual with legitimate beliefs and opinions. Professors know each student by name—both first and last—and offer all students personal attention. CMC students are graded as much on class participation as test scores, ensuring each student the chance to prove his or her own personal merit. Students are used to choosing their own topics for research papers, and busywork is nonexistent.

As a member of The Claremont College cluster, CMCers are offered a wide variety of courses from many different schools of thought. Class size is compact, even at other campuses within the cluster. Rather than sitting through lecture after lecture in oversized seminar courses, students are able to ask questions and engage in discussion directly with professors and other students. With the small classroom structure, many classes are able to break down into smaller groups of five or six for more in-depth conversations.

If the environment of CMC ever becomes claustrophobic, a student here may escape the campus and venture out into the other Claremont Colleges. Combined, the cluster has the feel of a large campus, with many opportunities for new activities and friendships.

Having multiple choices and the power to create one's own educational path are not what every college-bound person is searching for. CMC students must be strong of heart and unafraid to take hold of their own destiny. Only by taking charge of one's own life does one prepare to lead others.

❑ *Holly Vicente, B.A.*

COLBY COLLEGE

Colby College
Waterville, ME 04901

(207) 872-3168, (800) 723-3032 Admissions
Fax: (207) 872-3474

E-mail: admissions@colby.edu
Web site: http://www.colby.edu

Enrollment

Full-time ❑ women: 922
❑ men: 831

INTRODUCING COLBY

The happiest students in America! Inevitably, at some point during a Colby student's four-year tenure, another poll or article comes out proclaiming Colby as the bastion of joy in collegiate America again. It's easy to understand why. Students reappear on Mayflower Hill in the waning days of August, greeted by beautiful green grass, bountiful trees, and a wonderful view of Kennebec Valley from the steps of Miller Library. Frisbees and softballs clog the quad on Roberts Row and college-organized barbecues seem to be required before classes begin. This is when these articles are written and the polls are taken. Who couldn't be the happiest person on earth? Two days afterwards, it begins to snow and, quite intelligently, the pollsters are long gone. But seriously, Colby students have a lot to be happy about throughout the year.

With the great professors teaching you, thirty-two sports you might choose from, and beautiful places to visit, the questions of whom you will be sharing these four years with and where you will live become apparent. The Colby student body is primarily from the Northeast, with Massachusetts, Maine, and New York being largely represented. Like many New England institutions, Colby too has made significant progress in recent years in diversifying its population. The recently opened Pugh Multicultural Center (1996) is home to a dozen international and minority clubs, providing valuable office space for each and has helped in this effort.

At my exit interview, the dean of students asked me to summarize what defined my Colby experience. I sat back and thought about all that I had seen and done and said that I would tell someone that Colby truly allowed me to maximize my potential. I had taken a challenging set of courses from professors who honestly cared about my success and academic growth, I had taken leadership positions in some of the extracurricular activities I was involved with, I had developed long-lasting relationships with friends made over four years, and I had simply grown as an individual. At the risk of sounding trite, I told her I wouldn't have changed a thing. For that, I will forever remember my experience at Colby.

In general, Colby students often leave the campus after four years wishing commencement could be just another summer break from which they would return to Mayflower Hill in September. While it is true that many of the other New England schools will have similar stories, it is an unexplained warmness that most Colby students feel from their first days on campus that continues to earn the student body the title of "happiest in the nation."

ADMISSIONS REQUIREMENTS

Becoming one of these very happy students isn't getting any easier. In recent years, Colby has averaged more than 4,200 applications and just over 1,400 acceptances—a yield of just over thirty percent. The application itself offers no particularly unique aspects, but includes essays, recommendations, transcript requests, and personal data. Unlike its peer schools in Maine, Colby still requires the submission of scores from SAT I or the ACT. International applicants must also submit a TOEFL score of 550 or more. Average scores among successful applicants have climbed steadily each year, most recently at 650/650 for SAT I and 28 for the ACT. Other important considerations include AP and honors courses, leadership, extracurricular and volunteer accomplishments, and personal intangibles. An interview, while not required, is highly recommended as both an extra measure by which the college can judge candidates, as well as a measure for candidates to truly judge the college. As mentioned earlier, Colby is not shy in the use of technology, offering its application on disk on its Web site or by request.

And like many other of the smaller, liberal arts institutions, Colby gives extra consideration to students applying in one of the college's two Early Decision rounds. Statistically, slightly more than ten percent of applicants are Early Decision candidates and thirty-four percent of the final pool of admitted students was accepted in one of these two rounds.

I was nearing the end of my New England-school swing when I arrived on Colby's campus just after classes had begun in early September. Inexplicably, I got a feeling as I walked around that this was the place for me. I interviewed with an assistant dean of admissions who made me feel completely at home. The interview was less like a test—no "think like a tree" questions—and more like a conversation about who I was and how Colby and I matched up. I left the campus later that afternoon and headed home with my parents. My Early Decision application was submitted within two weeks. The sense of joy I got when Colby's acceptance letter arrived in my mailbox on December 7 was matched equally by the experiences I had and the friends I made during the four years I spent on Mayflower Hill.

Due partially to its location in central Maine, Colby has long had a mostly Caucasian, mostly Northeast-based student body. While male/female ratios have long remained relatively equal, minority recruitment, diversity issues, and a heterogeneous acceptance pool have remained a priority in recent years. Admissions staff actively recruit students from around the country and have successfully made inroads in achieving these diversity goals.

ACADEMIC LIFE

Colby students aren't only happy about the multitude of options available to them outside the classroom; the academic environment at Colby brings smiles to the face of nearly all undergraduates. Unlike a big university, where Social Security numbers are your most frequent means of identification, Colby professors and students are often on a first-name basis after a few weeks into the fall semester. Fellow students also work with you to make class exercises and homework meaningfully relevant. There are no fights to be "above the mean" when it comes to grading, as professors shun a grading curve for merit-based grades where an A is not limited to some percentage of the class.

The Faculty

The most important reason for the happiness of the student body lies in the college's most incredible asset: its faculty. Inside the classroom, professors preside over small groups of students—except for some large, introductory classes in the first year—and share insights and knowledge, rather than facts and textbook quotes. During fall and spring months, smatterings of students in upper-level courses escape to the grassy plateaus outside the library for changes of scenery. Outside the classroom, however, is where Colby's faculty outshines their peer groups at competitive institutions. Access to professors for both academic enrichment and social involvement is unprecedented. Office hours are flexible, home phone numbers are often made available, and extra-help sessions are the rule and not the exception. Additionally, it is nearly expected that residence hall events, athletic contests, and cultural happenings will include faculty members' attendance with regularity. Annual rituals such as Professors Bassett's and Boylan's rendition of Halloween stories always exceed the posted capacity in Lorimer Chapel.

Programs

Colby offers B.A. degrees in fifty defined programs, with an unlimited potential for creating combined or independent majors outside these defined boundaries. Newer programs include business, social, and such culturally relevant programs as computer science, environmental policy, French studies, and Latin-American studies. In addition, the 1996 completion of the $6 million F.W. Olin Science Center has given Colby a state-of-the-art edge in the natural science programs. Double majors, minors, and concentrations also abound throughout the student body, with heavy competition for admission into such programs as creative writing and education studies. The bottom line, however, is that Colby's distribution requirements challenge students to expose themselves to experiences across the curriculum.

While declaring myself a government major with a creative writing minor early in my sophomore year, I continued to enroll in courses that were outside these disciplines. My most memorable courses were studies of American music, analyses of classic short stories, and introductory chemistry because they challenged me to think about material that wasn't comfortable, but noticeably important.

Exchange Program

Another important and popular avenue of study at Colby is the off-campus/exchange program. More than sixty percent of the student body will spend at least one full semester away from Waterville in one of hundreds of approved destinations. Colby maintains its own programs in locations such as London; Salamanca, Spain; Cork, Ireland; and St. Petersburg, Russia. Additionally, students enroll in programs from peer institutions centered in large and small towns around the world, both domestically and internationally. An interesting aspect of Colby's support for off-campus study is the selected group of incoming students who are given the opportunity to enroll in a Colby-run international study program in London, Salamanca, or Cork for their first semester before beginning regular classwork on campus.

My off-campus study was spent at American University in Washington D.C. In the university's "Semester in Journalism" immersion, I spent three days in the classroom and around town, hearing guest lectures from respected national and international journalists covering domestic and international politics. The other two days were spent on a university-sponsored internship at NBC News where I worked with several national reporters and producers in tight-access locations such as the U.S. Senate chambers, the White House press room, and foreign embassies. Meanwhile, my roommate was spending his semester living in a convent in Rome studying Italian language, history, and arts while spending weekends on the Italian rail system witnessing the devastation in Pompeii or visiting the fashionable shops of Milan.

Integrated Semester Program

Colby has also instituted an Integrated Semester program, combining professors and course material across academic disciplines in topics such as "The Post-War World: 1945–1970" and "Enlightenment and Revolution: 1775–1800." These programs encompass an entire semester's course load and are geared toward first-year students.

January Semester

Despite all these improvements and additions, Colby's most innovative program continues to be the long-standing January Program—affectionately known as Jan Plan—that allows students a month to create an academic program of their choice. With virtually limitless boundaries, except for the requirement that students must complete three Jan Plan programs, with the first year being spent on campus, students have completed three-week Outward Bound programs, trekked across African countries researching gender relations, trained with Olympic rowers, and interned in nearly every imaginable professional role in preparation for life after Colby.

My Jan Plan programs truly ranged across a variety of countries and experiences. My freshman Jan Plan was spent simulating the role of Minority Leader Robert Dole in the Mock U.S. Senate. Sophomore year was spent with my roommate visiting a graduated senior in Vienna, Austria, during the weeks before the Gulf War. Junior year was a study of classic "film noir" with Professor Lubin. As if that wasn't enough, I opted to take on a fourth Jan Plan my senior year in Key West, Florida, on a thirty-foot sailboat run by Outward Bound. While not your traditional learning experiences, I can honestly say I learned just as much during each one of these months as I did during the eight semesters I spent in the classroom.

SOCIAL LIFE AND ACTIVITIES

Residences

Residence halls at Colby form the nucleus of the college's campus life. Choices range from Mary Low Commons—home to the crunchier students on campus—to Roberts Row, a favorite of the jock community. First-year students are mixed evenly throughout every residence hall on a random basis, except for those requesting chemical-free or "quiet" housing, all of whom are accommodated. Halls are grouped into four commons clusters, which maintain their own governmental bodies and sponsor activities for students residing within them. Each commons also has its own dining facility—although students are not restricted to eating in their own commons dining hall—that serve similar menus with unique twists. Tuesday's Wok Night at Foss Hall attracts students from Drummond Hall on the other side of campus with a high degree of frequency. It is not uncommon to see groups of friends sitting at tables in Dana Hall for a couple of hours during dinner, eating and talking over garden burgers, pizza, or ice cream.

Individual Internet connections (one per occupant) and telephone and cable television outlets were added in 1997 to each room on campus. These technology improvements earned Colby a top-fifteen ranking in *Yahoo Internet Life*'s 1997 "Best Wired" Universities survey. New residence halls opened in 1997, adding 141 state-of-the-art rooms to Colby's housing stock. Older halls are currently undergoing more than $16 million in renovations—scheduled for completion by the year 2000—to modernize and expand living space.

Come Friday afternoon, following a long week of classes and activities, students at Colby take to the fields, the town, and the campus for a plethora of athletic contests, local attractions, and cultural happenings.

Athletics

Athletics at Colby, while not the type of contests that draw 80,000 screaming, face-painted fans, is a respected part of Colby life, for both varsity athletes as well as intramural wannabees. One of the major reasons for the popularity of athletics is the facility in which students can participate. Colby's Alfond Athletic Center is one of, if not the most, exciting and feature-rich athletic centers on the East Coast, encompassing more than 9,000 square feet of fitness, weight training, and exercise areas, four locker rooms, a full-sized gymnasium, a hockey rink, an Olympic-size swimming and diving pool, and indoor fieldhouse for tennis, track, and indoor practices. Of course, there are fields galore, more than fifty acres, for outdoor sports that accompany the Alfond Center.

With such fine facilities, Colby boasts of more than thirty Division III intercollegiate teams—except squash, skiing, and women's ice hockey which compete at the Division I level—and over 600 student-athletes who consistently compete for regional and national recognition. In recent years, men's basketball has earned numerous trips to national tournaments, women's ice hockey has produced an Olympic competitor, and several individuals have earned national championships in track and field. All of this is, of course, done without the benefit of athletic scholarships, which are banned in Division III. Colby's White Mules are consistently competitive within the NESCAC conference and, at times, across the national Division III rankings.

As for the non-varsity types, Colby's I-PLAY (intramural sports) and club team programs fill any void that might exist. Students can often be seen throwing axes for the Woodsmens' team, battling in a scrum at the Swamp during a rugby match, or tossing the discus for the Ultimate Frisbee club. Additionally, friends, dormmates, and acquaintances join up each season to battle opposing groups of students in intramural contests of soccer, football, softball, and hockey. Points are added up for wins and losses as teams battle for the I-PLAY cup in each of the various sports.

Life outside the classroom at Colby is dominated by a love for the outdoors. Located within a couple of hours from mountains, national parks, and the scenic Maine coastline, students are constantly headed in each of these directions. Avid skiers enjoy the proximity of Sugarloaf and Sunday River, while hikers head off to Acadia National Park on weekends, and water lovers can trek to Camden and Rockport for an ocean breeze, or make the shorter trip to the Belgrade Lakes for recreational watersports access. The college helps students become familiar with the area using the COOT (Colby Outdoor Orientation Trip) Program prior to matriculation. Students are sent off on a choice of more than 100 four-day weekend getaways to meet one another and experience all that Maine has to offer on land and sea.

Extracurricular Activities

If sports of any kind don't tickle your fancy, you can get involved with the extracurricular activities both on and off campus. A strong student government manages the political and social calendar for much of the student body's day-to-day needs. Commons governments, comprised of leaders from the four groups of the college's residence halls, help to provide direction as well. In addition, more than fifty clubs align the interests of their members, pursuing religious, cultural, political, and volunteer agendas. Club day in the Cotter Union often sees students maxing out on club sign-ups because of the multitude of choices available to them.

Fraternity Ban

Away from school, Colby students love to have fun. It wasn't always fun for Colby students, however. In 1984 Colby's Board of Trustees took the risky measure of abolishing the college's long-standing fraternity system. Students burned furniture in the quad between Roberts Union and the library to protest the move and the college's social life in subsequent years revolved around a new commons-based system sponsored by the college and the underground members of the now-illegal fraternities. The unfavorable tug-of-war lessened with each passing year and is now all but extinct. And, with these troubles in the past, the evolution of social activities has continued.

Alcohol

If you're looking for beer bashes, those too have become memories as the college, like many of its peer institutions, has cracked down with increasingly stiff alcohol policies on campus. Twenty-one-year-olds can host parties, but are held responsible for underage drinking violations. The majority of student parties have now moved off-campus to houses that continue to be occupied by Colby students year in and year out. Designated drivers shuttle classmates to and from these parties and local beer and liquor purveyors deliver the goods with a phone call and proper ID. Seniors and older juniors also populate local bars for weeknight stress-relievers. All in all, students battled the movement of alcohol and parties off-campus at first but, as always, have adjusted and seem just as satisfied now as they once were.

Student-Sponsored Events and Other Activities

Of course, if drinking beer is not what you are looking for, alternatives have never been a problem at Colby. Student-sponsored events abound on weekends, including cultural parties, dramatic presentations, concerts, and second-run movies for a few bucks in Lovejoy Hall. Student government sponsors one or two major musical acts a year on campus, in recent years attracting major national talent such as Jewel, The Indigo Girls, Ziggy Marley and the Melody Makers, and Blues Traveler.

The Colby Museum of Art, open seven days a week (except holidays), houses the works of Alex Katz in the new Paul Schupf Wing, an exhibit named as "one of the seven most exciting museum exhibitions in the United States" by *Condé Nast Traveler* magazine. Other major artists, including Andrew Wyeth and William Wegman, have also brought their traveling exhibitions through the museum.

Off Campus

Waterville also offers the usual staples of bowling alleys, pool halls, movie theaters, and restaurants that attract the attention of the Colby community. Students with cars can even take a short ride to Freeport for some late-night action at L.L. Bean, or some big-city exposure in downtown Portland, or a longer weekend trip to Boston, New York City, or beyond. There are no limits on automobile ownership on campus and much of the student body takes advantage of this flexibility.

> *I never felt constrained by Colby's location in central Maine. The Colby community has so much to offer in the way of cultural events and social activities. Some nights I find myself partying all night with people down at Champions and others I spend with my girlfriend, a video rental, and a pizza in our residence hall. Still other weekends we head off to Sugarloaf or Boston to get away. I always felt that Colby's location gave me more access to this wide range of choices rather than placing a limit on what I could experience.*

FINANCIAL AID

The hefty price tag that accompanies that admission letter presents a financial challenge for a number of Colby students. Approximately forty-four percent of incoming first-year students, and thirty-eight percent of sophomores and beyond receive financial aid in the form of scholarships, grants, loans, and work-study contracts. Additionally, more than sixty-six percent of students hold one of hundreds of part time, on-campus jobs.

GRADUATES

Life after Colby, while not nearly as fun as life at Colby, is a world of possibilities in both the academic and professional worlds. If four years isn't enough for you, almost twenty percent of your class will feel the same as they head directly for the nation's top graduate programs in medicine, business, law, and other general disciplines. Indeed, more than seventy percent of Colby's alumni seek further education within five years of graduation.

For those who choose to spend a few years away from the classroom, the Office of Career Services maintains large and updated databases of Colby's alumni throughout the country, third-party reference books, and on-line services allowing students to search corporate and public-sector employer profiles and a hefty schedule of on-campus recruiting programs that connect students to employers. Résumé critiques and mock interviews are also conducted for seniors.

PROMINENT GRADS

Five Pulitzer Prize winners, including historians Doris Kearns Goodwin and Alan Taylor, authors E. Annie Proulx and Gregory White Smith and journalist Robert Capers, call Colby their alma mater.

Notable alumni attest to the value of a Colby education in the real world. Additionally, Colby students represent the school in nearly every imaginable professional role, including network television careers, Olympic ice hockey participation, and major international policy-making roles. Any of Colby's thousands of alumni are often more than willing to assist students with internships, full-time jobs, and simple advice both before and after graduation. Most importantly, Colby graduates acknowledge the importance of their education with generous gifts to the college, including twenty-four endowed faculty chairs during the past seven years and more than $100 million in pledges to The Campaign for Colby, a capital fund-raising drive designed to boost endowment, financial aid efforts, and campus redesigns and additions.

SUMMING UP

In short, there are many good reasons why Colby students are the happiest in the nation. They are academically challenged individuals who, both on and off campus, enrich their experiences across a wide variety of disciplines. They are athletically motivated, capturing ECAC championships in several team sports, excelling as recognized individual and team leaders, and earning the support of a dedicated and talented coaching staff. They are socially satisfied, making tight relationships with classmates over a beer in the campus Spa or a coffee at Jorgensen's in downtown Waterville. They are also culturally enriched, watching one of the many dramatic performances put on in Runnals Union, musical concerts in historic Lorimer Chapel, speakers on campus during the Spotlight event series, or catching an independent flick at Railroad Square Cinema.

True, life is not all about fun and good times. There is pressure to succeed. After all, an education at Colby is expensive and you (and your parents) want you to get the most for your money. There are also times you will wish that Colby's small size was expanded to one in which you could just disappear for a little while. There are times that your charisma in the classroom may take a slight vacation after a long night with the books, or maybe a longer night with your friends. A weekend tryst with a classmate may become the subject of lunchtime discussion for people you hardly thought you knew. The fishbowl that allows your hangovers to coincide with a multitude of questions from your professor, and your private relationships to be public knowledge, can truly make you wish for a campus four times larger. However, just like the time your mom found out that you lied about being at a friend's house studying, everyone forgets about your moments of weakness and life goes on.

In the end, if you are looking for four years in which you can challenge your mind, be exposed to beautiful surroundings, make life-long friendships, get to know professors who will serve as mentors long after you graduate, and earn a degree that maintains its value, Colby College is the place for you. As a graduate for whom all of the above is true, I can honestly say that a commitment to Colby will yield everything promised along with a host of other benefits that are unique to each individual.

❑ *Jeff Baron, B.A.*

COLGATE UNIVERSITY

Colgate University
13 Oak Drive
Hamilton, NY 13346

(315) 824-7401
Fax: (315) 824-7544

E-mail: admission@mail.colgate.edu
Web site: http://www.colgate.edu

Enrollment

Full-time ❑ women: 1,434
❑ men: 1,404

Part-time ❑ women: 2
❑ men: 2

INTRODUCING COLGATE

The first thing that strikes any visitor to Colgate is the beauty of its campus. Shaded quads, green hills, and the clear water of Taylor Lake form an idyllic environment in which to study and learn. But the school's greatest assets lie within the nineteenth-century limestone buildings that frame the upper campus—a top-rate faculty dedicated to teaching, and a student body that approaches life and learning with equal enthusiasm. Upon graduating, Colgate students will have received one of the nation's best undergraduate educations, along with a sound understanding of what it takes to succeed in the "real world."

With some 2,800 students, Colgate matches the ideal of a small, northeastern liberal arts school while maintaining an impressive array of academic, social, and athletic opportunities not found at many larger universities. In fact, the Colgate experience is distinguished by its contrasts. Students embrace a "work hard, play hard" approach to campus life; a day begun studying Plato could easily lead to an afternoon chemistry lab, followed by an acoustic performance in the on-campus pub, and ending in a party downtown.

One of the biggest reasons I chose Colgate over similar schools was its size. Most prestigious "small" liberal arts colleges have under 2,000 students, which made it seem that I would have been everywhere and done everything by the time I finished the first year. At Colgate I always saw someone I knew on the quad or in the coop (the student center), but I still never stopped meeting new people and having new experiences. I think Colgate achieves the perfect balance between size and intimacy that allows you to feel at home but never stifles your growth.

The Colgate experience is in no way defined by academics alone. Colgate students sustain an impressive number of organizations and activities that encompass almost every interest. More than one hundred groups afford students opportunities including deejaying a two-hour show on WRCU, kayaking with the Wilderness Adventure Program, or writing a humor column for the *Baker's Dozen* satire magazine, just to name a few. Sports also play a prominent role in the Colgate social scene, with about two-thirds of students participating in the school's twenty-six intramural, nineteen club, or twenty-three Division I varsity teams.

No discussion of Colgate would be complete without mentioning its rural surroundings. Hamilton is rightly called The Village. Farm markets outnumber fast food places by a wide margin. While there is no Starbucks within twenty miles, the college operates the Barge Canal Coffee Company downtown, a popular spot for town and college alike. But the absence of Broadway lights does have distinct advantages. Colgate students and faculty are integral parts of a tightly knit community that offers a lot of local flair. You won't find a better deli sandwich than one of Roger's specials.

When I first visited Colgate the big news was the installation of the town's second traffic light. Hamilton is surrounded by miles of farmland and wilderness, and those who can't survive without regular access to clubs, fine dining, and professional sports, probably won't feel at home. The college maintains a fine arts gallery, sponsors a concert orchestra and chorus, and mounts several theater productions (both dance and drama) each year. At the same time, Colgate's rural location makes it one of the most beautiful places I've ever seen. You can't beat the sight of the leaves during the fall, and even the snow can be spectacular. In addition to being physically beautiful, it's a relaxingly quiet place. Anyone who's ever wanted to live in or near a quintessential small town will love life in Hamilton.

In recent years the Colgate campus has undergone a dynamic transformation as the benefits of an ongoing $150 million fund-raising drive emerge. A spate of new construction has pampered students with a state-of-the-art fitness center, lavish new dormitories, high-tech classrooms, and a massive refurbishment of its art and student centers. Coupled with an increasingly competitive applicant pool, these changes have added special energy to the college and make Colgate one of the nation's top schools.

ADMISSIONS REQUIREMENTS

Getting into Colgate is an increasingly difficult task. Applications have risen twenty percent in the past five years for the same 720 spots. Forty-one percent of the applicants to a recent class were accepted, of which twenty-nine percent enrolled through Early Admission. Academic scores for incoming first-year students are predictably high: eighty-nine percent were ranked in the top twenty percent of their graduating high school class, their average SAT I scores were: Verbal—637, Math—644 (the ACT mean was 28), and it can safely be assumed that all had outstanding teacher recommendations.

However, impressive numbers alone will not guarantee entry into the first-year class. Successful applicants will also have demonstrated an ability to enliven the Colgate community through their intellectual curiosity, independence, imagination, and determination. To judge the most qualified students, Colgate's admission staff looks first at an applicant's transcript, followed by recommendations, standardized tests, extracurricular activities, and the personal essay.

While high test scores certainly help, a challenging high school curriculum and demonstrated commitment to a few interests or activities are often the key to an acceptance offer. Within the transcript, the admissions staff particularly looks to strong preparation in English and foreign language, history, math, and natural sciences. Advanced Placement courses are also used as indicators of a candidate's potential for success, and can count toward fulfilling graduation requirements.

I applied to Colgate as my stretch school. Although my grades and board scores were below the school's averages, I was involved in a number of extracurricular activities in high school, including running on the state championship track team and participating in the debate society. I think my acceptance at Colgate demonstrates that the admissions committee looks beyond the numbers and evaluates applicants as a whole. When I got to school I was surprised by the number of student leaders there were in all sorts of activities, but that is one of the things that makes Colgate such an exciting place to go to school.

Decision Plans

Another way Colgate hopefuls might improve their chances of receiving a fat letter is to apply Early Decision. All who submit applications identifying the college as their first choice by November 15 will receive a response within a month—and a significant number are accepted. Colgate accepted half of the Early Decision candidates into a recent class. A second Early Decision option allows students submitting applications by the normal deadline of January 15 to be considered on a rolling admission basis. Beyond making 215 winter vacations that much sweeter, high Early Admissions numbers indicate enthusiastic entering classes, with large numbers of students preferring Colgate over any other school.

Driving up Oak Drive on a gray January afternoon during my senior year of high school, I realized that Colgate was the one place I wanted to spend my collegiate years. What I really noticed, in addition to the beautiful campus and quaint village of Hamilton, was that the students were smiling and appeared to be happy despite the snow and ice piled everywhere. Coming from a public high school in Memphis, Tennessee, I wanted to expand my horizons and go to a liberal arts college in New England. I ended up applying to Colgate Early Decision, and it was one of the best decisions I ever made.

Interviews are not required for admission but campus visits are encouraged—if for no other reason than to introduce candidates to the stunning campus. Prospective students also have the opportunity to sit down with an admissions officer or student guide to ask any questions they have about the school or application process. The admissions staff genuinely urges applicants to learn as much as possible about the school, and students and faculty are more than willing to host visitors in their dorms and classrooms.

ACADEMIC LIFE

It is often said that education is what you make of it, but the maxim is likely truer of Colgate's academic environment than most. Built around a core of liberal arts courses, Colgate's curriculum allows for a wide degree of flexibility in choosing classes, majors, and learning opportunities outside of the classroom. The system rewards initiative and, as a result, the dedicated student can receive what is arguably the best undergraduate education in the country.

Intimate class sizes and an outstanding faculty are Colgate's greatest academic advantages. More than half of the courses have fewer than twenty students and fewer exceed fifty. Professors are exceedingly accessible and no classes are taught by teaching assistants. Moreover, while it is not uncommon to hear about the achievements of Colgate professors in the national news, their role and goal clearly is to teach.

Study Abroad

Another outstanding academic asset is Colgate's extensive study abroad program. While many competitive schools adopt the attitude that the best education can be found only within their hallowed walls, Colgate embraces the idea that worldly experience is often better than rote learning. For this reason students can choose from twenty-six separate off-campus study groups, from Sri Lanka to Switzerland, covering topics as diverse as urban education and Florentine art. Almost half of each Colgate class chooses to study off-campus at some time during their Colgate career.

Never having traveled outside the country before going to college, I was attracted to Colgate by the abundant opportunities to study abroad. I wasn't disappointed. During my junior year I studied international relations in Geneva with fifteen other Colgate students. The program included interviews with U.N. ambassadors, NATO generals, and parliamentarians in Prague, not to mention weekend trips to some of the most spectacular sites in Europe. Upon returning to campus I found our group had no monopoly on fun—friends told comparable tales of Russia, Australia, India, and Japan. It only added to the value of a Colgate education.

Work Load

Colgate is not Chicago or Caltech, where popular rumor has it that all work and no play are the academic norm. Colgate students can be found napping or exchanging gossip among the plush green chairs that dot Case Library's main reading room as often as they are found cramming. The laid-back atmosphere minimizes competition for grades and leaves ample time to pursue interests outside the classroom.

I think everyone was nervous about the work load when they arrived at school, especially a school of Colgate's caliber. Most of my classmates had graduated at the top of their high school classes and were accustomed to academic success. But although the work was challenging, I never encountered the kind of cutthroat competition I expected. Late night caffeine and cramming sessions became bonding experiences more than anything else, and I found that I learned from friends outside of class almost as much as from books or professors. I was challenged more than stressed by the classwork, which made the entire learning experience more rewarding.

Freshman Seminar

During the summer before matriculation all incoming students choose a freshman seminar from a tantalizing array of choices that in recent years have included Christianity and Money, The Architecture and Ideas of Frank Lloyd Wright, Nietzsche, and The Jazz Age. With fifteen other first-year students and a professor they may grapple with the intricacies of "Rhizomatic Structures—a Metaphor for Our Modern Era," as well as acquaint themselves with Colgate's extensive library resources and learn how to write the perfect college paper. Seminar professors are also students' academic advisors and their classes often serve as a social hub for the remainder of the year.

Core Curriculum

Colgate has one of the oldest liberal arts core curriculums in the country, consisting of four general education classes designed to provide a sound foundation of knowledge for the intellectual everyperson. The first two core classes examine the social, political, and scientific tenets of Western civilization, while the latter ones focus on non-Western cultures or philosophies and the significance of technological change. Added to the liberal arts core are six required electives, which are distributed among the three academic divisions: humanities, social sciences, and natural sciences. Students must take two courses from each of the academic divisions, a task that is usually easily completed by the end of sophomore year.

As a prospective political science major with little interest in math or science, I dreaded fulfilling my distribution requirements. Reluctantly, I enrolled in Physics and Philosophy, which boldly promised to explain quantum mechanics to the mathematically disinclined. To my surprise it was the most enlightening class I took at Colgate, and one I never would have taken otherwise. Colgate encourages you to challenge yourself by exploring fields you never thought of in high school, often with surprising results.

No one major stands out as the best at Colgate. Economics, biology, English, and political science are the most popular, but outstanding smaller departments like philosophy and neuroscience shouldn't be overlooked. All told, Colgate offers forty-eight majors (called concentrations), plus eight additional minors that together can satisfy just about any academic whimsy. It's also possible to arrange independent study courses with individual professors or even design an unique interdisciplinary concentration.

Resources

Colgate's academic resources are impressive. Its computer facilities are state-of-the-art, with all dorm rooms connected to the Internet, and the computer center has ample terminals for those who do not bring a machine to campus. Science majors at Colgate benefit from generous resources that enable students to work with lab equipment and projects reserved for graduate students at larger schools. And student research opportunities abound in all departments, often with exclusive access to professors who are leaders in their fields. More than one hundred students stay on campus each summer to conduct research with their professors full time.

Professors

Small class sizes also enable professors to engage students in the Socratic method of teaching, substituting questions and student participation for the lectures that usually accompany intro courses. Although frustrating for the unprepared, this interaction fosters provocative class discussions and close relationships with teachers and students that regularly extend beyond the classroom. Most professors have extremely flexible office hours that make it easy for willing students to engage their teachers on a personal level. Professors at Colgate act more as mentors than graders, which makes the educational experience all the more rewarding.

SOCIAL LIFE AND ACTIVITIES

Colgate students relish fun as much as their education and strive to strike a balance between the two. Although Colgate's party reputation has been overblown in recent years, Homecoming and the annual spring party weekend are still some of the best parties you'll find in the Northeast. But the social scene extends far beyond partying. Over one hundred student clubs and organizations exist to satisfy just about any interest, and whether your idea of college includes rugby or symphony, each can be had in abundance at Colgate.

Despite Hamilton's bucolic isolation, Colgate students rarely suffer from a lack of things to do. For relaxation students tend to drop the books in favor of less weighty pursuits. On the typical Friday or Saturday night one can choose from a range of private parties, student and university-sponsored events, fraternity and sorority parties, and the downtown scene. Together they provide ample and diverse options for anyone to choose from depending on their mood.

Private parties are usually held in the university apartments (where many upperclass students live) or downtown flats and can range from wall-to-wall crowds to more sedate video-and-popcorn fare. University- and student-sponsored events include frequent performances by bands or comedians in the on-campus Pub, student theater, and campus-wide theme parties like Casino Night and the Roaring 20's Party.

The Greek System

The Greek system is still a significant social organ on campus, although it has lost some of its influence in recent years. In 1996 the university instituted a policy prohibiting students from rushing until sophomore year, which drew protests from many that the school was trying to eliminate fraternities. That fear has proven false, however, and by most counts the Greek system is a more stable and mature organization. Now parties aren't nearly as outrageous as they were in the eighties, but usually several houses hold events on weekend nights. And while more than forty percent of the student body belongs to one of ten fraternities and five sororities, one's Greek affiliation is largely a nonissue on campus. Parties are usually open to everyone and friendships are seldom defined by who belongs to what house.

I feel that I evolved socially as well as intellectually at Colgate. My freshman year I went to a lot of fraternity parties and met a tremendous number of people. But by sophomore year I realized that Colgate offered so many different opportunities that making plans for nonstudying hours became more difficult. I joined an improv comedy group, was elected to student government, and discovered alternatives to the "row" like student theater, a renowned hypnotist, and casino night. Whether I was in the mood to shoot pool with some friends at the Jug or dance at the Edge, the options were always open.

Downtown

The downtown scene consists of several bars, a coffee shop, and a few minor restaurants that become quite crowded after midnight. Students usually end the evening with a slice (which comes plain only) at the New York Pizzeria and then either head to bed or hit a not-too-infrequent after-hours party on the way home. While these four choices seem distinct, the campus is small enough that everyone knows someone at each of them and a full evening can easily include them all. Weekends are never dull if you choose to be adventuresome.

Organizations and Events

During the week, student clubs, teams, and events provide an array of extracurricular activity. Most of the 100 or more campus organizations that are active at any given time were begun by students, from the school's own alternative rock radio station to the Kuumba Dance Troupe. With an enormous budget to spend on movies, speakers, and performers, the Colgate Activities Board is responsible for bringing events like Mikhail Gorbachev, Phish, Jesse Jackson, and Snoop Doggy Dog to Hamilton.

Athletics

Athletics are another prominent aspect of student social life. Colgate's varsity teams participate in Division I sports, with the men's basketball and hockey and women's soccer and volleyball among recent standouts. The school's most recent athletic boast is basketball star Adonal Foyle, who led the Red Raiders to its first NCAA Tournament appearance and was the eighth pick overall in the 1997 NBA draft. And locals and students alike crowd the raucous Starr Rink on weekends for ECAC hockey games.

In keeping with the school's entrepreneurial spirit, students are more prone to play sports themselves than watch from the sidelines. Whether it's spelunking with the Wilderness Adventure program or skeet shooting at the college's nearby range, it's possible to find a sport to satisfy every whim. Snow sports are another quintessentially Colgate diversion. Many take advantage of the harsh winter clime by traversing twelve miles of cross-country trails or downhilling at nearby Toggenberg Mountain. If athletics is your game, you will be able to play to your heart's content at Colgate.

Coming from Virginia, no one was more surprised than my parents when I told them I had signed up for the women's ice hockey team freshman year. The first practice was somewhat daunting since I had hardly put on a pair of ice skates before. But scoring in the championship game senior year was a triumph unlike any other athletic accomplishment because it was totally unimaginable when I began playing. The exhausting practices and long road trips became a special part of my college experience. Colgate offered me an unusual opportunity to try new things and expand my horizons beyond what I thought was possible.

Student Diversity

As for student diversity on campus, Colgate is not Berkeley (even after Proposition 209) but it does enjoy a vibrant ALANA (African, Latin, Asian, Native American) community. Fifteen percent of a recent class were students of color, a number that has been rising in recent years. The Cultural Center serves as a resource base for the ALANA community and often hosts lectures and meetings for a wide variety of campus organizations. Moreover, Colgate maintains a number of special interest houses where residents choose to live based on a common theme. These include the Asia, Harlem Renaissance, Spanish, French, Ecology, Peace Studies, and Creative Arts houses.

Volunteering

Colgate students are also involved in the Hamilton community, with Sidekick volunteers adopting little brothers or sisters in the community, SOMAC volunteers serving in the local Emergency Medical Service response team, and Volunteer Colgate organizing food drives for the needy during the holiday season. While Hamilton is limiting from a cosmopolitan point of view, it offers the chance to become involved in a small community in ways a large university never could. With so many things to choose from, students usually form circles of friends and activities tailored to their interests. But these patterns shift as the classes move up and it is refreshing to find new opportunities always available.

FINANCIAL AID

Like most selective private schools, Colgate's cost can be prohibitive, but rising costs have been matched in recent years by a rapid increase in available financial aid. Now sixty percent of all students receive some form of financial assistance, including forty percent who are granted Colgate scholarship aid. One quarter of the recent $150 million fund-raising drive was committed to financial aid resources, adding to the nearly $19 million annually that is awarded to students by the university.

What does this mean for individuals? Colgate does not provide any merit-based aid, but for those demonstrating need, the average grant is $17,800, while average total aid tops $21,000. Other, non-university sources of funds are available, including scholarships, grants, loans, and campus jobs. Through a combination of aid sources Colgate is able to offer assistance to virtually everyone who demonstrates need.

My senior year in high school, I was blown away by the prospect of paying for college—attending a private school just seemed out of the question. But Colgate offered me an aid package that included a grant, Stafford loans, and a work-study job. The people in the financial aid office were always extremely helpful in addressing my questions and concerns. For example, in my junior year when I wanted to study abroad, I found the total cost was much more than an average semester at Colgate. Colgate was able to increase my grant to make up the difference. Like most people I know, I'll be making loan payments for a long time to come. Was it worth it? Definitely.

Colgate offers access to federal Stafford loans, Pell grants, and Perkins loans, in addition to numerous university scholarships and selected New York State aid programs. To qualify for financial aid students must file the Free Application for Federal Student Aid (FAFSA) with the federal processor before February 15, and the financial aid PROFILE form with the College Scholarship Service (CSS) by February 1. Colgate relies on both forms to determine an applicant's financial need.

PROMINENT GRADS

- Charles Evans Hughes, 1884, Chief Justice of the Supreme Court
- William Rogers, '34, Former Secretary of State
- Andy Rooney, '42, Television Commentator
- Howard Fineman, '70, Journalist

Colgate graduates serve as a testament to the versatility of a liberal arts degree. Producing alumni who are leaders in science, academia, entertainment, politics, and on Wall Street, Colgate is committed to giving its graduates a solid intellectual foundation for future achievement.

"Real World" Workshops

The "Real World" workshops are a case in point. Pioneered by Colgate in 1996 and held for one week before school resumes in January, Real World programs offer seniors the opportunity to pick graduates' brains for career strategies and practical advice on how to find an apartment, finance a car, or select a wine that goes well with chicken. During the Real World, seniors attend workshops on how to find jobs in just about every professional field and, of course, practice the fine art of networking. It is the consummate example of how Colgate's career office strives to ensure that every graduate is well equipped to pursue post-college dreams.

Careers

The most popular career paths for recent Colgate grads have been in financial services, communications, consulting, and medicine. Nearly a quarter of students go directly to graduate school, with science, law, and medicine as the top three degrees. Most alumni are concentrated in commercial centers like Boston, New York, Washington, San Francisco, or Chicago but, as anyone who wears a Colgate insignia can attest, alumni seem to be everywhere and will not hesitate to let you know by calling out a greeting. More than anything, a Colgate education provides a broad foundation upon which graduates may build any number of careers.

I don't think that I truly appreciated the scope of Colgate's reputation until I began my job search in the fall of my senior year. Colgate graduates are everywhere and were exceptionally willing to help. It became clear after several informational interviews with alumni that four years in Hamilton forged strong ties that didn't end upon graduation. Whether on Wall Street or in Washington, I always found alumni to be exceedingly helpful in my attempt to find a job. I ultimately received an offer at the consulting firm where I had interned for a Colgate grad the summer before.

If you are looking for an internship or even just advice, chances are you can find a Colgate graduate among the school's 25,000 alumni who is at the top of his or her field. One way to tap this tremendous resource is to set up an externship through the Career Center during the January recess. Usually done during senior year, the Jan Plan is a great way to network and test out possible careers. In addition to the Jan Plan, the Career Center has vastly increased its alumni contacts and recruitment program in recent years, minimizing the handicap Hamilton's isolated location has on the employment search.

SUMMING UP

Considered by some to be a safety school for the Ivies, Colgate has emerged from their shadow as an excellent small college with big school amenities. Its greatest strengths are small class sizes and top-rate professors who concentrate on undergraduate education. At the same time, Colgate students enjoy athletic and extracurricular opportunities often found only at larger universities. Combined with a stunning hilltop campus, these qualities set Colgate apart from other competitive institutions.

Liberal arts form the core Colgate's curriculum and provide a broad foundation of knowledge upon which graduates build a limitless variety of careers. While some argue that a college's goal should be to provide professional training, Colgate's philosophy and graduates prove that a liberal arts education can open up the job markets. The Career Center and Colgate's vast and loyal alumni network combine to provide students in any major with ample job opportunities. With a Colgate education, biology majors may become investment bankers, and English majors med students.

Colgate's outstanding academics are grounded in its flexible liberal arts core curriculum and an outstanding faculty dedicated to undergraduate teaching. TAs don't exist at Colgate, classes are intimate and easily available, and professors are readily accessible. Colgate's academic resources are enhanced by state-of-the-art facilities that rival those of many large universities. Regular renovations have revamped almost every student space, including campus-wide access to the Internet, a new academic building, athletic and exercise facilities, dorms, classrooms, and art and student centers, which together give Colgate unsurpassed student amenities.

"The spirit that is Colgate" is a phrase often used to describe the intangible qualities of a Colgate education. It encompasses the quaint Hamilton community, the beauty of the surroundings, and the camaraderie that forms among students largely separated from most cosmopolitan amenities. Colgate is not a city school and those who can't go a semester without calling a cab probably would not enjoy the isolation. But at the same time the campus is always buzzing with activity and the small town atmosphere provides a relaxing environment where it is rare to walk to town or across the quad without seeing familiar faces.

The Colgate spirit is also captured by the intelligent, athletic, and active student body. *The New York Times* editorialized that Colgate basketball star Adonal Foyle proved that "one can be a good student, a devotee of Faulkner, and play first-class basketball too." The same could be said for the student body as a whole. Colgate students are steadfastly entrepreneurial and energetic, sustaining over a hundred teams, clubs, and organizations that offer an endless opportunity to explore new horizons.

At Colgate, students become adults. The transformation occurs gradually, in class, in the dorms, downtown, on the playing field, and abroad. Students arrive as naïve high school grad-

AN EVENING IN PARIS

While studying in Dijon for a semester on the Colgate French department program, three friends and I joined our group on a weekend trip to Paris. We filled our Saturday with extensive sightseeing and museum tours. As night fell we decided to treat ourselves to some truly fine French cuisine and sat down to dinner at Le Proçapé, an exquisite restaurant just outside the Latin Quarter.

To our surprise, an American couple was seated to the left of our table. We struck up a conversation with them, only to find out that the man had graduated from Colgate in 1979. What a small world. As we were paying our bill (which, somehow or another, ended up being nearly 1,000 francs), the gentleman leaned over with a smile and said, "Would you mind if an alum took you guys out to dinner?"

Graciously, we accepted, very content at knowing that Colgate is truly a global community. Later, we learned that the alum had graduated with a geology major and had gone on to start a record business and direct an office goods business. Who says majors mean something?

uates and leave ready to succeed in business or academia. In between, they are challenged by the work, meet great friends, and have a lot of fun. Graduates leave Colgate with an uncommon bond to the school and to each other that makes their education both special and unique.

❑ *Scott Worden, B.A.*

COLLEGE OF THE HOLY CROSS

College of the Holy Cross
Worcester, MA 01610-2395

(508) 793-2443, (800) 442-2421
Fax: (508) 793-3888

E-mail: admissions@holycross.edu
Web site: http://www.holycross.edu

Enrollment

Full-time ❑ women: 1,441
❑ men: 1,269

Part-time ❑ women: 13
❑ men: 7

INTRODUCING HOLY CROSS

The only Jesuit Catholic college in the country to offer an exclusively undergraduate liberal arts education, Holy Cross enjoys a well-deserved reputation as one of the preeminent schools in the United States. Small class sizes, devoted faculty members, and a challenging curriculum have made the college an increasingly popular choice for many top-notch high school students. Others are attracted to the beautiful campus, active student body, and friendly living/learning environment. Whatever their reasons for choosing Holy Cross, few students are disappointed when they arrive, as evidenced by the school's ninety-seven percent freshman retention rate and overwhelmingly positive student satisfaction statistics.

Holy Cross has grown in both size and stature since it was established in 1843 as an academic community where the Jesuit ideals of educational integrity and social justice could flourish among its male students and faculty. Founded by Benedict Joseph Fenwick, the second bishop of Boston, the school originally comprised only one wooden building and a half-finished brick structure on a hill overlooking the largely unsettled town of Worcester, Massachusetts. There was little evidence to suggest that such a prominent college would eventually arise from this undeveloped setting.

Coeducational since 1972, the college is today home to 2,700 young men and women and the campus is widely recognized as one of the most impressive in the country. Driving through the black, wrought-iron gates that form the entrance to Linden Lane, the tree-lined passageway that leads through the Holy Cross campus, visitors are immediately struck by the school's beautiful architecture and perfectly manicured grounds, which are spread over 174 acres. Ivy-covered residence halls and open green spaces are intermixed with technologically advanced academic buildings and state-of-the-art athletic facilities. There are three well-endowed libraries, two multi-sport recreational facilities, a recently renovated campus center, and a comprehensive art complex. With its outdoor sculptures and idyllic flower gardens, the award-winning campus is both peaceful and picturesque. Few who visit the school are disappointed by its physical surroundings.

Perhaps more impressive than the campus, however, are the strong traditions and deep loyalties that have taken root here for many generations. Each year, young men and women from all over the country come to Holy Cross to participate in a vibrant academic and residential community where the Jesuits' founding principles continue to flourish. These students experience an educational environment where intelligent dialogue is encouraged and scholarly exploration is rewarded. Along the way, they become part of a close-knit social atmosphere where lifelong friendships are fostered. Holy Cross graduates carry these meaningful lessons and experiences with them by continuing to seek ways to integrate their faith, their lives, and their value-centered education.

ADMISSIONS REQUIREMENTS

In a typical year, Holy Cross receives applications from more than 4,300 students who are competing for only 700 places in the first-year class. Though the Admissions Committee considers many factors before making its decision, those students who demonstrate a pattern of superior academic performance in high school do a great deal to improve their chances of gaining acceptance to the college. This is confirmed by the fact that nearly all of the entering students graduated in the top twenty percent of their high school class and an overwhelming majority come with Advanced Placement or honors coursework on their transcripts. In recent years, the average SAT I score has exceeded 1280, though few on campus consider this statistic a meaningful measure of success in either the admissions process or the school's curriculum.

Besides a high level of academic achievement, other characteristics that have been identified as common among those students offered admission to Holy Cross are an openness to different veiwpoints and ideas, a willingness to become engaged in the life of the college outside the classroom, a desire to grow not only intellectually, but socially and spiritually as well, and a commitment to helping others, both within the college community and beyond.

Unlike larger schools that rely on formulaic methods to make admissions decisions, the admissions staff at Holy Cross tries to remain focused on each individual and his or her unique talents. Before going through "committee," where the final decision is made, each application is read by at least two (and sometimes three) staff members who try to determine how well the applicant utilized the academic and extracurricular resources available in his or her high school. In this way, the team hopes to identify those students who will not only excel academically, but who will also make positive contributions to the vibrant intellectual, social, and spiritual life of the campus.

Requirements

Applicants are required to take the SAT I (or ACT) and three SAT II: Subject tests (one of which must be the SAT II: Writing test). In addition, prospective students are asked to write an essay on a question chosen by the Admissions Committee. Interviews, while not required, are highly recommended and should be considered an excellent opportunity to share additional insights about one's personality.

Early Decision

For those who have made Holy Cross their first choice, the school recommends applying Early Decision, which allows the Admissions Committee to spend more time reading the application and getting to know the student. An additional advantage of this option is the convenience of hearing a decision within three or four weeks of the school's receipt of all required application materials. One should be aware, however, that Early Decision applications are binding and therefore require accepted students to immediately withdraw all pending applications at other colleges.

Children of Alumni

Recognizing that there is no greater compliment paid to a college than an alumnus/a who wishes to send a son or daughter to his or her alma mater, Holy Cross does give special consideration to those children of alumni who are seeking admission to the school. The fact that more than ten percent of the student body qualify as such legacies offers testimony to the the loyalty of Holy Cross graduates.

Minorities

While the school has always been home to a distinguished and proud list of minority alumni—including U.S. Supreme Court Justice Clarence Thomas and James Healy, the Church's first African American bishop—it has had some difficulty in increasing minority enrollment percentages beyond the high single digits. However, since his appointment as president in 1994, Fr. Gerard Reedy has made racial diversity on campus one of his administration's highest priorities and the students and faculty have supported him in this initiative. As a result, the school has recently taken steps to more actively recruit and enroll qualified minority applicants to the school.

ACADEMIC LIFE

The academic atmosphere at H.C. is one of cooperation rather than cutthroat competition. Although some have complained that As are becoming increasingly scarce and, therefore, more highly coveted, most students are quick to assist their fellow classmates who are struggling with a concept. During exam periods, it is not uncommon to see large study groups congregating in Dinand Library's social lounge (often referred to as the Blue Room) or classmates sharing ideas in the Hogan Campus Center. As one premed student pointed out:

The great thing about the sciences at Holy Cross is that they are not as competitive as you might find at other colleges. Instead of competing with each other, we work as groups and encourage one another to do well. There is a real sense of teamwork among the students here. The professors also contribute to this environment by always being there for anyone who is seeking further elaboration on a lesson or an answer to a question.

Faculty

The Holy Cross faculty receives high marks from the student body. Recent surveys reveal that students find their professors to be both very intelligent and highly accessible, traits not often shared in today's academic world where scholars face increasing pressure to conduct research and publish regularly. While scheduled office hours for student visits are required by the college, most professors maintain an open-door policy and encourage their students to drop in frequently throughout the semester. Furthermore, it is not uncommon to hear of a professor holding class in his or her living room over wine and cheese or a home-cooked meal. Such hospitality is not lost on the students, who appreciate the opportunity to get to know their instructors outside the classroom and get away from the cafeteria for an evening. Just as it is a love of teaching that leads most faculty members to the college, it is this informal sharing of knowledge and ideas that makes H.C. so appealing to its students. As one senior commented:

I truly appreciate the philosophy of education at Holy Cross. My professors are more like friends. It's a shared intellectual atmosphere, and that is what makes this school such a great place to learn. It's not just learning for the sake of learning—it's learning for the sake of applying knowledge.

Distribution Requirements

This mature and open-minded attitude toward learning is the cornerstone of a liberal arts education. Though there is no core curriculum or specific set of classes required by the school, students must fulfill flexible distribution requirements entailing the selection of ten courses from six areas of study:

- The Arts, Language and Literature
- Religious and Philosophical Studies
- Historical Studies
- Cross-Cultural Studies
- Social Science
- Natural and Mathematical Sciences

Students must also demonstrate competence in a modern or classical foreign language, which can be achieved either by successfully completing an intermediate level language course or by "testing out" on a qualifying examination. Within this academic framework, students are encouraged to take classes that will both interest and challenge them. The curriculum trains students to think critically and independently, write succinctly and cogently, and communicate effectively. Holy Cross recognizes that these fundamental skills will provide graduates an educational foundation that is necessary to build successful careers in nearly any occupation.

One of the strengths of a liberal arts education is that it helps you to tie together fields as diverse as the classics and mathematics. It connects certain themes through all subjects of study and all themes of life. Many things seem to coincide. It's nice to step back every once in a while and look at the big picture, which is what an education like this enables you to do. I can go to law school, medical school, or become an engineer. Holy Cross really has provided me with many options and has expanded my intellectual capabilities.

Students are required to take four courses a semester, which does not seem too overwhelming until one considers the weighty reading list that usually accompanys each class syllabus. Athough students may spend fewer than fifteen hours a week in class, they are expected to do a great deal of reading and learning outside the classroom. While some majors (English, history, political science) are definitely more "reading/writing intensive" than others, it is not uncommon to hear of economics professors using seven or eight texts in a semester. As a result, most Holy Cross students either develop strong time-management skills early on or become very accustomed to pulling "all-nighters."

Classes

With class sizes that average fewer than twenty students and many with fewer than fifteen, professors are able to offer their students highly personalized instruction and individual attention. In return, students are usually expected to not only show up for class, but to come prepared to discuss that day's topic in some detail. One popular though somewhat eccentric classics professor has been known to walk across campus and wake up those students who dared to sleep through his 8:00 A.M. class. Upper-level seminars are particularly interactive, with professors often only facilitating the exchange of well-developed student commentary. Students rarely complain about H.C.'s faculty or curriculum, except to lament the lack of "gut" courses that might be taken to enhance one's GPA.

Research Projects and Internships

The faculty and administration grant a high level of academic autonomy to those students who are seeking opportunities to learn outside the classroom. By their junior year, many students are collaborating with H.C. professors on extensive research projects that are often presented at national symposia or in academic journals. Others gain valuable work experiences through school-sponsored internships that are offered either locally or in Washington, D.C. Additionally, each year more than 100 students study abroad and immerse themselves in the cultures and traditions of foreign lands.

Computers

In recent years, the admininstration has made a significant effort to enhance the school's technological capabilities by implementing new state-of-the-art information systems in the classrooms, libraries, and residence halls. As a result, there are now more than 4,000 locations on campus offering fully networked computer hookups. This effort appears to have paid off as the school was just named one of the top twenty-five most wired campuses in the nation by *Yahoo! Internet Life* magazine.

SOCIAL LIFE AND ACTIVITIES

Although a heavy workload generally keeps most H.C. students in the library from Sunday afternoon until Thursday evening, the weekends serve as a welcome opportunity to relax and catch up with friends. With more than eighty-two percent of the student body living on campus, dorm room parties can be found on nearly every hall and, not surprisingly, the consumption of alcohol (usually beer) often accompanies these social gatherings. Though the administration officially frowns on this activity, most resident supervisors simply preach moderation and tolerate such events as long as they do not get too loud or out of control. Fortunately, a mature and laid-back attitude toward drinking prevails at the school and few students report pressure to imbibe from their peers. Later in the evening, many students will head to the Crossroads Pizza Cellar, which offers inexpensive food and free on-campus musical entertainment until 2:00 A.M. For those who are legal, the Senior Pub offers a convenient and comfortable place to catch the latest sporting event or enjoy a beer with friends. Others walk a few blocks away to Caro Street or the Autumn Chase Apartments where off-campus students are frequent hosts of loud house parties. Afterwards, a majority of these revelers (regardless of age) end up flocking to crowded, local watering holes such as McGuire's, Rosie O'Grady's, or the White Eagle for hours of dancing and a final nightcap.

Dances and Shows

Holy Cross offers numerous social or entertainment options for almost any personality. In the fall, each dorm sponsors a semiformal dance known as a Blind Date Ball, or "BDB," where students are responsible for setting up their roommates with the "date of their dreams" or, at the very least, someone with whom they might enjoy spending a fun evening out on the town. Also well attended are the student-produced theater productions, popular concert performances, and stand-up comedy acts that are regularly sponsored by the Campus Activities Board. Those looking for something a little quieter (or cheaper) often decide to take in a show at the on-campus Kimball Theater where first-run movies can still be seen for under three bucks.

Whether tailgating at home football games or just going out for pizza and a movie, Holy Cross students tend to socialize in large groups. With everyone taking a diverse courseload and most participating in multiple extracurricular activities, acquintances are made easily and friendships forged quickly.

Off Campus

If one is in need of a change of scenery, the school's central New England location offers plenty of convenient day trips and adventurous outdoor excursions. Boston, with its excellent shopping and diverse cultural opportunities, is less than an hour away and can be easily reached by either bus or train. The beautiful beaches and quaint villages of Cape Cod offer another popular weekend escape for those who are feeling land-locked in Worcester. For those hoping to become one with nature, there is exciting skiing, challenging rock climbing, and excellent camping, all within short driving distance from campus.

Athletics

Although the college's athletic achievements have not captured the national headlines recently, there is a long and proud tradition of sports at Holy Cross. Many older alumni remember earlier decades when eventual NBA legends Bob Cousy and Tommy Heinson achieved tremendous success on the basketball court and helped the school win an NCAA championship in 1947 (the only New England college to achieve such a distinction). Others recall the Crusader football teams that dominated the college gridiron in the 1980s behind the offensive and defensive play of two-time All-American Gordie Lockbaum, a finalist for the Heisman Trophy in both his junior and senior years.

While an increased focus on academics and a limitation on athletic scholarships make a return to such national prominence somewhat unlikely, most of the college's twenty-five varsity teams still maintain strong winning traditions and loyal student followings in spite of being one of the smallest schools to compete at the Division I level. With nearly twenty-five percent of Holy Cross students participating in NCAA intercollegiate athletics, and many more participating in intramural competition, there are usually plenty of sports fans in the stands cheering their friends to victory.

Giving to the Community

Holy Cross students also find time to give something back to their neighbors in the Worcester community. Having heard the Jesuit mantra "Men and Women for Others" numeorus times while at mass or on retreat, students recognize the moral obligations inherent in a values-based education. More than thirty percent of the student body routinely volunteers time to those who are less fortunate. Most choose to do such work through Student Programs for Urban Development, an umbrella organization composed of twenty-four student-run outreach activities. As the largest extracurricular club on campus, with more than 700 participants, SPUD offers students the opportunity to serve food to the homeless, tutor in the public schools, visit the elderly, or counsel domestic violence victims. Moved by these experiences and the lives that they have touched, many participants choose to spend their spring breaks working on Appalachian service projects building homes for the poor.

Faith

Students actively contribute to the faith life of the college community. Though attendance at mass is no longer required as it was years ago, about half of the students choose to regularly attend the on-campus liturgies. The Jesuit priests and lay chaplains recognize the integral role that spirituality plays in a Holy Cross education and they typically deliver inspiring and thought-provoking homilies on topics or issues that resonate with young adults. As a result, it is not uncommon to see nearly the entire library empty out on Sunday evening as students attend the two crowded Sunday evening services. Also popular are the five-day silent retreats known as the Spiritual Exercises of St. Ignatius, which are led twice a semester by the chaplain's office. Many consider this week of solitude, prayer, and reflection to be among the most meaningful and rewarding experiences offered at the college.

FINANCIAL AID

Tuition, room, and board totaled just under $28,000 for a recent academic year; the cost of attending the college, however, should not deter anyone from applying. The college has a comprehensive financial aid program, with more than sixty-three percent of the student body receiving some form of assistance. Holy Cross makes every attempt to meet the demonstrated financial need of every admitted applicant through a mix of scholarships, work-study, and loans.

With the exception of the Bean Scholarship for study in the classics and the Brooks Scholarship for study in music, there are no merit-based sholarships offered by the college. Athletic scholarships are offered only in men's and women's basketball. All other financial aid is predicated on need.

To apply for assistance, an incoming student must indicate on the admissions application that he or she would like to be considered for Holy Cross financial aid. Also, a student must file both a Free Application for Federal Student Assistance (FAFSA) and register with the College Scholarship Service by filing a PROFILE document to be considered for both Federal Student Assistance and Holy Cross scholarships. The Financial Aid Form must be submitted as soon after January 1 as possible, and no later than February 1.

GRADUATES

Holy Cross students are frequently asked, "So what exactly do you do with a liberal arts degree?" An appropriate response to this question might be, "What can't you do with such an education?" A glance at the school's list of alumni reveals success in a diverse range of occupations.

Law, medicine, and business are the most common professions pursued after graduation. The college's science program maintains an excellent reputation among medical schools, which accept H.C. graduates at a rate of seventy or seventy-five percent, or nearly twice the national average. Holy Cross is also ranked in the top ten schools nationwide in graduates who have gone on to become CEOs of Fortune 500 companies, a noteworthy achievement for a college that does not offer an undergraduate business degree.

PROMINENT GRADS

- Clarence Thomas, Supreme Court Justice
- Edward Bennett Williams, Attorney
- Stanley Grayson, Managing Director of Prudential Securities, Inc.
- Robert Morrison, Chairman, President and CEO of The Quaker Oats Company
- Mary Berner, Publisher of *Glamour Magazine*
- Robert Wright, President and CEO of NBC
- Joseph Califano Jr., Former U.S. Secretary of Health, Education and Welfare
- David Anderson, Sports Columnist

Having enjoyed their time spent in service to others, many students choose to continue their social service work in a full-time capacity after graduation. Of the nation's twenty-eight Jesuit colleges and universities, Holy Cross consistently sends the highest number of students to serve in the Jesuit Volunteer Corps, a year-long postgraduate national service program. Many graduates also go on to volunteer through other organizations such as the Peace Corps, VISTA, and Teach for America.

By any measure, Holy Cross alumni are among the most loyal of any college in the country. They are also very generous with alumni participation in the school's annual fund-raising campaign, routinely placing it among the nation's top twenty undergraduate institutions. Another way in which they express their love for their alma mater is with the professional assistance they provide through the extensive alumni network. The school's Career Placement Office routinely puts both young and old job seekers in touch with fellow alumni who can offer guidance on a possible field or even identify specific employment opportunities. Their connection to Holy Cross has proven to be an invaluable resource for many alumni.

SUMMING UP

Holy Cross offers a superior values-centered, liberal arts education in the Jesuit tradition. Students here are bright, accomplished, and highly motivated. They are also excited by the diverse academic and social options that are available to them during their four years at the college. Many will take advantage of the opportunity to explore new interests and cultivate hidden talents. Some will discover that faith and spirtuality mean much more than simply attending mass.

Through their active participation in the intellectual, social, and spiritual life of the college, these students will receive a challenging and well-rounded education that provides a firm foundation for successful careers and productive lives. Along the way, they will also gain many wonderful experiences and loyal friendships that they will carry with them for the rest of their lives.

At the end of four years on campus, most will recall with great fondness their education on Mount Saint James. Like thousands who came before them, these students will recognize and appreciate the lessons that were learned and the values that were formed as a result of their experiences at Holy Cross.

❑ *Tim Keller, A.B.*

COLLEGE OF WILLIAM AND MARY

College of William and Mary
Williamsburg, VA 23187-8795

(757) 221-4223
Fax: (757) 221-1242

E-mail: admiss@facstaff.wm.edu
Web site: http://www.wm.edu

Enrollment

Full-time ❑ women: 3,312
❑ men: 2,307

Part-time ❑ 186 men and women

INTRODUCING WILLIAM AND MARY

When the letter I had been waiting for from the William and Mary Admissions Office finally came, I didn't want to open it—I was too afraid I would receive bad news. The amazing sense of joy I felt when I read the acceptance letter was the first indication to me of just how much I wanted to go to school here.

Not all students are certain about where they want to go to college but it doesn't usually take too much to convince prospective students that William and Mary is one of the greatest places around! Enrolling students come in with a wide variety of opinions about what William and Mary is like and what they are expecting to get out of it. Almost every person who sets foot on our campus can't seem to help but bubble over with Tribe Pride!

The College of William and Mary is named for King William III and Queen Mary II of England who granted the royal charter for the college's creation in 1693. In keeping with the traditional connection to Great Britain, Lady Margaret Thatcher was named Chancellor of the college in 1993. She usually visits William and Mary at least once a year at Charter Day or, as in 1997, as the commencement speaker.

Though the official title of the school is the College of William and Mary, it actually reached university status in 1967. It is still referred to as the college for historical and traditional reasons. It is the second oldest university in the nation and became state-supported in 1906 and coeducational in 1918.

Don't mistakenly infer from its 300-plus years that W&M is old-fashioned or out of date. Quite the contrary! William and Mary, which started out as only one building—the Wren Building, has grown over the years to its current size of approximately 1,200 acres. The historic Wren Building looks out into Colonial Williamsburg from the east side and onto campus and the beautiful Sunken Garden from the west. The bell atop the Wren Building was historically rung at the beginning of the year to signify the start of classes, and at the end of the year to signify their end. It is tradition that all seniors ring the Wren Bell on the last day of classes to signify the end of their academic studies at the college. The academic buildings and residence halls that make up Old Campus surround the Sunken Garden and lead off toward New Campus, the area to which the campus spread through the 1960s and 1970s.

The academic and social aspects of life at W&M are a mix of opportunities on and off campus, but by and large campus is where the action is, causing most students to choose to live on or near campus. There are now more students who want to live on campus than there are residence hall rooms available, but freshmen and seniors are guaranteed on-campus housing, and the number of sophomores and juniors who cannot be accommodated is minimal.

There are usually twelve or thirteen residence halls (the number depends on the sizes of the entering classes) reserved for first-year students so they can all go through the transition from high school into college together. Tight bonds almost always form between freshman year hallmates.

My freshman year I was assigned a roommate randomly by the Office of Residence Life. She and I talked on the phone a few times during the summer prior to beginning college and tried to get to know a little bit about each other and discuss who was going to bring what to outfit our room. She sounded nice, but I was still a little nervous about moving in with someone whom I had never met. Now I look back at my anxiety and laugh. Amy and I couldn't have been a better match. We lived together on campus all four years of college and she continues to be one of my very best friends!

Residence life at William and Mary is very progressive, specifically with its policy of self-determination. This basically means that students make their own rules with the help and guidance of their resident assistants. Hallmates work together to determine what their quiet hours will be, which lounges will be designated as study lounges and which as social lounges, and all other rules by which they want to live.

ADMISSIONS REQUIREMENTS

William and Mary is a very competitive school and seeks students who fit with the level of excellence for which it is well known. The qualities that define William and Mary students are far from set in stone: First and foremost, William and Mary is looking for students who will be able to both give to and take from the college as much as possible. Characteristics that aren't quantifiable such as leadership, creativity, or character, are as carefully considered as is academic performance.

Academic qualification, typically foremost in the minds of prospective students, is not based on any specific set of course requirements; however, most admitted students have taken the strongest courses available at their high schools. Usually included are four years of English, four years of math, four years of a foreign language, three years of history, three years of science, and other elective courses. Applicants from the state of Virginia are encouraged to strive for the Advanced Studies diploma as a minimum. The Admissions Office recognizes that course offerings are not consistent between schools so it is important to remember that there are exceptions to every rule.

I remember sitting in an information session after touring William and Mary when I was in high school. Several of the other prospective students in the room asked questions about their chances of admission, stating that they had taken five or six AP (Advanced Placement) courses; some had even taken classes at colleges in their hometowns. They played on sports teams or held offices in student government. I began to get nervous. I had only taken three AP classes. There was a college in my hometown but I hadn't taken any classes there. I didn't letter in any sports, and I wasn't class president. Sure I was pretty involved in other types of activities and organizations during high school, but they seemed to pale in comparison to the accomplishments of these other students. Not only that, but I was applying from out of state! What I realized after the fact (and after I had been accepted) is that it's not just a game of numbers. The Admissions Office doesn't decide to accept one person over another just because his or her GPA is a few tenths of a point higher, he or she took one more AP class than the other, or was involved in one more extracurricular activity. William and Mary doesn't just want to know what you've done and how well you did it—they want to know why you chose to do it, what you got out of it, what you will bring to the college as a result of those experiences, and what you will in turn hope to get out of your college experience in the future.

Standardized Tests

All applicants must take the SAT I or ACT in order to be admitted. Three SAT II: Subject tests are strongly recommended but none are required. Subject tests are used for advising. This type of testing must be completed by January of the senior year so that scores will be reported to William and Mary in time. Incoming students must also meet proficiency requirements in foreign language and writing. You can exempt yourself from these ordinarily required courses if you have already satisfied the requirements through successful completion of four years of one foreign language, a minimum score of 600 on the SAT II: Foreign Language test (650 on the Latin test), successful scoring on the AP English Exam, or with a combined score of 1350 on the English portion of the SAT I and the SAT II: Writing test.

The Intangibles

As mentioned earlier, things such as attitude, values, or leadership are just as important at William and Mary as grades and test scores. So how do they assess the intangibles? The process actually relies heavily on you, the applicant. It is up to you to present your activities and what you've accomplished through them, to tell the admissions staff about your interests and your values. Use the essay questions as your opportunity to really tell something about yourself. The William and Mary application has several creative questions for you to answer, one of which was introduced in 1996 and received nationwide attention for its innovation. The question asks applicants whom they would put on a twentieth-century Mount Rushmore. The admissions staff is always improving on their questions to give applicants more freedom to creatively tell about themselves and what they would add to the William and Mary community.

So what are your chances? William and Mary is a fairly small school, especially when compared to other schools of its caliber. Each undergraduate class is comprised of between 1,000 and 1,500 students. The entering freshman class in 1997 was made up of 880 Virginians and 464 out-of-state students out of close to 7,200 total who initially applied. Those can seem like some fairly intimidating numbers, but don't be discouraged. The first thing to do to get yourself moving in the right direction is to apply on time!

Deadlines

Like most other colleges, William and Mary offers an Early Decision plan for students who have already decided that William and Mary is their first choice. This plan is binding at William and Mary, which means that students who choose to apply Early Decision agree to attend if they are accepted. Students who want to apply early must have all application materials in by November 1 and will be notified in the beginning of December. Applicants not accepted Early Decision will automatically be reconsidered for Regular Decision.

There are two parts to the William and Mary application; both must be accepted by January 15 for freshmen, by February 15 for college students who would like to transfer for the fall semester, and by November 1 for transfers for the spring semester.

ACADEMIC LIFE

A college or university has truly succeeded if it is able to prepare its students for successful lives after graduation. William and Mary gives students the academic and social backgrounds necessary to make them competitive in the job market and accomplished scholars in graduate programs. Professionals and academics know how well prepared William and Mary students are and many specifically seek out W&M grads as a result. So how does William and Mary do it?

PHI BETA KAPPA

The national honor society Phi Beta Kappa was founded at the College of William and Mary, as was the first Honor Code system. The Honor Code is still in place and is taken very seriously by William and Mary students today.

Faculty

William and Mary encourages students to develop a very well-rounded educational base while at the college. It requires that students take classes in all of the different types of disciplines, but attempts to leave the students a lot of flexibility when it comes to choosing which specific courses to try. Because of William and Mary's smaller size, most classes are small enough for students to interact regularly with the professor and with fellow classmates. The student to faculty ratio is approximately 12:1. A few introductory classes have between 100 and 200 people, the most students in any one class. In these classes, the professor has teaching assistants who are available to answer questions and instruct labs, but a professor always teaches the class and also is very willing to help the students. At larger universities, you may have a graduate student teach your whole class and never see an actual professor all semester but at William and Mary you have easy access to your professors. The William and Mary faculty was recently ranked third in the country, and first among public schools by a *U.S. News and World Reports* poll. For W&M professors, research and publication are important, but teaching always comes first.

Starting freshman year, William and Mary students have classes taught by highly qualified professors who are well respected within their fields of expertise. To further enhance this experience, William and Mary has created a freshman seminar program that is guaranteed for all first-year students. These seminars are, for the most part, taught by full professors. The maximum number of students allowed in the seminars is fifteen. Freshmen are given top priority in enrolling for these classes. The seminars focus on a variety of interesting issues that are a part of the different academic disciplines. They give students a more detailed and personal view of a discipline early on while they are adjusting to college and trying to decide on a major.

Majors

There are roughly forty possible undergraduate majors, but William and Mary also gives students the opportunity to create their own majors if a combination of two or more different degrees' requirements fits the student's goals better. There are also opportunities within each major to explore personal interests through independent study or senior honors projects. Students work one-on-one with professors to choose and research their topics. William and Mary also provides opportunities for undergraduates to attend conferences related to their disciplines and present papers there. Some of these undergraduate papers have even gone on to be published!

I was nervous about the idea of presenting my thesis at a professional conference, but I figured I may not have the opportunity again. Despite being nervous, however, I was also looking forward to the experience. It was wonderful to meet so many professionals in my field, as well as undergraduates from other universities with whom I was able to compare notes.

Academic departments at William and Mary also provide students who have similar interests opportunities to gather through clubs or study groups. These clubs bring in prominent speakers from the different disciplines, and several also hold career seminars for students within a particular major to help students decide how to apply what they have learned.

SOCIAL LIFE AND ACTIVITIES

Because college is a place where students live and not merely a place where they go to class, the extracurricular and social activities available are just as important to the experience a student has during his or her college years. William and Mary has over 300 student interest groups, most of which are organized and run solely by students. There are several service-oriented clubs such as Circle K or Alpha Phi Omega (a coed service fraternity), clubs that focus on different ethnic backgrounds such as the Black Student Organization or the Indian Cultural Association, social fraternities and sororities, a literary magazine, the school newspaper, the yearbook, student government, the pep band, dance, and choir, to name only a few.

Delis

The majority of students' social lives are centered around the campus, campus activities, or other students they know from campus. A common weekend activity for several students is visiting different fraternities and their parties, and socializing with friends there. The delis are also a popular hang-out. These are restaurant/bars that are located within walking distance of campus. There are three different delis located next door to one another, and all are famous among students for their terrific submarine sandwiches and cheese fries. They are great places to casually hang out with friends and watch a game, listen to a band, or just talk and unwind from a busy week.

Performing Arts

The strength and variety of the performing arts at William and Mary does not leave much room for boredom either. The theater department puts on several productions a year, including some that are student directed. There is also a student-organized improvisational theater group that performs all over campus and is a favorite among the students. The Choir, which celebrated its seventy-fifth anniversary in 1997, continuously wows its audiences. It was asked to perform at the Presidential Inauguration in 1997, and was also honored by an invitation to sing at the funeral for Ambassador Pamela Harriman later that year. The Choir has performed for audiences all across the country and the world. William and Mary is also fortunate enough to have several student-run *a capella* singing groups. There are all-female, all-male, and coed groups that all sing a variety of styles of music—their concerts are incredibly popular among students and non-students alike.

Greeks

Somewhere between one-quarter and one-third of the William and Mary student body is Greek, meaning that they are members of a sorority or fraternity. There are thirteen sororities and fifteen nationally recognized social fraternities, all of which have their lodging on campus. These groups busy themselves with social, athletic, and philanthropic activities throughout the year.

Athletics

The athletics at William and Mary are also a big draw for students. William and Mary alumni and current students are very supportive of the twenty-three male and female intercollegiate teams. The club and intramural sports are also extremely popular among undergraduate and graduate students. At the varsity level, W&M has great teams in football, basketball, lacrosse, soccer, field hockey, and many more. Several William and Mary athletes have gone on to play at the professional level in sports such as football and soccer; in fact, a 1997 graduate of William and Mary was drafted by that year's Super Bowl Champs, the Green Bay Packers. William and Mary students aren't satisfied with sitting back and watching others conquer the athletic fields, however. Many students choose to get out and play through club or intramural sports. Club sports such as crew are a few steps down from the level of serious competition associated with varsity sports. Club teams compete against clubs from other colleges and universities in Virginia. Even more casual than that are intramural sports. Any students who can get enough of their friends together can form an intramural team that is then scheduled to play against other IM teams. Members of the same freshman hall, sorority members, fraternity members, or other associations come together to play each other in baseball, basketball, floor hockey, softball...the list is endless!

Along those same lines, the student recreation center is an attractive place that many students choose to spend some of their free time. There are basketball courts, racquetball courts, a pool, a weight room, exercise machine room, and more. It is a great facility for working out or for playing a pick-up game of basketball with a few friends.

Community Service

Students at William and Mary are also very involved in activities that help the community. There seems to be a large amount of interest from William and Mary students in volunteerism. The Office of Volunteer Services helps to publicize what opportunities exist, and where students can provide the most assistance:

- There is a Habitat for Humanity student club that helps to build homes for needy people.
- Several students also volunteer their time helping tutor children who live in Williamsburg or the surrounding areas. There is a Big Brothers/Big Sisters program in Williamsburg and some students have adopted a brother or sister to help mentor during their time at William and Mary.
- Blood drives are frequently held on campus through the Red Cross and sponsored by fraternities or sororities.
- There is also an annual bone marrow drive that is organized by students on campus.

The first bone marrow drive held on campus was a small effort organized by faculty in support of a professor who was in need of a bone marrow transplant. It was then picked up by Jay Bukzin, '94, who pulled together an incredible drive for which he was able to raise enough money so that no one who came to be entered into the registry of potential donors had to pay the normal $45 cost of tissue typing his or her blood sample. Jay was hoping to increase the chances for his younger brother to find a matching bone marrow donor to save him from his leukemia. Even though Jay has graduated, we still recognize the difficulty of finding a tissue type match that is accurate enough to make a bone marrow transplant possible. At last count, there were seventeen people who entered the registry at one of the William and Mary drives who have matched and donated their marrow to someone in need—that number has probably climbed even higher by now. That's a lot of lives that might not have been saved without our efforts.

FINANCIAL AID

The tuition and fees are definitely a great bargain for residents of Virginia, and a competitive cost for out-of-state students as well, especially when compared to the tuition fees of private colleges and universities. Nonetheless, the expense of a college education is a difficult burden to bear, and many students rely on financial aid for assistance.

As is the case at most other universities, financial assistance can come in different forms. Aid can be received based on need or merit. It is given out in the form of grants (money that does not have to be paid back), loans, or work-study opportunities. The Free Application for Federal Student Aid (FAFSA) is used to determine each student's need. Early Decision applicants should have their forms turned in by November 1; Regular Decision applicants should turn in their forms between January 1 and February 15.

Federally funded grants such as the Pell Grant and the Supplemental Educational Opportunity Grant are available at William and Mary, as are federally sponsored loans such as the Perkins Loan and the Stafford Loan. The State Council of Higher Education for Virginia (SCHEV) awards the Virginia Transfer Grant for minority transfer students. Some academic departments give scholarships to students who demonstrate outstanding scholarship in that field. There are several other unique opportunities for assistance such as $1,500 scholarships offered by the Order of the White Jacket for students who are working in food service to help put themselves through school.

GRADUATES

The College of William and Mary provides its students with an environment, not just an education, which prepares them for all aspects of life after college. To be competitive today, there is a lot more to success in the professional world than having book smarts. We have to know how to do the job, how to work well with co-workers, how our job and our company fits into the bigger picture. Memorizing a few formulas won't cut it. At William and Mary, students are given the well-rounded background they need to live life to the fullest once they graduate.

William and Mary graduates have become important members of the community by continuing the tradition they adopted at William and Mary of working hard to accomplish the goals they believe in, goals that improve their lives and the lives of others.

William and Mary students develop a loyalty to the college that extends far beyond their undergraduate years. Thousands of alumni come back every fall for Homecoming and thousands more remain connected to other William and Mary graduates through alumni chapters and clubs that are organized throughout the country and even abroad. Many William and Mary alumni remain very involved in the lives of current students as well. Several are willing to offer internships to W&M students at their places of business. Many of the companies who recruit at William and Mary have a large body of W&M grads already employed. They know the caliber of our students and come looking for more!

PROMINENT GRADS

- **Carter Braxton, Signer of the Declaration of Independence**
- **John Cannon, Tampa Bay Buccaneers**
- **Steve Christie, Buffalo Bills**
- **Glenn Close, Actress**
- **Benjamin Harrison, Signer of the Declaration of Independence**
- **Brian Hyde, Olympic Athlete**
- **Thomas Jefferson, President of the United States, Signer of the Declaration of Independence**
- **Linda Lavin, Actress**
- **James Monroe, President of the United States**
- **Darren Sharper, Green Bay Packers**
- **John Tyler, President of the United States**
- **George Wythe, Signer of the Declaration of Independence**

SUMMING UP

The College of William and Mary provides a superb liberal arts experience for all of its students.

- The on-campus living arrangements foster friendship building and self-discipline.
- The academic courses offer students the opportunity to take a focused look into a variety of different disciplines and subject matters within those disciplines. Better still, students are able to discuss these subjects with their professors, some of the best in the country in their given fields.
- Extracurricular activities such as sports, fraternities, sororities, service clubs, and religious groups allow students to relax and have fun with friends while developing their organization and leadership skills.
- The Office of Career Services holds a whole library of career information and hosts on-campus interviews with a variety of companies recruiting new employees.

William and Mary provides a very special situation for its students. Faculty and staff help every step of the way, but students are also allowed enough freedom to learn the independence and self-reliance they will need for life after college. Many people talk about William and Mary being very competitive and a very challenging place for students to maintain grade point averages they were used to having in high school. This is true, to a certain extent. At William and Mary you cannot sleep through class and expect to get an A. William and Mary has some of the best faculty members in the country and they know they have some of the best students; anyone intelligent and committed enough to be admitted to William and Mary will do just fine!

Students who consider William and Mary are looking for a university that isn't so large that they become lost in the crowd or just another number passed from one teaching assistant to another. They want a school that is big enough for a diverse student population and for a variety of academic and social options to be available, a school that has a personal touch and has a staff that is there to help with any problems the students face, yet they also want a school that allows its students the personal freedom to decide what classes to schedule and when, when to come and go from residence halls, and when to study and when to play. On graduation day, students can truly feel proud to have a diploma from the College of William and Mary. Remember, however, it is going to take a lot more than a college degree to get you a good job, regardless of the reputation of the school printed on your diploma. Your personal qualifications and your ability to present yourself are just as important, if not more so, and those are things you won't develop at just any university. The William and Mary experience won't let you down, academically, socially, or professionally, during college and the years beyond.

❑ *Kathleen McKeon, B.A.*

COLUMBIA UNIVERSITY/BARNARD COLLEGE

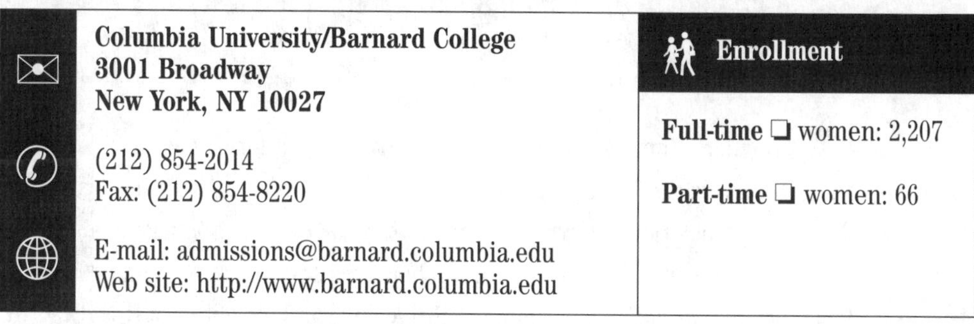

Columbia University/Barnard College
3001 Broadway
New York, NY 10027

(212) 854-2014
Fax: (212) 854-8220

E-mail: admissions@barnard.columbia.edu
Web site: http://www.barnard.columbia.edu

Enrollment

Full-time ❑ women: 2,207

Part-time ❑ women: 66

INTRODUCING BARNARD COLLEGE

Barnard College may not have a schmaltzy alma mater, but that doesn't mean its students aren't singing its praises or that the rest of the campus isn't whistling a happy tune. With applications soaring and physical plant renovations springing up all over the place, the college is moving and shaking in all sorts of ways. President Judith Shapiro is spearheading a major campaign for "Barnard of Tomorrow," the benefits of which are already being felt on campus.

Recently, the greenhouse, gymnasium, and major lecture halls were refurbished and upgraded, student computer consultants are available around the clock in each residence hall, and Elie Wiesel and alumna Suzanne Vega (among others) appeared before large and enthusiastic audiences. Not bad for a college whose mission is to educate and support the growth of some 2,200 students, all of whom are motivated and talented, all of whom are women.

Paradoxically, it is easy to forget that Barnard is a women's college, what with the intellectual excitement and the variety of activity on the campus. Barnard's unique relationship with Columbia University means that Barnard's women have access to a coed experience at all times, but on their own terms. It also means that the Barnard faculty and administration have as their main focus and attention the female Barnard student body, not the coed masses across the street (literally—Columbia's campus is just on the east side of Broadway). Therefore, the Barnard student is taught by faculty members rather than teaching assistants. These scholars are experts in their fields and have immeasurable resources that they share with their students. Or, as one young alumna put it:

> *As a graduate student at [Ivy League School X], I advised undergrads on their senior theses. I tried to be helpful, but I only know so much. My thesis advisor at Barnard was the chair of her department, a wealth of information, and an all-around inspiration.*

Add to this wonderful mixture Barnard's New York City location—now considered the safest major city in America by the FBI—and one begins to see what all the fuss is about. A stroll down Broadway, a bus ride uptown, or a subway trip to Greenwich Village enables students to experiment in the most diverse cultural laboratory this side of the United Nations (where students regularly intern). The glamor of Fifth Avenue and the glitter of Broadway are equally accessible. And, as in any urban setting, opportunities abound to make a difference in the community: Barnard women serve as legal advocates to the homeless, tutors in the America Reads program, and providers of hot meals through the Community Lunch Program. So nice they named it twice, New York is a great college town.

ADMISSIONS REQUIREMENTS

Barnard is, quite simply, "hot," which is both exciting and daunting. Everybody and her sister seems to be applying, creating a stir among prospective students and the admissions staff. In recent years, the college has barely utilized its waiting list, indicating that the "yield" of students initially offered admission has gotten to a point where the ideal number of new students can be attained in one fell swoop. The current admissions cycle reflects a seven percent increase in applications, continuing an upward trend that has more than doubled the applicant pool since 1991. Barnard has become America's most selective women's college.

Getting into Barnard isn't all that easy, but there is no single criterion a student can point and know, "THIS is the reason I was admitted." The application process is the usual, including personal data, high school transcripts, official copies of standardized test scores (either the ACT or the SAT I plus three SAT II Subject tests, including one in Writing or Literature), and three recommendations—one from a principal or counselor and two from teachers (preferably in academic subject areas). Barnard also accepts the common application. If Barnard is the student's first choice, she may apply for Early Decision (ED); the deadline is November 15. Applicants may be deferred to the general application pool if they are denied admission. The regular deadline for application is January 15.

The admissions staff at Barnard works hard to make sure that each student offered admission will thrive in her own way. The ideal applicant to Barnard has a solid record, pursues diverse interests, and shows promise that she will take advantage of the breadth and depth of experiences the college and New York City will offer her.

The High School Record

The high school record is the single most important part of the application. While overall achievement (that is, high grades) is important, the admissions staff makes it very clear that they care about a student's demonstrated effort to challenge herself in the classroom. This means an A in a less rigorous class doesn't mean as much as a B+ in one that is more rigorous. In addition, course availability is taken into consideration. For instance, if a particular high school offers twenty-five ways to exceed the minimum graduation requirements, and an applicant avails herself of only one or two, she doesn't seem to indicate that she'd take advantage of the thousands of opportunities that await her upon matriculation at Barnard. On the other hand, an applicant taking the only two AP courses available at her high school can't be expected to do any more, but those courses are important measures of her success. In addition, because the college expects students to study a broad range of subjects, evidence of that interest—four years of English, social studies, and math and at least three years of science and foreign language—is very important.

Other Criteria

That is not to say that the Barnard experience is solely an academic one! The college takes pride in the amazing collective talent of its actors and athletes, debaters and dancers. Indeed, its strength comes from its unparalleled diversity—students hail from forty-seven states and fifty-eight countries, from around the corner and around the world. One in three Barnard students identifies herself as Asian American, African American/Black, Latina, or Native American. Participation and leadership in extracurricular activities—clubs, teams, youth groups, or community service opportunities—are part of the admissions picture. Holding down a part-time job is also considered in this category, as some high school students are active contributors to their family's overall earnings. Multiyear commitment to an activity is always a plus; it shows your ability to stay with something for longer than it takes to get your picture taken for the yearbook. A liberal arts college wants to educate students to be good citizens, not simply good scholars. Participation in the community, which often translates into activity and volunteer participation, is a reality at Barnard, a positive reality.

Standardized Tests and the Essay

Now, about those pesky standardized tests. They are required, they count for something, and it's a good idea to do your best on them. They are the one measure that can be used to compare students no matter where they're from. That said, as the official admissions materials state, "no preconceived profile of an ideal student population limits the number of applicants accepted from any one group." So when it's time to fill out the personal part of the application, students should feel free to show some personality and let their individual quirks and interests peek through. The essays are a student's golden opportunity to express herself, her views, and her goals—and not knowing exactly what to do with one's life is a terrific place to start as a Barnard first-year student!

ACADEMIC LIFE

The admissions staff brings in class after class of students who dive into the curriculum. Graduation requirements ensure that a Barnard degree means something; all students must be competent in writing, quantitative reasoning, and in a foreign language. Beyond the depth provided by a major field (from which there are about fifty to choose, or students may combine or design their own), distribution requirements guarantee exposure to the humanities and social and natural sciences, as well as to a variety of cultures and societies. Several of the requirements overlap, however, and students always have a choice as to how to fulfill them. Although all students must take First-Year English, there are several topical areas from which to choose (American Identities and Writing Women's Lives are two of them). Its companion course, First-Year Seminar, is taught by faculty from all departments, allowing every first-year student the opportunity to discuss and write about subjects ranging from The Woman Warrior to The Psychology of Communication and from The Existence of Evil to The Crisis of Authority. Both of these courses are limited in size to promote active participation, lively discussion, and plenty of personal attention from the professors.

Faculty

Again and again, Barnard students and alumnae praise their academic experiences at the college.

> *Faculty members are great. They provide so much encouragement, are more than willing to provide a recommendation or just some encouragement and ideas. One history professor even helped me get my first real apartment!*

This kind of testimonial is available from virtually every Barnard student. Their close and productive relationships with the highly acclaimed Barnard faculty make Barnard a singular institution. Barnard students frequently collaborate with faculty as research assistants, so it is not unusual to hear a senior describe her work with an anthropology professor, or a junior discuss her experiences in the biology laboratory. Not long ago, a Barnard first-year student was asked to spend a semester at an astronomy station on Nantucket Island, where the other participants in the program were all graduate students.

During their first two years, Barnard students receive counseling from members of the faculty and the Dean of Studies Office.

> *My advisor helped me figure out what courses would be most useful to me in choosing a major and at the same time satisfying my general requirements. He also suggested I become a calculus tutor and helped me secure a summer internship at CBS news.*

Advisors are well versed in Barnard's policies and regulations, working closely with the Deans' Office and the Registrar to ensure that all students are on the right track for graduation. At the end of the student's second year, advisors are prepared to assist with the transition into the major. From then on, students are advised by a faculty member in their major department; a double major will have two advisors. Students can decide whether they want to establish a close relationship with their advisors or keep it strictly business. Advisors are prepared to provide the necessary and required parts of the job, but they have chosen this role because they want to be available to students in a more personal way. It is therefore not unusual for an advisor to write graduate school or other critical recommendations for students they never actually taught, but who they have come to know well over the course of several years together.

Affiliation with Columbia

Barnard's affiliation with Columbia means that the curricular offerings of one of the country's top research universities are available for the asking; courses in all departments are available for cross-registration. About equal numbers of Barnard and Columbia students do this, indicating a true academic parity between the two schools. Some celebrated professors have become major attractions; for example, Barnard's Richard Pious and Dennis Dalton are quite sought after, both as noted scholars in their fields (the American presidency and Gandhi, respectively) and as regular teachers of first-year students in introductory courses. Barnard students especially join their Columbia counterparts in courses taught by luminaries Edward Said and Robert Thurman in comparative literature and religion. While some departments are particularly focused on one campus or the other (theater at Barnard, for example, or computer science at Columbia), the offerings by popular departments such as English, history, and political science amount to nearly twice the number of courses as would be available otherwise. In every case, academic advisors can help students make informed choices about their course selection.

Senior Theses or Projects

Each Barnard student's academic endeavors are capped off by a significant culminating experience, which comes in the form of a senior thesis, project, or exam in her major. Preparing for and completing this terminal work presents true challenges, but that's part of the Barnard way. It understandably unifies the class; the buzz of activity in the library, labs, and studios keeps the midnight oil burning senior year. The idea is that if a student can succeed in such a project, she can do it in just about any field she chooses after Barnard. All things being equal, an art history major could just as easily land a financial services job as an economics major; they both certainly have the verbal, research, and critical thinking skills such a position might require.

Joint Programs

Other academic attractions include joint programs with the Juilliard School and the Manhattan School of Music, the Jewish Theological Seminary, and various graduate and professional schools of Columbia University such as the School of Engineering, the School of International and Public Affairs, the Law School, and the Dental School. While entrance into these programs is quite limited and often extremely competitive, the students who participate in them not only benefit themselves, but they contribute an extra degree of depth and diversity to their Barnard classrooms.

Exchange and Overseas Programs

About 200 students go on study leave each year, be it for one semester or two. Barnard's official exchange programs in the United States include Spelman College and Biosphere II in Arizona, while overseas programs are located in England, France, Germany, Italy, Japan, and Spain. These programs are structured so that, for example, students may bring their financial aid packages with them; however, Barnard students' diverse interests take them to such far-flung places as Russia, Israel, the Cameroons, Nicaragua, and Australia. The world, as they say, is their oyster. The Study Abroad Advisor meets with students individually and in groups, providing information and guidance before and after the experience.

After spending the spring term at the London School of Economics, I was feeling rather "out of the loop" at Barnard. When I attended Dean Szell's special meeting in the fall, my advisor helped me realize that I wasn't the only one feeling this way.

These kinds of touches mark the Barnard experience from start to finish. Whether it's the personal letter sent by the first-year class dean upon matriculation or the handshake from the college's president at graduation, the Barnard faculty and administration make a concerted effort to ensure that each student's experience at Barnard is individual and special.

SOCIAL LIFE AND ACTIVITIES

The past president of Barnard College, alumna Ellen Futter, often characterized Barnard by saying, "This is *not* a cloistered enclave," thus coining a slogan for the ages. While students find campus activities galore, they have never-ending access to the unquantifiable offerings of what is arguably the world's greatest city; moreover, the college tries to make the city's offerings affordable for the usually cash-strapped undergrad. Discount vouchers to first-run films and the performing arts supplement the popular Urban New York program, which takes students to events such as *Ragtime* on Broadway, opening day at Yankee Stadium, the New York Philharmonic, and even the circus, all for the price of the subway ($3.00 round-trip). Each trip is escorted by a member of the college or university faculty or administration, providing an extra opportunity to get to know a key member of the community in a relaxed, sometimes unconventional, setting.

Most students worry, to some degree or other, about making friends in college. If they can be generalized in any way, Barnard friendships are built to last. That said, the need for privacy inherent in living in New York City means that personal space is valued and respected. People don't run right up to you to get to know you here, but don't mistake that for unfriendliness. Attend any club meeting, event, or party and you're sure to make a new acquaintance. Whether it's the woman in your sponsor group during orientation, the friend of a friend from high school or summer camp who lives down the hall, or the person who wants to have coffee after orchestra practice, student life lends itself to the friendship-making process.

Housing

Barnard's residential focus means a great deal of programming takes place in the dorms. First-year students are clustered together in the quad, a grouping of (surprise!) four halls that situated on the south end of the main campus houses a total of about 900 students. The main dining room is located here, in Hewitt Hall, and the Quad Café is open late into the evening for that much-needed burst of energy courtesy of Starbucks Coffee. Beyond the quad, which primarily features the traditional corridor style of dormitory living, upperclass students live in suites of various configurations in six other residence halls surrounding the main campus. In every hall, Resident Assistants (RAs) sponsor floor programs and study breaks to foster social connections; movie nights and guest appearances by various peer education groups and speakers offer something for just about everyone. After the first year, students select their own living space through a lottery process. In addition, they may enter the lottery in groups, sometimes with their Columbia friends, for suite living on either campus. Another more competitive option is to participate in Special Interest Housing, meaning that students come together around a theme such as Community Service, Foreign Language, or Environmental Awareness, and sponsor programs in their residence hall for everyone's benefit. The Housing Office offers forums early in the spring semester to help explain the various options.

Outside Groups

The amount and quality of activity sponsored by and for the college is inspiring. While the faculty and administration present lectures and readings by prominent and emerging scholars and artists, students themselves create and invite a great deal of programming. Thus, you're likely to find both a classical musical recital and a concert by an alternative band, with a *Barnard Bulletin* (a news weekly) reporter on hand to interview the talent and audience as well. Barnard's radio station, WBAR, broadcasts a college/alternative format and there are traditional activities such as the yearbook and student government (called SGA), which is responsible for the eighty or so student organizations. Cultural organizations and various other community groups come under SGA's umbrella.

That said, there are at least as many groups at Columbia, giving Barnard students the opportunity to work on a daily paper (the *Spectator*) or a jazz-oriented radio station (WKCR), to get involved in religious, volunteer, and political organizations (most of which are jointly sponsored by Barnard, but whose offices are physically located on the Columbia campus), and clubs galore.

The Greeks

The Greek system, including both sororities and coed fraternities, is open to Barnard students who want to experience more "traditional" collegiate life. Those who take part in them tend to rave about their experiences; however, the SGA constitution prohibits groups that limit their membership and therefore does not recognize the Greek system. There's hardly a more concrete example of how student life at Barnard offers something for everyone!

Productions

Dance, theater, and musical productions abound. From improv comedy to *a cappella* singing, Barnard women regularly appear on stage. Two annual events are Acapellooza, an *a cappella* jamboree hosted by Barnard's own Bacchantae, which features groups from the university and selected others and results in a professional-quality CD, and Broadway Tonight, a benefit performance of Broadway selections that teams up Barnard students with professionals from the Great White Way. Off stage, students provide technical support and packed houses. This is one talented group of students, and a group appreciative of the efforts of their peers.

Athletics

Those who prefer their thrills on a court, arena, or stadium can participate on a number of levels. Barnard varsity athletes compete in Division I archery, basketball, soccer, field hockey, crew, tennis, lacrosse, cross-country, track and field, swimming and diving, and volleyball as part of the athletic consortium with their counterparts from Columbia College and the School of Engineering. We're talking Ivy League here—no athletic scholarships, just sheer love of the game. Club sports such as Ultimate Frisbee, sailing, and rugby offer unique opportunities for intercollegiate competition and comraderie. Intermurals provide a great way to let loose, either in soccer, basketball, or even bowling (at Barnard's on-campus alley). Finally, many students work out on their own or with friends by running in Riverside Park, taking a student-led aerobics class, or swimming a few laps in the Barnard pool. While obviously not an outdoorsy, let's-go-skiing-this-afternoon campus, Barnard students enjoy breaking a good sweat.

Off Campus

And, all right, let's not forget Barnard's location. From poetry readings to film screenings, cafés and restaurants to galleries and museums, concert halls to night clubs, this is the city that never sleeps and always has something to offer. Parades, street fairs, festivals, and impromptu concerts are year-round occurrences. Professional sports teams have crosstown rivals, bookstores have cappuccino, and there's nothing quite like a trip to Central Park, whether it's for a visit to the zoo, rollerblading around the Loop, or ice-skating at Wollman Rink. Even the lifelong New Yorker will find herself traveling to new places and trying new foods with her Barnard friends—and a welcome number of area restaurants deliver to the residence halls for snacking on sushi, tandoori, pizza, lo mein, or simply a nice deli sandwich.

FINANCIAL AID

Private colleges are expensive. Barnard's tuition falls in line with its peer institutions, but that doesn't make the bill much easier to swallow. Unlike many schools, however, Barnard admits students on a need-blind basis, meaning that students are admitted regardless of their ability to pay. Moreover, they are met with a full-need financial aid package in keeping with the federal government's formulas—once the Financial Aid Office has calculated the amount that a student and her family are able to contribute, it offers a package to make up the difference. Approximately sixty percent of the student body receives some form of financial assistance.

Generally speaking, this package has three parts. First, all students are expected to borrow money, but Barnard does not expect both the student and her parents to take out loans. Next, students are asked to work during the school year to contribute to their own education, with work-study awards focused on first-year and sophomore students in particular to assist in their getting to know the campus and its functionings; upperclass students are encouraged to find off-campus jobs relating to their majors or career interests. Summer earnings are also expected after the first year. Finally, the college provides grants—funds that need not be repaid—to bridge the gap. Half of the student body receives grant monies from Barnard.

New York state residents who meet certain financial and academic criteria may apply as Higher Education Opportunity Program (HEOP) students. This program, sponsored by New York state but largely funded by the college itself, provides intensive preenrollment preparation for Barnard academics as well as special counseling and support during all four years. About twenty-five students are admitted each year under the HEOP program and their graduation rate is on par with the overall Barnard student population.

GRADUATES

Barnard women are staunch and loyal supporters of their alma mater, leading to an "old-girl" network that spans the country and the world. Organized Barnard Clubs in many regions sponsor faculty lectures and receptions for admitted students, but even more prevalent is the individual connection—the women who make themselves available to assist current students and fellow alumnae through informational interviews, internships, job contacts, and relocation support.

Several times a year, alumnae appear on panels to discuss their career paths, in fields ranging from psychology to law, from education to arts management. The BEST program, sponsored by the Career Development Office, not only organizes these panels and helps seniors with résumé and interview tips, but also offers workshops on building a business wardrobe, following proper etiquette at business meals, and even how to find a New York City apartment.

Thanks especially to the high standards and personal encouragement of the faculty, Barnard is one of the leading producers of Ph.D.s in the country. The most recent study of private undergraduate colleges (done by Franklin and Marshall College for the decade of the '80s) ranked Barnard third overall—first in the fields of psychology and anthropology/sociology and in the top five in foreign language, English and history—in the number of its graduates receiving Ph.Ds. Not women graduates, *all* graduates. In terms of medical doctors, Barnard ranks fifth in the country in the number of women who become physicians, behind much larger institutions such as Cornell, Harvard, Stanford, and the University of Michigan. While no studies have been done on the field of law, Barnard boasts a remarkable array of graduates who go on to become lawyers and judges.

PROMINENT GRADS

- **Helene Gayle, Assistant Surgeon General of the United States**
- **Mary Gordon, Author**
- **Erica Jong, Author**
- **Jeane Kirkpatrick, United Nations Ambassador**
- **Margaret Mead, Anthropologist**
- **Joan Rivers, Comedienne**
- **Martha Stewart, Author, Television Personality**
- **Twyla Tharp, Choreographer**
- **Suzanne Vega, Singer, Songwriter**

A recent graduate who is currently earning her Master's in International Affairs at Columbia recently said, "At Barnard, I learned I could do anything!" and this sentiment seems to echo through the generations. Barnard alumnae have authored more than 3,500 books and such best-selling novelists as Erica Jong, Mary Gordon, and Edwidge Danticat are among the ranks. In journalism, Barnard alumnae have three times won the Pulitzer Prize, including Anna Quindlen and Natalie Angier at the *New York Times*, and most recently Eileen McNamara at the *Boston Globe*. In broadcast news, Cable News Network's Maria Hinojosa and National Public Radio's Susan Stamberg are prominent contributors to their fields.

Former Dean of the College Virginia Gildersleeve helped to charter the United Nations; alumnae Jeane Kirkpatrick and Sylvan Foa became its first female ambassador for the United States and its first female spokesperson, respectively. While their names may be less recognizable, the women who lead Rockefeller and Company and the Ford modeling agency, the presidents of Bank Street College and the American Museum of Natural History, and one of the founders of the National Organization for Women all graduated from Barnard. But whether they have made big names for themselves or have pursued goals more privately, Barnard women make a difference in the world, an aspiration inculcated in them during their years on campus.

SUMMING UP

Barnard's unique position as a small independent college for women closely linked to a first-rate research university and located in one of the world's major cities offers an extraordinary and unparalleled opportunity for those young women smart and savvy enough to avail themselves of it. The internship possibilities and cultural offerings of New York City are second to none, and the intimacy of the Barnard campus and student body provides a perfect home base from which to explore Manhattan. It is a literal and metaphorical oasis, a place where students can relax and learn to express themselves more and more fully.

Often described as "the best of both worlds," Barnard students have the advantages of a women's college—its nurturing and inspiring faculty, the sisterhood that stems from a unity of purpose in studying the liberal arts—while at the same time having full access to the facilities, activities, and social life of a large, coed, multipurpose university. Columbia provides research facilities, graduate programs, and a diversity of talents and backgrounds that no other small college can offer.

A recent article in *Town and Country* magazine featured women from the colleges still affiliated by their Seven Sister history. The interviewer asked a Barnard senior which one part of her education she would use most if she were stranded on a desert island. The student's response?

> *Barnard does not educate women to live on desolate islands. Barnard educates women to make a real difference in the real world.*

As this particular alumna now holds a master's degree in Public Policy and is currently spending a year in China as a Luce Fellow, she is certainly living up to the ideal she expressed.

Whether your interests lie in the humanities, the social and natural sciences, or the arts, Barnard College offers a fertile training ground for young minds and ideas. If the current generation has been described as apathetic, you'd never know it by meeting Barnard students or visiting the campus. The intellectual debates that begin in the classroom and extend into a dining hall or dorm room are reflective of the involvement and curiosity of the student body. Close academic relationships with faculty and peers, and a supportive environment that actively and tacitly provides a foundation for the intellectual and social development of an extraordinary group of young women makes for a wonderful home base from which to explore Columbia University, Morningside Heights, New York City, and the world. Small wonder it is experiencing such a surge in interest and excitement!

❑ *Catherine Webster, B.A.*

COLUMBIA UNIVERSITY/COLUMBIA COLLEGE

Columbia University/Columbia College
212 Hamilton Hall
New York, NY 10027

(212) 854-2521
Fax: (212) 854-1209

E-mail: ugrad-admiss@columbia.edu
Web site: http://www.columbia.edu

Enrollment

Full-time ❑ women: 502
❑ men: 474

INTRODUCING COLUMBIA

I first stepped onto Columbia's campus at nighttime. I was a senior in high school, visiting my cousin in the engineering school and had just arrived from Los Angeles. The sun had just set, but the campus buildings were brightly lit and aglow with white haze. They were intimidating with their red bricks and copper roofs and appeared as academic-looking as I had expected. My first thought was, "What's a poor girl from a Mexican neighborhood in L.A. doing at Columbia? It's Ivy League." Almost seven years later, graduated with both a bachelor's and a master's degree from Columbia, and with a good job in New York, I now know there was nothing I couldn't accomplish in college. I am the strong-willed free-thinker Columbia wanted me to become and New York is where I truly found myself.

THE FIFTEEN COLLEGES AND SCHOOLS WITHIN COLUMBIA UNIVERSITY

- Columbia College
- College of Physicians and Surgeons
- School of Law
- School of Engineering and Applied Sciences
- Graduate School of Arts and Sciences
- Graduate School of Architecture, Planning and Preservation
- School of Nursing
- School of Social Work
- Graduate School of Journalism
- Graduate School of Business
- School of Dental and Oral Surgery
- School of Public Health
- School of International and Public Affairs
- School of General Studies
- School of the Arts

Columbia University is a city within the City. Columbia College, one of four undergraduate schools on the university's Morningside Heights campus in upper Manhattan, is a small college within a large academic setting. Its liberal arts tradition, based on its unique core curriculum, aims to produce students learned not only in factual knowledge, but in the ways of the world, the social and political issues that affect people, and the critical thinking required for today's young leaders.

Founded as King's College in 1754, when America was still a cluster of colonies ruled by England, the school was the first institution of higher learning in the then province of New York. Its first alumni included John Jay, who would later become the first chief justice of the United States, and Alexander Hamilton, who would later become the first secretary of the Treasury.

Suspended during the American Revolution, the school reopened in 1784 as Columbia College, this time rechartered without ties to church or state. It remains the country's oldest independent institution of higher education.

Today, the face of Columbia's student body is as variegated as autumn leaves in Central Park. Going coed in the early 1980s, the college is split down the middle in its number of male and female students, and they come from all fifty states and more than thirty different countries. Every race, culture, and religious background is represented, which makes for a school founded on tolerance and understanding that knows how to celebrate its diversity. All this resides within the framework of New York City, the original melting pot of the nation.

Beyond Columbia's wrought iron gates lies a city brimming with energy, culture, and unforgettable, real-life experiences waiting to happen. Museum Mile, Restaurant Row, Lincoln Center, Broadway, Wall Street, Greenwich Village—upon arriving in New York City, the feeling that it is the center of the world becomes overwhelming! Which is why New York City becomes the perfect accompaniment to an education at Columbia; in many ways, it becomes its own classroom. An arts humanities class (one of the core requirements) might opt to study cathedral architecture inside the Cathedral of St. John the Divine, which is just down the street from campus and which happens to be the world's largest Gothic-style cathedral. A music humanities class (another core requirement) might understand opera a little better by attending Puccini's *La Bohème* at the famed Metropolitan Opera House. A student can visit the New York Stock Exchange to understand the mechanics of economics, and a drama student might learn something about acting technique by catching any number of off-Broadway plays.

But one need not venture outside Columbia's campus to breathe in a little culture or excitement. The surrounding Morningside Heights neighborhood is home to many ethnic restaurants, bookstores, and bars, where one can catch live jazz, stand-up comedy, or a local band any night of the week. There is a twenty-four-hour bagel shop and the all-night diner, of *Seinfeld* fame that has hosted many nocturnal cram sessions. There are poetry readings at cafes, used books being sold at every corner, and perhaps the largest slice of pizza anywhere in the city.

Columbia's students fit right into the neighborhood's bustle. During a leisurely stroll down College Walk, the school's main thruway, one might pass two students disagreeing over an interpretation of hell in Dante's *Inferno*, or a group of students jamming to hip-hop music on the steps of Low Library, the school's main administration building.

Such diversity at Columbia is a very valued component of its student body; therefore, the college's admissions process allows prospective students many opportunities to let themselves, their interests, and their aspirations shine through.

ADMISSIONS REQUIREMENTS

I think what matters more than aptitude to Columbia admissions officers is attitude. I was never a high scorer on standardized tests, and didn't do amazingly well on the SATs, but I was an active student in high school: I played two sports, was a member of a poetry club, and a class vice president. I did well in my English classes and knew right away that I would take a more literary path in college. I had some direction and think that I came off well in my admissions interview and that really helped me.

Columbia College values a student body filled with people from varying geographic, social, economic, and ethnic backgrounds because of the spectrum of perspectives and ideas each student will bring to a class. Therefore, Columbia's admissions selection of an applicant is based on a mixed bag of qualities. Aside from good grades in high school, the admissions officers are looking for extracurricular activities, an applicant's maturity and leadership capabilities, and his or her personal interests, talents, or hobbies.

For a recent first-year class, approximately 11,192 applications were received; of that amount, only 1,943 were accepted (a 17.3 percent admit rate). The odds are tough, but the general rule-of-thumb is that the more well-rounded the applicant, the better the odds.

The comprehensive application is designed to allow students many opportunities to document their achievements, interests, and goals. The regular admission deadline is January 1, and notification of the admissions office's decision gets mailed in April.

Recommendations for Admission

While the admissions office doesn't require a minimum SAT I or ACT score or have strict requirements on high school classes an applicant should take before applying, it does have some recommendations:

- four years of English, with an emphasis on writing
- three or more years of math
- three years or more of a foreign language
- three, but preferably four, years of social science
- three years or more of a lab science like chemistry (however, a student interested in science or medicine should take as much math and science—particularly chemistry and physics—offered in high school)

The required standardized tests are the SAT I: Reasoning test or the ACT Assessment test, and three SAT II: Subject tests (one of which must be the Writing test). The school recommends that these tests be taken in October or November of an applicant's senior year, but will accept scores taken during the junior year.

The Admissions Office will also heavily weigh an applicant's recommendations from a school principal, headmaster, counselor, and teachers, who are asked to comment on the applicant's personal qualities as well as academic stature and involvement in school activities. Interviews are also available with Columbia College alumni located worldwide. Candidates are contacted by Alumni Representative Committee members after the first part of the application is received.

Early Decision

Candidates can also submit their application for Early Decision consideration for admission. Columbia must be the first choice, and completed applications must be in by November 1 of the senior year. Applicants vying for Early Decision will hear from the Admissions Office by mid-December, at which point they are obliged to accept the admission offer and withdraw applications at other colleges.

Columbia College occasionally accepts transfer students entering their sophomore or junior year, who are admitted with advanced standing. The college also has a visiting student program that welcomes students from other colleges to spend all or part of an academic year in New York. However, the program is open only to students other than freshmen.

Once admitted, a Columbia entering class is designed to bring fresh, diverse ideas and opinions to its rigorous academic requirements.

ACADEMIC LIFE

The tie that binds Columbia's varied student population is the college's core curriculum, a rigorous series of required classes based on the contributions of Western civilization to the modern world. Through the core—which was developed after World War I and patterned by many other schools shortly thereafter—students are exposed to the works of Homer, Plato, Beethoven, and Picasso, among other greats.

What makes the core classes a more powerful exposure to the world's great achievements in literature, history, philosophy, art, music, and science, is class size—no seminar class holds more than twenty-two students. In such an intimate setting, students are expected to engage in intellectual observation, argument, comparison, and analysis, all in preparation for the life of the worldly freethinker Columbia would like all its students to become.

The two cornerstones of the core—Literature Humanities and Contemporary Civilization, or Lit Hum and CC as they are popularly called—are year-long classes that are usually taken during the first two years at Columbia. While students may complain about the vast amount of reading they'll do for homework, or each course's length (two-hour classes twice a week for an entire year!), they will in the same breath wish there was more time to spend with each work.

I made the mistake of taking CC during my first year at Columbia, before taking Lit Hum as it is recommended. You could say I delved into the course's subject matter more out of fear and intimidation than sheer intellectual curiosity. The sophomores in my class, well-prepared from their first year of Lit Hum, were assured, effective debaters of their own points and those of the authors we studied. I flopped with my first term paper and was asked to do it over again (perhaps because I did it in a few hours the night before it was due). But with my revision, I learned hard and quick how to dissect Plato's Republic *and find a point that I actually understood. I had to change completely the study habits that got me by in high school, and with that, realized I was no longer one of the elite, smart crowd in school—everyone at Columbia was smart and we were all peers that way.*

Lit Hum is designed to take a close examination of the most influential texts of Western culture. The class is light on lecture and heavy on the sometimes heated discussion of a text's themes that is expected in every class. Students soon enough find that it's not unusual for them to outtalk their professors.

CC was created in 1919 as a war-and-peace-issues course and has evolved into a class preparing students for lives as active, socially minded citizens in this great democratic country of ours. Intense class discussions centered around the works of some of the world's most influential political thinkers will engage students for most of their class time.

Often, teachers for both Lit Hum and CC will invoke the Socratic method to teach a point, provoking the "disputatious learning" so favored at Columbia. Along with the exploration of literary themes and philosophy that students will do as a class by sharing ideas and opinions, students on an individual basis will learn very quickly how to defend their own points of view. And defend them well, which is why it is always painfully obvious in class if a student didn't do the reading.

The rest of the core is composed of:

- the art and music humanities classes, formally called Masterpieces of Western Art and Masterpieces of Western Music (one semester each)
- three semesters of approved science courses
- two years of a foreign language
- one semester of Logic and Rhetoric (a comprehensive writing class)
- one year of physical education (with a mandatory seventy-five-yard swimming test)
- one year of "major cultures" classes, the one peek into non-Western culture and civilization required by the core.

Columbia strongly recommends that students complete all or most of their core requirements before the end of their sophomore year.

Both art and music humanities courses aim to produce visually and musically literate students. In Art Hum, students observe and also analyze the style and motifs of many great paintings, sculptures and monuments of the Western world, like the Greek Parthenon, Picasso's "Guernica," and Frank Lloyd Wright's Guggenheim Museum. Class lectures are supplemented by visits to many of New York's famed museums, galleries, and buildings.

In a similar way, Music Hum—a class that chronologically follows music from its earliest origins to its development of symphonies, opera, and jazz—is enhanced by the city's constant rhythm and beat. Students are expected to attend at least one musical performance, (and of course there are many to choose from in the Big Apple), and write about it for class.

After the Core

Once done with the core requirements, students can then focus the remainder of their tenure at Columbia with any one of the school's sixty-four majors offered in forty-nine departments, each having their own rigorous set of requirements. Majors range from Comparative Literature and African-American Studies to Neuroscience and Behavior and Film Studies. The college's departments most popular with students—English, history, and political science—are also its strongest departments academically.

Academic life for the Columbia student will include an average of about five classes a semester. But the college expects each student to balance school life with on- and off-campus activities and some semblance of a social life (this is where New York City plays a particularly crucial role).

Faculty

Whichever major a student chooses, he or she can expect to learn from the experts in that field. Columbia boasts a faculty that includes thirty-six members of the National Academy of Sciences, ninety-two fellows of the American Academy of Arts and Sciences, twelve recipients of the National Medal of Science, and fifty-five Nobel laureates, who now or at one point taught at or attended the university.

The Library

Here is some information about Butler Library, Columbia's main library:

- It currently holds one third of the university's six-and-one-half-million books (the remaining four million books can be found in any of the school's twenty-two other libraries).
- Butler is also home to the Rare Book and Manuscript Library that contains twenty-four million manuscripts and a half million rare books.
- Each semester at the stroke of midnight before the first day of finals (and whether you like it or not), the notorious Columbia Marching Band storms Butler Library and cajoles everyone present into singing the school's fight song, "Roar, Lions Roar."
- The library was named after former University President Nicholas Murray Butler, who coincidentally was the main force behind the development of the SAT.
- The names of renowned writers are etched onto Butler's facade: Homer, Herodotus, Sophocles, Plato, Aristotle, Vergil, Dante, Shakespeare, Cervantes, Voltaire.

SOCIAL LIFE AND ACTIVITIES

During my first year at Columbia I joined three clubs, did volunteer work with children in Harlem, and played intramural volleyball. Through many student organizations I met other students just like myself and, more importantly, learned from others completely unlike me. What I learned from Columbia's diversity matched what I learned in class. What was interesting was that, despite my involvement outside the classroom, my grades never suffered. I got the best of both worlds, socially and academically, that Columbia had to offer.

At Columbia College, there's a student organization or club for just about everyone—frisbee throwers, volunteers do-gooders, jugglers, *a cappella* singers, debaters, and aspiring comics alike. There are also groups representing just about every ethnic and religious background, political party, and career interest. Student groups plan social and fundraising events, but are also there to foster friendship and support among students who are dealing with being away from home and the things with which they identify. In all, there are over 200 organizations, which include fraternities and sororities, and student-run media outlets, including a daily newspaper, radio station, and cable television channel.

Athletics

Columbia, as part of the Ivy League, also competes in all NCAA Division I sports. Men's varsity teams compete in baseball, basketball, crew (both heavy and lightweight), cross-country, running, fencing, football, golf, soccer, swimming and diving, tennis, wrestling, and track and field, as do women's varsity teams in archery, basketball, crew, cross-country, fencing, field hockey, lacrosse, soccer, swimming and diving, tennis, volleyball, and track and field.

Less-serious athletes enjoy participating in intramural flag football, basketball, racquetball, soccer, softball, squash, swimming, tennis, and volleyball.

I came to Columbia with my high school best friend and we agreed to dorm together our first year in Carmen Hall. We ended up on the thirteenth floor, in room 1313, and while I thought that was a bad omen in the beginning, I could not have been proven more wrong. All of us on the thirteenth floor became one huge family, a giant pack that would dine together every night at the John Jay cafeteria, hop from party to party on Friday nights, and hold all-night cram sessions in the hallway of our floor. I've managed to keep in constant touch with some of those friends since graduation three years ago.

Housing

Most first-year students get housed in Carmen Hall, an all-first-year dorm composed of suites with two double rooms and a bathroom. There is also one TV lounge per floor that usually becomes the main congregation point for everyone. Some first-year students who get lucky will be housed in single rooms in John Jay Hall, some in doubles, and others yet are housed in Shapiro Hall doubles. Carmen, however, is the only dorm to exclusively house first-year students, and while the building may be a little more dated and institutional-looking than the other buildings, it's sure to provide a more fun, more interesting living experience.

New York Life

Beyond Columbia's undergrad dorms is a whole other world—New York City—to explore. Students from big cities will find in New York more of what they enjoyed back home—impressive museums, large sporting events, concert venues, and the like. Those from more suburban homes will find the vast amount of things to do in the Big Apple overwhelming. But every student will find the city invigorating, the subways both scary and thrilling, and the native "New Yawkers" unique and refreshingly uninhibited.

THINGS TO DO IN NEW YORK CITY (WHEN NOT STUDYING)

- ❍ Ice skate in Rockefeller Center.
- ❍ Throw a Frisbee on Central Park's Great Lawn.
- ❍ Make a wish atop the Empire State Building.
- ❍ Take a quick round trip on the Staten Island ferry at sunset (it's only fifty cents!).
- ❍ Shop at Macy's, the world's largest department store.
- ❍ Stroll across the Brooklyn Bridge.
- ❍ Eat dim sum in Chinatown.
- ❍ Catch a Broadway musical (discount tickets are always easy to buy).

True to the song, New York is the city that never sleeps. Nowhere else can you go to see a movie at one in the morning (and that's not the late show!), catch a variety of live bands on a single street (a good place to start is the Village), or dance the night away in any of the city's famed nightclubs.

More and more, however, students are finding enough things to do in Morningside Heights, Columbia's surrounding neighborhood. It's entirely possible during a quick study break to 1) grab a slice of pizza, 2) hear a set of jazz, and 3) play a round of pool at a local bar, and return in time to finish one's work.

At times, a student will go an entire week without setting foot off campus. Besides classes and homework, there are plenty of student-sponsored coffeehouses, musical performances, and drama productions to attend; the options never stop, not for at least four years!

FINANCIAL AID

Columbia's admissions policy is need-blind, meaning the school accepts students solely on their academic, personal, and extracurricular merits before even looking at their ability to pay for tuition and costs (however, this policy only applies to students who are U.S. citizens or permanent residents). The foundation of the college's funding program is its full-need financial aid package, meaning it tries in any way to match a student's demonstrated financial needs. More than half of all enrolled students at the college receive some form of financial aid, whether in the form of grants, loans, or work-study jobs (funding is more limited for transfer students).

Columbia made great pains to match what my parents and I needed to cover tuition costs. I was happy to bear most of that responsibility with Stafford and Perkins loans, and money I earned from my work-study job at the Graduate School of Arts (which was a whole other tremendous learning experience). Sure, now I owe a pretty sizable amount on my loans, but I know I'll pay them off gradually, like a habit, and will hardly notice when I'm done. It's a small cost to pay every month for what Columbia gave me—not only knowledge, but self-assurance, maturity, and loads of memories!

Determining a student's eligibility for financial aid is a multilayered process that will involve lots of frustrating paperwork and deadlines. A student's demonstrated financial need is the difference between tuition and costs and the amount the family can contribute. The family contribution, which includes what both the student and the parents will give, is determined by taking a close look at parents' income and assets, the family size, and the number of family members already attending college.

All entering students are expected to work during the summer and save a certain amount of money to be used toward their contribution ($1,600 for first-year students, $1,800 for sophomores, $2,000 for juniors and $2,100 for seniors). Once at Columbia, students will usually also earn an expected amount of money from an on-campus work-study job.

To receive grant aid (money from Columbia's trust that need not be repaid), students must stay enrolled for eight terms of undergrad study and register for a minimum of twelve points (usually four classes) each term.

Government-funded, low-interest loans (either the Stafford or Perkins loans) can be another source of funding in a student's package. After graduation, a student has a grace period (usually six months) before having to start paying back the loans in increments. The payback time is generally spread over ten years. Because the federal government allows upperclassmen—juniors and seniors—to borrow larger amounts of money, Columbia will usually increase the amount of government loans in their financial aid package.

Every year a student must reapply for financial aid, and any change in income or assets from the previous year will be accounted for in the financial aid package. Students will remain on financial aid only if they continue to do well academically.

GRADUATES

Applying to graduate schools during my senior year happened almost by rote—I just knew there was no other immediate path for me to take. Of course, I wavered on whether I'd get in, so I hoped for the worst from the two schools to which I applied. If I got accepted from either, I'd call it a "pleasant surprise." That acceptance phone call was an ecstatic climax to my four years. I'm halfway through getting my MFA in photography at the School of Visual Arts, and when I'm done with this, I'll start on my master's in art history at Columbia. My dream is to open up my own photo gallery in New York City that will spotlight younger, struggling artists. I'd say I'm off to a great start!

Ninety percent of Columbia College graduates eventually go to graduate school, either right after their four years, or after a few years of working in their fields. Which path a student takes can vary as much as Columbia's diverse student population.

The college's Office of Career Services hosts a comprehensive recruiting program, where many New York-based companies solicit graduating students for outstanding jobs in fields as diverse as publishing, marketing, moviemaking, and engineering.

Economics majors, for example, get aggressively scouted by most of Wall Street's brokerage firms and investment banks, where they can look forward to careers as stockbrokers, analysts, management trainees, or consultants. Many of them eventually wind up in business school, working on MBAs that will further advance their careers.

No matter what, Columbia alums always come back to the alma mater, some in bigger ways than others. In 1987 John Kluge, the media tycoon, donated $25 million for a minority-aid program. Morris Shapiro gave $5 million for the construction of Shapiro Hall, the newer dormitory overlooking the Hudson River. And some alums give back to Columbia and its students by giving on-campus seminars and speeches on their accomplished work.

The Young Alumni Club, created to bring together alums from the previous ten years, has brought many newer, younger faces back to Columbia as well, by organizing Happy Hours and Meet-and-Greets.

PROMINENT GRADS

- **James Cagney, Actor**
- **Art Garfunkel, Musician**
- **Lou Gehrig, New York Yankee**
- **Allen Ginsberg, Poet**
- **Alexander Hamilton, First Secretary of the Treasury**
- **Armand Hammer, Philanthropist**
- **Oscar Hammerstein, Composer**
- **Langston Hughes, Author**
- **John Jay, First Chief Justice of the Supreme Court**
- **Jack Kerouac, Author**
- **John Kluge, Entrepreneur, Philanthropist**
- **Alfred Knopf, Publisher**
- **Tony Kushner, Playwright**
- **Richard Rodgers, Composer**
- **Fifty Nobel Laureates are alumni or current or former faculty members.**

SUMMING UP

The combination of Columbia College's rigorous academics, esteemed faculty, diverse student body, and location within New York City make it easily the most well-rounded Ivy League school in the country. At least, this is the sentiment felt among everyone on campus. From the minute students step onto College Walk for the first time, to the moment they step onto Broadway as newly minted graduates, the whirlwind four years they've just spent will be filled with academic triumphs, unforgettable New York experiences, and relationships with professors and friends that will outlast even those first few years in the professional world.

The core curriculum, designed to embroil each student in the innermost workings of the world's greatest literature, art, music, and political and philosophical thinking, is matched by the world of knowledge waiting outside the school's wrought-iron gates. Required assignments of visiting some of the greatest art museums in the world or taking in a musical performance at any number of famed venues will hardly feel like tedious homework. Plus, the core is ultimately matched by the college's wide-ranging academic majors taught by the leaders in each of forty-nine fields.

Nary a moment is wasted in four years. The Columbia student knows how to balance schoolwork with the myriad social and student on-campus activities, as well as the vast number of goings-on in the city at any given moment.

Students are graduated with factual knowledge as well as street smarts. One student may have spent hours working on differential equations, but also balanced that with tutoring an inner-city high school student in algebra. Another might have composed a thesis on presidential-congressional relations while campaigning for a spot on the college's Student Senate. Columbia's legacy of student involvement and activism, recorded in the school's rich history, is unmatched by any other high-caliber institution of higher learning.

Columbia seeks out the nation's young leaders—those high school seniors who have made great strides in their school and community. The comprehensive admissions application is a canvas on which prospective students paint a picture of themselves, their goals, hopes, and interests. Once admitted, Columbia's Financial Aid Office will make sure all possible avenues are taken to finance a first-year student's education, and will continue to do so for the remaining three years.

Four years at Columbia College breeze by. Perhaps this is best reflected by the number of grads who stick around to pursue graduate work in any one of the university's remaining fourteen schools, or by the number of grads who pursue jobs in New York City. But far and wide, Columbia College alums share that everlasting something special—four years in which they were urged to find themselves and become freethinkers, ready to serve as leaders in their communities and beyond.

❑ *Anna Lisa Raya, B.A.*

COLUMBIA UNIVERSITY/SCHOOL OF ENGINEERING AND APPLIED SCIENCE (SEAS)

Columbia University/SEAS
212 Hamilton
New York, NY 10027

(212) 854-2522
Fax: (212) 854-1209

E-mail: ugrad.admiss@columbia.edu
Web site: http://www.columbia.edu

Enrollment

Full-time ❑ women: 312
❑ men: 866

INTRODUCING SEAS

Columbia University's School of Engineering and Applied Science (SEAS—pronounced *sees*) is a unique engineering school with the capacity to fine-tune one's analytical abilities and master technical principles needed to become a successful engineer. SEAS is an Ivy League school that provides far more than an impressive entry on one's résumé. SEAS invites and encourages students to learn theory through practice, which produces successful professional business and community leaders.

Life at Columbia is far more than an extension of one's academic career. The metropolitan microcosm, which reflects the diverse population of New York City, allows those in the Columbia community to have their own character while absorbing the culture of the Morningside Heights community around them. Living in dorms provides students with more than a place to live, study, and socialize; it prepares them to be part of a conscientious community. Generally, professors, advisors, and deans strive to instill in students a desire to aggressively make a place for themselves in the community—whether it be the SEAS community or the professional engineering community—both as a professional and a social contributor.

Retrospectively, I appreciate Columbia far more than I thought possible; conversations with friends, both recent graduates and not-so-recent graduates, seem to indicate that this is the norm. It is rare that one appreciates the intangible lessons and experiences of life—especially as an undergraduate—while they are being taught; rather one looks back to treasure the good times and internalize the experiences. SEAS exposed me to a rigorous technical engineering program, as well as an insightful liberal arts curriculum, but it also taught me to be resourceful and to be prepared to walk through any doors leading to opportunity.

One of the ideal aspects of being a student at Columbia is the foundation offered by exposure to varied academic subjects. SEAS encourages students to approach life with knowledge that will foster an open mind. Professors and students alike have a strong, common driving force that unites them as one body—a force based on mechanisms relying on analytical, problem-solving basics. These skills are essential in the field of engineering, and invaluable in life; however, another strong trait present in most of those who are successful at Columbia is the desire to be well rounded.

Life as a student at CU was probably far different than life would have been had I attended any other school. Before joining the CU community, I thought college would simply be an extension of my academic career. I had visited the atypical New York City green campus only a few times, but for some reason I always felt comfortable and excited while on campus. Columbia has prepared me academically and socially. Most of all, Columbia has been responsive to both technological changes and social changes providing effective tools to approach life with an open mind and great enthusiasm.

ADMISSIONS REQUIREMENTS

Admission to Columbia University, School of Engineering and Applied Science is generally competitive. Either SAT I or the ACT is required. Additionally, SAT II is required in the subject areas: Mathematics (either level I or II), Chemistry or Physics, and Writing. In addition to the standardized examination requirements, it is expected that each applicant has had sufficient preparation in high school to maintain competitive standings while enrolled at Columbia. It is recommended that the high school preparation courses include:

- mathematics courses including calculus
- one year of chemistry
- one year of physics
- four years of English
- three to four years of history or social science
- two to three years of a foreign language

In addition to coursework requirements, in consideration for admission to the School of Engineering and Applied Science, a written evaluation from a guidance counselor or college advisor is expected. Also expected as part of the applicant's file are two recommendations from teachers of academic subjects, including one from a mathematics teacher. A personal essay is also a required part of the application.

As in most other aspects of life at Columbia, admission is based on balance. Academic standing alone is not the only attribute used to measure a student's potential to be a successful and integral member of SEAS. While Advanced Placement or honors placement in high school are important factors, also weighted is the applicant's extracurricular activities record as well as evidence of special talent.

The School of Engineering and Applied Science of Columbia University offers programs with regional accreditation, as well as baccalaureate program accreditation with ABET; thus, all engineering students are required to attain a basic foundation in the first two years they are at CU. Generally, freshmen and sophomores take the same classes during their first four semesters at SEAS: general chemistry, physics, calculus, computer programming, and laboratories in both chemistry and physics. This homogeneity enables the engineers to quickly build a studying network.

One of the mandatory qualities that I was looking for in the institution I would attend is the competitive yet supportive academic atmosphere most apparent at CU's SEAS. While I was a top student in high school, I quickly found myself among fellow engineering students who were also at the top of their high school class. At first I found this intimidating, but I developed a driving force to excel and earn the respect of my peers and professors. Soon the sentiment of intimidation was erased by the supportive and reciprocated motivation between my fellow engineering students and me.

Majors

At the end of the second year, engineering students are required to declare a major. Foreshadowing the selection of a major, second-year students take introductory level courses. The courses include Principles of Applied Chemistry for potential chemical engineering majors, introducing ideas of matter such as statistical thermodynamics, and chemical thermodynamics, and for sophomores anticipating a major in electrical engineering, Introduction to Electrical Engineering, covering theories such as circuit laws and external behavior of diodes and transistors. Each major has introductory level courses that sophomores must take, not only to provide a foundation for higher level courses but also to introduce some of the concepts of their intended major and future profession.

General Liberal Arts Requirements

In the Columbia trend of diversity, the engineering students also fulfill general liberal arts requirements. Engineering majors are required to select either Contemporary

Civilization, a philosophy course examining the views of such prominent academics as Aristotle, Descartes, Galileo, Locke, and Marx, or Literature Humanities, a course discussing the works of such writers and philosophers as St. Augustine, Dante, and Homer. Also required is the selection of either Music Humanities or Art Humanities. Each of these classes examines the history of its subject matter and the basics of the significant theories put forth by the musicians and artists. In addition to these required courses, there is room for students to pursue their own interest; a total of twenty-eight credits in liberal arts is mandatory for completion of a bachelor of science degree.

SOCIAL LIFE AND ACTIVITIES

The engineering curriculum at Columbia is definitely demanding. Equally as demanding is participating in all of the extracurricular activities that might catch your eye. In addition to all of the commonly available activities on college campuses, such as sports—both varsity and intercollegiate—group publications, and student government, there are many active, thriving groups on campus. Various cultural groups, which welcome all students, organize spectacular fashion shows, buffet dinners, and dances that are known to sell out. There are also drama, comedy improv, and *a cappella* groups on campus to help satisfy your yearning to perform.

In addition to activities that offer entertainment and cultural education, there are groups that enable CU students to fulfill their need to help others. The community impact programs organized on campus are not only an important part of CU's community but the Morningside Heights community as well, providing tutoring to younger students of the neighboring schools, peer counseling, and numerous other services.

Student Enterprises

Student Enterprises is another group that supports independent, student-run, for-profit businesses where students run their own businesses such as the T-shirt stand on College Walk. All of these activities on campus are great outlets for meeting people, relieving stress from academic work, and developing a sense that one is giving back to the Columbia and Morningside Heights communities. Choosing one of these groups to be a part of is just one decision to make; however, life at Columbia reaches far beyond the grassy quads.

In addition to all of the social activities off campus, there are many social activities on campus. For instance, University Residence Hall (URH) organizes casual events such as dinners and lectures at professors' homes.

My social life was easily extended beyond the borders of our green campus bounded by the iron gates. The theater is only minutes from campus. Cuisine of almost any culture is only a hop, skip, and jump away. Any music—from classical at Lincoln Center to jazz down in the Village to rock played by various CU bands just across the street at the local hangout—can be heard in a heartbeat. Major sports arenas are just a subway ride away. The abundance of activities available in New York City always left me wishing I could be in more than one place on a Saturday evening.

FINANCIAL AID

A realistic and important consideration in applying to college is cost. Tuition, campus housing and board, books, and personal expenses are approximated to be $26,000 per year. In a recent year, ninety-three percent of all freshmen and sixty-three percent of continuing students received some form of financial aid. Financial aid packages are awarded in any combination of scholarships, need-based grants, loans, and federal work-study. On average, the freshman financial aid recipient recently received $18,000; $12,000 of the average quoted was accounted for in the form of scholarships or need-based grants. Approximately half of the undergraduate students work part-time; average school year earnings from campus work are $1,600. Campus work includes positions such as administrative assistants, library assistants, computer laboratory assistants, and numerous other employment opportunities.

A recent year's graduate had an average financial indebtedness of $11,000. Federal loans offered in the package help minimize postgraduate financial burden. In addition to an interest cap of 8.25 percent, the student does not accrue interest charges until repayment of the loan begins, which is typically six to eight months after graduation with various exceptions.

GRADUATES

Graduates of Columbia University, School of Engineering and Applied Science pursue various endeavors after completion of their undergraduate degrees, the most obvious being the practice of various disciplines of engineering. Many of the SEAS graduates go on to graduate school to continue their engineering education or to obtain professional degrees. Numerous SEAS alumni also can be found in business consulting and Wall Street positions. The education offered at the School of Engineering and Applied Science is far more than information handed to its students, rather it is a tool provided to each of its graduates enabling them to acquire, process, analyze, and dispense information given any circumstance.

PROMINENT GRADS

- Jeffrey Bleustein, President and CEO of Harley Davidson, Inc.
- Ed DiGiulio, President, Cinema Products Corp.
- Joseph Hoane, Software Engineer for IBM's Deep Blue Development Team
- Robert Merton, 1997 Nobel Laureate in Economics
- Pete Slosberg, Founder, Pete's Brewing Company
- Greg Smith, Chief Investment Strategist, Prudential Securities
- C.J. Tan, Senior Manager of IBM's Deep Blue Development Team

I don't think students realize what they are getting each day that they are sitting in class, studying in their rooms, programming in Gussman lab, or just talking with their professors. Only five months after graduating, I experienced a tremendous epiphany: Columbia has intensified my desire to learn and share my knowledge with all those around me. Everyone at Columbia has a thirst for knowledge, but you will know you have chosen the right place to continue your education when you can say your desire for knowledge has grown.

SUMMING UP

Many doors were opened for me as a result of attending Columbia. I not only earned a B.S. in biomedical engineering, I also received an education from an institution that demands its graduates enter the world with knowledge beyond the confines of their discipline. When talking with friends about Columbia, it was unanimous—being part of Columbia is a huge milestone in each of our lives.

Entertainment and relaxation are definitely important aspects of a Columbia education, but taking a break from lectures, laboratories, and studying does not necessarily mean defaulting to the neighborhood bar or campus party. The Columbia experience truly encompasses the principle of diversity in every sense of the word.

❑ *Kelly Lenz, B.S.*

CORNELL UNIVERSITY

Photo by Charles Harrington

Cornell University
Ithaca, NY 14853

(607) 255-5241

E-mail: admissions@cornell.edu
Web site: http://www.cornell.edu

Enrollment

Full-time ❑ women: 6,394
❑ men: 7,118

INTRODUCING CORNELL

Whenever my schedule got way too crazy and it seemed like I wasn't going to make it, I took the time to put everything in perspective. Sitting at the top of Libe Slope and taking in the breathtaking view of Ithaca and Cayuga Lake, or standing in the middle of the suspension bridge and jumping up and down to make the whole thing shake while watching water cascade over the falls, was the best cure for anything that was getting you down.

CORNELL LIBRARY TREASURES

- A copy of the Gettysburg Address handwritten by Abraham Lincoln in 1864, one of only five copies in existence.
- A vellum copy of the 13th Amendment to the United States Constitution, signed by Abraham Lincoln and members of the Senate and House who voted for the joint resolution, one of three copies known to exist.
- A complete set of the Shakespeare folios.
- The "Jade Book" of the second Manchu emperor K'ang-hsi (reigned 1662–1722), inscribed in Chinese and Manchu in blue and gold on ten tablets of solid jade.
- A witchcraft collection containing 3,000 books and manuscripts, one of the most comprehensive collections available for the study of European witchcraft.
- Five manuscript volumes of the famous Chinese fifth-century encyclopedia, *Yung-lo ta-tien.*
- Cornell's Human Sexuality Collection, established in 1988 to record and preserve the cultural and political aspects of sexuality, one of the few collections of its kind.

When the name Cornell comes up in conversation, people who've been there usually exclaim, "It's so pretty there," and after a visit, it is easy to agree. Cornell sits on founder Ezra Cornell's farm, overlooking Cayuga Lake, in the Finger Lakes region of New York State. The campus covers 745 acres with classic ivy-covered stone dorms and contemporary research labs. The *Cornell Daily Sun* is delivered every day, and there's probably a protest going on somewhere on campus. Ezra Cornell's educational philosophy, "I would found an institution where any person can receive instruction in any study," is the guiding force throughout campus where any person is free to found any organization, play any sport, practice any religion, and do just about anything they want without too much trouble.

Cornell is not solely a private or public school. It's both. Cornell is made up of seven undergraduate colleges, of which three are state-assisted schools and four are private (endowed), and four graduate and professional schools. The state-assisted undergraduate schools are the College of Agriculture and Life Sciences—the "Ag" school, the College of Human Ecology—"Hum Ec," and the College of Industrial and Labor Relations—"ILR." The endowed schools, whose nicknames aren't as exciting, are the College of Arts and Sciences—"Arts," the College of Engineering—"Engineering," the School of Hotel Administration—"Hotel," and the School of Architecture, Art, and Planning—"AAP." Together the faculty, staff, and students of these colleges form an eclectic mix and give Cornell its distinctive flavor.

Libraries

The seventeen libraries provide the best places for studying in whatever kind of atmosphere suits one best. The two most popular libraries are Mann and Uris. Mann is located on the Ag quad and is most frequented by students in Ag and Hum Ec. Uris Library is located on the corner of the Arts quad looking down the hill, affectionately known as Libe Slope. Uris can get pretty social at night, but within the library, the A.D. White Library, with its balconies and alcoves, provides a classic academic aura for studying. It's nice and quiet studying among the books in the stacks. The best-known spots in Uris are the Fishbowl and the Cocktail Lounge where wine isn't served, but wines may be studied.

Exams

Despite being the punchline of many Ivy League jokes, Cornellians are unfailing in their belief that they work just as hard as any other Ivy Leaguers, if not harder. Prelims, which are similar to midterms but take place two or three times a semester per class, are given on Tuesday and Thursday nights, and everyone has a few each semester. There's tons of reading to do and, with extracurricular activities, the schedule can seem like it's never going to let up.

ADMISSIONS REQUIREMENTS

Here's what it boils down to: If Cornell accepts you, you can make it. Every fall, thousands of applications pour into the Admissions Office. Over 20,000 students apply for admission to one of the seven colleges, thirty-three percent of whom were accepted in a recent year. UAO, the Undergraduate Admissions Office, collects and keeps track of all the applications and, once they are complete, funnels the applications to admissions offices in each college for decisions. The application is the same for all the colleges although extra essays or interviews are required for some. An applicant's first encounter with the uniqueness of Cornell's colleges is at this stage when applicants must decide which of the colleges to apply to. For example, one can major in biology and society in any of three schools, but the emphasis is different. In the Ag school, bio and society focuses on the natural world. In Hum Ec, bio and society looks at biology and human life, and in Arts, biology can be studied with anything from classic civilizations to anthropology to linguistics. (Don't worry—internal transfer between schools is possible if you decide you don't want to study biology and Latin and want to try meteorology instead.)

Requirements for admission vary by school and program, but basically excelling in any college preparatory course load in high school will get you in the front door. The SAT I or ACT is required with an essay. SAT II: Subject tests are specified by college and division. AP credits are accepted but will count differently depending on your major and score, so don't think you're home free just because you got a 5. Applicants who go to small high schools that don't offer AP classes shouldn't be concerned about being at a disadvantage. Some freshmen arrive with fifteen to twenty AP credits under their belt, and yes, they will probably be able to start out in higher level classes or maybe finish a semester early, but the majority of students have only a few, if any, AP credits and still graduate in good standing after four years.

In my freshman year, I had one of the lowest SAT scores on my floor, barely over 1200 combined, some of the lowest achievement test scores, and only AP Bio credit. But I was one of fifty Cornell National Scholars in the freshman class and became a Cornell Tradition Fellow at the end of my sophomore year.

Important Factors

One of the best things about Cornell admissions is that they look beyond the numbers. Special talents and leadership records are just as important as your SAT scores. Three percent of incoming students with an exemplary leadership record in high school are selected as Cornell National Scholars. Students who held jobs during their high school academic year may be selected as Cornell Tradition Fellows, an undergraduate loan replacement fellowship. In order to continue to be a Fellow, students must work, keep a certain GPA, and be involved in public service activities. Upperclassmen can apply to be Cornell Tradition Fellows in the spring of each year. Also, the new Presidential Research Scholars program is designed to recognize, reward, and encourage students who have demonstrated academic excellence and true intellectual curiosity.

Interviews

Regardless of whether your school requires an interview or not, the Cornell Alumni Admissions Ambassador Network offers the opportunity for applicants to meet with alumni in their local area for a casual interview.

The most important thing to remember is that if you get accepted to Cornell, the people who read the application believe you can make it and be a success. There's no need to change from the person you were in high school. Your record there led admissions officers to believe you would be a success at Cornell too. It doesn't all depend on the numbers.

Regardless of what school one is technically enrolled in, students can take classes from every school on campus, and there's no need to search in order to find the popular ones. The legendary Psych 101, incessantly discussed in tours and information sessions, is held in Cornell's biggest classroom, Bailey Hall, with a mere 2,000 of your closest friends. Despite its size, Psych 101 is educational and interesting. Offered only in the fall, one class in the semester is a live demonstration of a psychic telling one student everything about his or her life.

When I took Psych 101, Professors Bem and Maas selected Mindy from the class for their demonstration. Four years later, I would still hear people say, "There's that girl from Psych 101." In a class of 2,000, who says you don't get to know your classmates? Interested? It's offered Mondays, Wednesdays, and Fridays at 10:10 A.M. I'm sure you'll know someone in the class.

Other popular classes, though smaller in size, are Human Sexuality offered in Human Ecology, and Introduction to Wines in the Hotel School, which once a week offers an hour of tasting wines from around the world.

I would always see people carrying around these little black cases on Wednesdays. It seemed like they were everywhere. I had no idea what they were used for until one day, a senior opened up her case and I saw the three nicely packed wine glasses. From that moment on, I couldn't wait to have my own little black box.

Class Size

Cornell is big and you have to accept this fact to be happy there. Classes vary in size, but you will most likely have classes with at least 200 people. Depending on what you are studying though, it is possible that you may never have a class bigger than fifty people. Popular intro classes, such as Government 111 and Chemistry 207, can easily have 400 or more students in the class, but, as you move into upper-level classes, the numbers get smaller.

Language classes usually aren't much bigger than twenty students per section. Most large intro classes will also have a mandatory section held during the week, led by a TA (teaching assistant) or the professor, with much fewer students, rarely over twenty-five per section. These sections provide students with a time to ask questions and get to know the teaching assistants. TA's can be very helpful and are usually very willing to meet with and help the students in their section. Being nice to your TA will come in very handy when you need help on papers or problem sets.

Degrees

There are seemingly, to quote late Cornell professor Carl Sagan, "billions and billions" of programs of study at Cornell. You can graduate with a B.A., a B.S., a B. Arch, or a B.F.A., or any combination. Bachelor's degrees are awarded to any field from animal science, soil science and operations research, to ancient civilizations, textiles and apparel, and mechanical engineering. The largest enrollments (by major) are in biological sciences, economics, and mechanical engineering.

Trust me, you can major in anything and any combination of things you can find. Friends of mine had majors in classic civilizations, historic preservation, and linguistics and psychology.

Clearly, there are no boundaries to what you can study, even if it includes subjects that have never been put together or your areas of interest are in more than one school. That's one of the benefits of going to a school this size with a great deal of flexibility.

Required Courses

As for what's actually required of all students in addition to school or major requirements, the list is pretty short. Entering freshmen must take and pass the swim test, take two semesters of freshman writing seminars and two semesters of physical education. Now, there's no need to worry about these three requirements in the least. For the swim test, you have to swim three lengths of the pool, using any style you please. If you don't pass, you can take lessons, which also count as a phys ed requirement. Freshman writing seminars are just as varied as majors. Seminars are offered on such topics as:

- African American Women Writers
- Russian Literature
- Fairy Tales
- Writing About Film
- Writing From Experience (no books to read for that class)
- King Arthur's Legend.

There are countless others in fields as varied as biology, philosophy, and government, and just as many if not more phys ed classes to choose from to fulfill the requirements. Choices include the extremely popular ballroom dancing, tae kwon do, rock climbing, intro to ice skating, badminton, squash, Swedish massage, yoga, scuba diving, running, skiing, golf, and riflery. With this endless supply of choices, the requirements make up a fun exploration of specialized writing topics and gym classes where you may get and give massages.

Study Away

Getting sick of being on campus but think transferring is a little too drastic? It's easy to leave Ithaca, study somewhere else, and still graduate on time. You can study abroad in more than fifty countries, such as Spain, Sweden, Australia, and France. Engineers can take part in a co-op program and spend a semester earning some serious money. The Cornell in Washington program gives students in any college the opportunity to live inside the beltway at Dupont Circle in the Cornell Center (a four-story building with three floors of apartments and one of classrooms and a computer lab), take classes with Cornell and visiting professors, and have an internship in the nation's capital. Urban Semester gives students a chance to spend a semester in New York City working and studying.

One friend of mine spent a semester in Sweden and traveled all around eastern Europe. Four days after she got back for the summer, she headed to D.C. for an internship and stayed at the Cornell Center. I spent a fall semester with the Cornell in Washington program, interned at PBS Online, *and got a sneak preview of* Elmo Saves Christmas. *Being from Maine, it was my first time living and working in a big city. I took the Metro to work and experienced what rush hour traffic really meant! Other cool D.C. experiences were seeing the lighting of the Christmas tree, watching Bobby McFerrin conduct the National Symphony Orchestra, seeing the AIDS Quilt laid out in its entirety on the Mall, and spending an afternoon at the Supreme Court talking with Cornell alum and Supreme Court Justice, Ruth Bader Ginsburg.*

CORNELL FIRSTS

- Cornell's chimes, dedicated in 1868, were the first to peal over an American university.
- Cornell awarded the first Bachelor of Veterinary Science in 1871, the first Doctor of Veterinary Medicine in the United States in 1876, and the first DVM degree to a woman in 1910.
- Cornell granted the first Bachelor of Mechanical Engineering degree in 1871.
- Cornell appointed the first professor of American history in an American university in 1881.
- Cornell endowed the nation's first chair in American literature.
- Sigma Xi, the national science honor society, was founded at Cornell in 1886.
- Alpha Phi Alpha, the nation's first black fraternity, was founded at Cornell in 1906.
- Cornell offered the first college-level course in hotel administration in 1922.
- Cornell established the first four-year school of Industrial and Labor Relations in 1945.
- Cornell developed CUinfo, the first campus-wide information system, in 1986.

The academic life you have at Cornell is entirely what you make of it. Even though every student is allowed to do one or another of these programs, your program of study can make it difficult to spend a semester away. And yes, it can be hard to leave your friends at Cornell and spend a semester with Cornellians you've never met before, especially during your senior year. As for on-campus classes, don't let class size intimidate you. Go to office hours and discuss Pericles with the professor or talk to your TA about possible subjects for your term paper. No one wants you to fail or do badly. If you don't feel the need to talk with your professor or TA, that's okay too. Just make sure you get to know a few faculty members in case you ever need a recommendation for graduate school or any other application.

SOCIAL LIFE AND ACTIVITIES

Housing

All pre-frosh want to know about housing before they get here and the subject daunts every returning student for a few months each year. All freshmen live on campus in dorms located on two parts of campus, North and West. Most other students live off-campus in sorority or fraternity houses, in Collegetown and in the surrounding areas. There are a variety of off-campus options to choose from, from the high-tech (and expensive) apartment buildings to three-story houses with six apartments that include oddities like oval windows, sinks in hallways, and sit-down showers.

I guess I was a little naive about housing because I had never really looked into it—I just assumed everyone lived in dorms for all four years. Once one person mentioned apartment hunting, the race began. Those of us not living in fraternities and sororities started finding roommates and looking for apartments. As I look back, I'm now thankful for the chance to live off campus. My folks helped out with the bills, since they weren't paying for Cornell housing, but I got a sense of what it was going to be like after graduation. Off-campus living was one of the most practical experiences I had at Cornell, which successfully prepared me for the real world of bills, rent, and late fees.

Parties

The university doesn't really plan activities for the campus, so you're on your own for social activities, and trust me, you'll find plenty. As each weekend approaches, one is faced with an immense variety of choices. Since one-third of the campus is Greek (fraternities and sororities), there are always a collection of fraternity open parties, crush parties, after hours, and formals to attend. Fraternities are housed both off and on campus in just about every direction, so there is bound to be one nearby. Many other options exist outside of the Greek realm and cater to many different interests.

Campus Activities

Just glance at the *Daily Sun* on Friday and you'll find a plethora of activities going on all over campus. On any given weekend, you can attend a concert, a varsity sporting event, intramural games, an ethnic festival, or listen to a speaker. Because of its size, there are always people at whatever event you attend and you'll definitely find someone with interests similar to yours:

- Diwali, a celebration of the Indian New Year—"the festival of lights"—takes place every fall. It's put on by the Society for India and the Cornell Indian Association and features traditional Indian food and a performance of skits, traditional and modern dance, and instrumental music.
- In the spring, the Festival of Black Gospel brings famous gospel singers to campus and unites regional gospel choirs, like Cornell's own Pamoja Ni, in song and spirit.
- One weekend in every year, Lynah Rink is packed solid to watch the hockey team play their biggest rival, Harvard. Smuggled in under jackets and in shirts, fish of every size and color

as well as some frozen fish sticks and lobsters become airborne when Harvard players skate onto the ice.

- Some years, at the same time, Bailey Hall is packed with over 1,800 *a cappella* fans for Fall Tonic, the all-male Hangovers annual concert. Visiting *a cappella* groups who perform during Fall Tonic are undoubtedly amazed at the number of people at the concert and mention that there are more people in the audience than students at their school. We are dedicated fans and strongly support the groups or teams we enjoy.

Volunteering

Volunteerism runs like a raging river through Cornell as thousands of Cornellians find extra time in their crazy schedules to help others. For example, the Public Service Center, through related programs and projects, mobilizes over 3,000 student volunteers each year in both one-time and ongoing projects. That's over 170,000 hours each year of service to the community. For Into the Streets, a national day of service, there are close to 500 volunteers who work with 30 agencies. On that one Saturday, Cornellians do over 2,500 hours of service in the greater Ithaca area. Cornell's record of public service is one of the things that President Hunter R. Rawlings admires most about the university.

Movies

In the evening and weekends, Cornell Cinema offers at least four different films, playing either in the theater at the Straight (Willard Straight Hall, the student union) or in Uris Auditorium. Both are on central campus and are a short walk from any dorm or apartment. The movies can be classics that you never thought you would see on the big screen, such as *The Princess Bride* and *Psycho*, movies that have just left theaters across the country, foreign films such as *Il Postino* and *Like Water for Chocolate*, and every so often, the student film classes have a few nights to show their work. The admission is cheaper than for a matinee at a local theater and very accessible.

Sports

Sports at Cornell may not draw the television coverage of the Big Ten, but there are many teams doing an excellent job representing Cornell, and you have to admire student athletes for their hard work and hectic schedules. Hockey tickets are the only tickets that aren't free to students and where there is a high probability that a game may sell out. Cornell has varsity teams in basketball, cross-country, indoor and outdoor track, soccer, squash, tennis, polo, lacrosse, field hockey, rowing, gymnastics, and hockey. Known as the

Big Red, Cornell teams are of championship quality. Recently, the men's soccer team had two consecutive invitations to the NCAA Division I men's soccer championship, and the men's hockey team won two consecutive Eastern College Athletic Conference championships. Go Big Red.

Even though there are endless choices of what to do on the weekends, you may find yourself just hanging out with friends. You can pick up a movie at Collegetown Video, go out for dessert and coffee at Aladdin's, or go bar-hopping to any one of the ten or so bars in Collegetown. More often than not, you'll find the pleasure of your friends' company at your apartment or theirs is great for making many fabulous memories.

FINANCIAL AID

Cornell's need-blind admissions policy makes it affordable to attend this institution. Paying for college is often a burden for a family and Cornell's philosophy is that, even though paying for college is a burden, the burden shouldn't be one that kills you. Recently, some form of financial aid was given to sixty-five percent of all students and fifty percent of all students received need-based aid. The average freshman was awarded $17,400. Students always gripe about financial aid, but on the whole, Cornell assists those families who really need help paying for college. There are plenty of on campus and off campus jobs to be had as well as temporary jobs for crunch times.

The simplest way to think about it is this: If Cornell accepts you, they will find a way for you to meet the financial obligations. What sense does it make to accept all sorts of wonderful students if none of them can pay to come? If you get accepted to Cornell, Cornell will come up with a financial aid package based on your family's needs, whether it's loans or grants.

If you're a superstar athlete or have the best grades in your high school and think that will help your financial aid package, you are unfortunately wrong. Cornell's financial aid system is need based. Cornell (and all other schools in the Ivy League) doesn't give scholarships based on talent or ability.

The most important thing to remember is that paying for college isn't meant to be easy. It can put a strain on your resources. You are receiving a top-quality education, and the name alone will take you far.

The students who complain about financial aid the loudest are most likely ones that don't receive it; however, if they looked at how the system works, they might realize that they aren't getting any because their family is fortunate enough to have enough money to send them to Cornell.

A friend of mine said in conversation one day that he has a $10,000 check that he had to bring to the Bursar's Office. Another friend mentioned that he didn't have to pay anything thanks to his financial aid package. When the negative comments about financial aid started, I said that my parents would never be able to write a check for $10,000. Needless to say, the gripes about financial aid stopped right there. I am a strong believer in financial aid. It allowed me the opportunity to attend Cornell, and trust me, my parents were paying as much as they could.

Need-based aid also gives Cornell the kind of diverse community it desires to be a great institution. If only those who could afford it or only people on financial aid attended the university, it wouldn't be as interesting or stimulating a place as it is. The mix of income levels and economic backgrounds helps add to the greatness of the place.

Work-Study

When parents think about paying for college, work-study is always on the top of their lists. Work-study is a great thing. Your employer only has to pay half of your wage; the other half is paid by the government. Therefore, employers LOVE work-study students, and there are usually enough jobs to go around. Granted, it may not be your dream job, but in most jobs, there is plenty of room for advancement, and your salary usually advances too. If the job isn't research or something relating to your major, it gives you additional experience that makes you even more marketable once you leave, because all your experience isn't in one area. There's a student employment office to help you out, and job postings on CUinfo, Cornell's computer information system. It may be rough at first, but never fear. You will find a job.

When I first started hunting for a job, it was the worst. Every place I inquired at was full and none of the available jobs fit in with my class schedule. It seemed hopeless. I called my mother in tears and told her I didn't want to be on work-study anymore. Then I found a job at the Undergraduate Admissions Office as an administrative assistant. The job had great (and flexible hours), and an understanding staff. I stayed there for the rest of my four years, became a student personnel assistant—which meant I hired and coordinated all the students for the building—and still had a job after taking a semester off to go to Washington. The job gave me excellent experience that I put to good use after I left Cornell.

Packages

You can read all about the particulars of how financial aid packages are calculated in any number of brochures from the Undergraduate Admissions or Financial Aid Offices, but it really doesn't affect you negatively in any way while you're at Cornell.

During the senior class campaign, I found that many of my friends on financial aid were much more willing to donate to the university and to the scholarship our class was establishing than those students who weren't. Financial aid recipients are thankful for the assistance they received to come to Cornell and were willing to give back to Cornell at the drop of a hat.

GRADUATES

Friends who have had long hair since freshman year are getting haircuts and buying suits. Résumés are spilling off printers everywhere, and reality is starting to set in. What time is it? It's the fall of senior year, and recruiters are swarming over the campus. There are job fairs and information sessions every week, and everyone is talking about how to survive an interview. Don't be alarmed—not everyone goes through this.

Engineers, hotelies, and business majors are usually successful at finding jobs. The engineering school has a great recruiting program, and many Cornell alums come back from their respective companies to recruit more Cornell engineers. Not knowing too much about the hotel industry, any student at Cornell can tell you this one thing for sure: Cornell alums rule the hotel world. The statistics are fascinating. Because Cornell has the top hotel school in the nation, hotel graduates are in high demand. Business majors and anyone interested in areas such as investment banking are also pretty lucky when it comes to on-campus recruiting. There are lots of opportunities, and the Career Center is very helpful.

PROMINENT GRADS

- **Adolph Coors, '07, Beer Baron**
- **E.B. White, '21, Author**
- **Allen Funt, '34, TV Personality**
- **Harry Heimlich, '41, Developed the Heimlich Maneuver**
- **Kurt Vonnegut, Jr., '44, Author**
- **James McLarmore, '47, Burger King Founder**
- **Ruth Bader Ginsburg, '54, Supreme Court Justice**
- **Toni Morrison, '55, Author, Nobel Prize Winner**
- **Janet Reno, '60, U.S. Attorney General**
- **Lee Teng-Hui, '68, President of Taiwan**
- **Christopher Reeve, '74, actor**
- **Pablo Morales, '94, Olympic Medalist**

Of those who aren't interviewing for jobs, many of them are interviewing for graduate school. People are flying off left and right to go to med school, grad school, and vet school interviews—senior year of high school all over again, except much more intense. There's a breather after all the applications and interviews are over, but the decision letters start coming in the spring. There will be much rejoicing, but there may be a lot of disappointment too.

The rest of the senior class is made up of government majors who aren't prelaw, classic civilization majors, art history majors, bio majors who aren't premed and who don't want to do research, English majors, and women's studies majors, just to name a few. These people have their work cut out for them when it comes to finding a job. Basically, anyone who isn't going to grad school and isn't one of the aforementioned majors isn't going to benefit much from on-campus recruiting. There are jobs out there for these people, but they must be sought out. The Career Center is a great place to start, and they have lots of job sources and staff that can point you in the right direction. The Career Center offers Résumé Express, a service that scans your résumé for key words and keeps it in a database. When employers call and the key words in your résumé are what they're looking for, your résumé will be forwarded to them.

Public Service

Cornell's record of public service holds true after graduation as well as during undergraduate years. Cornell traditionally ranks in the top ten schools nationally in the number of alumni who are accepted into Peace Corps training. Many more work with AmeriCorps and VISTA in their postgraduate years. There are thousands of opportunities out there, and Cornellians are experiencing them and conquering them every day.

You'll do just fine with a Cornell degree.

SUMMING UP

After four years at Cornell, anyone is prepared to be a success in the real world. The road to success won't be paved for you, but you will have the knowledge and the experience to overcome the speed bumps and detours. Cornell successfully prepares its students by constantly challenging them both in and out of the classroom. It exposes them to different people, lifestyles, and experiences. It takes confidence to constantly seek out classes, clubs, and advice; you have to be able to stick up for yourself and to speak out. If you can't when you arrive, you will be able to by the time you leave. No one who goes through four years at Cornell will come out ill prepared for the real world.

As daunting as it may seem when new students arrive for orientation, most succeed and excel while at Cornell. While current students may seem like they are achieving the impossible, they aren't. The opportunities provided within its 745 acres and 400 buildings are unlike those available anywhere else. Cornell has been called by more than one Cornellian "the best place on earth to be."

❑ *Laura Barrantes, B.A.*

DARTMOUTH COLLEGE

Photo by J. Mehling

Dartmouth College
Hanover, NH 03755

(603) 646-2875

E-mail: admissions.office@dartmouth.edu
Web site: http://www.dartmouth.edu/admin/admissions

Enrollment

Full-time ❑ women: 2,063
❑ men: 2,222

INTRODUCING DARTMOUTH

If you're thinking of going to Dartmouth, smallest of the eight Ivy League schools, here's a few things to expect:

- First, you'll inexplicably have a sudden fondness for the color green.
- You'll begin wearing your winter coat in October, and you won't take it off until April. Then, you'll put on shorts to celebrate fifty degree temperatures—which you'll consider balmy.
- You'll be tempted to learn new languages and you'll probably study abroad at least once.

- You'll eat green eggs and ham.
- If you learn to ski, you'll do it at the Dartmouth skiway.
- You'll wonder why every school doesn't have a mandatory summer term.

Founded in 1769 by the Reverend Eleazor Wheelock, Dartmouth is the ninth oldest college in the United States. It's also one of the most beautiful. Nestled between the White Mountains of New Hampshire and the Green Mountains of Vermont, the 200-acre campus has its share of picture-perfect scenery. In fact, visiting the campus for a commencement address in 1953, Dwight Eisenhower commented that "this a what a college ought to look like." Affectionately termed "the college on the hill," Dartmouth's central green is adjacent to the cozy town of Hanover, New Hampshire. On campus, brick dorms and administrative buildings are adorned with ivy, and Baker Library's tower presides majestically over it all. If you listen carefully, every day at 6:00 P.M. the bell tower plays a recognizable melody. Selections range from show tunes to Beethoven.

Dartmouth, however, has a lot more going for it than aesthetics. A bona fide "college" rather than university, Dartmouth prides itself on this distinction. The whole issue was decided in 1819, during the now-famous "Dartmouth College Case," in which Daniel Webster, class of 1801, successfully convinced the Supreme Court that Dartmouth should remain a private institution instead of becoming a property of the state of New Hampshire. In what is an oft-quoted line around campus, Webster summed up his argument by saying, "It is, sir, as I have said, a small College, but there are those who love it." From then on, Dartmouth has fondly referred to itself in the same way.

ADMISSIONS REQUIREMENTS

Dartmouth's admission process is extremely selective and frankly, things aren't getting any easier. Recent years have seen a rise in applicant numbers, and of the 10,647 who applied for admission in a recent year, only 2,296 (or twenty-two percent) were accepted. Of those, eighty-nine percent were in the top ten percent of their class and approximately twenty-eight percent were valedictorians. Median SAT scores typically hover around the low 1400s.

Admission, however, is not based on book smarts or academic standing alone. What distinguishes the exceptional applicants from the merely solid is, according to a recent Dartmouth bulletin, "academic curiosity." Dartmouth, it says, seeks critical thinkers and creative problem solvers. What all this means, basically, is that Dartmouth is looking for students who display the tenacity to follow whatever pursuits—academic and otherwise—lie closest to their hearts. Energy, perseverance, and a sense of humor go a long way too.

Dartmouth's application is mostly standard fare, although there do seem to be an overabundance of essay questions, both short and long. One word of advice: Be as specific as possible, especially in your short answers. Although it seems like those questions are designed to make you squirm, they're a great way to showcase your writing talents.

There is one particularly unique thing about the Dartmouth application, however. In addition to three teacher recommendations, you'll also need to solicit one of your more eloquent friends to write you a peer evaluation. Dartmouth thinks having a friend write something is a great way to learn about you from someone who's really in the know.

Alumni Interview

Another influential, and generally positive part, of the application process is the alumni interview. Conducted by one or more alums in the applicant's home state, this personal conversation can go a long way toward helping your chances of admission.

> *I am still convinced that part of the reason I got into Dartmouth was because I wore a green shirt to my alumni interview. This was completely unplanned, but because the interviewers thought I was totally gung-ho, our session got off to a great start. We talked about everything from Clinton's presidency to my SAT scores. I even told them I felt that I could chat with them for hours! Afterwards, one of the interviewers called me to congratulate me on doing so well. Dartmouth scored very big points with me that evening.*

Early Decision

Finally, here's one more bit of advice. If you're completely psyched to go to Dartmouth, apply Early Decision by November 1 and you'll have a better shot of getting accepted. Although Dartmouth's admissions process is binding, meaning that you have to go if you get in, the percentage of applicants accepted for Early Decision is typically higher than that of the normal applicant pool.

ACADEMIC LIFE

Despite three top-notch professional schools (the Dartmouth Medical School, The Amos Tuck School of Business Administration, and the Thayer School of Engineering), as well as seventeen other graduate programs in the arts and sciences, Dartmouth prides itself on what seems to be an almost singular focus on undergraduates. Dartmouth students, consequently, have a unique advantage. With a few rare exceptions, classes are taught by professors with Ph.D.s, and not graduate students. Not surprisingly, Dartmouth consistently gets high rankings for its quality of teaching, as well as for the level of interaction between faculty and students.

The Dartmouth Plan

The Dartmouth plan is a unique year-round calendar that was instituted in 1972 when the school became coed (Dartmouth recently celebrated its twenty-fifth year of coeducation). Dartmouth's academic year is divided into four ten-week quarters (called fall term, winter term etc.), and students typically take three classes in each. This schedule works particularly well because not only is it difficult to get bored after a mere ten weeks, but students enjoy being able to focus on just three subjects at a time.

In order for the logistics of this to work out, students are required to spend at least nine terms on campus, including fall, winter, and spring of their freshman and senior years, as well as the summer between sophomore and junior year. Often a favorite term, summer allows for a less crowded campus, afternoons of studying outside in weather that's finally warm, and something called Tubestock where students float around the Connecticut River on inner tubes for the afternoon. Students then get to decide what they want to do with the other terms; choices range from staying on campus to doing a transfer term at another university to taking part in one of Dartmouth's forty-four off-campus programs in seventeen nations. International destinations include Prague, Costa Rica, and Beijing, and sixty percent of the student body will go abroad at least once during their four years.

I chose Dartmouth in large part because of its Russian department, and spent the spring of my sophomore year on the Dartmouth Foreign Study Program at St. Petersburg University in Russia. We were in Russia at a time when the country was changing every day and it was an unbelievable experience to witness these changes firsthand—and to have the language ability to speak to people about how their lives were affected. After it was all over, I came to back to Hanover and shared what I had learned with my classmates.

The year-round D plan is a ubiquitous force in the academic life of the college. Not only does it structure the length and duration of the classes, but in all honesty, it makes students hyper-aware of how much their studies relate to the seasons. This translates into such attitudes as, "It's winter term and it's really cold and I'm going to study really hard." It's always funny to see how students pick and choose classes based on what term they're offered in. Summer term, generally, is a popular time for some sanctioned slacking off.

Core Curriculum

The other important academic policy is Dartmouth's recent implementation of a structured set of graduation requirements. In its most thorough revision in almost seventy-five years, Dartmouth has brought back a more focused core curriculum. Parameters now exist for fourteen of the thirty-five courses it now takes to satisfy the graduation requirement, although no set list of required classes exists. Instead, the requirements are as follows:

- As always, students need to take a freshman writing seminar and demonstrate proficiency in at least one foreign language.
- Students also need three courses in world culture—one American, one European, and one Non-Western. Any type of class that deals with these subjects counts: music, history, or a foreign language. There is also a multidisciplinary requirement, meaning that the elected course must be taught by two or more professors from different departments. A class such as Literature and Business (jointly taught by an English professor and one at the Tuck School of Business) satisfies this requirement, as do others dealing with such topics as computerized music or the current health care system. The final component of the new curriculum also requires ten classes in the following areas—one art, one literature, one from either philosophy, history, or religion, one deemed international or comparative, two on social analysis, one considered quantitative or deductive, two natural sciences, and one technology or applied science. Additionally, one of the natural or applied science classes must have a lab.

Finally, students are now expected to engage in a "culminating experience" within their major, which can take the form of an honors thesis, an independent study project, an exhibition, or a performance. These new requirements, albeit more extensive than those of the past, were set up with an eye to making sure that the curriculum really did reflect the liberal arts focus that Dartmouth so prides itself on.

When I realized that I needed to fulfill an art distributive, I wasn't sure what I was going to do. I'm not exactly artistically inclined, but I found the perfect class. I enrolled in Greek Tragedy, which provided a unique alternative. Instead of creating or studying art in the forms of paintings or sculptures, we studied the art of performance in Ancient Greece. It suited me perfectly.

Faculty

Dartmouth has an incredibly strong faculty and student-faculty relationships are excellent. Although introductory classes in history, government, and biology tend to be large (about 200 students), classes for the most part are small. In fact, more than forty-one percent of the 1,350 courses offered in a recent year had enrollments of fewer than thirty. Also, the most popular departments at Dartmouth tend to be the strongest, so you can expect to find a lot of history, English, government, chemistry, and language majors.

Foreign Language Program

One particularly innovative academic program is Dartmouth's unique approach to foreign language instruction. The brainchild of famed professor John Rassias, the program is designed to make students comfortable speaking their new language. Each day, in addition to a regular class period, students have a one-hour "drill," which meets at 7:45 each morning. (Those who can't hack the early hours can elect to take a 5:00 P.M. drill instead.) There, they meet with an upper-level teaching assistant who puts them through the rigors of conjugating verbs and practicing dialogue. The session, accented by liberal amounts of pointing and clapping on the part of the instructor, is incredibly fast-paced and lively.

Although taking—and then teaching—drill got me up at 6:30 A.M. for most of my college career, I'm convinced that Dartmouth is an ideal and nurturing environment for anyone hoping to learn another language. Hundreds of students flock to drill each day to witness Professor Rassias' unique "in your face" approach, which is probably part of the reason I fared so well in my foreign language classes. It gave me such a good foundation, in fact, that now I'm fluent in French, in graduate school for Spanish literature and education, and learning Italian in my spare time.

Intellectualism and Special Programs

Another important part of the Dartmouth "character" is a continuing interest in intellectualism.

In keeping with this effort to increase intellectualism, a number of campus-wide programs have been implemented. In 1990 the Women in Science program began, specifically designed to encourage freshmen women who like biology, chemistry, or physics. (It was started after Dartmouth noticed the discrepancy between how many women arrived at Dartmouth intending to be science majors versus how many actually became science majors.) Thanks to the program, approximately 400 freshmen women are paired with a faculty member to conduct "hands-on" scientific research. Another popular option is the Presidential Scholar Program, which was recently endowed with enough money to keep it a permanent fixture on campus. The program allows approximately eighty to ninety juniors to work directly with professors and assist with research. After aiding the professor for two terms, most Presidential Scholars complete a senior thesis on the same, or a related, topic.

As a Presidential Scholar research assistant, I had the opportunity to assist my government professor on an article he was writing about the timing of presidential economic initiatives. He involved me almost every step of the way, providing me with first-hand exposure to the correct methodology for conducting political science research. I am currently using this knowledge to further my own research on media coverage of women gubernatorial candidates. In fact, my thesis proposal on this topic was accepted at the Midwest Political Science Association's Annual Meeting, and I presented my results at their annual convention in Chicago.

Dartmouth also awards between eight and twelve Senior Fellowships per year. Senior fellows spend their entire senior year doing research, and then complete a large-scale project—a book, film, or full-length production. (The big bonus here is that senior fellows get their own offices in the main library, instead of a lowly carrel where most honors students toil.)

Participating in the Senior Fellowship Program allowed me to study the life and work of a woman named Theodate Pope Riddle, one of the nation's first women architects. Because I was required to take only a couple of classes during the year, I had the chance to visit Riddle's buildings and travel to museums to do archival research. I also learned a lot from my advisor, a professor who specialized in architectural history. By the end, I had written a biography that was over 200 pages long and produced an accompanying video documentary.

Research Funding

It's not just senior fellows who fare well with research, either. As students will attest, funding at Dartmouth for almost any sort of academic endeavor is readily available. Much money is doled out by the Rockefeller Center, named for Nelson Rockefeller, class of 1966. The center houses the departments of economics and government, and has financially supported everything from internships at the U.S. Embassy in Ecuador to research on Dartmouth's role in the Civil War. The center also draws a number of prominent speakers for panels and discussions. In recent years, it has hosted famed African American Studies professor Cornell West, TV correspondent Lynn Sherr, human rights activist Harry Wu, and zoologist/geologist Stephen J. Gould.

DARTMOUTH MAKEOVER

The Dartmouth you visit on your prospective trip may not exactly be the one you will see four years later. Thanks to a $27 million donation from John W. Berry '44, the Baker Library (the largest on campus) will be expanded by about 125,000 square feet. Scheduled for completion in the year 2000, the Baker-Berry Library will host expanded rooms for books, maps, and manuscripts; a multimedia reserve room; new carrels and computer workstations; high-tech classrooms; and even a cafe. In the process of creating this library of the 21st century, the departments of psychology, math, and history will find new homes. And, sadly, an oft-snickered-at building will get the ax. Gerry Hall, aka the Shower Tower because of its 70s-esque blue-and-white tiled siding, is being removed to make room for the expansion. Guess the 70s really aren't coming back.

Libraries

The final thing to know about Dartmouth academics is that students spend a lot of time in one or more of Dartmouth's nine libraries, which contain over two million printed volumes. Baker is the largest and is an architectural wonder. The wood-trimmed Tower Room is a popular studying spot, as is the reserve corridor, which is framed by the murals of Mexican artist José Clemente Orozco. Painted between 1932 and

1934 when Orozco was the artist-in-residence, the famed murals depict the barbaric nature of the colonization of the new world. Dartmouth also has related libraries for biomedical science, math, business, physical science, engineering, art and music, and English. One thing to check out is the Sanborn English Library in midafternoon; every weekday at 4:00, students break for tea, cookies, and talk.

SOCIAL LIFE AND ACTIVITIES

"BLITZ ME"

Before freshman week is over, Dartmouth students are baptized into one of the school's most unique traditions—blitzmail. The Dartmouth version of e-mail, the on-line system, is so incredibly popular—in part because everyone on campus is required to bring a computer or purchase one prior to matriculation. As a result, phone calls between Dartmouth students are virtually obsolete. Instead of phoning your friend to see if she's free for dinner, you blitz her a message. (The fact that the word *blitz* is used as both noun and verb could cause linguistic confusion, yet oddly, it never seems to. Dartmouth students think it perfectly natural to get a *blitz,* and then *blitz* that person back.)

With everybody going to and fro so often, it might seem that Dartmouth would have a hard time fostering a sense of community on campus. Ironically, the opposite is true. Bonding begins early, in fact, before students even officially matriculate at Dartmouth. Over ninety percent of the incoming class elects to participate in a freshman trip sponsored by the Dartmouth Outing Club. Each group of eight to fifteen "shmen," led by an upperclassman, faculty member, or school administrator, take to the woods for three days of hiking, canoeing, biking, and rock climbing. There are few rules, but one remains firm: no showers. After the three days are over, students convene at the Moosilauke Ravine Lodge on Dartmouth's Mt. Mousilauke (still no showers) to practice singing the alma mater, learn the Salty Dog Rag, and pay tribute the Theodore Geisel, a.k.a. Dr. Seuss, class of 1925. (This is also where the green eggs and ham come into play.)

Dorm Life

Besides freshman trips, Dartmouth has an impressive network set up to unite incoming students. Organized by residence, each dorm floor has a U.G.A (undergraduate advisor) who organizes movies and ice creams sessions, plus dorm formals and barbecues. Dorm life tends to be incredibly social freshman year, although it undoubtedly lessens as the years go on. Surprisingly, however, even after freshman year, ninety-five percent of students remain in the dorms. Many Dartmouth students are surprised to find that the dorms, for the most part, are far more spacious than other living quarters. More than one person typically would share more than one room, and private bathrooms (although not showers) are not uncommon. Plus, many have fireplaces, which is an especially appealing feature as you're living through a long Hanover winter.

As if freshman trips, hall-bonding, and a host of common interests weren't enough, there's one more thing that tends to unify a diverse group of undergraduates: a fondness for their school. Student satisfaction ratings are among the top in the country, and tend to breed an odd phenomena: the "I love-everything-that's-green-and-related-to-Dartmouth" mentality. At first, anyway, it seems exceedingly hard to find anything you *don't* like. Of course, Dartmouth students do not love it blindly. In the past years, issues of race and sexuality have sparked debates, as has the age-old issue of whether or not the Greek system should be abolished. And despite impressive numbers of minority students (they compose around twenty-five percent of the campus), social and cultural activities often aren't as integrated as such statistics would suggest. It is safe to say, however, that Dartmouth students have a very real affinity for their school—not only during the years they attend, but in the years to follow.

Sports

More than seventy-five percent of the campus participate in either intercollegiate, club, or intramural sports programs. The athletic center's modern facilities include two pools, basketball courts, squash and racquetball courts, an indoor track, a weight-training room, a ballet studio, and a gymnastics area. Outside, there are tennis courts, an outdoor track, and the football stadium. Dartmouth also has its own skiway about twenty minutes from campus, and buses run to and from it six days a week during the winter. If you decide you want to ski, you can get a season pass to the skiway, a seasonal bus pass, and rent skis, all for about $200.

> *My skiing lessons were Tuesday mornings, and as I was headed up the lift, I always used to think how crazy it was that I was here skiing, when almost everyone else I knew was either in class or at work. Was I spoiled!*

Tucker Foundation

A host of other popular programs falls under the auspices of the Tucker Foundation, which organizes all the volunteer activities on campus. About one-third of the students devote time to programs like Big Brother/Big Sister, Adopt-A-Grandparent, Students Fighting Hunger, and Habitat for Humanity. To facilitate volunteering, the Tucker Foundation has cars that students can use to travel to their activities.

> *I see the Tucker Foundation as one of the moral and spiritual centers of Dartmouth. I volunteered as a book buddy, reading to and with a young boy, and then in the Adopt-A-Grandparent program, visiting a woman in a local nursing home. Both of these experiences taught me a great deal about the world beyond campus and also inspired me to spend a leave term volunteering full time. Funded by a Tucker grant, I worked at a legal services organization in Los Angeles. There I helped Holocaust survivors apply for reparations and counseled low-income people in need of free legal advice.*

In addition to organizing—and often funding— volunteer activities, Tucker is also the umbrella under which all the campus religious organizations fall. Most recently, Dartmouth dedicated the new Roth Center for Jewish Life, which will provide space for Jewish religious services, an annual Holocaust commemoration, and social events.

Racial/Ethnic Groups

Dartmouth students also spend a lot of time participating in groups organized by particular racial or ethnic affiliations. Group such as the Afro-American Society, The Dartmouth Asian Organization, The Korean-American Student Association, Africaso, Al-Nur, La Alianza Latina, and Native Americans at Dartmouth all have large memberships. The Dartmouth Rainbow Alliance, Dartmouth's gay and lesbian organization, also tends to be a vocal force on campus.

Publications

Working on student publications is also popular. *The Dartmouth*, said to be the oldest college newspaper in the country, resides in the same building as Dartmouth's AM and FM radio stations, which are completely student-run. The newspaper is supplemented by a number of specialty publications, including the *Stonefence Review* and *Snapshots of Color* (both literary magazines), *Sports Weekly*, *Easterly Winds* (the Dartmouth Asian Organization's publication), and *Black Praxis* (the Afro-American Society's publication). One recent interesting trend is the introduction of electronic magazines. Currently, there are two: *Sense of Place*, an environmental magazine, and *SANDpaper*, which is about the arts. *The Dartmouth Review*—the reason that so many outsiders mistakenly think of Dartmouth as a conservative bastion—is the mouthpiece of a small, but vocal few, but interest in it has been declining in recent years.

Campus Committees and Groups

Students also serve on campus committees, in the student government, and in organizations that try to educate the campus about problems that affect the Dartmouth campus, such as alcoholism, sexual assault, and eating disorders.

I was a member of SAFE, Students Against the Abuse of Food and Exercise. College-age women are so vulnerable about feeling that their bodies aren't good enough, and they fall victim to eating disorders. We wanted to get the word out that the campus has excellent resources, which include nutrition experts and body image counselors.

Many also sing in one of the four *a cappella* groups on campus. For those who don't sing, attending their shows is a favored pastime. (About now, you're probably beginning to understand why that daily planner comes in handy.)

Hopkins Art Center

The Hopkins Center, or the "Hop," designed by the architect who was responsible for both Lincoln Center and the U.N., is the hub of the arts on campus. Interestingly, it's also the home of the campus mailboxes. They were put there, goes the rationale, so that students would be forced to take notice of all of the Hop's artistic offerings. Besides housing three departments (art, music, and drama) and a jewelry studio, the Hop has incredible films, plays, and concerts. In a recent term, for example, the Hop played host to:

- Meryl Streep (on campus to receive a honorary award from the Film Society)
- the World Music Percussion Ensemble, famed choreographer Donald Byrd and company

- Sweet Honey in the Rock
- August Wilson (who directed a performance of his play *Joe Turner's Come and Gone*).

The hop also features movies; for a $10 pass, you could conceivably see about thirty-plus films per term.

Hood Museum

Dartmouth's other cultural center is the Hood Museum, which houses over 60,000 college-owned artifacts. The collection, which draws over 40,000 visitors annually, is particularly strong in African and Native American Art, nineteenth- and twentieth-century painting, and contemporary art.

Parties, Carnivals, and Fun

OK, so Dartmouth students are busy, you say. But, do they have any fun? The resounding answer to that question is yes. Dorm parties are a big deal freshman year, as are Homecoming (fall), Winter Carnival (winter), and Green Key Weekend (spring). Each fall, it's the responsibility of the freshman class to build a big wooden structure in the center of the green—and make sure that it's still standing on Friday night for the big bonfire. On that night, there's also an alumni parade, many speeches no one hears, and lots of parties. Winter Carnival, perhaps Dartmouth's most famous social tradition, is complemented by a huge snow sculpture on the green, keg-jumping, and for the very brave, a dip in the local pond.

Besides the dorms, fraternities, sororities, and coed houses there are central party areas. Freshmen are banned from houses during their first term, but after that, anyone can go to almost any party (there are few "closed" events on campus). No one joins a fraternity, sorority, or coed house until sophomore year, however, but those who do generally form close relationships with the people in them. The merits of the primarily single-sex Greek system are heavily debated on campus, although for the time being it seems to be here to stay.

For those who aren't into the Greek scene, there are a host of other social opportunities. The college often sponsors comedy clubs, hypnotists, concerts, and something called "casino night," which tends to be incredibly popular with the high rollers on campus. And, contrary to popular belief, people do date at Dartmouth. However, the on-again, off-again nature of the D-plan—you're there for nine months, and then gone for six—has been known to put a crimp in many a budding romance. Sorority and fraternity formals are popular date functions. Finally, right outside campus is the quaint town of Hanover, which has one good movie theater, a few bars, and a ton of reasonably affordable restaurants.

People always asked me what I found to do in Hanover, but the truth was, I was busy all the time. I loved the fact that my friends and I couldn't go anywhere particularly exotic: it made us all so much closer to one another. Had there been the distraction of a big city, I'm not sure I would have formed the fabulous friendships that I did.

FINANCIAL AID

First, the bad news. Dartmouth is *really* expensive, as in, you could take a few trips to Europe and buy a new car for the price of going to school there for one year. Thankfully, though, there is some good news. Not only will Dartmouth meet 100 percent of your demonstrated financial need, but they have a need-blind admissions policy. That means your application is kept separate from your financial aid forms, so that admissions decisions are in no way based on how much you can or cannot pay. Basically, if Dartmouth wants you there, they'll make sure you're able to afford it.

In fact, approximately fifty percent of each entering class receives money from the college or other sources. These funds come in the form of grants, loans, and/or work-study. Just to give you an idea of what kind of figures we are talking about, the average scholarship grant for a recent class was $15,966. Another interesting note: Dartmouth does not award academic, merit, or athletic scholarships. All aid is based solely on need.

Between my 10-hour-a-week work-study job in the cafeteria, student loans, and my family contribution, we were able to survive the first year at Dartmouth. The deal I worked out with my parents was that they'd cover the cost of the college bills not covered by loans, but books and spending money were my responsibility. I think it was a fair trade; they never sent me money, but I kept all that I earned.

Thanks to the fact that every incoming freshman is required to purchase a computer (or prove they have one compatible with Dartmouth's system), expect your freshman year bill to be particularly high but well worth the expense. Not only does Dartmouth have a good deal worked out with the computer company to get you really good prices, but it's virtually impossible to survive on campus without one.

Another thing that can complicate your financial future is the D-plan. Some students end up going to school for over a year without a summer break, and/or go abroad without having had sufficient time to earn extra money for the trip. Don't worry. A financial aid officer can work with you to increase your loans or scholarship for that time period, or figure out some other way for you to meet costs. Extra money is often allotted for students on financial aid to study abroad.

When I found out that my summer internship in publishing was virtually unpaid ($25 a week doesn't go far in New York), I had a meeting with my financial aid officer. Together, we worked out a schedule so that my loans would be a little higher for the coming term. I also spent two weeks in the spring working with Dartmouth's commencement and reunions. This gave me a lot of overtime, which was exactly what I needed.

GRADUATES

A few years ago, a rumor floated around campus that the average Dartmouth graduate makes $80,000 a year. While the figure was never completely confirmed, it's probably not far off base. On average, Dartmouth churns out large numbers headed for lucrative jobs in investment banking and consulting; recently, over 300 companies looked to Dartmouth to recruit prospective employees.

Of course, not everyone from Dartmouth heads off to the world of big business. Medical school and law school are both popular options for many recent grads, as are M.A.- or Ph.D-tracked graduate programs. In a recent year, about twenty-five percent of the senior class was headed right back into school. Additionally, by the time they've been out of school for five years, about seventy-three percent will have gone back to some school.

The working crowd, meanwhile, tends to be attracted to jobs in education, social services, advertising, and publishing. Others teach English in foreign countries or head off to parts unknown with the Peace Corps.

PROMINENT GRADS

- Salmon P. Chase, Former Secretary of State
- Louise Erdrich, Author
- Robert Frost, Poet
- Buck Henry, Film Director
- Laura Ingraham, TV Commentator
- C. Everett Koop, Former Surgeon General
- Norman Maclean, Author
- Robert Reich, Former Secretary of State
- Nelson Rockefeller, former U.S. Vice President
- Dr. Seuss (Theodore Geisel), Author
- Andrew Shue, Actor
- Paul Tsongas, Former Senator
- Daniel Webster, Orator and Statesman

Even with so many varied directions, the one thing you can be almost sure of with most Dartmouth graduates is that they'll come back to Hanover at some point. Dartmouth has an incredibly strong alumni network, and Homecoming and reunions are always well-attended. The alumni magazine is one of the strongest in the country. Each class produces a newsletter several times a year.

Dartmouth graduates don't just stay in touch with each other, either. They also stay in touch with the college. Over two-thirds of alumni contribute to Dartmouth's alumni fund, making Dartmouth's endowment one of the largest in the country. Alums also keep up with recent graduates. Dartmouth's Career Services keep extensive files on alumni who are willing to be contacted about their jobs, and the networking connections are consistently strong. Dartmouth graduates tend to like their school, and like others who went to their school.

Since I've been out of college for over a year, I'm surprised in a way by how involved I still am with Dartmouth. I recently attended the twenty-fifth Anniversary of Coeducation and was heartened simply by the sight of so many bright, articulate women who shared my alma mater. Dartmouth has exposed me to so many wonderful ideas and people that I'm realizing it's something I never want to give up.

SUMMING UP

If Dartmouth isn't the ideal campus, it's pretty much as close as you can reasonably get. With its northern location, year-round calendar, and focus on the undergraduate experience,

Dartmouth is perhaps the homiest of the Ivy League schools. Its intimate atmosphere breeds some of the highest student satisfaction rates in the country, which is probably partly due to the fact that everything balances so well. Dartmouth students are some of the smartest in the country, but they also like to have a lot of fun. The Dartmouth community is incredibly close-knit, yet, thanks to the fact that different students and professors come and go each term, it never feels stifling. Hanover is a beautiful, rural locale, yet the school manages to attract first-rate speakers, performers, and intellectuals. In fact, you'd probably be exposed to about as much culture at Dartmouth as you would in any major metropolis. It's just that Hanover is a heck of a lot quieter. Student activities see high participation rates, but the school is small enough so that you never get lost in the crowd. And finally, the school has just enough surprises so that even when you're feeling stressed, there's always something to appreciate.

Finally, Dartmouth is an intellectual powerhouse that offers incredible on-campus and international opportunities. Besides those tangibles, however, Dartmouth offers something ineffable. As evidenced by the fact that everyone puts their arms around one another as they sing the alma mater, there is something very special about going to school up in the mountains. Perhaps, in fact, this appeal is best summed up by the alma mater's cryptic last line, which speaks to the permanency of the Dartmouth experience. Dartmouth students, it proclaims, find themselves with "the granite of New Hampshire in their muscles and their veins." Go to Dartmouth, and by the end, you'll understand what that phrase means. I know I do.

❑ *Suzanne Leonard, B.A.*

DAVIDSON COLLEGE

Photo by Billy Howard

Davidson College
Davidson, NC 28036

(704) 892-2230, (800) 768-0380
Fax: (704) 892-2016

Web site: http://www.davidson.edu

Enrollment

Full-time ❑ women: 787
❑ men: 826

INTRODUCING DAVIDSON

With a strong dedication to undergraduate teaching and learning, Davidson, founded in 1837, has been recognized consistently as one of the country's most outstanding private liberal arts colleges. Davidson's 1,611 students, chosen not only for their academic promise, but also for their character, bring curiosity, initiative, and an enthusiasm for learning to every aspect of campus life. They stimulate each other with experiences such as researching the link between DNA and mental retardation, tutoring small children at an inner city elementary school, competing in Division I athletics, and studying South Asian culture and history in India. In and out of class, Davidson students respect each other and learn from their differences. Through a broad education across many different academic disciplines, Davidson encourages students to engage in an academic exploration that leads to a lifelong appreciation of learning.

Located in the town of Davidson, twenty miles from Charlotte, North Carolina, Davidson students, who come from forty-three states and twenty-one countries, enjoy the best of two worlds—the freedom and safety of living in a small college community with access to one of America's fastest growing cities. Davidson students are an active part of the town of Davidson, collecting their mail at the town post office, frequenting coffee shops and restaurants, and volunteering in the community at local schools and retirement homes. In Charlotte, students explore internships with businesses, hospitals, and law firms, and enjoy access to cultural, arts, and sports events. In addition, Davidson students broaden their horizons and enhance their learning experience by exploring internships and study programs across the United States and throughout the world.

THE CITY OF CHARLOTTE

The city of Charlotte follows New York City as the second largest banking and financial center in the United States. In addition to internship and service opportunities, Davidson students take advantage of cultural and arts opportunities at the Blumenthal Performing Arts Center and the Mint Museum of Art, enjoy attending Carolina Panthers and Charlotte Hornets games, and frequent the city's variety of restaurants and nightlife.

Davidson's 450-acre campus features seventy-six academic and residential buildings. Along with Chambers, the central academic building, the library contains 380,000 volumes, 2,000 periodicals, and 100 daily newspapers, and the Visual Arts Center, completed in 1993, adds extensive studio and exhibition space. Completion of the new life science wing in the fall of 1998 will enhance cutting edge science lab facilities available in the Charles A. Dana Laboratory and the Martin Chemical Laboratory. About ninety-five percent of students live on campus.

The Davidson Honor System forms a foundation for the campus community. The Honor Code represents a declaration by the entire college community—students, faculty, staff, and alumni—that an honorable course is the most just, and therefore the best. All students pledge to live by this creed that promotes trust and respect among all members of the community. The Honor Code at Davidson is much more than just a pledge; it is a way of life. As a result, take-home tests are common. Students are allowed to self-schedule exams, taking their exams in any order they wish during a week-long exam period. Library stacks are open, and students can feel comfortable leaving their books and papers unattended.

My favorite Honor Code story happened in the Baker Sports Complex. Over my four years at Davidson I swam laps in the pool in the Sports Complex each morning. I kept my goggles, swimsuit, and towel in a locker in the locker-room and I never thought to put a lock on my locker. In the rush of graduating, I forgot to clean out my locker. When I returned two years later for Homecoming, I went to visit my old locker. Although a little dusty after two years, I discovered all of my belongings just as I had left them. Indeed, the most important aspect of my four years at Davidson was the Honor Code. There is an immense sense of freedom derived from living and learning in a community where you know that you are trusted and you know that you can trust those around you.

ADMISSIONS REQUIREMENTS

In selecting a first-year class, Davidson seeks students who will contribute to the life of the college both inside and outside the classroom. Thus, as they shape a first-year class, the members of the Office of Admission and Financial Aid review each application with extreme care looking at the high school record, application essays, recommendations from teachers and counselors, test scores, and personal activities and achievements. Admission to Davidson is highly selective; typically a little over one-third of the applicants are admitted.

Nearly three-quarters of Davidson students graduated in the top tenth of their high school classes. The middle fifty percent of those accepted had SAT I scores of: Verbal—620 to 710, Math—620 to 700 (these scores representing the recentering). Of those students who submitted ACT scores, the middle fifty percent scored between 28 and 32. Students also demonstrated significant contributions in high school clubs and community activities.

One key to the admission process at Davidson is for students to challenge themselves academically. The rigor of the student's high school curriculum is of prime importance to the admission decision; therefore, Davidson encourages students to take advantage of the most challenging curriculum available to them in their high schools. Students entering Davidson must have graduated from high school, completing at least sixteen units of credit to include four, English; two, intermediate mathematics; one, plane geometry; two, of the same foreign language; one, history; and one, science. Electives should include additional courses in science, history, mathematics (ideally through calculus), and a foreign language (preferably continuing in the same language into the third, fourth, or fifth year). Students are encouraged to take at least five academic courses each year. In addition, Davidson requires that students submit either SAT I or ACT scores. While the SAT II: Subject tests are not required for admission, they are strongly recommended. Writing and Mathematics Level II are especially encouraged.

Davidson awards academic credit for up to four courses through the Advanced Placement exams for scores of 4 or 5, and also recognizes the International Baccalaureate Program and A-level examinations.

While high academics and extracurricular achievement are important, so are such qualities as motivation, leadership, and personal character. Thus, the admissions officers look closely at personal recommendations and essays to gain a view of the whole person. To put each applicant into perspective, they also take into account different ethnic, cultural, or economic backgrounds and the varying standards of individual secondary schools.

Decision Plans

At Davidson, first-year students are admitted for the fall semester; thus, the SAT I and II or the ACT should be taken no later than January of the senior year. Students may apply to Davidson under one of two Early Decision plans or under the Regular Decision plan. Early Decision is binding; therefore, it is for applicants who are certain that Davidson is their first choice college. To apply for Early Decision, students should take the SAT I or the ACT no later than October of the senior year, and along with the Davidson application for admission, submit the Early Decision candidate's agreement, which states that Davidson is the student's first choice and if accepted the student agrees to enroll at Davidson and withdraw applications pending at other colleges and universities. All application materials must be received by either November 15 for Round I of Early Decision or January 2 for Round II of Early Decision. Decisions will be mailed by December 15 for Round I Early Decision candidates, and by February 1 for Round II Early Decision candidates. For the Regular Decision plan, students must send all application materials to Davidson no later than January 2. Admission decisions for Regular Decision will be mailed no later than April 1. In addition to its own application, Davidson will accept the common application, provided that the student fill out special supplementary information.

The Davidson application was by far the most thorough application I had to fill out during my process of applying to college. More than any other application, it forced me to really think about myself and what was important to me. The application process convinced me that at Davidson I was more than just a number. The admissions staff cared about who I was as a person.

Campus Visits

While a campus visit is not required for admission to Davidson, it is strongly recommended because a visit to campus is the best way to get to know Davidson. In addition, it helps the Office of Admission get to know students better. The Office of Admission and Financial Aid is open from 9 A.M.–5 P.M., Monday through Friday and selected Saturday mornings in the fall and the spring. In addition to taking a tour of the campus with a current student tour guide, the Office of Admission offers opportunities for students to talk with admissions officers in group information sessions or through individual conversations. Students may also visit classes in academic areas of their choosing and talk with faculty, coaches, or other members of the Davidson community. Seniors may spend the night in a residence hall Monday through Thursday nights. To schedule a campus visit, call the Office of Admission and Financial Aid two weeks in advance.

Ultimately, my decision to attend Davidson rested upon my visit to Davidson's campus. The minute I stepped foot on the campus all that I had read and heard about the friendliness of the people, the beauty of the campus, the rigor of the academic program, and the openness and variety of campus activities suddenly became real. I knew Davidson was a place where I could excel and be happy.

ACADEMIC LIFE

Davidson encourages students to gain a lifelong appreciation of learning; at Davidson you will be engaged in exploring the life of the mind. This exploration begins in the classroom;

however, you will be challenged and directed down pathways of learning well beyond the bounds of the campus. Davidson's liberal arts curriculum is dedicated to allowing students to explore their interests while at the same time challenging students to discover new interests, strengths, and talents. Davidson's core curriculum requires that each student take courses across all disciplines—humanities, social sciences, fine arts, and science and mathematics. By the end of the sophomore year, students may choose from twenty different majors or may choose to create their own interdisciplinary major through Davidson's Center for Interdisciplinary Studies. In addition, students may supplement their major with one of Davidson's special interdisciplinary concentrations in applied mathematics, ethnic studies, gender studies, international studies, medical humanities, or neuroscience.

Approximately twenty students each year will design their own majors through the Center for Interdisciplinary Studies. Recent self-designed majors include: comparative literature, bioethics, international/medicine, and visual communications. Students may minor in anthropology, chemistry, economics, French, German, music, philosophy, Russian, Spanish, and theater.

One of my friends told me on our first day of class freshman year that she knew that she was definitely going to major in biology and go to medical school following Davidson. Her interests appeared to be completely focused in the sciences. Indeed, she majored in biology and attended her first choice medical school. However, during our first semester, as part of the Davidson's liberal arts core curriculum, she was required to take an art history course. Through the semester she fell in love with art history and over her four years continued to explore this newfound interest. Her exploration took her to France during the spring semester of our junior year. I'm convinced that her passion for art history will make her a much more interesting doctor.

Through reading and writing assignments across every discipline, Davidson students learn to think critically and communicate effectively, skills that will be integral to success throughout their lives. Davidson is recognized by graduate and professional schools for the rigor and high quality of its academic program, and Davidson students thrive on the challenges that the curriculum presents.

Faculty

Great teaching reflects the heart and soul of the Davidson experience. With a student-faculty ratio of 12:1, the capstone of the Davidson academic experience is the close relationships that Davidson enables students to develop with professors. All classes are taught by full professors, 96.5 percent of whom hold Ph.D.s. Eight Davidson faculty members have won CASE national teaching awards, more than any other college or university in the United States.

Davidson professors choose to teach at Davidson because they get their greatest professional satisfaction from teaching and guiding undergraduates. Thus, Davidson professors, accomplished in their fields, are teachers first, using their research and their publications as teaching tools.

I was amazed when I purchased my textbook for a history class my sophomore year—the main text for the class had been written by my professor. I knew then that I could never miss a reading assignment!

All classes are small with the average class size no larger than twenty students; therefore, at Davidson, individual attention is the norm. Small classes allow Davidson's 128 full-time faculty members to have engaging and thought-provoking discussions within the classroom, a time when students are encouraged to share their ideas and opinions and to actively participate in the learning process.

My friends had many opportunities to work one-on-one with our professors. One of my friends got to work in the neuroscience lab on a project that focused on a search for a cure for Alzheimers. Another friend traveled to England with a professor over the summer to help her do research for a book she was writing. Another student co-authored a U.S. Department of Justice report on the psychological impact on families of missing children.

Student-faculty interaction does not stop at the classroom door. Members of the Davidson faculty involve themselves in all aspects of student life, inviting students to their homes for dinner, fostering a friendly competition over intramural volleyball, working side by side on community service projects, cheering for Division I athletic teams, and attending student choral and symphony concerts.

One Saturday, I sheetrocked an entire house for Habitat for Humanity with one of my religion professors. While I'm not sure that anyone would want to live in the house we sheetrocked together, I developed a lasting friendship with the professor as we struggled with hammer and nails!

Off-Campus Study Programs

Davidson students are encouraged to enhance their learning experience by spending time at one of many campus-sponsored study programs in the United States or abroad. Through off-campus programs in the United States and many foreign countries, Davidson students further explore their interests. Among options in the United States, Davidson sponsors a marine biology semester on the North Carolina coast, exchange programs with Morehouse College and Howard University, a semester program in Philadelphia, and a summer program in Washington, D.C. Possibilities for expanding a sense of global understanding include studying art history in France, England, or Italy, attending a Russian university, immersing oneself in eighteenth century British history and literature at the University of Cambridge in England, or studying for an entire year in Tours, France or Wurtzburg, Germany, or for a semester in India. If Davidson does not have a study abroad program that covers a student's academic interests, or if the student is interested in studying in a country where Davidson does not have a program, the Study Abroad Office will help the student locate programs through other colleges and universities. In addition, the Dean Rusk Program in International Studies, named for former Secretary of State and Davidson graduate Dean Rusk, and led by former U.S. Ambassador Kenneth Brown, broadens Davidson's international offerings by sponsoring speakers and conferences on international topics. The Dean Rusk Program helps students formulate independent experiences across the world and gives students more than $35,000 annually in grants to pursue international research. Recent Dean Rusk Program conferences and speakers have addressed such topics as human rights, world hunger, global environment, the Middle East, and Central America.

I spent two summers abroad during my time at Davidson. During the summer between my sophomore and junior years I studied religion and political science in Switzerland, Italy, and East Germany (the wall had come down in Germany the summer before). I went to the Study Abroad Office and told them that I was considering religion for my major, I spoke some French, and had always wanted to live in Switzerland. They helped me find a program that surpassed my expectations; it was so much more than I had asked for. During the summer between my junior and senior years I studied on Davidson's program at the University of Cambridge. Not only did I get a taste of British university life, but I got to spend many weekends traveling throughout England and Scotland. Both programs greatly shaped and broadened my world view.

About sixty percent of Davidson students take advantage of Davidson's extensive study abroad options. Those options include programs in Germany, France, Italy, England, India, Ghana, Greece, and Turkey.

SOCIAL LIFE AND ACTIVITIES

Through opportunities to be involved daily in a myriad of activities that reflect a diversity of interests and talents, Davidson students lead well-balanced lives. Students come to campus with varied and diverse talents. They of course share these interests in the classroom, but they also find activities and programs outside of class in which they can share their talents. By participating in over 100 campus organizations, students make an impact on the community in many ways, influencing college policy and campus life, organizing campus events, and promoting social causes and multicultural interests.

The Student Union, a hub of campus activity and student life, is one of the important centers of social life on campus. The union serves as an umbrella for numerous student-run committees that plan campus-wide social events and cultural experiences. Union committees include Davidson Outdoors, Films, Artists' Series, Concerts, Gender Issues, Speakers, International, and Intimate Performance. The popular Davidson Outdoors program sponsors numerous trips to the nearby mountains and beaches for rock climbing, camping, biking, rafting, and sailing.

When warm weather arrives, students take advantage of the 106 acres of waterfront property that Davidson owns on nearby Lake Norman. The college provides boats for sailing and skiing and a beach area for swimming and sitting in the sun.

Patterson Court

The other important center of social life on campus is Patterson Court. Six national fraternities, three women's eating houses, and the Black Student Coalition are located on Patterson Court. Each house has both dining and social facilities, and serves as a place where members eat all meals and socialize. Students may join a house in the spring of the first year. The women's houses use a process of self-selection and the fraternities use an oral encouragement system. Approximately seventy percent of all students belong to either an eating house or a fraternity. In addition to sponsoring large and small parties open to the entire campus community, members of each house are actively engaged in a variety of community service projects.

Music and Drama

Davidson offers the student musician or thespian a wide array of options. Through small and large ensembles such as the concert choir, the symphony orchestra, and the jazz ensemble, students with musical interests share their talents. The Theater Department sponsors numerous student-run productions throughout each school year.

Singers with years of voice lessons and novice singers joined together each Tuesday and Thursday afternoon under the direction of a dynamic choral director. I lost myself in the music of Bach and Beethoven, Handel, and Vaughan Williams. Not only did I sharpen my music skills, but concert choir served as a wonderful outlet for self-expression.

Service Projects

Davidson has a strong tradition of contributing to the local community through service projects. Over 800 students each year get involved in community outreach programs in Davidson and the greater Charlotte community. Through the student-run Reach Out Organization, some students choose to do one-time activities such as the CROP walk for world hunger or the annual bone marrow drive. Other students may participate in service on a weekly basis, tutoring at the local elementary school, working with adult literacy, visiting prisons, and much more. Still other students are involved in daily service projects such as the on-campus recycling program. The Campus Community Service Coordinator, a full-time staff member, helps students design individual or group projects when students recognize a need in the community that is not being met.

THE BONE MARROW PROGRAM

New service projects at Davidson are often student-initiated. Several years ago a student who had recently undergone a bone marrow transplant joined with a group of friends to create Davidson's Bone Marrow Registration program. Since the program began, a number of members of the Davidson community have been matched as bone marrow donors. This program serves as a model for other colleges.

Athletics

Davidson offers a range of athletic programs for serious athletes or just for fun. Approximately eighty percent of students participate in intramural and club sports and about twenty-five percent play on one of the varsity teams. As one of the smallest colleges competing in the Division I of the NCAA, Davidson enrolls true scholar-athletes to play eleven different varsity sports for men and ten for women. In addition to varsity sports, students enthusiastically compete in club and intramural sports ranging from flickerball (Davidson's own version of touch football) to sailing. The Baker Sports Complex, opened in 1989, is impressive for a school of Davidson's size. While the Baker Sports Complex houses all of Davidson's varsity sports, the weight rooms, exercise equipment, pool, racquetball courts, and indoor tennis courts are all open to the entire student body on a first come first serve basis.

Davidson's recent athletic successes include hosting the NCAA Division I Men's Soccer Championship three years in a row, one national coach of the year, and one national player of the year. The field hockey team has won six consecutive Deep South Championships, and the men's basketball team has appeared in the National Invitation Tournament.

SPORTS AT DAVIDSON

- **Men's Division I Teams: Baseball, basketball, cross-country, football (Division 1AA), golf, soccer, swimming and diving, tennis, track and field, and wrestling.**
- **Women's Division I Teams: Basketball, cross-country, field hockey, lacrosse, soccer, swimming and diving, tennis, track and field, and volleyball.**
- **Club Sports: Crew, fencing, lacrosse, ranger challenge, rugby, sailing, soccer, tennis, water polo, and waterskiing.**

FINANCIAL AID

Davidson strives to keep costs moderate for all students. By a strong commitment to providing financial assistance to help those who need it, Davidson enables students of many backgrounds and circumstances to attend, giving all students the benefits of a diverse learning community. All admission decisions are made without regard to financial need.

Davidson helps students with financial need through a variety of financial aid programs. Approximately one third of each entering class receive some form of need-based financial aid in the form of grants, loans, and work-study programs. Recently, the average award was $12,250. Of this average total award, total need-based grants averaged $9,500, loans averaged $1,750, and work-study programs averaged $1,000.

To apply for financial aid at Davidson, applicants must complete the College Scholarship Service/Financial Aid PROFILE Application and the Free Application for Federal Student Aid (FAFSA). These forms are available through high school guidance offices. Davidson mails instructions on filling out these forms to each student who applies for admission. Following is the timetable for applying for need-based aid:

Early Decision:	CSS/Financial Aid PROFILE Registration	October 1
	PROFILE Application	November 1
Regular Decision:	CSS/Financial Aid PROFILE Registration	January 15
	PROFILE Application	February 15

Financial aid is normally renewable for four years provided the student makes satisfactory progress toward a degree and family financial circumstances do not change appreciably.

In addition to need-based aid programs, Davidson awards merit scholarships that recognize the academic promise, special talents, and personal qualities of students without regard to their financial circumstances (need-blind aid). A limited number of first-year students are offered merit awards based on the strength of their application for admission. For some scholarships, selection may also be based on the outcome of an audition, interview, art portfolio review, or writing sample. General scholarship awards are given on the basis of scholastic promise, ability, character, and potential to contribute to society. Awards range from $2,500 to $10,000 annually. No special application is required for the general scholarship awards. Special Competition Honor Scholarships are available to admitted students based on their application for admission. Finalists, selected by early March, must participate in a scholarship interview weekend.

THE SPECIAL COMPETITION HONOR SCHOLARSHIPS

- Thomas S. Baker Scholarship (full cost of attendance, two offered)
- John Montgomery Belk Scholarship (full cost of attendance, offered to one student from the southeastern United States)
- William Holt Terry Scholarship ($15,000 to full tuition, two offered)

Special Application Honor Scholarships recognize those students who wish to pursue specific study or career paths or further develop special talents. Awards are offered in the fields of art, music, creative writing, and Latin, among others. The special application required for these awards is included with the Davidson application for admission. In addition, Davidson offers North Carolina Legislative Tuition grants, athletic grants, ROTC Scholarships, National Merit Scholarships, and scholarships for children of Presbyterian ministers as a part of its program of merit awards.

GRADUATES

Davidson students are encouraged to use their time on campus to test themselves, focus their energies, and prepare for the future. Thus, Davidson graduates may be found in positions of leadership and service in communities across the nation and the world. More than eighty-five percent of Davidson graduates go on to graduate or professional schools within five years of graduation. Medical, law, education, the humanities, and the ministry attract the most students. Acceptances to law and medical schools have averaged eighty-five percent over the past five years.

Fortune Magazine recently ranked Davidson seventh nationally for proportion of alumni who are Fortune 500 and Service 500 CEOs, and twenty-two Davidson graduates have been named Rhodes Scholars in recognition of their outstanding leadership and academic talents.

With the help of an experienced counseling staff in the Career Services Office and over 700 alumni mentor volunteers, Davidson students are directed to explore career pathways. Davidson alumni, fiercely loyal, often serve as key contacts in the job search process for current Davidson students and younger alumni. A degree from Davidson will open many doors.

During November of my first year of law school, our Director of Career Planning made a presentation about searching for a legally related job following our first year. In the middle of her presentation she paused and said, "I want to tell anyone in the room who went to Davidson that using your Davidson contacts will help you immensely as you search for a summer position." She proceeded to say that she had never witnessed such a loyal alumni group at any other school. I took her advice and I'm convinced that making contacts with Davidson graduates helped me to find an excellent job at a law firm after my first year of law school.

The Office of Career Planning and Placement Services offers self assessment workshops, sessions in job interviewing and résumé writing, a well-stocked library of career planning resources, and visits by recruiters from businesses and graduate schools.

I vividly remember the Dean of Students telling my class during his welcoming address at our orientation that a Davidson education would give us critical thinking and communication skills, skills that would prepare us to do anything. I did not truly understand what this meant until I graduated and watched one friend travel to Japan to teach English, another friend pursue a career in politics in Washington, another classmate win a fellowship given by the German government to study economics. One of my friends is finishing her pediatrics residency, another worked for a consulting firm and then returned to pursue an MBA, another attended divinity school and is an Episcopal priest, and one friend earned a master's in English and teaches English at a public middle school. Davidson encouraged my friends and me to gain a keen understanding of our own particular gifts and to develop and use these gifts to the fullest.

SUMMING UP

At Davidson students meet the challenges of demanding professors who hold teaching and learning before all else, a grading system in which an A is really an A, a variety of community activities that need the strengths and talents of a diverse student body, and an Honor Code that forms a community based on mutual trust and respect.

The variety and flexibility of the liberal arts curriculum at Davidson allows the potential graduate to explore many subject areas, design majors, and explore interdisciplinary learning. Thus, students may be architects of their own educations. Small classes allow students and faculty to have an interactive dialogue in which everyone becomes an integral part of the learning process. Davidson-sponsored academic opportunities across the United States and the world allow students to carry academics far beyond the classroom. At Davidson learning is cherished as a lifelong enterprise.

Over 100 campus organizations, from athletics and the fine arts to community service and social events, allow students to lead balanced lives and to share their own unique talents outside the classroom. At Davidson students can do much more than simply attend campus events; they can be a part of them because most things that happen on campus are student-run and student-initiated. At Davidson the student-athlete finds a ready home because excellence reigns both in the classroom and on the playing fields.

Perhaps the most important thing about Davidson is the people. Students from forty-three states and twenty-one countries with their diverse talents and backgrounds share a common enjoyment for learning and being challenged. Faculty and staff are fiercely dedicated to the mission of guiding undergraduates and helping them discover their full potential. Davidson alumni, appreciative of the pathways that their Davidson experiences have forged, give generously of their time and efforts to the college and to their communities.

A day did not pass during my four years at Davidson when I did not face a challenge; however, all of these challenges were positive challenges and they taught me to strive for a sense of balance in my life. One day the challenge may have been struggling over a fetal pig dissection in biology, another day it was mastering the harmony in a piece of music, another day it was perfecting my blocking skills as a member of my flickerball team, another day it was composing the perfect paper on the Epic of Gilgamesh, *and another day it was helping one of the women on my hall work through a crisis. With each new day and each new challenge, I gained a better and stronger sense of self. I developed skills that help me face the many challenges that life brings.*

For the student with a serious commitment to learning and the desire to contribute to the wider world, Davidson offers outstanding opportunities in an environment of challenge and support.

❑ *Kristi Elaine Kessler, B.A.*

DUKE UNIVERSITY

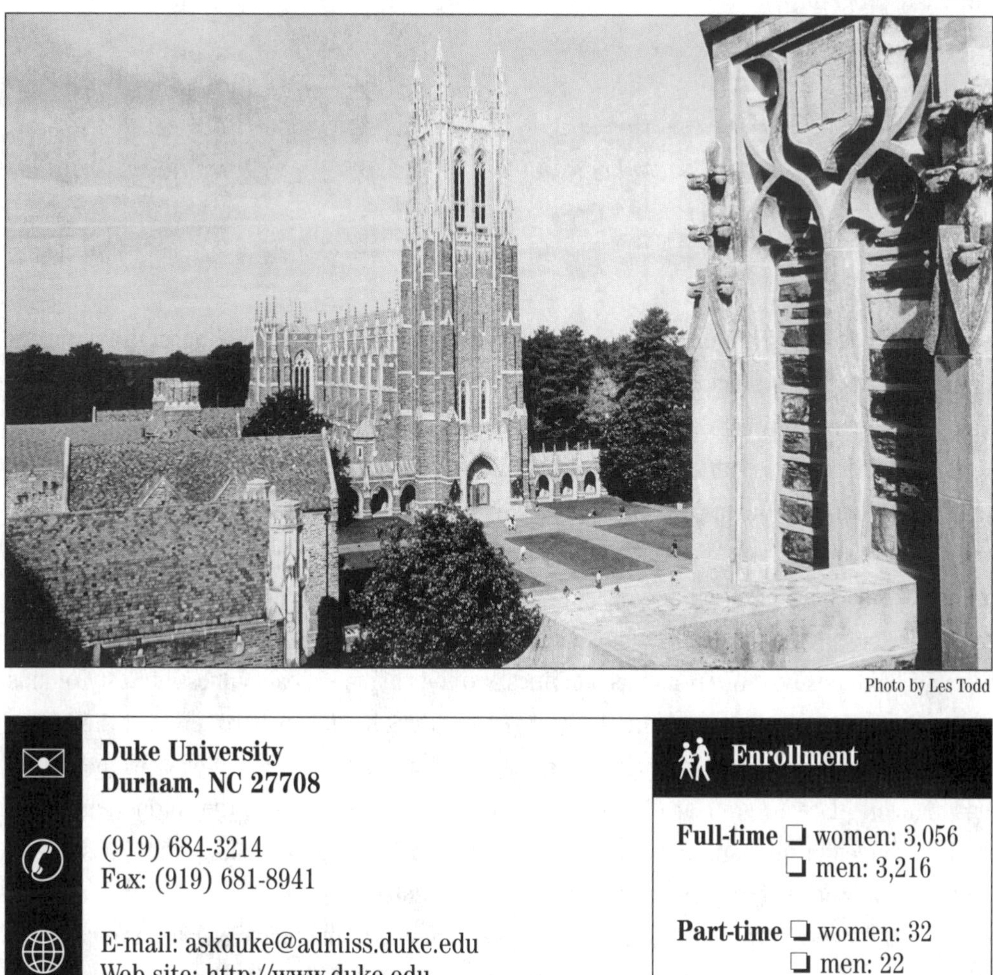

Photo by Les Todd

Duke University
Durham, NC 27708

(919) 684-3214
Fax: (919) 681-8941

E-mail: askduke@admiss.duke.edu
Web site: http://www.duke.edu

Enrollment

Full-time ❑ women: 3,056
❑ men: 3,216

Part-time ❑ women: 32
❑ men: 22

INTRODUCING DUKE

If Duke University's location in Durham, North Carolina, conjures up images of a stoic institution in a lethargic, southern town, a closer examination of Duke will change those impressions. Set in the middle of the state, this 8,500-acre campus exudes the same energy and entrepreneurial spirit of the Research Triangle Park area, Duke's home. Just as the region is a relatively recent hotbed for economic development and growth, Duke is a relatively young university that pulses with activity and enthusiasm.

Complemented by eight graduate and professional schools, Duke's Trinity College of Arts and Sciences and the School of Engineering have climbed to the very top tier of undergraduate programs.

There is a sense on campus that the best is yet to come. That expectation translates into energetic students and faculty pouring themselves into bettering the university and themselves.

Duke is an institution full of surprising and pleasant contrasts. The most dramatic and immediately apparent contrast is framed by the widely divergent architecture of Duke's West and East Campuses. West Campus features the soaring 210-feet-tall chapel at the heart of the Gothic buildings. It is difficult not to be academically inspired by the intricate angles and meticulous detail of the majestic buildings and landscape.

On the other hand, the Georgian architecture and long, lush lawns of the East Campus convey a sense of relaxation and peace. Weekends on East are often filled with outdoor concerts, Frisbee on the quad, and sunning students.

The intensity of West Campus buildings and the balanced peacefulness of East Campus' architecture work well to illustrate the well-known "work hard, play hard" ethic of the university. In the same way that the architectural styles of the campuses work together to create a magnificent place to grow academically, emotionally, and spiritually, the intense nature of Duke's academic program is enhanced by a sense of balance and perspective as students engage in a wide array of interesting activities and events.

With eighty-six percent of the student body coming from outside North Carolina, and a significant international presence, the university is a model of diversity. Student backgrounds vary from those arriving from America's top prep schools to those leaving large schools in some of the country's most impoverished areas. In the midst of this divergence of experiences, however, Duke has created a unique sense of "family" among its community members. This closeness is evident in the informal chatting of students crossing Duke's pristine quads or in the chaos of the Cameron Crazies cheering for Duke's revered basketball team.

Perhaps the men's basketball program has contributed to a "team mentality" among the students. It's great to feel a part of something bigger during your college years.

Some students cite Duke's friendly environment as the reason for this close-knit community. Others believe that the students attracted to Duke represent well-rounded, balanced individuals with common desires to excel in every activity they pursue while developing lasting relationships in the process.

It is not uncommon to walk from one end of the main quad to another and know the first names of most of the people around you.

This friendliness often stops at the campus gates during athletic seasons, however, as Duke is in close proximity to two of its primary *athletic* rivals, North Carolina State University and the University of North Carolina at Chapel Hill. But as an example of another contrast, outside of sports, Duke utilizes its relationships with these schools to benefit its students.

Enhancing Duke's impressive library collection of more than 4.4 million volumes, an inter-library loan program allows the three schools to share resources. In addition, Duke students can cross-register at the other campuses, expanding the number of available courses. These relationships have also translated into a large number of local internships available to students during the academic year or the summer.

Faculty

As another example of wonderful contrasts, the Duke faculty represents a demanding group of individuals who are known to expect incredible academic performance from students. The rigor of Duke's academic program is intense. In the midst of this push, however, Duke's faculty is made up of a group of wonderfully caring and interested scholars. Many are available for lunches with students and have a desire to know students personally.

A recently developed faculty associates program pairs top faculty with resident halls to encourage collaboration and student-faculty interaction. Many students also take on independent research with Duke's faculty members to develop relationships and experiences.

Faculty mentoring and interaction with the students seem to be genuine goals of the university administration. Many resources are funneled into creating opportunities to build relationships.

Operating in balance, these factors and contrasts work together to create an invigorating, friendly, competitive, challenging, and beautiful environment to spend the undergraduate years.

ADMISSIONS REQUIREMENTS

It works to Duke's advantage that the Admissions Office hosts its Accepted Students weekend in mid-April when the North Carolina spring is in full swing. Flowers are blooming, students are studying outside, and the sweet Southern air hovers at about seventy degrees. It is perfect weather, and the students who attend deserve it because they have made it through a tough cut.

Each year, around 13,000 students from across the country apply to Duke for a class of 1,600. Applications come from every state, and growing numbers of international applicants are discovering Duke.

Admitted students at Duke have an average SAT in the high 1300s and find themselves in the top ten percent of their high school classes. Like most of the top-tier institutions, however, grades and test scores don't serve as the only factors in the admissions process.

Duke students are simply amazing. They are leaders, and they possess a resilience that excites other people around them.

Applicants are evaluated on talent and active participation in learning. The Admissions Office focuses on six areas:

- quality of secondary school academic program
- performance
- recommendations

- personal qualities
- testing
- essays

To be admitted, most students must possess strengths in each of these areas. While these six areas are used to evaluate the candidates, Duke does a good job of assessing applicants in the context of their individual circumstances. Duke attempts to get a picture of the strengths of each high school to understand the differences in the rigors of secondary school programs through school profiles and guidance counselor reports. As one admissions officer has said, "We admit students, not schools." Therefore, a student's ability to excel in his or her own high school environment is of utmost relevance.

Duke's student body is active and engaged. The application should reflect a real desire to actively partake in the life of the community. Recommendations should point to a depth of interest in academics and an ability to translate intelligence and leadership into understanding among others in the university.

The Blue Devil's Advocates is a group of undergrads who serve in providing visitor programs and tours of the campus. These students provide wonderfully honest assessments of the university and also complement daily group information sessions offered by the Admissions Office. Those sessions are consistently praised as friendly and helpful.

My tour guide at Duke made the difference as I toured college campuses. He was positive, yet frank. When I enrolled, I felt I had a better sense of what to expect.

The Admissions Office can also arrange overnight stays with current students during the school year. This provides prospective students with chances to stay in the dorms and get a clearer picture of what to expect.

In the end, the admissions process is extremely competitive and similar to many other top-tier institutions, but the university has done a good job of making the process user-friendly and helpful. Under the leadership of Admissions Director, Christoph Guttentag, Duke has been able to recruit a first-rate group of scholars and leaders, while ensuring an open and encouraging applications process for almost all who apply.

ACADEMIC LIFE

ABOUT ACADEMICS

In a constant push to keep academics alive and relevant, Duke has worked diligently to attract "Professors of the Practice" to add new dimensions to classroom study.

Former White House advisor David Gergen and Pulitzer Prize-winning columnists William Raspberry and David Broder are famous people who have made their way into Duke classrooms in the past few semesters. Rather than just coming to campus to make speeches, these "professors" teach weekly classes, have office hours, and become an active part of the university community.

Some professors are not celebrities but are experts in specialized fields. For example, Tony Brown, former vice president at CS First Boston, complements the public policy curriculum by teaching courses in business leadership and public-private partnerships. Students love these courses because of their relevance and applicability to situations they will encounter after Duke.

Duke's motto is *Eruditio et Religio* (Erudition and Religion), and it signifies the university's commitment to infusing learning with the moral responsibility for using the educational experience to enlighten others and help communities. The nature and form of Duke's academic programs contribute to this spirit.

Students at Duke enter the Trinity College of Arts and Sciences or the School of Engineering. Both schools provide stimulating curricula that allow students to experience different courses across departments. In the first and second years, Duke's Pre-Major Advising Center encourages students to explore areas of potential interest.

I was really encouraged to take advantage of my first two years as an opportunity to get into some of the departments in which I had some interest. This opened my eyes to new ways to think about using the major.

Majors

By the end of the second year, Duke students choose one or two concentrations from thirty-six majors or pursue one of their own devising. The diversity of these offerings is also complemented by an offering of minors and certificate programs ranging from genetics to markets and management studies. While most students take approximately eleven courses within the major, there is plenty of room to fulfill Duke's requirement of courses in five of six major areas of knowledge: arts and literatures, civilizations, foreign languages, natural sciences, quantitative reasoning, and social sciences. This mix of required and major courses still leaves students plenty of room to explore the elective curriculum.

Credits

In order to graduate, Duke students must fulfill thirty-four credits. This means a normal semester load for undergraduates consists of four courses. While this often seems like few courses to new students, the amount and difficulty of the reading and work quickly prove that this is a rigorous number of courses to study.

> *Students should come ready to work. Professors expect a certain level of excellence that requires not only keeping up with the reading but adding creativity and new ideas to class discussions. It's an intense experience.*

Faculty and Programs

The faculty at Duke is made up of a renowned set of scholars that is surprisingly accessible to students. Formal office hours and after-class question periods are supplemented by regular meals and informal meetings. Some students complain that some professors are burdened, but most faculty members are willing to connect with students if students make the effort of stopping by and getting to know them.

Some of the first-year courses are large introductory lectures, with sections run by teaching assistants. Others, like those in Duke's Freshman Seminar Program, are courses for no more than fourteen students taught by senior faculty in specialty fields. A former Duke president and the dean of the college are regular participants. Freshmen build lasting relationships with faculty members and are encouraged to begin specialty research projects early in their academic life.

Duke has made its Freshman Focus program an integral part of its offerings. First-year students join together for semester or year-long tracks that tie together course curricula under an umbrella theme. For example, in the Twentieth-Century America Program, students take courses in history, religion, English, and the natural sciences with an eye toward thinking about the relationship of these fields to the modern American experience.

The Focus and Seminar programs are dynamic. Our small group studies the same materials, has fabulous interaction with leading faculty, and meets weekly for dinner discussions. This is what I came to college for!

A final, unique trait of Duke's curriculum deals with its emphasis on experiential learning and independent study. Rather than simply studying under Duke's faculty, students are encouraged to join with faculty members in independent research. The students are also given ample opportunities to take the ideas of the classroom into the Durham community and, to a greater degree, into the world. Community service, internships, and summer experiences are all used by the faculty to drive home lessons.

Duke's active environment doesn't end as students enter the doors of Duke's academic buildings. The vibrancy of the student body and faculty is demonstrated every day in the intense quest for learning in and out of Duke classrooms.

SOCIAL LIFE AND ACTIVITIES

After Duke students leave the classroom buildings, day planners and tight schedules are the norm as students balance wonderfully intense academic, extracurricular and residential lives.

In any week the pulse of Duke's campus is energetic and pounding. Almost 350 clubs and organizations meet at different times during the week. *A cappella* singing groups and orchestras rehearse. Students work in hospital internships, and community service groups plan outings into the local community. Duke is a busy place!

There is so much to do here. If an activity that interests you doesn't exist, the student government provides seed money to get the event up and running. My best college memories have been dashing from meeting to meeting making new friends.

Sports

Many students choose to participate in athletics, from fitness to recreational to intercollegiate. Although many of Duke's athletic teams are of national championship caliber (and students love to support them), other teams exist at the club and intramural levels. This array of opportunities gives students the chance to stay physically fit and to be spectators in first-rate athletics. New construction is underway for state-of-the-art athletic facilities on West Campus, and new facilities have already opened on East Campus.

During basketball season, the famed tents that make up Krzyzekskiville pop up outside Cameron Indoor Stadium. Students camp out for the best seats in the house as Duke takes on the finest teams in the Atlantic Coast Conference and the country. Tickets are free, but there is heavy demand for those courtside seats.

As students wait for games, study groups meet in the tents, some students put on musical performances, and others get caught up on neglected reading. Coach K is sometimes known to send pizzas out to the students waiting for the big game.

Consider having your parents visit during this time. It may convince them that you have resorted to living in a tent because they do not send you enough cash. The money will start flowing in!

Residences

Residential life at Duke is another draw for many of the students who choose Duke. Over ninety percent of the students elect to live on campus for all four years, so campus life is a crucial part of the undergraduate experience. All of the freshmen live together on Duke's East Campus. Activities, meals, and special campus programs are tailored to build comfortable interaction for Duke's newest community members. Many students cite class unity and quality of life as the best traits of the East Campus experience. To help students become acclimated to Duke and Durham, upperclass FACs (Freshmen Advisory Counselors) are assigned to the first-year students to help them adjust. In addition, upperclass quadrangles adopt freshmen houses as a way to introduce first-year students to the intricacies of campus life.

My freshman year was incredible. Imagine living with 1,600 of your classmates on a campus that allows you to know almost everyone's first name! It is wonderful to "come home" to our campus every night and find a comfortable place to grow. We had movie nights, arts events, and the all too often all-night academic discussions.. It was a great transition into college life.

Most upperclass students live on Duke's West Campus where they are assigned to sections of university housing. Most of the sections are randomly distributed through a lottery system. Extensive dining choices are available to replace the board plan of the first-year campus, and some students feel a letdown moving from the bonded first-year community to the larger, more individualized feel of West. As one way to counter this feeling of upperclass autonomy, Duke offers traditional fraternities (which may or may not be residential), sororities (which are not residential), and selective houses (which are residential).

Duke isn't a Greek or geek campus. Most of the students interrelate with each other at sporting events, weekend trips, and open campus parties.

While a majority of the students do not belong to Greek organizations, it is one outlet of community building at Duke. Most students find welcome places in their organizations, groups, and residence halls. Social life at Duke is vigorous and open-ended as most campus groups encourage all students to attend their parties. Durham is booming with new restaurants, a revitalized Ninth Street, Satisfaction's, and the Durham Athletic Park (home of the Durham Bulls AAA baseball team), but the city doesn't provide a particularly active college social scene. Therefore, students themselves are responsible for providing an atmosphere that has become less and less dependent on alcohol and more expressive of the students' creativity. Movies, Broadway at Duke, Springfest, and large quad events highlight the social calendars of Duke students each year.

In the rare event that I can't find anything going on at Duke, my friends and I can always go to Franklin Street in Chapel Hill for nightlife, but we just can't stand being that close to Carolina so, we'd rather stay on campus.

Recent administration attention to the upperclass housing system and social experience has put selective living groups under fire. As soon as one plan describing values and priorities in the upperclass system has been approved, some administrative departments of the university seem to reopen discussions on every aspect of residential life.

Vocal minorities of Duke students call for residential and social change at every turn. At the same time, most students and the alums crave stability after final decisions are made. Duke needs to make up its mind about which constituency to serve.

While the state of upperclass housing is in flux, Duke students don't let uncertainty deter them. They actively work with each other to create an unforgettable social climate where students meet new friends and build lasting relationships.

FINANCIAL AID

Duke's president and board have gone on record several times in the past few years, stressing their belief that the undergraduate admissions process should always be need blind. Therefore, when you apply to Duke, one form goes to the Financial Aid Office while the application goes to the Admissions Office. Ability to pay is not a factor in determining your admission to Duke.

Once accepted, however, ability to pay *becomes* a factor for students as they determine their ability to attend the university. Students receive their financial aid analysis with their acceptance letters. Duke's admissions materials say, "Duke admits students on the basis of academic ability, then provides one-hundred percent of their demonstrated financial need." It is important for accepted students and parents to remember that their perception of need may be vastly different from the "demonstrated need" calculated by Duke using federal and institutional guidelines. Parents and students are often aghast upon learning of their calculated ability to pay. Fortunately, the Financial Aid Office at Duke works well to alleviate this shock by putting together manageable financial aid packages to make a Duke education accessible for most accepted students.

Once I was accepted, the Financial Aid Office did everything possible to creatively work with my family to design a package to meet our needs.

More than forty-one percent of Duke undergrads receive financial aid of some sort. Aid usually consists of a package combining:

- federal and university grants
- loans
- work-study funds

Students and parents have the ability to pick and choose from the funding options offered to them. One thing to remember about financial aid at Duke is that the university has decided that cars are extremely valuable taxable goods. In order to discourage students from having cars, Duke factors a percentage of the value of a student's car into the family's calculated ability to pay.

The process for applying for financial aid can be a cumbersome one. Parents and students will find themselves filling out many forms throughout the four years at Duke. (Aid is granted one year at a time, so students must reapply annually.) On the whole, though, the Financial Aid Office at Duke is friendly and easy to work with. If a family situation changes during the year, the Financial Aid Office tries to adjust packages. In addition, good counselors often explain packages and changes to students and are accessible to parents. In this tiresome process, it is good to have helpful assistance.

Payment Plans

One of the recent developments in financial aid at Duke has been the increasing number of commercial payment plans available to parents and students. Rather than paying the bursar's bill in large, semesterly chunks, Duke has contracted with vendors to allow parents or students to spread out their payments to the university over ten to twelve months. Duke's bursar's office has one of the university's most resourceful and diligent staffs. Clerks and the bursar, herself, are willing to sit down and assist parents and students in choosing options that work best with individual needs.

Merit Aid

Many students are curious about merit aid at Duke. While many of the students who are accepted to Duke are eligible for scholarships at their state schools or other schools, *all* Duke students are extremely gifted; therefore, merit aid is used at a minimum to recruit students. Other than athletic and music scholarships, a very select group of outstanding applicants are considered for the A.B. Duke Scholarship, a full-tuition scholarship that includes a study abroad component. Students from the Carolinas are eligible for the B.N. Duke Leadership Scholarship. No additional applications are required for these two scholarships as every eligible student is considered.

Students at Duke are very resourceful as well. Many look for outside scholarships from local organizations. Students will find that the Duke name brings much attention from local organizations that provide scholarships funds.

Once my local Rotary Club found out I had been accepted to Duke, my chances for receiving its scholarship improved greatly.

While figuring out the financing of a Duke education may be the most painful part of the four years, most students find the process bearable by tapping into the resources of the university.

GRADUATES

Duke's reputation as a "hot" school has led to a demand for its graduates in the work force and at leading professional schools. As senior year approaches, most students don suits for job interviews or get ready to take graduate or professional school entrance exams. In the process, most find that the Duke name on their résumé can take them far.

All of the large management consulting, investment banking, and accounting firms flock to Duke each year hoping to pick up future grads. The well-rounded, personable style of the Duke students serves them well in interviews and most students have very little trouble finding jobs. One of the recent trends at Duke has been the increase of small, entrepreneurial companies recruiting at Duke. The nontraditional style of many of these start-up firms seems to be a good match for the energetic, active students at Duke.

PROMINENT GRADS

- **Elizabeth Hanford Dole, President, American Red Cross**
- **Grant Hill, NBA Star**
- **Jack F. Matlock, Former Ambassador to the USSR**
- **Charlie Rose, Talk Show Host**
- **William C. Styron, Author**
- **Judy Woodruff, Anchor, CNN**

Many of my friends decided to look for jobs at firms that allowed for maximum independence and creativity. I don't know if this is a need for most of our generation or a special characteristic of Duke students.

Most students get word of job offers in late February or March. So, a pleasant euphoria settles on the senior class for its final months in Durham. Seniors enjoy the peaceful spring months in North Carolina because, after graduation, most will flock to Washington, D.C., New York, and Boston (where many of them live) to begin careers in these large urban areas.

Graduate and Professional Schools

For those choosing to go to grad or professional school, Duke offers excellent counseling and preparation that allows the students to compete for spots at America's top graduate schools. For those applying to law school, Duke boasts a ninety-nine percent acceptance rate. Duke prelaw students are well advised under the tutelage of Dean Gerald Lee Wilson, the Pre-Law Advisor. Wilson gets to know these students well and is very effective at steering them to a law program best suited for them. He then becomes a grand advocate for helping the students achieve acceptance. Once accepted, Wilson aids students in choosing the school they should attend. Wilson and his assistants are well known around the campus as being extremely helpful and comforting to stressed prelaw students trying to figure their way through the law school maze. Their successes are recorded each year, as Duke is always well represented at Harvard, Yale, and Stanford, as well as at Duke.

Dean Wilson has the ability to comfort you yet challenge you about law school decisions. After my sessions with him, I knew I wanted to go to law school, and I knew where to go. He helped others realize that law school wasn't the best choice for them.

For premeds, the rate of acceptance is somewhat lower—seventy to eighty percent. This is due to fewer, more competitive spaces for medical schools and the recent reforms in medical practice, which have affected medical education. Dean Kay Singer, Duke's premed advisor, is effective at assessing students' options and helping them develop strategies to bolster their acceptance chances. Her organized and efficient style helps students stay on track in the process. Wilson and Singer are excellent examples of effective advising of preprofessional students. Conversations with graduates from other undergraduate colleges attest to this.

Students desiring to go to business school have access to the resources at the Career Development Center, which runs several prebusiness programs and has information on all of the best schools.

While Duke's Trinity College traces its origins to 1838, Duke University was created in 1924. Because of its relative youth as a university, Duke cannot boast of graduating Revolutionary War heroes or America's earliest presidents. However, alums like Judy Woodruff, Elizabeth Dole, Gary Wilson of Northwest Airlines, and Phil Lader, founder of the famed Renaissance Weekends and an ambassador to Great Britain, represent the current generation of political and corporate leadership. Duke is fast becoming a training ground for top participants in American and international affairs. The Terry Sanford Institute's Hart Leadership Program is a special program that brings together classroom, extracurricular, and internship experiences to prepare students from different majors to think about lessons of ethics and leadership. This is just one way that Duke instills a sense of responsibility and challenge in its graduates, and continues to produce tomorrow's leaders.

SUMMING UP

The energy and electricity of the Duke experience is reflected in and, in many ways, created by the dynamic leadership of Duke's president, Dr. Nannerl O. Keohane. Keohane came to Duke in 1993 and since her arrival there has been a renewed sense of real momentum that is felt throughout the campus. Keohane is actively involved and concerned about undergraduate affairs and actively tries to improve the quality of academic and cocurricular programs. She is incredibly accessible and warm. For example, every freshman is invited to dessert at her home in small, intimate gatherings that have affectionately become known as "Cookies with Nan." Keohane uses these opportunities and others like them to gauge students' needs and feelings. She then effectively acts on them.

This active, inclusive climate has given the campus a feel of constant momentum. Students are encouraged to share ideas and participate in the affairs of the university. There is a sense that Duke cannot rest on its laurels but must constantly and creatively think about ways to continue to grow and develop. Some students may find this unsettling, but most find it inspiring and interesting.

Duke has been a growing experience. Instead of being a part of a university community, I learned to become an active participant. Duke taught me to act after thinking, to encourage, and to constantly push.

Duke is uniquely positioned to provide students who want the opportunity to develop and learn. No other school in the country has such a strong sense of momentum and possibility throughout its campus. Under the leadership of Keohane, it is certain to become the leader in higher education for the next century. This aggressive positioning involves and excites students who are working to make Duke's vision of excellence a reality. In this strong move to preeminence, however, Duke never loses sight of its commitment to developing and fostering personal relationships among students, faculty, and the entire university community. It is common to find Duke grads congregating at parties or events around the country, watching Blue Devil basketball and sharing stories about "Dear Old Duke." Their loyalty to the university speaks volumes of the power of the Duke undergraduate experience.

Every March, I feel this strong urge to pack my bags and flee to Duke. My memories of the friendships I made, the classes I struggled with, and the ways I grew are intense and sweet. Returning to the glorious campus with friends reminds me of how we all grew up in those four years.

In the end, Duke is transforming. Students who are fortunate enough to enter the "gothic wonderland" will find challenge and reward. On the road to gaining these rewards, however, students also build the kind of relationships that last and will encounter opportunities to actively lead in all settings—laboratories, classrooms, athletic fields, organizations, and living groups.

After four years, you will feel refreshed, renewed, and ready to excel in new settings with a cadre of "family" members to assist you on the way. I can hardly think of more precious experiences to gain from college.

❑ *John Tolsma, B.A.*

GEORGETOWN UNIVERSITY

Georgetown University
Washington, D.C. 20057

(202) 687-3600
Fax: (202) 687-5084

E-mail: guadmiss@gunet.georgetown.edu
Web site: http://www.georgetown.edu
Electronic Application: http://guweb.georgetown.edu/admissions/appondisk.html

Enrollment

Full-time ❑ women: 3,144
❑ men: 2,907

Part-time ❑ women: 175
❑ men: 112

INTRODUCING GEORGETOWN

As freshmen we arrive one week before returning undergraduates. It is during this orientation week that we meet the people in our dorm, come to understand why Mom is the best cook in the world, and find that we are not the only number one student; in short, we begin the Georgetown experience. It was in freshman year that I formed the beginning of lifelong friendships. It was also the first time I met someone from every state. I was impressed by Georgetown's commitment to diversity. Orientation week is a fond memory for every Hoya.

Georgetown University, founded by the Jesuits in 1789, is one of the nation's oldest schools. Prior to the Civil War, Georgetown had a predominately Southern student body; after the Civil War, more students from the Northeast enrolled. To reflect this duality and promote the healing process within the academic community, Georgetown adopted blue and gray as the university's colors. This symbolizes the healing and reuniting of the campus and nation.

The first Catholic Church-affiliated institution of higher education in the United States, Georgetown is a private institution offering programs in arts, sciences, business administration, law, and medicine. Located in the heart of Washington, D.C., students are exposed, on a daily basis, to a highly stimulating environment, both culturally and politically—during every undergraduate's time at Georgetown, he or she will experience one full presidential election campaign. Opportunities abound for the industrious student to study the political process up close. International students also enjoy access to their embassies and other relevant political action groups.

The main campus is built on 110 acres of land, has 60 buildings, and is a mile and a half northwest of downtown Washington, D.C. The on-campus libraries contain more than two million books and microfilms; all libraries are Web accessible. Students also are in a city with more than 250 libraries, museums, galleries, and theaters, as well as classical and popular music, international cuisine, and research facilities. With the completion of the new MCI Center earlier this year, students now have Metro access to all home Hoya games as well as Capitals and Wizards games.

Diversity is one of the strongest elements of Georgetown. The diverse international and religious community of Georgetown is represented by students from 128 different countries and every major religion. These students contribute enormously to the international/multilingual community that Georgetown is recognized for.

ADMISSIONS REQUIREMENTS

There are no absolutes in the application process for Georgetown. Good SAT or ACT scores are expected, and they should be supplemented by a strong academic record in high school, a number of extracurricular activities and sports, and creative and sincere essays. Travel, an interest in foreign cultures, and/or a second language figure into an applicant's consideration.

Georgetown is represented by every state and also boasts a student body from more than fifty countries. It receives over 13,000 applications a year; the school accepts about 3,000 applicants a year. Again, diversity is key; if you have done anything out of the ordinary, highlight that in your essays. Many people are in Model UN, but only a handful have the personal fortitude to climb Mt. Everest. All applicants have a solid academic background, so it is in the alumni interview and personal essays that candidates will be given the opportunity to distinguish themselves.

ACADEMIC LIFE

Georgetown offers four undergraduate programs: the College of Arts and Science (which includes the faculty of languages and linguistics), the School of Foreign Service, the School of Business, and the School of Nursing. There are also four graduate schools: the Graduate School of Arts and Science, the School of Law, the School of Medicine, and the Graduate School of Business Management. What sets Georgetown apart is the small class size that allows for close interaction between students and faculty, both in academic and program areas; student participation represents a vital contribution to Georgetown's activities. Students are encouraged to hold positions on the Executive and Admissions Committees, and are taking an increasingly active role in organizing and planning academic programs and events, thereby helping to shape the role of students in the university community.

Applicants are asked to choose one of the four undergraduate schools when applying. Upon acceptance, the applicant will be enrolled in that school. If an applicant wants to apply to more than one school, he or she must submit separate applications for each school. While a transfer between schools is available after freshman year, nearly all students spend four years in their original school.

Majors

Majors are offered in: American studies, Arabic, biology, chemistry, Chinese, classics, computer science, economics, English, finance, fine arts (art history and studio arts), French, German, government, history and diplomacy, humanities in international affairs, interdisciplinary studies, international affairs, international business, international economics, international politics, Italian, Japanese, linguistics, management, marketing, mathematics, nursing, philosophy, physics, physics-engineering, Portuguese, psychology, regional and comparative studies, Russian, sociology, Spanish, and theology. Every student is required to take a core set of liberal arts courses. These include work in disciplines such as philosophy, social sciences, English and theology. Each school specifies its liberal arts core curriculum.

Class Size and Faculty

Class size has always been a concern to Georgetown; the average is fifteen to twenty students. To break up larger classes, smaller study groups are held with a professor and teaching assistants, which maintains the fifteen to twenty person ideal. Professors are also very generous with their time. All professors have office hours each week where they are available to the students. Genuine friendships often arise between students and faculty, especially when they choose a major and enroll in more advanced coursework.

> *I believe part of the uniqueness of Georgetown is its excellent faculty-student interaction. I have seen and spent time with many of my professors outside the classroom, in the halls, at the Tombs (a student pub located within two blocks of campus), chatting on the lawn, or at a sporting event. Our conversations were not limited to class and grades, but included other academic interests, goals, and politics.*

Georgetown's location enables some of the nation's and the world's greatest politicians, thinkers, and humanitarians to visit campus. Professor Richard Duncan always brought in former and current members of Congress to help students better understand the political process. Opportunities like these make Georgetown an experience that will last a lifetime.

SOCIAL LIFE AND ACTIVITIES

Georgetown is not a one-sided, academic-only institution; on the contrary, Georgetown offers a vibrant and dynamic student body. Best of all, Georgetown is located in the capital of the United States. If you could not fill your weekends at the university, you have an entire city with boundless opportunities. Georgetown is also located within an hour and a half of Shenandoah Valley, a beautiful national park. You need travel only five hours for skiing in West Virginia, two hours north or south for beaches, and a short plane ride to both Miami and New York.

As a student at Georgetown, I never lacked for anything to do. I was active in many campus organizations and also was able to enjoy many volunteer activities. Georgetown's diverse student body allowed me to meet people from every state and from many different countries as well.

Off Campus

The nightlife at Georgetown is a short walk from campus; numerous eateries, live entertainment, and bars are within walking distance. If you ever tire of the Georgetown scene, remember that you are in a city that is shared by seven other colleges, numerous band halls, and four professional sports teams.

On the fourth of July a group of us—along with about half a million other people—got together and had an all-day picnic on the Mall and listened to the National Symphony Orchestra concert. That night we laid on the lawn and watched the fireworks by starlight from the reflecting pool.

On-Campus Activities

The secret weapon for social activity at Georgetown revolves around the students who live on campus. Upperclassmen throw parties for the student body and all are encouraged to attend. Georgetown's Program Board brings many top-rated movies to campus—the Halloween screening of *The Exorcist*, which was filmed at Georgetown, is legendary.

Clubs

Georgetown offers a wealth of social and school-related clubs. Many have cultural themes: Arabic Club, Armenian Club, French Club, German Club, Japanese Club, Russian Club, and Spanish Club. Others take on a more theatrical tilt: Black Theater Ensemble, Friday Afternoon Theater, Mask and Bauble, and Nomadic Theatre. Still others fill the physical needs of the student body: Hockey Club, Intramural Sports, and Rugby Club. Journalistic opportunities also abound and include: *The Hoya*, Georgetown's twice-weekly newspaper of record, *The Voice*, a weekly news magazine, *The Independent*, a monthly conservative journal, and *The Anthem*, a primarily Web-based journal of opinion, art, and literature. Students will be able to find a club for just about any interest.

Georgetown has no social fraternities, sororities or eating clubs; for this reason many clubs take on an added social dimension. Some schools and clubs hold annual events: the Business School Ball, Senior Ball, Diplomat's Ball, Cherry Tree Massacre (an *a cappella* presentation from Georgetown and various universities), Casino Night, where students gamble the night away with "play money," Spring Fest (celebrating the coming of spring with a barbecue and live entertainment), and more. Thus, students are able to fill their weekends, while still receiving an unparalleled education at Georgetown.

Athletics

What fall Saturday would be complete without a visit to a Hoya football game at Kehoe Field? How can you have a March Madness without a strong bid by our Hoyas for the national championship?

Although Georgetown is mostly known for John Thompson's Hoyas, baseball, women's basketball, crew, cross-country, field hockey, football, lacrosse, soccer, swimming, tennis, and track also draw loyal contingents of fans. The Yates Field House is also open to all students. It contains a twenty-five-yard indoor swimming pool, indoor and outdoor track, tennis, squash, racquetball, basketball, and volleyball courts, rooms for dance and karate classes, weights, treadmills, rowing machines, and saunas. It is a modern, partially underground structure, and is open all year.

Volunteering

The character of Georgetown has always been one of balance; social activities have always been balanced by social responsibility. Numerous opportunities exist for those students who wish to give back to the community in the form of volunteer work.

> *I was an overnight volunteer for the Calvary Women's Shelter. The sense of pride I felt and the genuine thanks I received from those that I helped made that a truly special part of my college experience.*

FINANCIAL AID

I was ecstatic over my acceptance letter from Georgetown, but now I had the really hard decision of whether or not to accept it. I was unsure. I am not from a particularly wealthy family and I knew my parents would not be able to afford one year let alone four years of Georgetown. By working twenty-plus hours a week and with a generous financial aid program, I was able to graduate from Georgetown having taken only government loans. To this day I am happy that I made the decision to attend Georgetown and did not let the price force me to choose an inferior school. College happens only once—make the best decision that you can; receive the best education that you can; attend Georgetown.

Early applications are the first to be considered for scholarships; late entries suffer from many applicants already having received these grants. Tuition is about $22,000 per year with books, food, and housing additional. For a full academic year, you will need about $27,000 to $30,000. Parents are expected to make as much of a contribution as possible, about forty-five percent. Nearly half of all Georgetown students receive need-based financial aid. Many students also qualify for aid from outside sources, scholarships, Reserve Officer Training Corps, and other programs.

GRADUATES

What do the four hard years of stretching your academic potential bring? Some graduates head directly to graduate school to continue the process initiated at Georgetown, becoming lawyers, doctors, M.B.A.s, and scholars. Many volunteer in the Jesuit Volunteer Corps or Peace Corps, or become teachers, giving back to society before pursuing more personal goals. Others take the opportunity to travel, work, or pursue personal goals before advancing their career through further graduate studies. The vast majority begins work in the real world, applying the skills and techniques that brought them such success during their four-year stay on the hilltop.

After graduating from college I found a job within two months. Even though I was a liberal arts student, I was able to take my ability to learn and parlay that into a job in the computer industry. I have since found my strong background in liberal arts to be invaluable in the workplace. My ability to think and learn has advanced my career and has given me incentive to continue my education as an M.B.A. candidate. None of this would have been possible without the support of fellow Hoyas and the strong education afforded by Georgetown.

Georgetown's alumni network is extensive and consists of more than 90,000 alumni. The Hoya connection is one of the most significant elements of the degree. You become a member in a highly distinguished family that has succeeded in the business, political, and humanitarian arenas. Through the Alumni Association (http://hilltop.georgetown.edu), graduates are able to keep in contact, forge new friendships, and catch up on old ones. The Alumni Association has a network that is focused on helping new graduates find work in their field of choice and provides other opportunities for new and old alumni alike.

SUMMING UP

All good things must come to an end and life at Georgetown is no exception. Georgetown leaves its students with an unmistakable stamp of self-assurance and a strong moral character, but it is the student who must use that perspective to review his or her life's highs and lows.

Graduating from Georgetown brings membership in an exclusive alumni organization, with representation in the world's elite business circles. Graduates have access to an international network of friends and contacts and that, combined with their Georgetown connection, greatly enhances their chances for professional success. The prestige of the Georgetown degree will go a long way in opening doors and building professional friendships and the education obtained at Georgetown will enable graduates to meet and excel no matter what the challenges.

❑ *John Sikking, B.A.*

GEORGIA INSTITUTE OF TECHNOLOGY

Georgia Institute of Technology
Atlanta, GA 30332-0320

(404) 894-4154
Fax: (404) 894-9511

E-mail: admissions@success.gatech.edu
Web site: http://www.gatech.edu/admissions/undergraduate/index.html

Enrollment

Full-time ❑ women: 2,469
❑ men: 6,420

Part-time ❑ women: 208
❑ men: 574

INTRODUCING GEORGIA TECH

Georgia Tech was founded in 1885 in order to provide technological education to students from Georgia and the rest of the Southeast. The institute has long since surpassed this original goal and today provides superior technological education for students from around the world. The first and only major offered was mechanical engineering, but today students can choose from not only many types of engineering, but any number of degrees spanning a wide array of technically advanced fields of study. Located in the heart of downtown Atlanta,

Georgia Tech offers easy access to a variety of activities beyond those offered on campus. The campus itself is relatively secluded from the rest of Atlanta; even though there are 150 buildings on the 330-acre campus, students still enjoy streets lined with large, beautiful trees. Georgia Tech has several open spaces for afternoon football games, lying in the warm sun studying, or just relaxing.

I was afraid of the campus at first. It seemed so big and right in the middle of downtown Atlanta. That all soon changed. I realized that being in downtown Atlanta was incredibly convenient. If I wanted to go to a movie, visit a nice restaurant, or enjoy a ball game, it was all there at my fingertips. Not only that, Georgia Tech doesn't even feel like it's downtown. It seems to be in its own little world.

Georgia Tech's Atlanta location offers distinct season changes including mild winters, springs full of dogwood and azalea blossoms, sunny summer days, and beautiful fall foliage. Georgia Tech integrates the advantages of a big city with a safe, secluded campus where students have the opportunity to experience college life at its fullest.

Exactly what Georgia Tech offers beyond academics is something most current students and graduates have a hard time explaining. It is a feeling unlike any other. It is not pride, but Georgia Tech students and graduates are proud of their time at Tech. It is not familiarity, but they are familiar with what Georgia Tech means and provides. Georgia Tech pulls together people of different cultures, classes, races, and backgrounds and makes them one. They don't graduate, they "get out." They don't just study for finals, they scream and yell out of their residence hall windows at midnight. They don't leave Tech quietly, they steal the "T" from the Tech Tower. Nothing compares to the Tech experience. When people from Georgia Tech meet other people from Georgia Tech, they know each other. It is amazing how a group so diverse and so individualistic could produce this type of feeling. This feeling is Georgia Tech.

ADMISSIONS REQUIREMENTS

High school students today must face the reality that it is becoming increasingly more difficult to get into the nation's top universities. Georgia Tech is, unfortunately, no different. Due to more competition in and out of the United States, and Georgia Tech's desire to maintain a student body of between 12,000 and 13,000 students, it is more difficult for current high school seniors to be admitted to Tech than even five years ago. As expected, students must take either the SAT I or ACT; the average SAT I score for incoming freshmen recently was Verbal—580, Math—730. Candidates must have completed in high school: four years each of English and mathematics, three years of science, two years each of history and foreign language, and one year of social studies. Advanced Placement credit and honors courses are looked favorably upon and will also prepare students extremely well for their first year at Georgia Tech. As one Georgia Tech graduate put it:

I can't even imagine not having taken calculus in high school. As difficult as the first few quarters of calculus at Tech were for me, the people who didn't take it in high school struggled much more than I did. Advanced Placement Calculus BC was the only high school class I took that even comes close to comparing with classes at Tech.

Another important factor in determining admission can be whether a student's parent or sibling is a Georgia Tech alumnus. With so many applicants each year, Georgia Tech must use several different criteria to select the most qualified candidates.

Campus Visits

Prospective students are welcome to visit the campus any time, but a good time to come is for a Sunday-through-Monday visit conducted by the "Connect with Tech" program. On Sundays in this program, students and parents participate in a campus tour, question-and-answer session with Georgia Tech students, and a welcoming dinner. Each attending high school senior then stays overnight in his or her host's residence-hall room. On Mondays, the students go to classes, labs, lunch, and the library with their hosts, while parents meet with admissions, academic, and financial aid advisors.

Computers

One interesting new admissions requirement is that all incoming freshmen have at least a 486 IBM-compatible computer or the equivalent. This will allow all students to communicate more efficiently while at Georgia Tech and will better prepare them to function in tomorrow's world of electronic communication. The new computer requirement that

Georgia Tech has instituted truly shows the institute's commitment to staying on the leading edge of technology.

ACADEMIC LIFE

All the rumors are true. Georgia Tech's academic program is rigorous, challenging, and sometimes overwhelming, but ultimately well worth the time and effort invested. Incoming freshmen to Georgia Tech, each one among the top students at his or her high school, arrive at Georgia Tech to discover a very competitive environment, yet one that allows for accelerated learning and intelligent discussions about advanced topics. Georgia Tech's faculty is one of the best in the nation, with ninety-two percent of all faculty members having Ph.D.s. The student-to-faculty ratio of 13:1 provides students with much personal attention from the professors, which is particularly important to the advanced subject matter for which Georgia Tech is known.

The institute is comprised of five separate colleges: Engineering, Architecture, Sciences, Computing, and Management. Within the College of Engineering, students can choose from thirteen undergraduate degrees, some going beyond the more traditional mechanical or electrical engineering to include majors such as ceramic and textile engineering. The other four colleges give students the opportunity to study non-engineering subjects, yet maintain a technical background. The College of Architecture, consistently ranked one of the top in the nation, includes bachelor's degrees in architecture, industrial design, and building construction. The architecture building is a world of its own; it has its own library, computer lab, and even a snack bar, since the students must commit the majority of their time to their studio projects. The College of Sciences' degree-granting schools are: Biology, Chemistry and Biochemistry, Earth and Atmospheric Sciences, Physics, and Psychology. These majors allow students to study in-depth the pure sciences rather than simply taking them as core courses. The College of Computing offers only the computer science degree, as computer engineering falls under the College of Engineering. This program evolves constantly to keep up with the ever-changing pace of computer technology. The Ivan Allen College of Management, Policy, and International Affairs offers undergraduate degrees in Economics; History, Technology, and Society; International Affairs; Science, Technology, and Culture; and Management. Since these degrees are Georgia Tech's version of liberal arts, graduates receive a technological foundation, studying in-depth how technology and the liberal arts intertwine.

As in most colleges, freshmen begin with core courses such as calculus, English, physics, and chemistry. Many of these core classes are lecture-type classes of 200 to 300 students, but also meet in smaller recitation groups taught by graduate students to allow focus on homework, examples, and other specific problems. Once into upper-level classes, students are able to study in-depth their chosen major, normally with fewer than thirty students per class and frequently as few as ten. While most core mathematics and science classes are five credit hours, most other classes, including major classes, are three credit hours, which means that in any given quarter a student will take probably five or six classes. This is one reason Georgia Tech is more difficult than most other universities; juggling five or six college classes that each have numerous tests, quizzes, papers, projects, and homework assignments can sometimes be daunting. Incoming freshmen must seriously adjust scheduling and study habits to meet the new, formidable challenges Georgia Tech's faculty will throw at them. When students need help, various tutoring resources are available, including those sponsored by the math department, the Freshman Experience Program, and the minority student association, OMED.

High school never prepared me for the type of studying I needed to do for classes at Tech. I was used to looking over a few notes I had scribbled in class before any test or quiz in high school. I always made great grades in high school. That type of studying doesn't work here.

Academics are the focus at Georgia Tech and therefore the faculty makes it tough on their students. But this toughness ultimately rewards the students by making them more desirable to the employers who must make a choice from among thousands of graduates each year. A degree from Georgia Tech opens many doors that might otherwise remain closed.

The Co-op Program

Many students find the cooperative education program an important tool in gaining hands-on experience to prepare for the transition into their professional careers. Georgia Tech has the largest co-op program in the nation, employing students in their major field of study in alternating work/school quarters for eight consecutive quarters. Each student interested in participating in the co-op program is assigned to an advisor whose main goal is to match the goals of the students with positions available at companies. Prestigious companies across the nation seek out Georgia Tech students to fill specific needs and these students many times continue in full-time employment after graduation.

I look for bright, intelligent people when hiring. As the human resources director, I can't afford to choose the wrong people. In this day and age when training is so incredibly time-intensive and expensive, I need to make a good choice from the outset. Fortunately, when I see Georgia Tech on a résumé I know this is a person who is well educated and prepared to learn. I have hired numerous Tech grads and the outcome is always the same: success.

SOCIAL LIFE AND ACTIVITIES

Nerds. Computer geeks. Bookworms. Stuffed shirts. Students at Georgia Tech are often categorized by these names, but words like socially conscious, fun-loving, and ultimately well-rounded are much more accurate in describing Georgia Tech's diverse student body. Students come from all fifty states and 106 different countries to Atlanta, Georgia, in order to experience Georgia Tech. Hosting the 1996 Summer Olympic Games forever changed the city of Atlanta, bringing to it not only new sporting facilities, but also new energy, new people, new companies, and increased international awareness. Georgia Tech, as the site of the Olympic Village and the aquatic and boxing venues, benefited immensely from this once-in-a-lifetime opportunity.

Atlanta offers Georgia Tech students a wide array of activities. On any given night, students can see the world champion Braves, sip coffee at Cafe Intermezzo, listen to live music at a bar in Buckhead, visit an art exhibit at the High Museum of Art, or dine at any of the local restaurants. Atlanta's central location in the Southeast allows for easy weekend trips to the Appalachian Mountains or the beaches of the Atlantic and Gulf coasts.

On campus, more than 200 student organizations help students escape from the stress of their demanding schedules. Groups ranging from cheerleading, student government, and radio and television, to professional societies invite students to participate and meet others with similar interests. And these groups do not even include the thirty-one fraternities and eight sororities that line Georgia Tech's campus. Although the Greek organizations play an active role in student social activities (thirty percent of men and twenty-three percent of women are members), it is not necessary to join one to have an active and fulfilling social life.

Housing

Georgia Tech was fortunate to receive several completely new residence halls as well as renovations of all existing residence halls due to the Olympics. This gave Georgia Tech the facilities to house seventy percent of the student body on campus in modern dormitories. Unique living arrangements are also available, such as suite-style rooms with fully equipped kitchens and shared living rooms, coed facilities (by suite, not by room!), language halls where a specific language and culture can be experienced, and the very successful Freshman Experience program, which provides freshmen with extra opportunities for social and academic enrichment. The community surrounding Georgia Tech also offers excellent housing choices such as apartments and houses for rent.

Traditions

Another aspect of Georgia Tech's rich social life is the culture, traditions, and school spirit that are instilled in every student. Georgia Tech is not unusual in that it has spirit, rather that Georgia Tech creates a pervading sense of oneness among its students, even though they are from such varied backgrounds. This is true across the generations; students who graduated in the 1930s share the same sense of dedication and camaraderie as the graduates of recent years. All Georgia Tech students enjoy many traditions, such as the stealing of the "T" from the Tech Tower, Ramblin' Wreck parades at Homecoming, the fictitious student that everyone knows, George P. Burdell, and the long-standing rivalry with the University of Georgia. Any Georgia Tech student, when asked, "What's the good word?" will naturally respond, "To hell with Georgia!!" And at football games, one note from the band will strike up a rousing chorus of:

"I'm a ramblin' wreck from Georgia Tech
and a helluva engineer.
A helluva, helluva, helluva, helluva,
helluva engineer…"

FINANCIAL AID

Georgia Tech, being a public university, remains one of the last great bargains in higher education, especially for in-state students. Any student may apply for financial aid by completing a FAFSA and Georgia Tech's financial aid application. Sixty percent of recent freshmen and sixty-nine percent of non-freshmen received some form of financial aid.

Scholarships

Types of aid available include scholarships, grants, and loans and can be either merit-based or need-based. In addition to scholarships from external groups such as companies, clubs, and the government, Georgia Tech offers the President's Scholarship and the Dean's Scholarship. They are based on academic excellence as well as a series of interviews conducted over a two-day visit in which the candidate stays overnight with a current Presidential Scholar. In-state students must have a 1350 SAT score and out-of-state students must have a 1400 in order to apply. The Presidential Scholarship can be either a full or partial scholarship, whereas the Dean's Scholarship is only partial. The full Presidential Scholarship covers tuition, housing, books, and spending money; the partial Presidential Scholarship pays only for tuition. The Dean's Scholarship pays its recipients about $1,500 per quarter. Presidential scholars, or PSs, as they are known on campus, receive additional perks such as early registration, access to private study rooms, and invitations to PS social events.

The Hope Grant

In-state students are blessed with a scholarship from the state of Georgia called the Hope Grant. The Hope Grant is merit-based and can be used by any Georgia student who during high school maintained at least a B+ average. The Hope Grant provides the full tuition cost for any public university or college in the University System of Georgia, plus money for textbooks. This is important because Georgia Tech is a public university, not a private college, and therefore students can use the full Hope Grant toward fees at Georgia Tech. Students receive only partial grants for private colleges and universities. One important thing to note is that in order to maintain the Hope Grant, students must continue to have the B+ average each quarter. Once the student has dropped below this average, he or she cannot be eligible for the Hope Grant again.

Overall, there is much more aid available than most students and parents are aware. Every year thousands of dollars of scholarship money go unclaimed simply because no one knew about it. Counselors at high schools are good places to start researching possible sources of financial aid, but do not hesitate to contact the financial advisors at Georgia Tech for further assistance.

GRADUATES

> *My current job has absolutely nothing to do with my major. My boss told me after I was hired that there were two reasons he chose me: simply the fact that my degree is from Georgia Tech, and the way I presented myself in the interview, much of which I also attribute to the way Georgia Tech prepared me to cope in today's corporate world.*

This scenario is not uncommon. Georgia Tech prepares you for anything and companies are well aware of this. The beauty of a degree from Georgia Tech is that graduates are not confined to one field. Rather, with the variety of coursework required and the unique approach the faculty takes in teaching students, Georgia Tech alumni can easily adapt to the challenges presented by almost any profession. New graduates will find it helpful that there is such a strong alumni network in place, particularly in technical fields. These alumni know better than anyone the high quality of the graduates that Georgia Tech produces and this leads to a perpetual network of alumni who hire new Tech graduates. It is interesting to note that hundreds of the nation's top companies have graduates of Georgia Tech as CEOs, vice presidents, or other high-ranking officers.

Georgia Tech also has one of the strongest alumni associations in the nation. The alumni generate millions of dollars of funding each year in support of improving Georgia Tech, especially in the form of scholarship and other academic pursuits. Georgia Tech graduates share an uncommon bond, each having shared experiences such as "midnight" chemistry, senior design projects, and lunch between classes at Junior's Grill. Anywhere in the world, when one Tech graduate meets up with another, there is an immediate connection and desire to reminisce about those years spent in the shadow of the Tech Tower.

PROMINENT GRADS

- **Y. Frank Freeman, '10, Former Head of Columbia Pictures**
- **Bobby Jones, '22, Professional Golfer**
- **Randolph Scott, '23, Movie Actor**
- **Rufus Youngblood, '49, Secret Service Agent who protected Lyndon B. Johnson during JFK assassination**
- **John Portman, '50, Architect**
- **John W. Young, '52, Pilot of Gemini I, Apollo 16, Columbia Space Shuttle**
- **Admiral Richard H. Truly, '59, Former NASA Director**
- **Sam Nunn, '60, Former U.S. Senator from Georgia**
- **Dr. Kary B. Mullis, '66, 1993 Nobel Prize winner in Chemistry**
- **Antonio Lacayo, '71, Former Prime Minister of Nicaragua**
- **Jeff Foxworthy, '80, Comedian**
- **Susan Still, '85, Astronaut—piloted space shuttle**

SUMMING UP

Choosing a college is a very important decision, one that should be made only after first considering what subject to study, what price range, urban or rural location, and all the other pertinent factors. Prospective students should think long and hard before choosing Georgia Tech. This school is not for everyone. It is difficult from start to finish and very technically challenging, unlike anything most people have ever seen. But it is awesome, fulfilling, and unique. Georgia Tech students will never be able to find another group of people who have such diverse backgrounds, who come from such different cultures, and who possess such varying goals and interests, yet have so much in common. Graduates coming out of Georgia Tech will feel like they have conquered the world and that the rest will be a breeze. Georgia Tech is incredibly rewarding, from the friendships students will forge to the outstanding education they will receive, and ultimately the life for which Georgia Tech will prepare them. By choosing to attend the Georgia Institute of Technology, students embark on a journey to a bright and promising future.

❑ *Barbara Alexander, B.S.*
❑ *Brian Alexander, B.M.E.*

HARVARD UNIVERSITY/HARVARD COLLEGE

Harvard University/Harvard College
Cambridge, MA 02138

(617) 495-1551
Fax: (617) 495-8821

E-mail: college@harvard.edu
Web site: http://www.harvard.edu

Enrollment

Full-time ❑ women: 3,029
❑ men: 3,601

INTRODUCING HARVARD COLLEGE

Tour guides leading visitors around the Harvard campus are quick to mention that Harvard, founded in 1636, is the oldest college in the United States. In historic Harvard Yard, tour guides explain that Hollis Hall, a red brick structure built in 1763, housed Washington's troops during the Revolutionary War. In front of Widener Library, tourists learn that Harvard's library system is the largest university system in the world, containing ninety-seven libraries, more than thirteen million volumes, and some 100,000 periodicals.

Harvard's age and outstanding physical resources are among the college's most distinctive features. Yet, few Harvard alumnus will say that the best part of their Harvard experience was the fact that the college is the oldest in the country. It is more likely that they will mention the environment of daily life as the distinguishing aspect of their experience, an environment characterized by the cities of Cambridge and Boston, a unique residential life system, and the people who make Harvard tick.

LIBRARIES AT HARVARD

- **Harvard's Widener and Pusey Libraries contain millions of volumes on more than 57 miles of bookshelves.**
- **Harvard's libraries contain more than just books: a set of Harry Houdini's handcuffs; Charles Dickens's walking stick and paper knife; T.S. Eliot's panama hat; a set of George Washington's pistols.**

Harvard has called Cambridge, Massachusetts, home for all of its 360-plus years. Cambridge, located along the Charles River a few miles from downtown Boston, boasts beautiful tree-lined streets as well as numerous shops, cinemas, restaurants, music stores, coffeehouses, bars, theaters, and bookstores.

In addition, the city of Boston is only an eighty-five-cent trip away on the subway. The Boston area is home to more that forty colleges and universities and some 200,000 college students, five professional athletic teams, and all of the resources of a large city in a historic, scenic, and pedestrian-friendly package.

Boston was a considerable factor in my search for a college. Throughout high school, I'd said that I want to go to college in Boston because there are just so many colleges there. I really like Harvard's location because, while there are many opportunities and resources on campus, the entire Boston area is also still available. Public transportation makes it so easy to get to practically anywhere, and it's safe and inexpensive. Harvard Square in Cambridge is great for coffee, food, shopping, and even street entertainment; there just never seems to be a dull moment. I really like Boston for the cultural events that are there: I saw four musicals and one ballet last year in Boston. I'm from a large city, and I wanted to attend college in a place that would provide all the opportunities and experiences to which I was accustomed. I have yet to be disappointed.

Harvard students also enjoy the world beyond metropolitan Boston. The mountains of New Hampshire and the Maine seacoast are each a short drive away to the north; the beaches of Cape Cod are a short drive south of Boston.

Harvard students are amazing in the diversity of their backgrounds, interests, and perspectives. Students come from all fifty of the United States as well as more than 100 foreign countries, and nearly seventy percent of them come from public high schools. The college is entirely coeducational and has been since 1977, when Harvard and Radcliffe joined forces in a unique partnership (see Radcliffe College). Students hail from many different religious, ethnic, and socioeconomic backgrounds. It is impossible not to feel energized by the presence of so many different people and ideas.

I think the best thing about student life at Harvard is that, in a typical discussion, the topics of conversation could be anything from Kant's philosophy on morals to the thorough pummeling the New England Patriots received at the hands of the Green Bay Packers in last week's Monday Night Football game. It is really gratifying to be able to engage in a serious intellectual conversation whenever and with whomever one pleases. Also, because the Harvard community is saturated with such amazing talent, the atmosphere of high achievement and hard work around campus tends to motivate each of us to strive to be our very best.

Harvard's location, its residential system, and its many human resources create a unique environment for the college years. Regardless of your interests or goals, daily life in this environment is challenging, inspiring, and, in Boston-speak, "wicked fun."

ADMISSIONS REQUIREMENTS

Getting into Harvard is competitive. Only ten to twelve percent of the applicants in the past few years were admitted, yet more than eighty-five percent of the applicants were academically qualified. Harvard attracts some of the best students in the world: the class of 2001 includes 393 National Merit finalists and recipients of other academic and extracurricular honors. Statistics like these can be intimidating, but remember that about 2,100 people received good news from Harvard last year. It's hard to get in, but it's not impossible.

If you decide to apply, do your best to present yourself to the Admissions Committee with a complete, concise application. Keep this in mind if you are thinking of applying:

- Harvard accepts only the common application, and does not even have its own institutional form. The common application is fairly straightforward: send a transcript, write an essay on a topic of your choice, fill in some biographical information, provide a summary of your extracurricular life, and ask two teachers and a counselor to fill out recommendations. An alumns interview is also a required component of the application. After you send in your application, an alumns volunteer from your local area will contact you to arrange the interview. Finally, Harvard requires students to submit either the SAT I or ACT and any three of the SAT II: Subject tests. You will want to take these tests by November for Early Action consideration, and by January for the Regular Action pool.
- Early Action is nonbinding. If you apply for Early Action by November 1 of your senior year, you will be notified in mid-December. If you are admitted, you may apply to other colleges under the Regular Action programs, and tell Harvard in May where you plan to matriculate. If you choose to exercise this option, don't apply to any other colleges under early notification programs. If you are considering Early Action, you might want to check out the "Early Action Statement" in the admissions section of the Harvard Web page (www.harvard.edu). It provides some good insight if you are trying to decide whether to apply Early or Regular. The Regular Action deadline is January 1; decisions are mailed in early April.
- In making its decisions, the Admissions Committee considers all aspects of a person's candidacy. You will be evaluated on your academic performance and potential, your extracurricular talents, and your personal strengths. First and foremost, the committee wants to be confident that you can handle the Harvard coursework. Your high school transcript is important here; take the toughest classes your school offers and that you can do well in. Once it has been determined that you could swing it in Harvard's classrooms, the committee will look for what distinguishes you from the thousands of other qualified candidates. Some applicants set themselves apart from the rest of the pool based on their extraordinary academic promise. Others are distinguished because of their well-roundedness or their specific talents beyond the classroom. Personal qualities are important in every decision.

There is no formula through which one is admitted to Harvard and Radcliffe. The committee reads every application with great care and strives to identify and admit those students who will make an impact during their college years and beyond. Be yourself on the application and in the interview and let your strengths, talents, and accomplishments speak for you. You certainly can't get in if you don't apply.

ACADEMIC LIFE

Students at Harvard enjoy a great variety of academic offerings and resources. Pursuing their A.B. or S.B., undergraduate students choose from about 3,000 classes every year and over forty fields of concentration (or majors). Throughout the course of eight semesters, students are required to take and pass thirty-two semester-long courses to graduate. The concentration accounts for roughly half of the course load over the four years. Students major in such fields as engineering, folklore and mythology, computer science, linguistics, economics, history and literature, and biological sciences, to name just a few. Some students design their own concentrations or pursue joint concentrations in two different disciplines.

The Core Curriculum

The remaining half of the curriculum is divided between electives and the core curriculum. Through the core, students are able to explore eight semester-long courses that have nothing or very little to do with their concentration. With the help of your advisor, you decide when to take the core courses and which ones to take. Many students end up taking more classes in the core curriculum than they are required to take for their diploma. The core courses are lively and interesting; they provide an opportunity to explore areas outside of your concentration.

Electives

The last part of the curriculum is composed of electives, which allow students to explore any other interests they might have. For example, some students concentrate in a nonscience discipline and use their electives to complete the premedical requirements. Others become fluent in a foreign language or take studio art classes as electives. Many students use their electives to take classes that will be fun and that will provide them with a different academic experience.

The curriculum offers students a great deal of choice and flexibility, and it includes special opportunities such as cross-registration at M.I.T. and study abroad. In a recent year, Harvard students studied in

EXAMPLES OF CORE CLASSES

- Caribbean Societies: Socioeconomic Change and Cultural Adaptations
- Individual, Community, and Nation in Vietnam
- Medicine and Society in America
- The Warren Court and the Pursuit of Justice
- Tragic Drama and Human Conflict
- The Modern Jewish Experience in Literature
- Majesty and Mythology in African Art
- The Hero of Irish Myth and Saga
- Ethics and International Relations
- Matter in the Universe
- The Biology of Trees and Forests
- Children and their Social Worlds

thirty-five different countries in Europe, Asia, Africa, and Latin America. Physical resources, such as the world's largest university library system, enhance the curriculum by providing students with world-class facilities. Yet it is the human resources, namely the faculty and students at Harvard, that have the largest influence on the academic experience at the college.

Faculty

The student body benefits from a great human resource—the faculty. For the most part, the professors are kind, approachable people, as well as remarkable scholars. They make themselves available to students through office hours, by leading students in research, and by chatting informally before or after class or in the Yard during the school day. The enthusiasm of the professors is a perfect complement to that of the students they teach.

My favorite professor is Peter Burgard, who is also the Head Tutor for my concentration (German Cultural Studies). As a freshman, I took one class each semester with Professor Burgard. He really seemed to care about what we thought of the class by periodically asking the students for feedback. Professor Burgard encouraged us to see him during office hours, which I frequently did. He was always very helpful in answering my questions, and he helped me to think about which classes would be most beneficial for my interests, in addition to providing information on study abroad programs.

The Harvard professors are terrific scholars, but they also prove to be caring and devoted teachers. Ninety-eight percent of the faculty teach undergraduates, and the average class size is smaller than you might imagine (about sixteen or seventeen students, according to a recent survey). Students take advantage of the small class sizes provided by numerous seminars and tutorials. Many students are involved in research at some point during their college years, which might include one-on-one work with a professor. A senior thesis project is an option for most concentrations, although a few of the departments do require a thesis.

Freshman Seminars

Freshman Seminars bring together faculty members and small groups of freshmen to investigate specialized topics. About a quarter of the entering class takes advantage of this early opportunity to work closely with professors in an area of mutual interest. Some recent Freshman Seminars:

- Chaos in the Solar System
- Research at the Harvard Forest
- Victorians and the Theatre
- Perceiving Works of Art
- Comedy and Laughter
- Eighteenth Century London
- Baseball and American Society

Academically, the experience at Harvard depends to a certain degree on what you decide you want to do with your time in Cambridge. Small classes, accessible, friendly professors, helpful advisors, and top-notch physical resources are yours to enjoy; ultimately, it's up to you to take full advantage of the opportunities.

SOCIAL LIFE AND ACTIVITIES

Residences

The exciting atmosphere of the area surrounding Harvard's campus complements the college's unique residential system. Students are guaranteed on-campus housing for each of their four years at the college, and about ninety-eight percent of them choose to live on campus. First-year students live in Harvard Yard, the historical, academic, and administrative center of the campus. This first year is fun, and living with all of your own classmates in the heart of the campus is a great way to create class unity and to adjust to college life in a friendly, supportive environment.

The housing system is an enormous part of my life here. I have forged some of the most wonderful friendships with the people from my freshman year entryway. The house masters and tutors really create a family atmosphere. It's a good feeling to be able to go to the dining hall and know among all those eating there—there is certainly not a dearth of friends.

Sophomores, juniors, and seniors reside in one of the twelve residential houses, which are large dorms accommodating 350 to 500 students. Each House has its own dining hall, library, computer lab, weight room, music practice rooms, and other facilities. Faculty members are in residence as well as a team of advisors or tutors. House spirit is strong, as students represent their houses on intramural sports teams and spend hours socializing in the house dining halls and common areas. In sum, while students at Harvard College enjoy all of the resources of a university, the residential system provides the feeling of a smaller college. The communities of the Yard and of the houses give students access to one another, and to the educational benefits of the college's diverse population.

I have absolutely loved the way [freshman] housing is done. Because so much effort went into arranging first-year rooming groups, I got along really well with my suitemates (I had four). My entryway—the people who lived near me in the same dorm—was really close, and we often went to meals and to Boston together. My proctor always had his door open, and he made the transition into college life a lot easier. I also really felt that I was able to get to know people in my class who were not in my dorm or classes because all freshmen live and eat together. I doubt that I would have had as much class pride if it weren't for this factor.

Everyone in my blocking group this year was from my entryway last year. Now that I am in a house, I am still with wonderful people, plus there are the benefits of having numerous tutors, an extremely helpful house staff, and a library right in the house.

Harvard Square

The second tier of social life, after the houses, is Harvard Square and Cambridge. On the weekends, students flood the Square, taking full advantage of this unique urban atmosphere. Even during the week, the Square offers a refreshing break from the books; a study break might include a movie, a cup of coffee with a friend, or an hour of listening to Cambridge's fantastic street musicians.

The City of Boston

The final tier of the social life at Harvard is the city of Boston, where students might attend the theater, go to museums or concerts, visit other local colleges, or walk and shop in the city's historic neighborhoods. While the Harvard campus itself provides all students with social options, many do like to explore the surrounding environment in their free time.

Student Organizations

Harvard students like socializing and relaxing, but they also tend to be busy, as most are involved in two or three extracurricular activities. All told, there are more than 250 official student organizations on campus, including five orchestras, two jazz bands, a marching band, a gospel choir, a glee club, over ten *a cappella* groups, a daily newspaper and dozens of other political and literary publications, more than eighty theater productions per year, and student government, debate teams, religious groups, and minority public service organizations.

> *I'd like to say I chose Harvard because I thought it was the best fit for me in terms of size, location, student-professor ratio, etc. I have to honestly admit, however, that I came here mostly because of Harvard's reputation. I knew my academic needs would be met here but was actually worried I wouldn't be musically stimulated. My worries were unfounded, however, because Harvard gave me musical opportunities that I probably wouldn't have found at another institution. Not only was I able to sing a lead in an opera, but was able to sing solos with full orchestras and tour around the world. Only at Harvard are undergraduates given this much opportunity at such a young age.*

Athletics

Harvard boasts forty-one varsity athletic teams, more than any other college or university in the country. If you don't think of Harvard as a jock school, think again. In recent years, Harvard athletes have won Ivy League championships in men's and women's soccer, women's basketball, men's tennis, baseball, football, men's and women's squash, and men's and women's crew. Harvard athletes have earned NCAA Division I championships in women's lacrosse, men's hockey, crew, and squash. In addition, intramural, club, and recreation-level sports are extremely popular; about two-thirds of undergraduates are involved in some sort of athletic endeavor. You can take aerobics, learn a martial art, row novice crew, or play soccer for your house or dorm intramural team. Even if you are a non-athlete, you'll probably enjoy the Ivy League rivalries and the school spirit they inspire. The Harvard-Yale football game continues to be one of the highlights of the school year.

The example of athletics demonstrates the scope of extracurricular life at Harvard; it is astounding if not sometimes overwhelming. You will probably never be able to take part in as many activities or groups as you would like; however, you can rest assured that the opportunities for involvement will be numerous regardless of your level of ability.

The energy of Harvard's campus is one of its most distinctive features. That energy originates from the wide range of extracurricular and cocurricular activities and from the committed, enthusiastic students who keep them going. Some people perceive all Harvard students to be "grinds," interested only in their academic pursuits. This is one of the biggest myths about Harvard. Daily life is full of occasions for involvement, and it's hard, if not impossible, to find a Harvard student who isn't passionate about something beyond school work.

> *My problem is trying to narrow down what I really want to do extracurricularly because there are so many groups and programs that interest me. I am currently involved in varsity cheerleading, the Black Students Association, undergraduate recruiting, and the Undergraduate Admissions Council. I have also been involved in the Harvard Entrepreneurs Club and tutoring elementary school students. I find that I need to be involved in activities; it's just an important aspect of who I am.*

FINANCIAL AID

Harvard is committed to a need-blind admissions process. This means that an applicant's candidacy for admission will be evaluated without regard for the family's ability to pay. So, let's say you've been admitted; now, how to foot the bill? College is expensive, and Harvard is certainly no exception. Fortunately, Harvard is also generous in its use of funds to support students.

Once you have been admitted, Harvard will meet your family's demonstrated need to make it possible for you to matriculate. All of the financial aid is based solely on need. Harvard believes that all of its students make valuable contributions to the college; therefore, the college offers no merit-based scholarships. In addition, as part of the Ivy League, Harvard offers no athletic scholarships.

Approximately seventy-percent of Harvard students receive financial aid, and that aid is usually significant. Recently, the average scholarship was around $13,000; the average financial aid package, including a grant, a loan, and a campus job, totaled over $20,000. Harvard usually devotes some $74 million to undergraduate financial aid.

Applying for Financial Aid

Logistically, it's important to have your act together and to submit all of the forms required for a financial aid application on time (by February 1 of your senior year).

- You will need to fill out the CSS Profile, a form that you actually file directly with the College Scholarship Service. Don't forget to designate Harvard and Radcliffe as one of the schools to which you are applying.
- You need to fill out the Free Application for Federal Student Aid (FAFSA), a form that is available in your school guidance office.
- You are also required to submit your own and your parents' federal income tax returns.
- Students applying from countries other than the United States should fill out Harvard's own Financial Statement for Students from Foreign Countries instead of the CSS Profile. This is the only difference for international students in the financial aid process.

The financial aid officers are some of the most helpful people at Harvard. They want to work with you and your family to make it possible for you to come to Harvard once you have been admitted. Stay organized so that you always give the Financial Aid Office the most accurate, up-to-date information. It's also a good idea to photocopy all of the forms you submit as part of your financial aid application.

GRADUATES

The commencement ceremony is Harvard's most spectacular annual event. I remember every detail of that day vividly—the beautiful crimson, black, and white flags and banners in Harvard Yard, the music, the smiling graduates draped in caps and gowns, my own friends and family sharing in my excite=

ment. This extraordinary celebration of the university community was the perfect way to end the college experience.

Students leave Harvard well prepared to head off in many different directions. Many of my own close friends went into graduate programs; some went right to work. They pursued work in investment banking, consulting, advertising, and teaching. Now that we have been out of college for a few years, many of my close friends are starting to make changes, such as going back to school for an M.B.A. or graduating from medical school and beginning their residencies. It is exciting to see all the different opportunities my classmates are pursuing.

PROMINENT GRADS

- **John Adams, President of the United States**
- **John Quincy Adams, President of the United States**
- **Leonard Bernstein, Composer, Conductor**
- **e e cummings, Poet**
- **W.E.B. DuBois, Educator, Writer**
- **T. S. Eliot, Poet**
- **Ralph Waldo Emerson, Writer, Philosopher**
- **Al Gore, Vice President of the United States**
- **Oliver Wendell Holmes, Jurist**
- **Henry James, Author**
- **Tommy Lee Jones, Actor**
- **John Fitzgerald Kennedy, President of the United States**
- **John Lithgow, Actor**
- **Yo-Yo Ma, Cellist**
- **Franklin Delano Roosevelt, President of the United States**
- **Theodore Roosevelt, President of the United States**
- **George Santayana, Author**
- **Henry David Thoreau, Writer**
- **Paul Wylie, Skater**

Harvard's liberal arts curriculum provides students with a base on which to build their futures. Students graduate from Harvard with a comprehensive understanding of their concentrations, and with an appreciation for other disciplines. In recent years, the most popular concentrations have been economics, government, and biology. This may reflect many students' interest in business, law, and medicine, respectively. But many graduates who were government concentrators are not aspiring lawyers; they are pursuing various career paths. The message here is that it is impossible to generalize about Harvard students and graduates.

Students receive excellent career counseling from the Office of Career Services, where they are encouraged to explore possible career paths. More than 300 companies recruited on campus in a recent year. These facts illuminate the degree to which students are exposed to different possibilities before they leave Harvard.

SUMMING UP

When you think of Harvard, think of its many resources, both human and physical. Think of Cambridge and Boston and New England. Think of the vibrant extracurricular life. Think of the special benefits of the residential system.

At the same time, Harvard isn't the ideal school for everyone. For one thing, Harvard is urban and it might not be a good place for those looking for a small, quiet, college town. Cambridge has a lot of trees and lawns and a beautiful river, but it also has traffic and a lot of general activity. Harvard might not be great for those who want a small college environment. Although the college is considered medium-sized, you probably won't be able to learn everyone's name. Moreover, although you will work closely with an advisor, Harvard is more suited to those who are excited about taking some of the responsibility and initiative to make their education a success. Finally, Harvard might not be a good choice for you if you have a clear idea of what field you want to pursue in college and want to pursue a strictly professional program. Having said that, come visit Harvard. It's worth seeing as an historic site even if you never decide to apply.

What is so great about Harvard? More important than the prestige (though perhaps because of it), it is the resources and opportunities that Harvard places within your reach that shrink your four years into fleeting moments. What you have at Harvard is an unmatched opportunity to discover and rediscover, in and outside class, who you are and what motivates you.

❑ *Brooke Earley, A.B.*

HARVARD UNIVERSITY/RADCLIFFE COLLEGE

Harvard University/Radcliffe College
Cambridge, MA 02138

(617) 495-1551
Fax: (617) 495-8821

E-mail: college@harvard.edu
undergraduate@radcliffe.edu
Web site: http://www.harvard.edu/
http://www.radcliffe.edu/

Enrollment

Full-time ❑ women: 2,918
❑ men: none

Part-time ❑ women: 15
❑ men: none

INTRODUCING RADCLIFFE

It's very easy to wonder why you'd choose to focus on Radcliffe when you have all the resources of Harvard to consider. Very simply, because Radcliffe is a treasure. As a Harvard-Radcliffe student I have the vast resources of Harvard University, and the individual opportunities and network provided by Radcliffe College. It's a great bonus to have Radcliffe; it's not simply a women's center, the location of an outstanding library and theater, or a set of student activities. Though it has all these things, the sum of the parts adds up to much more. No other university I know of has anything like Radcliffe.

Whenever anyone asks me what I have liked best about Radcliffe, I always answer: the college community. It has provided me with a circle of peers and mentors that helped develop me both intellectually and personally. This community is a place where I have had the chance to learn from so many amazing women: I've worked side-by-side at a computer with a well-known scholar, discussed leadership theories with fellow students over coffee, and shadowed an alumna both at work and at home for a week. All of these experiences created learning opportunities that extended far beyond the classroom and extracurricular activities. These are some of my college experiences I will remember most fondly, and the people I shared them with have come to be some of my best friends, whether they were peers or mentors.

The Radcliffe community brings together distinguished scholars and high-powered students to create an atmosphere that supports personal and intellectual growth, risk-taking, and leadership development. This community, unique within the Harvard University environment, enhances the experience of being a woman undergraduate at Harvard and Radcliffe Colleges. Unlike a single-sex college or a women's student center within a larger university, Radcliffe College provides many resources and contacts that contribute to a comprehensive coed undergraduate educational experience.

The college that supports this lively community is a unique educational institution. Located in Cambridge, Massachusetts, Radcliffe College was founded in 1879 as the "Harvard Annex" and was incorporated in 1882 as the Society for the Collegiate Instruction for Women. The college obtained its charter from the Commonwealth of Massachusetts in 1894 and was named for Ann Radcliffe, who established the first scholarship fund at Harvard in 1643.

Over the years, Radcliffe has broadened its initial mission, which was to promote women's education with the assistance of instructors at Harvard University. The 1894 charter added to this a dual purpose: to furnish instruction and opportunities of collegiate life to women, and to promote higher education for women. Today, Radcliffe's mission is to advance society by advancing women. According to Radcliffe communications, "Radcliffe empowers women through education across the lifespan, mentoring and transforming experiences. Radcliffe enables society to value, accommodate, and benefit from women through its research and public policy programs." The college works toward its mission through its undergraduate programs in leadership, research, action, and mentoring; its postbaccalaureate programs for educational interests of women and men of all ages; and its Institutes for Advanced Studies, which make up the college's four academic research and policy centers. The educational programs and institutes provide undergraduates with resources and opportunities that add to the Harvard classroom educational experience.

DEFINING RADCLIFFE

Radcliffe is:

- **a community of women—students, scholars, artists, and activists—with whom you can connect**
- **a wealth of resources that you can use**
- **a place to go for mentorship, hands-on experience, community support, and even employment**
- **an environment that encourages productive partnerships among women and men**
- **the home of the Lyman Common Room, the Externship Program, the Radcliffe Dance Program, and many significant avenues for experience, fulfillment, and self-expression**
- **a tradition of opportunity for women**

Source: Radcliffe College Web site

Harvard and Radcliffe Colleges collaborate in a relationship that is often called, "the nonmerger merger." Though not actually a merger, the 1977 agreement between the two colleges delegated to Harvard the responsibility for instruction and day-to-day management of undergraduate life. The two colleges maintain a joint Office of Admissions and Financial Aid that admits women undergraduates to Radcliffe College and men undergraduates to Harvard College. Women undergraduates who are admitted and enrolled in Radcliffe are "thereby enrolled in Harvard with all the attendant rights and privileges accorded by Harvard College enrollment," according to the agreement. Women undergraduates receive diplomas signed by the presidents of both Harvard and Radcliffe, while men receive diplomas with only a Harvard signature.

Few undergraduates comprehend the exact relationship between Radcliffe and Harvard, either on paper or in practice. Having a great college experience does not require a full understanding of the relationship, as long as women students realize the benefits of their dual Harvard-Radcliffe citizenship. Many of the programs and research centers open their doors to men students, so it is beneficial for them too to know how their studies and activities can be enhanced by the theaters, libraries, and other programs Radcliffe has to offer. It is the women, though, who stand to gain immeasurably from the network Radcliffe can provide them, both as undergraduates and as alumnae.

ADMISSIONS REQUIREMENTS

Radcliffe and Harvard share a central Admissions Office, and have the same requirements. Please see this section in the previous Harvard College essay.

ACADEMIC LIFE

The intellectual horsepower of the students at Radcliffe and Harvard Colleges ensures that academic life is always lively. Courses are taught by professors of the university, sometimes from the graduate schools such as the Kennedy School of Government or the Graduate School of Design, or from Radcliffe but, for the most part, from the Faculty of Arts and Sciences. These professors, regardless of their university affiliation, are distinguished scholars, many of whom teach first-year or core courses.

The Core

The core is the core curriculum and is similar to a distribution requirement. To fulfill the core requirement, students are required to select and take eight courses from specific areas of study (one from each area) such as moral reasoning, literature and arts, and foreign cultures. With some of the most prominent professors in their fields leading core courses, even students with little background in a specific area can learn from the best. For instance, Neil Levine teaches an outstanding course on Frank Lloyd Wright, Michael Sandel a course on justice, and Marjorie Garber a class on Shakespeare. Students give mixed reviews to the core as a whole, and the current system is under review. Changes are currently being made to ensure that there will be a greater number and range of classes offered each semester in each area of study. In addition, the current quantitative reasoning requirement (QRR), which most students test out of, will be replaced by a new quantitative requirement.

Informal Interaction

Academic life extends beyond coursework and reading. Students learn a tremendous amount through more informal interaction. Whether it's casual conversations over coffee with other students about a professor's latest book, or a deeply intellectual discussion with a professor during one of the official faculty dinners, Harvard-Radcliffe students do as much learning away from the classes and books as they do sitting in class or the library.

One of my best academic experiences didn't occur inside a classroom at all. In fact, it happened all over campus, but mostly in a renovated former house that now houses the Radcliffe Public Policy Institute. During the spring of my sophomore year I participated in the Research Partnership Program, which was established in 1991 by President Linda Wilson. I was paired up with a labor economist who was writing an article about students' attitudes and expectations about labor force participation and the division of labor in the household. Basically, we were interested in whether students have realistic expectations of how they would divide up housework and childcare in their future households, and whether they would need to take a break from working full-time in order to fulfill their childcare expectations. I thought I would be doing only number crunching or be buried in the library the whole time. To my surprise I helped in writing the survey that we sent out to students, analyzing the results, and editing the article. I enjoyed the experience so much that afterwards, I was pretty sure that I wanted to go to econ grad school after college, and I undertook my own survey and research project, using the skills I had learned.

Programs Outside the Classroom

Outside of the classroom, there is an abundance of programs to enhance the Harvard academic experience:

- The Radcliffe Research Partnership Program matches undergraduate women with female scholars to provide meaningful research and mentorship experiences in fields varying from math to domestic violence and French history to breast cancer art. The Research Partnership Program draws on the resources and scholars of Radcliffe's Bunting Institute, Murray Research Center, Public Policy Institute, and Schlesinger Library.
- The Bunting Institute is the home to approximately forty scholars who come to the institute for a one-year fellowship to pursue an independent project, on topics ranging from biology to performance art, novel-writing to social activism. During the year, these women continue their research, present their work at weekly forums, and work with undergraduate students as research partners.

- The Murray Research Center houses data sets and other resources on the study of human lives over time. Many economic, sociological, and psychological studies from all over the country reside in the center's archives, and students may access the data and records for use in independent projects, course research, or summer jobs.
- The Public Policy Institute is a research-and-action program that brings together policymakers, scholars, educators, students, members of the media and business community, grassroots organizations, and the public. Together, these constituencies work to shape policy and public thought on social, political, and economic issues.

The Schlesinger Library houses a superb collection of books, manuscripts, oral histories, and photographs that document women's lives and achievements from about 1800 to the present. These extensive resources allow undergraduates to expand their academic experience beyond the classroom whether through independent research or formal study.

THINGS TO DO AT RADCLIFFE

- **Students can explore Amelia Earhart's papers or Susan B. Anthony's original diaries at Radcliffe's Arthur and Elizabeth Schlesinger Library on the History of Women in America.**
- **Undergraduates can enroll in Radcliffe Seminars, which offer graduate courses in liberal arts, management, and landscape design.**
- **Radcliffe Union of Students, the Radcliffe College student government, organizes events such as "Take Back the Night" and advocates for gender equity at Harvard and Radcliffe.**
- **Radcliffe offers the Radcliffe Publishing Course, a six-week summer training program that is recognized throughout the publishing industry as one of the nation's foremost print publishing training courses.**

Radcliffe provides other programs that help to support academic life at Harvard-Radcliffe. The Harvard-Radcliffe Science Alliance gives entering first-year students a week-long introduction to science professors, university facilities, and other students interested in the sciences. The Alliance aims to build a network and familiarity with Harvard's science resources and encourage women to pursue or maintain their interest in the sciences. Other organizations such as Women in Economics and Government and Women in Science at Harvard and Radcliffe provide a network for women interested in specific academic fields, interaction with professors in those fields, and upper-class students who can serve as mentors to younger students. These organizations provide regularly scheduled dinners, receptions, and study breaks where students can gather in an informal setting to discuss their studies and research with professors and other students or listen to a speaker or scholar discuss her own work.

SOCIAL LIFE AND ACTIVITIES

If classes alone aren't enough to keep students busy, they can easily find something else to keep them occupied. It's quite safe to say that there is never a shortage of things to do at Harvard-Radcliffe. From newspapers to clubs to public service to intramurals to just plain hanging out, Harvard-Radcliffe students are always busy with something. There's an organization for almost any topic—and if there's something of interest that's not represented here, someone will start a club for it. For instance, for those students who are musically inclined, there are three orchestras, chamber orchestras (including a cello orchestra), and many quartets and other chamber music groups that meet casually.

There is truly something for everyone at Harvard-Radcliffe, whether your interests include mountaineering, flamenco dancing, political canvassing, or tutoring inner-city children.

Together my three roommates and I were involved in many different activities. We played in musicals, led the First-Year Urban Program, managed orchestras, rowed intramural crew, laid out pages of the Crimson, ran a leadership conference, mentored first-year students, deejayed classical and jazz music at the radio station, researched culinary history, shadowed an architect for a week, taught cello lessons, took dance classes, raised money for the senior class gift... not to mention spending hours reading the newspaper, doing the crossword, and writing e-mail messages to friends (read: procrastinating).

Extracurricular Activities

The beauty of Harvard-Radcliffe is that you can try to do everything or you can do nothing at all—but you won't be doing nothing for very long. In fact, at the beginning of first year, many students find themselves involved in more activities than they have enough time for. By sophomore year, however, most students have figured out how much they can handle at one time and are able to try new activities without feeling overwhelmed. For many students, extracurriculars take up more time than classes do and often become the defining experiences of undergraduate life.

One extracurricular of note is the Harvard-Radcliffe Women's Leadership Project, which sponsors a six-day leadership training conference at the beginning of the school year, a mentor program for first-year women, and other projects to promote women's leadership on campus. Sponsored by Harvard and Radcliffe Colleges and the Institute of Politics at the Kennedy School of Government, the project was founded in 1987 by undergraduate women who noted the lack of women in prominent undergraduate leadership positions and the findings from a study that women at Harvard-Radcliffe were speaking up in class less than their male counterparts. The project brings together undergraduate women leaders with women leaders in diverse career fields from across the country to engage in an intergenerational dialogue about leadership, gender, and career issues. The six-day conference introduces participants to leadership theory and practice, enabling the undergraduates to become more effective leaders in college and beyond.

Social Life

As for the social life at Harvard-Radcliffe, it's a mixed bag. Because students throw themselves into their activities, extracurriculars often form the core of students' social circles. The undergraduate population is large enough that any student will be able to find a niche to call her own, but small enough that she will not be bumping into the same people at every party across campus. There is something for everyone at Harvard-Radcliffe, though most students still complain that there's not enough of a social life in general. The rap is well deserved; it's the obvious consequence of the fact that undergraduates often overextend themselves both academically and extracurricularly, making it difficult to find enough time to simply relax and have fun. It's not uncommon to find at least a few students in the library on a Friday evening, not because there's nothing to do, but because there's always work to be done.

Most students are able to pull away from their studies to take advantage of a variety of social activities. On most weekends there is an abundance of opportunities, from house parties to *a cappella* concerts, 80s dances to final club parties, theater and music concerts to hockey games. In addition, many students venture into Boston to visit the music and dance clubs, theaters, and restaurants, or travel to other nearby colleges for parties or performances.

While there are always events going on across campus and in Cambridge and Boston, most students' social lives revolve around their residential house. Most sophomores, juniors, and seniors live in one of the twelve on-campus residential houses; they take their meals in the dining hall, play intramural sports, and volunteer in the community with housemates. Committees of house residents organize events throughout the year, from toga parties to house formals, Secret Santa to ski trips, and these events contribute to the loyalty that residents feel toward their house.

Back when students had a say in where they lived, each house developed a reputation or personality, each house known for the general character (some would say stereotype) of the students who lived in the house. Various houses became known as the jock house or the artsy house. (What's interesting is that over the years, one house evolved from the artsy house into the jock house.) Nowadays, students don't have a choice; they choose a small group of friends to live with, and, as a group, they are randomly assigned to a house. With housing randomization, the administration hopes to increase the diversity of all the houses and, as a result, the undergraduate social experience as a whole.

FINANCIAL AID

Becoming a Harvard-Radcliffe student requires not only superior academic and extracurricular performance, it often requires a hefty amount of financial assistance from Harvard-Radcliffe. Fortunately, Harvard-Radcliffe selects students on a need-blind basis, which means that it admits first-year students without regard to the candidates' financial situations. For those students who require financial aid, the actual cost of attending college is much less than the full $30,900 and is made possible by a combination of loans, jobs, and scholarships and grants if necessary. Students are first given a job and loan of about $6,000–7,000; if further financial assistance is required, outside scholarships, federal grants, or scholarship funds make up the difference. This year, approximately forty-six percent of undergraduates will receive some scholarship assistance.

If a family can't afford to pay anything, Harvard-Radcliffe expects the student to contribute about $1,800 from summer earnings plus one-third of the student's savings. Most families, however, are able to contribute more; the average family contribution for scholarship recipients is about $11,000 and the average aid package is more than $20,000.

Approximately two-thirds of the undergraduate student body is eligible for some form of financial assistance, which means that as many students work during the year as part of their financial aid package. Undergraduates take jobs all over campus; in fact, there's something to suit each student from the slacker to the studious. Jobs range from stacking books in the library to researching topics for professors, soliciting graduates for donations to videotaping classes. The Student Employment Office maintains a list of jobs that are available both on- and off-campus. The listing, which is available on-line for students to browse through, contains jobs for students on financial aid as well as jobs for those who simply want to earn some extra cash.

GRADUATES

HIGHEST HONOR

The Captain Jonathan Fay Prize, Radcliffe's highest honor, is awarded each year to the graduating senior woman whose academic achievement and personal conduct have made her an outstanding member of the community.

Radcliffe graduates are found all over the world, doing everything from organizing unions to running coffee bars, editing magazines to treating emergency room patients, running for mayor to playing cello professionally. Radcliffe graduates' careers are as diverse as their interests. Along with the usual large number of doctors, lawyers, and businesswomen, there are Radcliffe graduates in public service positions, research labs, churches, and many other careers and jobs around the world.

Researching Career Interests

Seniors as well as underclass students have a wealth of resources to use in researching potential career interests. At Harvard there is the traditional Office of Career Services (OCS) which provides a vast collection of books and on-line resources for students to use in researching potential employers and fields. Summer and full-time job listings, help with résumé writing and job interviews, as well as information on alumnae who are willing to speak to undergraduates about their careers can be found there. OCS offers workshops and individual appointments with career counselors to help students define their interests, skills, and goals with a personality test, learn from a panel of graduates who work in a specific field, or simply weigh job offers. For students looking for full-time jobs, Harvard's extensive recruiting process helps hundreds of seniors find jobs. Many different organizations come to campus to hold interviews. Although many recruiters are looking for staff for investment banks, management consulting companies, advertising firms, or information technology houses, an increasingly larger number of recruiters are coming to find private school teachers and fill public service positions.

Mentors

Radcliffe offers unique opportunities for undergraduate women to explore career interests and learn from the college's most valuable resource: its graduates. The Mentor Program and the Spring Break Externship Program both connect undergraduate women with alumnae in their field of interest. The Mentor Program pairs undergraduates with alumnae during the academic year, providing a forum for the undergraduate to learn more about her mentor's career, and how she balances her personal and work lives. At the beginning of the year the mentor/mentee pair agree on a schedule for meetings; they might meet for coffee, take a tour of the mentor's office, attend a conference together, eat dinner in the mentee's dining hall, or just exchange phone calls during a busy period. Throughout the year the program holds workshops, panel discussions, and social events to encourage more formal discussions of topics such as ethics in the workplace, leadership issues, and women in government. Social events give undergraduates the opportunity to interact with many different graduates and to learn about a variety of careers, and they provide a network for the undergraduate women as well as the alumnae.

PROMINENT GRADS

- Tenley Albright, Skater
- Benazir Bhutto, Former Prime Minister of Pakistan
- Stockard Channing, Actress
- Ellen Goodman, Journalist, Columnist
- Helen Keller, Lecturer
- Gertrude Stein, Writer

Undergraduates and Alumnae

The Spring Break Externship Program matches undergraduate women with alumnae during the week of spring break. The student shadows the alumna both at work and at home and, in most cases, lives with the alumna (and her family if possible) for the week. The Externship Program offers a more concentrated view of the day-to-day requirements of a possible career or field. Through an intensive one-week look into aspects of work and personal life of the alumna, the undergraduate obtains a more concrete picture of her potential career and its accompanying lifestyle. Both the Mentor Program and the Externship Program offer students a more complete view of potential career options than simply reading a job profile or flipping through books and binders at OCS, and students should take advantage of opportunities to meet and get to know alumnae as much as they can.

I found my experiences with Radcliffe graduates to be extremely valuable to the development of my thoughts on what I'd do after college—much more valuable than any book in OCS. My mentors in the Mentor and Externship Programs talked with me about the pros and cons of various careers, helped me put together my résumé, even introduced me to summer job opportunities. Having that connection with the real world helped keep me grounded.

Harvard-Radcliffe has a strong network of graduates, which serves both undergraduates and the graduates themselves. Both Radcliffe and Harvard provide information on graduates who are willing to speak with others interested in their field. More informal networks exist beyond Cambridge; after all, the Harvard-Radcliffe name is an instant connector. For younger grads there are Radcliffe Recent Graduate Committees in Los Angeles, San Francisco, New York, Boston, and Washington that plan social events for graduates who have been out of school fewer than ten years. Through Radcliffe and Harvard Clubs throughout the world alumnae can remain in contact with grads of all ages. And, in this electronic age, there is always e-mail. Recent graduating classes have e-mail lists so that grads can send messages to all the members of their class who have registered their e-mail address with the alumnae office.

For a high school student considering various colleges, it's difficult to look ahead to what comes after college graduation. It's easy to look at colleges and compare their campuses, departments, dorms, and so forth, but it's harder to figure out how life after college will be different as a result of choosing one college over another. When I chose Harvard-Radcliffe, I chose it because of the superior academic environment. My thinking was: At Harvard-Radcliffe I would learn from the best professors and be motivated by my peers. While I was in college, however, when people asked me whether I was glad I chose Harvard over my other choices, I always was, but for different reasons. I had discovered Radcliffe: the Women's Leadership Project, and the Mentor Program, but most importantly, the Radcliffe community, and I knew that nothing like it existed elsewhere. Now that I've been out of school for a year, I treasure my college experience and the friendships I made there, but my connection now, and from now on, is as an alumna. Coming back to Cambridge to visit now, meeting other grads at a Radcliffe Club meeting—these things energize me and remind me why I liked being an undergraduate so much: always feeling as if I'm among old friends.

The feeling of community remains as strong as ever for Radcliffe alumnae. In addition to the committees and clubs that bring alumnae together with each other, there are the many programs that connect them with the next generation of graduates, such as the Mentor Program and the Externship Program. An ever-changing institution, Radcliffe holds a biannual conference called Alumnae Council so that graduates can stay in touch with the college and all its changes.

SUMMING UP

The biannual conference may not come often enough for all to understand Radcliffe, as it is so constantly changing. As female undergraduates have become more completely integrated into the academic and social structure of undergraduate life at Harvard, Radcliffe has sought to update its mission. Though the undergraduate programs continue as strong as ever (both the Women's Leadership Project and the Mentor Program recently celebrated ten-year anniversaries), Radcliffe's emphasis in the future, according to many observers, is moving toward the research and public policy institutes and away from undergraduate activities. While some undergraduates and alumnae find this to be a natural and logical evolution, others are disturbed by the transition of concern away from undergraduate life and the original mission.

This debate is nothing new; the question of Radcliffe's role in undergraduate life has stirred questions among undergraduates since the 1970s. Articles about what Radcliffe should be (a college, a research center, etc.) appear regularly in campus newspapers, though many students consider the issue closed. Radcliffe has an established place in the minds of many undergraduates, both male and female, as a relic of a time gone by, a time when women weren't allowed to enroll at Harvard. Nowadays, women undergraduates see themselves more often than not as Harvard students rather than Radcliffe students. Certainly it is more accurate that Harvard can and does have more influence on undergraduates' academic, social, extracurricular, and personal lives in the aggregate. But that is not to say that Radcliffe's role is minimal. For those individuals who choose to uncover its attractions, Radcliffe enriches the Harvard experience, through its undergraduate programs, research and policy institutes, and network of alumnae.

For someone who is examining colleges and attempting to distinguish the differences among them, there is only one more thing to add: Radcliffe's presence in undergraduate life bestows on Harvard a benefit found at no other undergraduate institution. Though Radcliffe has a reputation of its own and is an experience unto itself, it adds immeasurably to the undergraduate experience of women at Harvard.

❑ *Lauren Young, A.B.*

HARVEY MUDD COLLEGE

Photo by Chuck Chaney

Harvey Mudd College
Claremont, CA 91711

(909) 621-8011
Fax: (909) 621-8360

E-mail: admission@hmc.edu
Web site: http://www.hmc.edu

Enrollment

Full-time ❑ women: 161
❑ men: 483

Part-time ❑ women: none
❑ men: 1

INTRODUCING HARVEY MUDD

Harvey Mudd College is a funny little school with a funny little name that could probably bill itself as "the best college in America that most people have never heard of" if it bothered to take itself that seriously. The college does not show up in the Final Four or try to market itself as the Harvard of anywhere. What it does do is attract some of the nation's brightest students and offers them a unique, rigorous, and liberal technical education that is as good as or better than the more famous colleges that some turn down to matriculate here. There are two key aspects of HMC that set it apart from other top colleges and give the school its often touted one-of-a-kind status: Harvey Mudd College is an intensely small college and has a narrow academic focus on math, science, and engineering.

For most prospective students Harvey Mudd seems like a big enough place engulfed in the larger Claremont Colleges Consortium. In reality, HMC is a close-knit community, a place where everybody knows your name, or at least everyone recognizes your face. The entire student body of around 650 "Mudders" is smaller than the high school graduating class of many incoming students. With ninety-five percent of the school living in the seven dorms (and the other five percent regularly crashing with friends on campus), getting to know your fellow Mudders is not difficult. The core math and science curriculum ensures that most freshmen are taking a nearly identical set of classes. All of this community interaction means that the same group of people you sit with in class in the morning will be eating with you in the dining hall at lunch, dropping by your room to work on homework that evening, playing intramural floor hockey with you later that night, and going out to have a good time together on the weekend. And it stays that way for four years. With this amount of inter-campus intimacy, Mudd is a good place to make great friends and a terrible place to make any enemies.

With no graduate students, no TAs, and a faculty dedicated to a high level of student interaction, few Mudders fall through the cracks or blend into the woodwork. Even the administration and staff take an active role in campus life. The chef in the dining hall and the building attendants on the night shift are some of the best-liked and most well-known personalities on campus, regularly chatting with students. Faculty/staff/student interaction is supported on all levels through "Wednesday Night Prof Things" (where professors spend an evening hanging out in the dorms talking about anything other than their courses) and the Activities Planning Committee (APC for short), a student group that sponsors trips to cultural and fun events throughout Southern California that are open to all members of the HMC community. It is common for a student—any student—to be seen eating lunch with the president of the college, playing Frisbee with a professor, or dropping in to the office of the dean of students to talk about which campus policies need to be reformed. This camaraderie and immediate access to the people who make the college run (from the maintenance staff to the professors to the president) gives Harvey Mudd a sense of community unthinkable in the large research-oriented institutions that most Mudders turn down to come here.

Some students find Harvey Mudd's small size a bit smothering, and most students need to take a break from HMC every now and then. For these Mudders, the other four colleges in Claremont provide a convenient distraction from the unique culture, cliques, and atmosphere that make up HMC. Within the five undergraduate colleges in Claremont, there are innumerable clubs, organizations, concerts, art shows, sports teams, and coffeehouses to take your mind away from the academic rigor of a small science and engineering school. Anyone with a car has the unlimited distractions of Los Angeles just a quick freeway drive away. Students looking for nationally televised football games, fraternity/sorority parties, and large government-funded research laboratories, however, will be sorely disappointed if they come to Harvey Mudd College. What can be found instead are afternoon pick-up football games, impromptu dorm parties, and small labs where talented faculty involve their undergraduate students in every aspect of their research.

ADMISSIONS REQUIREMENTS

Getting into Harvey Mudd College can be as much fun (and as difficult) as graduating from the place. Over the past several years, Mudd's Admissions Office has worked hard to put a human face on the sometimes cold and judgmental world of college admissions. The school's infamous "Junk Mail Kit" (a satirical mailing introducing Harvey Mudd to prospective students) adds much needed levity to the college recruiting process, poking fun at the way most schools try to market themselves, while at the same time drawing in the type of savvy but not humorless student that Harvey Mudd seeks to attract.

I got way more personal attention from the Admissions Office at Harvey Mudd than any other college I applied to. I liked the fact that every letter I received was signed in ink, not laser printed or photocopied. Any time I had questions I was able to talk to someone directly and not just get brushed off in favor of some pamphlet dropped in the mail. I felt that I was a welcome part of the college before I ever saw the campus.

Harvey Mudd is a highly selective college and the applicant pool is dominated by students in the top five percent of their high school class. Each year around one-third of the incoming class is made up of National Merit scholars. As opposed to some larger schools, the HMC Admissions Office avoids hard-and-fast admission requirements or formulas. Instead, the staff at HMC favors reading each application and determining if the individual applicant is the sort of student who will thrive at Mudd. The staff does, however, insist that every incoming freshman at Mudd has had chemistry, physics, and calculus as part of a rigorous and successful high school career.

SAT scores among applicants tend to be extremely high. Aptitude in math, as demonstrated by test scores and grades, is an important admissions criteria, as the science and engineering curriculum at Harvey Mudd is, by necessity, very math-intensive. Verbal scores, however, are not neglected in the admissions process. The college seeks to educate scientists and engineers who can think, write, and express themselves, as well as perform laboratory research and engineering calculations. Students who show strong math skills but weak verbal skills often have a difficult time getting past the HMC Admissions Committee.

The college has been successful in adding more diversity to its student body in the last several years but still has more than its fair share of white males from Southern California. Extracurricular activities, unique talents, interests, hobbies, and a diversity of geographic and cultural backgrounds are all taken into consideration in the admissions process, although academic aptitude remains the essential component in each admission decision. Interviews are optional, although visiting the campus and experiencing its unique atmosphere is highly recommended for prospective students.

ACADEMIC LIFE

Although Mudders tend to be extremely talented and have widely varying interests and hobbies, everyone's course load at HMC revolves around a heap of rigorous courses in math, science, and engineering. The core curriculum demands that every student take courses in physics, chemistry, biology, computer science, engineering, and a lot of math. Coincidentally, these are the same six fields that you can choose to major in at Mudd. Students with a distaste for one of these fields will find themselves sitting in tough classes with high expectations, a motivated professor, a steep grading curve, and a room full of classmates who are engrossed in the subject matter. Almost everyone suffers through at least one such course during the freshman or sophomore year before settling into more comfortable classes required for their chosen major.

Humanities-Social Sciences

The significant humanities and social sciences requirement (around one-third of the total graduation requirements) makes the curriculum at Harvey Mudd far more interesting and challenging than the typical tech school. A past president of Harvey Mudd College often described the school as "a liberal arts college of science and engineering." Indeed, the educational approach at Mudd is to provide young scientists and engineers with a broad, liberal education including courses in a variety of technical and nontechnical fields. Although no one without a strong affinity for the sciences and engineering should enroll at HMC, those who cannot stomach reading books and writing papers are well advised to stay away as well.

Few Mudders can fill the requirements for their technical classes anywhere other than HMC, but it is common for students to take advantage of the vast course offerings in the humanities and social sciences at the other four colleges in Claremont. The Claremont Consortium provides Mudd students with a wide array of course offerings including music, fine arts, and foreign languages, which would otherwise not be available at a small engineering college. The strong academic programs at the other colleges in Claremont allow Mudders to study nontechnical fields in depth and even double major if they so desire.

One of my classmates double majored in chemistry at Mudd and literature at Scripps College; another was the concertmaster for the Pomona College orchestra and double majored in music. Next to them I felt like an academic slacker completing my physics major from Mudd with an economics concentration.

Some of the best and most interesting "hum/soc" (humanities and social sciences) professors in Claremont, however, teach right at Harvey Mudd and every Mudder is required to take several of their classes from the HMC hum/soc Department. Although students lament the limited selection that the on-campus hum/soc department can offer in any given semester, there are several extremely popular hum/soc courses at HMC, including an annual Shakespeare seminar, The Media Studio (a course in media production), and a business course entitled Enterprise and Entrepreneurship. Mudders tend to dismiss their humanities courses as less work-intensive than their technical course load, although at the end of each semester the computer labs are filled through the night with as many students writing term papers as students running computer simulations of chemical processes.

Majors

After three well-regimented semesters of the core curriculum, students complete their career at Harvey Mudd taking classes in their major and completing the humanities requirements. The six majors at Harvey Mudd are all academically broad in their own right. The most popular major, engineering, shuns the specialization seen in other top engineering programs for an emphasis on core design principals, mathematical modeling, and a cross-disciplinary "systems" approach to the ever-broadening field of engineering. The chemistry, physics and biology majors are largely focused on producing top-caliber graduate students who will go one to become career scientists, although in recent years more and more Mudd science majors are studying and pursuing applied fields. Math and computer science makes the most popular double major option and both majors are widely recognized as top undergraduate programs.

All students at Mudd must have a concentration in a humanities or social sciences field in addition to their technical major. This concentration (which may as well be termed a minor) may be in any nontechnical field from dance to political science to religious history. The vast array of course offerings in Claremont gives Mudd students a lot of options in choosing their hum/soc course of studies, although students must take about half of their nontechnical courses from HMC faculty members.

Projects

During the junior and senior years students are required to get involved in either a research or a clinic project. The faculty at HMC has a variety of ongoing research projects, especially in chemistry, biology, and physics, in which students can get involved either as a summer job or toward a senior thesis. Many students, however, opt to organize their own research project for their senior thesis with a faculty advisor providing guidance and advice. Faculty and student research at Mudd ranges from analytical modeling and computational projects to field observation of wildlife and measurement of seismic activity. Laboratory and computer facilities at Harvey Mudd College are unrivaled among undergraduate institutions, and students have access to these facilities around the clock via passcode protected locks and the strength of the HMC Honor Code.

The clinic program (pioneered by HMC over twenty-five years ago) brings blue-chip corporate sponsors to campus to "hire" teams of four to six HMC engineering, math, and computer science majors for one-year projects that solve a problem or fill a need for the company. The clinic projects give students at Mudd the opportunity to deal with the real world issues of working with a client, facing deadlines, writing reports, presenting and defending their work, and finding solutions to problems that do not appear in a textbook. The nature of the clinic projects varies widely both in scope and in subject matter. Conceptual designs, research projects, detailed analysis, and software development are all common in clinic projects that may incorporate mechanical, electrical, structural, or chemical systems, depending on the problem as defined by the clinic sponsor. Biology, chemistry, and physics majors who are oriented toward professional careers often elect to participate in a clinic project in lieu of a research project. Numerous patents have come out of work done by HMC clinic teams over the years, and many companies return to sponsor clinic projects year after year.

The Honor Code

The strong, student-administered Honor Code at Harvey Mudd has broad implications on the academic end of campus. Cheating of any kind is not tolerated but there is a high level of trust between the faculty and among the students due to the Honor Code. Open-book, proctorless, and take-home exams are all common at Mudd. Students are encouraged to study and work in groups but are also instructed to acknowledge their classmates who help them on homework assignments. The horror stories that come out of some institutions of sabotaging lab experiments, classmates refusing to share lecture notes, and stealing homework assignments are foreign concepts at Mudd. Mudders scorn the cutthroat attitudes that mark some highly selective colleges, preferring cooperation and camaraderie.

Course Load

A typical course load at Mudd is five courses per semester. At least one lab per semester and one or two hum/soc classes per semester is the norm. Those who choose to double major often enroll in six classes each semester. Those who can get away with taking four classes (through summer school, advanced placement, or shear luck) are ridiculed by their friends for slacking off. At the other four colleges in Claremont—and most of the rest of the civilized world—three to four classes per semester is the accepted norm.

Grades

The grading scale at Harvey Mudd can be brutally harsh although most Mudders exaggerate the cruelty of their grades. GPAs average around 3.0 at graduation, although many freshmen and sophomores suffer through much lower GPAs before pulling them up during their junior and senior years. Counter to the notoriously high grade inflation at some prestigious schools, at Harvey Mudd students who do not perform in the classroom receive the appropriate grade—and that does not mean a B+! Around one quarter of the students fail a course at some point during their time at HMC.

Failing freshman physics was one of the best things that ever happened to me at Mudd. Although it was a real blow to my ego at the time, it forced me to get serious about my homework and not let things slide until an exam came along as I had in high school. The study habits I adopted in order to get through physics became part of my routine for every class and helped me keep my grades up for the rest of college—although to this day I still hate physics.

Midterms and finals, always administered proctorless under the HMC Honor Code, can be three-hour nightmares, designed to ensure that there is a broad range of scores and that no one aces the exam. Class average scores of fifty to sixty percent on an exam are common with some students who had 4.0s in high school scoring in the twenty to thirty percent range. Fortunately, most of the faculty at Mudd grades on a sliding scale and there is an abundance of academic tutoring resources available for students who fall behind in their studies.

Freshmen at Mudd do not receive letter grades for their first semester classes in order to give incoming students a chance to adjust to the raised academic expectations of a fast-paced and demanding college course load. The Freshman Division is a joint faculty-administrative body dedicated to ensuring that every freshman at Mudd makes it through the year without failing out or slipping through the cracks.

Students at Mudd are expected to work hard, study hard, and do an abundance of homework each of their four years at HMC (and few take more than four years to graduate). The work load is heavy but the competition between students is not. Studying in groups is standard, peer tutoring is widely offered on both a formal and informal basis, and the faculty keep long office hours and offer extended review sessions before exams.

SOCIAL LIFE AND ACTIVITIES

Dorms

Social life at Harvey Mudd revolves around the seven on-campus dorms in which nearly the entire student body resides.

HMC Dorms: The Quad:	*East (Mildred Mudd Hall)*
	West
	North
	South (David X. Marks Hall)
The new dorms:	*New (Atwood Hall)*
	Case
	Linde

Each dormitory at Mudd has a distinct personality and set of traditions. The social atmosphere in any given dorm (and indeed on the entire campus) evolves somewhat with every group of new students but there is a surprising amount of continuity in the types of students found hanging out in certain dorms at Mudd year after year. Dorm stereotypes are plentiful: West Dorm is rowdy and obnoxious, Case is secluded and quiet, South is eclectic, New dorm is where the athletes live, etc. Mudders often identify themselves by which dorm they live in and hence what sort of people they socialize with. The dorm images are (like all stereotypes) only partially grounded in the truth. Mudd is small enough (and homogeneous enough) that students are generally comfortable regardless of which foreign dorm they end up in for a review session, study break, or weekend party. Of course, due to space limitations, many students take up residence in a dorm that is not their first choice, and Mudders tend to have friends scattered across multiple dorms. Most students at Mudd reside in more than one dorm over the course of their four years.

The dorms are all coed and include a mix of students from all classes. Freshmen are required to live on campus with a roommate and are placed in all seven dorms. The quad dorms, the four older dorms on campus, are named for the four points of the compass although in a Mudd-esque twist of logic, South Dorm is north of West Dorm and west of North Dorm. The quad dorms are each constructed in the 1950s vintage cinderblock style that dominates the architecture on the campus. The atmosphere tends to be more social in the quad dorms, even if less aesthetic and less air-conditioned than the newer dorms where suite arrangements are typical and students are more likely to stick with their closest friends and less likely to wander throughout the dorm. All of the dorms have central lounges with TVs and VCRs (perfect for weekend movie festivals), and all of the dorm rooms are hard-wired into the campus computer network for modem-free access to the central file servers and the Internet.

Proctors (seniors trained in first aid, crisis management, and handing out candy) are placed in each dorm. There is no non-student presence on campus after hours, except for the bike-pedaling five-college campus security force, and the campus is therefore largely egalitarian. There are a host of official and not-so-official student government organizations on campus that set student policy, organize events, discipline those who step over the line, and promote the general welfare.

Parties and Competitions

Parties of all sizes, from small spontaneous gatherings to well-hyped five-college extravaganzas, take place at frequent intervals in the dorms on the HMC campus. Mudd parties are revered throughout the Claremont Colleges as the biggest, most creative, and most fun parties in Claremont. As on all college campuses, alcohol is a prominent part of the social fabric, although drinking and driving is not, since all of the parties are within walking distance on campus. Claremont as a community is short on places for college kids to get a drink, although the Harvey Mudd College campus is not. It is commonly said that at Mudd "there is no pressure to drink, only to drink more." In truth, HMC's rigorous academic curriculum ensures that students who do not understand when to stop partying and start studying will not last very long on the campus.

There is a sizable portion of the student body at Mudd (around thirty percent) that does not drink at all and there are always a myriad of nonalcoholic events at HMC including regular movies, concerts, and off-campus trips. The "Muddhole," an on-campus pizza parlor, pool hall, and dive is a popular hangout seven nights a week, occasionally offering up live music and other events. Mudders are as good at coming up with creative and unique extracurricular activities for themselves as they are at throwing parties. The Etc. (extremely theatrically confused) Players produce original plays as well as old standards as often as they can get a willing cast together (three or four times a year). Other Mudd clubs plan outdoors events, race the school yacht *Mildred* (a nineteen-foot class boat named for Mrs. Harvey Mudd), and coordinate volunteer opportunities for Mudders looking to use up the last remaining ounce of their valuable spare time.

The five-class competition (there are a handful of fifth-year masters degree students at Mudd) is an annual event with little or no redeeming value besides being a great time. The event is a giant relay race that crisscrosses the campus with representatives from each class performing in such events as whistling with peanut butter in one's mouth, computer programming under pressure, a seven-legged race, and mass eating. Faculty and staff serve as judges for the events, although stretching the rules is a time-honored tradition. After the race is over (it takes about thirty-minutes), the entire campus settles in for a picnic and celebration of all things great about being at Harvey Mudd College.

Dating

The dating scene at Harvey Mudd is as unconventional as the rest of the school. Students at Mudd frequently lament "the ratio," referring to the fact that Mudd is roughly seventy-five percent male. The ratio is hard on the men at the school, many of whom give up quickly on ever finding a girlfriend there. The ratio can also be very hard on the women at the school who get an inordinate amount of amorous attention and sometimes have trouble making friends with other females at Mudd. The Claremont Colleges Consortium is the saving grace that takes the edge off the ratio. Scripps, a women's liberal arts college, is literally across the street from HMC. Naturally, many Mudd men find dates at Scripps and most Mudd women are relieved to have more women around watering down the predominantly male atmosphere on campus.

Sports

Despite the emphasis on academics, Mudd is a very athletic campus. Many Mudders achieve in varsity sports, although for some students it is difficult to find time to participate in the NCAA Division III athletic program HMC shares with two of the other Claremont schools. Intramural sports are popular and help promote dorm rivalries. Pick-up games of volleyball, basketball, soccer, and softball are daily occurrences at Mudd, as most students are looking for any chance to put aside their homework, soak up some sun, and release some stress. HMC is in the shadow of Mt. Baldy, one of Southern California's highest peaks, which means that quality mountain biking, hiking, and skiing are less than a half hour away.

Trips

Claremont is well located for weekend and spring break road trips. Los Angeles, Las Vegas, the Joshua Tree National Monument, Santa Barbara, San Diego, and Tijuana are all within three hours by car. San Francisco, the Grand Canyon, and resort towns in Baja are all popular locations, well within the reach of road-tripping HMC students with a few days break. Perhaps the most popular road trip among Mudd students, however, is to DonutMan (a.k.a. Fosters), home of world-famous strawberry donuts. Mudders make the fifteen-minute drive nightly, bypassing numerous other inferior donut shops along the way. For those who prefer their cholesterol spicy, not sweet, the Sanaumlang Cafe offers up the best Thai food around, at reasonable prices, until 2:00 in the morning. This is the popular eating spot for Mudders who are studying late (or taking a break from studying late).

FINANCIAL AID

Harvey Mudd is, unfortunately, an expensive place to go to college. The school is young (founded in 1955) and has an impressive endowment for its age, but does not bathe in the financial resources that much older institutions enjoy. However, most of the students (around seventy percent) receive financial aid of some form and most of the students (around one hundred percent) would like to receive more financial aid. As at other prestigious private institutions, students and parents alike often accrue a sizable debt over their four years at HMC. The consistency of Mudd graduates being placed in high-paying jobs and prestigious graduate school programs, however, makes all of this debt a little easier to stomach.

Fortunately, Harvey Mudd is the type of small institution that can give students personal attention, even in financial aid matters. It's common for parents to call and discuss their child's financial aid package with the college's director of financial aid or with the college vice president overseeing the financial aid office. Mudd will work with parents and students to adjust financial aid awards and to establish payment plans that help ensure that any student who has been admitted to HMC has every opportunity to attend the college.

GRADUATES

Perhaps the greatest testament to Harvey Mudd College is the success of its alumni body. Although the average age of the alums is around thirty, Mudd has produced a greater percentage of graduates who go on to receive Ph.D.s (over forty percent) than any other institution over the last several years. An astounding percentage of HMC alumnus own their own businesses (around six percent), alums litter the faculty ranks at top colleges across the country (including three alums who teach at HMC), an HMC alumnus was an astronaut for NASA, another produces the James Bond films, and still another alum currently serves as U.S. Ambassador to Lebanon. Not bad for a college with around 3,500 total alumni, fewer than many universities produce in a single year.

PROMINENT GRADS

- **Richard Jones, Ambassador**
- **Pinky Nelson, Astronaut**
- **Lust Puppy, Rock Group**

Roughly half the students at Mudd step directly into the top graduate programs in the country. Students from all majors regularly make the choice to go immediately to graduate school out of Mudd, but the chemistry and biology majors are especially valuable commodities and generally can write their own ticket into the graduate program of their choice. In the past several years, numerous highly prized NSF fellowships, Churchill scholarships, and Thomas Watson fellowships have been handed out to Harvey Mudd College graduates.

Due to the HMC clinic program and the continuing success of Mudd alums in the work force, dozens of companies come to campus each year to recruit HMC engineering, physics, computer science and math majors. Most of these companies are located in Southern California or the Silicone Valley although Mudd is gaining increasing national exposure in the professional world. HMC graduates leave college with a set of skills and experiences that are unique to the Mudd philosophy of education, and invaluable to employers. These experiences include working in randomly selected teams of peers, tackling open-ended problems with no clear solution, exploring the intersection of different technical fields, and generally working hard with limited resources under unreasonable deadlines and undue stress.

In my first year out of Mudd working for a big Silicone Valley software firm I was amazed at how most of the guys I started with would complain about the long hours and difficult project assignments that they felt were way over their heads. All I could think was "this stuff is fun and interesting and a hell of a lot easier to manage than my clinic project back at Mudd was." I was certainly challenged in my new job but I wasn't overwhelmed like the other new guys.

A few Harvey Mudd College graduates go on to business, law, or medical school, although most pursue more traditional careers in math, science, and engineering. Medical school applicants from HMC often face the disadvantage of a lower GPA than most of the competing applicant pool who have not endured HMC's rigorous curriculum and take-no-prisoners grading curve. A growing number of Mudd students are pursuing volunteer service appointments upon graduation including programs in the Peace Corps, AmeriCorp, and Teach for America.

SUMMING UP

Harvey Mudd College is a distinctly small school where some of the top undergraduates in America come together to study science, math, and engineering in an academically rigorous, but extremely fun, environment. The technical curriculum is broad with an emphasis on the humanities and social sciences as well as core science, math, and engineering principals. The residential campus is vibrant with a student body that is widely talented, dynamic, and eccentric in addition to being academically gifted. HMC is bolstered by its participation in the Claremont Colleges consortium, which gives Mudd students access to academic resources, course offerings, athletics, and other opportunities that could not otherwise be supported by a small technical college. The student-run Honor Code demands integrity and honesty from every student. In addition, the general pace and atmosphere of the college demands a healthy sense of humor in addition to a healthy work ethic and a strong affinity for math, science, and engineering.

❑ *Erik Ring, B.S.*

HAVERFORD COLLEGE

Haverford College
370 Lancaster Avenue
Haverford, PA 19041-1392

(610) 896-1350, (general info) (610) 896-1000
Fax: (610) 896-1338

E-mail: admitme@haverford.edu
Web site: http://www.haverford.edu

Enrollment

Full-time ❑ women: 590
❑ men: 557

INTRODUCING HAVERFORD

Once a well-hidden gem tucked away in leafy, suburban Philadelphia, Haverford is breaking out of obscurity and into the forefront of the country's top liberal arts colleges. And why not? Haverford embodies what most people associate with college: an arboreal campus dotted with historic stone halls, professors and students chatting away on the steps after class, people reading or throwing a frisbee on the main green. But there are many things about Haverford that go beyond that, that break the mold and make it a unique place. An Honor Code brings trust and respect to the campus community both in the classroom and at Saturday night parties. Only 1,100 students means that even intro courses average fifteen or fewer students, giving you close contact with a challenging and accomplished faculty. And Haverford has the top collegiate cricket team in the nation (also the only one). It's no wonder Haverford is no longer a secret.

The college covers 216 acres about ten miles from Center City Philadelphia; however, you could easily be convinced that you were in the middle of nowhere. Shrouded by a wall of trees on all sides, the campus consists of rolling fields with buildings concentrated around a square in the middle. The campus itself is an arboretum, and there is a duck pond (complete with ducks). Founded in 1833 by the Society of Friends, Haverford was intended for Quaker men, but soon thereafter opened its doors to all comers (except women, who were admitted in 1980). The Quaker tradition is strong but not overbearing in typical Quaker fashion. Meeting is held weekly for those who choose to attend, and aspects such as consensus decision-making and the Honor Code are direct results of the Quaker background.

Liberal arts is the important thing to remember when talking about academics. Haverford is truly committed to the idea, meaning that physics majors cannot hole themselves up in lab for four years, just as philosophy majors will end up stepping into the Sharpless Science Building once or twice during their college career. A few basic requirements, such as a year of foreign language, freshman writing, and a social justice class, are designed to ensure this, but don't prove to be restrictive. That's not to say Haverford students will do well only in Trivial Pursuit; the past few classes have produced prize-winning physicists and published economists, among others. Be prepared to roll up your sleeves right away—the work is rigorous to say the least. The thirty-page reading assignment that you were shocked to get in high school will seem like a night off.

Of course it's not all work and no play. Haverford offers a broad range of activities for such a small college. More than half of the student body plays sports at either the varsity, club, or intramural level. Students can choose from seventy-five clubs and groups ranging from theater to the Zymurgy Club (beer-making). Haverford also has the highest per capita number of *a cappella* groups in the nation, making for a lot of harmony on campus.

The surrounding towns offer the usual fare of movie theaters, restaurants, book stores, and twenty-four-hour Wawa convenience stores, which come in very handy when you want a hoagie at 2:30 A.M. Downtown Philadelphia is a fifteen-minute ride away on the local train; Swarthmore and Bryn Mawr can be reached through regular van and bus service.

The Honor Code

Underlying life at Haverford is the Honor Code, one that goes beyond not copying off your neighbor's exam book. All incoming students have to sign the Code, pledging to live by the academic and social responsibilities it assigns to all students and faculty. What this translates to is take-home tests, and unproctored, self-scheduled final exams that can make the stress-induced angst of finals week a bit easier to take. The more blurry and controversial side of the Code is its social expectations. The basic premise is that all students must treat each other with respect and work out their differences through dialogue. Enforcing such a vague idea can be difficult. The social Honor Code has been a big topic of discussion the past few years at Plenary, the town-meeting style biannual gathering. The Code is a work in progress, constantly being changed and remolded by students who propose amendments and then plead their case at Plenary. All resolutions are put to a vote, and if passed, become part of the Code.

If what you are looking for is academic excellence combined with a strong sense of community, then look no further. A strong emphasis on the liberal arts and the trust and respect implicit in the Honor Code teach Haverford students not only how to be a complete intellectual package, but also how to be well-rounded people.

ADMISSIONS REQUIREMENTS

Gaining admission to Haverford is not an easy task, but it's also not one that should be discouraging. Only thirty-four percent of the students who apply are accepted, but being in the top of your class with great SAT scores doesn't guarantee you a spot nor does that C+ you got in tenth grade geometry seal your fate. The Office of Admission uses the numbers as a benchmark, but is also interested in more than just an applicant's statistics. It is looking for students who will not only excel in the classroom, but also contribute to the Haverford community, either on the athletic field, on stage, at club meetings, or even in a conversation in the dining center. So keep up the piano lessons, join the French club, and maybe take a weekend day or two to volunteer.

Now for the numbers. A total of 2,769 students applied to Haverford during a recent year; 946 were accepted from which 299 chose to attend. Of those who enrolled, 97 percent were in the top fifth of their high school class, and 80 percent were ranked in the top tenth. The median range for Verbal SAT I was between 640 and 720; Math was 630–730. Women make up fifty-one percent (152 students) of the class of 2001, and twenty-one percent of the class are students of color. Almost all the enrolled students have been officers of one or more school organizations or have lettered in a sport, illustrating the emphasis Haverford places on complete candidates. Volunteer service was also high among the class of 2001.

The Office of Admission requires the standard materials from applicants: SAT I and II, high school transcript, recommendations, and a personal writing sample. Students are welcome to use the Common Application in lieu of Haverford's forms. Interviews are required for students living within 150 miles of Haverford, and are strongly encouraged for those outside of the radius. Any additional material sent with an application is welcomed, but make sure it is relevant to your admissions information. You might want to hold onto the tape of you scoring the winning goal in last week's soccer game. If you're seriously considering Haverford, an overnight visit is also a good idea to get a good feel for the place. Admissions has a cadre of nonthreatening hosts ready to show any prospective students around for a night.

Haverford has been making a concerted effort to increase the diversity of the college. Nineteen percent of the students are students of color, and Haverford offers scholarships such as the José Padín Fund for students from Puerto Rico and the Ira DeA. Reid Fund for minority students. The college has also been addressing other areas of diversity, including class differences. Haverford students tend to come from upper middle-class backgrounds, a trend that the Office of Admission is trying to change by seeking out talented students from lower income families. This is a difficult task because it means putting a heavy burden on the already limited amount of financial aid the college can provide, but one that Haverford has committed to.

ACADEMIC LIFE

The freshman orientation week used to include a session with a long-time chemistry professor on balancing work. The bow-tied chemist would break down, to the hour, the daily schedule of the average Haverford student in an effort to impress upon the freshmen the amount of planning they needed to keep up with their studies. Eight hours a day were allotted for sleeping, three for meals, four for class, and three for any extracurricular activities, which, according to his calculations, left a reasonable six hours of the day for homework. Needless to say, this left many already apprehensive freshmen wondering what they had gotten themselves into.

While few if any Haverford students follow these recommendations for time budgeting, most take their studies very seriously. There are no stereotypical students; the captain of the basketball team might also be a philosophy major who reads Kant when not at practice. The work load is heavy, and often the faculty members seem to forget that you aren't taking only one course each semester. The library is one of the most popular places during the week, which also makes it one of the most social spots on campus. Students looking for some serious studying can hole themselves up in one of the numerous carrels that are scattered throughout the stacks, leaving the main floor for those more interested in being seen.

The competition that is rampant in high school does not carry over to Haverford. With the academic responsibility of the Honor Code as a backdrop, the academic life at the college is refreshingly noncompetitive; that is, people are only interested in their own work and don't snap their neck trying to see how their neighbor did on an exam. Haverford supports this by intentionally avoiding a competitive environment; there is no dean's list or honors program, and students of high academic achievement are not publicly recognized until graduation.

I remember the summer after my freshman year at Haverford, returning home after one of the most stressful years of my life. It was the first time that I had really been home since the school year began, and the first time I had seen many of my high school classmates since graduation. I was really taken aback when one person asked me what my GPA was. Maybe I was reacting as any Haverford student, not used to asking people about their grades, and not being asked about mine, or maybe I thought it was a judgment of my success in college. The fact is I had become part of a community in which grades are not the measure of a person's worth (nor a point of competition or separation within the student body), a community that looks at each member as an individual and values what that individual brings to the community. I am a lot more than the ten-page paper I stay up all night writing, and I am glad to be at a school where the community (and not just my close friends) realizes that.

The Value of Liberal Arts

Haverford heavily stresses the value of liberal arts, meaning that there are a set of academic requirements. Students must take at least three credits (one class equals one credit) in each of the three major disciplines: the social sciences, humanities, and natural sciences. A semester of freshman English is required for all first-year students, and two semesters of a language is necessary to graduate unless a student can test out of the requirement. There is also an oft-forgotten gym requirement that can haunt seniors who need gym credits to graduate. Rumor has it that the athletic department comes up with last-minute workouts to let some students off the hook. Students can choose from twenty-six majors, and also have the option of majoring at Bryn Mawr College.

The bi-college relationship with Bryn Mawr is designed so that one school picks up where the other might be weak. For example, Bryn Mawr offers a major in growth and structure of cities while Haverford provides astronomy. Some majors, such as comparative literature, are bi-college, sharing faculty and campuses. Class size is generally small, averaging fifteen to twenty students. Introductory courses can reach thirty and the occasional night survey course can reach seventy-five students. However, by the time students are seniors, they have most likely been a part of more than one seminar that numbered from five to ten.

Faculty

Small classes mean that students get to come into close contact with professors, and Haverford has some of the best around. Not only are many at the top of their fields, but they are also interested in teaching as well as research. The biology faculty welcomes juniors into their labs over the summer to assist them in their research, and many biology majors use that experience as part of their thesis or to get published. Most Haverford professors encourage classroom discussion, which both enlivens courses and means that if you haven't done the reading for the day, there's nowhere to hide. Professors are very accessible, with ample amounts of office time, and they are willing to stay after class to talk. Faculty members will invite students over to their homes for dinner at the end of the semester, and some hold class in their living rooms.

The summer after I graduated, I drove across the country with five friends of mine from Haverford. We were crashing with friends as much as possible, but we didn't know any people in the Upper Midwest, so we called up one of the history professors who spends his summers in Montana. The seventy-year-old professor met us at the end of his dirt road on a dirtbike complete with boots and helmet. He put the five of us up for the night at his cabin in the middle of a national park and cooked us dinner and breakfast. He even took us on a tour of the woods and told us about the family of moose that lived nearby and the bear that tried to break down his door.

Study Abroad

By junior year, many students feel the urge to try something new for awhile and to meet some new people. Study abroad programs are enormously popular and the junior class is gutted each semester when students head off for all corners of the globe. The most popular programs are the European ones, but Haverford has also established ties with universities in Nepal, Ghana, and Chile, among others. Junior year abroad serves two purposes: students get to see the world, and they also tend to return to campus with a fresher view of the college after their time away.

SOCIAL LIFE AND ACTIVITIES

The Haverford experience begins with Customs Week, basically five days of intensified summer camp. Freshmen are divided into groups of ten to fifteen according to their dorm and hall, which becomes their Customs group. Upperclass students, usually sophomores, guide first-year students through a gauntlet of games, get-to-know-you activities, and general orientation to the college. The week includes a dorm Olympics, where each of the three freshman dorms compete against each other in games ranging from the human knot to egg tossing. Dorm Olympics is also one of the few times the president can be seen on campus in a toga. Customs groups tend to be tight-knit during the first semester, usually traveling *en masse* to and from the dining center. This mentality can slow down the process of meeting new people, but it also is easier to make some close friends within the group.

Housing

For those who enjoy their personal space, housing at Haverford is ideal. Most of the dorms have all single rooms, usually grouped together in suites with a common room. There is a good chance that a student can go through all four years of college without having to share a room. If you are looking for a college roommate with whom you can share stories at your twenty-fifth reunion, the several houses on campus and the Haverford College Apartments (HCA) are the way to go. HCA is a complex located on the edge of campus that the college bought to handle the influx of students after women were admitted. It now houses a third of the freshmen and a large part of the sophomore class. Apartments are shared by three or four students, each with two bedrooms, a bathroom, and a kitchen. The only drawback is that you have to clean the bathroom yourself. HCA develops its own social scene throughout the year, since the third of the student body that lives there is in relative isolation from the rest of the campus.

Parties and Bars

Haverford has no Greek system, but party-goers still tend to gravitate toward the several houses on campus for their Friday and Saturday night activities or to Lloyd dorm for traditional Thursday night parties. The same scene can get old midway through the first semester, so the more adventurous and legal fun-seekers head out to some of the area bars. Actually, most don't make it any further than the five-minute walk to Roache and O'Brien, more affectionately known as Roaches. About the size of your average walk-in closet, Roaches is a bizarre mixture of seedy locals and Haverford students, complete with a life-size poster of Willie Nelson, a jukebox that hasn't changed a record in twenty years, and a bartender who dishes out insults along with drinks. It's no wonder why it is such a popular hangout. Bryn Mawr is also five minutes away by Blue Bus, the shuttle that runs between the two campuses. Haverford men have the distinct advantage of the famed 3:1 ratio, that is, three women between the two schools for each Haverman, although this is no guarantee that romance will be found. The dating scene can get a bit claustrophobic at a school as small as Haverford, and a general complaint is that there is no casual dating—most relationships tend to be intense. However, many students find their future spouses in the bi-college community.

Traditions

The college also has some long-standing traditions, the most notable being Class Night, a variety show in which classes compete with each other to put on the most ridiculous and often offensive skit. Alums will get teary-eyed remembering their Class Night shenanigans, but in the past few years, participation has flagged, and some classes don't get organized enough to put in an entry.

Going Off Campus

Finding places to go off campus is not too hard. Vans run between Haverford and Swarthmore every day, and UPenn is a twenty-minute car ride away. Right across the street from Haverford is a commuter train stop that goes directly into Center City Philadelphia, opening up a whole world of restaurants, theaters, clubs, sports, stores, parks, and, of course, historical Philadelphia. New York is also a three-hour ride away and Washington, D.C. can be reached in two hours. Or, if you're interested in risking your student job earnings, Atlantic City is only an hour away.

Sports

Athletics are a big draw at Haverford, ranging from the varsity athlete to the intramural badminton player. Forty percent of the students play intercollegiate sports and another fifteen percent play on club teams. There are twenty-two varsity teams that compete in the NCAA Division III and in the Centennial Conference, which includes schools such as Swarthmore, Bryn Mawr, and Johns Hopkins. While some teams are up and down each year, both the men's and women's track teams are perennial powerhouses, advancing to the national championships virtually every year. The college does not have a football team, so Haverford has a unique Homecoming with soccer as the centerpiece of the weekend's events. One requirement to play or watch sports at Haverford is a passionate hatred for Swarthmore. The academic camaraderie is left at the door whenever there is a game against Swarthmore, and the schools compete for the Hood Trophy, given annually to the winner of the most games.

Clubs or Groups

If you're looking for a club or group to join, there is a smorgasbord to choose from. Interested in boats? Sign up for the sailing club. Want to learn how to make films? Try the Bi-College Filmmaking Club. If you have an interest that you want to pursue or organize, the college will help you get it started.

For the past few years, people had been talking about how Haverford needs a pottery studio. Every now and then someone would put up a sign about organizing a club, but nothing ever got off the ground. Two friends and I decided to finally do something about the one wheel covered with dust in the basement of the dining center, and last year we began to organize a pottery club. We received a large donation from an alum to buy another wheel, and with budgeting funds from Student Council we bought a third wheel, a kiln, clay, glazes, and tools. When we advertised at the Student Activities Fair, 120 students signed up to use the room or learn how to throw on the wheel. It is tough to accommodate so many people with three wheels, but we try to let everyone use the studio and we can keep getting more equipment. It took a lot of time to go through all the necessary paper work and finances with the college to set this up, but it was definitely worth it. We finally have a completely functional pottery studio that anyone can use. I think we found out that if you want to make something happen at Haverford, you can do it as long as you organize.

Haverford shares a weekly newspaper with Bryn Mawr, and the entirely student-run *Bi-College News* is a favorite Saturday morning brunch reading material. Lighted Fools is a popular student theater group that produces several comedy skits each semester, and Horizons Unlimited Musical Theater puts on two musicals each year. Four campus *a cappella* groups regularly square off against each other in joint concerts as does the Bi-College Chorale.

In accordance with its Quaker roots, Haverford also encourages students to take part in service activities. The 8th Dimension Office is a resource for students looking to do some volunteer work, and the office has a goal of getting every student to take part in at least one activity before graduation. That goal has never been realized, but a good number of Haverford students do take time out to volunteer. This can simply be spending one Saturday afternoon helping to fix up an abandoned row house in Philadelphia, or a Big Brother/Sister pairing that lasts for all four years of college. The Quaker student group on campus also runs several service events and each spring break Haverford sends small groups of students throughout the country to help build or repair housing for low-income families.

FINANCIAL AID

Haverford is not cheap. With a price tag that hovers close to $30,000 a year, many students need help to cover their expenses. The Financial Aid Office is as generous as it can be, providing aid of some form for thirty-seven percent of all freshmen and forty-five percent of the entire student body. Admission is need-blind, and financial aid is addressed only after a student has been accepted.

Financial aid decisions are made solely according to a need-based allocation formula developed by the college. In other words, Haverford does not offer any financial aid on the basis of academic, musical, athletic, or any other merits.

Financial aid at Haverford comes primarily in the form of grants and scholarships. The college has around 120 scholarship funds that students are awarded as part of their aid packages, and can be general or directed at students with particular interests. Campus jobs are plentiful, and range from monitoring the field house during evenings to writing press releases for the Public Relations Office. Students often use work-study as résumé-builders for summer internships or even jobs after graduation. Students receiving financial aid are given preference in hiring for campus jobs.

GRADUATES

The real test of the value of a Haverford education and experience comes after students walk across the stage to receive their diplomas. For some it is directly on to graduate or professional school, while others want to take some time to breathe before continuing their education. Roughly thirty percent of all graduating seniors head straight for school right after college, with five percent attending law school and seven percent going on to medical school. Another thirty-five percent spend some time in the work world before going back to school within five years of graduation. Those who do start the nine-to-five life do so in a wide variety of fields. Recent graduates tend to find jobs in business, education, scientific research, and journalism—basically most types of employment. Some students receive fellowships for overseas programs. Haverford is a perennial recipient of at least one Watson Fellowship, which provides money for a student to pursue a self-designed research project overseas. Recent grads on Watson Fellowships have played baseball in Russia and traveled throughout Scotland taking photographs.

PROMINENT GRADS

- **John Whitehead, '43, Former Deputy Secretary of State**
- **Gerald M. Levin '60, Chairman and CEO, Time Warner**
- **Joseph Taylor, '62, Nobel Laureate in Physics**
- **Norman Pearlstine, '64, Editor-in-Chief, Time Inc.**
- **Dave Barry, '89, Humorist**

The bi-college career development office has a wealth of information on jobs, careers, and internships for those who get over the apprehension of even thinking about finding a job. Recruiters from many major companies and firms come on campus each year in search of future employees, and job-seeking students are also able to interview off-campus through programs established by career development. Those who try the word-of-mouth approach of networking can draw upon an alumni body of roughly 15,000, a small but tight-knit and very accomplished group eager to help out a fellow Haverfordian. Younger alumni tend to congregate in the major cities of the East Coast, a large contingent move a whopping ten miles away to Philadelphia, many succumb to the lure of New York, and Washington, D.C. is often referred to as Haverford's southern campus because of the large number of alumni living there.

SUMMING UP

I never really appreciated the effect that Haverford had upon me until I graduated. Comparing myself now to who I was when I arrived as a freshman is like looking at two different people. When I was a student, I never took the time to step back and realize what a fantastic experience I was having; I was more concerned with my work, my social life, the here-and-now. It wasn't until I left the comfort zone of college and joined the "real world" that I began to realize what Haverford had done for me. Not only was my brain crammed with more information than I knew what to do with, but I also had picked up a lot of valuable tools. I could write, express myself, carry on an intelligent conversation, and think critically. I found myself more aware of the world around me and how I could affect it. The Honor Code had opened my eyes not only to larger-scale social issues, but also to my interactions with people on an everyday basis. I would say the best thing Haverford did for me was to make me a complete person.

Haverford offers its students an experience that they will carry with them long after graduation. It is also a rare example of a school where the word community can be used without stretching the truth. With only 1,100 students, most of whom know everyone on campus, Haverford is like a small town, and even has Plenary, its own form of the old-fashioned town meeting. This is exactly what some students are looking for, while others find it too stifling. Whatever their perception on the size, most would agree that the best aspect of the Haverford community is the healthy environment, one with intelligent, thoughtful, and respectful people.

And let's not forget education—Haverford offers one of the best around. Top-notch professors challenge the limits of their students, and classes are intimate academic experiences only a small college can offer. Students work hard, but in return are given the best available resources, the opportunity for independent work, and a thorough education. Haverford will forever remain committed to the liberal arts, choosing to produce intelligent, capable people rather than those trained to occupy a niche.

Each year Haverford sends its graduates out into the world, and in the fall, welcomes another batch of freshmen. While the faces are constantly changing, the college remains the same, and so do the values and education it imparts to its students. Trust, respect, and excellence will forever be the cornerstones of the Haverford experience.

❑ *Steve Manning, B.A.*

THE JOHNS HOPKINS UNIVERSITY

The Johns Hopkins University
3400 North Charles Street
Baltimore, MD 21218

(410) 516-8171
Fax: (410) 516-6025

E-mail: gotojhu@jhu.edu
Web site: http://www.jhu.edu/~admis

Enrollment

Full-time ❑ women: 1,479
❑ men: 2,177

INTRODUCING HOPKINS

On moving-in day, my parents and I drove right up onto the quad in front of the freshman dorms and instantly an army of upperclassmen descended upon our minivan and started to unload my belongings and carry them up the three flights of stairs to my room. Before I knew what was going on, another upper-classman grabbed my arm, pulled me out of the car, and introduced me to

President William Brody. The president of The Johns Hopkins University was standing right in front of me. He wasn't wearing a gray suit or carrying a briefcase—he and Mrs. Brody were both wearing helmets, knee pads, and roller blades and looked pretty silly! I giggled when I saw them. He leaned against the minivan trying to get his balance and stuck out his hand and said, "Hi, I'm Bill Brody" and warmly welcomed me to the Homewood campus. He pointed in the direction of their house, which is right on the campus, a two-minute walk from where I was going to be living. And as they took off to greet another of my classmates, I thought—boy, this place is going to be fun!

The Johns Hopkins University prides itself on being the best of all worlds. Usually, high school seniors have to choose between a small liberal arts school and a major research university—or between a rural or urban campus. Hopkins has it all. It is the unique combination of a small liberal arts school with a major research university wrapped around it, set on a 140-acre parklike campus called Homewood, located in the middle of the city—about three miles north of downtown Baltimore.

The Homewood campus is home to the two undergraduate schools of Hopkins, the Krieger School of Arts and Sciences and the Whiting School of Engineering. With only about 3,400 full-time undergraduates and 1,400 full-time graduate students studying at Homewood in four different areas of study—Humanities, Social and Behavioral Sciences, Engineering, and Natural Sciences—Hopkins definitely has a cozy feel. On the other hand, it also has an inescapable BIGNESS of which students can also take advantage. There are seven additional divisions that make up Hopkins: the School of Medicine, the School of Hygiene and Public Health, the School of Nursing, the Paul H. Nitze School of Advanced International Studies (with international centers of study in Bologna, Italy, and Nanjing, China), the Peabody Conservatory of Music, the School of Continuing Studies, and the Applied Physics Lab. Though most undergraduate students will spend most of their time at Homewood, they can easily hop on a free shuttle that will take them to east Baltimore where they can take classes at the School of Hygiene and Public Health or do research at the School of Medicine. Students can also take the shuttle to Peabody where they can take advantage of classes in music theory or private lessons in classical guitar. A 45-minute train ride to the nation's capital, and Hopkins undergraduates are sitting in classes with some of the most renowned scholars in international affairs at the School of Advanced International Studies. Hopkins students have it all at their fingertips.

ADMISSIONS REQUIREMENTS

The Hopkins admissions process is a highly selective one. It naturally competes with many of the Ivies for top high school seniors each year. There was a time when only the top natural science/premed students came to Hopkins, but in recent years outsiders are realizing what Hopkins insiders have known all along. Hopkins has more than a dozen nationally ranked departments in the humanities, social sciences, and engineering. Now, top high school seniors who want to major in English, writing seminars, international studies, and electrical engineering are placing Hopkins as their first choice. The Hopkins admissions process is a unique one because students are not required to apply to a particular school. Students apply to Hopkins and are accepted to *all* of Hopkins, and they don't officially have to decide in which division they would like to enroll until the end of their sophomore year.

Hopkins basically looks at five elements for each applicant. (The following is in order of importance.)

1. Academic Record: Hopkins is a rigorous academic environment. The Admissions Committee wants to make sure that each admitted student can handle the academic rigors. The best indication of that is the high school record, and the most important aspect is the coursework. Challenging coursework (AP and Honors, for example) is an indication to the Admissions Committee of the ability to think independently and creatively.
2. Standardized Test Scores: Yes, those dreaded SATs are required, but they don't count more than your coursework and grades. Test scores help the committee evaluate candidates on a nationally consistent scale. Students can submit either the ACT or the combination of the SAT I and three SAT II: Subject tests (Writing plus two others).
3. Extracurricular Activities: College is not about studying all the time. Hopkins is an active campus with a diverse student body and the Admissions Committee is looking for high school seniors who are going to contribute to campus life. The best indication of that is involvement at the high school level. What's important is commitment, leadership, and creativity.
4. Recommendations: Two recommendations are required, one from an academic teacher and one from a guidance counselor. Supplemental recommendations are also welcome.
5. Essays: Two essays are required. One is fondly called the match question and basically asks why the student and Hopkins would be a good match. The other is one of a choice of four and allows for more creativity.

Diversity

Hopkins doesn't accept or deny applications strictly on the basis of grades or test scores. It is important to the university to form a diverse class of approximately 950 students each year. Diversity on every level is important at Hopkins, not just for the sake of diversity itself, but because diversity richly enhances the intellectual and social experience. Who wants to be at a place where everyone is the same and has similar interests? Not only would that be boring intellectually and socially, but it would also not reflect the real world. The Hopkins student population has historically been dominated by men; women joined the student body only in 1973. However, in recent years, the university has made considerable strides in this area. In the past year, the Kreiger School of Arts and Sciences has enrolled a higher percentage of women than men, and with 23 percent women, the Whiting School of Engineering has one of the highest percentage of women among engineering schools in this country. The current student body is made up of students from all 50 states and over 30 foreign countries. Ethnically, Hopkins boasts of a 31 percent minority rate (21 percent Asian, 6 percent African American, 3 percent Hispanic, 1 percent American native). Hopkins enrolls students with diverse academic interests (33 percent natural science, 33 percent humanities/social sciences, 33 percent engineering).

ACADEMIC LIFE

INTERSESSION

Intersession is the optional mini-session during the month of January when many students return to campus to pursue coursework, personal development, or just plain fun. It's a relaxed time of year where students participate in all sorts of activities and where the possibilities are endless:

- **Ice-skating at Rash Field (the Inner Harbor's outdoor skating rink)**
- **Taking ballroom dancing lessons**
- **Brushing up on French in a conversation class**
- **Doing an internship at Merrill Lynch in downtown Baltimore**
- **Traveling to Egypt with Professor Betsy Bryan on an archeological dig**

Discovery Learning

Hopkins was founded in 1876 as the first American research university modeled after the German type. The institution was founded on the idea that education should be more than just the transmission of knowledge; it should be the discovery of new knowledge, information, and ideas. This philosophy of education is still at the heart of Hopkins. Every faculty member and student at Hopkins is constantly striving to push the frontiers of knowledge. This type of discovery learning does not take place only in the fields of sciences and engineering that most people associate with research; at Hopkins there is fascinating and cutting-edge research taking place across all disciplines from anthropology and English to biomedical engineering and neuroscience.

Premed and Other Majors

Hopkins will always be known for its world-renowned premedical education. The natural science departments are without a doubt tops when it comes to professors, research, and state-of-the-art equipment, but Hopkins also is home to nationally ranked humanities and social science departments. International Studies is the third most popular major on campus and the Hopkins undergraduate program is nationally ranked at number 2. English, art history, Italian, writing seminars, Near Eastern studies, history, and German are all nationally ranked top ten undergraduate programs. Biomedical engineering, a field that was pioneered at Hopkins, continues to be the number 1 undergraduate program in the country. Many of the engineering, humanities, and social science departments are small—but there lies their strength. With strong faculty and resources, students receive individual attention in many of these small departments.

When people would ask me which college I was going to attend and I replied that I had decided to go to Hopkins, they immediately assumed that I wanted to be a doctor. All I knew was that I wasn't sure what I wanted to do. Upon arrival, I discovered that there were lots of premeds, but there were also plenty of writers, political scientists, psychologists and others who didn't know yet what they wanted to major in. In the end, I ended up majoring in art history and loved every minute of it. I never felt that I was a second-class citizen because I wasn't a premed, but since the department was small, I felt I was a part of a close-knit community. I knew every one of the professors in the department.

Research and Creative Scholarship Opportunities

Research and creative scholarship opportunities for undergraduates abound at Hopkins. There is no formal program set up for students to do research nor is there any requirement but the great majority of Hopkins students take advantage of research to enhance their classroom experience. Being involved in an attempt to find a cure for AIDS, building human prosthetics, discovering new information about eighteenth-century authors, or producing your own independent film are commonplace experiences at Hopkins.

I got involved in research my freshman year. I hadn't declared a major yet and was still exploring various options. When my sociology professor mentioned her research on the effects of media during her class, I was fascinated by the subject and ended up talking with her after class for 20 minutes; she invited me to become part of her research team right then and there. I didn't realize until a month later that I was working side by side with one of the world's foremost scholars. A year later, our findings were published in a national journal. I was published before I turned 20 years old!

Class Size

Hopkins is unlike many other major research universities where classes are extremely large and impersonal and taught by teaching assistants. This is where the smallness of Hopkins has many advantages. Over 85 percent of Hopkins classes have fewer than 50 students, and over two-thirds enroll under 20 students. Close to 98 percent of classes are taught by a professor and not a teaching assistant. Hopkins isn't a place where the professors are interested only in their research and not teaching undergraduates. Every professor teaches at least one undergraduate course a year, which encourages faculty-student interaction and collaboration.

My largest class in four years at Hopkins was about 100 students and that was during my freshman year. After the introductory classes, I didn't have a class with more than 50 students enrolled in it. My senior year I didn't have one class with more than 15 students enrolled and one of my classes had only three students. Sometimes I was the only one who showed up for class and the professor and I would end up discussing the readings over coffee and bagels.

Academic Curriculum

Hopkins' academic curriculum is extremely flexible. Students have the power to shape their education into what they want it to be. There are no university-wide core requirements—what many other colleges call a core curriculum—with the exception of a four-course writing requirement. Hopkins believes in giving students the flexibility and power to create individual programs to meet individual goals. It encourages exploration and interdisciplinary work. Each major has its own departmental and distribution requirements that students fulfill in order to graduate. Because of the lack of a core curriculum, students can easily minor or double major and over two-thirds of students at Hopkins do. Hopkins students are also very creative when it comes to preprofessional programs. At Hopkins, you don't have to be a biology major to be premed or a political science major to be prelaw; the Homewood campus is filled with English majors who are premed, mechanical engineers who are prelaw, and chemistry majors who are prebusiness. Students are not limited to taking classes in either the Kreiger School of Arts and Sciences or the Whiting School of Engineering. Anyone can easily take classes in either school and students have even been known to double major in an engineering field and an arts and sciences department or switch schools completely. At Hopkins, there are hardly any rules or restrictions on forming an academic program.

Satisfactory/Unsatisfactory

All Hopkins freshmen take their first semester on a satisfactory/unsatisfactory basis, which most students absolutely love. It allows students to adjust to college life without the pressure of grades and also encourages curricular exploration.

The satisfactory/unsatisfactory semester is great. My freshman year I didn't know what I wanted to major in so I signed up for all sorts of classes, even a philosophy course that I didn't know anything about. I had never taken philosophy in high school because my high school didn't offer any but I always wanted to. I decided to go for it since there was no pressure on my GPA. I ended up loving the class. Who knew? Now, I'm double majoring in philosophy and international studies. The first semester also gave me the chance to learn how to take college-level exams. I'm glad I had a whole semester to learn how to study, take exams, and write papers.

Hopkins' academic climate is often described as competitive. It is indeed a place where academics are stressed and people work hard but the competition is not overwhelming nor is it negative. It's a healthy competitive spirit that pushes students forward rather than down.

The academic spirit at Hopkins is definitely one of independence and where students take initiative. This is not a place for students who need hand-holding or spoon-feeding for four years. Professors expect you to be an adult and they treat you like one. No professor is going to knock on students' doors asking for a research assistant but if students go knocking on doors and contact professors, the possibilities are endless. Hopkins students don't just dream about discovering cures for diseases or coming up with new economic theories; they actually do.

SOCIAL LIFE AND ACTIVITIES

Hopkins students don't do anything without intensity, whether it's work or play. The Hopkins social scene is as diverse as its student body. There are students who love staying on campus; there are others who venture downtown every chance they get. Some love the Blue Jays and never miss a men's lacrosse home game and there are others who don't even understand the game. Each Hopkins student finds a niche and makes a mark there.

Residences

During the first two years, social activities revolve around the campus to a large degree. Freshmen and sophomores are required to live on campus in either suite-style or traditional hallway-style residence halls. Strong friendships are usually formed during this first year of living, eating, and going places together. During the junior and senior year, about 25 percent of upperclassmen live in university-owned apartments that are located right off campus. All of the university apartments have been recently renovated and are very popular among juniors and seniors. There is typically a competitive lottery process to get into one of these apartments. The other 75 percent choose to live in commercially owned apartments or row houses in the surrounding neighborhood. Affordable and safe housing is readily available around campus.

Student Groups

There are more than 170 student groups on the Homewood campus—an extensive list that continues to grow and is limited only by the imagination and drive of the students. The list of clubs is extremely diverse and includes seven different *a cappella* singing groups, more than 20 ethnic and religious groups, literary magazines and newspapers, a nationally ranked debate team, and popular men's rugby club. Each of the groups was founded by students and is directed by students.

> *When I first arrived at Hopkins, there was a huge activities fair where all the student groups set up tables and the freshmen walked around to see what kinds of clubs there are to join. I felt overwhelmed. There must have been more than 100 groups—each one seemed more exiting than the next. I knew I wanted to do theater so I signed up for the* Barnstormers, *the main student theater group on campus. But I also found out about the* Buttered Niblets, *an improvisational comedy troupe. I ended up registering for about 30 more clubs before the day was over. I was super busy my first two years with theater, student government, and my other activities. Then in my junior year, a few of my friends and I wanted to start a new club, a volunteer group of Hopkins students that go into Baltimore inner-city schools and teach elementary school children about health and science through theater. We got some funding from the university and named ourselves the* Germbusters. *Now we've got our own table at the student activities fair and are signing up new freshmen who want to join our group.*

Arts and Music

The arts flourish at Hopkins and music is everywhere. The Hopkins Symphony Orchestra is popular and auditions are competitive. Hopkins recently hosted the Collegiate East Coast *a cappella* Competition in Shriver Hall, the largest auditorium on campus. At the Peabody Conservatory, Hopkins students can catch a free performance of the world-renowned Peabody Symphony. Undergraduates at Homewood can also take advantage of classes at the Peabody Conservatory of Music and, by audition and on a space-available basis, can also take private lessons with a Peabody faculty member. Theater, photography, dance, and other forms of performing and visual art also thrive at Hopkins. With the increased involvement in such activities, the Hopkins community is eagerly awaiting the building of a new Student Arts Center. The new facility will house an auditorium, dance studios, music practice rooms, dark rooms, art studios, and student group offices, as well as a cafe where students can meet and relax between classes.

Athletics

More than three-quarters of the student body participate in some sort of athletics at Hopkins, whether it's on the varsity level, club, or intramurals. Intramural sports are popular, with intense competition between freshman dorms and fraternities. On the varsity level, men's lacrosse is definitely the biggest sport on campus, filling the stadium to 10,000 plus for home games. The Hopkins nationally ranked Division I team is a source of intense pride among Hopkins students, faculty, and alumni. The women's lacrosse program will join Division I in 1999. In addition to lacrosse, there are 12 other varsity teams for men and 12 for women that compete at the Division III level. With the increase in athletic participation, everyone on campus is anticipating the renovations of the athletic center and the addition of a new recreational center in the next year.

Fraternities and Sororities

About 30 percent of Hopkins students are members of one of the 13 fraternities or three sororities on campus. Greek life doesn't dominate the social scene as at many other universities but there are plenty of parties on the weekends at various fraternity houses in the neighborhoods surrounding the campus. Hopkins has an open Greek system so students don't have to be Greek to go to fraternity parties and many non-Greek students take advantage of this. More than two-thirds of the student body participates in Greek-sponsored events during their years at Hopkins.

Hot Spots and Social Events

Though some students complain that there is nothing to do on campus, there really is plenty to do. E-Level, the on-campus student pub whose name is a spoof on the four levels of the library (A-Level through D-Level), is a hot spot on campus for live music and sporting events on the large screen TV. The active film society shows movies on campus every weekend and the HOP (Hopkins Organization for Programming) brings comedians, concerts, and special shows to campus on a regular basis. The large grassy area nicknamed "the Beach" is a popular hangout on warm spring nights. The two largest on-campus events of the year are The M.S.E. Symposium and Spring Fair. Both are student-organized and involve hundreds of student volunteers. The Symposium is the longest running student lecture series in the country. Each year, two student cochairs choose a topic of national interest and invite world-renowned speakers to give their insight on that particular topic. Past topics have included First Amendment rights, sexuality and defining Generation X, and religion's role in our society. Past speakers have included the Reverend Jesse Jackson, Phil Donahue,

Archbishop Desmond Tutu, Dr. Ruth, and Tyra Banks. What is so amazing about the Symposium is that it is completely student-run. Two undergraduate students are given a budget of $75,000 and they put a three-week lecture series together that raises awareness and discussion. The biggest and most popular social event of the year is the annual Spring Fair. It is totally student-run and attracts more than 150,000 visitors to the Homewood campus for three days of live entertainment, ethnic foods, crafts, and amusement park rides. The weekend takes tremendous teamwork on the part of 60 student organizers and more than 200 student volunteers.

Off Campus

There are students who desert the Homewood campus on the weekends, preferring other parts of Baltimore to the residential neighborhoods that surround the campus. Downtown Baltimore and the famed Inner Harbor are only about 10 minutes away. Fells Point is also a popular weekend hangout for Hopkins students, with streets lined with bars, clubs, and shops. Camden Yards, home of the Baltimore Orioles, and the recently built stadium for the Baltimore Ravens are both located in downtown. Shuttle buses are available regularly from campus to downtown. Many students complain about the lack of a college-town atmosphere in Baltimore. The university and the city are striving to remedy this with the revitalization of Charles Village, the neighborhood directly east of campus. Several shops and small restaurants have popped up and the Hopkins community is also anticipating a mini mall on the first floor of the Homewood Apartment Building, one of the university-owned apartment buildings located in the heart of Charles Village.

FINANCIAL AID

With the total cost of Hopkins in the $32,000 range, it's understandable that more than 60 percent of the current student body are receiving some sort of financial aid from Hopkins. Hopkins' endowment is among the top 25 in the country at just over 6 million, and it strives to meet the full demonstrated financial need of virtually every admitted student. The great majority of aid offered by Hopkins is need-based; however, there are a growing number of merit-based scholarships being offered each year. Hopkins awards about 25 students with the Beneficial-Hodson Scholarship, worth $17,000 per year and renewable every year as long as the student maintains a 3.0 grade point average. The scholarship is awarded purely on the basis of academic and extracurricular excellence with no regard to financial need. Athletic scholarships are also available for students who participate in Hopkins' Division I sports, including men's and women's lacrosse.

GRADUATES

Hopkins is definitely a place where the students are preprofessionally oriented. Many are certain of what they want to do before they even arrive on campus, having their hearts set on medical school, law school, or an MBA, even before registering for freshman classes. But there are a growing number of students who take advantage of all that Hopkins has to offer and explore various fields of study before deciding on a career path.

PROMINENT GRADS

- Morris Tannenbaum, '49, AT&T President/CEO
- John Astin, '52, Actor/Director/Producer
- Donald Henderson, '60, Scientist
- Madeleine Albright, '63, U.S. Secretary of State
- Bert Roberts, '65, MCI CEO
- Allan Huston, '66, PepsiCo President
- David Schneiderman, '69, '70, *Village Voice* President/Publisher
- Andre Watts, '72, Pianist
- Jody Williams, '84, Nobel Peace Prize (eradication of landmines)
- Marcia Miller, '81, ITC Commissioner
- Lori Esposito Murray, '81, '90, Presidential Special Advisor
- John Cooke, Disney Company Senior VP

About 65 percent of Hopkins students immediately go on to graduate school or to preprofessional programs after graduation; the others go directly into the work force. Approximately 80 percent of Hopkins graduates earn an advanced degree within 10 years of graduation, the highest percentage among Hopkins' peer institutions. Among those who pursue higher degrees, about one-quarter go on to medical school; Hopkins boasts a 75 percent acceptance rate to medical school, one of the highest rates of acceptance among its peer schools. About 15 percent pursue a law degree, applying to and being accepted at top law schools across the country. In recent years, Hopkins had close to 100 percent of applicants accepted to law school. About 10 percent of the graduating class apply to business programs.

Preprofessional Advising

Hopkins pioneered preprofessional advising, a specific advisor (separate from a faculty advisor) who helps students get into the preprofessional programs of their choice. For students who want some work experience after graduation, the Office of Career Development and Planning provides services from résumé-writing workshops and mock interviews to an extensive alumni career network that can put students in touch with alumni in their field or city of interest.

Staying at Hopkins

Some students choose to stay at Hopkins to continue their education. Besides the prestigious medical school, Hopkins also has nationally ranked schools of Hygiene and Public Health and of Nursing. These three academic institutions along with the Johns Hopkins Hospital make up the Johns Hopkins Medical Institutions in east Baltimore. Located in Washington, D.C., the Nitze School of Advanced International Studies (SAIS) is one of the country's foremost schools of international affairs and government. Each year, international studies majors apply for the combined BA/MA program, where students spend three years in Baltimore at the Homewood campus and two years in D.C. at the SAIS campus. The great majority of Arts and Science and Engineering departments offer combinations of bachelor's/master's degrees in four or five years. Many students apply for such programs within individual departments.

There are Hopkins graduates all over the country and world, with large and active alumni chapters in every major metropolitan area from New York to Los Angeles as well as internationally in such cities as London, Seoul, and Tokyo. Graduates can take advantage of an extensive alumni career network and programs like Lunch and Learn, where alumni are paired with a graduating senior who is interested in the alum's field.

SUMMING UP

It seems as though Hopkins will always be known as a school for premeds and lacrosse players and no fun, but Hopkins is actually a place where humanists and scientists alike pursue creative scholarship with passion and intensity. It's not a place where the humanities and social science departments are overlooked by the university because of the world-renowned natural sciences; rather, the Hopkins community knows the strength of the humanities, social sciences, and engineering departments. The rest of the world is slowly discovering that

Hopkins has much more to offer than just stellar premedical studies and cutting-edge medical research.

Students are challenged in every area to develop individual convictions and philosophies. They choose their own courses and are expected to develop their own ideas and thoughts and to express them effectively. Each student's program is different, whatever the major; the focus is on whatever each student chooses to make it. Hopkins students are ready for the world—ready to think independently and creatively.

❑ *Judy Chung, B.A.*

MASSACHUSETTS INSTITUTE OF TECHNOLOGY

Photo by Donna Coveney

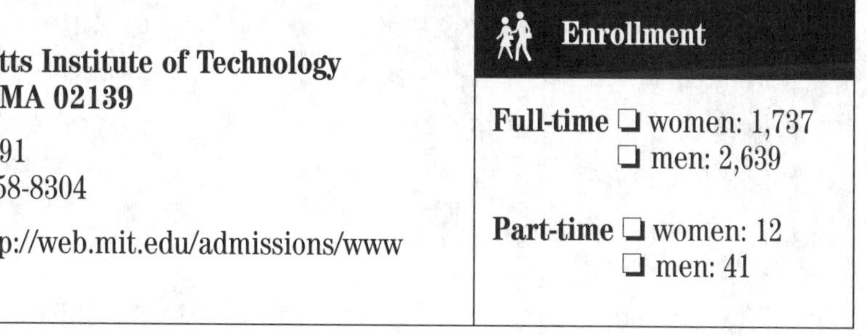

Massachusetts Institute of Technology
Cambridge, MA 02139

(617) 253-4791
Fax: (617) 258-8304

Web site: http://web.mit.edu/admissions/www

Enrollment

Full-time ❑ women: 1,737
❑ men: 2,639

Part-time ❑ women: 12
❑ men: 41

INTRODUCING MIT

The MIT educational experience is like a series of "ah-ha!" revelations that students build into an arsenal for attacking problems—and it will happen to you no matter what you major in. Everyone—this includes philosophy majors as well as physics majors—must take a year of calculus, a year of physics, a term of chemistry and a term of biology. There are other institute-level requirements (such as eight humanities classes and a laboratory course) but it's really the science core that sets a quantitative ability standard for all undergraduates. This standard makes MIT students extremely attractive to graduate schools, professional schools, and potential employers. And it provides for an unusual sense of community—how many other schools can you name where *everyone* is able to solve a reasonably complex kinematics problem?

This doesn't mean that the only people who belong at MIT are mathematicians, physicists, and engineers. Quantitative thinkers don't necessarily manipulate equations for a living, and there's certainly a need for more of them in policy-making positions. John Deutch, an MIT alumnus and professor, lamented the lack of technical literacy in the higher levels of government during his tenure as Director of the CIA:

> *...probably two people in the Cabinet could solve quadratic equations. If you include deputies, you might have four. And three of them will have gone to MIT.*

ADMISSIONS REQUIREMENTS

> *From the time Early Action applications arrive in early November, until Regular Action decisions are made in early March, each admissions staff member will have read close to 950 applications. It seems that most MIT applicants have high standardized test scores and very good grades. Our pool is very self-selecting, so a lot of the applicants are quite similar. We turn down a surprising number of straight-A students.*

The take-home message is that you need to be distinctive. MIT is fortunate enough to be able to pick and choose from a very large pool of academically superior applicants. Distinction comes in many forms; athletes, musicians, chess players, and debaters are all distinctive if they achieve at a high level. Applicants who work on a farm for thirty hours a week and still manage to get straight As are distinctive. Students who have gone out of their way to take college courses or participate in independent research are distinctive. And of course, *extreme* academic talent or achievement is distinctive.

A word about how MIT defines "extreme" for academics—straight As and 800s on your SATs are *not* enough to guarantee admission (more than a third of MIT applicants have at least one 800). MIT is far more likely to admit a student with scores in the 700s, a few Bs in English classes, and a Westinghouse science fair project that made it into the semifinals. Why? Because the Westinghouse applicant has demonstrated initiative, a passion for learning, and a degree of competence in a very competitive field. That last bit is important. No matter how brilliant you are, if the Admissions Committee can't see your brilliance, then it won't help your application one iota. And the SATs alone are not enough to prove brilliance.

So, if you're truly gifted academically, make sure that the committee has some way of knowing that.

- Take the AHSME (American High School Mathematics Examination).
- Get into an academic competition or science fair at the state (even better, national) level.
- Find a local university professor and get involved in independent research. It helps if you include a letter of recommendation from that professor with your application.
- For those of you who spend a solitary forty hours a week hacking on the internals of some compiler, *please* make sure that you have some way of providing verification of this work in your application.
- Get your independent programming projects supervised by teachers at your high school and then choose these supervisors to write your letters of recommendation.

This touches nicely on another point: how to present yourself in the application. Pick teachers who know you well (preferably, ones who like you) to write your evaluations. Ask them to relate some anecdote that they think captures you as a student. It's very difficult to get a feel for an applicant from a list of adjectives; "intelligent," "motivated," and "curious" all have different meanings, depending on who is using them. A story, on the other hand, provides context for the reader of the application, and has the nice side effect of making you appear more of a living, breathing, human being.

Description of Activities

Also, when you list your extracurricular activities, be very descriptive. The Admissions Committee probably doesn't know a lot of specifics about your high school, so if you write that you are the president of the National Honor Society, the reader doesn't know if there are five people in the NHS or 500. Detail is good. Detail is also important in writing your application essays. Expounding on some formative event in your life is a reasonable start, but remember that you're not just telling a story—you're trying to convince the reader why you belong at MIT more than 7,000 other students. MIT allows you to make up your own essay question, so take advantage of this to show off your creativity. If you choose to take a humorous route, be witty, not just funny. Above all, try to display some element of intellectual curiosity in your writing. Speak to the reader.

The Interview

As for the interview, it can be a mixed bag. In most cases, the interview lasts for about an hour and consists of fairly low-stress questions. The questions will probably be reasonably vague (as in, "Why do you want to go to MIT?"), so it helps to think about these types of questions in advance. You should also come up with a set of meaningful questions to ask, something beyond "How good is the food?" because it will indicate to the interviewer that you're serious about your decision to apply. Questions turn the interview into a two-way conversation, which will help to make it less stressful. In reality, a negative interview report is unlikely to hurt your application very much, but a good interview can give you an extra edge in gaining admission.

Highlights

There are a few more highlights you should probably know about the MIT admissions process.

- Of the 8,500 applications received in a year, 1,800 students are admitted, so competition is tough.
- MIT is Early Action, not Early Decision (if you're admitted early, you don't have to enroll).
- MIT admissions are need-blind, so the admissions staff has no idea how much your parents make or whether you're applying for financial aid.
- MIT has an affirmative-action policy, so all qualified underrepresented minorities who apply are admitted.
- Finally, international applicants go through a more competitive admissions process.

All of this factual information, plus a lot of other detail, can be found in the MIT admissions literature.

ACADEMIC LIFE

First, a general overview. MIT is divided into five schools: Architecture, Engineering, Humanities, Management, and Science. Within those schools there are sixteen academic departments (such as Brain and Cognitive Science, Electrical Engineering, Computer Science, Mathematics). Most departments offer several majors, all of which are variations on a theme. Students aren't expected to declare a major until the end of their freshman year, so you don't need to apply to a particular school or department as an undergraduate; when you're admitted to MIT, you're admitted to all of MIT. Here's one student's perspective on the importance of this:

It didn't really occur to me that the lack of administrative hassle would turn out to be such a vital thing. I switched majors twice: from architecture to biology and from biology to chemistry, and each time all I needed to do was get a signature from my advisor. I was horrified to hear stories from friends at other colleges who needed to write a long petition to switch majors, or go through a mini-admissions process to get into another department. If I had been asked to choose a major straight out of high school, it would have been a random choice, at best.

This lack of bureaucracy pervades MIT's entire approach to education. With the exception of a few humanities courses, students never have to deal with being lotteried out of oversubscribed classes. You can add a class as late as five weeks into the term and drop a class as late as five weeks before the end of the term. After freshman year, there are no limits on the number of classes you can take per term or the number of majors you can declare, as long as your advisor approves the decision (which is a rubber-stamp process for students who are performing well). Many students double major at MIT, and a few manage to quadruple major in four years. Undergraduates can also register for graduate-level classes, which offer a very different type of educational experience: most graduate courses meet in a small room with very few students and one professor. The topics in these courses are usually closely related to the professor's current area of research, and the class feels more like a discussion than a lecture.

Classes

As for the undergraduate classes, there's a lot of variation in the presentation format. Most of the freshman science core courses consist of three lectures and two recitation sections per week. Lectures for these courses have between 200 and 300 students, but recitations are limited to about twenty students per instructor, giving a lot of opportunity for individualized instruction. Departments also offer variants on the basic core courses, so while the standard freshman calculus class has the format described above, the theoretical version of freshman calculus has far fewer students in its lectures. In addition to the other flavors of the science core classes, MIT has different versions of the freshman year program itself. Concourse, the Experimental Studies Group (ESG), and the Integrated Studies Program (ISP) all offer alternative, innovative approaches to teaching the freshman curriculum. These programs are limited in size (between forty and sixty students in each) and are first-come, first-served, so if you're interested in learning more about them, do your research before showing up on campus.

Credit

The institute gives Advanced Placement credit for some classes if you score well enough on your AP exams, and in many cases will accept transfer credit from another college. Advanced standing exams are also offered by MIT, and if you pass them you receive credit. More than three-quarters of MIT's enrolling freshmen receive some sort of advanced credit, but no matter how much credit you have, MIT does not offer sophomore standing to first-term freshmen (although second-term sophomore standing is offered).

Grading

There is a limit on the number of classes freshmen can take and there is one other major difference between the freshman year and the remainder of the MIT undergraduate experience: Pass/No Record. This refers to the grading system used for freshmen. If you earn an A, B or C in a course, it appears as a P on your transcript. Ds and Fs do not appear on the external transcript at all—it will simply look as though you had never even registered for the course. There are two reasons why MIT has this system of grading: to level the playing field for students from different high school backgrounds, and to allow students to explore a little (academically or otherwise) without fear of receiving a bad grade.

Many prospective students want to know if the freshman year is difficult. "Different" would be a better word. Generally speaking, if you're bright enough to be admitted to MIT, you're more than bright enough to handle the material. For students with advanced high school preparation, most of the core classes will feel like accelerated versions of the material in high school with slightly more complicated homework, longer tests, and some interesting stories thrown into the lecture. If you're truly bored with the standard fare, try one of the theoretical versions of calculus or physics; even the brightest, most academically prepared students find these courses to be quite challenging.

Seeking Help

Students with less rigorous background training might have more of a shock; if you've never seen a vector before, freshman physics might appear somewhat alien to you at first. Here's a hint: If you don't understand something after fifteen minutes, ask someone. More often than not, it will take a knowledgeable person five minutes to explain something that could take you hours to extract from a book. MIT does offer one-on-one tutors for the science core classes, but it's usually easier to grab the first available upperclassman for help. In fact, upperclassmen often look for freshmen working on problem sets. That may sound bizarre, but there are a few reasons for this apparent selflessness:

- All upperclassmen have taken the core courses, so they are familiar with the material.
- There's no freshman dormitory, so upperclassmen and freshmen occupy the same living space.
- Realistically, all MIT students are a touch egotistical at heart; they enjoy being able to demonstrate their knowledge.

So even though they're not necessarily altruists, the upperclassmen are a fantastic resource for the freshman class.

After freshman year, it's difficult to make sweeping claims about academic life. What people choose as a major drastically affects their experience. Generally speaking, the classes become much smaller and more specialized. Engineering courses, design courses, and laboratory courses will be very different from anything you're likely to have seen in high school. They'll be more time consuming as well (some classes are notorious for this). One student had the following comment:

> *I had never touched a computer before coming to MIT, so the first time I took a programming class, I had a lot to learn: how to use a text editor, how to move files around—some really basic stuff. Many of the other students in the class had been programming for years, which was sort of intimidating, and on the first problem set, I spent all night (from 5:00 P.M. to 8:00 A.M.) in front of a computer and accomplished literally nothing. I was going to drop the class, but a friend offered to come in and show me the essentials, so I took her up on the offer. We spent about four hours working, and it was enough to give me an overview of what I needed to do. I stayed with the course, and ended up earning an A in it. Looking back, it's hard for me to imagine why I thought it was so complicated at first, but I guess that's because I actually learned something.*

Programming

MIT classes tend to be heavier on the theory side than many people expect. This is the reason why a person with no programming experience can do as well as, if not better than, a veteran coder in the same class. MIT is one of the few places where students can major in computer science without being required to learn C or Java or any other programming language in popular use. Instead, they learn Scheme and CLU and languages that few people outside of academia have ever heard of. But all of these languages are chosen with a purpose: They are ideal for teaching good engineering principles and good design techniques. So MIT students find that when they go to learn a more common language it takes them very little time to do so because they are able to easily apply the fundamental ideas they've learned to a specific case. As a result, when technology changes, MIT graduates are able to adapt with it. This phenomenon isn't specific to computer science; the same holds true across all MIT disciplines.

Engineering Contest and Other Projects

Some MIT courses are so different, they're famous. One of the mechanical engineering design classes requires students to build a small robot, which they ultimately operate against other robots in a huge contest. This is a cult experience at MIT; many of the people who take the class are not even mechanical engineering majors! The contest itself is held in a large lecture hall in front of a packed audience, and it's televised for the viewers at home. There's an electrical engineering version of the same contest in which the robots must be equipped with an automatic controller. For one of the architecture design courses, students develop visual projects that they display publicly. So, for a few weeks during the term, sandboxes, statues, performance artists, and thought-provoking signs can be found everywhere on campus.

Nonengineering Classes

MIT is often thought of as primarily a science and engineering school, but in reality it's more of an analytical thinking school. MIT's economics, management, political science, and philosophy programs are all top-notch. In particular, economics and management are always ranked as one of the top three programs in the country. For some reason, math and music go hand-in-hand, so the music department is phenomenal; moreover, MIT students can cross-register for classes at both Harvard and Wellesley, so if you're really dying to take a course in Sanskrit, that's not an adequate reason to avoid MIT.

IAP/UROP

There are two other very unique elements to MIT academics: the Independent Activities Period (IAP) and the Undergraduate Research Opportunities Program (UROP). IAP takes place during January, and it's like a miniature, optional, month-long term. Students can decide for themselves whether they want to be at MIT for those four weeks, but the vast majority of students stay. Some students choose to do a wide variety of one-day seminars and projects, some students take classes (often for credit), and others work. Here's a small sampling of the non-credit activities offered last IAP: the 18th Annual Paper Airplane Contest, Basic Darkroom Techniques, Blackjack 101, Computers and the Human Genome Project, Hebrew Reading Literacy in Eight Hours, Intro to British Politics, Practical NMR Spectroscopy. For-credit classes included: Intro to Special Relativity, Special Problems in Architecture, IAP Japan Workshop (which included a three-week stay in Japan), Intro to Neuroanatomy, Experiencing Health Policy: A Week in D.C., Foreign Currency Exchange, Intensive German. There are hundreds of course offerings during IAP; for a complete listing of last year's activities as well as detailed descriptions of the events, check out <web.mit.edu/afs/athena.mit.edu/activity/i/iap/>.

The majority of students who work during IAP will probably do so through UROP, which is quite arguably one of the best things about MIT. In this program, undergraduate students work on a research project at MIT. UROP isn't limited to a select few, nor are the projects watered-down pedagogical tools. More than eighty percent of all students choose to get a UROP at some point in their undergraduate careers. The projects themselves are ongoing research efforts, so undergraduates work together with professors, graduate students, and "postdocs." With a little motivation, undergraduates can even coauthor research papers with the group, and there's no better way to cultivate a good faculty reference for later use. UROP enables students to interact with professors as colleagues, not just teachers; it also gives undergraduates an excellent sense for what graduate studies in a particular field would be like. On top of all this, students actually get paid for their work in UROP so they don't have to choose between meeting financial need and doing undergraduate research. For a listing of current UROP openings and their descriptions, look at <web.mit.edu/afs/athena.mit.edu/project/urop/www/openings.html>.

The summer after my freshman year, I got a UROP with the Communications Biophysics Group working on a speech aid for deaf-blind people. We built a device that decomposed sound waves into different spectral regions, and then mapped each region to one of twelve buzzers. When you strapped the device on your forearm, you were able to "feel" people talking. The engineering was cool, but working with the deaf-blind test subjects was probably the most interesting part. They had been deaf and blind since birth, yet could speak pretty well and were able to "hear" me talk by placing their hand across my face. Listening to their perceptions of the world was absolutely fascinating.

SOCIAL LIFE AND ACTIVITIES

Housing

The first bizarre thing you'll notice about MIT's social life is the housing situation. There is no assigned housing at MIT; students choose where they live. You also get to choose a roommate if you meet someone who's compatible. When freshmen arrive on campus, they're placed in temporary housing for about a week while they check out the various living options available. There are many to choose from: ten dormitories and over forty Independent Living Groups (ILGs). The dorms differ in both facilities and personality—some dorms are modern and strictly maintained; at others you can paint the walls of your room black. The personality of the dorm tends to match its physical appearance to some extent, and the residents range from quiet to social to well...alternative.

As for the ILGs, there's a lot of variation there, too. Some are affiliated with the Greek system (fraternities and sororities); others are simply groups of students who prefer to live in a more cohesive setting (there are between thirty and forty students in a typical house). Approximately one-third of the students choose to live in an ILG.

The system works, and many students like the idea of choice—loyalty to one's living group is common at MIT. As a result, undergraduates find that the dorms and ILGs are a great support network, academically, socially, and otherwise. Students are guaranteed on-campus housing for all four years; almost all of them decide to remain in their initial living group choice until they graduate.

Athletics

MIT has an amazingly large athletics program—there are about forty varsity teams at the institute. In many of these sports, MIT is quite competitive, even by national standards. Athletics at MIT are accessible; it is not uncommon for a person with no rowing experience to join the crew team as a freshman and then stay with it at the varsity level for four years (the Charles River is literally across the street from MIT). Club and intramural (IM) teams are also very common; at last count there were more than 1,000 IM teams participating in thirty different sports. D-league ice hockey is a great example of the IM spirit. It's hockey for people who don't necessarily know how to skate. The A-league teams, however, are considerably less forgiving.

Student Activities

There are more than 200 student activities at MIT, including cultural groups, student government, journalistic organizations, performance groups, and clubs for people interested in games. Getting involved at the institute is very easy—just ask. MIT students are about as anti-elitist as people can get; they're usually thrilled to find someone else who's interested in what they do. They're also enthusiastic teachers, so even if you know nothing about a particular game or skill, you'll probably be able to find someone who will spend hours showing you the ropes. Free of charge.

MIT students are famous for the elaborate practical jokes that they manage to pull off. Cars, telephone booths, makeshift houses, and plastic cows have all appeared on the tops of MIT buildings at various points throughout MIT history. While many hacks require what seems to be a small miracle of engineering, others are just really good ideas put into action:

One of my all-time favorite hacks was pulled at a football game, but it's not the famous Harvard-Yale inflating balloon prank. Every day for several months before the game, an MIT student would show up at the stadium, blow a whistle, and then throw handfuls of seed onto the field. On the day of the game, right before play started, the MIT student blew the whistle. Hundreds of birds descended onto the field, delaying the start of the game for some time. Of course, in order to start the game they needed to blow a whistle again...

I think that the simplicity of this hack is what appeals to me—the student didn't have to resort to complicated technology to pull this off, just raw cleverness and some birdseed.

FINANCIAL AID

MIT is expensive but the good news is that MIT is committed to meeting the financial need of all admitted students (although sometimes the institute's definition of "need" differs from the definition students' families have). More than half of all undergraduates receive some sort of financial aid.

Packages

Unfortunately, there's no quick formula to give you an estimate of what your financial aid award would be. Evaluations are made by financial aid staff on a case-by-case basis. If you disagree with the amount of aid offered, you can always contact the Financial Aid Office to try and renegotiate, but unless they've missed something egregious, this is unlikely to change your aid package very much. Bottom line: The median loan debt for students in a recent graduating class was $18,150; only ten percent of those students borrowed more than $26,000. Even so, this seems like a staggering amount of money to many people.

You may think that you don't receive as much financial aid from MIT as you would have from other universities. This is not your imagination, and it doesn't mean that MIT cares less than other colleges about whether you enroll, but because MIT is committed to need-blind admissions, financial aid packages are very conservative. Moreover, MIT offers no merit scholarships of any kind—there are no academic, athletic, or music scholarships. MIT will accept outside scholarships, but then deducts fifty percent of the scholarship amount from whatever grant money was awarded to you. At this point, you're probably wondering when this gets better.

It eventually does, but you won't see the improvement until you leave the institute. Here's the upside: MIT graduates are absurdly employable people. Companies need to fight just to get space for a booth at MIT career fairs. The job placement rate, as well as the average starting salary for MIT students, is incredibly high in comparison to other universities; in a recent survey, students graduating with a bachelor's degree reported an average starting salary of well over $40,000. It's probably difficult to believe this when you're faced with the prospect of massive debt, but in all likelihood you won't have any trouble repaying your loans. MIT graduates have the lowest student loan default rate in the country. Read that sentence again.

GRADUATES

Many extraordinarily bright people have attended MIT. The institute has had more than its share of Nobel Laureates, National Medal of Science recipients, and the like. Rattling off a long list of MIT's all-time stars would be interesting but probably wouldn't tell you much about how the average graduate fares.

PROMINENT GRADS

- Richard Feynman, '39, Nobel prize winner
- I.M. Pei, '40, Architect
- Kenneth Olsen, '51, DEC founder
- Sheila Widnall, '61, former Secretary of Air Force
- Shirley Jackson, '68, U.S. Nuclear Regulatory Commission
- Kofi Annan, 72, Citicorp CEO
- Benjamin Netanyahu, '75, Israeli Prime Minister

MIT students have very high acceptance rates into postbaccalaureate programs, and more than fifty percent of graduating seniors choose to go directly to graduate, medical, or law school. Industry and government employers heavily recruit students seeking jobs after graduation. A nice side benefit of MIT is the name recognition—simply saying you're a graduate commands a certain level of respect. Of course, it also sets a pretty high expectation level for your abilities.

MIT prepares its graduates to be more than just cogs in the machine, unless you like being a cog, in which case that's your choice. In 1997, the BankBoston Economics Department prepared a report titled "MIT: The Impact of Innovation." Here's what was reported.

If the companies founded by MIT graduates and faculty formed an independent nation, the revenues produced by the companies would make that nation the twenty-fourth largest economy in the world. The 4,000 MIT-related companies employ 1.1 million people and have annual world sales of $232 billion. That is roughly equal to a gross domestic product of $116 billion, which is a little less than the GDP of South Africa and more than the GDP of Thailand.

MIT graduates excel at whatever they choose to do, primarily because they can often think circles around people with less quantitative backgrounds. While they're here, students may complain about the work load, but it's unlikely that you'll ever hear the phrase "I regret getting an MIT degree."

SUMMING UP

If you're still trying to figure out whether MIT is the place for you, consider the following two questions: Does "fuzzy thinking" bother you? Do you want to learn how to critically assess problems in whatever discipline interests you (whether it's mechanical engineering or political science)? If you can answer both with an enthusiastic "Yes!" then there's no better place for you academically than MIT.

❑ *Stacy McGeever, B.S.*

MIDDLEBURY COLLEGE

Photo by John McKeith

Middlebury College
Middlebury, VT 05753

(802) 443-3000
Fax: (802) 443-2052

E-mail: amit@panther.middlebury.edu
Web site: http://www.middlebury.edu

Enrollment

Full-time ❑ women: 1,076
❑ men: 1,021

Part-time ❑ women: 32
❑ men: 19

INTRODUCING MIDDLEBURY

As it prepares to celebrate its 200th anniversary in the year 2000, Middlebury, one the nation's best small liberal arts colleges, is positioning itself to become *the* best. Already secure in a growing international reputation, with Middlebury Schools Abroad in Florence, Madrid, Mainz, Moscow, and Paris, Middlebury has set its sights on being "the college of the future, the college of choice" for students who want to compete in the global economy of the twenty-first century.

Middlebury's president, John M. McCardell, Jr., who came to the campus in the mid-1970s as a young professor of American history, has inspired two decades of students with two favorite phrases that perhaps best reflect Middlebury's challenge: "*Be bold!*" but also remember that "*One is not entitled to praise, nor to condemn, until one first understands.*"

Students who enter over the next few years will ride a wave. For its bicentennial, Middlebury has embarked on the most ambitious fund-raising campaign in its history: seeking to raise $200 million by 2000. Construction of Bicentennial Hall, a new interdisciplinary, state-of-the-art, high-technology science center, began in 1997. The college library, with more than one million items, is slated for renovation and expansion, and its athletics master plan will be brought closer toward completion. Significant investments in the academic program, including the hiring of more faculty, will continue, and the college remains committed to a need-blind admissions policy.

Education is an experience broadly defined, and Middlebury is committed to an ideal for residential life in which every encounter is an education. In 1993 the college decided to increase the student body gradually from 2,000 to 2,350, and recently it unveiled a new commons plan, which envisions, among other things, decentralized dining facilities. The plan still is subject to refinement. Students who enter Middlebury over the next few years will live in a community undergoing dynamic, positive change, but the college's small, close-knit character can be expected to remain an essential part of its academic and residential life.

Competition with Other Schools

Middlebury often is considered to be in competition with Williams and Amherst Colleges, but most Midd students see their choice, and themselves, as different from those schools. They consider Middlebury special and unique, and reflect a deep sense of community pride. Bowdoin College, which ties with Middlebury in *U.S. News & World Report* rankings, views Middlebury as a principal competitor, but in Middlebury minds, Bowdoin often seems more like an afterthought.

Academically, the school that Middlebury would most like to beat is Princeton. There is also Dartmouth, but some prospective applicants may consider the Dartmouth community too elitist or politically conservative. Swarthmore and Brown University also compete for Middlebury applicants (indeed, Middlebury and Swarthmore maintain a student exchange program), but their more urban/suburban environments make them different in their own right.

Geography

What makes Middlebury unique? In large part, geography. Vistas from the 350-acre main campus, particularly the Adirondack Mountains to the west, are spectacularly beautiful, and at times genuinely breathtaking. Located on the edge of the Green Mountains, the college also is not far from Lake Champlain, where students can learn to sail for physical education credit or ply the waters in a thirty-two-foot research vessel, conducting biological surveys. Middlebury also has an 1,800-acre mountain campus where it runs its own ski area, the Snow Bowl, the Bread Loaf School of English, and the Bread Loaf Writer's Conference meet each summer.

> *Vermont attracts a certain kind of person. Midd kids are thought to be more independent than their counterparts at other schools. Academic pressure is high, but Midd students compete more against* themselves, *striving to achieve personal bests, rather than against each other. They respect each other's individual strengths and talents, and support each other's endeavors. A close sense of community and mutual respect distinguishes them, cutting across academic, athletic, political or social differences.*

Middlebury's small, rural character, Vermont's topography and climate, and the relative remoteness of northern New England are factors that applicants clearly should weigh, both positively and negatively, in considering the school, but the negatives should not be exaggerated. Middlebury exists as a self-contained microcosm and laboratory, but still enjoys relatively easy access to several metropolitan areas. By car, Montreal is two and a half hours away, Boston, four hours, and New York City, five hours. Burlington, Vermont, is forty-five minutes away and provides access to airline connections. Middlebury also attracts frequent and prominent visitors from all around the United States and the world. In fact, ten percent of Midd students come from more than seventy different countries.

Vermont's geography also provides a metaphor for Middlebury's overall academic profile. Like the Green Mountains themselves, the college takes special pride in five "peaks of excellence," grounded in the bedrock of a traditional liberal arts curriculum. Each peak represents a unique strength:

- environmental studies and awareness
- international studies and perspectives

- language studies
- literary studies
- real world experiences.

This does not mean, however, that only students who want to study Robert Frost, learn Chinese, or save Boston Harbor should apply. Most Midd students select traditional majors, and only fourteen percent actually major in a foreign language. In fact, some students choose *not* to study a foreign language or take any science courses (although one can wonder: "Why *waste* the opportunity?"). No matter what their individualized Middlebury experiences, students graduate with a solid, highly rated academic education that includes strong practical skills and a broad international perspective, along with a sense of adventure, community, and bold horizons, that will serve them well in meeting future challenges.

ADMISSIONS REQUIREMENTS

Just as the Middlebury experience varies for each student, applicants accepted for admission are likely to have unique backgrounds or interests that help to set them apart. The college tries to assemble classes marked by diversity and extraordinary potential. Admission is a highly selective process. The college's prospectus declares that Midd students generally:

> *...take their studies seriously, are intellectually curious, seek creative challenges, are friendly to and supportive of each other, enjoy sports and the outdoors, serve as advocates for many causes, and volunteer their services to the local community.*

Middlebury considers applicants relative to six areas:

- academic ability
- achievement
- community citizenship
- leadership
- character
- other personal qualities.

No one area is decisive, but the overall quality of an applicant's academic record is most important.

Deadlines and Decision Plans

The regular deadline application is December 31. Early Decision I applications must be filed by November 15, Early Decision II Part One by December 15, and Part Two by December 31. Applicants must submit three SAT II: Subject tests, three Advanced Placement (AP) tests, three International Baccalaureate (IB) tests, three scores from any mix of the SAT II, AP, or IB tests in different areas of study, as long as they include one English test and one quantitative test; or the American College Testing (ACT) assessment test. Applicants also generally are expected to have taken advanced or honors level courses in their secondary school program, including four years of English, four years of a foreign language, four years of mathematics or computer science, three or more years of laboratory science, three or more years of history and social science, and some study of art, drama, or music. Middlebury also leaves room for the unconventional. Supplementary materials such as art portfolios (on slides), music tapes, dance or theater videos, or student-produced videotapes are welcome as part of an application.

Geographical Distribution and Minorities

One of Middlebury's caricatures is as a college for northeastern preppie elites, or as one alumnus declared, "A training school for the ruling class." But statistics show a much different reality.

> *Not everyone at Middlebury is blond, blue-eyed, and from Connecticut. Not everybody drives a BMW or a Saab with a ski rack on top, or even owns a car. Those are just the people who stand out. The rest of us are pretty average. You have to look beyond appearances.*

About seventy percent of Middlebury's student body comes from outside New England, representing all fifty states and the District of Columbia, and more than seventy foreign countries. About sixty percent of Midd students have graduated from public high schools.

Twenty percent are students of color, most of whom are from the United States. Minorities are a part of Middlebury's heritage. Alexander Twilight (class of 1823), who became a Vermont educator and state legislator, was the first African American to earn a degree from a U.S. college. During the era of the civil rights movement, the late Ronald H. Brown (class of 1962), who later became the first African American Secretary of Commerce, was the first

African American pledged by a Middlebury fraternity. Brown and a fraternity brother, William David Delahunt (class of 1963), who is now a member of Congress from Massachusetts, also co-chaired John F. Kennedy's 1960 presidential campaign in Vermont.

Need-Blind Admissions Policy

As part of its commitment to diversity, Middlebury maintains a need-blind admissions policy. In any one year, about forty percent of the students receive financial aid. Midd students come from a broad range of socioeconomic backgrounds: from high-income, middle-income, or low-income families, and from big cities, suburbs, small towns, and rural villages.

Legacies

Children, grandchildren, and siblings of Midd alumni also have a slight edge. It is not unusual to find Midd classmates and friends who are the children of former classmates and friends; only about five percent of any class, however, are legacies. A Middlebury education may be a privilege, but it is not the province of a privileged elite, nor a hereditary right.

Middlebury also may be more closely within the reach of exceptional applicants than they might think. Students who have struggled to overcome hardships, disadvantages, disabilities, prejudices, or other challenges in their lives while maintaining faith in the human spirit, or who simply believe they have what it takes in some special way, should not hesitate to apply. Middlebury favors students who demonstrate independence, character, courage, and a sense of adventure.

ACADEMIC LIFE

> *Middlebury pushes me to do what I want to do, to be the best that I can be. Middlebury has always met me halfway while challenging me to rise higher.*

Facilities

Middlebury offers breadth, depth, and flexibility in its curriculum, and its faculty and facilities are considered world class. Alumni envy current students the opportunities the college offers, and wonder whether they themselves, if they could do it over again, still could master the challenge. To name only a few facilities, Middlebury has

- a language center with multimedia workstations, a television studio, and satellite reception of international broadcasts
- a center for the arts with a concert hall, studio theater, dance theater, and art museum
- a computerized cartography laboratory
- a roof-top observatory with a computer-controlled sixteen-inch telescope.

Students also have access to the college computer network from their dormitory rooms.

Terms

Most students take four courses in the fall and spring semesters (thirteen weeks each). During winter term (January) they focus exclusively on a single course, internship, or independent project. Some students also select "J-term" courses with an eye toward maximizing time to ski on nearby slopes. Nonetheless, winter term's work loads (particularly reading lists) usually are rigorous. Moreover, winter term provides an important experimental dimension to the Middlebury experience. Faculty members try out topics and ideas that sometimes are refined and later offered as part of regular semester curricula. Students take greater intellectual risks and explore fields in which they might not be willing (at least initially) to invest a full semester. Internships off campus also provide real world experiences that enable students to try out professional fields, gain specific skills, or apply academic knowledge in practice.

Faculty

One of the best features to Middlebury's academic life is the personal attention students receive from professors. The ratio of students to full-time faculty is eleven to one. Small classes and seminars are common, with about seventy-five percent having less than twenty students. Professors and students come to know each other well (which also means that it's hard to hide if a student isn't prepared or doesn't turn in a paper on time).

Faculty members are teachers first, but also advisors, mentors, and collaborators with students on research. They frequently develop friendships with individual students that extend beyond graduation. Indeed, Middlebury serves as a resource and intellectual home for many alumni throughout their careers. Some return as guest speakers or to help teach winter-term courses; a few even return as members of the faculty.

Degree Requirements

Since the 1970s, Middlebury gradually has increased the number of formal requirements for its A.B. degree. Some were controversial at the time of adoption, but largely reflect patterns of distribution and concentration that students used to select on their own when left to their own devices. In other words, Middlebury's requirements are not onerous or restrictive; instead, they provide a clearer road map by which students structure their education, while retaining a broad degree of individual flexibility and choice.

First and foremost, Midd students must fulfill a distribution requirement by taking courses in seven out of eight academic categories: literature, the arts, philosophical or religious studies, historical studies, physical and life sciences, deductive reasoning and analytical processes, social analysis, and foreign languages. Courses taken to fulfill this requirement also count toward other requirements.

During freshman year, every student also takes a first-year student seminar that involves intensive writing and an interdisciplinary, thematic perspective. By the end of the sophomore year, every student also must take at least one college writing course, which similarly involves an intensive writing component.

Students also must fulfill a cultures and civilizations requirement by taking three different courses—one focusing on the United States, one on Europe, and one on a region of the world other than the United States or Europe. Distribution courses, first-year student seminars, winter-term courses, and courses that count toward a student's major or minors all can be applied toward this requirement.

Majors

By the end of junior year, Midd students need to declare a major out of almost forty academic fields, ranging from American Civilization to Women's Studies. Most of the fields offered reflect a traditional liberal arts curriculum, while others reflect Middlebury's peaks, such as East Asian studies, environmental studies, international politics and economics, or literary studies. The three most popular majors on campus are English, history, and political science.

One of the greatest secrets about Middlebury is its natural sciences, perhaps because they often are overshadowed by the college's language, literary, and international peaks. Nonetheless, the biology, chemistry, geology, and physics departments are superb. A physics textbook authored by Professor Richard Wolfson is one of the standard texts used in colleges across the country. Middlebury also was a pioneer with its environmental sciences curriculum, establishing the first formal major in the field in the United States in 1965, well before Earth Day.

More than forty percent of Midd students pursue double or joint majors. Truly outstanding, creative, and innovative students may design special curricula to be pursued as Independent Scholars under a faculty advisor. Middlebury also recently initiated an international major, in which a few select, focused students study a foreign language and specific courses over three years and two summers at the Vermont campus and one of the Middlebury Schools Abroad.

Study Off Campus

More than fifty percent of each class spend at least one semester off campus, usually in the junior year. Time away is an important dimension of the Middlebury experience. Many attend the Middlebury Schools Abroad: in Florence, Madrid, Mainz, Moscow, Paris, Voronzeh, and Yaroslavl (the latter two sites in Russia serve as an alternative to Moscow). Others enroll in approved programs in Australia, China/Taiwan, Ireland, Japan, Latin America, and the United Kingdom. Some students stay closer to home, but study off campus through American University's Washington Semester program, SEA Semester, or a semester at the Marine Biological Laboratory in Woods Hole, Massachusetts, the Williams College Mystic-Seaport program in American Maritime Studies, or exchanges with Berea College in Kentucky, St. Mary's College in Maryland, and Swarthmore College in Pennsylvania. Students who return each semester from such interludes create a special dynamic in the college's academic life. New ideas and energy are injected into classroom discussions, and new enthusiasms fuel campus activities. Students who scale the peaks of international perspectives and real-life experiences ultimately enrich college life overall.

SOCIAL LIFE AND ACTIVITIES

Two myths exist about Middlebury social life: one is that the college's isolation means there is none; the other is that two-thirds of Middlebury graduates marry Middlebury graduates.

Students who want to go to a school where the diversions of Boston, New York City, or San Francisco remain close at hand probably shouldn't look too closely at northern New

England, but that doesn't mean that Middlebury lacks a rich social life or a broad range of activities and entertainment. The key to contentment at Middlebury is for students to make their own social life, especially through extracurricular activities. It also helps to enjoy the outdoors and to like winter sports.

Athletics

Middlebury sometimes is caricatured as Kamp Middlebury or Club Midd because of its truly awesome athletic facilities and the overall Vermont environment. Students who lack athletic dimensions when they arrive at Middlebury will find it difficult to avoid developing them — the college makes it easy. For example, students who don't know how to ski can take ski lessons to fulfill half of their physical education requirement (two courses). Besides the Snow Bowl's alpine trails, the college has fifty acres of wooded ski-touring trails on Bread Loaf Mountain, as well as a lighted cross-country trail near the main campus. There is also an eighteen-hole golf course, an eight-lane all-weather outdoor track, eighty acres of playing fields, a football and lacrosse stadium, a hockey rink, two field houses (basketball, volleyball, badminton, tennis, squash, racquetball, and track), a fitness center, outdoor tennis and platform tennis courts, and a new fifty-meter swimming pool. Vermont's mountains, forests, lakes, streams, and roads also provide opportunities for bicycling, canoeing, hiking, kayaking, rock-climbing, sailing and scuba diving. For many Midd students, the entire state, as well as the campus, is their playground. But don't get the wrong idea—if Midd kids play hard, it's because they also study hard.

Middlebury emphasizes lifetime sports but varsity, club, and intramural team sports also abound. Middlebury participates in the National Collegiate Athletic Association (NCAA) Division III, Eastern College Athletic Conference (ECAC), and New England Small College Athletic Conference (NESCAC).

Residences

Most Midd students (ninety-seven percent) live on campus in single-sex or coed residences that house from three to 240 students. Coed social houses replaced fraternities in 1989, and there are no sororities at Middlebury. Five large student dorms are organized into commons, each of which has its own social and cultural events and system of self-governance. If implemented, the new commons plan announced in 1997 will add decentralized dining facilities and other features. The college also offers housing options based on academic or cultural interests. Le Chateau, an impressive eighteenth century French-style residence, is designated by floor for speakers of different foreign languages. Weybridge

House is for those with environmental interests. An African American-Latino Center has residential space for about twenty students.

Men and women often live in close proximity and, in some cases, on a *de facto* basis (in other words, not by college policy); even bathrooms are coed. Overall, the social environment is informal, but respectful. Weekend social house parties attract large crowds, but small parties also occur. As is the case at most schools, alcohol, drugs, and sex also are factors. Some students may put themselves at risk or create community problems, but for the most part, Middlebury students take themselves and their responsibilities seriously. It is *not* a party school.

Middlebury gives students the opportunity to study together, eat together, work out together. You see people at their best and worst. How they handle exams or stress gives you a pretty good idea of how they handle life itself.

Clubs and Events

Most student activities are campus-centered. In a single academic year, Middlebury estimates that 500 club meetings, 400 films, 350 special lectures or symposia, 125 videos, 100 professional or student concert or dance performances, 90 dances and parties, 20 theater productions, 20 poetry and fiction readings, and 10 gallery exhibitions occur. There are almost 100 different student social organizations, including a weekly student newspaper, *The Campus*, WRMC-FM radio, and the Middlebury Mountain Club. Overall, they generate a rich, diverse, social and cultural life, and many opportunities for leadership.

I am a member of both a women's group and a social house, which at Middlebury is not an oxymoron. Come to Middlebury and you'll be someone. If you go to Stanford or Yale, you'll be just a face in the crowd.

Even during winter, it's hard to get bored. Middlebury's biggest social event of the year is Winter Carnival in February, which includes intercollegiate ski races, ice sculptures, a nightclub, a ball, and a big name concert.

FINANCIAL AID

All Middlebury financial aid is need-based. There are no merit, academic, or athletic scholarships. Each year, between thirty-six and forty-seven percent of the students receive some level of assistance for an overall average of forty percent; the variation reflects the fact that in some years the college overspends its financial aid budget because of the commitment it makes to students through its need-blind admissions policy. The comprehensive fee also represents only two-thirds of the cost of each student's education, including tuition, room, and board. The remaining third is a hidden scholarship to each student, and comes from the college's endowment and annual alumni gifts.

Based on a student's financial aid application, Middlebury first calculates a family contribution, then determines a grant to the student, in combination with a self-help requirement. Self-help may include taking out a subsidized student loan or working at a campus job. The recent average family contribution ranged from $1,300 to $17,000, and depended on a family's income, size, and the number of children in college at the same time. Under the right circumstances, it therefore is possible for a student with a family income over $100,000 to get financial aid. The recent average grant ranged from $7,500 to $24,000. In addition to the comprehensive fee, students also should budget $2,000 for books, supplies, and personal expenses, plus travel to and from campus.

GRADUATES

Middlebury alumni remain bonded to the college by a sense of home and family that endures long after graduation. As a result, every Middlebury student has an extended family that stretches throughout the world. The college also is aggressive in establishing networks and opportunities to help recent graduates (or those shifting in midlife) to find and get started on their career paths.

Many Midd students find that issues or themes encountered in their coursework resonate throughout their professional careers. Each student's academic work at Middlebury provides a long-term, but flexible career foundation. In a rapidly changing global economy, Middlebury's goal is to prepare its graduates "not just for the first job, but the fifth, sixth, and seventh job as well."

The Career Services Office is driven by a desire to provide excellent customer service for both students and alumni. That includes staying ahead of the curve with the latest in technology and job information. As society and the economy keep changing, student and alumni needs will change. Our job is to be here always for them.

Middlebury's Office of Career Services helps students to assess their personal aptitudes and goals, write résumés, and prepare for interviews. It also brings alumni speakers and employers to campus, and regularly cosponsors recruiting programs in Boston, New York, and Washington, D.C. Middlebury's extensive alumni database also offers students contacts in more than sixty career fields, including the arts, business, education, government, journalism, law, medicine, publishing, sports, and television and film. About sixty percent of Midd alumni eventually go to graduate or professional schools, and over ninety percent say they are satisfied or very satisfied with their Middlebury experience.

Middlebury alumni include a respectable share of big names. What is perhaps more characteristic, however, are the number of Midd alumni with relatively low profiles, who nonetheless contribute in important ways to their professions and communities. Middlebury produces citizens first, celebrities last. Success is measured not necessarily by career, fame, or wealth, but rather a sense of self-worth. Just as Midd students tend to be independent and laid back, Midd alumni are relatively self-assured and low key. They try to maintain well-balanced lives, and in their career paths, they are prone to experiment and to take risks, and are guided by conscience and community service.

PROMINENT GRADS

- **The Honorable Robert Stafford, '35, Retired U.S. Senator**
- **William David Delahunt, '63, U.S. Representative**
- **Donald M. Ellman, Jr., '67, President/Publisher, *Sports Illustrated***
- **Charles Moffet, '67, Art Historian**
- **Frank Pallone, Jr., '73, U.S. Representative**
- **Michael L. Tolkin, '74, Screenwriter, Novelist**
- **Frank W. Sesno, '77, Bureau Chief and Vice President, CNN**
- **Edie Magnus, '79, Television Reporter**
- **Kevin Kelleher, '80, CFO, Sony Music, Inc.**
- **Mary Polk Gitlin, '81, Movie Producer**
- **John Tinker, '81, Movie Producer**
- **Juliet Lambert, '86, Singer/Actress**
- **Ann Battelle, '89, Olympic Skier**

SUMMING UP

Middlebury is poised to become the nation's "college of the future, the college of choice" for the twenty-first century. Even if it falls short of that goal, it still offers one of the best liberal arts educations in the nation. The college is also committed to a need-blind admissions policy, and offers financial aid to about forty percent of its students. Don't worry about the price tag until you first know whether or not you actually can get in.

Middlebury chooses applicants with solid academic records, but who also demonstrate ambition, independence, character, and a sense of adventure. The college seeks broad geographic, socioeconomic, and cultural diversity.

Vermont's geography determines much of the college's character and educational opportunities. Students who get the most out of the Middlebury experience tend to be athletic, enjoy the outdoors, and like (or at least tolerate) winter, snow, and ice. The college's overall environment is breathtakingly beautiful, scenic, and idyllic.

Middlebury's academic peaks of excellence are environmental studies and awareness, international studies and perspective, language studies, literary studies, and real world experiences, grounded in the bedrock of a traditional liberal arts curriculum. The three most popular majors are English, history, and political science. Middlebury's science departments also are superb and probably its best-kept secret. Only fourteen percent of Midd students actually major in a foreign language; half of each class spends at least one semester off campus—many study at Middlebury's Schools Abroad and others in programs such as the Washington and Woods Hole semesters.

Middlebury seeks to produce graduates who are informed citizens, independent thinkers, committed to service, with the courage to follow their convictions. Alumni tend to be citizens first, celebrities last. Self-assured, they seek well-balanced lives and in many cases are family-oriented. Their pride in Middlebury runs deep. Most of them think it was an absolutely terrific place to go to school.

❑ *Robert J. Carolla, A.B.*

NEW COLLEGE OF THE UNIVERSITY OF SOUTH FLORIDA

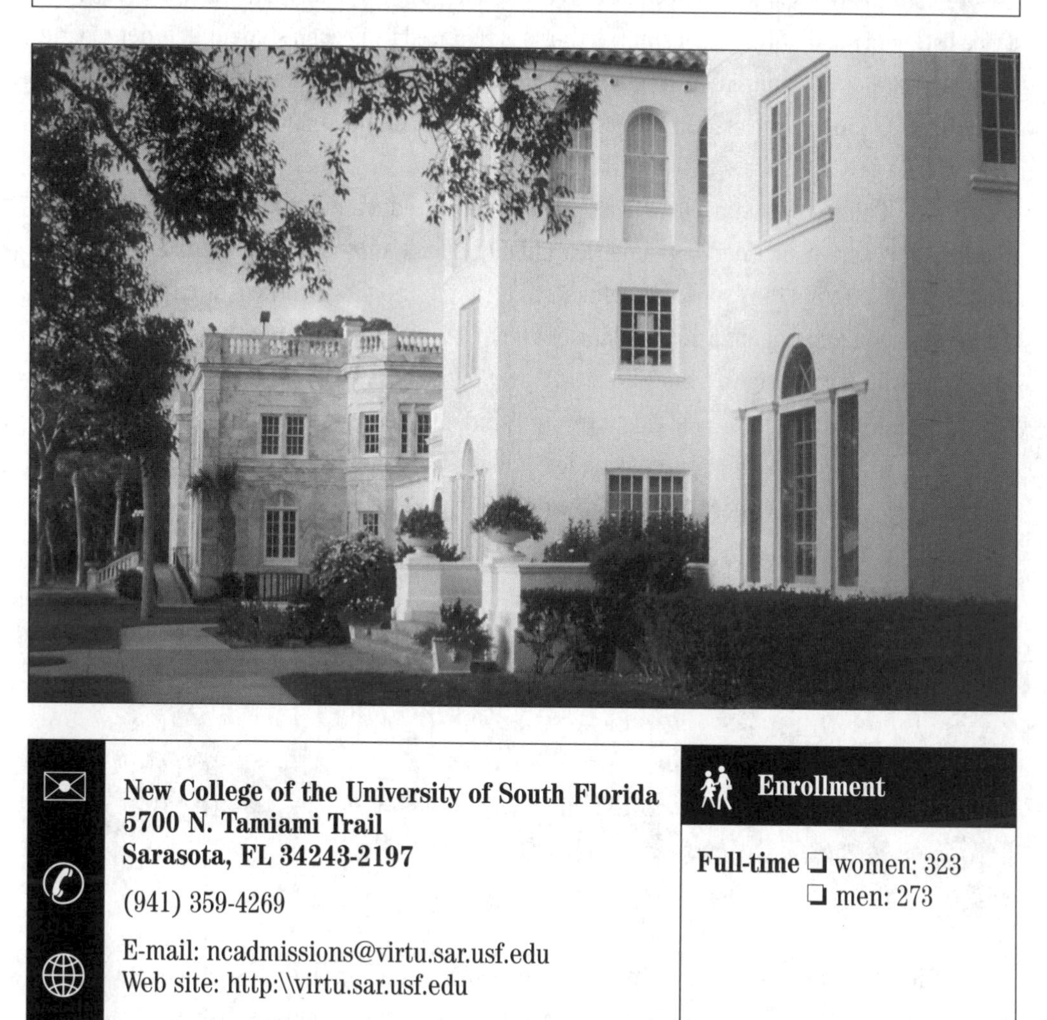

New College of the University of South Florida
5700 N. Tamiami Trail
Sarasota, FL 34243-2197

(941) 359-4269

E-mail: ncadmissions@virtu.sar.usf.edu
Web site: http:\\virtu.sar.usf.edu

Enrollment

Full-time ❑ women: 323
❑ men: 273

INTRODUCING NEW COLLEGE

Most New College students and graduates (novocollegians) have their own version of the answer to the question "New College, what kind of school has that funny name?" They take a deep breath and start with the easiest response that New College is an extremely small liberal arts college in Florida. In fact, it's so small that living on campus can be likened to an experience in communal living. If pressed further, tantalizing details emerge, such as the absence of shoes, the absence of grades, and the fact that it's harder to get in than to get out.

New College students look like they were caught in a time warp from the 1960s—bare feet and tie-dyed shirts are common. Despite the free-wheeling atmosphere, students work very hard. Once listeners find out that a substantial thesis is required from each student in order to graduate they are either impressed or glad they didn't go there. If they are further intrigued, it takes a much longer conversation to fully appreciate the unique education that one receives at New College.

New College was started in 1964 by a group of educators and citizens in Sarasota, Florida, who were concerned that American higher education was losing its focus on the student. Using land from the Charles Ringling estate (of the Ringling Brothers circus fame), complete with a pink marble mansion on Sarasota Bay, New College got its start as a different kind of college with a great view of the water.

Beaches are only a bicycle ride away and students frequent them often. Signs of "beach studying" can be found when purchasing used books from the bookstore—you have to shake the sand out of them. Others prefer to confine their studies to the laboratories and library, retreating to the beach only for rest and relaxation.

After particularly busy days at school, one of my favorite things to do on beautiful warm days was to pick up some Chinese food, get in a car, and race the sun; we wanted to get to the beach before the sun had set. If we were successful, the reward was the most spectacular pink and purple sunset I've ever seen. Then it was back to the books after such a wonderful respite.

One of the most striking differences between New College and most other small liberal arts colleges is the no-grades policy. Students either complete a class satisfactorily, called a "Sat," or fail the class, called an "Unsat." They always receive an extensive written evaluation of their performance from the professor. This narrative evaluation provides some positive reinforcement but also frequently discusses areas in which the student needs improvement. Some professors have said that they consider a Sat to be in the B+ range or higher. To complicate matters even further, students are judged against their own performance, not against some artificial standard. Some overachievers find this uncomfortable, as it's sometimes hard to tell how one is doing compared to one's peers. And, students frequently find out that they can always do better. Students who want to coast through college are in for a rude awakening.

I remember taking an economics course and getting the highest score on the midterm exam. Of course, I was very proud that I had done so well, and went on to perform only reasonably well for the remainder of the semester. I knew that I had done enough to Sat the class. I was expecting a great evaluation, but was I in for a shock! The professor observed that I had cruised through the semester and proceeded to point out all the work that I had done in a mediocre fashion. It turned out to be a painfully honest reminder that I was judged by my own abilities, not by my standing compared to the rest of the class. I was used to getting all As in high school and not having any incentive to strive any further. New College rewarded excellence and achievement in a way that did not have a ceiling.

The individual reigns supreme at New College, which makes for an eclectic and sometimes downright weird student body. In four years at New College, a student will come across people from vastly different backgrounds and experiences. While this may be true for most colleges, the extremely small size of New College keeps students from becoming too cliquey and forces them to interact with others who are not exactly like themselves. It is hard to graduate without having your horizons broadened even a little.

New Facilities

New College has undertaken a building and planning spree that has significantly improved the learning and social environment for the students and faculty. Below are some of the buildings that have been added in the past few years and are planned for the new two years—just in time for entering classes to enjoy.

- The Caples Art Complex. This quadrangle building, built in 1992, has radically changed the working space for the fine arts students. The four parts of the building, centered around a courtyard, contain a performing arts theater, a music wing with offices, classrooms, practice rooms, and an electronic music lab, a painting wing with studio space and office space, and a large sculpture studio with high ceilings and roll-up doors to accommodate the largest of sculptures. Attached to the quad is a new two-dimensional art building with gallery and painting studio.

- New student dormitory. In order to accommodate more students and to keep upper-level students on campus, a new dorm features apartment style living. Private bedrooms are situated around a living room, bathroom, and kitchen. These dorms are meant to be competitive in price with rentals in the area. This new dorm, opening in fall 1998, will house approximately seventy students.
- The ground breaking for a second section of apartment-style dorms will be underway in the near future, with room for another seventy students.
- New natural sciences building. This state-funded complex is one of the most anticipated new construction projects at New College. A new building for marine sciences will contain a teaching auditorium, offices, classroom, and laboratories. This was made possible by a grant from the National Science Foundation matched by private donations. The NSF was impressed with the high quality of student research coming out of New College and wanted to make it even better with new facilities. The ground breaking for this new building will take place in the near future.
- Marine sciences building. Capitalizing on New College's location near Sarasota Bay, a new marine sciences building will be constructed. Saltwater tanks on the bay are planned, to allow students to do research on bay and ocean life. This is scheduled for construction in the next two to three years.

While the location near the beach in sunny Florida and the lack of grades may make New College attractive, it is not for most students. Its unique characteristics bring incredible flexibility to design one's own curriculum. It is not always apparent at first just how difficult this flexibility and personal responsibility can be for those who choose to come to New College. The high degree of autonomy combined with the exacting academic standards proves to be too much for some. The survivors emerge from New College with an unparalleled education and set of experiences unlike any other.

ADMISSIONS REQUIREMENTS

Although New College is a public school, it behaves like its private counterparts. It was expressly created as an honors college for academically talented, intellectually active students (even the Ivies cannot claim that!). Within this context, the admissions process is personal, with no minimums or maximums applied to admit or reject an applicant automatically. Every application receives careful evaluation from the admissions staff. Key criteria are:

- Strength of course selection. This criterion is extremely important, and the applicant's record is examined closely. The GPA is important, but the bottom line is whether the student consistently attempts the *most* challenging classes available. A student who strives to be challenged academically is the type of student who will be successful at New College.
- Ability to write well. The application to New College requires four essays and a graded, analytical paper. To make it through New College you have to be willing to write—and not just a thesis, either. In most courses, even in the natural sciences, students are required to write a lot. For example, a course often will require two major papers plus a final take-home essay exam. Lab courses can involve precision note-taking and academic journal-style reports.
- SAT I, ACT, and GPA. Because New College doesn't offer grades or a CPA, it should not be a surprise that no number will get you an automatic acceptance or rejection at New College. New College, looking, as noted, for academic talent and intellectual drive, recalculates an applicant's GPA, removing noncollege prep courses, and adding points for Advanced Placement, international baccalaureate, and honors courses, for example.

New College has what it calls a "holistic applications process," which means no one element will automatically accept or reject an applicant; however, here are some basic statistics about the New College: fifty-seven percent of a recent class were accepted (615 applied, 353 accepted). Of those admitted fifty-one percent enrolled. These figures suggest that New College applicants tend to self-select, responding to the distinctive nature of the school. Fourteen percent of the freshmen were National Merit Scholars. The average weighted freshman high school GPA was 3.9, and well over half (fifty-eight percent) were in the top twenty percent of their high school class. The average SAT I scores were Verbal—701, Math—644, for a total of 1345. Twenty percent of the class was made up of transfers; as a public honors college, New College has a special commitment to working with the honors programs at the public community (two-year) colleges.

It must be noted that the State University System of Florida has academic requirements for admission into any of its state universities, New College included. New College has no discretion on these requirements. They are four years of English, three years each of social studies, math, and science, and two years of the same foreign language. In addition, the applicant must have enough other academic courses to bring the total semester long courses to nineteen. If applicants are lacking these courses from high school, they are encouraged to remedy this at a community college or junior college before applying.

Because of the unique nature of New College's academic environment and social life, prospective students are strongly encouraged to come to the campus and stay overnight. This option is open to those students who have an application on file; calling two weeks in advance is recommended. Applicants stay with students in the dorms and are encouraged to sit in on any classes that may interest them. It is important to make sure this unique environment is one in which an applicant would want to immerse himself or herself for four or more years.

The application deadline is May 1. For additional information, the admissions director can be reached at ncadmissions@virtu.sar.usf.edu. You can access the new admissions web page through *www.newcollege.usf.edu.* URL application sites include *www.weapply.com* (order free disk containing a New College application).

ACADEMIC LIFE

The academics at New College are ruled by one phrase: "Each student is responsible in the last analysis for his or her own education." Students negotiate their curriculum on a one-on-one basis with a faculty advisor, called a "sponsor," and always a full-time regular faculty member. There are few rules. Some students have been known to design their own courses and pursue independent study instead of taking formally scheduled classes. Accordingly, students must think long and hard about what they want out of college from the moment they set foot on campus. This also puts the burden of success or failure squarely on the students' shoulders. The key relationship in a student's stay at New College is with the faculty advisor, or sponsor. Everything academic flows through and around the sponsor—especially since most academic decisions are complex.

Given New College's student body of under 600, it is not surprising that the academic environment is personal and reachable. The faculty does the teaching, the grading, and the evaluation. As the college adds students, it adds faculty, so that the faculty-student ratio remains relatively constant, at approximately one to eleven. The average class size is eighteen; sixty-three percent of classes have under twenty students. Science labs average twenty students. There are almost 600 individually arranged tutorials per semester. Members of the faculty know each student's work thoroughly. An intimate knowledge of the student's progress is required for the written evaluations that students receive instead of grades.

Concentrations

New College offers the bachelor of arts degree. Majors, which are called areas of concentration, are offered in over twenty liberal arts disciplines: in the humanities, art history, fine arts, classics, French, German, literature, music, philosophy, religion, Russian, and Spanish; in the natural sciences, biology, chemistry, mathematics (minor in computer science is available within math), and physics; in the social sciences, anthropology, economics, history, political science, psychology, and sociology. Interdisciplinary concentrations in environmental studies, gender studies, international studies, Medieval and Renaissance studies, and urban studies are offered. Students can do divisional (humanities, for example) concentrations. They can fashion their own special topics and interdisciplinary concentrations, as well. Each concentration has required coursework that a student must complete in order to graduate.

Requirements for Graduation

To graduate from New College, a student must satisfactorily complete each of the following:

- Seven contracts with the advisor
- Three Independent Study Projects (ISPs) during the month of January
- A substantial year-long thesis project
- An oral defense of his or her thesis in front of a baccalaureate committee

Each semester, the contract with the sponsor is the backbone of the academic life at New College. Its purpose is to list the classes a student will take during the semester, like a registration form, but also to lay out the terms of a satisfactory contract. For example, if a student is taking four classes, the terms of the contract may be that he or she satisfactorily complete three out of the four, two out of the four, or four out of the four—it all depends on what is negotiated with the sponsor. The importance of the contract lies in the fact that if the terms of the contract are not successfully met, one is not any closer to graduation. The classes that a student has Satted (or passed) show up on the transcript, but the student still needs seven satisfactory contracts to graduate.

The ISPs are done during the month of January when there are no classes, and are equivalent to a full semester-long class. The topic is negotiated between the sponsor and the student, and is supposed to be completed before the second semester begins, but they can be incompleted and turned in up to a year later. ISPs allow students to immerse themselves in a topic for a month. They do not have to be done on campus, which provides the flexibility for research projects using other libraries or in other labs.

The thesis is the pinnacle of the academic journey at New College. It is usually done over the entire final year, along with coursework needed for the student's concentration, and generally involves original research or creative work. While many college and universities have a thesis requirement for honors graduation, every New College student does a thesis. The thesis teaches students to grapple with a research problem or creative work in depth over an extended time period. Many theses become the backbone for work later pursued in graduate school.

In conjunction with the sponsor, a thesis student has a baccalaureate committee that gives feedback as the thesis progresses. Most importantly, the committee constitutes the student's oral baccalaureate examining board. Depending on the strength of the thesis, the bac exam can be an exhilarating experience, or one of the longest two hours in a student's career.

After the grilling of the bac exam, I had to step into the hallway while my committee decided my fate. I paced back and forth kicking myself for not bringing up a salient point or for becoming tongue-tied. I felt that I had done a good job and had prepared myself well, but, of course, they found the spots in my thesis that I knew were the weakest and pointed them out. Fortunately, four years of written evaluations taught me to look for the strengths and weaknesses in my work. When I was called back into the room, my heart was pounding but when my sponsor smiled at me, I knew that I had passed. Some students did not pass their bac, which made the experience more than just a rubber stamp of the thesis. I think I let it go to my head because I swore that I walked about two inches above the ground for the next few hours. First year students were used to seeing wild-eyed thesis students come running into the student center to be congratulated. It was a bigger moment for me than graduation.

Once the thesis is approved, it is bound and shelved in a special room in the library.

SOCIAL LIFE AND ACTIVITIES

"Walls"

Nothing else compares to a "wall" in terms of importance to the social life of New College students. This needs a bit of explanation. A wall is a Friday and Saturday night dance party that takes place under the stars in a palm tree-lined court (thus its name "Palm Court.") Its name comes from the low wall around Palm Court on which everyone sits to observe the scene or rest when not dancing. The student government purchased the sound equipment, which generates a fairly loud party that starts late and can last until sunrise. Students check out the equipment and control the music. Very few students ever regularly go to bars around Sarasota, choosing instead to socialize at walls or in student-rented houses and apartments near campus. Thus, graduates may find many traditional university rituals quite foreign, especially sororities and fraternities. These groups are not only nonexistent, they are generally openly ridiculed.

On- and Off-Campus Interests

When not dancing the night away, students find much to do both on campus and off. The outdoor pool with the sand volleyball court next to it gets a lot of use all year. A new fitness center was built that contains indoor facilities for Nautilus equipment, racquetball, aerobics, and dance. For those students who like outdoor activities, the student government purchased sailboats, canoes, sailboards, camping equipment, and scuba equipment for student use. Certification on the sailboats and sailboards is provided at the campus's part of the Sarasota Bay. Scuba lessons are given on campus for a minimal cost, allowing students to use the equipment all around Florida.

Sarasota boasts some of the most beautiful sugar-white beaches in the United States. The sunsets are stunning displays of pink and purple against the blue water. The Long Boat Key and Siesta Key beaches on the Gulf of Mexico are popular destinations for many students, who are always in search of cheap entertainment. In the fall and winter, students compete for towel space with many tourists from Europe and the "snow birds" from the United States. Since Sarasota is the winter home for many retired folks from up north, restaurants and roads become quite clogged from Thanksgiving to Easter.

Few off-campus activities are easily accessible on foot, through mass transit, or by a bicycle. Most students find life difficult without a car, although having friends with a car helps. New College is directly between the centers of both Sarasota and Bradenton, with the beaches between fifteen and thirty minutes away by car.

FINANCIAL AID

New College has the same tuition as other public universities in Florida. This is because, in 1975, the then-independent New College—successful academically but failing financially—made a deal with the state. Under the terms, the Tampa-based public University of South Florida, which needed a Sarasota base to serve local area students, paid New College's debts and, in return, got its campus on Sarasota Bay. Then, if the New College Board of Trustees, newly evolved into a "New College Foundation," each year paid the state the extra cost of providing the New College curriculum, USF would continue New College. The deal worked. New College continues, a highly autonomous college with USF, with its own faculty and student body, its own distinctive curriculum, even its own diploma. New College students and faculty have full access to the vast library resources of a major research university. Students are eligible for many of the university's scholarship programs, such as its grants to National Merit Scholars and to top out-of-state students. The Foundation continues to provide the annual grant that offsets some of the cost of operating New College and, most importantly, provides additional scholarship money. Today, the Foundation scholarships and much of the annual grant come from endowments held on behalf of New College by the New College Foundation.

New College offers the same federal, need-based financial aid programs as do other colleges. The average need-based financial aid package for freshmen in a recent year was $5,996; in-state tuition was $2,387; out-of-state tuition was $9,387.

GRADUATES

New College has an extremely high percent of graduates go on to earn a Ph.D. in the social sciences. After their intense research and extensive writing, and the individual academic program, New College graduates are quite prepared for the rigors of graduate school. In fact, it has been said that writing a master's thesis is easier than writing a thesis at New College. In any case, whether a student decides to go on to graduate school or into the work environment, the academic rigors of New College continually work in the student's favor. Not having grades usually requires some additional explanation, especially in the fill-in-the-blank forms for graduate schools and tests. It is customary for graduates to send copies of their evaluations to prospective employers or graduate schools, which forces a more subjective evaluation of the student's qualifications and potential. Given the stellar successes of New College alums, this process does not hinder them.

The New College alums make up a tight-knit network. There are only a little under 3,000 of them all around the United States and the world, but they support New College's efforts in a large way. Contributions from alums fund a program that defrays some of the cost of research projects. Over $11,000 was recently awarded directly to students, and, in addition, there is a program for faculty development and research. The alums funded a study on the condition of the natural sciences facilities that was the impetus behind the new building. The alumnae/i also sponsor a program of Alumnae/i Fellow visits: distinguished graduates come to campus for up to a semester to offer courses, workshops, and for talks in their fields.

In a recent school year, 122 degrees were awarded. Psychology, literature, and biology are still the most popular areas of concentration with twelve, eleven and nine percent of total grads respectively. If you add environmental studies, technically an interdisciplinary area, to biology, it becomes number one at twelve percent

Graduate School Attendance

The overall rate for graduate school attendance for all classes is fifty-four percent, which includes older grads who attend many years after graduation from New College. As for the recently graduated, many novocollegians have followed the national trend of working a year or two before continuing with graduate school.

Not surprisingly, New College alums include quite a number of entrepreneurs. Surprisingly, for a school with hardly any computer science classes to speak of, many alums work in computer fields, with many owning their own companies. The single employer with the most New College employees (eight) is in Sarasota. It's the second very successful software company built by an alum with a philosophy degree!

PROMINENT GRADS

- **Esther Barrazone, '67, President, Chatham College**
- **John Cranor, '67, President and CEO, Long John Silver Restaurants**
- **Bill Thurston, '67, Director, Mathematical Sciences Research Institute**
- **Lincoln Diaz-Balart, '76, U.S. Congressman**
- **Carol Flint, '78, Television Producer, Scriptwriter**
- **Gregory Dubois-Felsmann, '81, Physicist**
- **Karen Volkman, '90, Poet**

SUMMING UP

It is not surprising that graduating from New College is part of a lifelong, unique experience. The net effect of being constantly challenged on a personal basis is a feeling that one can do anything; however, having made it through four years of a fairly unique experience necessitates constantly having to explain and justify the undergraduate experience. If you want a pedigreed degree, New College is the wrong school for you to attend. Fair or not, many employers classify people on the basis of where they went to school, and use it as a filtering criteria. It is generally not meaningful to hear "I went to New College," versus hearing "I went to Harvard, Brown, Duke, etc." With the latter, the student/graduate is instantly classified as being smart, ambitious, or successful, whether or not it is deserved. New College students must be prepared to constantly prove and reprove themselves in new situations. Given that New College professors are constantly challenging students, this should be a situation with which graduates are quite familiar.

In addition to the challenges of going to a fairly unknown school, attending New College does have some weaknesses and pitfalls. With the small size of New College comes the traditional small school difficulties. There are only a few professors in each discipline, making the course choices rather slim. Pity the poor students whose advisors take a sabbatical the year that a thesis is supposed to be completed. Pity them further if they do not connect well with the other faculty member in that discipline who could sponsor the thesis. While the administration is moving to eliminate the very small disciplines, and add faculty to others, a strong recommendation is that a student plan to take a semester or even a year off campus (including studying abroad) to get the classes that might not be available at New College. This is especially true in the hard and soft sciences, such as economics, where technical, nonliberal arts courses are needed, but not offered at New College. Given that one only technically needs three and one half years of classes to graduate, a semester off campus fits in very well.

Overall, four years at New College will create a lasting way of looking at the world and overcoming challenges. While four years is a short amount of time when compared to the rest of one's life, they come at an influential and formative juncture in a young person's life. No matter how a student chooses to experience college life at New College, his or her outlook will be vastly expanded.

❑ *Ann Burget, B.A.*

NORTHWESTERN UNIVERSITY

Northwestern University
Evanston, IL 60208

(847) 491-7271

E-mail: ug-admission@nwu.edu
Web site: http://www.nwu.edu

Enrollment

Full-time ❑ women: 3,908
❑ men: 3,701

Part-time ❑ women: 12
❑ men: 24

INTRODUCING NORTHWESTERN

Northwestern, a private liberal arts and research university, is two campuses along Chicago's Gold Coast. Most of its graduate programs are located on the downtown campus, while the campus for the six undergraduate schools and the J.L. Kellogg School of Management stretches for almost a mile along Lake Michigan in Evanston, the first suburb north of Chicago. The undergraduate program offers study in the arts and sciences, education and social policy, journalism, music, speech, and engineering and applied science.

My education at Northwestern started before I even entered my first class as a freshman. My new friends and I ventured downtown on Chicago's elevated train, the "el," during New Student Week. We happened upon the Art Institute of Chicago, where a Monet exhibit was on display.

I spent the afternoon drifting from one work of art to another, trying to synthesize everything around me. Eventually, I stood mesmerized, looking at three wall-size murals of Monet's famous Waterlilies. *It was amazing and almost overwhelming that this cultural opportunity was so accessible.*

In time, my years at Northwestern would teach me how to seek out, utilize, and appreciate the many resources and opportunities available to me. Whether it was visiting one of Chicago's housing projects to help develop solutions to urban problems for my sociology class, or reporting at the Chicago Board of Elections alongside a professional reporter during the 1996 presidential election, I was challenged by the faculty of Northwestern to take the strong academic foundation it had laid for me and put it into practice.

The requirements for the six undergraduate schools vary, but all students must take a core of academic classes to complement their majors. Often referred to as the Midwest's alternative to the Ivies, Northwestern prides itself on its strong liberal arts foundation. An English major may grumble at having to take a statistics class, or a voice major may question why she's learning the different types of fungus for a biology class, but students realize that they are receiving a well-rounded education.

Northwestern treads a careful balance between tradition and innovation. Upholding and seeking to strengthen the traditions and high academic standards set by its founders in 1851, Northwestern is continually evolving to equip its students with the skills to succeed in an unprecedented world, where the explosion of communications and technology has opened an unlimited number of resources.

Students amble to their Friday afternoon classes, talking to friends as they walk up the well-worn stairs of Harris and University halls, two of the oldest lecture buildings on campus. Inside, a professor begins his lecture in one of the newly renovated classrooms, dubbed a "smart classroom." Equipped with ceiling projectors, sound systems, computers, VCRs, laser disc players, and slide projectors, these classrooms bring learning to a new level by integrating computer, multimedia, and network technologies.

Real-World Experience

Real-world experience is a core concept at Northwestern. A career development office and multiple placement offices make internship and employment possibilities a reality for students. Some of the schools' programs even include internships as part of their curriculum. Students in the Medill School of Journalism choose from a selection of fifty newspapers, fifteen magazines, and thirteen television stations nationwide in which they are interns during a Teaching Media quarter. The McCormick School of Engineering and Applied Science offers a five-year co-op program where engineering students work with professional engineers and researchers. Each of the six schools also provides students the option to do independent research, participate in field-study programs, or work with a professor.

Northwestern's close proximity to the nation's third largest city provides students with a multitude of educational opportunities. Theater majors are constantly seeing theater productions; art history majors have a wealth of museums to choose from. But enjoying the city does not end at just learning possibilities.

Piling into a cab after seeing the musical Miss Saigon, *my friends and I talked excitedly about the wonderfully choreographed acts and stage sets of the production. As we sped up Lake Shore Drive toward Evanston, I looked to the left to see the city lights of Chicago and then to the right to see the beaches of Lake Michigan. Chicago, a mecca of cultural and entertainment possibilities, definitely was a big factor in my decision to attend Northwestern. Studying so close to a major metropolitan area has only added to my college experience.*

ADMISSIONS REQUIREMENTS

As part of the Student Admission Council, I am privy to the prospective students, or "prospies," as we call them, who walk through the doors of the Admissions Office. The first time I sat on a student-life panel, I was expecting questions about the quality of dorm food and the size of dorm rooms, but instead I was thrown questions about the internship opportunities Northwestern provides students through its placement office and the percentage of students who go on to graduate school after graduating from the university. At first I was surprised by the highly motivated students who were just interested in applying to Northwestern, but now it's something members of the Admissions Office and I have come to expect.

Northwestern's admissions process has always been highly selective but even more so in recent years. The Cinderella story of the Wildcats, Northwestern's football team, catapulted the Purple Pride into living rooms across the country during the 1995 football season. Northwestern went from the underdog of the Big Ten Conference to become the 1995 undisputed Big Ten Champions and went on to play in the 1996 Rose Bowl, their first since 1949.

This additional coverage and recognition has caused a thirty percent increase in applications for admissions. In 1994, 12,918 students applied; in 1997, while other prestige schools experienced a drop or leveling off in applications, Northwestern's went up to 16,700.

Applicants must have completed sixteen units, including four of English, three of math, two or three each of a foreign language and history, and two of sciences. The SAT I or ACT is required. For the class of 2000, the mean combined score was 30 on the ACT and 1363 on the SAT I. SAT II: Subject tests are only required for the accelerated Honors Program in Medical Education (HPME) and in the Integrated Science Program (ISP), but it is a good idea for anyone applying to Northwestern to take them. Auditions are required for the School of Music but not for the School of Speech.

Northwestern does have the option of Early Decision, but be forewarned: the Admissions Office does not make it a practice of deferring its Early Decision applicants into the Regular Decision pool. Admissions standards for the two periods are identical. If Northwestern is your first choice without a doubt, it would make sense to apply early.

While grade point averages and test scores are important to the Admissions Office, a great emphasis is put on students' high school courses, teacher recommendations, and extracurricular activities. Attitudes toward learning and special talents can also be determining factors. And the more personal contact you have with the Admissions Office—such as an interview—the better off you will be.

In a dean's convocation for the Medill School of Journalism during New Student Week, an orientation for incoming freshmen, the assistant dean asked how many students had been the editor of a student publication during high school. Practically everyone raised their hands.

That's what amazed me about Northwestern. Many of my friends were not the valedictorian of their high school class, but they all had some characteristic that made them outstanding students. Be it the editor-in-chief of their school newspaper, the lead coordinator in starting a recycling program during lunch, or an actor in numerous community theater productions, all Northwestern students I have met have been involved with a project that they truly believe in. This self-motivated student body benefits the learning environment; everyone has earned the right to be here and knows the value of this acceptance.

ACADEMIC LIFE

It was the Sunday night before another finals week of fall quarter. The only noises coming from one study room in the university library were a few sighs and the shuffling of papers. Each cubicle and table was crammed with harried students.

And then it came out of nowhere.

At first, it was just a rumble in the distance. Slowly, the noise grew louder and louder. When it reached the students, the once-quiet area was now a place of chaos. They joined in the yelling, trying to relieve the stress of finals. The tension was broken, and while it took a long time for the room to quiet down, everyone felt a little more relaxed. And the freshmen smiled, knowing that they had just experienced their first "Primal Scream," a time-honored Northwestern tradition to start off finals week.

Because of the high standards that professors demand in the classroom, most Northwestern students push themselves to excel. This entails studying two to three hours for each hour spent in class. It is sometimes hard not to get caught up in studying, but events such as the Primal Scream act as leveling factors.

Students rely on each other for support. Study groups are never difficult to form. Competition between students is honestly almost nonexistent; the only competition that occurs is between students and themselves, as they try to better their personal academic records.

Academic Distributions

Each undergraduate school has its own set of academic distributions that students must fulfill. CAS, the College of Arts and Sciences, has the largest student enrollment of the six schools. Besides CAS major requirements, students must take two classes from each of the following areas: natural sciences, formal studies (such as linguistics and statistics), social and behavioral sciences, historical studies, values (such as anthropology, philosophy, and religion), and literature and fine arts. The schools also vary on the amount of classes a student can take P/N (pass/no credit); this option is not available to fulfill requirements for a major.

Accelerated and Combined-Degree Programs

Northwestern offers many accelerated and combined-degree programs. The seven-year Honors Program in Medical Education (HPME) is a big draw for some students. B.A.-B.S. degrees in liberal arts and engineering, liberal arts and music, and music and engineering cater to students' quest to integrate their specialized interests into a concentrated major. A highly selective group of students may participate in the Integrated Science Program (ISP) that follows a curriculum of combining the natural sciences and mathematics in small classes at an accelerated pace. Students may also apply for an interdisciplinary study in Mathematical Methods in the Social Sciences (MMSS) that provides the training to build mathematical models and apply them to the study of the social sciences, such as economics and political science.

Class Size

Classes range from large introductory lectures to small advanced-level discussions. The average class size of an introductory class is thirty-seven, a lab, seventeen, and a regular class offering, thirty. Underclassmen should not be discouraged by the sight of a class of one-hundred students—large lectures are often the most captivating of classes. A favorite is Introduction to Sociology taught by Professor Charles Moskos, who has been an advisor to President Clinton and is a renowned scholar on the sociology of the military. Introduction to Macroeconomics is also popular; few professors can describe the concept of opportunity costs by quoting from the movie *It's a Wonderful Life*, as Mark Witte does.

Typically, larger lecture classes break up into small discussion groups during the week, which makes it possible to work in a more intimate academic environment. And while many professors are working on their own research, they are extremely accessible to their students. Most have posted office hours, and all are willing to set up individual appointments.

Computer Programs

Professors will also often utilize web sites customized for their classes and e-mail to interact with their students. Some classes will use the computer program First Class, which is basically an electronic bulletin board where students can post notes to their fellow classmates.

As a side note, all of campus housing has Ethernet hookups. Northwestern is one of the only institutions to provide a full suite of Internet software customized for each student, including the Netscape's web browser and Eudora Pro e-mail.

SOCIAL LIFE AND ACTIVITIES

It's a Wednesday night, and the yearbook editor-in-chief and I are sitting in our third floor office at Norris University Center, where a number of student groups' offices are located. Down the hallway, I can see members of the College Democrats sprawled out on the lobby couches, throwing out possible ways to contact Secretary of State Madeleine Albright to get her to speak at Northwestern. In the neighboring office I can hear the frenzy of the Daily Northwestern, *which has won numerous Hearst Foundation and Society of Professional Journalists awards for its journalistic endeavors, as the staff tries to put the paper to bed for the night.*

Northwestern has more than 160 activities and organizations that students can join. Being part of some sort of group is important to almost all students. Some view it as a means of promoting their personal cause in the more liberal, accepting environment of academia. Others, particularly those who participate in political or journalistic organizations, see it as a stepping-stone to future career aspirations. Because academics are so rigorous, those who participate in extracurricular activities must plan their time carefully. Ultimately, these activities play a huge role in a Northwestern education.

Service Groups

In recent years, service groups have become more popular on campus. Students volunteer through organizations such as Northwestern Volunteer Network (NVN) and Special Olympics. One rapidly growing organization is Alternative Spring Break (ASB), which gives students the opportunity to do volunteer work in sites across the United States, from working with AIDS patients in San Francisco to planning programs in the world's largest homeless shelter in Washington, D.C. ASB participants help others while learning about a culture they've never been exposed to.

Sports

Northwestern is the only private school in the Big Ten Conference. Seventeen varsity teams compete for championships through the Big Ten and NCAA. In 1997 the newly renovated Ryan Field, which underwent a $20 million facility upgrade, was opened for the Wildcat football season. Northwestern also provides numerous opportunities for students who are looking for a less intensive sports level. From participating in intramural and club sports to working out at SPAC, the state-of-the art sports and aquatic center that boasts an Olympic-sized swimming pool, indoor track, racquetball, squash and basketball courts, and a private beach on Lake Michigan, students have many fitness options.

Student Government

Students can also experience the drama and theatrics of the Associated Student Government (ASG). ASG comprises an executive group of elected officers and senators representing various dorms and student organizations. While a lot of pageantry and disputes surround this student governing body, ASG does manage to get some useful policies passed during the school year.

Performing Groups

The School of Speech attracts many aspiring actors and directors. That translates into a competitive performance arts program. Campus performing groups include improvisational comedy, *a cappella* singing groups, and ethnic theater troupes. More than sixty theatrical productions are put on each year. While the School of Speech provides its fair share of participants in Northwestern's theater scene, students from the other undergraduate schools gain roles on a regular basis as well.

THE WAA-MU SHOW

One highly revered tradition at Northwestern is the acclaimed Waa-Mu show, a musical revue of student-produced and -written skits and songs. Named for the collaboration between the Women's Athletic Association and the Men's Union, this show spoofs campus life and pop culture. Extremely popular not only in Evanston, but in the nation since its beginnings in 1929, Waa-Mu has been deemed by the Associated Press as "the best college show in America," and, according to *Sports Illustrated*, "a pastiche of knock-'em dead production numbers." Throughout the years, more than 10,000 students have been involved with this all-original musical.

Other Outside Activities

There are many venues for those students who are interested in writing and photography. Besides the more mainstream publications such as *The Daily Northwestern* or the *Syllabus*, Northwestern's yearbook, there are many specialized publications like the entertainment magazine *art+performance* and the literary journal *Helicon*.

Other media opportunities include WNUR-FM, the nation's largest student-run radio station. Broadcast students also utilize the newsroom in Louis Hall, which uses NEWSTAR II, the professional newsroom computer system. The Northwestern News Network (NNN) produces a thirty-minute weekly news program that can be seen on local cable access channels.

The Greek Scene

Forty percent of the student body belongs to the twenty-two fraternities and eleven sororities on campus, most of which are nationally affiliated. While a substantial percentage of students are Greek, there is no big pressure to rush. Most students do not get caught up in the Greek system; loyalties are not divided between Greeks and non-Greeks. Moreover, there is no great stigma attached to being in a fraternity or a sorority, as might be the case at other schools. Recently, Northwestern's fraternity system has undergone an evolution. In the coming years, many fraternities will become technically substance-free. The future success of these policies, however, is debatable.

Northwestern students' daily planners are well used and dog-eared as students try to keep track of the meetings and appointments that are involved with being in any student organization. While a lot of work and time is invested into these activities, the friendships formed through common interest and the experience gained are invaluable.

> *The skills I've acquired as yearbook managing editor, such as knowing the computer program Quark XPress, have helped me more to find internships than any grade point average can. It's that real-life experience gained from being involved in any student organization at Northwestern that catches the eye of potential employers.*

Residential Colleges

An alternative to living in a regular residence hall at Northwestern is the residential college system. Each residential college is thematic, such as the Thomas G. Ayers Residential College of Commerce and Industry, the Communications Residential College, or the College of Culture and Community. Students who live in these colleges participate in fireside gatherings, build closer relationships with faculty members, and partake in tutorials in specific fields of study.

There are eleven residential colleges at Northwestern, ranging in size from three dozen to 300. Each college is headed by a faculty member who serves as college master.

The residential colleges plan an array of social and intellectual events during the school year. Some highlights of the residential college system include:

- Willard Residential College's annual Polka Party.
- the collaboration of members from Shepard Residential College and the Humanities Residential College (Chapin) for "Shakespeare at the Rock," an outdoor Shakespeare festival held during Northwestern's Mayfest activities.
- the Communications Residential College (CRC) with its own in-house radio stations where residents hold their annual forty-eight-hour radiothon as a fund-raiser.
- Jones Fine and Performing Arts Residential College and its own theater, dance studio, literary magazine, and CD of residents' musical performances.

Dance Marathon

Dance Marathon, which gathers more than 200 Northwestern students to dance thirty consecutive hours, is the second largest college philanthropy event in the nation. Planning for this event begins a year in advance. In 1997, 330 student volunteers worked on 11 committees to coordinate this event. During the marathon, there are activities held in Norris University Center are open to the public, including a Las Vegas-style casino, health and beauty spa, and performances by singing and dance groups. Dance Marathon has raised almost $3 million for eighteen different charities since its beginnings in 1974.

FINANCIAL AID

With two younger sisters in college at the same time as I was, I would not have been able to attend Northwestern without some financial aid assistance. In fact, the generous grant the financial aid office offered me made attending Northwestern less expensive than the state schools I was looking at as a high school senior.

Northwestern is committed to a policy of need-blind admissions. Once a student is accepted, the Financial Aid Office finds a way to meet a student's financial needs. Financial aid packages comprise federal and Northwestern-sponsored loans and grants, and federal work-study options. In every case, a Northwestern grant will bridge the gap between a student's family contributions and the other financial assistance a student has qualified for. In 1997 the university completed a $60 million fund-raising campaign to endow its grant program.

As the twenty-first century nears, the administration of Northwestern has undertaken several educational initiatives for the new century, including instituting more small-class seminars, improving study abroad opportunities, building new residence halls, and enhancing academic and career advising. While a planned fund-raising campaign will bring in a portion of the revenue needed for these initiatives, students will bear a substantial part of this much-needed funding.

While costs to attend any university are continually climbing, Northwestern's Financial Aid Office works to ensure that students are able to attend the university. Sixty percent of undergraduates receive some form of financial aid; forty-seven percent receive aid from Northwestern funds.

Some students worry that their aid from Northwestern will be reduced after their first year of school. However, the school will continue to meet a student's need for the duration of the four years. In many cases, grants increase as students become upperclassmen.

Face it, when you have two midterms and a paper due, the last thing you want to worry about is the status of your loans. The counselors at the Financial Aid Office provide quick solutions to any problems that may arise—anything from making sure a loan paper is signed to ensuring that a student can finance off-campus living. The counselors work in an extremely organized and timely manner to meet the needs of the students.

GRADUATES

As part of the Student Alumni Advisory Board (SAAB), I take part in planning projects to strengthen relationships between students and alumni. One of SAAB's most successful programs has been the Northwestern University Externship Program (NEXT), where freshmen and sophomores spend a day shadowing an alum. Students gain a firsthand perspective of their interested career field and receive useful guidance from the alumni.

Northwestern has approximately 150,000 living alumni from its undergraduate, graduate, and professional schools. According to a study of a recent graduating class, thirty-seven percent planned to enter a graduate or professional program immediately after graduation, fifty-three percent began full-time employment, and ten percent intended to pursue other endeavors, such as working for the Peace Corps. The most recent survey of alumni revealed that eighty-one percent eventually undertook advanced study.

The Northwestern Alumni Association (NAA) is actively involved in the Northwestern community with programs such as Homecoming, Wildcat Welcome, Senior Week, and summer welcome parties for new students. By building strong relationships with current students, NAA hopes to gain active alumni in the future.

Alumni remain involved with Northwestern by participating in NU clubs in more than fifty major metropolitan areas around the world, educational seminars, travel/study programs,

Young Alumni events, and reunion parties in fall and spring. With the NAA's renewed support in these programs, alumni interest has grown rapidly in the past few years.

Organizations such as SAAB utilize the Alumni Network, a database of 3,500 alumni, which allows students to contact alumni in a particular company or field. It circumvents students making a lot of phone calls to get in touch with alumni. This valuable resource is available to all students.

Besides SAAB, the NAA has several other constituent organizations. The Council of 100 is made up of prominent women alumni. Established in 1992, the current chair is Ruth Reinke Whitney, editor-in-chief of *Glamour* magazine. The Council's objective is to provide positive role models for women and to build a network for career counseling, job placement, and mentoring.

PROMINENT GRADS

- **Warren Beatty, Actor**
- **Cindy Crawford, Model**
- **Richard Gephardt, U.S. House of Representatives Minority Leader**
- **Bob Greene, Author, Syndicated Columnist**
- **Charlton Heston, Actor**
- **Ann-Margret, Actor**
- **Garry Marshall, Producer, Director**
- **Brent Musburger, Sportscaster**
- **Tony Randall, Actor**
- **Ruth Reinke Whitney, Editor-in-chief of *Glamour* Magazine**
- **Kate Shindle, 1998 Miss America**
- **Cloris Leachman, Actor**

Each undergraduate school has an alumni program as well. The Medill School of Journalism Alumni Board established a mentoring program between current Medill students and professional journalists in Chicago and New York. The Schools of Speech and Music and the School of Education and Social Policy plan to follow suit in the upcoming years.

Some other quick facts about Northwestern alumni:

- According to the most recent Financial and Economic Information Company survey, Northwestern ranked ninth among the universities educating the majority of the nation's leading business executives.
- In 1989 *Business Week* reported that Northwestern ranked fifth nationally in the number of alumni heading America's top 1,000 companies.
- In 1990 *Fortune* magazine reported that Northwestern was the fourth most frequent alma mater of 1,891 present and former CEOs of Fortune 500 and Service 500 companies.

SUMMING UP

The primary goal of Northwestern's six undergraduate schools is to provide their students with a strong liberal arts foundation. While carefully devoting time in the classroom to theory, professors also stress the importance of putting those lessons into practice. Not only utilizing the multitude of resources available to them in Chicago, students take the skills they learn nationwide, which is evident in the success of Northwestern's alumni.

While it's difficult to put a label on such a heterogeneous group, it can be said that Northwestern students are extremely motivated and focused. These traits have their good and bad points. This desire to succeed can often lend itself to a stressful academic environment. On the other hand, students go out of their way to find internships and gain real-world experience before graduation. It's very common for students to graduate with two or three internships on their résumé. Simply put, this experience translates into successful employment and graduate school acceptance rates.

Recent improvements, such as revamping classrooms to equip them with top-notch video equipment and hooking every dorm room up to the Internet, reflect Northwestern's readiness to prepare its students for the twenty-first century. Educational initiatives set by the administration will augment the already competitive learning environment at the university.

Situated twelve miles north of Chicago along the shores of Lake Michigan, location is key for Northwestern. Professors turn this major metropolitan area into a working laboratory for students. Instead of just hearing about an issue, students can experience it firsthand.

Today's Northwestern students know that competitive higher education is a privilege that they've earned. Because Northwestern practices need-blind admissions, no one can buy their way into this school, which is a leveling factor for all students. They are accepted to Northwestern because of their high merits and achievements, from volunteering at inner city schools to being a National Merit scholar. This acceptance is becoming more competitive as the number of applicants continues to increase each year.

With one more year until graduation, I already can appreciate the high-quality education that I've received. While the book knowledge is extremely important, I must admit that it's only been one facet of my Northwestern education. By being part of this community, I can talk knowledgeably about race relations because I've seen student groups wrestle with them and have heard Dr. Khalid Muhammed and Maya Angelou address these issues. I know what Princess Diana looked like in person because she toured our campus during a visit to Illinois.

I've seen the Chicago skyline, dotted with the city lights, from the top of the Sears Tower with my friend, just because we wanted to one Wednesday night. I've seen the 1996 Olympic torch passed, scoured the city for scene locations from The Blues Brothers *and* The Untouchables, *stood by the green Chicago River on St. Patrick's Day, and worked at the Chicago Board of Elections during the 1996 presidential election.*

These opportunities both in and out of the classroom have greatly impacted my four years as a college student.

❑ *Jennifer Caruso*

POMONA COLLEGE

Photo by Philip Channing

Pomona College
Claremont, CA 91711

(909) 621-8134

E-mail: admissions@pomona.edu
Web site: http://www.pomona.edu

Enrollment

Full-time ❑ women: 668
❑ men: 753

INTRODUCING POMONA

I came to Pomona seeking an atmosphere that was ferociously intellectual, but at the same time, more open and friendly than colleges back East.

Pomona College is a coed, residential, nonsectarian liberal arts college located thirty-five miles east of Los Angeles. Its mission is "the pursuit of knowledge and understanding through study in the sciences and the humanities...[its curriculum prepares] students for lives of personal fulfillment and social responsibility in a global context." (*Pomona College Catalog*) Like most things in life, students get out of a Pomona education exactly what they put into it. They can spend four years thinking hard, taking a broad variety of classes, and stretching their intellectual experiences and capabilities, surrounded by other highly motivated people in one of the world's most pleasant climates.

Pomona was founded in 1887 by New Englanders affiliated with the Congregational Church. They named the school after the Roman goddess of the harvest, and conveniently forgot she was also a goddess of wine. The founders wanted to provide a liberal arts college "of the New England type" for the youth out West. They also took the then-radical step of making Pomona coeducational from the start. Today, students come from all over the country and some foreign countries as well, and the Congregational heritage survives only in some restriction of alcohol consumption on campus. People still have fun—they just do it without kegs. The educational goals have also been refined, most recently in 1994, when the college adopted new general education requirements aimed at giving students the skills "to live resiliently in a changing world." Pomona is the founding and largest institution of The Claremont Colleges, a consortium of six colleges and Claremont Graduate University. The Claremonts share some facilities and work together to provide students with expanded classroom and extracurricular opportunities.

Just looking at the beautiful campus, you could guess that Pomona offers a lot of resources to its students. The chemistry, biology, and physics labs are among the finest available to undergraduates anywhere. The Seaver Theatre complex has large and small stages, studios, and classrooms housing The Claremont Colleges' theater program. It's a stone's throw from the Oldenborg Center, a combination international study center and residence hall, with its own dining room and international film and colloquia series. Three computer labs, one on north campus and two south, provide students with word processing, printers, on-line course materials, and candy: free e-mail, Internet access, and multi-user games. Pomona's administration has housed itself in Alexander Hall, where students can walk in air-conditioned comfort from pleading for classes at the Registrar's Office, to pleading for money in Financial Aid, to pleading for time at the Business Office, to pleading for mercy from the Dean of Students.

ADMISSIONS REQUIREMENTS

If this sounds good so far, start planning for the application process. Applicants are required to submit an application form, recommendations, a transcript, and either ACT or SAT results. The admissions staff is interested in people who have done strong academic work, and have stretched themselves in some way. The high school transcript shows academic strength. Pomona expects applicants to have spent four years in high school English, three each in mathematics and foreign languages (but four is better), and two years each in laboratory sciences and social sciences. This doesn't leave much room for electives. Those nonacademic courses show that applicants have lots of interests, but grades from electives don't count in helping determine if they will do well at a demanding college. Admissions officers also consider whether they took Advanced Placement or honors courses if available, where their grades may not have been as high, but they received a great deal of preparation for college academics.

The application form asks some basic demographic information, a few more personal questions, and requires two or three essays that indicate to the admissions staff the special things the applicant has done. They are looking for applicants who took on challenges, acted in a play, did community service, edited a publication—anything that asked the applicant to take on a new project and see it through. Not all Pomona students were valedictorians, but the vast majority of them played sports, participated in student government or community service, or were performing or studio artists in high school. Applicants can use the common application if they don't have Pomona's own, which is available on Pomona's Web site.

Recommendations

Three recommendations are also required, one from the applicant's high school principal or guidance counselor, and two from teachers in core academic subjects. Core academics are English, math, social sciences like history and anthropology, languages, and laboratory sciences like biology, chemistry, or physics. Applicants need recommendations stating that they are the most outstanding students ever encountered, because that's the caliber of the competition. The SAT I or ACT is also required. The average incoming Pomona student has a verbal SAT I score of 710 and a math score of 710.

Other things that are recommended, but not required, for applicants include achievement tests, interviews, visits to the campus, and supplemental application materials. Achievement tests are another way to demonstrate mastery of a broad range of subjects. Applicants can interview either with admissions officers on campus or with a Pomona alum in their area. In addition, applicants can send samples of what makes them special along with their applications. Videotapes of their performances, clippings of news stories they wrote, slides or photographs of their paintings or sculptures will all stand out and help the admissions staff see the applicant as unique.

ACADEMIC LIFE

Before applying, students should know some of the demands Pomona will place on their time. Students at Pomona need to pass thirty-two courses to receive the Bachelor of Arts, the only degree Pomona confers. (Even science majors are BAs here. Then again, at Harvard, computer science majors receive the Bachelor of Arts, too.) The classic student will complete courses in four years, taking four courses each semester. Pomona doesn't count credit hours, but some nonacademic classes, such as foreign language conversation and physical education, count only as half a course. Time demands vary from subject to subject, instructor to instructor, but most students won't want to take much more than four courses at a time. There's extensive lab time for science classes, hours of language lab each week for introductory foreign language classes, and huge amounts of reading and writing (and rewriting) in almost every class. Classes are kept small so everyone gets plenty of attention from the instructor. After freshman year, most classes have ten or twelve students, the biggest classes having about twenty-five students.

General Education

Most colleges and universities require all of their students to demonstrate basic knowledge of a few academic subjects, and the choice of subjects and the level of achievement demanded varies from school to school. Some call it breadth of study, others general education. The Pomona faculty in 1994 defined a common core of intellectual experiences and skills their students should have. Supposedly, these skills in perception, analysis, and communication will enable students to explore ideas, evaluate evidence, draw balanced conclusions, and communicate their findings throughout their college career and in their life afterward. The ten skills are

- read literature critically.
- use and understand the scientific method.
- use and understand formal reasoning.
- understand and analyze data.

- analyze creative art critically.
- perform or produce creative art.
- explore and understand human behavior.
- explore and understand an historical culture.
- compare and contrast contemporary cultures.
- think critically about values and rationality.

There's a list of courses that teach each of these skills, and in order to graduate, students have to complete a course in every one. Some of these courses will fall within their field of concentration, but they'll have to broaden their intellectual pursuits for others, at least for the four and one-half months it takes to complete the course.

Writing

Every Pomona student has to complete at least two writing-intensive courses, in which several drafts of every paper are submitted to the instructor for comment before a final grade is given. The required Critical Inquiry seminar every student takes in the first semester at Pomona counts for one of these.

My second writing-intensive course was Economic History with Professor Hans Palmer. There were only eight students in the class. Professor Palmer required us to turn in four drafts of every paper, and he reserved the right to require more revisions when necessary. I was in the second semester of my senior year, so I had plenty on my mind besides my courses and was a little taken aback when I got the first draft of my first paper back with three pages of comments and suggestions, in red ink. When the second draft came back with just as much red ink, I was downright dismayed. But my writing improved, and while I was rethinking my written ideas over and over, I was also sharpening my analysis of what I learned.

Foreign Language Proficiency

Another requirement for a Pomona degree is proficiency in a foreign language, defined as speaking and writing the language at the level of a third-semester course. Pomona is serious about this requirement, and it has even kept a few bright people from graduating on time. Plan ahead. Students can test out of this requirement by scoring a 650 or better on a language SAT II test, or by scoring a 4 or 5 on an Advanced Placement exam. Students are also required to complete one course defined as "speaking-intensive." This is a new requirement; the catalog defines it as "frequent, extemporaneous oral presentations, discussion, or debate that are carefully evaluated by instructors." With all these requirements, it would seem that there isn't much room to do your own thing, but in truth, a single course can often satisfy more than one graduation requirement. An advanced language class can also be writing- or speaking-intensive. A philosophy class can also involve learning about a modern or historical culture.

Majors

On admission, students are asked what academic subject they intend to study, and they may be assigned to a faculty advisor based on this initial concentration, or major. Don't worry too much about your initial choice. Pomona has a number of great academic programs, and you can change your mind a lot later in your college career than you think. If the introductory courses in a subject don't light your fire, you'll be taking classes in other subjects that might. No one will look back at your admissions essay when you declare an English concentration and say no, you can't do this, because you said you wanted to be a diplomat. Honest!

When you decide which subject you're interested in, choose a permanent faculty advisor who teaches in that concentration. Pomona offers top-notch courses in forty-one concentrations, in the natural and laboratory sciences, mathematics, social sciences, and humanities. Read the catalog for complete listings and course descriptions. The foreign language concentrations are also extremely demanding, so, as mentioned, plan to start studying the language in high school.

Studying Off Campus

Students can take two courses at the other Claremont Colleges every semester, though in order to graduate there are a few courses they absolutely must take at Pomona. Some concentrations are offered jointly among all Claremont Colleges. If you choose to pursue Neuroscience, Women's Studies, Black Studies, Chicano Studies, Asian American Studies, Media Studies, or Science, Technology, and Society, you'll automatically be taking a number of your courses at other campuses. You'll become acquainted with new professors, new students, and new ways of thinking by doing so, and with any luck, your social life will also be enhanced.

If The Claremont Colleges don't offer enough variety of experience, students can also study as exchange students at Colby, Spelman, Smith, and Swarthmore colleges; Fisk University; or Caltech. Students can pursue five-year joint engineering degree programs with Caltech and Washington University in St. Louis. Every year, about twenty juniors and seniors spend a semester in Washington, D.C., where they serve as interns in government or national organization offices, write research papers, and attend seminars. There's also a semester internship with the California state government in Sacramento.

About half of Pomona's students choose to study abroad during their undergraduate years, for one or two semesters. The college strongly encourages study abroad, sponsoring thirty-nine programs in thirty-five cities located in twenty-one foreign countries. At each of these sites, there's a program director who acts as an advisor to the students and a liaison between the foreign school and Pomona.

I went to Strasbourg, France, for a semester in a Pomona-sponsored program run jointly with Brethren Colleges Abroad. The American and French staff associated with BCA helped me register for classes, found housing for me, sent my friends to doctors and dentists who spoke English, held get-togethers that supplemented my pitiful food budget, and generally made integration into a new culture much easier. My Pomona liaison took us out to dinners, the opera, and local museums, all on Pomona's dime! I had a great experience studying abroad although it was tiring speaking another language all the time, and I had to think really hard about the business of everyday life. It wasn't just because of cultural differences, but also because I wasn't living on campus anymore, so I was doing a lot more on my own. I learned a lot.

In general, people have had a much easier time on study abroad by going on Pomona-sponsored programs. They don't require people to set up their own living arrangements; they usually involve taking real classes at real universities, and Pomona makes sure they're reputable. Truly adventurous students have found independent programs in places like the Dominican Republic, South Africa, and Indonesia, with widely varying results.

While I was studying abroad, I took a vacation in Ireland, and I stayed in a youth hostel in Limerick where I met up with a group of unlucky young Midwesterners whose study abroad program had promised them housing with local families, but hadn't delivered. For three months, they'd been staying in a dingy building, sleeping dormitory-style with total strangers every night, with no on-site laundry facilities. Every night, five or six of them would sit in the hostel lounge, tune the TV into Baywatch, *and talk about how they couldn't wait to get home. What a waste!*

SOCIAL LIFE AND ACTIVITIES

Life in a Pomona residence hall is nothing like a youth hostel. It's more like an elite summer camp. Everyone there was a high achiever in high school. Everyone wants to do something important in the world upon graduation. Almost no one is there because "Oh, well, Mommy and Daddy went here, and it's something to do between prep school and joining the family firm." People really think and talk about what they're learning, and are active in the community, on campus and off.

Housing

Everyone lives in residence halls as a first-year student. The first-year students are placed with a core group of ten or twelve other first-year students and two sponsors, one male and one female, who are sophomores or juniors. The members of a core group live in neighboring rooms, or adjoining hallways but men and women have separate bathrooms. Upperclassmen can always spot first-year students because they travel in packs. Entire core groups arrive together at the dining halls, swimming pools, concerts, even dances.

My core group lived in Oldenborg, the foreign language dorm. We had a great mix of people who had lived abroad, were first-generation Americans, spoke English as a second language, or were just interested in languages and international studies. My sponsors were great people. They spent a lot of time with us, clueing us in to all kinds of essential Pomona facts, and making the transition to a new lifestyle a lot easier.

There are a few important facts to know about the residence halls. Of course, they have developed personalities over the years. Oldenborg is the only hall with air conditioning, so people living there tend to get more work done in the daytime, while everyone else is taking late-afternoon naps to avoid the heat. Oldenborg in particular has a reputation for being very insular. People enter "the Borg" and don't often come out, since it has its own dining hall, a library, and a movie theater in the basement. The International Theater shows foreign language films several times a week, drawing people from all Claremont Colleges and the community. Walker residents live the closest to what most people imagine the Southern California college lifestyle is. They tend to be laid back, playing a lot of Frisbee in the day and partying hard into the night. Lots of stressed-out first-year students and sophomores choose to live in Mudd-Blaisdell because there's a computer lab in the courtyard; they can work late into the night and have a short walk back to their rooms.

Students can apply for permission to live off campus in their sophomore, junior, and senior years, but only a few students are permitted to go every year, and it's hard to stay involved with campus life if you do. However, there are a few good reasons to move off campus. If you live in the residence halls, you have to eat at the cafeterias, or at least pay for the meal plan, whether or not you eat there. Also, in the words of the Pomona College Catalog, "The College attempts to maintain a campus environment conducive to the personal and intellectual development of its students." Over the years, the administration has concluded that a hard-core party culture on campus is inconsistent with encouraging personal and intellectual development. Alcohol consumption in the residence halls is regulated. Private parties can have alcohol only in single servings—no kegs. So, if you want to throw wild parties, you can either move off campus, or register your event with the Office of Campus Life and hold it in one of the six designated social rooms on campus.

Off-Campus Life

It is a good idea to cultivate friendships with people who own cars, because the sidewalks roll up at 9:00 P.M. in the village of Claremont. There is no movie theater, fast food, late-night restaurant, or shopping mall in the village, though there are a few smart little clothing boutiques and a video store or two within walking distance, and the Rhino Records store and Starbucks, source of all good things. Anybody can have a car at Pomona, although registration is required and parking areas are restricted.

Sports

The administration realizes the limits placed on their students by the suburban location, so to keep them from stagnating in their personal development, any number of activities to keep them occupied outside of class have been organized. Pomona fields nineteen men's and women's intercollegiate sports teams. The sports facilities are really first-rate, especially the brand-new Olympic-size Haldeman swimming and diving pool. The twenty-five-yard recreational pool behind Mudd-Blaisdell residence hall is a favorite spot for unofficial late-night visits, as are the Scripps and Harvey Mudd pools to the north. There's also an eight-lane all-weather track anyone can use and the Rains Center, a $16 million facility built in 1992 that houses the weight room and CV equipment, squash, racquetball, basketball, and volleyball courts, aerobics studio, and locker rooms and coaches' offices. The dance department has its studio on south campus, and students can cross-register for any physical education class at the other Claremont Colleges as well.

Student Union

Pomona is constructing a new Campus Center to provide a centrally located space for student activities both organized and disorganized. In the meantime, the college has a full complement of performing arts, political, cultural, and community service groups, honor societies, and any other activities that you'd expect from an extremely wealthy small college. They're just scattered in offices and rooms all over the campus.

Clubs and Organizations

The hosts of clubs and organizations spend lots of time recruiting new members in the first few weeks of every semester. Most announce their activities to the wider community in *The Student Life*, Pomona's student-run newspaper; *Collage*, the five-college paper; *Chirps*, the Office of Campus Life's activities newsletter, and various flyers and posters around campus. KSPC, Pomona's student-run independent FM radio station, is also a good source of information about things to do.

Performances and Socials

Almost everyone joins at least one significant extracurricular activity, but there are plenty of other ways to pass time on campus. The Committee on Campus Life and Activities, made up of elected student representatives and staff from the Office of Campus Life, has a huge budget dedicated to making sure that students have a good time and occasionally expand their minds when they're outside class. They help sponsor performances on campus from such acts as the Violent Femmes, No Doubt, Bobby McFerrin, and the Kodo Drummers. They sponsor screenings of second-run films, parties and dances in the residence halls, the spring formal dance, the spring carnival, and even a few lectures here and there. Individual residence halls also sponsor their own activities, such as ice cream socials and movie nights.

There are six social rooms scattered among the residence halls that can be reserved in advance for any social event. There are a few social fraternities to join, but no sororities, although some of the fraternities are coed. No recognized Greek organizations are allowed to maintain houses for their members, so fraternity parties are also held in the social rooms, or off campus. Greek parties in the social rooms are subject to the same regulation as everyone else's, including a requirement to have security officers for events with more than fifty people.

Getting Away

If the attractions of Claremont wear thin, there are always the Pacific beaches, about an hour and a half away by car. The San Bernardino mountains are an hour in the opposite direction, with camping, hiking, and even skiing at Big Bear. Adventures in downtown Los Angeles are also an hour's drive away, and Disneyland is just forty-five minutes away. L.A. has a wide variety of cultural, shopping, and entertainment experiences to offer, what you'd expect from a huge city filled with hundreds of ethnic and cultural groups.

FINANCIAL AID

If you are wise in the ways of the world, you have been asking yourself how much a college with so much to offer will cost. The budget (tuition, fees, room and board, and personal expenses) was about $30,000 a year in a recent year, which is comparable with costs at other private schools of its caliber. If you can afford this out of pocket, great! Skip ahead.

For the rest of the population, the Financial Aid Office will be a significant part of your college life. The Financial Aid Office at Pomona is extremely knowledgeable and helpful. Pomona is committed to meeting the financial need of all enrolled candidates, so applying for financial aid has no effect on admissions decisions.

Financial aid applicants file the Free Application for Federal Student Aid to determine their eligibility for federal programs such as Pell Grants and Perkins and Stafford loans, as well as Federal Work-Study funds. They also file the College Scholarship Service's Profile application to determine their eligibility for funds administered by Pomona. Pomona gives away or loans a lot of its own money every year to students who have financial need, which is a big help because there isn't much money available from the federal government. California residents also file the Cal Grant GPA Verification form. Students with divorced parents will be asked to send a Non-Custodial Parent's statement, giving financial information about the parent they do not live with, along with their Profile application.

The information gathered on all these forms does two things. First, it shows how much money your family can contribute toward the costs of your education. Second, it gives the financial aid officer an idea of what kind of person you are, which shows what aid money you're eligible for. If there is anything on any of these forms that confuses you (most likely, there will be), or if the picture of your family's finances that comes out of the form doesn't look right, contact the Financial Aid Office and ask them about it. They have seen thousands of students and awarded millions of dollars in aid. Chances are they will know exactly how to help you, as long as you keep them informed.

The Financial Aid office maintains databases of scholarships and sources of aid that you can apply for on your own. If the money doesn't come from Pomona, the state of California, or the U.S. government, they don't award it to you from the Pomona Financial Aid Office—you have to apply for it yourself. The Financial Aid staff will help you with applications, though.

GRADUATES

Pomona graduates often go into public service—teaching, government, nonprofits, congressional internships—right after graduation. Then, when the thrill of working long hours for poverty-level wages wears off, they pursue advanced degrees and move into more lucrative fields, such as management consulting, medicine, and the law. Pomona is well represented in scientific research, publishing, and business marketing as well.

PROMINENT GRADS

- **John Cage, '30, Composer**
- **Frank G. Wells, '53, Former Disney President**
- **Richard Chamberlain, '56, Actor**
- **Kris Kristofferson, '58, Songwriter, Singer**
- **Myrlie Evers, '68, NAACP Chairman**
- **Mary Schmich, '75, *Chicago Tribune* Columnist**
- **George C. Wolfe, '76, Playwright, Producer, Joseph Papp Public Theater Director**

SUMMING UP

Pomona College is a coed, residential, nonsectarian liberal arts college located thirty-five miles east of Los Angeles. It is academically rigorous and attracts highly motivated people as students, staff, and faculty. Its location is both a blessing and a curse, with a great climate and easy access to mountains, beaches, and city life, but very little cultural life off campus (and within walking distance). The college is aware of this and outdoes itself providing on-campus activities and resources for students, funding student projects, building recreational facilities, and bringing distinguished performers and lecturers to campus. Graduates can rely on their skills to go anywhere they want and do whatever they dream.

❑ *Christina Caldwell, B.A.*

PRINCETON UNIVERSITY

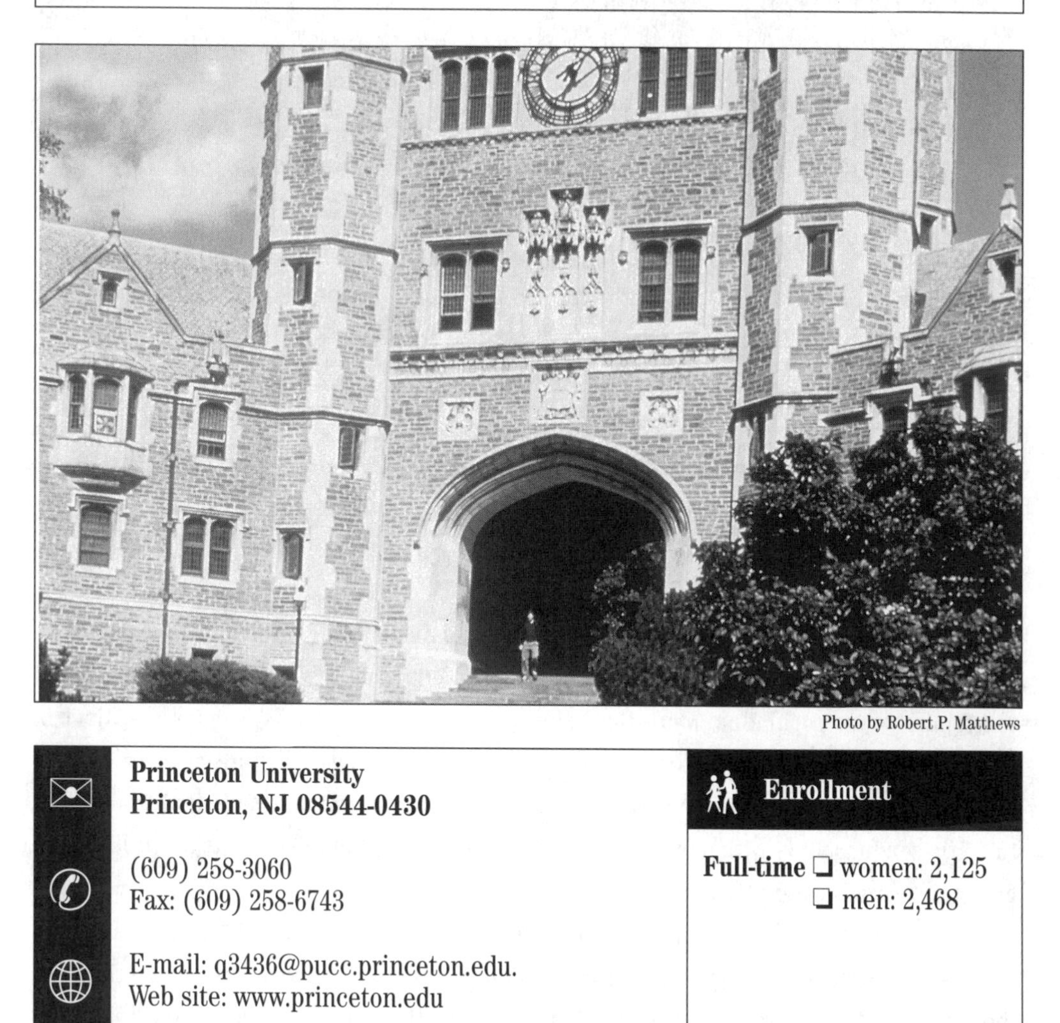

Photo by Robert P. Matthews

Princeton University
Princeton, NJ 08544-0430

(609) 258-3060
Fax: (609) 258-6743

E-mail: q3436@pucc.princeton.edu.
Web site: www.princeton.edu

Enrollment

Full-time ❑ women: 2,125
❑ men: 2,468

INTRODUCING PRINCETON

One of the leading universities in the world, Princeton is impressive on all levels and deservedly appears at or near the top of all of the ranking reports you might read. Like other Ivy League schools, competition to get in is stiff: in a recent class, ninety-eight percent of the enrolling students had been in the top fifth of their high school class and two-thirds of them had scores higher than 700 on both Math and Verbal SATs. Like other Ivy League schools, the faculty members represent the best in their fields, from professors whose novels win the National Book Award to those whose achievements in molecular biology win a Nobel prize.

I graduated from a public school in a small town where all the teachers were neighbors and not only knew the students, but knew the parents, too. I didn't have a lot of choice about courses, but I was used to getting high grades pretty easily and getting along with my teachers really well. When I first got to Princeton, I was nervous—the campus seemed huge, I was taking an introductory course in philosophy in a lecture hall with more kids than had been in my whole high school, and the professor was down on a stage and seemed as far away from me as a famous rock star in a concert. On top of that, I didn't do very well on my first paper. My roommate told me to go to see my preceptor for the course. My preceptor went through the whole paper with me, and helped me to broaden my thinking about how to tackle different concepts. She really cared about helping me learn how to learn. Not only did I write better papers after that, but I wasn't nervous anymore. Princeton wasn't so different from home after all.

What sets Princeton apart, however, is its dedication to undergraduate education. The undergraduate population of approximately 4,400 students comprises over seventy percent of the total student population. More than ninety years ago, Woodrow Wilson, as president of Princeton, implemented the preceptorial system; even the largest lecture courses meet in small class groups once or twice a week. As early as your first year you could find yourself sitting at a seminar table with only ten other students arguing the finer points of *Hamlet* with one of the world's leading Shakespearean scholars.

Not surprisingly, this commitment to undergraduates results in both flexibility in devising academic programs and greater access to faculty members for independent study. Between the two bachelor's degree programs (A.B. and B.S.E.), the university offers more than sixty department and interdepartmental programs. Students may also apply for independent concentration outside of the already existing programs. In fact, independent study is an important part of every undergraduate's academic life. For A.B. candidates, all departments require a combination of upper-level courses and independent study during both junior and senior years, and all A.B. candidates (as well as most B.S.E. candidates) must write a senior thesis. The thesis averages 100 pages and is the culmination of a year's study (outside of regular coursework) on a topic of your choice under the direction of a faculty advisor.

In a world where some colleges require no core courses and others require course plans structured toward practical applications, Princeton remains a fierce proponent of a balanced liberal arts education. All A.B. candidates must meet a one-term writing requirement and show proficiency in a foreign language. In addition, they must take one course each in the recently revamped distribution areas of epistemology and cognition, ethical thought and moral values, historical analysis, and quantitative reasoning, and they must take two courses each in literature and the arts, science and technology (with laboratory), and social analysis. Nor are engineering students off the hook. They too have to satisfy a writing requirement and take a number of (although not as many) courses in the various areas of study.

The change in the nature of the distribution areas came as Princeton studied ways to advance into the twenty-first century. There are other signs, in both enrollment and governance, that the Princeton of today is not the elitist tradition-bound school of past portraits. The undergraduate student body comes from all fifty states and seventy foreign countries. American minorities (including African American, Latino, Asian American, and Native American students) make up twenty-five percent, and an additional five percent are foreign citizens. Almost forty-five percent of all undergraduates receive some kind of financial aid. Students also play an active role in policy-making at the school, sitting on committees right along with faculty and administration. Each spring a graduating senior is elected to serve a term on the university's Board of Trustees.

Of course, you can still find plenty of tradition at Princeton, from Opening Exercises in the Gothic University Chapel to the locomotive cheer at football games to Class Day festivities on Cannon Green behind Nassau Hall, the home of the president's office and for several months (in 1783) the capital of the United States. Princeton seems to connect its preparation for the future with its affection for the past in so many ways that, no matter how diverse the community, anyone can find a place to feel at home there.

ADMISSIONS REQUIREMENTS

For an Ivy League school, Princeton is relatively small: it enrolls approximately 1,130 freshmen of the 1,700 it accepts. Yet nearly 15,000 applications come into the Admissions Office. In other words, almost ninety percent of those who apply will receive that dreaded thin envelope.

It's not easy to get into Princeton. Among those admitted, more than seventy-five percent had SAT I scores over 680, and one-third of those had scores over 780. On the other hand, Princeton has only three mandatory admission requirements—SAT I, SAT II tests in three subject areas, and the application form itself. While the Admissions Office recommends that applicants take four years each of English, math, and a language, as well as two years each of history and a lab science, it also insists that there are no fixed unit or course requirements that must be completed before admission. The school gives "full consideration to any applicant who has been unable to pursue studies to the extent recommended if the record otherwise shows clear promise."

Of course, the key words are "clear promise"—and the admissions process itself can seem far from clear. There is no formula for getting in. Like other highly competitive schools, Princeton wants to see how candidates have excelled, not only in their coursework but also in their extracurricular activities. Because Princeton is a residential university, the committee takes an interest in candidates' roles in their communities. Special talents are also considered, whether the talent is on the athletic field or on the stage. The Admissions Office encourages candidates involved in the performing and creative arts to submit audition tapes or portfolios. Legacies (children of alumni) are given a certain amount of special consideration. (In 1997, forty-one percent of the 423 alumni children who applied were admitted; eighty-one percent of those admitted enrolled, accounting for 132 of the class of 2001.)

Decision Programs

Princeton has two decision programs: Early Decision and Regular Decision. (The university has discontinued its Early Action program. You may apply Early Decision only if you are not applying Early Decision or Early Action anywhere else.) Early Decision applications must be mailed by November 1. You will hear from the Admissions Office in December whether your application has been accepted, denied, or deferred for review in the Regular Decision process. All admissions are for September enrollment; however, Princeton allows you to defer enrollment to travel, work, perform military service, or participate in special year-abroad programs. You cannot request a deferral until you have actually been notified that you have been admitted.

My mother was a whiz at Latin in high school and got a really high score on the Latin Achievement Test. When she was accepted at Princeton, the Classics Department wrote her a letter saying that if she wanted to major in classics she could start as a sophomore. She said, "No way! I worked hard to get into Princeton and I'm not going to shortchange my time there by a year!"

Some students joke that it is harder to flunk out of Princeton than it is to get in. There is some truth in that. You could spend your four years cruising, making full use of pass/fail options and easier courses, doing the minimum amount of work, getting by with Cs. But what a waste that would be. Princeton has so much to offer that these can also be the most intellectually stimulating years of your life. If anything, the tough part for a new student is trying to absorb all of the information about department offerings, programs, and seminars.

The undergraduate course catalogue is more than 400 pages. Princeton has thirty-three departments, supplemented by twenty-nine interdisciplinary programs ranging from African American Studies to Musical Performance to Women's Studies. New students can start right in on their special interests through Freshman Seminars, small groups of students chosen on the basis of a short essay who meet with a professor on a specific topic. A few years ago, there were as many as forty-six freshman seminars, including The Aims of Education, led by the president of the university.

Off Campus

Princeton is flexible with off-campus opportunities. The Field Study Program lets students substitute, for one semester, a full-time job or research assignment closely related to their academic interests. For example, if you major in biology, you could apply to do biological research in a private lab. The field study doesn't have to be near Princeton: people have done work from San Francisco's Bay Area to the Woods Hole Oceanographic Institute on Cape Cod. Although Princeton doesn't run any of its own foreign study programs, the university will allow students to receive credit for a semester or a full year in an approved program. Students on financial aid even continue to receive support.

Special Schools

There are also some special schools on the undergraduate level. In addition to the School of Engineering and Applied Science, Princeton has a School of Architecture and the Woodrow Wilson School of Public and International Affairs. The official word is that the Woodrow Wilson School "prepares students for participation and leadership in public affairs on the local, national, and international levels." Most Princetonians will tell you, though, that it is a breeding ground for budding lawyers. The Woodrow Wilson School limits its enrollment to eighty students a year and the competition is pretty intense. (Good practice for trying to get into law school.)

Advisors

If this already seems like too much to take in, there is help. Academic advising is available to all freshmen and sophomores through the residential colleges. The masters and directors of studies in the colleges are also available for counseling.

I didn't pay any attention to my advisor my freshman year; I figured that all he had about me was a file. How could he know what I might want to do? Well, by sophomore year I realized that I had been pretty arrogant. He might not have known me, but he did know Princeton. The suggestions he had made would have been much more sensible for me. Instead, I just did my own thing and ended up taking some courses that were just not right for me. I wish I had paid more attention to him—and I sure wish now that I had that time back.

Graduation Requirements

Graduation requirements are based on the number of courses taken, not the number of credits. Students in the A.B. program must complete thirty courses. (Students in the B.S.E program must complete thirty-six courses.) Normally, students take four courses a semester during their first three years, and then three courses a semester during the senior year. Most students try to take care of the distribution requirements in the early years so that they can have as much flexibility as possible in structuring their majors. (Majors are usually declared in the spring of sophomore year.) Be aware: You may be able to use a high score on an Advanced Placement test or an SAT II: Subject test to satisfy the language requirement, but all students must take one of the university courses to satisfy the writing requirement—even if you did get a 5 on the English AP.

Classes

Courses usually meet three times a week, with two lectures and a class (precept). (Engineering and science courses may meet more frequently and have required lab periods.) You might notice, however, that as you start taking upper-level courses the size of the lecture gets smaller, or you have two precepts and only one lecture, or you meet as seminar groups. You will have more and more individual contact with professors, whose accessibility is one of Princeton's hallmarks. All professors have weekly office hours, open time when any student can go in and just talk.

Papers and The Thesis

You will get to know some of the professors in your department especially well during your junior and senior years when you are doing the required independent work with an advisor: the J.P. (Junior Paper) and the senior thesis. The J.P. is in many ways practice for the thesis. It is usually a long paper written each semester on a topic of your choice. Work on the senior thesis, part of Princeton's student lore, is intended to take the time you would spend on a course. (This is why seniors take only three courses per semester, not four.) Many students very diligently allocate their time that way, regularly holing up in a carrel in the basement of Firestone Library, accumulating several shelves of texts for references, filling out box after box of index cards, handing in chunks of a rough draft periodically to their advisors. Several unfortunate students have been known to endure several very unpleasant weeks with little or no sleep right before the spring due date for the thesis.

Faculty

Princeton has more than 700 full-time faculty members and all of them teach undergraduates, making the student-faculty ratio 7-1. The faculty is top-notch. At any one time there may be six Nobel prize winners teaching, or eighteen MacArthur Fellows. (MacArthur Foundation grants are sometimes referred to as "genius grants.") And, yes, it can be exciting to bump into novelists Toni Morrison or Joyce Carol Oates coming out of the English department office. But it can be equally exciting to be on an adventure of discovery with a new assistant professor in the biology department. Because of its prestige, Princeton attracts the best and the brightest of candidates out of graduate schools, people who are doing the most up-to-the-minute research in their chosen fields.

I kept telling my roommate how much I enjoyed the preceptor of my United States and World Affairs course. She was young and had terrific energy and seemed to know everything. My roommate told me to invite her to dinner at our eating club. I didn't think she'd come, but I asked her anyway. She said sure! A bunch of us sat around a table with her, all talking at once and having a great time. For that hour or so she seemed just like one of us—only a lot smarter!

Facilities

Princeton's facilities are top-notch, too. The main library, Firestone, provides easy access to more than five million books and 30,000 periodicals as well as manuscripts, maps, coins, prints, and microform. All but the rarest of materials are in open stacks. There are an additional eighteen satellite libraries associated with various departments. Princeton has two museums on campus, the Princeton University Art Museum and the Natural History Museum, as well as a variety of exhibition spaces. There are four major venues for the cultural and performing arts, from a 200-seat recital hall to Tony Award-winning McCarter Theatre. Princeton also provides an extensive computing environment. Students can go to hundreds of workstations in two dozen computing clusters around campus. Students who bring their own computers can subscribe to Dormnet, a data service available in every undergraduate dorm room on campus that connects to campus and Internet resources. In 1996, seventy-five percent of first-year students took advantage of this resource.

Academic life at Princeton can be as rich as you choose to make it. The array of opportunities is far more than you will be able to explore in your four years, and there is the danger that, in trying to do it all, you will feel stressed and pulled in too many directions. But it is all there for the taking, and the rewards are well worth the risks.

The hardest thing for me to get used to at Princeton was the different sense of time. In high school, my days and weeks were pretty structured (usually by someone else!) and we had specific assignments almost every night. At Princeton, courses meet only a couple times a week, sometimes leaving big blocks of time during the day. Many professors just hand out a syllabus at the beginning of the course and you are on your own to keep up with the reading and to remember when papers are due. At the end of each semester is "reading period"—about two weeks with no classes scheduled just before exams. At first it seemed as though I had unlimited free time, and I confess I spent a lot of my first semester goofing off. Then, when I had three papers due at once and got into a jam, I realized that it wasn't that it was free *time; it was* my *time. I had to learn to be responsible for my own time now. No one else was going to do it for me.*

SOCIAL LIFE AND ACTIVITIES

Whenever something exciting happens in the borough of Princeton (which is not very often), the newspapers always refer to it as a "genteel college town." The 300-year-old town (population of about 30,000) is charming. Shops range from the local hardware store to Laura Ashley and The Gap. More restaurants and coffee shops have appeared over the last twenty years as the area right outside of Princeton has become home to several corporate headquarters. Students can get fries at Burger King, and parents can splurge at a fancy French restaurant right around the corner.

But Princeton is not a party town. The few "hang-outs" are strict about checking IDs and they close early. New York and Philadelphia are only an hour away, with regular bus and train service to New York City, and the university often subsidizes student trips for various cultural and athletic events in both cities. Nevertheless, there is hardly a mass exodus to either city on the weekends, or at any time. Princeton really is a residential college, with more than ninety-seven percent of undergraduates living on campus, and it is on campus that most students experience their social life.

Residential College, Dorms, and Clubs

For freshmen and sophomores, life generally revolves around their residential colleges. Each college houses between 440 and 490 students and is made up of a cluster of dorms, a dining hall, lounges and study rooms, a library, computing facilities, and game and television rooms. Some of the colleges even have theaters and exhibit spaces, and all have an extensive intramural athletic program. Students themselves plan most of the activities, so that each college takes on the character of the group of students in it. This residential college system is relatively new for Princeton (it was instituted about ten years ago), and freshmen particularly like it. It's a lot easier to be a new person in a group of 440 than in a universe of 4,400.

Upperclass students live in dorms that are not part of the residential colleges, and seventy-five percent of juniors and seniors belong to one of the twelve eating clubs that line Prospect Avenue. Each club has between 120 and 180 members who meet and eat and socialize in large houses that the clubs themselves run. Run by student officers under the guidance of independent alumni boards, the clubs are more than simply a place to eat. While each club has study and computer areas, they really are a haven for a tight community of friends to relax together. On any given weekend, several—or all—of the clubs will be having parties and the Street (as Prospect Avenue is called) is alive with activity, windows lit up, music streaming out of open doors, groups of people wandering from one club to another to visit friends and to see who has the best band that night.

Alternatives to the clubs do exist. Stevenson Hall is a university-sponsored nonresidential dining facility on Prospect that has its own extensive social program and is open to juniors and seniors. Upperclass students may also choose to remain in the residential colleges or to be independent—to make their own arrangements for meals. Several of the dorms have special facilities for independents who want to cook their own meals, including one house that has been converted to a dorm for those who want to shop and cook vegetarian meals as a co-op. Princeton is constructing a major (170,000 square-foot) Campus Center that will provide food, meeting spaces, and activities of various kinds for undergraduates in all four classes, as well as graduate students, faculty, and staff. It is scheduled to open in the year 2000.

Extracurricular Activities

Princeton provides a remarkable choice of extracurricular activities. In athletics alone, there are sixty teams and crews, men and women compete in thirty-seven varsity sports, and there are another thirty-one men's, women's, and coed club teams. Nearly forty-five percent of the undergraduate student body competes in intercollegiate sports. While Princeton may not be known as an athletic powerhouse, during the past several years the school's varsity teams have won eight national championships. *Sports Illustrated* recently ranked Princeton the number ten jock school in the country. The basketball, lacrosse, and squash and field hockey programs rank at the top of anyone's list.

One of Princeton's most famous extracurricular activities is Triangle Club. Each year students write and produce a musical that they perform in McCarter Theatre and take on tour. Prominent Triangle alumni include Josh Logan, Jimmy Stewart, and, of more recent vintage, Brooke Shields. Theatre Intime, one of three other student production facilities, offers a student-produced drama series every year. Students interested in music have numerous outlets for their talents: the Orchestra, the Opera Theatre, the Jazz Ensemble, the Band (well known for its irreverent attitude at football games), the Glee Club, the Chapel Choir, and the Gospel Ensemble. Nine *a cappella* singing groups perform their own arrangements regularly around campus and in concert tours during vacation breaks.

Publications

Writers will find all kinds of publications on campus. Students publish two regular newspapers, the *Daily Princetonian* and the *Nassau Weekly*. The *Nassau Literary Review* is the nation's oldest student-run literary magazine. There are at least ten other publications, from the yearbooks to *Business Today,* which has a national circulation. (Princeton also has its own radio station, WPRB, which is affiliated with the Associated Press.)

Organizations

The American Whig-Cliosophic Society (known as Whig-Clio) is the oldest college political, literary, and debating society in the United States. (When a school has been around for more than 250 years, it's bound to have many of "the oldest" organizations!) This organization brings about twenty speakers to campus each year and sponsors a variety of programs related to public affairs. Those thinking of going into public affairs themselves can practice by participating in the Undergraduate Student Government (USG). In addition, twelve undergraduates sit on the Council of the Princeton University Community. The Student Volunteers Council and Community House provide service opportunities in which more than a thousand students participate each year.

These organizations may be the largest, but they are not the only ones on campus. The Office of the Dean of Student Life recognizes more than 200 official student organizations, and new ones are started all the time. These include more than twenty minority organizations on campus. On a far larger scale, the Third World Center, founded in 1971, emphasizes the cultural, intellectual, and social issues of students of color. Its mission is to be a readily accessible resource to all students interested in minority and Third World issues. The International Center, the Center for Jewish Life, and the Women's Center all represent the university's commitment to educational, cultural, and social programs that speak to a diverse student body. The Dean of the Chapel and Religious Life and various denominational chaplains on campus provide many opportunities for religious inquiry and expression—and Princeton surely has one of the most glorious college chapels in the world.

As with the academic programs, there is something for everyone in the abundance of extracurricular activities. Just pick one...or ten.

I was scared about the workload at Princeton, so I decided that I wouldn't do anything else but study. I had a pretty dull freshman year, and my grades weren't even that good! Then I missed singing too much and decided to audition for Triangle and one of the a cappella *groups. I got into both and started having fun. It also turned out that having other commitments helped me organize my study time better and—surprise!—my grades went up. That might not work for everybody, of course, but I have found since graduation that the people I keep in touch with most are the ones I sang with.*

FINANCIAL AID

Princeton admissions are need-blind, and the university pledges "to provide aid to all enrolled students judged by the Financial Aid Office to be in need of assistance." In a recent year, Princeton allocated almost $23 million in direct support through endowed scholarships and general funds to more than 2,000 undergraduates. That's almost forty-five percent of the student population. The Financial Aid Office looks at not only the parents' contribution, but also the potential contribution from the student, from savings, student loans, summer jobs, and campus jobs. Princeton is also very flexible in helping families who are not typical candidates for financial aid. The Student Employment Office helps undergraduates find jobs on and off campus. Financial aid students are given priority, but there really are jobs for anyone who wants one and almost seventy percent of the undergraduate student body works part-time. There is also a Princeton Student Loan program for students who don't qualify for financial assistance. And there is even a loan program, called the Princeton Parent Loan, for high-income families who do not need financial aid but who want to extend their payments over a much longer time than the four years.

In other words, if you are admitted to Princeton, Princeton will work with you and your family to figure out a way to pay for your four years there.

GRADUATES

My father was an alumnus of Princeton, and I was the first girl (woman!) in the family to be accepted. During the spring of my senior year in high school, he and I spent a lot of time going over the catalog and talking about all of the things we would do together. Then that summer my father died suddenly. Everything changed. Not only did I miss my father terribly, but it was also too late for me to apply for financial aid for that year. I knew my mother was worried about the costs. Instead of arriving on campus for Freshman Week bouncy and eager, I arrived sad and anxious. I hadn't been there more than a few days when I got a call from one of my father's classmates who was in the administration. I had never met this gentleman before, and I didn't remember my father ever having mentioned him as a good friend. Somehow, though, he had heard about my father's death and knew that I was starting at Princeton. He invited me to a home-cooked meal with his family. Within a few weeks he had helped me find the right people to talk to in the Financial Aid Office and had helped me find a part-time job. Later that year, he nominated me for a scholarship established by my dad's class. I was awarded that scholarship for my remaining three years. In June he invited me to stop by the class's tent at Reunions, where I met many of my father's college pals who made me laugh—and cry—with stories about my dad when he was my age. These men didn't know me at all, but they made me feel part of a family when the strongest link in my own family was gone.

I honestly believe no other school can claim the intense alumni loyalty that Princeton generates—loyalty both to fellow Princetonians and to Princeton itself. This speaks volumes about just how remarkable the Princeton experience is.

Over the past decade or so, there has been a slight shift in the postgraduate choices of Princeton seniors. The number choosing to go straight into the job market has steadily risen. In a survey of a recent graduating class, fifty-two percent said that they were going to get a job right away. Of the twenty-seven percent who answered that they were going to continue their education, half were going to graduate school and the other half to professional school. Of those choosing professional schools, most were going to medical school (twenty-four percent) or law school (twenty percent). Only a handful were going on for degrees in education, business, or public policy.

PROMINENT GRADS

- Woodrow Wilson, 1879, Thirteenth President of the United States
- Adlai Stevenson, '22, Former Governor of Illinois; former Ambassador to the United Nations; Presidential Candidate
- Josh Logan, '31, Broadway Producer
- Jimmy Stewart, '32, Actor
- Jose Ferrer, '33, Actor
- Claiborne Pell, '40, U.S. Senator (Rhode Island)
- James Baker, '52, Former Presidential Advisor
- Frank Carlucci, '52, Former Secretary of Defense
- Ralph Nader, '55, Activist
- Frank Deford, '61, Sportswriter
- Bill Bradley, '65, Former NBA star, U.S. Senator
- Steve Forbes, '70, President and CEO, Forbes, Inc.
- Queen Noor (Lisa Halaby), '73, Queen of Jordan
- Brooke Shields, '87, Actress

What do all these numbers mean? Because of its former elite reputation, Princeton is still often thought of as a place that churns out only doctors and lawyers. In fact, however, less than twelve percent of the Class of 1996 planned to go into those fields. Princetonians can be found in all walks of life, and the university has a number of resources to help graduates explore many kinds of prospects. Those interested in teaching or school administration can turn to the Program in Teacher Preparation, which maintains a placement service for all Princeton students and alumni. The Princeton-in-Asia program places interested students in short-term teaching assignments in China or Japan. Career Services offers a full range of programs and counseling, including workshops on résumé-writing and interviewing. Staff members can arrange interviews with representatives of professional schools and corporations. Career Services also coordinates with the Alumni Careers Network, which is made up of over 4,500 alumni around the world who have volunteered to give guidance and job-hunting assistance.

It's no surprise that Princeton has an incredibly loyal alumni body. Of the nearly 70,000 living Princeton alumni, both undergraduate and graduate, at any given time ten percent are involved in some kind of volunteer work for Princeton, whether in regional associations, the job placement network, or community service. And every spring more than 5,000 alumni return to Princeton on the weekend before Commencement for Reunions, to walk again the paths between the dorms, to catch up with classmates, and to parade through the campus, smiling at the cheers of current students and proudly wearing their orange and black. Also, more than 10,000 alumni keep up with the university and each other through an electronic alumni network known as Tigernet.

By the time I was a sophomore, I didn't think too much about being at Princeton. It was old hat. Then on the last Friday of October that year, the school celebrated its 250th anniversary with a big Convocation. It was one of those fall days when the sky is so blue it hurts your eyes and the sun was making the walls of Nassau Hall look almost golden. I was walking from the library and had stopped under one of the arches of a class building to watch the crowd breaking up from the ceremony. There were all kinds of people—I saw my history professor in his black academic gown, and I saw families with little kids pulling the orange and black tassels out of the programs, and I saw white-haired men moving slowly through the crowds. All of these people were heading toward a stage that had been put up in front of one of the dorms for a free Sheryl Crow concert. Sheryl Crow to celebrate 250 years! And I thought to myself, what a great place.

SUMMING UP

Princeton University successfully combines the best of several possible worlds. It has a world-renowned faculty, yet its primary focus is on its undergraduates. It has a range of activities that rivals even the largest universities in the country, yet the undergraduate population of 4,400 gives it an intimacy similar to that of a small liberal arts school. The diverse student body is drawn from all corners of the United States and the world, yet the students all share one thing—the intellectual potential to achieve at the highest level.

This is not to say that Princeton is for everyone; however, the students who have been disappointed tend to be those who expected something that Princeton never attempted to offer. If you are a star running back and want to play your college football games in front of rows of scouts and national television audiences, Princeton is not for you. On the other hand, the Princeton Tigers regularly get to the NCAA Basketball Championships and have defeated such powerhouses as UCLA. If you want to get a B.F.A. in film or creative writing, Princeton is not for you. On the other hand, you could design your own interdisciplinary major under the auspices of the Film Studies Committee or write a novel for your senior thesis in the English department and go on to a career in entertainment or the arts.

What you can expect from Princeton is one of the finest educations in the country. In this you won't be disappointed. You will also get something more: experiences that will stay with you a lifetime. You may have the chance to hear a famous Chaucer scholar recite *The*

Miller's Tale in Middle English to a packed lecture hall, making everyone laugh in the right places just by the judicious raising of an eyebrow. You may have the chance to work with a new preceptor in microbiology who will win the Nobel Prize in 2019. You may have the chance to dance in a Triangle Show kickline next to a skinny young man who will go on to become the next Jimmy Stewart.

The Princeton experience can be as unique as each student chooses to make it. Most graduates look back on their four years as a wonderful time of unlimited opportunities. This combination of the unique and the universal creates a bond among Princetonians that lasts far beyond graduation day.

❑ *Kathryn Taylor, B.A.*

RICE UNIVERSITY

Rice University
Houston, TX 77005

(713) 527-4036, (800) 527-OWLS
Fax: (713) 737-5646

E-mail: admi@rice.edu
Web site: http://www.rice.edu

Enrollment

Full-time ❑ women: 1,202
❑ men: 1,438

Part-time ❑ women: none
❑ men: none

INTRODUCING RICE

Entering students at Rice get their first taste of college life during the one-week orientation program at Rice known (appropriately enough) as Orientation Week (or O-Week). This intense, occasionally wild (and frequently messy) week proves amazingly effective at drawing the incoming students into the social and intellectual environment that will be their home for the next four years. The week itself is a blast, and it seems to instill an enthusiasm that lasts through the next four years of six-hour exams, twenty-page papers, and long nights spent on problem sets and difficult reading. If you are not careful, you may find yourself enjoying them!

As at most of the other top universities, Orientation Week at Rice is the time for new students to learn the ins and outs of their new home: the rules, the people, the procedures, and the expectations. But O-Week at Rice is unique in its structure and its flavor. In the first place, Orientation Week is planned and executed primarily by Rice students. For most of the summer, twenty-some-odd students have been working (volunteering) long nights in preparation for O-Week, and when late August finally rolls around, some three hundred students return to campus a week early to act as freshman advisors. The benefits of this system are threefold (at least):

- The intense Orientation Week forges strong bonds among freshmen that last for the next four years (and beyond).
- Since upperclassmen and freshmen are in an older sibling/younger sibling relationship from the start, strong bonds exist among the classes as well as within them.
- Orientation Week, like many other activities and events at Rice, is student-run and therefore responsive to student needs.

Why do some of the brightest students from around the country decide to come to Rice? Prospective students often get swamped with statistics about the universities they hope to attend, but statistics alone are seldom sufficient to convey the unique flavor of a university. Accurate statistics are often dull, and entertaining ones are frequently wrong. As an example of the latter, Rice was recently ranked by a southern gentleman's magazine as the fourth best university in the country for young people looking for "an easy and laid-back college experience." The magazine cited Rice's unusually high graduation rate and its congenial atmosphere as being among the reasons for their rating.

Of course, the magazine has gotten it more or less completely wrong. The eighty-eight percent graduation rate that Rice boasts is not a measure of the ease of the coursework, but a measure instead of the impressive quality of the student body and the individual attention that is given to each of the 2,700 undergraduate students that make it up. Far from being "easy and laid-back," students at Rice tackle their coursework and other activities with an enthusiastic vigor. A significant fraction of the student body graduates with a double major, though we are reminded time and time again that only one major is needed to graduate. Although the increasing number of students who enter Rice with a full semester's worth of Advanced Placement credit (or more) could easily get away with a reduced academic load, most of these students use those credits to take more challenging courses right away. Yet they still manage to play a dozen intramural sports and twenty club sports, support over 200 active groups on campus, and find time to hang out on Saturday afternoons.

It has been almost forty years since Rice University was known as the Rice Institute—a somewhat wild institution known for its strong technical program. Rice has continued its strong programs in the sciences and engineering, but has developed strong programs in the social sciences and humanities as well. Most newcomers to Rice are surprised to find that Rice's architecture and music schools are considered among the best in the nation. Add to this a large number of intramural fields and a tree for each student on campus (and a male to female ratio of five to four), and you find you have a beautiful and well-balanced intellectual oasis sitting on Main Street in the biggest city in Texas. And since Rice is still an up-and-coming university and not yet a topic of common conversation, you may still have a chance to get in.

ADMISSIONS REQUIREMENTS

Getting into Rice is hard. Recently there were nearly 7,000 applicants for only 665 positions in the incoming freshman class at Rice. The statistics of last year's incoming class at Rice are quite impressive as well. Twenty-five percent of the admitted students had verbal SAT I scores of 760 or higher; twenty-five percent had math SAT I scores of 780 or higher. Nearly two-thirds came from the top five percent of their graduating high school class, and National Merit scholars now comprise a full third of all currently enrolled students at Rice. But Rice students have to show that they have gotten more out of high school than simply good grades and test scores. In their deliberations each spring, the Admissions Committee weighs heavily how much students have challenged themselves in high school by taking advanced or honors classes, and is also impressed by students who have demonstrated talents in areas beyond the classroom. In short, the Admissions Committee is looking for, and has the luxury of choosing from some impressively well-rounded students.

The student body as a whole is diverse, too. Though many students were Texans before matriculating at Rice, the rest represent all of the other forty-nine states and sixty-eight foreign countries. Sixty-three percent of the Rice student body is Caucasian, fifteen percent is Asian American, eleven percent is Hispanic, and six percent is African American. Twenty-five percent are intended engineers, twenty-three percent are natural scientists, twenty percent are social scientists, humanists, musicians, or architects, and the remaining third is some combination of the above.

For the past couple of years, more accepted students have enrolled in Rice than the Admissions Committee has anticipated. In 1997–98, nearly fifty more students decided to attend Rice than projected by the Admissions Committee. Many attribute the increased numbers of entering students in the science and engineering programs to Rice's two 1996 Nobel Laureates in Chemistry, Richard Smally and Robert Curl, or perhaps to the national interest in Randy Hulet's research group and the physics of Bose-Einstein condensation. Others feel that these numbers are likely to continue to increase. Rice, though well known in the South, does not seem to be nearly so well known in other parts of the country, for reasons that may have more to do with the size of Rice's football program than anything else. But this is changing, and Rice may be forced to become even more selective as the years progress.

Rice recognizes that the students they admit are choosing among the other top schools in the country; as a result, prospective students are strongly encouraged to visit the Rice campus. Rice sets aside two days during the spring semester for prospectives to visit the university and to get a feel for the social and academic environment. This extended weekend has been affectionately named "Owl Day" after the fearsome Rice mascot, and prospectives who visit on that weekend are affectionately called "Owls." For many students it is this weekend that clinches the college decision in favor of Rice. No article can hope to fully convey Rice's distinctive character, so plan to visit!

ACADEMIC LIFE

On my honor, I have neither given nor received any aid on this examination.

Perhaps the most important aspect of academics at Rice is the Honor Code, a policy adopted by a vote of the student body in 1916, and one that has been cherished ever since. Developed by students at Rice, the Honor Code continues to be entirely student-enforced. It enables professors to give timed, closed-book, take-home exams (or unproctored, in-class exams), and it offers the students a significant amount of respect and responsibility. Incoming freshmen learn the details of the Honor Code in their first few days at Rice; its importance is internalized over the next few weeks; and its philosophy pervades their next few years.

When I got to Rice I found myself pleasantly surprised at the intellectual generosity of my fellow classmates. I still remember taking a rigorous calculus class my freshman year with seventeen other intended science and mathematics majors. The nights just before the midterm found no less than ten of us all working together to learn the material for the exam. I especially remember that two students who really knew the stuff made a special effort to help the rest of us, and I have marveled at consistently finding that same selfless attitude during my years at Rice. As a result, whenever I found myself in the fortunate position of being able to explain something, I tried to follow the model that was set before me my freshman year. It is a cycle that seems to continue itself, and probably one that was started a long time ago.

Peer Tutoring Program and Professors

Academic help at Rice also exists in the form of a peer tutoring program, but most students begin by taking full advantage of the accessibility of their professors. Because Rice is relatively small with a student-to-faculty ratio of nine to one, students find a number of opportunities to interact with professors both inside and outside of the classroom. Although some of the introductory classes at Rice are unavoidably large, most of the classes at Rice are no bigger than that calculus class I took my freshman year.

The residential halls on campus that house over 1,700 of Rice's undergraduates also house a couple dozen of the best Rice faculty, who are on hand to offer academic advice when you are eating lunch with them in the college, an informed opinion on a topic that has recently captured your attention as you stroll across campus, or just general words of wisdom, wherever you happen to be. Because these professors know the students outside the classroom and see them nearly every day, it is rare for a student to fall through the cracks of the academic advising structure at Rice.

Variety of Courses

In the true tradition of a liberal arts school, Rice offers an impressive variety of classes, and many students take advantage of the chance to take a course in a field they know nothing about from one of many excellent professors. Most students choose to take five classes per semester, which can be a heavy load even for students who are academically well prepared. A significant number of students also double major, though this is certainly not required.

I have had many chances to share undergraduate stories with students at some of the other top universities. Occasionally the subject of "all-nighters" will surface during the course of the conversation, and out of interest I usually ask how many they have had to pull. To date, the average answer is fewer than five over four years. When they ask me in return, I usually reply "about twelve," and do not bother to mention the fact that I am only counting my freshman year!

Grades

Not only do students at Rice work hard, but the grade inflation that seems to have hit most of the nation's top schools has so far completely missed Rice. If you do fairly well in a class, you get a B. Rice does offer As (which count as a 4.0) and A+s (which count as 4.33), but the latter is especially difficult to earn, and in some time-consuming classes an A- may be the highest grade awarded. Quite a lot is expected academically from students at Rice, but the strong support network and advising system that exists at Rice enables most students to do quite well.

Research

Another advantage of attending Rice is the opportunity to become involved in research as an undergraduate. Getting into graduate school is becoming increasingly dependent upon demonstrating the ability to do research. Rice, in addition to its strong program in undergraduate education, is home to some impressive research projects as well. Ties to NASA, the Texas Medical Center (the largest concentration of health-care facilities in the world is literally right across the street from campus), and many companies in the private sector result in terrific opportunities for students. Because so many research groups exist on campus, becoming involved with one is as simple as knocking on a professor's door. If the professor's door happens to be open, as is usually the case, it is even easier.

Accessibility

Finally, since Rice is located on a single (285-acre) block in Houston, getting to anyplace on campus requires at most a ten-minute walk. The computer labs, your professors, your classes, and over 1,700 other students are all well within walking distance. It may not seem like that big a deal, but the fact that everything is right there means that you will be saying hello to architects, social scientists, scientists, humanists, engineers, professors, researchers, athletes, and administrators, all in the three minutes that it takes you to walk to your nine o'clock class.

SOCIAL LIFE AND ACTIVITIES

The College System

Many of the social events at Rice occur within the structure of Rice's college system—a residential system instituted in 1957 and the brainchild of Rice's first president, Edgar Odell Lovett. Partially patterned after the system at Oxford and Cambridge, Rice's college system is nonetheless unique and distinguishes a Rice experience from one at any other institution. Each undergraduate at Rice is a member of one of eight residential colleges on campus, so each college has slightly more than 300 students and is physically home to over 200. Each college has its own Cabinet which makes policy and spending decisions, its own dining commons, its own study areas, its own faculty and community associates, its own intramural sports teams, its own drama productions, and its own unique character and traditions that have been developed over the years.

The college system is particularly important for incoming students, since it acts as the catalyst that brings so many students within hand-shaking distance. After Orientation Week, students find that they know most of the other freshmen in their college, and after another couple of weeks they generally find that they have gotten to know nearly everyone else in their college. Each college is also home to a faculty member (the college master) and his or her family. The master at various times will act as counselor, advisor, intramural football coach, party thrower, idea generator, student-administration liaison, and someone you know you can count on if something serious happens at three o'clock in the morning. The college also has two residential associates who function in a similar role, and who are often as much a part of the social life of the college as they are an integral part of the academic life of the university.

Each college has its own dining facilities, and students often eat breakfast, lunch, and dinner together in the common area of the college. This provides another opportunity for interaction among students (and also with faculty and administrators), and frequently students learn nearly as much at such a lunch hour as from that day's lectures. Though much more could be told, suffice it to say that the college system at Rice offers to students a welcome alternative to fraternities, sororities, and large freshman dorms.

Of all the many social activities I took part in during my time at Rice, one of my personal favorites was sitting in our college master's house every Sunday evening with about sixty other people to watch that week's episode of "The Simpsons." Our college master, in addition to studying the process of protein folding, winning teaching awards for his Socratic-style approach to freshman chemistry, and functioning in many roles around the college, invited us all into his living room (snacks in the dining room) to hang out for an hour or so, catch up with friends, and see what Bart was up to that week.

Traditions

A spirited rivalry exists between many of the colleges, and at no time during the year is this spirit more apparent than during those days immediately preceding Beer Bike. This appropriately named event, which usually occurs in mid-March, is a combination bike and beer-chugging race. (Water, though an acceptable substitute for boiled beer, is more difficult to chug.) Ten individuals from each college bike a mile sprint, and ten chug—the goal of the race simply being to finish first. Beer Bike is a long-standing tradition at Rice, and there are few students on campus who are not guilty of participating in the fun. We note in passing that, although each team is required to field ten bikers and ten chuggers, most teams consist of fewer than twenty people. (Some rugged individuals, in true Rice style, do both.)

Baker 13 is another of the long-standing traditions at Rice. Some time ago a group of students got together and decided to run almost naked around the university on the 13th, 26th, and 31st of each month. Almost naked in this case means naked except for about a half a can of shaving cream smeared in appropriate places. On these nights, starting at about ten o'clock, they run around campus, often through the student center, many of them stopping down in Willy's Pub to grab a beer, and at times walking through the president's house. After running several minutes, whatever shaving cream you had originally applied has probably ended up on the ground somewhere behind you. But by that point, generally, you don't particularly care.

Alcohol

Whether we wish it so or not, the alcohol policy on campus and its use by students does a large part to shape the social scene at most universities. As a result, many incoming students, drinkers and nondrinkers alike, are justifiably interested in the university's alcohol policy. Rice is unique among schools in Texas (and rare among schools nationwide) in having a wet campus and an alcohol policy that was originally constructed by, and is continually enforced by, the student body. Though liability issues have forced most universities to adopt a dry campus policy, a strong push to keep the social life at Rice on the campus itself has led the administration to place a lot of faith in the responsibility of Rice students. In short:

- The alcohol policy is a student policy that keeps social life on campus while complying with Texas state law.
- Almost all of the social events at Rice occur on campus, which makes getting to them a matter of a five-minute walk.
- Because everything happens right on campus, students have a wonderful opportunity to meet most of the other students there.

Clubs

Most Rice students are involved in at least one of the many clubs on campus. These clubs vary in defining activity and temperament from the campus Karate Club to the Chinese Student Association to the nationally known debate team to the Rice Student Volunteer Program (RSVP) to the Rice Association for Biologically Inclined Students (RABIES) to the Rice Association of Transfer Students (RATS) to the Marching Owl Band (MOB) to more than 200 other groups that space requirements don't permit listing here. Each year most of the residential colleges put on plays and musicals of surprising quality, and woe to you if you pass up the opportunity to watch your friends perform.

Sports

After spending all night putting the finishing touches on a paper, sleeping through your nine o'clock, and acing a chemistry exam just after eating a hurried lunch, nothing beats sweating the last of your strength away in a good intramural soccer game. Due in part to the long sport season in the Houston area (sports such as football, soccer, and tennis are played year-round, though usually only after four o'clock in the summer months), and due in part to the large number of good intramural fields that lie right outside your door, over sixty percent of the Rice student body participates in a strong intramural program.

An inter-college competition exists for many team sports—these so-called "college sports" are a level above intramurals in terms of their competitiveness and the number of fans that come out to watch the games. At yet another level of ability are the club teams, which at Rice exist for twenty sports including soccer, crew, Ultimate Frisbee, rugby, lacrosse, cycling, fencing, and cricket, and that provide an intense experience for several hundred students at Rice. Considering the small number of students the club teams have to draw from, Rice is remarkably competitive: the men's lacrosse team missed advancing to the league finals by an overtime goal against a team that outweighed them three to two, the men's rugby team earned the right to compete at nationals last year, the Ultimate club team finished seventh at the national tournament last year, and several other club sports have been similarly competitive. We may be small, but we tend to be scrappy.

Rice, now a member of the sixteen-team Western Athletic Conference, also has the honor of being the smallest Division I-A school in the nation. In spite of its size, Rice does well in the sports in which it competes. While no one ever really expects Rice to dominate the conference in any sport, the last few years have been especially good for Rice athletics—last year saw the Rice baseball team in the College World Series, and saw one of the team's stars chosen as the #1 draft pick in the major leagues. This is especially impressive when one remembers that varsity athletes at Rice are held to the same rigorous academic standard as the rest of the student body. And going to a sporting event is especially fun at Rice since you find yourself rooting for your hallmates and classmates.

Politics

Speakers come to Rice frequently to give talks, and these guest lectures often end up being a fine one-hour crash course in an area you previously may have known nothing about. As an example, listening to Yassir Arafat talk at Rice last semester gave many of us an appreciation not only for the problems that are being addressed in the Middle East, but also for the security measures that are taken to ensure the safety of one of the world's most important heads of state. The James A. Baker III Institute for Public Policy, which was responsible for bringing Yassir Arafat to Rice, also enabled Rice to host the 1990 Economic Summit of the Industrialized Nations, which, among other things, gave major political figures from around the world the chance to experience Houston in July. And, of course, within Rice's 70,000-seat stadium lies the spot from which President Kennedy made his historic announcement of our nation's mission to the moon some thirty-five years ago.

If you think that world politics may be your cup of tea (or if you are interested in politics at any level), you might consider playing a role in the student government at Rice. As you might expect, the Rice administration is especially receptive to students' comments on curricula and university policies. If you think you have come up with an especially good idea, odds are good that you will be given a chance to see what you can do with it.

FINANCIAL AID

For the last three years Rice has ranked in the top three on *Money Magazine's* list of best college buys. Everything detailed above provides only half of the reason for this ranking; the other half is Rice's low tuition. Discovering Rice is sort of like finding the best model of your favorite product in a half-off sale.

Rice is able to offer all that it does while costing as little as it does because of its massive endowment, now over $2.3 billion and growing. Though the true cost of a Rice education is actually quite high—over $40,000 per student, per year—the size of the endowment enables Rice to keep tuition at a third of that, and to continue its policy of need-blind admission. Rice's financial success is due largely to the foresight and wealth of William Marsh Rice, the founder and namesake of the university, and to shrewd investments since then. Rice's healthy financial state means that it can continue to expand its programs while keeping tuition low, as evidenced by the current construction of three major buildings on campus.

Rice offers additional merit- and need-based financial aid when possible. In a recent academic year, Rice offered $22 million in financial aid to over 2,200 students, for an average award of $9,600 to eighty-five percent of the student body. In the charter of the university, Rice commits itself to providing any qualified student the opportunity to receive a first-rate education, regardless of his or her financial situation. Through a low tuition, additional financial aid packages, and many opportunities for loans and work-study, Rice continues to honor this commitment almost a century later.

GRADUATES

Rice graduates only some 620 undergraduates per year, so the number of currently enrolled students at some of the bigger public schools in the country actually exceeds the number of living Rice alumni! As a symbol of the individual attention given to each student at Rice, the university has always prided itself in recognizing each student individually during the graduation ceremony. Exiting the academic quadrangle through the sally port that you had matriculated through just four short years before leaves a bittersweet taste; yet many of the good-byes said on graduation day contain the unspoken but confident assurance that the odds of running into that person again are actually quite good.

Of this last year's graduating class, roughly twenty-five percent applied to, and are now attending, some of the best medical schools in the country. According to a recent COFHE

PROMINENT GRADS

- Charles Blair, '31, Chemist
- Seth Morris, '35, Architect
- Marshall Gates, '36, Chemistry Educator; First to Synthesize Morphine
- Bill Archer, '46, Republican Congressman; Chairman of the House Ways and Means Committee
- Robert Curl, '54, Nobel Laureate in Chemistry
- Robert Wilson, '57, Nobel Laureate in Physics
- Nancy Cole, '64, Educator; ETS President
- William Broyles, '66, Journalist, Screenwriter
- John Doerr, '73, Venture Capitalist
- Larry McMurtry, Writer

report, the twenty-five percent going on to graduate school or law school are more successful in getting into their top choice school than students at any other elite university. The twenty-two students from the school of architecture are now in their fifth year preceptorships in world-renown firms in cities like Vienna, Milan, New York, San Francisco, and Paris. The 200 graduates who interviewed for engineering, consulting, and computer science jobs now hold challenging and well-paid positions in companies such as Microsoft, McKinsey & Co., Intel, and Exxon.

Admittedly, some graduates of Rice end up being a bit of a disappointment. A friend who lived down the hall from me is postponing her entrance into the political arena in order to spend two years at Oxford on a Rhodes scholarship. Another is deferring admittance to the M.D./Ph.D. program at Harvard in order to study at Cambridge on a Churchill scholarship. Another is heading to Cambridge to study classics on a Marshall scholarship. Another was admitted to only six of the top seven graduate schools in physics, so he is spending this year at the Niels Bohr Institute in Denmark on a Fulbright scholarship with his better half (a Rice graduate in biology, also on a Fulbright scholarship), who had recently been forced to decline over $100,000 in scholarship money since she could only accept one of her three national fellowships. We all felt really sorry for them.

Many other Rice grads are grabbing the opportunity to study or to do research abroad—some on fellowship, some on a whim, many on both. Some of the best in recent years have decided to join the Teach for America program to help teach disadvantaged kids, and others are taking up other educational positions around the country.

In addition to all the prestigious and socially responsible roles that Rice graduates appear to be filling, it should be noted that Rice's $2.3 billion endowment alone is not sufficient to keep Rice's tuition as low as it is. The advantage of a Rice education is further evidenced by generous contributions from successful alumni.

SUMMING UP

Having just recently graduated from Rice, I can still recall my college search experience. The position most of us find ourselves in, unfortunately, is one of incomplete information. It is really hard to decide whether or not you want to spend four years at a place until you have actually spent one there, and that is clearly not something that you will be given a chance to do. The main reason I decided to go to Rice was just because it felt right. Now, almost five years later, I look back on that decision as one of the best I have made so far. Others have had different experiences in their time at Rice—many good, some not.

You are now in the fortunate position of having the opportunity to choose among some of the best colleges in the country. If anything just feels right about the academic program, the academic atmosphere, the social life, the sports, the clubs, the college system, the size, the campus, the cost, or whatever, I think that you will find that Rice is a great place to be. I have very fond memories of Rice, and I am afraid, like many alumni, that I will not need much of an excuse to go back to Rice every now and then. On those occasions that I do, I hope to see you there.

❑ *Bruce Knuteson, B.A.*

STANFORD UNIVERSITY

Photo by Stanford News Service

Stanford University
Stanford, CA 94309

(650) 723-2091
Fax: (650) 725-2846

E-mail:
undergrad.admissions@forsythe.stanford.edu.
Web site: http://www.stanford.edu

Enrollment

Full-time ❑ women: 8,056
❑ men: 8,786

INTRODUCING STANFORD

It was about 8 A.M. on the first day of my freshman orientation at Stanford. I was an East Coast transplant to California, and I knew nobody at Stanford. It was kind of a terrifying feeling, knowing that after my mom left, that same afternoon, I would basically be entirely on my own for the first time. I trudged up to my assigned dorm, Lagunita Court, dragging two huge suitcases behind me. There were about thirty people gathered around a row of tables talking and laughing, and my heart sank that I didn't have a single friend to talk to. I was almost convinced that this whole thing—committing myself to four years 3,000 miles away from home—was a big mistake. Then, all of a sudden, all these people were pointing at me and yelling my name! A couple of guys came over and took my bags from my hands, and introduced themselves as the resident fellow and the resident assistant. I found out later that the staff of my dorm had memorized the faces and names of all the freshmen, and singled out each as they came up to the dorm to welcome us! Orientation week was a blur; I went to so many meetings, parties, and events that I don't think I slept more than a few hours a night because there was so much to see.

The most often-heard description of Stanford is that it's laid back. Like any other superlative, it's got a little bit of truth in it and it leaves a lot out at the same time. As at any other top university, you'll find quite a few people stumbling out of the library at midnight, only to be back at the same desk the next day after classes end. The courses are demanding, and there are few students who don't spend at least a few sleepless nights in the computer centers or in the twenty-four-hour study room attached to Meyer Library. But at Stanford, the perpetually shining sun makes it hard to stay indoors and stress over school all the time.

Far removed from the cold winters and deep-rooted tradition of the Ivy League, Stanford, just over 100 years old, is a young institution still creating its identity and traditions. Academically, one of the best things about the school is that it is constantly expanding its offerings for its 6,500 undergraduate students. In 1997 a set of eighty new seminars was offered for the first time to the incoming freshman class. A three-year-old program called "sophomore college" lets sophomores apply to take one of a set of intensive small seminars with a faculty member for a few weeks before regular classes start in the fall. The academic programs are constantly changing and being modified, and student input plays a role in what is kept and what is discarded.

Physical Description

Outside of the academic sphere, Stanford offers a huge amount of activities as well. The campus is known for its beautiful architecture and layout and is home to the largest collection of Rodin sculptures in the United States. The weather is also something that non-Californians tend to marvel over; shorts and T-shirts are the school uniform year round. The beauty of the surrounding area occasionally convinces entire dorms to brush off assignments and take off for the weekend. There's skiing up at Lake Tahoe, kayaking in Monterey Bay, hiking in Big Sur, or camping at Yosemite; none of these activities is more than about four and a half hours away.

Student Activism

Students sometimes take a very active role in Stanford's educational direction. This is demonstrated by the recent case of Akhil Gupta, an anthropology professor who was approved for tenure by his department, then denied tenure by the School of Humanities and Sciences. A group of students, upset by the decision, helped take Gupta's case to the media and to his colleagues at other schools, and turned the debate over the makeup of the anthropology department at Stanford into a national issue. Student activism at Stanford also played a role in the recent national uproar over *U.S. News and World Report*'s yearly ranking of colleges. Stanford's decision to offer an alternative to the *U.S. News* rankings by establishing a site on the Internet that offers data on the school came after Stanford students started a national organization to protest *U.S. News'* ranking methods.

One Stanford T-shirt reads "Stanford—Why any other place?" It's a sentiment shared by most of the student body. Where else could you start the day with a class with Richard Zare, who was part of the science team that stunned the world by announcing that they had found what they believed to be evidence of past life in a Martian meteorite, and end it at a secluded High Sierra campground in Yosemite?

ADMISSIONS REQUIREMENTS

I remember being really intimidated by the other students here when I started; it seemed that everyone had all these awards and achievements, and that I really didn't. But I came to realize that, like everyone here, I had my strengths, and, as I got involved with my classes, I found that I sometimes contributed to classes and activities in a way that others couldn't. Stanford finds the strengths in its applicants, I think, and they realize it when your strengths make you a good fit with the school.

Getting admitted to Stanford is a complex process; as with many other high-caliber schools, it is difficult to discern what it is about an application that makes one student stand out to the Stanford admissions staff in a crowd of high achievers. Stanford states that for all the qualified students who are admitted, there are other, similarly qualified students who are turned down.

Stanford states that academic excellence is the primary criteria for admission; in the freshman class of 1997, eighty-nine percent of students were ranked in the top ten percent of their graduating classes. A rigorous academic program is also important. Most Stanford students have chosen and excelled in the most difficult courses offered; however, Stanford will occasionally turn down even students at the top of their classes.

After high academic marks, Stanford looks for personal achievement outside the classroom in applicants. Students who show dedication to furthering their education outside the classroom make a favorable impression. It is difficult to find a student at Stanford who didn't spend a good deal of time challenging himself or herself further through extracurricular activities. Stanford looks for students who will add to the Stanford community both academically and through their nonacademic interests.

Early Decision and Interviews

Stanford now offers two Early Decision application options with application deadlines of November 1 and December 1. These applications are binding, should the student be accepted. The deadline for regular applications is December 15. Stanford does not offer interviews, either on campus or in the applicant's hometown area, stating that interviews can be misleading, and as such do not really add to the application. Applications may be reviewed by as many as five admissions officers.

There is no magic formula for admission, but the undergraduate admission home page at: http://www-leland.stanford.edu/group/uga/html/admission.html gives some additional basic information on how Stanford evaluates its applicants.

I was in a class called the Psychology of Mind Control, and we were all put into sections that met to discuss more parts of the class in depth. I was placed in the cult section, and each week we studied cults: how cults attract people and how they get them involved and keep them. For our final project we were supposed to present something to the class to teach them about what we learned about cults. Well, we didn't think that we would be able to start a cult in the ten weeks that we had the class, so we started thinking what else we could do. Someone came up with the idea of seeing how many people we could get to drop their pants in White Plaza at noon on a Friday. We called it "Moon at Noon" and put together a series of presentations and flyers based on what we had learned about cults to convince students to do this pretty bizarre thing. We posed it as an antiestablishment activity and said that if enough people mooned, Stanford might make it into the Guinness Book of World Records*. In the end, over 200 people mooned! We wanted to do something interesting and different, something fun for the project. It was definitely the most interesting group project I've ever done.*

Stanford has undergone many changes in its academic programs and offerings through its first 100 years. Its core curriculum is in a constant state of flux, with graduation requirements changing three times in the past five years. An example of this is the old western civilizations requirement, which was changed to the more inclusive and global cultures, ideas, and values, which is now also undergoing revision. Although all the changes are confusing, they also reflect the commitment that Stanford has to responding to student and faculty input on its courses.

Class Size

Many new students share the fear that they will be trapped for their first year in huge lecture classes with little hands-on experience. It was student desire for more interactive classes that led to the creation of small introductory seminar classes for freshmen and sophomores in which students work with a professor in a group setting. Topics cover many fields, from engineering applications in medicine, to the evolution of voting rights in the United States. It is a great opportunity to meet professors who specialize in fields that students have an interest in, or just to indulge an interest.

While there are classes that number in the hundreds, there are also classes that give new and old students alike a chance to try their hand at producing tangible projects. Mechanical Engineering 101 is an example of this. Frosh and upperclass alike struggle with this introductory course, which involves designing and creating projects from an original musical instrument to a device that shoots a Twinkie twenty feet across a table through a pair of doors, unwraps it, and cuts it in half. As one student puts it: "Half the fun is watching everyone else's project self-destruct. Then you don't feel so bad about yours."

Courses

Stanford's constantly expanding offerings give students a chance to expose themselves to different fields, and often the people teaching introductory-level classes are at the top of their profession. One example is a course offered for the first time in 1997 called Nobel Perspectives on Ethics in Science. The class, developed by an undergraduate student who wanted other students to hear from some of Stanford's most respected professors, brought in five of Stanford's Nobel Laureates who discussed ethical concerns in their fields of physics, chemistry, and biology.

Faculty

Professors also draw on student talent to improve their classes; upperclass students often give a great deal of time to a course as a teaching assistant or section leader, thus giving students another resource to go to when they are having difficulty.

Computer science is an exciting major at Stanford, especially considering that we are smack in the middle of Silicon Valley. Stanford is kind of a model school when it comes to teaching computer science as well, and that was what made me get involved with a class called Teaching Computer Science. About two-thirds of all Stanford undergraduates take a beginning computer science class. Since those classes are pretty big, and computer science is a pretty difficult subject, we have small sections taught by undergraduates to give students one-on-one help when they need it. When they hand in a programming assignment, we don't just grade it and throw it in a box, we have individual sessions with each student to discuss each program, how they did, and what could be improved. It's great because the undergraduate teachers are an enthusiastic group, and help students get the most out of the class.

Faculty also interacts with students in many ways outside of class: as advisors, as lab heads, and as speakers. The faculty often goes a step past lecturing, bringing in experts in the field of study of the course to talk about their work.

I was in a class on twentieth century African American fiction, and we were reading Terry McMillan's book Waiting to Exhale. *The book had started a debate among students as to whether McMillan's work belonged in the same literary category as Toni Morrison, James Baldwin, and other authors we were also reading, or whether it fell short of that distinction. Well, Professor Porter came in one day and told the class that instead of him lecturing about* Exhale, *Terry McMillan would be giving the talk that day! She got up on stage and discussed her work for about an hour, and then took questions and comments from the class. It was incredible to actually have the author on stage talking about what I had read the night before. I definitely got a deeper understanding of the work from McMillan than I would have with someone else lecturing on it.*

Interaction with faculty members is a wonderful way to learn more about a field that you are considering majoring in, and for the most part, members of the faculty are very receptive to student inquiries about their research and interests. Not only excellent lecturers, the faculty at Stanford often guide students through honors projects, research, or lab work.

As a sophomore, I took my first journalism course at Stanford. I wanted to be a reporter, and I was taking a class on writing and reporting the news with Dale Maharidge, a professor who was also a Pulitzer Prize-winning reporter. I was terrified when he returned our first assignments to us with slashes of red editing all over them and the comment "These were awful." But he was determined to make our class into better, or at least tolerable, writers. With his encouragement, I went on to write stories on the development of AIDS drugs and on egg and sperm donation among college students, and discovered that journalism was my calling. My junior year, Professor Maharidge helped me land a summer internship as a reporter for a daily paper in New York. He was a mentor as well as a teacher, and I will always be grateful for his help.

Overseas Programs

To fully take advantage of all that Stanford has to offer, students must take the initiative to explore the variety of courses and programs. For instance, Stanford offers a number of overseas studies programs, with programs in Kyoto, Japan; Florence, Italy; and Oxford, England, to name just a few. Students with interests in subjects such as French literature or Japanese can take a quarter or two in another country to learn; many students feel that this is a wonderful way to enhance their academic experiences. At Stanford, the hardest academic choice is usually how to narrow down all your interests to fit them into a manageable courseload.

STANFORD FACULTY

The caliber of the faculty at Stanford is unmatched almost anywhere, and faculty shares the same wide variety of interests and achievements as its student counterparts.

Among the 1,455 faculty at Stanford, there are fourteen Nobel Laureates, including physicist Steven Chu and economist Myron Scholes, who were honored with the award in 1997. In addition, there are 108 members of the National Academy of Sciences, 191 members of the American Academy of Arts and Sciences, 69 members of the National Academy of Engineering, 19 members of the National Academy of Education, and 20 winners of the National Medal of Science.

SOCIAL LIFE AND ACTIVITIES

The first weekend of my freshman year, my dorm and I were taken by the residence staff to San Francisco for a scavenger hunt. I had never been to San Francisco, and I didn't know the people in my dorm too well at that point, but we were dropped off in Union Square with lists of items to pick up. We were told to return that evening with a box of Rice-a-Roni, a picture of us in front of Jerry Garcia's former apartment, and an optional body piercing (no ears), to name only a few of the items. It was completely insane—a great time.

Dorms

For new students, social life revolves around the dorm. Dorm staff, made up primarily of students, is one of the unique features about student life at Stanford. The staff includes a resident assistant, academic advisors, tutors, a computer consultant, and a peer health educator—all students, whose job it is to make life at Stanford as exciting and interesting as possible. Dorms take ski trips, head out for midnight romps on the beach, compete against each other in scavenger hunts through San Francisco, and have intramural teams that take on other dorms. Students also make the most of the beautiful area around Stanford. Dorm hiking and whitewater rafting trips are frequent in the fall and spring, and most dorms go on at least one ski trip up to Lake Tahoe in the winter.

Athletics

A unique feature of Stanford is its nationally known athletic program. The biggest question at Stanford involving another school isn't "Should I have gone Ivy?;" it's "Do you think Stanford will whip the Weenies again this year?" in reference to the biggest athletic event of the year: Stanford's 100-year-old football rivalry with U.C. Berkeley. In 1997 Stanford took home six NCAA titles, and had seventeen varsity teams nationally ranked in the top five.

For the most part, the statistics speak for themselves: Stanford was the winner of the Sear's Cup, an honor given to the top athletics program in the nation, for the third year in a row. Stanford teams are no strangers to national championships: as mentioned, in 1996–97, Cardinal (the color, not the bird!) teams took home NCAA championships in men's and women's cross-country, men's and women's volleyball, and men's and women's tennis. Nine other teams finished in the top-four nationally. A year ago, Stanford won an unprecedented six NCAA team championships, the most ever won by one school in an academic year.

Stanford's dominance extends to international competition as well. Cardinal members made quite an impression in the 1996 Atlanta games; past and present Stanford athletes accounted for sixteen gold medals, one silver, and one bronze.

Home football games were always a huge event my freshman year. Imagine sitting under the burning sun completely wrapped in aluminum foil with a huge red "S" painted across your chest and back, and screaming your lungs out for three hours straight. And I wasn't the craziest person there, either.

Games are livened up by the irreverent—and occasionally reprimanded—Leland Stanford Junior University Marching Band, and Stanford's beloved mascot, the Tree. After football games, overheated masses of students often "fountain-hop" around the campus, splashing from fountain to fountain until they cool off.

The Greek Scene

On the Greek scene, Stanford has six housed fraternities and nine unhoused, and seven sororities, none of which are housed. These groups don't play a huge part in campus life, although students flock to their weekend parties, with themes such as "Arabian Nights" and "Jello Bash." About a fifth of the campus is involved in these organizations, and many hold community service events and fund-raisers for organizations.

Outside Activities

Although inundated with classwork, most Stanford students manage to squeeze out some time to follow up interests outside of classes. Stanford holds the diversity of backgrounds and interests in its student body as one of its greatest strengths. The diversity of interests that students bring to the campus is evident in the endless activities and organizations that students create, develop, and maintain.

I think my biggest problem with Stanford was that there were so many things to do in the four years that I was here that it was impossible to do them all.

Students at Stanford are expert organizers and great recruiters, drawing their peers into activities like the yearly mud volleyball tournament where dorms and groups of students team up to benefit a chosen organization by playing (or at least attempting to play) volleyball in a pond of mud. Stanford offers a huge variety of community service groups and organizations dedicated to everything from peer HIV/AIDS counseling to tutoring to spending time with children undergoing treatment at the Lucille Packard Children's Hospital.

Publications

The large number of student publications on campus are also a draw for many students. You can try your hand at creative writing, poetry, and even hard-core news reporting if you join the staff of the student-run newspaper, the *Stanford Daily*. Student activism often calls attention to deficiencies on campus. In 1997 a group of disabled students took the initiative to rank buildings on campus according to their accessibility. The poor marks of many of the buildings caused an outcry that led to a dialogue with the administration to remedy the problem.

Traditions

Stanford traditions are rooted in irreverence.

As traditions go, it's impossible to ignore the Full Moon on the Quad, a frosh right of passage where new students are smooched by their departing counterparts, the seniors. A quick kiss in the dark under the first full moon of the school year is considered a prerequisite for becoming a Stanford woman or man. FMOTQ is a gathering complete with music and entertainment from the Band and the Tree, and other student groups. But frosh should beware of lonely sophomores and juniors trying to get in on the action!

Sunday nights, students head out in droves to Flicks, a student-run evening of recent movies that traditionally starts off with a huge paper fight. Seniors are treated to a special showing of *The Graduate*, and sit in their caps and gowns to watch Dustin Hoffman take a stab at the real world after he graduates from college.

Another campus-wide event is the annual Viennese Ball, which has students entering a raffle and sleeping out to get tickets. The dance, which gives students a chance to hone their waltzing skills, has been a tradition at Stanford since 1977.

There are an immense number of nonacademic student organizations at Stanford, and many students will tell you that 6 A.M. workouts with the crew team or Thursday afternoons tutoring an elementary school student were among their best memories of Stanford.

FINANCIAL AID

As if the tuition at Stanford wasn't bad enough, the Palo Alto area is also a pretty expensive place to live. I decided to get a job my freshman year to keep up with my bills. I applied to be a tour guide, and I was still working there four years later as a senior. I got to give a tour to the ambassador from the Ivory Coast and helped the CIA search bags when Secretary of State Warren Christopher came to speak at Stanford, not to mention talking to tons of prospective students about how great Stanford is. Guiding ended up being one of my best experiences at Stanford.

With the cost of tuition, room, and board rising, it's not a surprise that just under two-thirds of Stanford students get some form of financial aid. According to the Department of Undergraduate Admissions, all students applying for aid at Stanford are required to fill out the Free Application for Federal Student Aid (FAFSA) to establish eligibility for aid such as Pell Grants, Cal Grants, and Stafford Loans. Self-help is another component of financial aid at Stanford; students are expected to work and borrow up to twenty-one percent of their budget, which came out to about $6,500 for a recent academic year.

Stanford has a policy of need-blind admission in which admission decisions are made independent of financial need. Stanford makes an effort to provide aid for students who demonstrate financial need, but the process of applying for and receiving aid can often be quite confusing. Many students go outside the Stanford system to win scholarships or grants from private organizations to finance their education, and students often look to work as another way to offset the expenses of being a student.

I received almost no financial aid from Stanford. I won two outside scholarships in high school, and that took a little of the edge off the bills, but it is still an incredibly expensive place for a middle-class family to send their kid.

The Financial Aid Office makes information available to students and also has people on hand to make the process of paying for college less confusing, for Stanford offers a variety of long- and short-term payment plans and options available to help students meet their financial obligations. There are also several parent loans, including the Parent Loan for Undergraduate Students (PLUS), a government-guaranteed loan that is not need-based, which students and their families can apply for.

For more information on financial aid and admissions at Stanford, a good resource is the undergraduate admission home page on the web at: http://www.leland.stanford.edu/group/uga/uga.html.

GRADUATES

I was an economics and public policy major at Stanford, and most people in those majors either went to law or business school after graduating, or went into consulting. I didn't know if I really wanted to do that, and a few friends of mine had been talking about starting a company. I realized that I was at a rare point in my life when I was surrounded by amazing people who had all these amazing ideas, and I decided, if they weren't going to succeed, who was? So I decided to take a risk. We started a consulting company in 1994 that was focused on Internet technologies. At that time, the market for Internet consultants was untapped and growing, and there was a lot of room for new consulting companies. We started out in someone's living room, moved to a tiny office, and now, three years later we are moving to a really nice, huge office! We had only four people in the beginning; we now have fifteen, and expect to keep on growing.

That Stanford students take a variety of paths after graduation is not surprising, considering the diversity of experiences that Stanford prepares them with. Many stay after their undergraduate degree to take advantage of Stanford's co-terminal program, which allows students to work on their masters degree while still an undergraduate, and get a master's degree in a year. Others travel far from Stanford to work in the Peace Corps. Stanford is currently the tenth-ranked university nationwide to provide the most volunteers to the Peace Corps.

PROMINENT GRADS

- **Stephen Breyer, U.S. Supreme Court Justice**
- **John Elway, NFL Quarterback**
- **Robert Hass, U.S. Poet Laureate**
- **Anthony M. Kennedy, U.S. Supreme Court Justice**
- **Ted Koppel, ABC *Nightline* Anchor**
- **Sandra Day O'Connor, U.S. Supreme Court Justice**
- **William H. Rehnquist, U.S. Supreme Court Justice**
- **Scott Turow, Author**
- **Sigourney Weaver, Actress**

The Career Planning and Placement Center at Stanford brings in employers from Microsoft to the American Heart Association to the Rainforest Action Network who conduct interviews and recruit on campus. Because Stanford is in the heart of Silicon Valley and on the cutting edge of computer science and engineering academically, students are heavily recruited by Silicon Valley firms. Nonengineering majors often complain that the CPPC's offerings lean too heavily toward engineering students, but with a number of job fairs throughout the year, and help from their departments, many students find employment well before graduation.

Stanford also has its share of premedical, law, and business students, and others who choose to continue their education after they receive an undergraduate degree. Student groups offer talks and information sessions for students interested in medical, law, and business school, and the Undergraduate Advising Center will aid students in planning out their four undergraduate years to meet their pregraduate school requirements. Many students enjoy their undergraduate experience so much that they remain at the university for graduate studies, or as employees. University departments act as a network for job-hunting students as well, informing them of job openings through mailing lists.

After graduating, I joined the staff of the Stanford Human Genome Center. I realized that I was really going to miss being in the loop of student life, so I decided to become an undergraduate advisor. Now I try to help new students make the most of everything that there is at Stanford, especially the things that I missed while I was here! Many of the advisors are Stanford graduates themselves, and they bring an enormous amount of enthusiasm and knowledge about the workings of the school to their incoming students.

Stanford alumni often keep in close touch with the school, and offer their assistance to graduating students who are looking for direction. The Career Planning and Placement Center keeps information on alumni who are willing to be contacted by Stanford students who are interested in similar careers. When young alums get together with current students, there are some differences in memories of Stanford—but sometimes older alums might almost have gone to different schools, Stanford has changed so much in its first 100 years!

SUMMING UP

Stanford has come a long way from the stock farm that Leland and Jane Stanford decided to turn into a small university in 1891. Just over 100 years later, the university continues to grow and change to make the most of its faculty and students.

Not surprisingly, the rigorous academic program at Stanford often brings students a large measure of stress. In the weeks before midterms and finals, the libraries are packed until closing with worried students. But students at Stanford don't keep it all locked up inside. Whether you're walking home from studying at midnight, or just sitting in your room as the clock strikes twelve during "Dead Week," as students call the week before finals week, you'll hear a shrill, campus-wide scream wash through the dorms. It's called "Primal Scream," an energy- and stress-releasing shriek that reminds students that they are not alone in feeling overwhelmed at times.

Stanford makes every effort to ensure that students don't get lost among the variety of opportunities that the university offers, with an incredible orientation program, and through freshman advisors, who help new students sort out their choices. But in the end, it is other students whose knowledge and advice guides new students through the maze of courses, seminars, and extracurriculars that Stanford offers.

I came in freshman year as a hard worker, but not at all what you would call a stress case. After my first week of classes, however, I was a wreck, terrified that there was no way I was going to be able to handle all the work, and staying up all night trying to keep up with my classes and my fellow students! I would stand in the hallway of my dorm at three in the morning, juggling tennis balls with other late-night studies—about half the dorm—to calm myself down. My resident assistant, a senior, saw me one night, and basically told me to slow down, that I wasn't going to learn anything if I was stressing so much. He helped me plan out my time and classes so that I didn't have to cram everything in at the same time, and told me that I had four years to figure things out. I needed perspective as a new student, to be told that it was normal to feel that it was tough to keep pace, and I was lucky to have him there to give me a hand.

Students provide their own brand of support and encouragement for each other. The diversity of interests and backgrounds among Stanford students expose Stanford students to new ideas and new worlds to explore. It is worth noting, however, that while Stanford affirms its commitment to diversity, there is no doubt that the exorbitant cost of attending the school is a limiting factor for many applicants. In addition, there has been an outcry among students recently regarding Stanford's commitment, or possible lack of, to tenuring minority and women professors, a charge that the university is currently dealing with. Stanford students, however, have committed themselves to expressing their beliefs, using methods such as rallies and speakers to remind their fellow students that minority groups are still sometimes ignored at Stanford.

Most Stanford students will tell you that they made the most out of Stanford through the help and guidance of their peers and professors. As role models, as teaching assistants, as professors, and as friends, the people at Stanford never stop pushing each other to achieve. It is this dynamic environment of learning that carries outside the classroom that makes Stanford such an exciting place.

There is so much going on at Stanford that sleep becomes a low priority on most students to-do lists. It's an exciting and occasionally exhausting atmosphere, but the academic and personal growth that most students take away with them after four years is well worth the price. Add endless days of clear blue skies and sunshine to that, and the package is unbeatable.

❑ *Libusha Kelly, B.A.*

SWARTHMORE COLLEGE

Swarthmore College
Swarthmore, PA 19081

(610) 328-8300
Fax: (610) 328-8580

E-mail: admissions@swarthmore.edu
Web site: http://www.swarthmore.edu/Home/Admissions

Enrollment

Full-time ❑ women: 720
❑ men: 650

INTRODUCING SWARTHMORE

When I first came to Swarthmore, a lot of little things around the campus struck me as very intellectual. Phrases like "Use well thy freedom" and "To thine own self be true" were carved into the walls of its buildings. Every tree, shrub, and flower on the campus was labeled—in Latin. And best of all, there were dozens of fantastic places on campus to sit alone and read, the grandest of which was the amphitheater, with its grassy terraces and canopy of ancient trees.

But even though I basically had the right idea about Swarthmore—that it was, indeed, very intellectual—I hadn't a clue what that meant, or what four years at a place like that might mean. What I didn't get yet was this: Being genuinely committed to learning isn't about sitting alone under a tree absorbing the wisdom of the masters. It isn't about sitting at all. It's much more than that. Swarthmore, for me, was about arguing passionately, questioning constantly, pushing my limits, failing, and, eventually, succeeding. And it happened among the students themselves as much as between the students and the professors—in the dorms, on the playing fields, and in late-night meetings of virtually every imaginable activity, Swatties teach each other, and they pull each other through.

Founded by Quakers in 1864, Swarthmore College is a diverse community of some 1,400 students and 156 professors in southeastern Pennsylvania. Despite being an easy twenty-minute commuter-rail ride from Philadelphia, the campus itself is a lushly suburban, 330-acre arboretum. And even though it might look like a country club, its clientele isn't quite the country club set—students from all fifty states, more than forty foreign countries, and an exceptionally broad range of backgrounds call this green haven home. They also call it, affectionately, "Swat."

Swat is a very small place. When you sign on as a Swattie, you commit to four years of what might be called, for better or for worse, intimacy. On the bright side, classes are usually marvelously small. With a student:faculty ratio of nine to one, everyone can speak in class and everyone can claim a sizable hunk of the professor's attention. On the slightly dimmer side, everyone at Swat seems to know everything about everybody else. Questions like, "Hey, did you hear that thing about Dave?" are usually answered in the affirmative.

Swat does liberal arts like no one else does liberal arts. This is, in part, because Swat is liberal like no one else is liberal. Of course, it's also due to the exceptional range of courses, majors, and concentrations that are available, from Interpretation Theory to Psychobiology. While majors like English and biology seem to be perennial favorites, it's never unusual to see students double-majoring in physics and philosophy, or creating their own majors. In addition, unlike most other liberal arts colleges, Swat has a very highly regarded engineering program.

As you might have heard, Swat is tough. The unbridled pursuit of knowledge seems to be, in fact, its primary purpose for existence. The two main libraries on campus probably get more foot traffic per day than those of most schools twice its size. Because professors tend to assign more work than students can possibly do, a pall of perpetual academic humility tends to cover the campus. Raising the stress factor, around twenty percent of all Swatties elect to undergo the unique External Examination Program, taking only tiny, double-credit seminars for their last two years, and facing ultimate evaluation at the end of their senior years by experts from other universities.

Yet, as much as Swatties lament the amount of work they have to do, it's tolerable; virtually everyone makes it through just fine. Despite what some jaded seniors might tell you when you first arrive, you don't have to spend every weekend behind the bars of McCage (proper name: McCabe Library). But there is no denying that being a student at Swarthmore is an intense experience. The intensity spills out of the classroom and into the hallways after class, into political debates in dormitory lounges, into numerous campus activities and activist organizations, and into energetic athletic rivalries. And as far as interests go, there seems to be something for everyone (not to mention someone for everyone, considering that nearly one in five Swatties eventually marries another Swattie).

If students who come to Swarthmore have anything in common, it's that they want to be in the middle of things academically. They have intentionally avoided the anonymity of large universities because they want to know each other, and their professors, very well. It becomes clear over the course of four years that this is a school where everyone has an opinion on everything. During the course of four years, you will develop an opinion on everything, too. At Swarthmore, you cannot hide. You also cannot ever be lost.

ADMISSIONS REQUIREMENTS

There's a rumor afloat that the hardest thing about some prestigious schools is just getting in—the four years thereafter, presumably, are a breeze. Though few graduates would argue that this is the case at Swat, the competition for admission may still seem daunting to potential applicants. One recent freshman class's average SAT I verbal and math scores both hovered around 700, and ninety-four percent of them were in the top fifth of their high school class. But it's hardly a lost cause; not as many people out there have heard of Swat as have heard of the big Ivies, so year after year, Swat accepts about twenty-four percent of those who give application a try.

The secret to admission is being yourself, and being it in excruciating detail. The admissions officers aren't just number crunchers. They ask for the usual stuff, of course, like an essay, recommendations, transcript, and SAT I and II tests. But beyond that, they look for students with remarkable talent, creativity, passion, or motivation. You may impress them if you're a student council president or a valedictorian, but you may impress them a lot more if you taught yourself Greek or started a community organization or took college physics for fun while still in high school. Or, they may see something in you that you don't even see quite yet—a significant proportion of Swatties spend their first year wondering why exactly they were admitted to this assembly of minds at all.

If you're considering a four-year immersion in Swat, you may want to test the waters for a couple of days first. The Admissions Office encourages applicants to visit the campus, sit for an interview, observe classes, and maybe most importantly, stay the night in a dorm with real, live Swatties to see what the place is all about. Prospective students, dubbed warmly "specs," regularly make their way to parties, club meetings, and (of course) the cafeteria alongside their Swattie hosts. If you can't visit campus, you might want to schedule an interview with an alumnus or alumna who lives near you. In general, the Admissions Office wants applicants to find out as much about Swarthmore as Swarthmore wants to find out about them.

When I was considering Swarthmore in my senior year of high school, I stopped by Swat's table at a local college fair. I approached reluctantly, expecting to be intimidated. When it became clear to the man from the Admissions Office that I didn't really know what I was supposed to ask, he started asking me questions: what I wanted to study, what I liked to do outside class, and what I was looking for in a college. More at ease, I had a nice discussion with him and left feeling good about the school. I felt even better when, to my surprise a week later, I got a packet in the mail with more information about everything we had spoken about, and a handwritten personal note from him, thanking me for my interest.

Tucked in a little pocket of suburban Philadelphia, Swat is home to precious few students actually from Pennsylvania. Though the mid-Atlantic states are well represented, Swatties hail from every state in the union and from a whole host of foreign countries. Many first-year roommates and hallmates find that they come from almost different worlds. Unlike at many other top private colleges, around sixty-five percent of the student body comes from public high schools. And, also unlike at many other top private colleges, approximately twenty-nine percent of the students are nonwhite, due in part to the college's extraordinary outreach efforts.

Decision Plans

Fully eighty-five percent of students accepted at Swat in 1997 applied in the regular admissions round, in which applications are due January 1. The remaining students applied through one of two available Early Decision plans: the fall plan, in which applications are due November 15 and decisions made by December 15, and the winter plan, in which they're due January 1 and decisions are made by February 1. If Swat is indeed the one and only school that you want, it is generally in your favor to demonstrate it to the Admissions Office by applying early. Of course, these Early Decision plans are binding, so you need to be very sure about your decision. You are required to withdraw all of your other applications if you're admitted to Swat—it may be a strict policy, but it gives you the pleasure of sending Princeton and Harvard a few rejection letters of your own.

ACADEMIC LIFE

If you're really serious about applying to Swarthmore, you probably turned to this section first—after all, this is what it's all about. Swatties think; therefore they are. They elect to spend their college years at a school that has a long-standing, well-deserved reputation for being academically grueling, and most of them love it. Well, perhaps more accurately, most of them have a love/hate relationship with it. The only thing Swatties seem to do more than study is complain about how much they have to study. Sometimes they're just grumbling, but sometimes there really does seem to be more reading and writing and thinking to be done than hours in the day to do it in.

Luckily, there are enough things to study that most students can find something they really want to devote hours to. Swat offers B.A. degrees in the more than two dozen fields in the arts and sciences and a B.S. degree in engineering, which a little less than ten percent of the student body pursues (usually a very bonded and very clever group, the engineers posed on stage at graduation a few years ago with a large sign that read, "Now our B.S. is official.") In addition, students can add one of almost a dozen concentrations onto their majors, with themes like public policy, women's studies, peace and conflict studies, and black studies. If none of the above appeal to them, they may also work with faculty members to create their own interdisciplinary special majors. The largest departments on campus seem to be English Literature, Political Science, Economics, Sociology/Anthropology, and Biology. About a third of all students choose to escape Swat altogether for at least a semester, either studying abroad in the country of their choice or participating in a domestic exchange.

Of course, students are required to try a little of everything first. In addition to taking at least twenty classes outside their majors, Swatties have to take at least three courses in each of the three divisions—humanities, social sciences, and natural sciences. Two classes in each of these divisions have to be what the powers that be have named Primary Distribution Courses, or PDCs—usually broad, introductory classes with a special focus on writing. Before graduation, Swatties also have to fulfill a foreign language requirement (which can be fulfilling in itself, since Swat has exceptional language classes), pass a swimming test (we're not kidding), and complete phys ed classes.

Class Size and Professors

While some first-year classes can have thirty students or so, most classes and labs have fifteen or fewer. Due in part to the quality of the students and in part to the efforts of the professors, the classroom experience is both challenging and familiar. A majority of classes are quite small, discussion- and question-oriented, and heavy on reading and writing. Swatties pass a common milestone the first time they discover that they have to read not just particular sections from a book, but the entire book, before the next class. In addition, professors assign frequent papers, with which students often find competent help from Swarthmore's Student Writing Associate Program, the largest of its kind at comparable liberal arts schools.

Academics at Swat are very personal, in part because of the extraordinary way students and professors relate. Professors choose to teach at Swarthmore because they are more interested in their students than in potential research opportunities at a larger university. Over the course of my four years at Swat, I formed genuine and lasting friendships with many of my professors. Because they really have respect for their students, discussions with them often seem more like an interchange of ideas between equals than a lecture from someone who knows to someone who doesn't. Since I've graduated, I've found that Swarthmore professors look out for their former students more than I could have possibly anticipated. They invest a lot in them and want to see them do well. They honestly see maintaining these connections with students as one of the great joys of their jobs. That's part of what makes my Swarthmore education the most valuable experience I've ever had.

External Examination Program

About one in five students chooses to spend the last two years at Swat in the External Examination Program, a plan of study unique to Swarthmore that's colloquially called "honors." Instead of regular classes, honors students take double-credit seminars (and often write double-credit theses and create their own double-credit class combinations), usually with fewer than eight students per seminar. Sometimes held in special seminar rooms and sometimes in professors' living rooms, seminars meet once a week for several hours, focusing discussion on papers written by the seminar participants. Between weekly meetings, students are usually assigned upwards of 500 pages of reading and are encouraged to explore all of the other literature on the special shelves in the library reserved for their seminars. After two years of this, the program culminates in one very manic, anxious week when professors from other universities administer both oral and written tests to honors students. Although honors students do receive grades from their professors every semester, the final level of honors they graduate with (highest honors, high honors, honors, or none) is determined entirely by these outside examiners.

The honors program has its pros and cons. As an introduction to the kind of writing and thinking students will need to do in graduate school, it's second to none. Students develop a kind of intellectual independence through the program that's hard to come by elsewhere, and the program is well known and respected among graduate schools. In electing to go honors, however, students sacrifice breadth of study in favor of depth. In addition, because seminars are so uniquely student-led, seminar quality depends less on the professors and more on the quality of the students who choose to take them. Plus, the final week of exams is terrifying. For all of its weaknesses, though, the program offers students the absolutely unique educational experience of sitting in a professor's living room with one another for five hours every week, eventually arguing their way to their own personal truths.

SOCIAL LIFE AND ACTIVITIES

The first person to say, "Life is what happens while you're making other plans" must have been a Swattie. At Swarthmore, social life is what happens while you're doing everyday things like checking your mail in Parrish at noon or gathering around the dinner table at Sharples in the evening, both of which you can expect do upwards of a thousand times in four years. It also happens in dorms (in which ninety percent of all students live), in the midst of meetings of all kinds of organizations, at weekend parties, and at sports matches and practices. As a rule, socializing is both informal and intimate.

Even outside of classes, Swarthmore challenges its harried students' convictions in every way possible. It's not uncommon for a classroom discussion to spill over into an analogy-filled debate in the dining hall about topics as common as income taxes and as obscure as exactly how mimsy were the borogroves. Because Swat is such an academic institution, its whole atmosphere is born of the students' shared need to learn and to teach.

Student Organizations

On this campus of some 1,350 people, there are 150 student organizations. As a point of comparison, Penn State University's main campus has 30,000 undergrads and 400 student organizations. Of course, like everything at Swat, many of its organizations are pretty small. Vocal and instrumental music groups, student publications, and ethnic and gay/lesbian groups attract a loyal following, as do less traditional groups such as men's and women's rugby, the volunteer firefighters, Motherpuckers (ice hockey club), Swarthmore Warders of Imaginative Literature, Vertigo-go (improvisational comedy), and Ultimate Frisbee. Every fall, these and other campus organizations gather at the Activities Fair, where they set up their tables in a big circle and recruit new students. This happens, like most everything else at Swat, on Parrish lawn, or beach, as the locals like to call it. It gets its name in part because people tend to read, sleep, and sunbathe on it in the warmer months, and in part because it's equipped with massive white Adirondack chairs in which to see and be seen.

In general, campus clubs and organizations thrive because they involve almost everyone. Aspiring professional musicians and actors obviously won't be turned away, but most people who participate in these activities are aspiring doctors, economists, and writers who just happen to be amateur singers and actors. In general, Swat isn't very preprofessional in its activities or in its curriculum, unless the profession you happen to be interested in is academia. Instead, it focuses on nurturing cultured, thoughtful people, and trusts that they'll eventually figure out what they want to be when they grow up.

Politics

When they're not studying or playing, some Swatties are off trying to change the world. By any measure, Swarthmore is politically active. Environmental, human rights, and women's groups write letters and organize boycotts while several volunteer groups travel to nearby Chester and Philadelphia to offer food and tutoring to those in need. Politically, the students (and faculty) are legendary for leaning to the left—in fact, sometimes the Socialist Club has a lot more members than the College Democrats. In a case that amused the local press a few years ago, there was heated debate among the students over whether to raise an American flag over Parrish; some students said it represented values they did not share. Of course, some groups, like the Swarthmore Conservative Union, aim to change the world by first changing Swat. Through their organization, such prominent conservatives as William F. Buckley, Jr. and Phyllis Schlafly have made their way to campus on speaking tours.

Sports

If they still have any free hours in the day, Swatties have the opportunity to compete in twenty-two varsity teams in the NCAA's Division III. Needless to say, these aren't nationally televised games, but many of the teams advance to regional and even national competitions. Just as impressive is the fact that almost a third of the campus competes in interscholastic play. The swimming, tennis, field hockey, and women's lacrosse teams are perennial winners, while football isn't always as fortunate. In addition to the varsity teams, there are club teams (which compete with other colleges and clubs, but are student-run) and a whole host of intramural sports on campus. All students who don't participate in interscholastic sports are required to spend two semesters taking such physical education classes as weight training, swimming, or dance.

Parties

Finally, Swatties let off steam every weekend at parties. As with on-campus lectures, performances, and other events, parties at Swat are almost always free of charge. Most parties are hosted by clubs or informal groups of friends. (There are two fraternities on campus, but they're tiny, nonresidential, and nothing like *Animal House*.) As far as parties are concerned, the good news is that there are several interesting get-togethers each weekend, and the bad news is that they are usually at the same half dozen places with all the same people. During your first few years at Swat, you will probably enjoy these places and these people and everything will work out fine. Sometime around junior year, you and your friends may choose instead to spend your precious free time at off-campus parties and in coffee shops in Philly, a short ride away on the train. And, in case you wondered, there's little in the way of bar-hopping to do in the village of Swarthmore.

PLACES TO EXPLORE

There are some interesting places to explore at Swat when you're not in the library.

- **The extensive Crum Woods, featuring Crumhenge, a large circle of stones that are there for no particular reason.**
- **The nineteenth-century Sproul Observatory, featured last year in the film *Addicted to Love* with Matthew Broderick and Meg Ryan.**
- **The verdant Scott amphitheater, in which everyone eventually gets a diploma.**
- **The Arboretum's prized rose garden outside Parrish.**
- **The "ruins garden" outside Kohlberg, built where the old Parrish Annex once stood.**
- **Philadelphia and the surrounding suburbs, via Swat's on-campus train station.**

Swarthmore has been nicknamed "the Quaker matchbox," but that's not entirely accurate—even though the college maintains some Quaker philosophies and traditions, I've noticed few actual Quakers here, and even though some people make matches and go on to marry each other, there is very little casual dating. In general, I think Swatties would probably rather spend two hours talking about the business environment in Hungary with a friend from their economics seminar than head out to a fraternity for a few beers. That doesn't mean we don't have social lives; it just means our social lives are a little unusual at times.

FINANCIAL AID

With a $750 million endowment and a commitment to completely need-blind admissions, Swarthmore's not a bad choice for those whose finances aren't quite as stellar as their SAT scores. As part of its commitment to diversity, Swat tries to attract bright students from all kinds of financial backgrounds, and retain them with rather generous aid. In fact, more than half of the student body—including many international students—receives some kind of financial aid, whether in the form of grants, loans, or work study. And the campus jobs students use to pay the bills aren't that bad either; working at the libraries, as tour guides, and as assistants in administrative and academic departments, students get pretty useful work experience along with much-needed cash.

The average financial aid package at Swat is valued at $21,425. To give you an idea of how far this aid goes, in a recent year, tuition, room, and board together totaled $29,500. Some students do graduate with significant debt, though, which is often compounded by the fact that many of them choose to spend the first few years after graduation teaching, working for non-profit organizations, or doing something similarly poorly paid.

In addition to regular aid, Swat offers two major scholarships: The McCabe Achievement Awards are given every year to incoming students with superior leadership qualities (and are not necessarily based on need), and the Lang Opportunity Grants for Social Action (part of the $50 million Eugene Lang has donated to date) provide full need-based aid, plus up to $10,000 to carry out a social service project, for students with strong community service backgrounds.

GRADUATES

Having made the transition to adulthood together in classrooms, dorm rooms, and Sharples dining hall, Swatties tend to grow in the same directions even many years after graduation. Almost a quarter of current alumni have chosen academic careers of some kind, be they as professors, researchers, teachers, or authors. Others land jobs in government, medicine, journalism, and business, often in offices and agencies alongside one another. Whatever their individual experiences may have been at Swat, most alumni expect that students coming out of Swarthmore are first-rate; a lot of Swatties get their first jobs (and even summer internships) from older Swatties. It may be a kind of nepotism, but it's not a bad route to take.

Immediately after graduation, about twenty-seven percent of grads go directly to graduate and professional schools. Among those who don't go to graduate school right away, jobs in research, consulting, and teaching are popular. The college's Career Office has extensive resources and coordinates several rounds of on-campus recruiting for seniors. Within five years, a stunning eighty-seven percent of Swatties are back at the books, whether at graduate school, law school, medical school, or business school. Clearly a cerebral bunch, alumni of Swarthmore include five Nobel Laureates, nineteen recipients of MacArthur genius grants, thirty-six members of the prestigious National Academy of Sciences, and more Ph.D.s per capita than any other school in the country. Not bad for a group of less than 17,000.

PROMINENT GRADS

- **Michael Dukakis, Former Governor of Massachusetts and Presidential Candidate**
- **Eugene Lang, Founder of the I Have A Dream program**
- **Carl Levin, U.S. Senator**
- **James Michener, Author**
- **Alice Paul, Suffragist, Author of the Equal Rights Amendment**
- **Molly Yard, Former President of the National Organization for Women**

Just as admirable is the fact that alumni all over the country regularly make their names and addresses available to other, especially young, alumni who may want a place to stay while traveling through. They're a closely knit crowd, probably because there just aren't that many intensely studious, liberal, somewhat neurotic people out there in the general public.

Every June, between 300 and 400 people join the ranks of Swarthmore alumni. A few leave intellectually exhausted, wondering whether they might not have fared better as bigger fish in smaller ponds. But despite being pushed to their limits, most Swatties are energized by the experience, and roll that energy into building promising careers.

SUMMING UP

As with most everything else in life, what you get out of Swarthmore depends a lot on what you put into it. Tiny, liberal, and intense in every way, Swarthmore requires of its students a very personal, four-year investment of time, creative energy, and, above all, self. In return for this investment, Swatties get a diploma, a set of friends for life, an acute understanding of themselves and their fields of study, and a profound sense of accomplishment at having done it all. That's the deal.

That said, it is perhaps just as important to understand what you *won't* get at Swat. Even though Swat was recently number one on *U.S. News and World Report's* list of liberal arts colleges, a Swarthmore degree won't command the kind of immediate respect from the general public that a degree from a big Ivy League school will. If you choose Swarthmore, you won't always feel confident, and you won't leave college with exclusively sunny memories of carefree days and wild parties. And no matter how much Swatties try to explain their experience to friends and colleagues, some people out there will never appreciate what a challenge this low-profile little Pennsylvania college can be. In general, if you want to get the greatest acclaim for the least possible pain, you might want to avoid Swat. Similarly, if you don't really enjoy losing yourself in your reading, your writing, or your calculations, Swarthmore isn't the place for you.

But despite what you hear from guidebooks like this one, there's a lot more than just dry studying going on on this campus. Beyond the memories of papers, exams, and stress, Swat alumni treasure the memories of certain little ceremonies and traditions, some of which are so much a part of everyday Swat that they go unappreciated until after graduation. For instance, at midnight the night before finals begin every semester, all 1,500 people on campus lean out their dorm windows and join the primal scream. Every April Fool's Day, a set of students (often the engineers) puts together a programmatic plan of pranks that affect—and amuse—the whole campus. At the end of every semester, professors invite all of the students in their seminars to their houses for homemade seminar dinners. And every year on graduation day, the seniors pick roses from the Arboretum's prized rose garden and pin them onto their graduation gowns.

When it's all said and done, Swarthmore remains highly admirable year after year primarily because of the special batch of young people it attracts. Energetic, diverse, imaginative, and always inquisitive, the students of this little college consistently teach each other—and often their professors—a lot about both books and life.

When things got tough academically, and they did get tough, my father liked to remind me why I had chosen Swarthmore in the first place. I wanted, for the first time in my life, to be average. I wanted to be around people who performed better than I did, people from whom I could learn. I wouldn't recommend Swarthmore to everyone, but for those made of Swattie material, it's right, and it feels like coming home.

❑ *Sylvia Weedman, B.A.*

TUFTS UNIVERSITY

Tufts University
Medford, MA 02155

(617) 627-3170
Fax: (617) 627-3860

E-mail: uadmiss_inquiry@infonet.tufts.edu
Web site: http://www.tufts.edu

Enrollment

Full-time ❑ women: 2,330
❑ men: 2,174

Part-time ❑ women: 16
❑ men: 19

INTRODUCING TUFTS

When Charles Tufts put "a light on the hill" in 1852, he set the framework for what has become one of the top universities in the country. As President John DiBiaggio and Provost Sol Gittleman point out, Tufts is a teaching institution where the faculty does research, meaning that Tufts offers all the benefits of a liberal arts college—small classes, student interaction with the faculty—while also providing the positives of a large university—research laboratories, large-city cultural experiences, and internationally recognized faculty and facilities. Located just five miles northwest of Boston, the school offers the best of all worlds; students can remain in the suburban Medford setting or hop on the subway to Harvard Square or downtown Boston; they can study in classes of less than twenty students and still assist professors with important research, study in the library, or experience history through the Museum of Science or the Museum of Fine Arts in Boston. The options are limitless.

Set on 140 acres, the Medford campus's 167 buildings are an architect's delight with some dating back to the college's inception while others have been recently constructed or renovated, including the Tisch Family Library. Tufts recently completed a $20 million overhaul of the library, which was long in need of an upgrade, making it another attractive, and research-friendly, site on the lush campus. The campus is unofficially divided into two parts: Uphill and Downhill. Many of the Uphill buildings are the original red brick residence halls and academic departments. These buildings have been added to and modified to now include dining halls, a computer center, the Fletcher School of Law and Diplomacy, and more dorms and classrooms. Many students' favorite parts of Uphill are the quads—open, grass-covered spaces where students study, lie in the sun, and play Ultimate Frisbee. Downhill consists of more recently constructed buildings, such as the recently renovated chemistry building and the South Hall dormitory, and some of the athletic facilities.

Approximately 3,500 students live on campus in single-sex and coed dormitories, on-campus apartments, and fraternity and sorority houses. In addition, there are special-interest housing options, including the African American, Asian American, Hispanic American, Jewish, French, Spanish, German, and Substance Free Houses. All freshmen and most sophomores are required to live on campus.

With both the College of Liberal Arts and the College of Engineering, Tufts welcomes a student body interested in diverse areas of study and career paths. The nine graduate schools, including medical, dental, veterinary, and the Fletcher School, attract the brightest students from around the world who are interested in furthering their education. Past Tufts students have gone on to successful careers in such diverse fields as acting, politics, and writing.

I had my first experience of Tufts one summer while in high school. I spent six weeks there taking a few summer courses, living in one of the dorms, and eating in the dining halls. I fell in love with the campus and the environment then and knew I would be applying to Tufts when I was a senior. When the time came for me to make a decision among the universities that accepted my application, the choice was easy—and I never regretted my decision. Tufts offered me a wide range of academic options, a friendly, open environment, and numerous career-developing opportunities, including extracurricular activities and internships.

As a double major, I had a wide-ranging course of study. This gave me the opportunity to meet many professors, all of whom were readily available to talk to students about their coursework. My advisor, for example, was often in his office with the door open well beyond his office hours and always invited students in to talk about some reading material or the best way to plan out one's academic career.

It's this special care that Tufts provides that separates it from the other top schools. The professors, ninety-nine percent of whom have a Ph.D., teach nearly every class, not like other universities where the graduate students step in for the professors. The faculty cares about the students and the professors want to help their students do well. And still the faculty has time to conduct research; eighty-six percent find the time to do research in addition to teaching their regular classes.

ADMISSIONS REQUIREMENTS

Admission to Tufts has become much more competitive during the past few years: just thirty-two percent of recent applicants were accepted for admission to Tufts. Over the past two decades, Tufts has gone from being a small, New England liberal arts school to a major international university thanks to the work of former Tufts president Jean Mayer and current president John DiBiaggio. They worked to attract the brightest students from the United States (all fifty are represented) and around the world (students from sixty-five foreign countries attend Tufts).

All applicants to Tufts must submit results of either the SAT I: Reasoning test and three SAT II: Subject tests or the American College Testing Program (ACT). While the Admissions Office does not require that the testing be completed by a specified date, it is suggested that the testing should be completed by January of the applicants' senior year. If an applicant repeats any test, the higher score will be used in assessing the application for admission.

For applicants to the Liberal Arts school taking the SAT tests, students should take the Writing test in addition to two other subjects. Applicants interested in pursuing medical, veterinary, or dental school programs or a science concentration should take Subject tests in science and mathematics Level I or IIC with the Writing test as the third exam score submitted. While scores from sophomore year may be submitted, at least two of the scores should be submitted from junior and senior years. Engineering applicants are recommended to take either physics or chemistry, mathematics Level I or Level IIC, and the Writing test.

Applicants are expected to achieve high marks on these exams. In a recent freshman class, seventy-six percent scored above 600 on the Verbal and eighty-seven percent scored above 600 on the Math portions of the SAT I.

Those submitting ACT scores for the same class scored as follows: three percent below 21, nine percent between 21 and 23, twenty-one percent between 24 and 26, twenty percent between 27 and 28, and forty-seven percent above 28.

Students are expected to perform well while taking a challenging course of study in high school. Eighty-six percent of freshmen were in the top fifth of their class while ninety-seven percent were in the top two-thirds. Applicants are expected to have taken four years of English, three years each of humanities and a foreign language, two each of social and natural sciences, and one year of history.

In addition, the admissions officers require a personal statement as part of the application. Other areas that will be considered are recommendations by high school officials and extracurricular activities.

For those applicants who do not attend schools where English is the language of instruction or for whom English is not their first language, a Test of English as a Foreign Language (TOEFL) should be submitted in addition to the other required exams.

Tufts also accepts AP credits. For results to be considered, they must be sent to the Admissions Office for review. Generally, a 4 is required for credit to be earned through an Advanced Placement exam.

Tufts uses the common application plus the Tufts Supplemental Form for both the liberal arts and the engineering programs. Applicants are required to submit the common application and the supplemental form, two short-answer questions found on the supplemental form, and the $55 application fee.

Deadlines

Tufts offers three application deadlines for freshmen beginning school in the fall: Early Decision rounds I and II (both binding) and Regular Decision. The deadline for submitting application materials for Early Decision I is November 15; for Round II it is January 1. Students applying for Round I are notified by December 15; Round II applicants are notified by February I; and Regular Decision by April 1. Early Decision applicants are eligible for the waiting list.

Five-Year Programs

Tufts offers a rare opportunity for liberal arts students to participate in five-year programs in conjunction with either the New England Conservatory (for those with a specific focus on music), the School of the Museum of Fine Arts, or the Fletcher School of Law and Diplomacy. Those who wish to enroll in one of these five-year programs must submit separate applications to both institutions they wish to attend. The application forms and literature must be requested separately from the different institutions. If a student is admitted into only one of the two programs, the applicant may matriculate into that school and then reapply for admission into the five-year program at a later date.

International Applicants

Tufts has a special interest in attracting the best students that other countries have to offer and looks closely at the applications of international students, who are required to submit the common application like American students. In addition, the Admissions Office requests that applicants submit a certified English translation of all academic credentials.

The admissions officers realize that education systems and extracurricular opportunities vary around the world; therefore, these criteria are placed in the proper context when being evaluated. Also, Tufts requests that all international applicants take the standardized American exams, but primary emphasis is placed on each country's methods of education evaluation.

First-year applicants are also required to submit the following: secondary school reports from all schools attended, a midyear school report, and a teacher's report. Applicants may submit any supplementary materials to bolster their applications, but these materials may not be returned to the applicants.

Interviews

Most applicants, once their Supplemental Form and application fee have been received, will most likely be assigned an alumni interview. The university depends on its Tufts Alumni Admissions Program (TAAP) for conducting interviews with applicants for two reasons: It allows students who live all across the country to have an interview, and it allows applicants to learn more about Tufts from people who went to school there. In cases where a TAAP interview cannot be scheduled, the applicant's chance will in no way be diminished.

Last year I took part in the TAAP program for the first time. Before my first interview I was very nervous because I was afraid that I wouldn't ask the right questions or I might scare the person off. But in the end everything went well—I led a very easy-going conversation about the applicant's experiences in high school and what she expected out of college. And at the same time I found myself selling the school, persuading the applicant why Tufts is the best college. TAAP truly sets the Tufts admissions process apart from other schools. Not only does it keep alumni involved, but, unlike many other schools, applicants are given an opportunity to talk with people who know the school better than anyone else.

Transfer applicants go through a competitive admissions process with primary consideration going to those with superior college and secondary school achievement records and a history of personal involvement. Seventeen of thirty-four courses must be completed at Tufts.

ACADEMIC LIFE

A Tufts liberal arts education stresses enhancing students' ability to think independently and express themselves clearly. Students are taught how to develop both written and oral presentations through interpretation and analysis of evidence. The faculty expects students to challenge the conventional wisdom and develop independent opinions.

Tufts requires liberal arts students to take a wide range of courses in order to broaden their areas of knowledge. Liberal arts students must take a minimum of thirty-four courses over eight semesters, approximately ten of which must be in one area of concentration. In some departments this concentration number may vary. For example, the political science department requires students to take slightly fewer courses within the department and three additional courses in related fields, such as history, philosophy, or economics.

Students, with the assistance of an advisor, are required to choose a major or concentration before the end of their sophomore year. Students have the option of pursuing a double major or a minor in another field if they choose. Approximately twenty-five percent of students complete a double major. If a student is interested in exploring an area of study not offered through the departments, he or she may also work with an advisor to develop an independent course of study, mixing various areas of thought.

All liberal arts students are required to fulfill the basic requirements, some of which may be done through AP exams. The core curriculum consists of two freshman writing courses, three semesters of a foreign language and three of a foreign culture, one non-Western civilization course, and two courses in each of the following: humanities, the arts, social sciences, natural sciences, and mathematics.

As a double major in English and political science, I took a wide variety of courses, not only in my two areas of concentration but also in other departments I might not have explored if it weren't for the basic requirements. Thanks to those courses, I now have a better understanding of economics, the Russian language, the sciences, and cultures other than my own. The interest my professors showed helped me increase my desire to learn and understand more. The learning environment at Tufts is second to none.

The Tufts faculty also believes that engineers must be well versed in various subjects. That is why students in the School of Engineering must take English, humanities, and social sciences courses in addition to the engineering curriculum. These students must complete thirty-eight courses, twelve of which are in a specific area of concentration. Approximately one-quarter of the courses will most likely be in math and science while another twenty percent is devoted to engineering science and other foundation courses.

First-year engineering students must take two half-courses that provide in-depth study in a specific field. These courses are designed to assist engineering students in choosing their majors. Some of these half-courses have included From Trail Bikes to Nintendos: The Use of New Materials; Exploring Laser Light; and Skyscrapers, Architecture, and Engineering.

Bachelor's degrees are offered in biological science, communications and the arts, computer and physical science, engineering and environmental design, and social science. The most popular majors are English, international relations, and biology.

The Experimental College

The Experimental College is one of Tufts' great educational innovations, offering about thirty courses each semester designed to expand students' knowledge in an interactive setting. Among the programs offered through the Ex College is Education for Public Inquiry and International Citizenship and Communications and Media Studies. EPIIC provides students the opportunity to immerse themselves in global issues and help run a renowned annual international symposium bringing together experts in the field from around the world. CMS is an interdisciplinary minor allowing students to better understand the media through internships, courses, and special events.

The Ex College also provides first-year programs designed to assist students in the transition to college. First-years can take a course taught by upperclassmen or just join advising groups run by older students. These upperclassmen help guide students through their first year of school and give them a better understanding of the academic setting at Tufts.

Special Study Opportunities

Tufts offers a number of special study opportunities. Tufts students are eligible for cross-registration at other Boston-area schools: Boston College, Boston University, Brandeis University, and Swarthmore College. The students who take advantage of this opportunity are looking for specific courses not offered at Tufts. The university also has a number of study abroad programs for students to take advantage of during their junior year. Students may study in England, Spain, France, Moscow, Ghana, and Germany. Furthermore, if a student wishes to study in a different country than those Tufts formally offers, arrangements can be made to study through another program. For example, many Tufts students have in recent years begun to study in Australia. For students interested in politics, Tufts has a semester in Washington, D.C., program through American University.

Faculty and Class Size

Tufts has a very dedicated faculty, forty percent of which is female. All members of the faculty teach and conduct research while maintaining office hours so that students always have an opportunity to further discuss reading material, lab experiments, or a course of study. Graduate students do assist professors, but they do not teach introductory classes. While some introductory classes, such as biology, could be quite large, the average class size is twenty-five, and some seminars can be as small as ten or twelve students.

SOCIAL LIFE AND ACTIVITIES

Being just a few miles from Boston, Tufts offers many social opportunities. One can take a short walk to the subway (the "T") and ride into Cambridge or Boston in just a matter of minutes. Or students can stay on campus and take advantage of the many social activities Tufts has to offer.

Greeks

About fifteen percent of male students and four percent of female students are part of the Greek system, which includes nine national fraternities, four national sororities, and a coed house. Each of the fraternities and sororities hosts or sponsors various social and educational events throughout the year in which all students may take part. For example, one house holds a softball marathon each year, inviting other groups to pay small fees to play. The money then goes to a worthy charity and everyone has fun playing softball. Another student favorite is Greek Jam, in which the fraternities and sororities perform skits in the school's main auditorium, conducting singing and dancing sets whether they are skilled to do so or not.

Student Organizations

Aside from the Greek system, there are approximately 130 student organizations covering diverse interests: student government, cultural events, media, religion, ethnicity, community service, and political and social action. There are various segments of the student government, depending on people's interest and time available. The largest arm of the government is the Tufts Community Union Senate, whose main responsibility is allocating the budgets for the other student organizations. There is also the judicial board, an election board, and student-faculty committees dedicated to improving various aspects of academic and social life at Tufts.

Performing Groups and Cultural Events

There are a number of performing groups at Tufts, some that do large musical performances, one that is a comedic sketch group, and one that produces plays for young people in the area. All these groups are student-directed and produced. Past performances include *Into the Woods*, *Hamlet*, *Godspell*, and *Candide*. The musical organizations are also among the most popular groups at Tufts. The school has a number of *a cappella* groups including two—the all-male Beelzebubs and the all-female Jackson Jills—that have won national recognition. Their concerts are always packed. Tufts also offers many instrumental groups, including the Wind Ensemble, Jumbo Marching Band, Jazz Ensemble, Third Day Gospel Choir, and the Tufts University Chorale.

CAMPUS NEWSPAPERS

- **Student journalists at Tufts take great pride in their accomplishment of providing the main source of campus news, information, and entertainment. Every weekday morning, students grab the paper on the way to class or the dining hall to catch up on campus happenings, get a movie recommendation, or read the comics. Tufts is not only the smallest school in the country with both a daily (*The Tufts Daily*) and weekly (*The Observer*) newspaper, but it is the smallest school with just a daily paper.**
- **As a former editor of *The Tufts Daily*, I still read the paper every day when it is posted on the Web site (www.tufts.edu/as/stu-org/tuftsdaily) because I share a bond with the current staff and I enjoy watching how the paper evolves, as do many other *Daily* alumni with whom I stay in touch.**
- **While serving as editor-in-chief, I had the opportunity to interact with other student leaders as well as members of the Tufts administration. While it was these communication skills as well as my writing and editing skills that have helped me succeed after college, it was the social bonds I developed that made the *Daily* even more enjoyable and forged strong, lasting friendships.**

The university provides students with a wide variety of other special cultural events throughout the year, including concerts, comedy shows, and guest speakers. Past performers and speakers have included Adam Sandler, Natalie Merchant, Queen Latifah, B.B. King, They Might Be Giants, George Bush, Margaret Thatcher, Joycelyn Elders, Alice Walker, and Spike Lee.

Publications and Other Media

Perhaps one of the reasons the new Communications and Media Studies program is quickly growing is the students' interest in all the media opportunities available at Tufts. There are two student-run newspapers, *The Tufts Daily,* which prints Monday through Friday, and *The Observer,* a weekly that comes out Thursdays. The two papers share a friendly rivalry that extends to the softball field and basketball court. Among the other publications are *The Primary Source,* a journal of conservative thought, *The Zamboni,* a humor magazine, *Queen's Head and Artichoke,* a creative writing journal, and the yearbook *Jumbo*. There are also some cultural publications, such as *Hemispheres,* a journal on international affairs, *Onyx,* the publication of African American students, and *Voices,* which features Asian American students' works.

In terms of nonprint media, there is Tufts University Television and the radio station WMFO, which broadcasts music, news, and sports. TUTV underwent a recent revival when the campus dormitories were wired for cable TV. The students who run the television station are now creating the programming, which will include student-written production, as it begins broadcasting across the campus.

Religious and Ethnic Groups

With a diverse student body, there are many religious and ethnic groups catering to the various groups represented at Tufts.

- Tufts Hillel offers many Jewish activities including Sabbath and holiday services, kosher dinners, and social and community activities.
- The Catholic Center provides religious programming, Sunday Mass, and social events.
- The Protestant Ministry conducts counseling, services, and special programming.
- The Islamic Center, besides holding weekly Friday prayer services, also has social and educational activities.
- The Tufts Orthodox Christian Students Fellowship provides liturgical worship and support and guidance programs.
- Other religion-oriented students groups include the Asian-Christian Fellowship and Episcopal Student Fellowship.

Minorities

Besides the various special-interest housing, there are also a number of organizations dedicated to minorities at Tufts, ranging from the African-American Center to the Lesbian, Gay, and Bisexual Resource Center. There are also student-run groups like the Armenian Club, Asian Community at Tufts, Hellenic Society, International Club, Latin American Society, Pan-African Alliance, and the Vietnamese Students Club. These groups provide support for their members as well as campus-wide educational and social activities.

Athletics

There are a number of athletic opportunities for Tufts students. As a Division III school, Tufts does not offer athletic scholarships, but that doesn't diminish the students' desire to compete and it preserves the idea of student athletes. As a member of the NCAA and the New England Small College Athletic Conference (NESCAC), Tufts competes against the best schools in New England and, in some cases across the country. With seventeen intercollegiate sports for men and sixteen for women, Tufts athletes have excelled against the competition, and in some cases (including men's soccer, women's field hockey, men's basketball, and men's tennis) have qualified for NCAA post-season competition. In fact, the sailing teams are repeatedly ranked among the top five in the country and so often dominate the competition that it is rare they don't win national championships.

While Tufts may not have a UNC basketball team or Notre Dame football team, there are few experiences as wonderful as watching Tufts play Williams College in basketball at home with the gym packed well beyond capacity and 2,000 Jumbos literally hanging from the rafters, cheering their team to victory or the soccer team playing Johns Hopkins in the NCAA tournament with fans lined twenty feet deep all around the field, screaming and shouting with every shot on goal.

During my four years at Tufts, one of the big causes for student activists was "school spirit." And thanks to student organizations like the Trample Zone, originally formed to support the football team, most Tufts squads could count on an extremely animated cheering section at every home game and many on the road as well. With colorful cheers, cow bells, and boundless enthusiasm, Tufts fans are often just as important in defeating the opponent as the players on the field. It's hard for the opposing team to set a play during a half-time huddle when fifty people are standing ten feet away, drowning out the coach.

And for those not looking for the varsity level of competition, Tufts offers many club sports and intramurals. The club sports depend on both the university and their own resources for funding for these competitive yet instructional sports, which include rugby, equestrian, skiing, volleyball, and Ultimate Frisbee. Like the varsity and club sports, there are three seasons of intramural sports, which feature fraternities, dorms, clubs, and friends who form their own teams to compete against their fellow students. Among the intramurals are indoor soccer, tag football, basketball, hockey, and softball.

For the competitors and those just interested in keeping in shape there are a number of facilities available. Besides the eight-lane, 440-meter outdoor track that often hosts New England championship events, there is an indoor 200-meter synthetic track, an indoor six-lane swimming pool, many playing fields, and two gymnasiums, Cousens and Jackson, in which teams train or friends meet to shoot around. But the crown jewel of Tufts' athletic facilities is the Chase Gymnasium, recently renovated to include state-of-the-art workout equipment for teams, weight-training classes, and other students to use at their leisure.

FINANCIAL AID

As many high school students are aware, college has become an expensive proposition, especially at the competitive New England universities. And like the schools Tufts measures itself against, Tufts does its best to provide financial assistance to as many students as possible. Unfortunately, many parents and applicants see it as too expensive for their family incomes, but Tufts urges everyone to apply, regardless of financial resources and promises to do its best to assist academically qualified students afford a Tufts education.

In the past, Tufts has not been able to grant aid to all the students who request assistance, but thanks to the ongoing $400 million capital campaign, the number of students receiving financial assistance is growing. Tufts students are eligible for a wide range of sources of financial aid: university, state, and federal grants; long-term federal Perkins, Stafford, and Tufts loans; and campus employment through the Federal Work Study program. Recently, Tufts students received over $33 million in these forms of aid as well as other government and foundation grants.

In a recent year, forty-eight percent of all freshmen received some sort of financial aid; forty-four percent of all freshman received need-based aid. Furthermore, forty-one percent of continuing students were granted financial aid; thirty-seven percent of continuing students receiving need-based assistance. The average level financial debt following the graduation of the Class of '95 was $12,227.

The average freshman financial aid award totaled $17,400 including need-based grants or scholarships, which averaged $15,000 with a $25,000 maximum. In addition, student loans averaged $3,200 ($3,265 maximum) and work contracts averaged $1,560 ($1,800 maximum). Nearly one-half of Tufts students work part-time, earning an average of $1,350 but up to as much as $1,800 or more based on number of hours worked.

As a member of the College Scholarship Service (CSS), Tufts uses the CSS Profile Application, the Free Application for Federal Student Aid (FAFSA), and families' tax returns to determine each student's award package of grants, loans, and jobs. In some cases, Tufts' Office of Financial Aid may also require additional information, such as the Noncustodial Parent's Statement.

Students should be aware that financial aid packages can vary year to year for each student based on the family's financial circumstances, the student's educational goals, and the availability of financial aid funds. For example if an older sibling graduates from college, the family may be expected to contribute more money to its Tufts student's education now that only one child is still in college.

GRADUATES

There are many statistics used to measure universities against each other, but one of the most telling is retention rate, the percentage of enrolled students who stay at a university through graduation. This is one of the areas in which Tufts truly stands out. Eighty-nine percent of the average freshman class graduates within four years and nearly ninety percent of all students (including transfers) graduate within six years. The vast majority of colleges and universities would be envious to have numbers like these because they demonstrate that students enjoy the education and opportunities that Tufts provides.

PROMINENT GRADS

- Leo Rich Lewis, 1887, Composer
- Arthur Anderson, '12, Financier
- Vannevar Bush, '13, Scientist
- John Holmes, '29, Poet
- John Ciardi, '38, '39, Poet/Editor
- Daniel Patrick Moynihan, '48, Senator
- Dorothy Skinner, '52, Scientist
- Nancy Schons, '53, Sculptor
- Bette Bao Lord, '59, Author
- Frederick "Rick" Hauck, '62, Astronaut
- Peter DeFazio, '69, U.S. Congressman
- Ambassador William Richardson, '71, Diplomat and Former Congressman
- Steven Tisch, '71, Producer
- William Hurt, '72, Actor
- Arthur Sulzberger, '74, Publisher, *The New York Times*
- Peter Gallagher, '77, Actor

In a recent year, Tufts conferred 1,118 bachelors degrees to its students. The most popular majors among Tufts students were international relations (ten percent), English (ten percent), and biology (eight percent). And after graduation, Tufts students often tend to continue their education beyond a bachelor's degree as approximately forty percent of graduates go on to graduate school. Among the most popular professional programs for Tufts students are law school (twelve percent), business school (ten percent), medical school (eight percent), and dental school (one percent). Additionally, many students pursue graduate degrees in the arts, sciences, and engineering. Even those who do not go directly to grad school indicate that they plan to do so in the future: seventy-eight percent of Tufts graduates predict they will attend graduate school further down the road.

Tufts graduates pursue a wide range of careers: science, literature, politics, the media, and many others, but when they leave Tufts, they never leave for good. Besides the Tufts Alumni Association, which includes every person who has graduated from Tufts, there are many other alumni associations, some targeting specific groups of alumni, some targeting specific regions. For example, the university boasts a Tufts Alliance in nearly every large city in the country as well as some international locations. Each of these organizations provides educational, social, cultural, and community service activities.

As a member of the Washington Tufts Alliance steering committee, I help develop and implement activities for alumni in the D.C. area. Some of our past activities have included a reception at the Russian Embassy, a holiday party, monthly happy hours, painting a soup kitchen, helping at a food bank, and attending lectures given by nationally recognized people. As more people graduate, our membership base is growing and our ties to Tufts become even stronger.

Every year at Homecoming, thousands of alumni show up at Tailgaters Village to cheer the teams on and remember the great times we all shared as Jumbos. After all, elephants never forget.

SUMMING UP

Tufts is unique in that it can offer just about anything a student can look for in a college. It's not as large as the University of Pennsylvania and not as small as Williams College but it provides the benefits of both. It's not thrust into the middle of a city like New York University or relegated to the boonies like Cornell University, but, again, Tufts offers students both environments with its easy access to Boston while sitting in the quiet suburbs just a few miles outside the city.

Almost every class is taught by faculty members, not graduate students, who care about their students' academic, cultural, and social growth as they move through their four years at Tufts. And if a student can't find a specific class among the many diverse options, there is always the opportunity to take a course at one of Tufts' fellow consortium schools. Students are encouraged to study a wide range of issues in order to be ready when they graduate from college to move on to either graduate school or the "real world."

In the past, many freshmen at Tufts have had a feeling that is something like an inferiority complex, caused by being in the shadow of the better-known northeastern schools—Harvard and MIT. But over the last four or five years, Tufts has grown in stature and students are no longer using Tufts as a "safety school;" in many cases it is the first choice of many top high school students. Jumbos no longer see themselves as being lower than their Ivy competitors, but as equals in the academic community. And in many competitions, Tufts proves to be superior.

Tufts provides opportunities from the very beginning of college for new students to make friends and meet upperclassmen who can provide a great insight into life at college. Through freshman orientation and introductory programs like Perspectives and Explorations—two freshman classes taught by upperclassmen—Tufts students get together in social and educational activities to build relationships and discuss their progress at Tufts. These programs, coupled with residential hall activities, grant students many opportunities to grow socially. And with easy access to Harvard Square and Boston, it is very common to see packs of Tufts students heading off campus for a busy night in the city.

Despite the cold and snow associated with New England, if you ask a Tufts alumnus/a if he or she enjoyed his or her time at Tufts, you would most likely get an enthusiastic yes—their memories of their time at Tufts are among their most cherished possessions.

If Charles Tufts were alive today, he would be very proud of his light on the hill.

❑ *David Meyers, B.A.*

UNITED STATES AIR FORCE ACADEMY

United States Air Force Academy
2304 Cadet Drive, Suite 200
USAF Academy, CO 80840-5025

(719) 333-2520, 1-800-443-9266
Fax: (719) 333-3012

E-mail: n/app
Web site: http://www.usafa.af.mil

Enrollment

Full-time ❑ women: 647
❑ men: 3,436

INTRODUCING THE UNITED STATES AIR FORCE ACADEMY

"Sir, the mission of the United States Air Force Academy is to develop and inspire air and space leaders with vision for tomorrow!"

I still remember my first day at USAFA. The volume knob on campus was cranked beyond max to the "melt your eardrums" position. Yelling and screaming filled the air as upperclass cadets began to crunch 1,200 civilians through what seemed like a mental, physical, and emotional meat grinder to become military officers. What had I gotten myself into? Many of my friends from home thought I was nuts and would never make it through. But, when they cut my long, brown hair, I knew I would finish. My reflection in the mirror looked ridiculous, and all I could do was laugh—I could never quit and go to another school sporting this "do!" I figured it would take another four years for my hair to appear normal again, so it looked like I was there to stay.

Established in 1954, the United States Air Force Academy—aka USAFA—is the youngest of the three military service academies. Its first graduating class of 1959 commissioned 207 officers into our nation's armed forces. These first graduates have now been joined by 38 other classes and are serving to build upon the heritage and tradition of an ever-increasing Long Blue Line.

The four-year odyssey begins at the base of the Rocky Mountains in Colorado Springs, Colorado among 18,000 beautiful acres of evergreen forest and situated at 7,258 feet above sea level. The Air Force Academy prides itself in being "far, far above" the other academies at West Point and Annapolis.

The class sizes change with the needs of the Air Force. For example, in 1964 President Lyndon Johnson authorized the size of the population to 4,417. Following the Gulf War, however, military drawdowns dropped the total cadet population to 4,000. Currently, the academy hosts approximately 4,000 cadets with an average of seventeen percent minority students and forty foreign national students from a variety of countries.

Women have also played a major role in the development of the history of USAFA. In 1976 the academy accepted 157 women into its ranks. Now, between sixteen and eighteen percent of every incoming class is comprised of female cadets. Since 1980 the academy has graduated more than 2,000 women to exciting assignments all over the world.

The Air Force Academy is based on four pillars of instruction: academics, professional military training, athletics, and the Honor Code. There are also a published set of core values that all cadets are expected to internalize, which include "Integrity First, Service before Self, and Excellence in All We Do." The academy strives to develop officers who will choose the right courses of action and provide respect to all human beings. It challenges cadets to act decisively and take full responsibility for their actions and creates a spirit of self-discipline and selflessness. Through these four areas of training and the core values, the academy endeavors to develop professional military officers and a professional officer corps.

ADMISSIONS REQUIREMENTS

The four-year academy program is difficult to complete. To ensure the lowest attrition rate, the academy has strict eligibility requirements and offers suggestions to precandidates regarding preparation. All applicants must be U.S. citizens; unmarried, without dependents, between the ages of 17 and 23 on July 1 of the year they wish to enter, and have excellent moral character. Because the academy strives to select individuals on the "whole person" concept, students should be well-rounded in terms of academic discipline, athletic skill and participation, leadership experience, and community service-oriented activities.

Academic Requirements

The academy suggests that preparation to attend USAFA should begin as early as junior high school by ensuring that the high school academic requirements include:

- four years of English, with a college preparatory course in composition
- four years of mathematics, with algebra, geometry, trigonometry, calculus and functional analysis
- basic sciences, such as biology, chemistry, physics and, computers
- social sciences with history, economics, government, and behavioral sciences
- two to three years of a foreign language.

Ninety percent of the accepted students graduate in the top fifth of their high school class. Historically, many of the students have been valedictorians or salutatorians. It is in a candidate's best interest to maintain a high and competitive grade point average (GPA) as it is an indicator of potential performance. The academy requires the candidate to submit the entire scholastic record, to include transcripts from high school and preparatory schools, or college if applicable, along with class ranking if available.

Testing Requirements

High school guidance counselors will help schedule the Preliminary Scholastic Aptitude Test (PSAT) during the sophomore year to give ample time to improve specific areas before taking the SAT I or the ACT in the junior year. It is important to understand that the academy strongly believes that the scores of these tests reflect the academic potential of an individual, so every candidate is encouraged to take the tests as many times as needed to meet the requirements or to improve scores. The academy will take the best scores to create the highest composite; however, applicants may not mix and match scores from different tests.

> *Between the ACT and SAT I, I ended up taking the standard tests seven times. My parents even had me take it on a vacation to attempt to improve my math scores. The hard work pays off. Don't give up!*

Physical Requirements

The academy expects cadets to maintain high physical standards. To ensure that precandidates can handle the physical load, a Candidate Fitness Test (CFT) is required. It consists of overhand pull-ups, sit-ups, push-ups, and a 300-yard shuttle run. Men average ten pull-ups, sixty-nine sit-ups, forty-one push-ups, and sixty seconds on the shuttle run. Women average two pull-ups, sixty-eight sit-ups, twenty-four push-ups, and sixty-nine seconds on the shuttle run. This test is an indicator of how future cadets will do on the strenuous physical fitness test that the academy administers once a semester.

All of these fitness items can be improved with practice, and it is in the candidate's best interest to get in as much practice as possible before taking the CFT. If candidates fail any part of this test, they are ineligible for acceptance. If candidates do not pass the CFT on the first attempt, they will have one additional opportunity to pass the test before they are disqualified. In most cases, women have a problem with the pull-ups due to lack of development in upper body muscles. This is more a result of female physiology than a matter of being out of shape. To strengthen the development of upper body muscles, women should practice reverse pull-ups and lat pull-downs to strengthen these muscle groups. Although they are only required to do one pull-up on the CFT, the academy considers women candidates to be more competitive if they are able to complete a greater number.

Like most girls trying to get into the academy, I had trouble doing pull-ups. In fact, I failed my first CFT because I couldn't even do one. From then on, I practiced every day. My dad put a pull-up bar outside my doorway so that every time I walked into or out of my room, I could do a pull-up. By the time I took the next CFT, I was able to do three. By my senior year, I could max the event!

Cadets are also required to participate in intramural, intercollegiate, or club sports. During the high school years, precandidates should participate in strenuous team sports to develop strength, coordination, and endurance. The academy is also interested in the skill a precandidate possesses in terms of athletic prowess and leadership exhibited on the field. Part of the candidate questionnaire asks if the applicant was a team captain or was recognized for athletic achievements.

Courses in swimming are helpful to prepare a cadet for the required aquatic classes. In addition, a daily physical routine will help prepare a candidate for daily runs conducted by the candidate's squadron (the unit to which a candidate is assigned when entering the Academy) during Basic Cadet Summer. Preparation through long-distance running will also speed a candidate's adjustment to the high altitude in Colorado, which traditionally proves to be one of the greatest challenges of basic training. The name of the game is endurance.

Medical Requirements

All commissioning sources use one general standardized physical examination to determine medical qualification. Examinations are scheduled by the Department of Defense Medical Examination Review Board at either military or civilian medical facilities throughout the admissions cycle.

Extracurricular Activities

The academy strives for the "whole person" concept. Along with scholastic and physical qualities, it looks for people who take part in a variety of service organizations or support groups. These activities can range from the local chapter of Key Club to Honor Society, or from singing in the church choir to aiding as a candy striper at hospitals. Along with participation in these activities, the selection panel will look to see if a candidate held leadership offices in any of these clubs.

Employment is another sign of responsibility. Summer jobs or part-time jobs show that, along with their academic and athletic commitments, candidates are still able to successfully hold a job. Being able to balance these types of commitments is an everyday battle in the life of a cadet. During the school year, every cadet has a military job to manage as well as giving his or her all in academics and sports.

Essay

The academy requires every applicant to submit a 300- to 500-word, handwritten essay that will discuss the individual's ability to adopt the academy Honor Code: "We will not lie, steal, or cheat, nor tolerate among us anyone who does." It also encourages applicants to make reference to whom or what most influenced them to apply to the academy, a personal experience that has contributed to their own character, and a social issue that most concerns them. This essay should be succinct in nature and should effectively communicate the applicant's ideas and feelings to the selection panel.

Interview

An Admissions Liaison Officer (ALO) is assigned to every applicant. The ALO guides the student throughout the application process by answering questions and reminding candidates of deadlines. In addition, the ALO interviews each candidate to ensure that the student's character matches the standards set by the academy and that he or she understands the commitment it takes to make it through the four years of academy life. Finally, the ALO ensures that the student understands the requirements of active duty military commitment and that the decision to apply to the academy is being made with a free conscience and without undue influence from family or friends.

Nomination Process

In order to be eligible to compete for an appointment, a candidate must receive a nomination from a legal nominating source as specified in Title 10 of United States Code (Public Law). These sources are members of the United States Senate and House of Representatives. Some candidates may also be eligible in one or more military-related nominating categories. Instructions for requesting a nomination and descriptions of the various categories are provided in the academy's application materials.

All of these sources are looking for individuals who possess aptitude in scholastic, athletic, leadership, and extracurricular activities. Each requires a letter requesting nomination before October 1 of the senior year. After reading the applicant's letter and, reviewing the transcripts, test scores, and extracurricular activities, they will set up an interview to meet with a selection board. This board will ask very challenging questions to determine a candidate's character and potential for military leadership. After the interviews are completed, the nomination will be awarded to candidates who best meet the academy's qualifications out of those who competed for the limited number of available appointments.

There is also a military affiliated nomination process. To request a nomination in the Presidential, Children of Deceased or Disabled Veterans, Military or Civilian Personnel in a Missing Status, or Children of Medal of Honor recipients categories, individuals must meet the specific requirements within those categories.

Prepare yourself before your interview with the Senator's or State Representative's panel. Dress and act professionally. First impressions count! Male candidates should wear a suit or a coat and conservative tie. Female candidates should wear a business suit or dress with conservative makeup and jewelry. Be mentally sharp, because panel members (usually congressional staff members and military advisors) will be asking you hard questions to test your intentions and character. Before meeting the panel, make sure you go over all the questions you anticipate they would ask and have a general idea as to how you would answer them. Maintain eye contact *and even though you have every right to be nervous, it is important to appear calm, cool, and collected by minimizing excessive body movement, squirming in your chair, or playing with a piece of jewelry. This kind of stuff really happens, so do your best and be very honest with all of your answers.*

ACADEMIC LIFE

USAFA is a four-year struggle in time management. There simply is not enough time to complete all academic work, military work, or athletics, so you have to battle each day with prioritizing and accepting the fact that one person cannot do everything. The curriculum is heavily weighted in the hard sciences and math, so even if you are more inclined to social or behavioral sciences, you had better whip out the calculator because you'll be doing a little bit of everything.

The Air Force Academy has one of the most challenging regimens in the country. Unlike most other institutions, cadets must complete the academic requirements within four years. During the freshman and sophomore years, cadets will spend a majority of their time taking core courses, during the junior and senior years, elective courses that correspond to a major are available. Students are required to choose their academic major before the spring break of their sophomore year. Academic counseling and major's fairs are available to freshmen and sophomores to help them make this decision.

Classes run from 7:30 A.M. to 3:30 P.M., Monday through Friday in fifty-minute periods. There are forty-two lessons in each semester with a six-day exam week at the end of the semester. Students are normally given two weeks of leave in December, one week during spring break, and three weeks of leave during the summer. Students also have the option of giving up summer leave to take academic classes.

Each class consists of fifteen to twenty students. This small student-to-teacher ratio provides excellent opportunities for students to ask as many questions as they need to fully understand a topic. If students are having trouble with certain concepts, they can schedule extra instruction with their instructors during academic free periods or after school hours. Student tutoring is also available in many of the core classes.

The Air Force Academy has made great strides in creating facilities to enhance learning. It has a local area network (LAN), which provides access to the Internet at no cost to the cadet. Cadets can access the LAN from their microcomputers in their rooms. The cadet library has over a half-million volumes, numerous magazine and journal subscriptions, and visual equipment to aid in study and research. Within the library, there is also a cadet self-help area that provides tools for the cadets to prepare projects and briefings.

During the school week, at 7:00 P.M., the trumpets sound the "Academic Call to Quarters" (ACQ). From 7:00 to 11:00 P.M., cadets are expected to study quietly in their rooms or the library. Signs are posted in the hallway to remind cadets that it is study time. All military training ceases during this time.

Each student is assigned an academic advisor. During the freshman year, one officer from the dean of faculty is assigned to the freshman class of each squadron. As cadets choose their major, however, their academic advisor will change to an officer working in the department offering that major. Academic advisors play a significant role in helping students organize their semester class loads and aiding them in applying for different summer programs and scholarships.

USAFA is a fully accredited academic institution. The standard Bachelor of Science degree is accredited by North Central Association of Colleges and Schools. All students who graduate receive a Bachelor of Science, regardless of their academic major. USAFA offers twenty-nine academic majors including aeronautical engineering, astronomical engineering, behavioral science, civil engineering, computer science, English, history, humanities, legal studies, operations research, and space operations, among others.

Military Training

Along with each semester's full academic load, cadets are also required to take military arts and science classes to improve their professional development. These classes help the cadets understand and appreciate the history of the Air Force and give them insights into professional skills of great leaders. Tactics and joint military concepts are also taught in these courses.

During the summer, cadets continue their military training. Following the freshman year, a cadet will take a survival course and may then choose between free-fall parachuting and a soaring aviation program. Following the sophomore year, cadets will spend three weeks shadowing an Air Force officer at an actual Air Force base to gain real life experience and knowledge about the Air Force. They will also choose between a leadership position in either Basic Cadet Training or Survival Training. Qualified cadets will teach soaring, jump, and navigation classes to the lower classes. Following the junior year, rising senior cadets assume officer roles in the different leadership programs. Those who are qualified to attend Undergraduate Pilot Training may also participate in the T-3 flight screening program.

Exchange Programs

> *Imagine studying for a month in Morocco. The countless hours of hard work in my Arabic minor program definitely paid off. Three cadets from the program were selected to visit the Moroccan Air Force Academy and tour throughout the country. It was great to be immersed in their culture, practice Arabic, and learn valuable lessons about their academic and flying programs. The trip wasn't all hard work. We did get to spend a weekend in the famed Casablanca and visit the Moroccan version of European nightclubs. We even had a stopover in Paris on the trip home. C'est la vie!*

Cadets can participate in numerous exchange programs. During the summer, one- to two-week trips are available to several foreign countries. During the fall semester of the second class (junior) year, USAFA also participates in an inter-service academy exchange with the U.S. Military Academy at West Point, the U.S. Naval Academy at Annapolis, and the U.S. Coast Guard Academy in New London, Connecticut. In these inter-service programs, cadets spend a semester at a sister academy. Additionally, first class (senior cadets) with French minors can apply to spend fall semester of their senior year at the French Air Force Academy.

During my junior year I spent fall semester at West Point. It was probably the most enjoyable and memorable time during my cadet career. Thank goodness Air Force beat Army that year and kept the Commander in Chief's trophy. If they had not, I would have lost a lot of privileges and had to pay back a lot of push-ups for all of the bets I made with the Army freshman and my host Army company. I made many lifelong friends while I was there and still run into people I met at West Point all over the world.

Achievement

USAFA has an academic recognition program similar to most colleges and universities. If a cadet maintains a semester academic grade point average (GPA) of 3.0 or greater, the cadet is placed on the Dean's List, symbolized by wearing a silver star. If a cadet maintains a 3.0 or greater military performance average (MPA) over a semester, he or she earns the Commandant's Pin, a silver wreath. Finally, excellence in athletics is rewarded by the director of athletics with a silver lightning bolt. This is achieved by maintaining a 3.0 in physical education classes. Cadets able to achieve all three lists in one semester are placed on the Superintendent's List. Special privileges and passes are granted to cadets that are on any of the lists to reward them for their hard work. The more lists the cadet attains, the greater the recognition and number of privileges the cadet receives.

Since the academy curriculum and activities are very demanding, not all cadets have a "pin collection," and some find it very difficult to make it through each semester. If a cadet receives a failing grade in one or more classes or falls below the required 2.0 cumulative GPA by mid-semester, he or she will be placed on academic probation. All test scores, quiz scores, and study hours per week are then documented. Cadets are given until the end of the semester to bring their grades up. If the grades do not improve, the cadet meets an Academic Review Committee. The committee can recommend that the student retake a class during summer school or the following semester, if time permits. They can reduce a student's academic load during the school year by allowing him or her to take two summer school classes. If a cadet is seriously deficient, then the committee can recommend disenrollment. Cadets can also be placed on probation for poor military and athletic performance.

All cadets must take the Aerobic Fitness Test (AFT)—a one and one half-mile run for time—each semester. They are also required to take the Physical Fitness Test (PFT) consisting of pull-ups, push-ups, sit-ups, broad jump, and a 600-yard dash. Special allowances are made for cadets who are injured or sick on the day of the test who can take a make-up test later during the course of the semester.

Cadet Honor Code

The Honor Code states: "We will not lie, steal, or cheat nor tolerate among us anyone who does. Furthermore, I resolve to do my duty and live honorably, so help me God." This is a code that all cadets live by each day and continue to hold sacred as a pillar of their character after graduation. Cadets accept this code during Basic Cadet Training and receive Honor training continually during the next four years. The Code is owned by the entire Cadet Wing and maintained by the cadets elected to serve on the Cadet Honor Committee. It is everyone's responsibility to protect his or her personal honor and character.

SOCIAL LIFE AND ACTIVITIES

Sports are a part of everyday life at USAFA. Everyone is required to participate in either intercollegiate sports, club sports, or intramural sports. The highly rated coaching staff at USAFA trains athletes in twenty-seven different varsity teams, all of which compete at the National Collegiate Athletic Association Division I level.

Club sports also play a large role in cadet daily life. Cadets can participate in rugby, team handball, squash, rifle and pistol, women's lacrosse, boxing, power lifting, triathlons, Nordic skiing, judo, karate, flying team, soaring team, Wings of Blue (parachute team), and many more. In fact, cadets participate in eighty-seven extracurricular clubs and teams each year. Involvement in these competitive sports helps develop officers and prepare them for the challenges of an active duty officer.

I played competitive rugby all four years of my cadet career and loved every minute of it. Of course I had never even heard of this sport in Georgia, and my Dad couldn't believe that his little girl who played touch football in the backyard was now breaking through a line of rugby players tackling other girls. It made me a stronger person mentally and physically. I loved the thrill of the kickoff and the first hard hit! My teammates really made all hard work, long runs, and endless practices in the snow, rain, and mud worthwhile. The proof of the effort we put into the sport was in our reward. While I was there, we won the Women's National Rugby Championship in 1994 and continued to finish in the top three. It was a truly wonderful experience!

Not all teams are competitive in nature. The academy also supports recreational clubs such as Big Brother/Big Sister, Way of Life, ski club, and amateur radio. It includes mission support clubs such as the different religious choirs, Honor Guard, Media, and Civil Air Patrol. Finally, it also encourages professional clubs such as the Arnold Air Society, Institute of Electrical and Electronic Engineers, and Asian Studies. Taking part in these activities benefits the civilian community as much as the cadet and promotes a spirit of civilian and military cooperation. It also helps a cadet internalize the core value of "service before self."

Off-Campus Activities

The ability to actually possess a social life lies in the delicate balance of time management. The setting itself provides many opportunities. Colorado Springs is a thriving community with two large shopping malls and a growing number of restaurants. With ski resorts and white water rafting only two and a half hours away, there is never a lack of things to do; there is simply only a lack of time.

As fourthclassmen (freshmen), the only weekend passes granted during the first semester are Labor Day (Parent's Weekend) and Thanksgiving. As time increases, so do the privileges. During the secondclass (junior) year, cadets begin to have enough passes to go out periodically. It is during this year that cadets are also authorized to have a car on or off campus. During the firstclass (senior) year, passes are most generous. If cadets want to exercise an independent social life, this is the year that they have to enjoy it, providing that they are not on any type of probation.

Religious Services and Support Programs

One of the most prominent and awe-inspiring features on the Air Force Academy's campus is the Cadet Chapel. The Chapel and Chapel clergy host religious services for Protestant, Catholic, Jewish, and Muslim faiths, sponsor choirs that sing at the religious services, and offer programs for cadets seeking religious activities, discussion, guidance, and support.

> *The pressure at USAFA is always present and the demands on you from the time you wake up until you go to sleep can really take their toll. I found the Chapel clergy and programs to be extremely helpful in restoring my faith and relationship with a much higher authority than my military chain of command. The clergy and staff really understood what I was going through and offered me a sense of familiarity and home, even though I was far away from former school friends and family. The freshman year experience is hard on anyone who is separated from his or her family for the first time. The academy freshman year only adds to this pressure. The Chapel can be a refuge for those who seek the peace and comfort afforded by their religious beliefs.*

FINANCIAL AID

Upon admission to the academy, every cadet is required to make a $2,500 deposit to cover expenses for a personal computer and clothing allowances. This deposit will be collected during the initial in-processing of basic cadets. If a new (basic) cadet is unable to pay the full amount of the deposit, an allotment will be made from the cadet's monthly paycheck until the balance is paid. Some national and local scholarships allow a cadet to use the money toward the deposit. There is no financial aid given at the Air Force Academy because none is needed.

Appointees will be contacted on procedures to make travel arrangements to the academy. The travel allowances will be credited to the cadet's checking account during in-processing. If however, a basic cadet refuses to take the Oath of Allegiance upon arrival at the academy, or is disqualified for admission because of the cadet's fault, the academy will waive the cadet's right to reimbursement of travel expenses.

GRADUATES

As stated earlier, all cadets graduate with a Bachelor of Science degree and are commissioned into the United States Air Force as second lieutenants. Upon graduation, they must complete five years of active duty before becoming eligible to separate from the Air Force. If a lieutenant separates before the five-year mark, he or she will owe a monetary portion of his or her education to the government. Those who attend Undergraduate Pilot Training (UPT) incur an eight-year commitment upon completing UPT.

PROMINENT GRADS

- Ronald R. Fogleman, '63, Air Force Chief of Staff
- Lance P. Sijan, '65, Medal of Honor Winner, P.O.W.
- Susan Helms, '80, Astronaut
- Alanzo Babers, '83, Olympics Gold Medalist
- Chad Hennings, '88, NFL Player, Outland Trophy Winner

Graduates with outstanding academic achievement may win scholarships immediately upon graduation from the academy. They will earn their masters degree while being paid as a second lieutenant. Some fortunate graduates will also be accepted directly into medical programs. They can attend the military medical school or civilian schools. Other graduates may wait three years and apply for Air Force scholarships once on active duty.

Most graduates compete for training slots to pilot or navigation training. Other graduates will attend training in their desired career path. Whether it is communication, maintenance, personnel, intelligence, or services, each individual must complete training before earning the qualification badge. After training, they will report to their assigned bases to begin work in an operational squadron.

SUMMING UP

In retrospect, USAFA was a really great experience. One cannot just say its a great college, because the academic portion is only a small part of the whole picture—so much more goes into creating a professional Air Force officer.

The admissions process is long and tedious and it should be, considering that USAFA offers every student a $250,000 scholarship. It is a year-long struggle of taking standardized tests and retaking them to improve one's standing with the admissions panel. Not only is the panel looking for students who can handle the academic, military, and physical pressures, but it has to carefully judge the character of all applicants and their potential to become professional Air Force officers.

The academic programs and support are fantastic. The academy has the most up-to-date technology to support the learning needs of the 4,000 cadets. The small class sizes encourage students to interact with the professors and optimize the time spent in the classroom. Extra instruction from teachers and other students is available to all cadets to help them understand concepts that escape them during class. Finally, study periods during the evening are observed and regulated by the cadet squadrons.

Extracurricular activities are some of the USAFA's greatest strong points. There is definitely an opportunity for everyone to "find that niche." Whether you're an avid sports nut or you thrive on community service projects, you will find there is something for everyone. These activities not only help cadets learn to tame the time management beast, they help develop a cadet's character, an essential element of the four-year odyssey.

The Colorado setting overflows with social and recreational opportunities. Mountain climbing, skiing, horseback riding, and white water rafting are available through the services support provided by USAFA. There are many tourist areas such as the Royal Gorge, Seven Falls, and Garden of the Gods, which are favorites of cadets and their parents. Colorado Springs offers two shopping malls, dozens of new restaurants and clubs, movie theaters, and concerts. If Colorado Springs is too small for your liking, Denver and Boulder are a quick drive up I-25.

Finally, graduates not only complete a four-year degree, they complete a four-year journey. It is a challenge to make it through each day. They are continually forced to push themselves past paradigms of what they believe is physically possible. Tossing the hats as the Air Force Thunderbirds race across the sky is a sign of a huge accomplishment, but, in actuality, it is really only the beginning of a new life adventure as a commissioned officer in the United States Air Force.

When asked if I could do it all over again, would I still make the same decision to go through it all? My answer is a definite YES! I wouldn't do it for the free education. I wouldn't do it for all of the opportunities I'd been given. I'd do it for the friendships and experiences I've shared with my squadron mates and teammates. The friends I made here are friends for a lifetime. These are friends I'd sweat and bleed with, friends I'd shared my greatest fears and hopes with. Time will never erase all the hell we went through together, with ties that bind us together, with blood that sticks.

❑ *Lt. Melissa S. Cunningham, B.S.*

UNITED STATES COAST GUARD ACADEMY

United States Coast Guard Academy
New London, CT 06320-4195

(203) 444-8500, (800) 883-8724
Fax: (203) 437-6700

E-mail: uscgatr@dcseq.uscga.edu
Web site: http://www.cga.edu

Enrollment

Full-time ❑ women: 240
❑ men: 608

INTRODUCING THE UNITED STATES COAST GUARD ACADEMY

The Coast Guard Academy is not a college; it is an experience unto its own. It is a place where the magnitude of the adversities before you only intensifies the joy of overcoming them. It is a place where you will make the best friends you will ever have, a place where you can be truly alone on a ship with 200 people on it, kissing the commissioning pennant at the top of a 147-foot mast. It is a place of unyielding routine: the daily pipe of reveille, the formations, the New England winters, and the color blue. It is a place of passionate idealism, of young men and women seeking perfection in a less than perfect world. It is a place of paradox and tradition, where the rules constantly change but things always seem to stay the same. It truly is the best of times and the worst of times for four years, and then there goes your hat—it is over.

The United States Coast Guard Academy, founded in 1876, is the primary source for commissioned officers in the United States Coast Guard. It is similar in many respects to the military, naval, and Air Force academies, except that it is a lot smaller. With a cadet corps of only 848, the Coast Guard Academy has the benefits of both an Armed Forces Service Academy and a small, focused college or university with a strong academic program.

The decision of whether or not to attend a U.S. service academy has plagued countless high school seniors. The benefits are immediately apparent: the freedom from financial burden, an outstanding four-year education with the guarantee of employment and subsequent job security, the development of character and self-discipline. Accepting the appointment to serve is often hindered by a host of persistent, nagging thoughts; the five-year commitment is imposing, as are frequent transfers and sea time. Self-doubt exists as to the possibility of actually surviving, and how can anyone put up with haircuts, uniforms, and taking orders? These are all issues that must be considered, and considered carefully. The decision of what to do with the next nine years of a promising future is a weighty one to be made by a seventeen-year-old. However, a person who is truly committed will not regret the fateful summer afternoon when the right hand was raised and the oath was uttered. It's not the path of least resistance, to be sure, but it's exciting, and the service is enriched by the fact that the U.S. Coast Guard is an honorable profession, and a superior organization.

TRADITION

When a fourth class cadet is asked, "How's the cow?" the correct response is: "Sir/Ma'am, she walks, she talks, she's full of chalk! The lacteal fluid extracted from the female of the bovine species is highly prolific to the nth degree, Sir/Ma'am!"

So, which high school seniors actually do take the plunge? They tend to stand out a little from their peers at the top of the class. They are all incredibly qualified with respect to grades, test scores, athletics, and activities—that goes without saying. Yet, they have a certain boldness that dares them to take on such a formidable challenge, but that boldness is tempered with a desire to make a positive contribution to the world in some way. They are drawn to the discipline of the military lifestyle, the grandeur and tradition associated with a maritime academy, and the romantic ideal of saving lives at sea. The typical academy cadet is extremely intelligent, remarkably well-rounded, and fiercely idealistic. Still, these traits are shared by an incredibly diverse group of scholars, athletes, musicians, and artists from across the country.

THE CADET REGIMENT

The cadet regiment is divided into eight companies—Alfa, Bravo, Charlie, Delta, Echo, Foxtrot, Golf, and Hotel—and each occupy a section of Chase Hall. The cadets in each company remain together for all four years. Naturally, each company begins to develop its own personality.

Swearing-in Day

The journey begins the second week of July on swearing-in day. The new cadets are fitted for uniforms, relieved of the burden of carrying so much hair around, and get a crash course on marching in formation. Then, in the late afternoon New England summer sun, the incoming class is paraded before families and friends, and simultaneously sworn to "protect and defend." Following that, the new fourth class cadets get about fifteen minutes for pictures and last good-byes, and the upperclass cadre and their charges disappear into Chase Hall. That first evening in the barracks generally is quiet, with some more instruction on stowing new uniforms and issued gear, the cadre issuing quietly stated expectations to a very captive audience of swabs.

The reality hadn't really set in at all during swearing-in day. I remember lying in my rack that night, feeling a little nervous, but mostly swelling with pride about the select company that I had just joined, the tradition, all that stuff. And then...it was morning. Really early in the morning, too, and my ears were filled with reveille and bellowing upperclass. That's when the reality set in.

BASIC DEFINITIONS

- Zoomie: Air Force Cadet
- Grunt: Army Cadet
- Squid: Navy Midshipman

The Difficulty of the Military Program

The academy's real strength in its military program lies in its focus on character. The standard of conduct for academy cadets continues to remain a few notches above expectations of other college students. "Who lives here reveres honor, honors duty" is set in stone on the quarterdeck in the front entrance to Chase Hall, home to the corps of cadets. The academy's honor concept is: "Cadets neither lie, cheat, steal, nor attempt to deceive." These are lofty-sounding phrases, but the wonderful thing is that cadet culture embraces these ideals, rather than blindly following them. Honor education begins in Swab Summer and continues until graduation. There is even an exceptional Morals and Ethics class that examines various moral philosophies and applies them to a social or academy context.

Outward Appearance

The outward appearance of the academy can be somewhat austere. Despite the tumult within, the academy grounds are always enveloped in a certain quietude. Buildings fit a definite architectural motif: brick and square. The grounds are immaculately kept, and the lush green expanse used every Friday afternoon in the fall and spring for regimental drill is breathtaking. A tour through the academy during the day allows you to catch a glimpse of the cadet corps doing what they do. Fourth class march to class in section, brandishing briefcases. Upperclass file along the sidewalks, grimacing, looking severe. There's very little standing around or idle conversation. There certainly isn't any sitting cross-legged in the grass in the afternoon sun, studying and drinking Snapple, no modern art sculptures scattered throughout the campus, no cadet couples walking and holding hands, and no cluster of cadets sipping espresso at a campus cafe. The prospect of attending an institution that appears so commanding is somewhat daunting. Even at a glance, there's no doubt that it's not your ordinary college experience.

MEALS

The corps of cadets—all 850 cadets—eats a sit-down breakfast and lunch together simultaneously each day. The average time one has to eat breakfast: seven minutes.

The Average Day

It is difficult to describe how demanding a cadet's schedule really is. The day generally begins around 5:45 and continues well into the night. It consists of at least two military formations and possibly a personnel inspection. There's one hour of military training allotted each morning. Most cadets carry an eighteen- or nineteen-credit load (some as many as twenty-two), so nearly all of the day is occupied with classes. Free time throughout the day is as rare as an arctic fox. Following classes is sports period, and after a good, hard sweat, a shower, and a big dinner (the food served in the cadet wardroom is of excellent quality and quantity), coffee is necessary before sitting down to tackle the evening's work. One Friday evening each month is occupied with preparing for a formal room inspection. In addition, Saturday mornings are filled with training and other activities. Although there is no formal daily or weekly physical training program, cadets must take and pass a physical fitness exam once every six months that consists of pull-ups, sit-ups, standing broad jump, 300-yard shuttle run, and a 1.5-mile run. The overall effect of four years of non-stop activity is this: each day seems to last forever, yet each successive year passes more quickly than the one preceding it.

ADMISSIONS REQUIREMENTS

The Coast Guard Academy has long been regarded as one of the most selective schools in the country. The average SAT scores and academic performance of an incoming class are not quite as high as the Ivies or some of the better-known academic powerhouses, but the acceptance ratio is always among the most competitive. The size of any given incoming class averages around 270, and the academy receives five to six thousand applications each year. The critical thing to remember is that academics alone will not earn an appointment; neither will outstanding achievement in athletics, music, or community service, without evidence of leadership to complement it. A well-rounded application is perhaps more important to the Coast Guard Academy than to nearly any other college or university.

There are a few basic requirements for admissions. Applicants must have reached the age of seventeen but not the age of twenty-three by July 1 of the year of admission, be citizens of the United States, and be single at the time of appointment and remain single while attending the academy. Required secondary school courses include three years each of English and mathematics.

Points

Unlike the other service academies, which require a congressional appointment or a similar endorsement, Coast Guard Academy admissions are completely free from political influence. The process is entirely merit-based. Each candidate is evaluated based on his or her high school class rank, SAT I or ACT scores, transcript, essays, letters of recommendations, and extracurricular activities or sports. It's an unfortunate reality that each year there are numerous applicants with a great desire to serve who must be turned away. Admissions officers at the academy are not just shaping a talented corps of cadets. They have an additional burden—the decisions that they make have an impact on the Coast Guard for years to come. In evaluating an individual's potential to contribute to the academic environment of the academy, they must necessarily infer a candidate's willingness to serve and potential long-term value to the Coast Guard from a written application. It's not an easy task.

ACADEMIC LIFE

TRAINING AID

As a training aid to future seagoing officers, the academy professional development department operates a $5 million bridge and radar simulator.

Coast Guard Academy academics have a surprising degree of intellectual freedom for a military institution. Government majors debate the latest, most controversial issues in public policy. Engineers design new classes of ships and make advances in electronic navigation. Marine science majors are at the forefront of the fields of environmental protection and remote weather sensing. The classes are conducted with a refreshing openness. The academic halls are a place where cadets can truly be liberated from the daily routine if they so desire.

Majors

There are eight majors at the academy: naval architecture/marine engineering, electrical engineering, civil engineering, mechanical engineering, operations research, government, management, and marine science. Fourth class cadets all take introductory level classics, and the intended major must be declared by the end of the first year. To graduate, cadets must pass at least thirty-seven courses, twenty-five of which are core curriculum. one-hundred twenty-six credit hours must be accumulated, ninety or more with a C or better. Physical education classes are required each semester.

Faculty

The faculty at the academy is roughly equal proportions military and civilian; members of both populations are excellent. Being an academy instructor is extremely competitive in all academic disciplines. Each year, officers throughout the Coast Guard apply for a few academy instructor positions. They are prepared for their assignment by some of the nation's best graduate schools. These officers are not only experts in their field, they can apply the relevance of the academic experience to the future careers of the cadets with a few good sea stories. The civilian faculty are the Ph.D.s, and tend to hold the senior positions in the departments. They enjoy teaching cadets and provide continuity as officers transfer in and out.

Class Size

The academy's small size facilitates plenty of individual attention. There are *no* large lecture hall-style classes whatsoever, no graduate TAs teaching classes. Introductory-level courses, mostly taken by fourth class, tend to be only slightly larger than the average of twenty for all academy classes. Depending on the popularity of the academic major, upper-level courses may be populated with as few as six or eight cadets. Both civilian and military instructors aggressively take advantage of the small student/faculty ratio (8:1) with fourth-class cadets and constantly seek their involvement. The most popular phrase heard throughout academic buildings is "ask questions!" It can be difficult, at first, to draw out the intellectual creativity of fourth class cadets who, only months earlier, had it frightened out of them. Before too long, everyone reverts to their own inquisitive selves and enthusiastic participation becomes the norm.

SQUARE ROOT CLUB

Legend has it that members of the square root club (if you take the square root of your GPA and it comes out *higher*, you're in the square root club) must sleep on the grave of Hopley Yeaton, the Coast Guard's first commissioned officer, the evening before an exam.

Grades

As tough and unforgiving as the academy may be, there's plenty of help available. There are few professors who will not go out of their way to aid a cadet in academic distress. In addition, there are plenty of sympathetic upperclass who volunteer to tutor underclass in various subjects. Cadets are sympathetic to each other's academic woes and will go to great lengths to render assistance; it's always tragic when a potentially great officer can't hack the academics and reverts to civilian status.

Class Rank

One would expect the academic environment to be fiercely competitive at a military academy; to the contrary, the atmosphere is one of cooperation. There are always the few cadets in every class gifted enough to scuffle it out in the thin air of the 3.98 stratum, but most cadets find their niche somewhere between there and 2.0.

Core Curriculum

The academy's academic program has relatively few weaknesses. The curriculum can be a bit restrictive at times; the staggering amount of core courses required reduces the number of free electives available. The core curriculum is important from a professional development standpoint. Cadets take four semesters of nautical science, as well as courses in maritime law enforcement, criminal justice, organizational behavior, and electrical engineering, to name a few. All of these become relevant immediately following graduation.

SOCIAL LIFE AND ACTIVITIES

Sports

Athletics tend to be the main focus of extracurricular activities at the academy. Cadets are required to participate in athletic competition at either the varsity or intramural level in two of the three sports seasons. For only having a student body of 850, the academy fields a surprising number of athletic teams: thirteen for men and nine for women. Despite the relatively small pool of talent from which the sports teams draw, nearly every team is a fierce competitor at the Division III level.

With or without the emphasis placed on sports by the administration, athletic participation would still be hugely popular in the corps. At 1600, the beginning of sports period, a mass exodus begins from the Chase Hall barracks to Roland/Billard, the primary athletic facility, and the "lower field." Cadets take out their frustrations on the wrestling mats, the soccer fields, or in the weight room, and emerge two hours later refreshed and renewed.

The athletic facilities are fabulous. The Jacob's Rock sailing center makes it into just about every admissions publication, and the academy's boats are in superb condition. The crew team enjoys similar conditions with their boathouse. The main athletic facility, Roland/Billard, as it is commonly known, is the center of cadet activity from 1600 to 1830 each day. It sports two enormous weight rooms packed with equipment, one consisting entirely of free weights that would be worthy of a Division I university. There are two gymnasiums, two swimming pools, five racquetball courts, a wrestling room, an indoor track/field house, and even a rock-climbing wall.

Intercompany sports are the main attraction for amateur athletes and varsity athletes out of season. IC sports fulfill a sports credit, and the light playing schedule leaves enough time in the week to train hard for a varsity sport. The companies in the regiment each field IC teams in a multitude of sports. There's the usual fare, like softball and basketball, but there are some oddball sports, too, including an academy creation called flickerball. The amount of spectators at IC championships rivals that of some varsity events.

Other Activities

There are still plenty of other escapes and diversions available for cadets. The cadet drill team is entirely cadet-run and competes with other schools in silent trick drill. *Tide Rips*, the academy's yearbook, has a long tradition and is worthy of a much larger university in terms of size. Student government is very active in the form of class officers and company representatives; they organize many of the class events that take place throughout the year. In addition, there are social service and religious organizations, as well as special interest clubs (snowboard club, paintball club) that spring up from time to time.

The cadet music program puts forth a valiant effort each year to produce high-quality cadet music despite all the competing interests. A large percentage of the corps are musicians who actively participate in the variety of cadet musical activities. The Regimental Band exists to provide martial music for the weekly regimental reviews. Many members of the Reg Band also participate in the newly formed Concert Band. The Windjammers, the academy's drum and bugle corps, is perhaps the largest musical organization. They perform a full field show at all home football games, and travel to various locations throughout the Northeast to perform as exhibition at marching band competitions, attracting legions of fans wherever they go. The Nitecaps Jazz Band is an incredibly talented group that performs dozens of times a year at various functions up and down the East Coast. Vocal music thrives; the Glee Club and its associated Idlers and Icebreakers are especially good.

Social Opportunities

Apart from sports and activities, social opportunities are rare and precious. The amount of liberty time one is afforded off-base correlates with seniority. As a fourth class cadet, you don't get much.

Although I had no liberty and no cash, I always managed to find fun my fourth class year, often in the weirdest of ways. I spent Friday nights down at the old Billard pool with a few of my classmates from Foxtrot company, trying aerials off the diving board (and the balcony) and goofing around in general.

The true adventures were on long weekends. Imagine six guys crammed into a Chevette going to Boston with no idea where to stay or what to do, and ending up with photographic evidence that Woody Harrelson was induced to wear a Coast Guard Academy sweatshirt during a concert on Boston Commons.

If there is one thing about the academy that everyone agrees on, it's that incredible friendships are made in each class. There's something about spending four years in close company with your peers under difficult circumstances that forms very strong bonds. A tour through the first class pages of Tide Rips will reveal a trend: nearly every graduating first class cadet devotes their page to the friends that they made.

I had a roommate from West Virginia—a football player who cried every time he heard "Take Me Home, Country Roads." I had a six-foot six-inch roommate from Washington, D.C. who started learning Tae Kwon Do at the Academy and left with a black belt. I had a roommate from the extreme northeast corner of Montana whose high school burned down his senior year because all the fire-fighting water in the town had frozen. I had another roommate who lived within walking distance of the academy.

I had a classmate who played eight-man football in Idaho, a graffiti artist from Sacramento, a prior Air Force enlisted musician, basketball players from Arizona, tobacco-chewing football players from North Florida, a globe-trotting intellectual from La Jolla, California, an Irish EMT from Boston, a snare-drumming wildman from Hawaii, and a playwright/soccer player from Cameroon.

I shared some incredible experiences with all of these people. I am closer to some than to others, but I could meet any of my classmates for lunch thirty years from now and we would still have this thread of unique experiences that we've shared.

Off-Campus Activities

If liberty is available, most cadets do not stay within the boundaries of the reservation on the weekends. New London itself may be small, but cadets are extremely resourceful when it comes to sniffing out a good time. The academy is in between New York and Boston, with Interstate 95 running right by it. If you're not a firstie with a car, and you can't manage to scam one, there's a train station downtown. New York, Boston, and Philadelphia are all accessible within the span of a weekend. Even short trips to Baltimore and Washington, D.C. are not unheard of.

Not that there isn't anything to do in southeastern Connecticut. The area is probably best known for its cultural activities. The Garde Arts theater in New London hosts many national dance, musical, and dramatic acts. There are a host of other regional theaters, including Long Wharf in New Haven, the Goodspeed Opera House in Haddam, and Summer Music at Harkness Park in Waterford. The coastal towns of Connecticut are a tourist attraction in themselves, especially Mystic with its seaport and aquarium. But even if you're an underclass cadet with no ride and no civilian clothes, the nearby mall and movie theaters are available via liberty van.

Mixers

Social life on the academy grounds can be interesting. The cadet social committee manages a number of events each year, including mixers where invitations are posted to a number of the smaller colleges in the area. Although the mixers are attended almost exclusively by underclass, they can be a convenient way to make acquaintances, or perhaps to arrange dates to any one of the several formal dinner/dances held throughout the year. Of course, Connecticut College is right across the street. Formerly a females-only institution, Conn College is just too conveniently located next to the formerly all-male Coast Guard Academy. Conn does still retain a majority of women, and the academy is just over two-thirds male. Members of Conn and CGA may eye each other with suspicion (political differences) when they do interact, but the fact that many marriages have emerged between Coast Guard officers and Conn College graduates illustrates the fruits of this juxtaposition.

CLASS RINGS

Cadets earn their class rings at their second class ring dance. At the dance, the cadet's date takes the ring and dips it in a bowl containing water from each of the seven seas and places it on the cadet's finger. The act is sanctified with a kiss (and an expensive photograph).

FINANCIAL AID

As with the other service academies, the U.S. Coast Guard Academy is essentially free. After graduation, a five-year service obligation is incurred. Except for an entrance fee of $3,000, the federal government covers all cadet expenses by providing a monthly allowance of approximately $550. Only a small percentage of the monthly allowance is available to cadets as spending money. The majority of the allowance is managed by cadet finance for the purchase of books and uniforms. The amount of spending money is increased (as are other privileges) with each year of seniority attained.

PROMINENT GRADS

- G. William Miller, '46, Secretary of the Treasury
- Dan A. Colussy, '53, CEO, UNC Inc.
- ADM Robert E. Kramek, '61, Commandant, U.S. Coast Guard
- RADM Richard W. Schneider, USCGR, '68, President, Norwich University
- John A. Gaughan, '70, Head, Maritime Administration
- CDR Bruce E. Melnick, '72, Former Astronaut

GRADUATES

The Coast Guard Academy continues to be the primary source of career officers in the Coast Guard. Upon graduation, a five-year obligation to serve in the fleet begins, the first two years of which must be spent afloat on a cutter 157 feet or larger.

A career in the Coast Guard presents continual challenges; it's not a "nine-to-five" job. Nearly any field that you may enter requires you to maintain an odd schedule. If you stay afloat, you're gone for six months of the year. The aviation and marine safety fields also impose certain demands. The work is hard, and it sometimes becomes difficult to balance "work" and "life." The career of a Coast Guard officer is really a lifestyle unto its own, and it's not for everybody.

But the adventures you'll have! You're a junior officer, and no matter where you go, you'll gain experiences that you'll later say you wouldn't trade for anything.

In the fifteen months following graduation, I've boarded factory trawlers in the Bering Sea while conducting fisheries enforcement, and participated in counter-narcotics operations off the coast of Mexico. Just two months ago, my ship interdicted 69 illegal Chinese migrants. I've sailed through eighty-knot winds and thirty-foot seas. I've participated in Fleet Week in San Francisco where my blue uniform in a sea of black ones earned autograph requests. I'm one of the good guys in blue, part of the same team that I hear making major drug busts in the Caribbean or rescuing victims of an overturned ferryboat.

An academy education has many tangible and intangible benefits. The most apparent is probably the freedom from a financial burden imposed by the high cost of a college degree. While others are hacking through student loans the first five years following graduation, Coast Guard ensigns are starting to invest. The 20-year retirement is also something to consider. You may never be rich as a Coast Guard officer, but you'll always be financially secure.

As an added benefit, doing well academically at the Academy opens doors to the possibility of free graduate education. Officers compete annually for graduate program openings in fields ranging from electrical engineering to finance or operations analysis. There is a three-to-one payback for graduate school; that is, each year of education creates another three years of obligated service. Even if one desires to "pull chocks" and start a second career, academy graduates tend to rise to the top of every field they enter. The Coast Guard Academy degree carries a certain amount of prestige, especially in engineering circles. A quick perusal through the alumni directory will reveal that, in time, an increasing percentage of graduates finds success as CEOs, lawyers, and other professionals. This is no accident. The habits made in work, study, and character are at least partially the result of a Coast Guard Academy education.

SUMMING UP

The mission of the United States Coast Guard Academy is to graduate young men and women with sound bodies, stout hearts, and alert minds, with a liking for the sea and its lore, and with that high sense of honor, loyalty, and obedience that goes with trained initiative and leadership—well-grounded in seamanship, the sciences, and the amenities, and strong in the resolve to be worthy of the traditions of commissioned officers of the United States Coast Guard, in service to their country and humanity.

The Coast Guard Academy is not for everyone. With all its rewards, it can be a claustrophobic, nasty place at times. It takes more than a "stout heart" to make it. It takes a level of commitment that few are prepared to make. It takes the idealism to seek utter perfection and the maturity to understand it isn't possible. It takes strength of character and a strong will, tempered by patience and understanding.

If you've got what it takes, then not only is it a great place to be from, but it's a great place to be.

❑ *Lt. (J.G.) Jared Dillian, B.S.*

UNITED STATES MILITARY ACADEMY AT WEST POINT

United States Military Academy at West Point
West Point, NY 10996

(914) 938-4041
Fax: (914) 938-3021

E-mail: admissions @www.usma.edu
Web site: http://www.usma.edu/admissions

Enrollment

Full-time ❑ women: 579
❑ men: 3,531

INTRODUCING WEST POINT

What do I remember most about West Point? It would be impossible for me to choose just one event. Perhaps it was marching with my class onto the parade field at the end of the very first day and taking the oath as my family and friends watched anxiously from the stands. Or maybe it was the exhilarating feeling of parachuting from an airplane 1,250 feet in the sky and the shock of seeing my parents waiting for me on the drop zone! Or it may very well have been the day I found out I passed physics. Or perhaps the day we beat Navy in football for the fifth straight year. Or the day I scored two goals in our Army-Navy lacrosse game and we won by one goal in the last second. Or it could have been when I was a squad leader and my squad successfully completed squad stakes competition and found our way home. Or perhaps the day I became platoon leader at CTLT (cadet troop leader training) at Fort Campbell, Kentucky. Or it might have been when I shook the hand of the President of the United States after receiving my diploma. Now that was a day to remember. ...

Founded in 1802, West Point is our nation's oldest service academy. Graduates of West Point "serve this nation honorably, sharing a strong sense of purpose, pride, and satisfaction that comes from meaningful service to others."

Attending the United States Military Academy is a wonderfully unique and challenging experience. West Point is a four-year college with a mission to develop leaders of character for our army—leaders who are inspired to careers as commissioned officers and lifetime service to the nation. The students of West Point (called cadets) are selected from the most talented, energetic, and well-rounded young people in the country. Located on 16,000 acres in the scenic Hudson Valley region of New York State, West Point is conveniently situated just fifty miles north of New York City. The year-round pageantry and tradition make the Military Academy a national treasure and a popular tourist spot. People come from all over the world to see cadets in action, and there is so much to see.

Choosing West Point opens the door to countless opportunities. Cadets receive a top-notch education, training in leader development, and numerous professional opportunities. They learn first how to be a follower, and then to be a leader—skills that will carry them in all of their life endeavors. Not to mention the fact that they are guaranteed a five-year job in the military.

So what makes West Point such a special place? West Point is more than a school; it is a tightly knit community. The officers and noncommissioned officers who serve as instructors at West Point share a special bond with the cadets. The students and their instructors at West Point are members of the same profession and are dedicated to the same principles of "duty, honor, and country."

Cadets at West Point live under an Honor Code that states that "a cadet will not lie, cheat, or steal, or tolerate those who do." The penalty for those who violate this code is serious. The Honor Code is meant to develop cadets into true leaders of character. Cadets internalize the importance of living honorably and carry this value with them into the army.

ADMISSIONS REQUIREMENTS

Admission to West Point is highly competitive, and the application process is much more involved than that of a civilian school. Of the approximate 13,000 candidates who start files each year, only about 1,600 are offered admission. While most colleges and universities look primarily at a student's academic background, West Point is interested in the whole package. Not only must candidates be of high academic caliber, they must qualify physically and medically as well. Candidates must also earn a nomination from a U.S. representative, senator, the president, vice president, or from the Department of the Army (these nominations are service-related).

The admissions committee seeks students who are bright, athletic, and have "demonstrated leadership potential" throughout their high school years. To determine the academic strength and potential of a candidate, the admissions committee examines both the high school transcript and the SAT/ACT scores. To determine the physical fitness and potential of a candidate, the committee looks at the athletic activities in which the candidate participated during high school. In addition, candidates are required to take a physical aptitude examination (PAE), which consists of several events such as a 300-meter run, pull-ups, and a broad jump, designed to determine athletic ability and potential.

Leadership Potential

Because West Point strives to be the premier leader development institute in the world, it is important that the academy admit cadets who have leadership potential that can be built upon. With that in mind, the admissions committee looks for students who were part of the student government in their school, primarily student body or class president. Other indications of exceptional leadership potential might include participation in boys/girls state, scouting, debate, school publications, and varsity athletics. In a recent class of 1,192 new cadets, 1,054 had earned varsity letters in high school and 741 were team captains. Over seventy-five percent of the class graduated in the top fifth of their high school class. The mean SAT I score for the Class of 2001 was 620 Verbal and 644 Math. Over forty-seven percent of the class scored above 29 on the ACT, and 142 members of the class earned National Merit Scholarship Recognition.

Candidates must also be at least seventeen and not older than twenty-three years of age on July first of the year they enter the academy. They must also be U.S. citizens, be unmarried, and not be pregnant or have a legal obligation for child support.

Steps in Applying

There are several steps in applying to West Point.

- Make a self-assessment. Determine if you qualify for West Point and if this is something that you would be interested in doing.
- Start a candidate file. This is done by contacting the USMA Admissions Office.
- Seek a nomination from the representative in your district and your senators.
- You must complete all of your SAT and ACT testing, as well as your physical and medical examinations.
- You then have the option of visiting West Point and spending the day with a cadet on a candidate orientation visit. This is optional, but highly recommended. An orientation visit is the best way to get a feel for academy life and if it's for you.
- If you complete all of these steps and are admitted into the incoming class, your final step is to enroll in the academy on Reception Day.

For those candidates who consider USMA to be their top college choice and are interested in applying early, West Point offers an Early Action plan. Under this plan, applicants are informed of their admissions status by January 15. Persistence is "key," as about thirty percent of each incoming class are second-time applicants.

ACADEMIC LIFE

I'll never forget my first day of classes as a plebe (freshman). I was astonished to see that each of my classes had only about fifteen cadets in it, about half the size of my high school classes. The first thing each professor did was write his or her home phone number on the blackboard. "Call me at home anytime, day or night," each one said. The classroom experience at West Point is unlike any other. There simply are no crowded lecture halls or graduate assistants. Each class is taught by an instructor whose primary responsibility is to teach cadets. Each class has a maximum number of eighteen students. You just can't get that kind of personal interaction at other universities—many of my friends at other schools had as many graduate assistants as they did professors. My professors taught every lesson, were available for additional help at all hours of the day or night, and even came out to support me at my athletic matches!

The Core Curriculum

Academics at West Point are tough, but with the amount of assistance available, cadets are set up for success. The overall curriculum contains classes in both science and the arts. Unlike most colleges and universities, the core curriculum is very extensive. In other words, during the first two years, there is not much flexibility in course selection. The core curriculum consists of thirty-one courses. This broad base of classes serves several purposes. Cadets not only get a solid foundation before specializing in one area, but have also studied in all of the academic departments and have a sound basis for selecting a major. Cadets can choose from nineteen majors and twenty-five fields of study. To major, cadets take ten to thirteen electives; to complete a field of study they must take nine. Besides their major or field of study, all students take what is called a five-course engineering sequence. This sequence strengthens the cadet's engineering background and in a sense gives him or her a second major. The engineering sequences include electrical engineering, environmental engineering, civil engineering, mechanical engineering, nuclear engineering, systems engineering, and computer science. All graduates receive a bachelor of science degree.

Resources

The resources available to cadets are very impressive. The library contains over 600,000 volumes of resources and 2,000 academic journals and newspapers. All cadets have desk-top computers in their room and full access to the Internet. In addition, the Center for Enhanced Performance assists cadets in achieving their potential in all aspects of academy life, offering classes, open to all students, in reading efficiency and student success. One-on-one additional instruction is available to cadets from their instructors and is what sets the military academy apart from other schools.

Physical Education and Military Development

Part of the overall curriculum includes physical education and military development. The physical education curriculum spans the four years. Physical education classes are incorporated into the grade point average, which highlights the importance of physical fitness in the army. Cadets receive grades in each physical education class as well as the Army Physical Fitness Test and the Indoor Obstacle Course Test. The physical program is quite challenging, but rewarding and fun as well.

Military development is also part of the curriculum. Cadets are graded based on military performance within their cadet companies as well as their performance during summer training and military intersession. The heart of the military training takes place during the summer. During their first summer, new cadets are introduced to the academy through the rigors of Cadet Basic Training, a six-week experience that transforms the new class from civilians to cadets, and gives the upper two classes the opportunity to practice small unit leadership. During Cadet Basic Training—also called "Beast Barracks"—new cadets learn what it means to be a cadet as well as what it means to be a soldier.

The summer after plebe or freshman year, cadets participate in Cadet Field Training. At Camp Buckner, sophomores or "yearlings" complete seven weeks of advanced military training including weapons, tank, and aviation training. During this time, cadets are also introduced to the different branches of the army and how their focus contributes to its overall mission. They apply the skills they learned in the classroom as they practice tactical exercises in small units. Like Cadet Basic Training, upperclass cadets serve as the cadre for this training.

Camp Buckner is also a time for recreation and class bonding. During the summers before junior ("cow") and senior ("firstie") year, opportunities for cadets broaden significantly. During these summers, cadets must participate in either Cadet Troop Leader Training or Drill Cadet Leader Training. This involves being assigned to an active army unit for six weeks and acting as either platoon leaders or drill sergeants. For most cadets, it is their first experience in the regular army and it is both exciting and rewarding. A cadet must also serve as a leader or cadre member for either Cadet Basic Training or Cadet Field Training during one of these summers.

This leaves two periods open for cadets to participate in Individual Advanced Development (IADs). Some military IADs include Airborne School (parachuting), Air Assault School (rappelling out of helicopters), Combat Engineer Sapper School, Mountain Warfare School, and Special Forces Scuba School. There are also physical IADs such as training at the U.S. Olympic Center and Outward Bound. Very popular among cadets are academic IADs. These are similar to internships students at civilian colleges might participate in. Some academic IAD cadets participate, including duty with the Supreme Court, Crossroads to Africa, the Foreign Academy Exchange Program, NASA, and the National Laboratories.

Perhaps this is a curriculum unlike any you've ever seen. A cadets total QPA (quality point average) is based on fifty-five percent academics, thirty percent military, and fifteen percent physical. Cadets must be well rounded. The curriculum is meant to develop "enlightened military leaders of strong moral courage whose minds are creative, critical, and resourceful." It was Thucydides who said "The Nation that makes a great distinction between its scholars and its warriors will have its thinking done by cowards and its fighting done by fools."

SOCIAL LIFE AND ACTIVITIES

A few years ago, a couple of seniors painted "West Point is a party school!" on the side of their R.V. in an attempt to rouse spirit among the corps. The irony of this statement roused more than a few chuckles, because cadets know that nothing could be further from the truth, but, while the rowdy fraternity party scene is not alive and well at West Point, don't be fooled into thinking that being a cadet isn't fun. With the number of available activities, it can be an absolute blast!

One of the toughest things about being a cadet is deciding what activities to become involved in. From sports to dramatics to religious activities, West Point truly has it all.

Athletics

Because "every cadet is an athlete, and every athlete will be challenged," all cadets must participate in sporting activities throughout the year. West Point has a highly competitive varsity program, with sixteen men's varsity sports and eight women's, each competing at the Division I level. More than twenty-five percent of the corps participates at this level. Some examples of varsity sports are football, basketball, baseball, softball, soccer, track, lacrosse, and swimming. For those cadets not involved in varsity athletics, there are twenty-nine competitive club sports. Some examples of club sports are crew, equestrian, fencing, mountaineering, rugby, sport parachute, marathon, martial arts, skiing, team handball, water polo, and women's lacrosse. Competitive club sports are great leadership opportunities as cadets do the majority of the planning and executing of team practices and events. Yet another portion of the corps is involved in intramurals. Intramural competitions occur twice a week at 4:00 P.M. and are between teams fielded by each cadet company. There are seventeen different intramural sports for cadets to choose from. Intramurals foster company spirit, sportsmanship, and competition. Whichever level of sports a cadet chooses to participate in, each cadet is truly challenged. Sports at West Point are highly competitive, a great deal of fun, and a welcome break from the rigors of the academic day. School spirit and support for sporting teams at West Point are outstanding.

Clubs

In addition to sports, there are countless other activities for cadets to enjoy. For instance, there are over 100 recreational clubs for cadets to participate in:

- There are clubs that support the corps such as the cadet band and the cadet radio station.
- There are clubs that are academic in nature such as the debate club.
- There are clubs that are geared toward the arts such as the Theatre Arts Guild.
- There are numerous religious groups and activities. Religion plays a large part in the lives of many cadets and cadets are the backbone of the churches on post. From singing in the choir, to teaching Sunday school, cadets find plenty of time to grow in their spirituality both personally and as a member of the larger community. Almost all religious denominations have services on post for cadets to attend.

There are also many social activities for cadets to attend. There is an on-post movie theater, frequent dances, a golf course, a ski slope, a bowling alley, boat rides, and tailgates. You'll very rarely ever hear a cadet say that he or she is bored!

FINANCIAL AID

Because there is no tuition cost associated with attending the United States Military Academy, all students have an equal chance of attending. This creates a diverse population within the corps of cadets. Because we wore the same uniforms and none of us paid tuition, we really didn't know how well-off our fellow cadets were, nor was it our concern. We accepted one another for who we were, not for our family's background.

All cadets at West Point are active-duty soldiers in the regular army. As such, they receive approximately $6,500 a year in pay. They are provided medical and dental care, and room and board. For this, cadets perform assigned duties and agree to serve as commissioned officers for a minimum of five years following graduation. From the cadet salary, deductions are made in order to pay for uniforms, textbooks, a desk-top computer, laundry, grooming, and similar necessities. Upon acceptance of the appointment, cadets are asked to make a one-time, nonrefundable deposit of about $2,500. The total cost of a cadet's full education is about $275,000. This is quite an impressive national investment!

GRADUATES

Some of my fondest memories of West Point involve marching in the alumni parades. Marching along an endless line of distinguished alumni and trying our hardest not to let them down was just an awesome experience. I recall one time when I was moved to tears as an "old grad" in a wheelchair struggled to his feet as my company marched by. We were his old company, and he was not going to sit in his wheelchair as we passed his position. As he applauded and cheered, "Looking good H-4! Go Hogs!" I could not help but get choked up. I was so proud to be even the smallest part of this amazing place. I was part of a tradition, part of history, and someday I too would be standing there facing the corps, recalling my days as a cadet, and cheering them on.

Graduates of West Point tend to be very proud of their alma mater; it seems that the older they get, the prouder they become. Alumni weekends are always very inspiring and very crowded. Grads come decked out from head to toe in paraphernalia that indicates their year of graduation. The alumni are known as "old grads" and the funny thing is, one is referred to as an "old grad" the second he or she tosses that hat in the air on graduation day. The common joke is that "old grads" are always complaining that the structure and discipline at West Point is simply not as rigid as when they were cadets. But most agree, it is the values and traditions that make West Point an enduring national treasure.

West Point has had more than a handful of distinguished graduates. Much of the U.S. Army leadership since the Civil War were members of the Long Gray Line—and the tradition continues. West Point graduates have, and will continue to make wonderful contributions to our nation. More than 100 graduates have competed on various U.S. Olympic teams. West Pointers have served as everything from presidents of corporations to presidents of the United States. Service is what West Point is all about, and our graduates serve our nation well.

PROMINENT GRADS

- Robert E. Lee, 1829
- Ulysses S. Grant, 1843
- George Goethals, 1880
- John J. Pershing, 1886
- Douglas MacArthur, '03
- George Patton, '09
- Omar Bradley, '15
- Dwight D. Eisenhower, '15
- Matthew Ridgway, '17
- Leslie Groves, '18
- Maxwell Taylor, '22
- Creighton Abrams, '36
- Doc Blanchard, '47
- Glenn Davis, '47
- Alexander Haig, Jr., '47
- Brent Scowcroft, '47
- Frank Borman, '50
- Fidel Ramos, '50
- Edward White, '52
- H. Norman Schwarzkopf, '56
- Peter Dawkins, '59
- Mike Krzyzewski, '69

SUMMING UP

West Point is indeed a special place. Where else can you eat virtually every meal in less than twenty minutes with the entire student body? Where else can you march into a stadium on national television and be a part of the Army-Navy rivalry? Where else can you stop on the way to class and pose for a picture with tourists? Where else can you make so many friends for a lifetime? At no other school does the word classmate mean so much. The bonds that are formed at West Point are unparalleled. On the very first day cadets are advised to "cooperate and graduate." This mantra follows them through victories and defeats, through successes and failures, from reception day until graduation day. The West Point Experience prepares cadets for all that life has to offer. When they throw their hats in the air, they are truly ready to be all that they can be.

❑ *2LT Megan Scanlon, B.S.*

UNITED STATES NAVAL ACADEMY

United States Naval Academy
Annapolis, MD 21402-5018

(410) 293-4361, (800) 638-9156
Fax: (410) 293-4348

E-mail: candidateguidance@nadn.navy.mil
Web site: http://www.usna.edu

Enrollment

Full-time ❑ women: 625
❑ men: 3,404

INTRODUCING THE UNITED STATES NAVAL ACADEMY

If life is measured by unique experiences, you just can't pick a better place. In my four years, I went to Navy firefighting school, spent six-weeks of one summer in San Diego training on an amphibious vessel, sang for the president five times as a member of the Men's Glee Club, skippered a forty-four-foot sailboat from Annapolis to Newport, Rhode Island, and back, spent another month one summer with an F/A-18 squadron in Virginia Beach, went to Dublin, Ireland, to watch the Navy football team play Notre Dame, got my scuba qualifications, was in four musical productions, did aerobatics in a T-34 (one of the Navy's training planes) in Pensacola, Florida, and went under the waves in a submarine for a few days. Sound fascinating and eclectic? It was. And I recommend it to any of you.

The United States Naval Academy was founded in 1845 to provide a place where young men could learn the ways of the sea and the necessary traits of a future combat leader in an environment where a misstep could be tolerated here and there. *Here and there*, mind you. Not often. More than 150 years later, Navy offers both men and women undergraduate degrees in eighteen majors. While math and engineering receive the primary emphasis academically, there are several majors offered in the social sciences and humanities, including history and English. Everyone who is offered an appointment to Navy is admitted on full scholarship. The Navy pays for your room and board, tuition, medical and dental bills, and even gives you a modest monthly stipend. The academy has baccalaureate accreditation with both ABET and CSAB to go along with its regional accreditation. The Nimitz Library, built in 1973, acts as a second home for many of the academically taxed midshipmen at the Naval Academy. It has 530,000 volumes and subscribes to 2,000 periodicals, as well as possessing such computerized library sources and services as the card catalog, interlibrary loans, and database searching.

Special learning facilities include a learning resource center, art gallery, planetarium, radio station, TV station, propulsion laboratory, nuclear reactor, oceanographic research vessel, towing tanks, flight simulator, and a naval history museum called Preble Hall.

The Campus

The Navy campus, known by the Brigade of Midshipmen as the "Yard" is located in Annapolis, a small Chesapeake Bay sailing mecca and the capital of Maryland. The city is located about thirty miles southeast of Baltimore and thirty-five miles east of Washington, D.C. The Yard covers 338 acres, and is home to twenty-five historic buildings including Bancroft Hall, in which all midshipmen live, which happens to be the single largest dormitory in the United States (4.8 square miles of hallway).

Classmates

One thing you can look forward to if you become a midshipman at the Naval Academy is making some of the best friends of your life. Your classmates will hail from all fifty states and more than twenty foreign countries. A recent high school graduate will have classmates here who have spent some time at other colleges or in the operational Navy as enlisted sailors or marines. The diversity is extraordinary, and refreshing. Religiously, fifty percent of the Brigade is Protestant, forty-nine percent Catholic, and one percent practice other religions. Whatever else may happen, you can be sure that your horizons will expand tremendously.

ADMISSIONS REQUIREMENTS

Requirements for getting into the Naval Academy are much stiffer even than those at many of the nation's other top schools, because, at least in part, Navy looks at other things. While other institutions will examine you closely academically, the academy, because of its affiliation with the federal government and the U.S. Navy, will want to know more about what they are getting. To enter, you have to be between the ages of seventeen and twenty-three, unmarried, with no children, and pass the Department of Defense Medical Review Board physical exam. You must also score high on SAT I or ACT. Of the applicants for the Class of 2001, only 11.6 percent received appointments. Of those finally admitted, seventy percent had scored higher than 600 on the Verbal section of their SAT and eighty-six percent had done at least that well on the Math section (twenty-five percent exceeded 700 on the Math).

The Nomination

Once you've met these requirements, the next step is to attain a nomination. This can be done through a couple of different sources, the most common of which is the congressional nomination. This means that you put your name and information in the hands of your congressman and both of your senators, and they decide whether or not to grant you an interview. If you are successful in gaining an interview and impressing the proper people at these events, you may receive a nomination. If a nomination is given, it is up to the academy whether or not they will give you an appointment, which is the final acknowledgment of admission. (Note: if you are the child of a career military officer or enlisted person, or if your parent was disabled or killed in the service of our country, there are special categories under which you can be nominated; more information is available on this from the

Candidate Guidance Office). One little hint: you will put yourself in the best position to get a good look from your congressman and senators and the academy if you get your admissions materials in early.

What to Submit

There are a few things that you need to submit. In the spring of your junior year of high school you should write to the Candidate Guidance Office at the academy and ask for a Pre-Candidate Questionnaire (PCQ). They will send you one, and when you complete and return it you will officially be on the list of potential candidates. Then, sometime in the late summer or early fall of your last year in high school, you will receive the rest of the academy's admissions packet. Send it back quickly and you will jumpstart the process.

Extracurricular Activities

To make yourself most competitive for a nomination and subsequent appointment to the Naval Academy, there are a few things you can do. First of all—and this is true for all the good schools—-get involved in all that you can and do it well. Prove in various activities that you have what it takes to be a leader. Load up your plate with Advanced Placement and Honors courses and perform favorably in them. These courses, along with faculty recommendations from your high school, play a sizable role in the selection process. Also, play varsity sports. The vast majority of each class entering the academy each year lettered in at least one sport in high school. These accomplishments, combined with good grades, show that you are a well-rounded individual, just the kind of person the military is looking for to make up its corps of officers.

ACADEMIC LIFE

Suffice it to say, if you are seeking academic challenge, you won't be at all disappointed by the Naval Academy—it is undoubtedly one of the most stressful and taxing academic programs found in our country. On top of that add the fact that military activities take up much of your free time, and you have a true time-management crisis. Study time simply isn't plentiful, and it takes a great deal of self-discipline to maximize your effectiveness. Over time you learn to cope, however, and are a better person for it.

There is also a great deal of academic opportunity at Navy.

Degrees

The Naval Academy offers the Bachelor of Science degree in three major areas. Engineering, Mathematics and Sciences, and Humanities and Social Sciences. Every midshipman is required to complete 140 semester hours to graduate, and to pass core courses in mathematics, engineering, natural sciences, humanities, and social sciences.

Physical Education

Physical Education is another staple of the curriculum, with everyone taking three semesters of swimming, a semester of boxing and wrestling, a semester of judo, and three semesters of free electives. The Physical Readiness Test (PRT) is taken each semester and tests the midshipmen's fitness by measuring their performance in push-ups, sit-ups, and a one-and-a-half-mile run. All midshipmen also take mandatory professional development courses during their four years that include Naval Leadership, Naval Science, Tactics, and Navigation. Class attendance is mandatory for all midshipmen, making it pretty difficult to slack off in general.

Class Size and Faculty

Class size and student-to-faculty ratio are advantages that you will truly appreciate if you attend the Naval Academy. In the absolute largest plebe chemistry lecture section you might have fifty people. The average size for an introductory lecture is twenty-three students; for a regular course it's about fifteen, and for a lab, ten. The student-to-faculty ratio is seven to one.

The faculty, you'll find, is impressive in its own right. It is composed of both civilian professors and military officers, with ninety percent of its members holding Ph.D.s.

Educational Options

Last but not least, if you make it through all the rigors of the program and come out with top grades, there are several special options open to you at the academy. First, a group of seniors begin graduate work at educational institutions in the Washington, D.C./Baltimore area like Georgetown and Johns Hopkins each year. This is called the Voluntary Graduate Education Program, and is a great deal for the academically motivated. A small number of midshipmen are also named as Trident Scholars, allowing them to spend their last two semesters doing an independent research project. The Trident program culminates in a presentation given by the Scholars, attended by the faculty of their department, and open to the public. There are ten national honor societies active at the Naval Academy, and five of the departments on the Yard have honors programs in their majors.

SOCIAL LIFE AND ACTIVITIES

Want to be busy? Don't worry about that for a second if you receive an appointment to the Naval Academy. Activities aren't even really an option—they're an imperative. Everyone marches in parades, everyone plays a sport (either intramural or intercollegiate), everyone attends all home football games, everyone attends guest lectures by high-level speakers—everyone gets exhausted.

Sports

On the athletic front, the possibilities are endless. Navy offers twenty different intercollegiate sports for men, and nine for women. Men's and women's basketball, water polo, men's lacrosse, rugby, boxing, swimming, and crew are some of the sports in which Navy has traditionally been very strong.

In the fall, the football team is the center of all nonacademic activity. Before every home game, midshipmen march to the stadium and conduct a brief parade on the field; after the game they hold tailgaters. But during the game, they sit as a group. There is no sight quite like that of more than 4,000 young men and women in full uniform leaping up and down in celebration of a big play by the team. And keep in mind that the chance to cut loose only comes once in a blue moon at the academy. It gets crazy at Navy-Marine Corps Stadium in the fall, and, in the last couple of years there has been plenty to cheer about. In 1996, the team finished 9–3 and defeated the University of California in the Aloha Bowl in Honolulu. And since we're on the subject of football, we must mention the annual Army-Navy game. Is it a big event? Read this and you'll see. Both West Point and Navy pack their *entire* student body into buses and cart them to either Philadelphia or New York, depending on where the game is being held that year. So you've already got 4,000 plus students from each school there in uniform. Add countless alumni from both schools and national television coverage and you have a truly BIG event. And, for the upperclassmen it's the biggest party weekend of the first semester. Juniors and seniors usually head up on the Friday night before the Saturday game and paint the town. More celebrations of even higher intensity ensue if Navy wins. If it's not a Navy win, the weekend usually takes a major downswing and becomes a time of commiseration with friends. Either way, it's an unforgettable thing to witness. And the game is ALWAYS great. It seems that every year, no matter what the records, rankings, or anything else, the game is a grudge match that comes down to the wire.

Club sports of the more exotic variety like Ultimate Frisbee, ninjitsu, and karate are also available and are part of some intercollegiate competition as well.

Organizations

Nonathletic activities at the Naval Academy are just as varied as the athletic offerings, if not more so. For the adventurous spirit (as are many that look into attending one of the service academies) there are organizations like the Freefall Skydiving Club and the Scuba Club, offering basic training sessions as well as more advanced opportunities to their members. Those interested in the fine arts will find the program, especially in the field of vocal music, significantly more rewarding than they might have expected at a service academy. The Men's Glee Club is one of America's best-known and critically acclaimed groups of its type, and Navy's annual winter musical productions are the largest-drawing nonprofessional theatrical events in the Baltimore–Washington area. The Women's Glee Club, Gospel Choir, and Protestant and Catholic Chapel Choirs round out the varied offerings for singers at Navy.

Players of brass instruments and percussion may find a home in the Naval Academy's Drum and Bugle Corps, which generally travels with the football team on road trips and plays every day for a flock of tourists as the Brigade of Midshipmen marches in from noon meal formation.

The Masqueraders are the Naval Academy's thespian troupe; they present a full-length dramatic production in the fall of each year.

If none of this sounds good, maybe mountaineering, cheerleading, competing in triathlons, or one of the host of other options available will. The possibilities are nearly endless.

Social Life

Now to your social life at the Naval Academy. It should be said right off the bat that if your goal at college is to strengthen your liver and go to wild parties five days out of the week, while appearing only to take your exams each semester, Navy is *not* the place for you. Of course, you are reading this book, so this is not presumably the path you have chosen. You won't be highly successful at any of the other schools in this book by modeling your life after John Belushi's character in *Animal House*, but depending on your innate ability and resourcefulness you might be able to graduate. Forget it at Navy. You will be challenged with the restrictions, and the academic demands, accompanied by the fact that you have to stay in pretty darned good physical shape throughout your four years.

With that little disclaimer out of the way, the best way to explain social life at the academy is that you start out with none and it slowly gets better. One of the intentional pillars of the rigid training that one undergoes at the academy is self-sacrifice, and one of the big ways that this is hammered into you is through the withdrawal of many social privileges during your four years. You start out as a plebe (freshman) and go through your summer of basic training (known as Plebe Summer), in which you are not allowed to leave the Yard at all. Then the year starts.

I made what were, undoubtedly, the best friends of my life at the Naval Academy. They say misery loves company, and I guess that was one bond we had…but there was more. We all had a common thread of altruism and principle that we could see and appreciate in one another—not to mention that we had a heck of a lot of fun jetting off to D.C., Baltimore, New York, Philadelphia, and various away football games with each other.

An average day as a plebe? How about a morning? Wake up at 5:30, study your rates (required memorization), read the three newspaper articles that you'll be asked to report on at meal, go report your knowledge to your upperclass at 0630, fix your shoes and uniform for formation, do a chow call (stand out in the passageway and scream out the breakfast menu, officers of the watch, and a million other memorized items), and run off to 0700 formation. Morning classes feel more like sanctuary than a grind, since they mark the only time when you can sit quietly. Relax in Bancroft and an upperclassman will gladly remind you of the laundry bags to be delivered, newspapers to be collected for recycling, and various other menial jobs to do. Some plebes escape to the library during their free periods but there aren't any bells there, and fourth class midshipmen are notorious for dozing. Nod off in Nimitz and you might sleep through the rest of your classes for the day…and a plebe on restriction is significantly more unhappy than a plebe delivering laundry. The gist of all this: the kinder and gentler era we live in has had no effect on the level of activity that punctuates an academy plebe's mornings.

Once the academic year starts you can go out only on Saturdays from 10:00 A.M. to 1:00 A.M. Sunday as a plebe. When you do venture away from the Yard, you can't drive, have to wear your uniform, and can only go a certain distance away from the grounds of the academy. Pretty limiting.

During sophomore year, known as youngster year, midshipmen can go out on Saturdays *and* Sundays and if they happen to have really good grades, Friday night as well (until 10:00). Once or twice a semester, they might be allowed to leave on a Saturday morning and come back Sunday evening, but this sort of overnight liberty is rare until second class, or junior, year.

As a second class midshipman, you can go out every Friday, Saturday, and Sunday that you like, and for the first time you don't have to be in uniform when you do it. You still have to come in at midnight on Fridays and 1:00 on Saturdays (it's 6:00 P.M. for evening meal formation on Sundays) unless you are on an authorized weekend. You get about five of those per semester (give or take one or two depending on your grades, physical shape, and conduct). Those glorious weekends allow you to take off Friday afternoon and not come back until Sunday for formation. Second class with top grades and military performance marks get to go out on Tuesday nights until 10:00 as well.

Firstie (senior) year gets pretty reasonable: weeknight liberty on Monday, Tuesday, and Thursday is possible until 10:00 for good performers, and many of your weekends will be the kind where you can take off and leave the place behind for a couple of days.

Social Opportunities

While social life is, to say the least, not traditional, there ARE some social opportunities at the academy that are quite impressive. Every year popular music groups as well as renowned classical musicians come into Alumni Hall, the Naval Academy's arena and theater complex. Popular concerts of the past few years have included shows by INXS, Blues Traveler, and The Steve Miller Band. The Bolshoi Symphony, the Kirov Ballet, and the traveling company of the New York City Opera have recently appeared as part of the Distinguished Artists Series, a classical program conducted each year in Alumni.

Dances

Some of the traditionally highly anticipated nonperforming arts social events of each year are just as impressive. The Ring Dance, which takes place at the end of the second class year to celebrate the new firsties' right to put on their class rings for the first time, is basically super-prom. It's a formal dance, and the second class midshipmen spend much of the year prior to the event agonizing about who they will bring, often from all the way across the country, to the event. The night includes dancing, a formal dinner, and fireworks to top it all off. Most people arrive in limos and stay at luxurious hotels in Washington, D.C., or Baltimore for the weekend. It's a nice reward for three years of hard work—and good motivation to put up with one more.

Commissioning Week

Then there is Commissioning Week, an indescribably exciting time each year that leads up to the graduation ceremony and the hat toss that mark the end of the road for the departing seniors. It's a week filled with formal parades, concerts, ship tours, a special performance by the Navy's Flight Demonstration Team, the Blue Angels, and many other nice events. Annapolis is so packed with people during Commissioning Week that it is advisable for parents to get hotel reservations at least one year in advance.

FINANCIAL AID

Financial aid at the United States Naval Academy is a given. Everyone at the school has room, board, and tuition paid for all four years by the federal government. Midshipmen even receive a modest (very modest) stipend each month for any extraneous expenses. At the end of the second class year, all members of the Brigade are eligible for the "career starter loan." This is a loan of up to approximately $20,000 (the ceiling gets a little higher every year) that you pay back at incredibly low (in the neighborhood of two percent) interest rates over the time that you serve in the Navy or Marine Corps after graduation. And that brings up another point: in exchange for these various little perks, all graduates of the Naval Academy owe the Navy or Marine Corps at least five years serving as officers in the operational force.

GRADUATES

The effect that graduating from a place like the academy has on a person is interesting and a bit humorous. You spend four years grousing and complaining at every turn about the limitations that have been put on you and how you wish you could just be "normal" and such. Then you toss your hat up into the azure skies on graduation day and develop an instant and puzzling fondness for almost everything about the place. Navy grads are like a huge extended family. They can be found in all walks of life and are always ready to lend friendship and a help-

PROMINENT GRADS

- James E. Carter, President of the United States
- Admiral William Crowe, Former Chairman of the Joint Chiefs, Ambassador to Britain
- John Dalton, Secretary of the Navy
- Admiral William "Bull" Halsey, World War II Hero
- Admiral Ernest King, World War II Hero
- Jim Lovell, Former Astronaut
- John S. McCain, III, U.S. Senator from Arizona
- Admiral Chester Nimitz, World War II Hero
- H. Ross Perot, Entrepreneur
- Alan B. Shepard, Jr., Former Astronaut, First American in Space
- Roger Staubach, NFL Quarterback and Heisman Trophy Winner
- Admiral Stansfield Turner, Former Director CIA
- James Webb, Former Secretary of the Navy, Novelist
- Virtually all of the notable admirals of World War II fame and dozens of Congressional Medal of Honor winners.

ing hand to another alum. And, as it might seem would be the case, they've got more exciting stories to tell than the average grad from a "normal" school. Where the average homecoming gathering at another school will undoubtedly be filled with tales of business deals and house remodelings, a Navy homecoming is filled with anecdotes concerning such atypical topics as night landings on aircraft carriers, being shot at by surface-to-air missiles, or a weekend spent on liberty in Bahrain. It's a whole different world....

SUMMING UP

What the academy did for my classmates and me was that, through all of its stifling regulations and regimentation, it set us free on the playground of life. It opened up to us a wealth of opportunities that will take some of us to the top of the military profession and to the highest levels of government, and others in altogether different but exciting directions. And we all set out on our journeys armed to the hilt with weapons not often found in our society today: self-awareness, self-reliance, and determination. We were forged in the fire of four years by the waters of the Chesapeake Bay, four years that often hurt, but also purified and strengthened the good in us, and gave us the tools to attack life and its hurdles with gusto and confidence.

Attending the United States Naval Academy is a decision that, if you come expecting a challenge, you will never regret. It is a small, insulated, often unforgiving place that pushes you to your limits. For twenty-three hours, fifty-five minutes a day in a regular school week during your four years there you might hate it. But that other five minutes comes about once a day when something happens that reminds you of how much you owe to the place. Maybe it happens walking to class in the morning and looking out at the beautiful campus for a minute, or seeing one of the many close friends you've made there, or going into Memorial Hall and seeing the memorial register of past graduates who sacrificed their lives for our country in all of the major wars that America has been involved in since 1845. Those moments are special. They make it all worthwhile.

And let's face it...there are more pluses than you could hope for at most other schools: Your education is paid for, you are in a great and historic town, you make lifelong friendships, visit exotic places, try things you've never previously dreamed of, and get a degree out of all of it. You'll have all the tools you need to be a success once you are done here. So how could you really go wrong?

The single biggest thing that attracted me to Annapolis was my awe for the extraordinary heroism that so many graduates of the school had exhibited throughout our nation's history. Only a few of us will ever be called on to perform in situations that dire. But the way we prepare for that is the same way that we must prepare for roles more typical but no less important. The essential thing is that we ready ourselves, whether we are preparing to give our life for our men and women or just be a figure that works for general improvement in the quality of life in our community. This preparation must be intrinsic, but there are a few institutions left in America that can give you invaluable tools with which you can further sculpt yourself into that which you ultimately desire to be. The Naval Academy is one of them, because no matter what one's personal experience, good or bad, it is a place that you leave self-aware. You know what your strengths and weaknesses are, and you know that you can put up with a great deal of hardship compared to the average person you run into on the street who spent four years at fraternity or sorority parties, having the time of his or her life. Any way you slice it, if one is serious about making a difference, whether it be as a submariner, a pilot, a businessperson or in any other career, this is still the best school in the United States to attend. There's no question in my mind.

❑ *Ensign Anthony Holds, B.S.*

UNIVERSITY OF CHICAGO

University of Chicago
Chicago, IL 60637

(773) 702-1234, Admissions: (773) 702-8650
Fax: (773) 702-4199

E-mail: college-admissions@uchicago.edu
Web site: http://www.uchicago.edu

Enrollment

Full-time ❑ women: 1,613
❑ men: 1,902

Part-time ❑ women: 23
❑ men: 23

INTRODUCING THE UNIVERSITY OF CHICAGO

I was going to begin: "When I look back on my four years at the University of Chicago, they seem to me like a blissful dream." But that is precisely wrong. I should say: "When I look back on my four years at the University of Chicago, they seem to me years of waking up and of being intensely awake." I say "awake" because the University of Chicago, especially its college, is a community committed to the life of the mind, so that inquiry, whether in laboratories or libraries, tends to be intertwined with life.

The University of Chicago has a deserved reputation for an almost single-minded devotion to the theoretical as opposed to the practical. Isn't this a contradiction? To be oriented away from the practical and yet toward life? The nature of self-reflection gives rise to this paradox, which, if you come to the University of Chicago, you will certainly confront in your humanities class, one of the classes required as part of the common core (more on that in a moment). For instance, Human Being and Citizen, the most popular of the humanities courses, takes its title from a question raised by Socrates as he defends himself to the Athenians: "Who is a knower of such excellence, the excellence of a human being and the excellence of a citizen?" The course devotes itself to this question for an entire year, and, naturally, there is time for pursuing the questions that this question spawns, such as, "Are the excellence of a human being and the excellence of a citizen identical or different, and, if different, can they come into conflict?" Such a question is not of merely theoretical interest! On the other hand, the pursuit of such a question is not really a practical matter. Even if one arrives at a satisfactory answer, that answer will not put food on the table or cure cancer.

The University of Chicago is dedicated to the proposition that education consists in serious and communal inquiry into such questions, under the guidance of teachers who have reflected at length upon them. The university provides the teachers and the community that make such an education possible. This experience is like waking up; via such questions, one is not transported to a theoretical and remote world, but rather finds oneself in the familiar world, revealed by a new light.

The Common Core

Another distinctive feature of a Chicago education is the common core, first instituted by president Robert Maynard Hutchins and a cohort of idealistic and erudite faculty in the 1930s (see Academic Life for specific requirements). At the same time, Hutchins eliminated the football team, permanently removing the University of Chicago from its position as a Big Ten powerhouse. (It's little known that the Heisman trophy was modeled after its first recipient, Chicago player Jay Berwanger.) Meanwhile, athletics at the University of Chicago have been resurrected (both men's and women's soccer teams played in the NCAA final four tournament in 1996), and the common core lives on alongside them, although its current form is much more flexible and greatly reduced from the original four-year curriculum.

The common core is very different from so-called distribution requirements. It provides, among other things, common ground. Not all students have read all of the same books, but almost everyone has acquaintance, for instance, with Plato's *Apology of Socrates* (and very often also the *Republic*), basic writings of Adam Smith, Karl Marx, and Max Weber, at least some Shakespeare, the *Federalist Papers,* and often Thucydides' *Peloponnesian War* and Virginia Woolf's *To the Lighthouse,* as well as calculus, elementary genetics, and elementary physics. Not only does the common core provide a fertile common ground for conversation both in class and out; it's courses are designed by the faculty specifically to ensure that these four years of college culminate as a coherent whole, not simply a jumbled accumulation of marked time. The Core, combined with courses in one's concentration (major) and electives, educate whole persons, once called "Renaissance men," who exemplify the virtues of a thinking human and a caring citizen, staunch in their convictions, humble in their acquaintance with great books, curious in their daily life, and capable in their achievements.

ADMISSIONS REQUIREMENTS

Admission to the University of Chicago is competitive. All admissions decisions are need-blind. While every credential helps, no credentials guarantee admission. If there is a difference between Chicago's Admissions Office and those of other highly competitive schools, it is perhaps that the University of Chicago is more ready to take a chance on a student whose credentials are relatively modest, but whose essay is carefully written, original, and thoughtful. Because of the distinctive curriculum and intellectual atmosphere, the admissions process considers not only an applicant's cleverness but also seriousness, reflectiveness, maturity, and perseverance. These atypical criteria are reflected in the atypical essay questions on the application. The questions are not single sentences, but paragraphs that introduce broad concepts and ideas. Whatever your record, if you are the type of student who thrills to such quirky questions and can offer a sincere and thoughtful answer, you're a promising candidate for the University of Chicago.

ACADEMIC LIFE

The atmosphere of shared intellectual excitement is what I have missed most since I left the University of Chicago.

The ferment and fervor of intellectual life at the University of Chicago begins right away. During the orientation program, the annual Aims of Education address is given in the grand old Rockefeller Chapel, where every member of the entering class comes to hear a well-established teacher talk about the ends of the education on which the assembled are about to embark. A chief feature of this intellectual community manifests itself in the conversation that follows the lecture. The hundreds of assembled students return to their houses where a professor leads a discussion of the ideas and questions presented in the lecture. For a picture of the depth and diversity of the thinkers who, at the University of Chicago, are also teachers, you might want to read the collection of these lectures just published under the title, *The Aims of Education,* and available from the college for $14.

Common Core

These speakers frequently discuss the aims of the Chicago curriculum, which embodies the special character of a University of Chicago education, namely the commitment of world-class thinkers to formulating an educational program, arousing in students a passion for human questions, and helping students to find their way through books that formulate and confront those questions. The core is only

TWO EXAMPLES OF ESSAY QUESTIONS FROM RECENT YEARS

- **For a Chinese bureaucrat in imperial times, a citizen of ancient Rome, a South Sea Islander, or an Onondaga clan mother among the Iroquois, precise knowledge of one's descent from an ancestor was essential for understanding his or her role in society. However, in the modern United States, it is possible to have a role in society with little or no knowledge of one's ancestors. Write an essay about one or more of your ancestors and try to imagine what it means that you and this ancestor are kin. Alternatively, what does it mean that you, like some of us, are without knowable ancestors or that you feel no meaningful connection to those ancestors whom you do know?**
- ***Elvis is alive!* Okay, maybe not, but here in the Office of College Admissions we are persuaded that current Elvis sightings in highway rest areas, grocery stores, and laundromats are part of a wider conspiracy involving *five* of the following: *the metric system, the Mall of America, the crash of the Hindenburg, Heisenberg's uncertainty principle, lint, J.D. Salinger,* and *wax fruit.* Help us to get to the bottom of this evil plot by constructing your own theory of how and why five of these items and events are related.**

in part a plan to give students skills and facts they will need when they depart; it is also in part an understanding of intellectual traditions, of the contemporary American situation, and of the highest needs of the human spirit. As such, the core is necessarily controversial and subject to revision, and is, in fact, incessantly revised.

EXAMPLES OF COMMON CORE COURSES

- **Humanities—Human Being and Citizen; Form/Problem/Event; Readings in Literature; Philosophical Perspectives**
- **Social Science—Classics of Social and Political Thought; Self, Culture, and Society; Wealth, Power, and Virtue**
- **Civilization Studies—History of Western Civilization; Introduction to East Asian Civilization; Science, Culture, and Society in Western Civilization; Introduction to African Civilization.**

The core now encompasses twenty-one of the forty-two courses required for graduation, although almost all students are exempted from some coursework through placement tests. The twenty-one common core courses are as follows (note that one year is three terms): one year of humanities, one term of art or music, one year of social science, one year of civilization studies, two terms of mathematics, one year of biological science, one year of physical science, and one year of a foreign language. One year of physical education is also required, but a placement test exempts most students from some or all of that requirement.

More information on the courses that fulfill each requirement can be found at the University of Chicago Web site.

Concentrations

The thoroughly planned structure of the common core is complemented by a variety of highly flexible concentrations. You might be surprised to learn that a university so strongly committed to a particular educational program allows any student who so desires to choose a concentration that is essentially self-designed. Four examples are:

- fundamentals: issues and texts
- history, philosophy, and social studies of science and medicine
- law, letters, and society
- general studies in the humanities.

These four concentrations offer a self-motivated student who has conceived an unorthodox project the resources and freedom to carry it out.

Graduate Students

The happiest students at Chicago tend to be those who have an intellectual passion and vision that helps them to find their own way. This is partly because of the significant graduate presence at Chicago. While at some universities graduate students teach undergraduates, at Chicago graduate students are the classmates of undergraduates almost as soon as one leaves the common core. It is a rare undergraduate who leaves without having this experience, which is almost always challenging, frustrating, and enriching. Because undergraduates have to compete with graduate students for attention, the undergraduate who lacks a definite drive and project, and thus follows the path of least resistance, can occasionally find it difficult to win the attention of teachers.

The economics department, for instance, attracts many, undergraduates because, amazingly, it has five Nobel Laureates as currently active teachers. Indeed, a degree in economics from the University of Chicago will garner a hefty salary, but only the brightest and fastest students are noticed by the professors. Smaller programs like mathematics or classics afford students more personal attention. At all the larger universities there is some competition between undergraduates and graduate students, but there is perhaps no other school that accords such respect and freedom to passionate, imaginative, and disciplined students. All of the majors mentioned above, and many others too, require students to write a major paper in the junior or senior year. Such sustained intellectual work, under the guidance of a professor, helps students mature so that they can do more than absorb what they are taught by others, but can actually think things through for themselves.

Faculty

> *Above all, it was my excellent teachers who brought me to love the University of Chicago, to love learning, reading, and study, to feel so strongly about the university that I would be asked to write a published essay about it. In your decision about where to go to college, I urge you to consider no factor more important than the presence of caring, excellent teachers.*

At the University of Chicago, as at any institution, one must seek out the best teachers. This is made easier by the Quantrell Award, the oldest award in the nation for undergraduate teaching. If you visit the campus, you will find a plaque listing the winners of this award since 1938 in the hall in Harper Library. A few remarkable teachers have won it twice. Norman MacLean, author of *A River Runs Through It,* won it three times.

The mathematics department is especially rich in Quantrell winners; no fewer than four currently teach undergraduate courses on a regular basis. This makes Chicago an excellent place to study mathematics as an undergraduate, particularly for talented students whose background in mathematics is strong but not outstanding. There is room for such students to make good on their talent without being shut out by students who happen to have attended science magnet schools.

> *Of all the college students I have ever met, those students who found caring teachers loved their colleges and their years in college; those who were not blessed with caring teachers were dissatisfied, often downright unhappy.*

The general intellectual excitement also leads to the formation of student-led discussion groups, some running in tandem with classes, others simply pursuing the interests of a few curious people. But excited and curious students are always seeking one another out for further conversation, over lunch or dinner or coffee, in regularly scheduled meetings or at a chance moment. The work load and intensity are not for everyone, but those who like it come to love the place and thrive.

SOCIAL LIFE AND ACTIVITIES

The University of Chicago does not deserve its reputation for dull social life; this myth is perpetuated by a student body that indulges the natural penchant for complaining and loves to work hard. But one must acknowledge that, if you want large parties (hundreds of people) on a weekly basis, the University of Chicago is probably not for you. Some students do wish that the school had a busier party scene, and many of them congregate in the Shoreland dormitory (see below) or in the nine fraternities and two sororities, where large parties are thrown often. One wonders why certain students didn't redirect the energy expended complaining about the lack of parties into hosting a party themselves. And once you turn twenty-one, the night life of the third-largest city in the United States is at your doorstep.

The university's social life is interwoven with its intellectual life, and is generally focused on interaction and conversation rather than drink, dancing, and "socializing." Various social activities are associated with the dormitories: trips around the city to cultural events and notable places, study breaks, dinners with special guests. The Reg (short for Joseph Regenstein Library) has for years been a social center on campus, both for meeting old friends and making new ones though it now has serious competition from the newly renovated Reynolds Club. Study groups, whether formal or informal, meeting on a regular or impromptu basis, can gather in the numerous seminar rooms, many equipped with blackboards. Or, if your conversation starts to annoy nearby readers, you can retire to Ex Libris, the coffee shop in the basement where you will find muffins, bagels, strong coffee, and the chance to procrastinate as long and loudly as possible.

Coffee Shops

A conversational social life is fostered by fourteen coffee shops on campus. Not only the Reg, but also Harper Library, the Classics Building, Cobb Hall, the Divinity School, the Business School, and the Reynolds club have coffee shops (the Reynolds club has two!), each with an ambience and cuisine of its own.

The coffee shop in the Divinity School is run by graduate students who use the proceeds to underwrite their expenses and provide scholarships to needy students. It has the widest array of food on campus, including Thai, Mexican, and Middle Eastern dishes from local restaurants, and, being in the basement, has a close and shadowy feel conducive to heartfelt talk. It also sells mugs and T-shirts that boast: "The Divinity School Coffee Shop—Where God Drinks Coffee." The Classics coffee shop offers delicious coffees and sweet morsels. Most important, it has a very high ceiling and a row of high windows at one end that welcome in an abundance of light, which in turn brings out the wood paneling along the walls. The Reynolds Club renovation has turned it into the de facto student center, with lounges, a marketplace, the offices of dozens of student organizations, and foosball and pool tables installed in the coffee shop upstairs. This coffee shop, along with the Taco Bell and Pizza Hut on the first floor, are open until 2 A.M., and have become a favorite hang-out for many.

Just down the street there are cafes built just for hanging out. Most popular are Café Florian (named after an old cafe in Venice, Italy) and the Medici on 57th Street.

Movies

You can also see a movie any night of the week. There is one commercial movie theater in Hyde Park, but the university is home to no fewer than three film societies, Doc (short for Documentary Film Group), Outlaw Films, and I-house (short for International House). Doc, the oldest film society in the country, shows at least one movie every night, more on the weekends when recently released films are on. On weeknights, they run various series, such as a Kurosawa film or a Western every Tuesday for the whole term. Outlaw Films (formerly Law School Films) shows old movies on Saturday and Sunday—*Arsenic and Old Lace*, *High Noon*, *Casablanca*. I-house shows foreign-made films, usually not in English, such as *Cinema Paradiso* or *Red*. Afterwards, you can discuss the movie with your friends over an espresso or great mocha shake at the Medici on 57th Street.

Festivals

There are also three major festivals during the year: Kuviasugnerk, Summer Breeze, and the Folk Festival. Kuviasugnerk runs for a week during January. It is an attempt to beat the cold by getting out into it at six o'clock in the morning. Hundreds and hundreds of students attend various activities, including aikido classes taught by sociology professor David Levine. On the final day, this class takes place at the lakefront. Until 8:30 or 9 A.M., one can get free hot cocoa, coffee, and doughnuts from a stand in the center of the quads. Those hardy souls who come every morning win a T-shirt that proclaims "I survived Kuviasugnerk '99!" Summer Breeze, as you might expect, is less demanding but also less rewarding. It's a week of dances and blues and rock performances by the best local bands (and they are good), and free drinks of all kinds. The Folk Festival draws together performers from around the country and students from throughout the university for a weekend of performances, master classes, and jam sessions. Then there's the annual Scavenger Hunt. Teams circle the Henry Crown Field House with paper clips, shave their heads, and drive to other states to retrieve items ranging from circus elephants to Canadian traffic signs.

Organizations

Amidst the storm and stress of classes, Chicago students somehow manage to run more than two-hundred student organizations and thirty-five sports clubs. An impressive seventy-five percent of undergraduates participate in intramural sports.

Model United Nations—University of Chicago (or MUNUC), started in the late 1980s by a few independent and very capable students, has blossomed into the largest student organization on campus, hosting an award-winning model-U.N. conference for high school students from around the United States. More than a thousand visitors annually descend on the Palmer House Hilton for a weekend of intensive meetings simulating the activities of the U.N.

The student-run radio station, WHPK 88.5 FM, offers a dizzyingly eclectic variety of programs, from avant-garde rock to political commentary. The theater groups are particularly strong, staging about ten full-scale productions per year. Off-off Campus is a student improvisation group that continues the tradition begun by the students who went on to found the Second City comedy club. Students can act, direct, produce, and even write their own shows. Because there is no theater major at the university, any student can audition for any role in any play; a science major can direct a show. Yet classes on acting and directing are taught by professionals active in the Chicago scene. The student-run University Theater has a new internship program with the university's professional and critically acclaimed Court Theatre, the third largest professional theater in Chicago. Many students join the University Orchestra, the Chamber Orchestra, the University Chorus, or the Motet Choir, which makes an annual tour during spring break. There are two student-led *a capella* singing groups, The Unaccompanied Women and The Acafellas.

Recent years have seen the flourishing of several organizations that help students use their abilities to help Chicago. The university is in the heart of the south side of Chicago, a sprawling and economically disadvantaged region of the city. The Community Service Center was started by students in the early nineties, but is now an official part of the university, with a director who is also an associate dean. The center links hundreds of students with volunteer opportunities around the city. A tutoring program run by the Blue Gargoyle facilitates weekly one-on-one meetings between university students and children who need help in school. Actors from University Theater perform and lead workshops in local schools. Student Teachers runs an after-school program, which this year will expand to involve three local elementary schools, where students teach reading and creative writing in discussion courses that they themselves design. Habitat for Humanity regularly brings together large groups of students to build or repair homes, and a program called "Turn A Lot Around" puts students to work alongside residents in cleaning up vacant lots and transforming them into gardens.

Housing

As for living conditions, the university guarantees every student four years of housing, and the accommodations are generally good. Particularly nice is the easy availability of single rooms, even for first-year students. To some people, this won't sound like an advantage, but if you are eager to rise to the challenge of living with a stranger, double rooms are plentiful as well. Sometimes roommates become fast friends. Many young people, however, underestimate just how difficult a difficult roommate can be, and how rejuvenating they would find a private space for exhausted sleep or newfound pensiveness. The Shoreland, with several hundred students, is by far the largest dorm, and also, being a renovated luxury hotel, the most palatial. First-year rooms are nice, not extraordinary, but after four years there, students can enjoy suites with huge living rooms, kitchens, and views of Lake

Michigan. Burton-Judson is a particularly sociable dorm, despite—or rather, because of—the numerous single rooms. Single rooms, far from isolating students, make everyone interested in meeting their neighbors.

The dorms are subdivided into Houses, some named after famous professors. Each large dorm has a master, usually a senior faculty member, and each house has a resident head, usually a senior graduate student. The masters and resident heads host discussions, trips, and study breaks for the dorm. But the houses don't constrain your social life. In some houses, there is a marvelous, synergetic mixture of students who desire nothing more than to spend every waking minute together; in some houses, the residents couldn't care less whether they ever speak to one another. The presence of the resident heads, who often are married, provides a steadying influence; and, if there are children, their serene good will can be a blessing after a long day. The resident heads handle discipline problems and, if they are severe, the master becomes involved too.

Off-Campus Living

About a third of Chicago's students live off campus. This means that almost everyone lives off campus for the fourth year, some also for the third or even second. Despite all the hassles of bill paying and grocery shopping, students who live off campus love the independence and self-sufficiency. Affordable apartments are available near campus and, if one wishes to maintain links with a dorm, one can buy into a meal plan, which is fairly expensive but rather tasty and nutritious. The occasional student even lives on the north side, commuting daily to campus, in order to take better advantage of the city. And what a city!

The city of Chicago is one of the original jazz and blues centers of the nation. Anyone with the least taste for blues should visit the Checkerboard. The Chicago Symphony is world class; tickets to concerts at the newly renovated Orchestra Hall are inexpensive and easy to get, whether for full orchestra concerts or intimate chamber music. The major theaters (the Schubert and the grand, old, Louis Sullivan-designed Auditorium Theater) put on new and classic plays and musicals. The Shakespeare Repertory Theater is widely acclaimed. (As mentioned, the University of Chicago itself is home to the Court Theater, one of the finest small theaters in the city.) There is also an array of small, inexpensive, experimental theaters on the north side, where one can see *Too Much Light Makes the Baby Go Blind* or an avant-garde production of Aeschylus' *Agamemnon*. Chicago is also a city that loves to eat: Chinese (try dim sum at Hong Minh in Chinatown or the new Lulu's on the edge of campus), Japanese (try Renga-tei at Touhy and Crawford), Thai (four restaurants in Hyde Park alone!), Korean, Vietnamese, Polish, Italian, Indian, French, Cajun, or down-home American.

Students with a taste for professional sports have options year-round, from the Chicago Bulls to the Bears, Cubs, White Sox, and two hockey teams.

It's been years since I left the U of C, but the performances of Shakespeare's Othello *and Sophocles'* Elektra *that I saw at Court Theater still live in my memory.*

Like any American city, Chicago requires caution, and the neighborhood around the university is not the best. A student who walks alone after eleven every night for four years is unlikely to escape mugging. But keeping safe is just a matter of common sense. The university knows that some students come from small towns and may not know what common sense is in a big city, so part of Orientation is devoted to tips for big city living: stick to lighted streets, what to do if you feel threatened, how to use the emergency police phones located on most corners in Hyde Park. The precautions are particularly confining for women, and, in January and February, it gets dark before five o'clock. The university is aware of the difficulties and is trying to help. There are several free shuttle buses running from the Reg around parts of Hyde Park, so that one can safely travel between the quads and one's room. And a new express bus runs every thirty minutes nightly from campus to the North Loop, the heart of the city's nightlife. (The buses don't just go to the university's dorms, so they're also useful for students living off campus.) But relying on buses can be frustrating. One must run one's schedule by the buses. This means waiting sometimes, and often confronting the choice between waiting for the bus or risking the walk home in the dark. A bicycle can be liberating. Biking alone is safer than walking alone, but one must be prepared to accept either the precautions or the risks.

Above all, the university is a place that fosters fast friendships (meaning strong, not speedy). Because so many classes are teacher-led discussions, one often gets to know fellow students with a special but strange intensity that comes from discussing questions that are, in a way, deeply personal, such as what attitude one ought to take toward Anna Karenina's adultery, toward King Lear's madness, toward St. Augustine's faith, toward Socrates' comportment (did he corrupt the young?). Such conversations naturally continue outside the classroom, and naturally lead to friendship. I have met many students who attended elite colleges and universities, but, according to their reports, no institution has such a thriving intellectual life outside the classroom as the University of Chicago. For many students, this is the most precious aspect of social life at Chicago, and the friendships whose bonds were forged by that intellectual heat are the strongest you will have.

FINANCIAL AID

The cost of a University of Chicago education is high, but comparable to other outstanding private institutions. More than half of students receive some form of need-based financial aid. The University of Chicago offers, besides need-based aid, several purely merit-based College Honors Scholarships. (The application for this scholarship is included with the usual application materials.) These range in value from a few thousand dollars per year to full tuition for four years, and they succeed in attracting some extraordinary students. Whether or not an applicant wins such a scholarship, the presence of such scholarships enhances the intellectual community for everyone and represents an admiration for outstanding abilities.

GRADUATES

A degree from the University of Chicago can take you anywhere. Graduates work in government, business, law, academia, entertainment, and public service. A surprising number of graduates, about one-third, continue in school after they graduate, either in graduate or professional school, and ninety-five percent of graduates say that they plan to enter graduate or professional school within five years (although presumably some do not carry out their plans). When graduation approaches and seniors begin to consider their opportunities and ambitions, the Career and Placement Services (CAPS) office helps students make the transition into the wider world. Their career counselors have information about a whole array of opportunities for further study or employment, in the public or private sector, whether for-profit or nonprofit, and they talk with students to help them figure what their ambitions are, what the next step after graduation should be, and how best to present themselves and their credentials. The CAPS Web site (at http://caps1.uchicago.edu) provides twenty-four-hour access to a range of information, including an internship database with more than 1,000 listings.

Many students start to take advantage of CAPS long before graduation. The University of Chicago has an innovative set of internship programs, that reflect the importance that employers of all kinds place on real world experience. During the summer of 1997, students worked as interns with researchers in several Smithsonian institutions in and around Washington, D.C., including the Museum of Natural History, the National Portrait Gallery, and the Smithsonian Environmental Research Center. Also in Washington, students participating in the Paul Douglas Internship Program (named after former faculty member and U.S. senator from Illinois, Paul Douglas) worked in each of the Illinois U.S. senators' offices, while others served as White House interns. In Chicago, students selected as Jeff Metcalf interns worked in for-profit firms such as Goldman Sachs, as well as nonprofits, such as the Joffrey Ballet and the Museum of Contemporary Art. Undergraduates selected for the Mayoral Internship Program worked as paid interns in the office of Mayor Richard M. Daley during much of the past academic year.

Chicago students have always done well in job placement after graduation, and in the last few years employers have sought to hire Chicago graduates more and more eagerly. During the 1996–97 academic year alone, the number of employers recruiting on campus through CAPS increased by over forty-three percent, one of the largest one-year increases for any liberal arts college in the country. The number of interviews scheduled between students and recruiters increased more than forty-eight percent from the previous year. Employers scheduled nearly three times as many information sessions (a way of attracting job candidates to industries and firms) as in 1995–96.

PROMINENT GRADS

- **Ed Asner, Actor**
- **Jay Berwanger, First Heisman Trophy Winner**
- **David S. Broder, *Washington Post* Journalist**
- **Henry Steele Commager, Historian, Author**
- **Katherine Dunham, Dancer, Choreographer**
- **Katherine Graham, Former *Washington Post* Chairman and CEO**
- **Seymour Hersh, Journalist, Author**
- **Mike Nichols, Director, Actor, Producer**
- **Charles Percy, Former U.S. Senator from Illinois**
- **Carl Sagan, Astronomer, Author**
- **Susan Sontag, Writer, Critic**
- **Studs Terkel, Writer**

SUMMING UP

If, after reading this article, you think the University of Chicago might be for you, but you aren't sure, do arrange a visit through the Admissions Office. Nothing can give you a more vivid sense of what life would be like there.

No matter where you go to college, you will find yourself impressed with the distinctiveness of your alma mater. After four years steeped in its special atmosphere, exploring its nooks and crannies, relishing and bemoaning its quirks, you will have learned what makes your college special. The same is true, of course, about the University of Chicago, but it also has an up-front distinctiveness that deserves your careful consideration, since it may or may not be what you seek. Few people have lukewarm feelings about Chicago—the university evokes love or hate, not tepid good will. Most of the students love the place, but there are some exceptions, often people who did not consider carefully whether they desired such academic intensity. One factor in this intensity is the calendar, consisting of three eleven-week terms. Sometimes it feels as if one always has midterms or finals. On the other hand, students receive (for the same price!) far more time in class with their teachers than at many comparable institutions, since the University of Chicago has thirty weeks of classes (plus three weeks of exams), whereas schools that spread out their exams and reading period over several weeks may have only twenty-four.

Some prospective students worry that the Common Core would be confining, but in fact hardly any students object to those constraints once they're in class. Although Chicago, unlike the vast majority of American institutions, requires all students to become educated through a certain program of courses, these constraints are balanced by the freedom allowed by concentrations such as fundamentals, HiPSS, LLS, and GSHum. It is a sign that most students do not find the Core constraining that these majors are all quite small. And while the Common Core can evoke a few gripes and groans along the way, most students are profoundly satisfied with the unity of their educations and even proud to have read, say, ancient Greek writers or famous philosophers like Kant, even if now heading toward medical school or a consulting firm.

Even the very brightest students do not run out of challenges: The university really has a liberal arts college housed within a world-class research university. The great resources of the research university are in most departments at the students' disposal, and students often have close contact with the world of graduate students. The intellectual diversity of the students and faculty sustains endlessly stimulating debates. The wealth of diversity in the university is complemented by the wealth of diversity in the city: music, theater, shopping, dining, museums, movies, parks, ethnic neighborhoods, night life, and Lake Michigan.

These surroundings enrich and enliven the concentrated atmosphere of the university campus, where learning, discovery, hard work, and thoughtful conversation create an atmosphere that, for an intensely curious student, is exhilarating and inspiring.

❑ *Jonathan Beere, B.A.*

UNIVERSITY OF NOTRE DAME

University of Notre Dame
Notre Dame, IN 46556

(219) 631-7505

E-mail: admissions.admissio.1@ND.edu
Web site: http://www.nd.edu

Enrollment

Full-time ❑ women: 3,450
❑ men: 4,250

INTRODUCING NOTRE DAME

Every year in late August, freshmen converge upon Notre Dame's campus in South Bend, Indiana, rushing from one freshman orientation event to the next. During the Graffiti Dance, the Alumni Hall Tie Dye Party, and the Orientation Mass, a certain phrase resonates throughout the campus: "the Notre Dame family." This one phrase, which has a slightly different meaning for each student and alum, is a distinctive element of the University of Notre Dame.

I experienced "the Notre Dame family" immediately during my initial days at the university. I first sensed the friendliness among the students when my parents and I arrived on campus. As we pulled up to my dorm, a number of my hallmates descended upon our car, fully packed with all the essentials for college, and helped us carry all my stuff to my room. But the Notre Dame family is more than just friendliness; the campus has a sense of togetherness to it. During those first days on campus my parents and I immediately felt at home in my new surroundings and we began to realize that my Notre Dame experience would not only be for me, but would include my parents in many ways as well; they too would become part of the Notre Dame family.

The phrase "Notre Dame family" embodies three of the main characteristics of Notre Dame: community, tradition, and Catholic heritage.

The campus setting makes it easy to foster a close-knit community. With its tree-lined paths and two lakes, the sprawling 1,250-acre campus seems to be isolated from the rest of the world. The university is located ninety miles east of Chicago and has more than one hundred buildings on campus. The dorms in particular are an integral part of the campus and enhance the feeling of community. Eighty-five percent of students live on campus, and most remain on campus for three or four years.

Notre Dame's Catholic roots are a vital part of life at the university. Even the buildings on campus, such as Sacred Heart Basilica, the Grotto, and "Touchdown Jesus" on the side of the library, demonstrate the Catholic character and influence at the school. Eighty-five percent of Notre Dame students are Catholic, and the Catholic nature of the school is emphasized in all aspects of life at the university, including classes. In fact, one of the main social activities of the week for dorm residents and off-campus students is Sunday night mass in the dorm chapels.

The Notre Dame family can trace its roots back 150 years to when Fr. Sorin and his fellow Holy Cross brothers founded Notre Dame du lac (Our Lady of the Lake) with a small log chapel. The campus has grown significantly since that time, but the strong desire to educate students in the classroom and beyond remains. By the time freshmen reach graduation day, they will realize that they are part of a unique group that extends past South Bend. And although the students may have different memories of what makes Notre Dame such a special place, each will have been shaped in some way by the elements of the Notre Dame family.

ADMISSIONS REQUIREMENTS

The University of Notre Dame looks for students who are Renaissance individuals—intellectuals, leaders, athletes, artists, and volunteers. Basically, Notre Dame wants the best all-around students.

In a recent freshman class, 9,452 students applied for entrance, 3,766 were admitted, and 1,885 enrolled. On average, the students who enrolled graduated in the top five percent of their senior class; in fact, twenty-five percent of that class finished in the top one percent of their high school class.

As one recent Notre Dame grad put it:

> *I remember attending a freshman orientation program with my entire freshman class and their families. The Dean of Student Affairs asked those students who had been valedictorians or salutatorians of their high school classes to raise their hands. As I looked around, I was surrounded by a sea of raised arms. That's when I realized my class was packed with students who were all accustomed to being number one.*

So, how does Notre Dame evaluate all of the applications it receives every year? There are five areas on which students are judged: high school record, standardized tests, teachers' evaluations, extracurricular accomplishments, and the essays and personal statement submitted with the application.

From a student's high school record, Notre Dame considers the quality of the school's curriculum. Notre Dame recommends that applying students take four years of English, math, science, foreign language, history, and electives. The admissions counselors especially look at students who have pushed themselves by taking honors and AP level classes, in addition to courses such as precalculus or calculus, chemistry, and physics. A current Notre Dame student said:

> *The only reason I suffered through physics in high school was so it would be on my transcript when I applied to Notre Dame, even though I knew I was going to be an English major.*

Notre Dame also considers a student's class rank, grades and the academic competition at the high school.

Standardized Tests

Notre Dame, which requires either the SAT I or the ACT, candidly admits it places a great deal of emphasis on standardized tests. The university believes that these tests are an accurate measurement of how students will perform in college. On the Verbal section of SAT I, seventy-six percent of a recent freshman class scored above 600, and eighty-four percent scored above 600 on the Math section. The average range for the ACT is 28–31.

Recommendations

Because Notre Dame does not interview candidates, teacher recommendations are one way for the admissions counselors to learn about the applicants personally. Students should have a variety of teachers, who have worked with them extensively, write their evaluations.

Extracurricular Activities

As mentioned earlier, Notre Dame seeks enthusiastic students who have developed themselves inside and outside of the classroom; therefore, the university weighs extracurricular activities heavily. Students are judged on leadership positions in clubs and student government, school and community involvement, and special talents. Also, because service work is an important aspect of life at Notre Dame, the university looks for students who have volunteered at social service organizations such as nursing homes, soup kitchens, and day care centers.

Personal Statements

Finally, a student's essays and personal statements are thrown into the evaluation mix; these compositions are vital to providing the admissions counselor with an inside look at the student. For instance, one essay asks students to reflect on how a book, poem, play, or piece of music has influenced their life. Also, Notre Dame has two long essays and three shorter essays, which is more than many schools' applications.

Application Plans

Notre Dame has two application plans, Early Action and Regular Action. With Early Action, a good option for people who have exceptional grades and standardized test scores, applications are due the beginning of November. If admitted through Early Action, students do not have to withdraw their applications from other schools and they have until May 1 to inform Notre Dame of their decision. Most students still apply Regular Action, however, in which applications are due at the beginning of January.

International and Minority Students

The student body at Notre Dame is geographically diverse, representing all fifty states, more than seventy-five countries, and five continents. Notre Dame believes international students add a unique perspective to the campus and make the university an international center of teaching and research; however, due to the Catholic heritage of the school, Notre Dame is not very mixed ethnically. Only about fifteen percent of the student body are minority students.

Similar to many highly competitive colleges, Notre Dame has made a serious commitment to recruiting minority students; for example, Notre Dame hosts two events every year to introduce minority students to life at the school. One is the Fall Open House, which has become a popular event for prospective students. Later in the year, after acceptances are sent out, Notre Dame brings admitted students and their families to Notre Dame for a three-day campus visit to help them with the decision process.

Women

Notre Dame also has increased the number of women in its student body. About five years ago, the ratio of men to women was three to one; now it is almost one to one. To accommodate the increased number of women students, Notre Dame converted some male dorms into female dorms and constructed several new residence halls.

Children of Alums

Part of the reason Notre Dame has maintained its traditions and family feeling is the fact that twenty-five percent of the students are children of Notre Dame alums. Each year the university aims to admit the appropriate number of daughters and sons of alums to maintain this statistic.

Although it is not unusual to have three generations from one family attend the University of Notre Dame, my grandfather, father, and I share a unique experience in that we all graduated exactly thirty years apart ('34, '64, '94). And while it is true we had individual experiences and memories spanning over half a century, we share a timeless bond with every other member who makes up the much larger "Notre Dame family": an overwhelming sense of community, tradition, and pride.

Visits

For applying students who wish to visit the campus, Notre Dame will arrange an informational meeting with an admissions counselor and an overnight stay in a residence hall with a student host. To get the feeling of attending Notre Dame, the prospective student sits in on classes and eats at the dining hall. The program is a great way for students to learn the campus and decide if Notre Dame is the right fit for them.

ACADEMIC LIFE

For many students, Notre Dame marks the first time they are required to question and articulate their feelings about their faith, social beliefs, and politics. No longer are students asked to simply regurgitate information as they did in high school; instead, as students learn world history, finance, and calculus, they begin to define themselves and what is important to them. A Notre Dame graduate once stated, "In the Notre Dame classroom, the spirit and the intellect culminate."

As a Catholic school, the university could easily expect that students believe only what the Catholic church teaches, but often, the required theology and philosophy core classes force students to take a serious look at what they believe and why. The Notre Dame learning environment is a unique combination of faith and questioning.

The Colleges and Majors

Notre Dame is divided into five colleges: Arts and Letters (the largest), Business, Science, Engineering, and Architecture. Overall, the most popular majors are government, finance, and accounting, with majors such as history and economics growing in popularity. Notre Dame also has strong preprofessional programs, which combine medical school prerequisite courses with a liberal arts major or additional science classes. Each college also has its own academic organizations and honor societies, including the Arts and Letters Business Society and the Management Club.

First Year of Studies

Before selecting a college, all students are enrolled into the First Year of Studies (FYS), a program created to help freshmen adjust to college-level academics. The FYS assigns each student an advisor, who guides students with course selection, choosing a college and/or a major, and with concerns about classes. The FYS center also provides students with tutors and study groups if necessary. Students must fulfill the core requirements of the FYS before they can enter sophomore year. Usually, students do not have any difficulty completing the required classes since approximately half of each incoming freshman class receives class credit for AP classes and SAT II test scores.

Although taking calculus for a future government major might seem like sheer agony, Notre Dame adheres to the philosophy of a well-rounded education, and offers its core classes as a way to achieve this purpose. For example, while in the FYS program, all students must complete one semester of Freshman Seminar and Composition and Literature (Comp and Lit). Freshman Seminar is a literature class that addresses any topic the professor selects, from reading Plato's *Republic* the entire semester to studying the subject of leadership through reading books about Ghandi. Comp and Lit is more of a grammar class that focuses on improving the overall structure of a student's writing through rewriting and peer evaluations.

By the end of their sophomore year, students are required to declare a major, but at this point, most students have created a program of study simply by taking electives that interest them.

The Core

If students declare Arts and Letters as their college, they are required to complete a unique course called core, a year-long class with approximately thirteen to twenty students, guided by an Arts and Letters professor. Although there is a recommended course list, with the first semester addressing "self" and the second semester focusing on "God," professors are given the freedom to direct the class in any manner they choose.

My class was lead by Professor T. R. Swartz of the economics department, a man of unmatched energy. The first action he took was to move our class from the uncomfortable, stiff chairs in O'Shaughnessy to the inviting lounge of a residence hall. Next, he limited our writing assignments to one page, exactly, no eight-point fonts and no wide margins. He forced us to write briefly, concisely, and weekly. Our class, a diverse group of students, became fast friends. No one missed class, and it was at 9:00 A.M., which is considered early in college. After an intense year of discussion and thought, T.R. told us, "Choose a theme for your life. Find a purpose and direct your actions toward it." Never in my life have such simple words had such profound affect on me.

Faculty

Similar to core, the majority of classes at Notre Dame have fifteen to twenty-five students. With classes that size and a student-teacher ratio of thirteen to one, students and teachers develop close relationships, a crucial element of the educational experience at Notre Dame. Teachers often invite students to their homes for dinner to hold class discussions or simply socialize.

Academics at Notre Dame is a two-part machine, student and teacher, and when they are functioning in sync, they create the spirit of Notre Dame. Professors at the university guide their students, but allow them the necessary freedom to discover their interests and strengths.

Internships

Students have the opportunity to apply for internships that pique their interest, both on and off campus. For example, the local NBC affiliate, WNDU-TV, and the Notre Dame Public Relations office offer internships to qualified students. Many students apply to be teachers' assistants their senior year, a rewarding experience that allows upper- and lower-class students to work together closely.

My senior year I had the opportunity to design, implement, and write a thesis in psychology that incorporated my interests of children, minority populations, and psychological experience. Through the university's strong connections to the community (in my case, Head Start of South Bend) and the guidance of the faculty, my work had an established framework in which I could create an experience that was meaningful to me. There was room for individuality and independence within a supportive structure, which is sometimes a tough balance to achieve, but an example of how the academic experience at Notre Dame is broader than the limited space of a classroom.

Study Abroad

Many students go abroad their sophomore or junior year. Notre Dame encourages students to participate in study abroad programs, and offers quite a few programs through the university itself. Some of the popular year-long programs are in Angers, France; Innsbruck, Austria; and Toledo, Spain. Students who participate in the year-long programs tend to go during their sophomore year and are required to take intensive language courses before they go. The favorite semester-long programs include London; Jerusalem; Santiago, Chile; and Fremantle, Australia. All of the abroad programs are competitive to get into, so often students end up enrolling in other universities' programs, although it does sometimes affect class credit.

Physically Challenged Students

To further diversify Notre Dame academics, the university provides programs to accommodate students with disabilities. For example, students with challenges can get note takers, have extended time on exams, or use textbooks on disk to ensure equal access to all disciplines and facilities.

Libraries

Students also have access to the 2.1 million volumes in the eight libraries located on campus. Most of these facilities have late hours and are open twenty-four hours a day during exams. In addition, there are ten computer clusters throughout the campus, many of which are always open.

Because Notre Dame is a highly competitive college that requires students to put in long hours of studying, it is common to see students heading off to the library on Friday and Saturday nights to do class work. Notre Dame students are dedicated to their education and are willing to put in the extra hours on the weekend if necessary, even if they are only going to be studying on the extremely social second floor of the Hesburgh Library.

After four years of intense learning at Notre Dame, students are armed with the tools of the Notre Dame academic environment, independence, questioning, and discipline, and are prepared to commence learning in the real world.

SOCIAL LIFE AND ACTIVITIES

Students at Notre Dame are as busy with club meetings and sports during the week as they are with their normal course load.

Although Notre Dame does not have a Greek system, students reside in the same dorm throughout their stay at Notre Dame and are often identified by the dorm they live in. For example, it is common to hear students refer to each other by saying, "She lives in Walsh" or "He used to live in Carroll Hall." The dorms organize a large number of students activities, including volunteer tutoring at local schools, dinners with Brother/Sister dorms, and resident hall councils.

Athletics

Tradition is an important aspect of life at Notre Dame, and the most famous tradition at the university is football. From the "1812 Overture" played at the beginning of each game's fourth quarter, to the world's oldest marching band, to the legends of Knute Rockne and the Gipper, "Fightin' Irish" football is rich in tradition. Because of the team's national reputation, many believe Notre Dame is much larger than its average enrollment of 7,700 undergraduates.

Intramural sports are very popular. Each dorm usually offers football (men), flag football (women), basketball, and soccer. Since the majority of students played varsity sports in high school, and most were captains of their teams, intramural sports are extremely competitive. In fact, Notre Dame may be the only school where students play intramural football wearing full gear. Women's flag football is equally competitive; injuries such as concussions, broken wrists, and cuts requiring stitches are not uncommon. In line with Notre Dame's love of football, the championship games for both of these football teams are played at Notre Dame stadium.

After classes, students work out at the athletic facilities available on campus, including the Rockne Memorial (the Rock), the Joyce Center, Rolfs Sports Recreation Center, Rolfs Aquatic Center, and Loftus Center. Students are able to swim, run on tracks and treadmills, ride stationary bikes, lift weights, or participate in aerobics classes at these fitness centers. In addition, Notre Dame has a nine-hole golf course open for students and alumni to play on from May through October.

The traditions of Notre Dame extend past the football season. Events such as the Keenan Review, a "talent" show performed by the residents of Keenan Hall; An Tostal, the student spring festival; Bookstore Basketball, the world's largest five-on-five basketball tournament; and the Blue and Gold game, the spring inter-squad football scrimmage, all contribute to traditional life at Notre Dame.

Volunteering

On the non-athletic side, the Center for Social Concerns (CSC) runs more than thirty-five community service clubs and residence halls that offer students the opportunity to participate in volunteer programs in the South Bend area. Last year, about a quarter of the Notre Dame student body participated in programs coordinated through the CSC, including Big Brothers/Big Sisters, Habitat for Humanity, Neighborhood Study Help Program, and Recycling Irish. The CSC epitomizes the Notre Dame spirit. The center uses a holistic method by enhancing students' spiritual and intellectual awareness of today's social realities through service opportunities and seminars. The center also identifies volunteer programs to participate in around the country with service trips to areas such as Appalachia and the inner cities. In addition, each summer, more than 125 Notre Dame alumni clubs sponsor 200 Notre Dame students in Summer Service Projects around the United States. Said a recent graduate, who participated in a Summer Service Project while at Notre Dame:

> *I spent the summer before my senior year living in a Jersey City homeless shelter for women and their children. I was given the opportunity to see the tough realities of the world. One woman I clearly remember was a twenty-year-old mother who was wise beyond her years, struggling to find a job while being supported by the welfare system. Through her I learned what really matters in life: unconditional love, trust, and spirituality. I didn't need to know anything else.*

Special Interest Clubs

Notre Dame has more than twenty special interest clubs including College Republicans, College Democrats, and Knights of Columbus. In addition, the university offers twenty-three ethnic organizations such as the African American Student Alliance, the Hispanic American Organization, and the Korean Club.

Performing Programs

Although Notre Dame historically has not been known as a performing arts school, students have a variety of programs to choose from. There are a range of music groups, from Shenanigans, a song and dance troop, to the Liturgical Choir, and nine instrumental music groups, including Concert Band. If students are interested in drama, a number of different troupes put on performances throughout the year, including The Freshmen Four, St. Edward's Hall Players, and four plays produced by the Communications and Theatre Department.

Publications

For future Pulitzer Prize winners, Notre Dame has several student-run publications: *The Observer*, the daily newspaper; *Scholastic*, the weekly news magazine; and *The Dome*, Notre Dame's yearbook. All of these publications have positions for students interested in copywriting, design, and photography. Students with a strong interest in music have the opportunity to be DJs at WVFI-AM, the alternative music station, and WSND-FM, the classical music station.

Additional special annual events on campus include the Sophomore Literary Festival, the Collegiate Jazz Festival, and the Black Cultural Arts Festival.

POPULAR SOCIAL EVENTS

- **Junior Parents Weekend**
- **Morrissey Film Festival**
- **Sophomore Sibs Weekend**
- **Fisher Regatta**
- **Beaux Arts Ball**
- **Glee Club Christmas Concert**
- **Bengal Bouts**

Weekend Activities

The weekends offer Notre Dame students plenty of social and recreational activities as well. In the fall, weekends are dominated by Notre Dame football games, both home and away. Students often have family and friends visit on these weekends to tailgate before the game, follow the marching band across campus, and dine by candlelight at the dining halls. Many people say that life at Notre

Dame ends after football season, but, since Notre Dame has joined the Big East, other sports, such as men's and women's soccer, lacrosse, and men's and women's basketball games, have become popular events. In fact, women's soccer games often sell out since their 1995 National Championship.

Although traditional dating is not common at Notre Dame, dorms host dances and formals throughout the school year. The dances are similar to giant parties in the dorms and tend to be more casual. Formals are at off-campus locations and are dressier.

The first few years at Notre Dame, students generally go to dorm parties. Notre Dame does allow students to drink in their dorm rooms, but the university has strict penalties if underage students are caught drinking in the halls or carrying alcohol across campus. On-campus parties usually end by 2:00 A.M. when parietals, or visiting hours, end. As a university that is based on Roman Catholic values, Notre Dame has single-sex dorms and enforces visiting hours. If a student is found in a dorm of the opposite sex after parietals, there are severe consequences.

Upper-class students often host parties at off-campus student housing complexes, such as Campus View and Lafayette Square, or hang out at popular bars, such as Club 23, Corby's, and Alumni Senior Club, the bar located on campus.

Many students enjoy dining out on the weekends at favorite local restaurants, such as Macri's Deli for sandwiches, Bruno's for pizza, Rocco's for pasta, and CJ's for burgers. Also, the Student Union Board (SUB) and the Snite Museum show recently released films on campus.

FINANCIAL AID

When compared to other Catholic and private universities that are nationally recognized for academic excellence, the overall costs for Notre Dame tend to be lower.

For a recent academic year, Notre Dame expected tuition and academic fees would be around $21,000, and room and board approximately $5,400. For books, students can expect to pay about $800 per year. To cut back on the cost of books, students often purchase course materials from each other or buy used books from Pandora's Books, located on the corner of Howard Street and Notre Dame Avenue, about three blocks south of campus. The university reminds students to expect costs to increase annually in order to maintain Notre Dame's solid academic environment.

As for personal expenses, the overall cost of living in South Bend is less than in other cities, but students typically spent $1,000 to $1,500 per year for incidentals as well as social and weekend activities, such as going out for dinner, movies, and other social activities.

In the last few years, the university has made aggressive efforts to substantially increase its financial aid funding.

According to Joe Russo, Director of Financial Aid:

> *In 1990, Notre Dame had $5.5 million for financial aid, and in 1997, the amount has increased significantly to over $19 million. The goal of the Financial Aid Department is to reach the point where every student who gets into Notre Dame can afford to attend Notre Dame and experience the Notre Dame family.*

This growth in funding stems from programs including post-season football bowl games, the affinity credit card (each time alums use their Notre Dame credit card, money is donated to Notre Dame's financial aid fund), the NBC contract to televise Notre Dame home football games, and licensing income from Notre Dame paraphernalia sold around the United States.

The Package

When a student receives financial aid from Notre Dame, the university works with the student and his or her family to create a financial aid package, often a combination of low-interest loans (Perkins Student Loans and Stafford Student Loans), scholarship money, and work-study. The university encourages work-study for students on financial aid to help cover their personal expenses. Options for on-campus employment include working in the dining halls, computer clusters, at the athletic department, and in the library. Also, the Notre Dame alumni clubs across the country provide hundreds of scholarships annually, now totaling more than $1 million, to incoming students.

Grants and Other Options

As part of Notre Dame's efforts to increase the ethnic and socioeconomic diversity at the school, the university offers the Holy Cross Grants. These scholarship programs are awarded to students from disadvantaged backgrounds.

Other financial aid options include two-, three-, and four-year ROTC scholarships with the Air Force, Army, or Navy (includes Marines). These scholarships sometimes cover full tuition, and books, and provide a $150 monthly stipend. A little more than five percent of Notre Dame's students are on one of the above ROTC scholarships. In fact, Notre Dame's Navy ROTC unit is the second largest in the country (the Naval Academy is first).

To apply for financial aid, students are required to submit the standard Free Application for Federal Student Aid (FAFSA) and the PROFILE of the College Scholarship Service (CSS) by February 15, but are encouraged to file them as early as possible.

GRADUATES

Every home football game, Notre Dame alumni wander around the campus, remembering the days when the university belonged to them. Wearing their green shamrock-covered pants, they visit the bookstore, stop by concession stands, and stroll past their old dorms. As the current students pass the old alums on their way to tailgate, Notre Dame students promise themselves they will never become sentimental graduates, but when graduation day arrives, they find themselves reminiscing about their time at Notre Dame as well. The recent grads might be wearing jeans instead of plaid pants, but suddenly they also become nostalgic about their alma mater. Notre Dame alums are known for being maudlin when it comes to the university, and are the butt of many jokes as a result, but it is difficult to leave Notre Dame and not realize that it is a special place. Once someone attends Notre Dame, whether it was in the 1940s or in the 1980s, that person is always a member. It isn't a coincidence that Notre Dame boasts one of the largest and most loyal alumni networks of any U.S. college. The university has more than two hundred clubs in the United States and more than thirty alumni clubs worldwide.

PROMINENT GRADS

- **Rabbi Albert Plotkin, '42, First Rabbi from Notre Dame**
- **Robert Galvin, '44, Chairman of Motorola**
- **Regis Philbin, '53, Television Personality**
- **Phil Donahue, '57, Television Personality**
- **Daniel Lungren, '68, Attorney General of California**
- **Ernesto Perez Balladares, '67, '69, President of Panama**
- **James Weatherbee, '74, Astronaut**
- **Judge Ann Williams, '75, First African American Woman Appointed to Federal Bench**

In 1996 the Office of Institutional Research at Notre Dame conducted a survey of the undergraduate Class of 1986. The survey intended to find how satisfied those graduates were with their Notre Dame educational experience, if they felt prepared for life after college, and if they would select Notre Dame again if they could relive their college experience. In all of the questionnaire areas, student satisfaction indicated that the overwhelming majority (eighty-five to ninety-five percent) of alums had positive and enthusiastic feelings about their experience at Notre Dame.

After graduating from Notre Dame, alumni locate all over the world and enter a wide array of professions. Every year, Notre Dame sends the largest percentage of its graduates into the career world. Notre Dame alumni rank first nationally among Catholic universities and seventh among all private universities in the number of leading business executives in the workforce. The most popular fields graduates enter into include, law, marketing and sales, engineering, medicine and accounting.

Career and Placement Office

To help students secure positions in the business world, Notre Dame's Career and Placement Office holds seminars about writing résumés and preparing for interviews, and also counsels students on what professional careers fit their interests. Career and Placement tries to invite a range of companies to the campus; however, many of the companies tend to be better matches for business and engineering students than for liberal arts majors.

Advanced Degrees

Many students go on to pursue advanced degrees, in law, medicine, MBA programs, or other graduate programs. Almost half of all Notre Dame grads eventually go on to complete at least one advanced degree.

Service Programs

After graduation, social service continues to be an integral part of many students lives. In recent years, about ten percent of each graduating class has entered into a one- or two-year service program, domestic and abroad. The Center for Social Concerns, which brings numerous postgraduate service programs to campus, advises students on what programs are available and would be a good match in terms of structure, location, and activity. Some of the more popular programs include Jesuit Volunteer Corps., Alliance for Catholic Education (ACE, a Notre Dame-founded program), Inner City Teaching Corps, and the Peace Corps.

Alumni Support

In terms of alumni annual giving, Notre Dame ranks third in the nation, but alumni are dedicated to Notre Dame more than just financially. Approximately 161,000 alums participate in events organized by the alumni clubs, such as golf outings, happy hours, and vacations. There are also activities meant to enhance the spiritual, educational, and professional aspects of alumni's lives. For example, the Alumni Association has started a program that brings graduates back to South Bend to rehab houses in the area and the Chicago Alumni Club frequently hosts networking meetings for graduates.

When a student graduates from Notre Dame and is unclear what area he or she wants to enter or is looking for a career change later in life, the Notre Dame alumni make up a strong support network. Graduates often look to each other for career guidance, resources, and connections, even if they graduated generations apart.

Alums permeate every field worldwide, from politics and the film industry to medical research and education, yet they all share the moral, ethical, and spiritual framework of the Notre Dame family.

SUMMING UP

The plethora of activities, programs, and facilities at Notre Dame allows students to create their own experience while at the university. As the phrase "Notre Dame family" has a different connotation for each student and graduate, so does the "Notre Dame experience." Although the school encourages students to be involved in all aspects of university life, students can choose if they want to focus more on academics, service, student government, or the arts. It is the same for social activities, where there is something for everyone.

The spirit of Notre Dame students and graduates proves that there is something special about the place. The fact that people affiliated with Notre Dame call it a family shows that students and graduates really care about the school and the people involved with it.

When I think about all of my experiences at Notre Dame, a certain image comes to my mind. No matter where we were, at a football game, mass, or special function, every time students and faculty heard the Notre Dame alma mater played, we put our arms around each other and swayed. Friends, strangers, teachers, students—it didn't matter. It was always such a powerful and unifying sight to have everyone together for that moment and exhibiting what the "Notre Dame family" really meant.

All in all, it is the last lines of the Notre Dame alma mater, "Notre Dame, Our Mother," which truly summarize how its students and graduates feel about the school: "And our hearts forever, Love thee, Notre Dame."

❑ *Meghan Case Kelley, B.A.*

UNIVERSITY OF PENNSYLVANIA

University of Pennsylvania
Philadelphia, PA 19104

(215) 898-7507
Fax: (215) 898-9670

E-mail: info@admissions.ugao.upenn.edu
Web site: http:\\www.upenn.edu

Enrollment

Full-time ❑ women: 4,671
❑ men: 4,789

Part-time ❑ women: 794
❑ men: 605

INTRODUCING UNIVERSITY OF PENNSYLVANIA

The University of Pennsylvania is entering a new era as it approaches the year 2000. The twenty-first century is redefining Penn's original goal of theory and practice, the very tenet upon which Benjamin Franklin founded the university. In order for students to succeed in the increasingly competitive professional world, and become more effective leaders, Penn continues to add to Franklin's tradition by granting a vast field of opportunities for students to use what they learn in the classroom. Penn is committed to graduating only the best of the best.

The University of Pennsylvania is the perfect place to get a top-notch education, develop lifelong friendships, experience everything college could possibly offer, and graduate confident, enthusiastic men and women who are determined to face whatever challenges the future may hold.

Penn is plagued with the criticisms common to an Ivy League school: a highly competitive atmosphere, difficulty in balancing academics, cocurriculars, and a social life, and more particular to Penn, the fear of its size. Although Penn is large, it feels surprisingly like a smaller school. While possibly a bit overwhelming at times, the environment is never impersonal. Penn offers a diverse environment, which gives every individual the possibility of finding a comfortable and enjoyable niche.

On the whole, Penn students are laid back and friendly, and they embrace a "work hard, play hard" attitude. Despite the competitive admissions process, the natural environment is generally in tune with the attitude of the students. If you happen to visit Penn on a warm and sunny day, you may think it is a national holiday, you're bound to find several hundred students gathered on College Green, either sitting with a few friends, "hacking" in a large group by the Peace sign, playing Frisbee between the Ben Franklin statue and the trees in front of College Hall, or simply passing the time between classes.

Penn students are truly fortunate to enjoy the best of both worlds—a suburban campus nestled in the fifth largest city in the country. Though downtown Philadelphia is only a five-minute subway ride away, College Green (the center of the campus) seems miles away from the city streets. The city is in the midst of a revival, with numerous new residential and commercial developments in progress. The South Street area, where green-haired weirdos hang out in front of quirky stores, has often been compared to Greenwich Village. Vibrant ethnic neighborhoods have charmed many an adventurous Penn student who has taken the time to trek beyond Center City. Sports fans may attend professional baseball, football, hockey, and basketball games, and concerts, dance clubs, restaurants, movies, theaters, and a wealth of shops provide endless distractions from studying.

ADMISSIONS REQUIREMENTS

Getting into Penn is not as easy as it used to be. The average SAT II score is 1359 (666 Verbal, 693 Math) and approximately fifteen percent of each class are students who were either the valedictorian or salutatorian of their high school graduating class. Though these facts may intimidate applicants, they shouldn't; Penn carefully selects each incoming class to include a diverse range of students—academically, socially, culturally, geographically. A good portion of each class still hails from the Northeast, but the demographics are rapidly changing. California, Florida, and the Midwest are well represented, mainly because of strong recruiting across the nation. The number of foreign students has increased dramatically over the past few years. The undergraduate population is forty-nine percent female and, according to university literature, nearly thirty-five percent are racial minorities.

Penn's application allows students the creativity and freedom to present themselves in the way they want to be perceived. On recent applications, questions have included: "If you could spend an evening with one person, who would it be and why?" "In your 300-page autobiography, how does page 209 read?" and "If you could take three things to a desert island, what would they be?" The Admissions Office has also received a deluge of videotapes displaying applicants' skills, but unless you have something that can be conveyed only on videotape (and this doesn't include a personal plea to admissions officers), you should probably stick with paper. However you apply, avoid anything overly contrived, and whatever you do, don't lie or even exaggerate; admissions officers read enough applications to spot insincerity when they see it.

The Admissions Office does not seek any one specific quality. Almost everyone who applies was a newspaper editor, class president, or debate champion. The challenge is to separate yourself from the masses without seeming arrogant. If you are certain that Penn is your first-choice school, then consider applying for Early Decision. This may prevent you from getting lost among the thousands of applications, and it will show your commitment to Penn.

The University of Pennsylvania requires the SAT I and three SAT II exams, including SAT II: Writing. Although no specific high school courses are required, the admissions material states that Penn "recommends a thorough grounding in English and foreign languages, social science, mathematics, and science."

ACADEMIC LIFE

The curriculum of the College of Arts and Sciences covers the spectrum of academic areas. Though it requires a core program, the college allows students freedom to choose their course of study. Proficiency in a foreign language is necessary, although students may waive the Penn exam by scoring well on the achievement test. They may also receive class credit for high scores on most AP tests.

Majors

There are more than forty majors in the College of Arts and Sciences, covering almost every conceivable subject. History, biology, math, and English are among the most popular majors, and each department is top-rated, with internationally acclaimed professors teaching undergraduate courses. Nobel prize winner Lawrence Klein teaches in the economics department, and the psychology and anthropology departments are among the best in the country. Being at a major research university allows undergraduates to work with professors on projects and to be taught by those on the cutting edge of scientific development. Opportunities for students to work individually with professors abound in the liberal arts, as well as in the science departments.

In addition to the common majors, students may also choose some that are more unusual: folklore, environmental studies, history and sociology of science, architecture, linguistics, urban studies, women's studies, and South Asia regional studies. One of Penn's specialty area is the Biological Basis of Behavior, a unique program that allows premeds and others to take an array of science courses from various departments. The Annenberg School for Communication offers an undergraduate major. Individualized majors are also popular and relatively easy to get approved.

Internships and Study Away from Campus

Penn also awards credit for some internships and encourages students to spend time studying in a foreign country. Many departments take advantage of the city by incorporating Philadelphia's resources into their courses. Students may visit the Philadelphia Art Museum, take a tour of historical architecture, or meet with city leaders as part of a class. The steady stream of important and famous people into Philadelphia also enables student and university groups to attract interesting speakers to campus.

Other Undergraduate Schools

Students are permitted to take courses in the other undergraduate schools. Many College of Arts and Sciences students, for example, take marketing or legal studies in Wharton. The college also permits undergraduates to take graduate-level classes with permission from the professor, and independent studies are a convenient way for students to work closely with a professor in an area of particular interest to them.

The requirements in the Wharton, Engineering, and Nursing schools are quite different from those in the college, although each school requires its students to take some liberal arts classes. Wharton students must take finance, accounting, management, and marketing, and most of their work is group-based. Due to the fact that Wharton's core requirements are so extensive, a major is actually a concentration of about four classes. Students often have more than one concentration, such as finance and strategic management or finance and accounting. In the School of Engineering and Applied Science there is a good balance between technical requirements and electives. In order for students to get a complete education, it is mandatory to take any seven humanities and/or social science classes from the College of Arts and Sciences. Engineering students seem to work harder than anyone, and they are notorious for spending all night in the computer lab working on independent studies or senior design projects. A few enterprising students enroll in the management-technology program, which enables them to obtain degrees from both the School of Engineering and Applied Science and the Wharton School.

Penn is the only Ivy League school with a nursing program that has an entering class of approximately 100 students each year. The Nursing School, affiliated with the Hospital of the University of Pennsylvania, has rigorous requirements for its students and is ranked among the top programs in the country.

Faculty

Very few Penn classes are taught by teaching assistants, a rare occurrence at a large school. Professors are surprisingly accessible; they are not at Penn solely for graduate students and research. After freshman year and the completion of introductory level classes, students find most upper-level courses have fewer than forty students. It is not uncommon for Penn students to take a series of graduate level or M.B.A.-level courses beyond their freshman year. These classes tend to be smaller, ranging anywhere from five to forty students.

Academic Advising

Because Penn doesn't require students to choose a major until the end of the sophomore year, one can take a little extra time before committing to a specific course of study. The flip side of this is that academic advising in the College of Arts and Sciences is not great. Not only must one actively seek it out, but many people do not feel the advisors provide much guidance. Once you declare your major, you will be assigned an advisor in the student's department, which helps but college students are largely left on their own. Ultimately this may work to your advantage, but people who need to be nurtured, who want someone telling them that they're taking the right course and that they're on the right (or wrong) track, may feel a little neglected.

Academic advising in the other schools is similar yet a bit different since the number of enrolled students is fewer.

As an engineering student, I never had a problem trying to find my advisor when I needed to speak to him. Most class advisors along with professors have specified office hours when they are available; otherwise, they are somewhat flexible about setting up another time which is more suitable to one's schedule.

Registration

Is registration at a large school a nightmare? Registration at Penn is no longer done in the classic way that we're all used to seeing—waiting on long lines in a hot and sweaty gymnasium for five hours on a Sunday. The registration system has been automated and is called PARIS (the Penn Automated Registration and Information System). Each semester, there is a period where students can preregister for classes that they know they have to take or classes that they simply want to take during the upcoming semester. Hope is not lost for students who are too lazy to get their act together early. Registration officially begins a few weeks prior to the start of each term, when most of Penn registers for their classes.

Certain classes such as graduate courses, M.B.A. courses, seminars and independent studies require permission before students can register. The actual act of registration is done over the phone so technically, you could register for classes while still in bed.

SOCIAL LIFE AND ACTIVITIES

What is the social life like at such a large school? Well, it may be a bit overwhelming at first, but for most students, by the midpoint of their Penn career, a balance is struck between their academic duties and having a social life. At a school with nearly 10,000 undergrads, it is wise to become involved in as many activities as possible. The Class Boards, a branch of student government, has a board for each class and is primarily responsible for planning events throughout the school year that try to integrate the class and foster a sense of school spirit, but most students rely on themselves and their friends for their social activities—something that is key in creating their own unique Penn experience.

The Quad

There are some 2,500 students in the entering freshman class. For most, freshman year is spent in the quad, a massive ancient structure that houses nearly 1,200 students in separate, but connected dorms. If college means loud music, spontaneously erupting parties, closet refrigerators stocked with beer, volleyball in the center courtyard, late night feasting at McClelland Hall, and Spring Fling, the quad is where you want to be. Other housing is available either through being assigned or through an application process, but anyone and everyone puts down the quad as their first choice for freshman housing.

Fraternities

A large part of the freshman social scene revolves around the on-campus fraternity parties. My recollection of the first few months of freshman year was as follows:

We traveled in packs of twenty roaming the entire campus—going to fraternity parties making sure to always bring our own beer—going to Murph's (you'll know where that is when you get to Penn) where of course every freshman was already twenty-one—late night Billibob's, which was the first indication of a change in diet—we went from enjoying brown-bagged lunches that our mothers prepared to only requiring the nutrition offered by a beer and a cheesesteak at 4 A.M.

By sophomore and junior year, most students either live in their respective fraternity or sorority houses, one of the three high-rises, or off campus. By this point, students have generally found a core group of friends and the fraternity party scene no longer holds the same charm as it did freshman year. Off-campus parties and small gatherings among close friends is much more the popular thing to do.

Off-Campus Action

Philadelphia offers many options if staying on campus is not your thing. Whether it be the movie theater at 38th and Walnut Street, one of the dance clubs on Delaware Avenue, one of the countless number of bars on South Street, or one of Philadelphia's famous restaurants, there is always something going on that will catch your interest. Don't forget that one of the largest outlet malls in the country, Franklin Mills, is only a twenty-five minute drive away and that Philadelphia is home to the steps of the Art Museum, the famous *Rocky* steps. The City of Brotherly Love provides many alternatives when you need a change of scenery.

Being in a major metropolitan city provides students with ample opportunities to fulfill their interests. I spent all of my four years doing research for a doctor at the Children's Hospital of Philadelphia, while friends of mine worked in the mayor's office in City Hall or for investment banks in the Liberty Building downtown. Philadelphia complements the natural preprofessional attitude fostered by most Penn students very well.

Traditions

Penn, like many other schools, is an institution with several old traditions. One of the most outrageous—and for most students one of the most memorable—Penn experiences, is Hey Day. On the last day of classes in April, all of the juniors dress in red T-shirts and Styrofoam skimmer hats and carry bamboo canes. The entire 2,400-member class marches from the corner of 34th and Walnut Streets through the center of campus to the Junior Balcony in the quad, a term you probably didn't understand as a freshman, and back through campus to College Green. This is the day when juniors officially become seniors. The president of the university and the senior class president-elect address the huge crowd of enthusiastic juniors. Most everyone is in such good spirits that one of the only things remembered about Hey Day are the final words that ring out over the crowd: "Congratulations, we're finally seniors!"

Senior year is a time of joy for some and a time of sorrow for others. Your Penn career comes to a close before you know it, but not before a final farewell to Dear Old Pennsylvania. Senior year is spent with friends you haven't seen since your freshman year hall in the quad or friends you have made along the way, interviewing for jobs and graduate schools, at Senior Screamers in campus bars, at Sink or Swim, at Smokey Joe's (the toughest bar to get into for underclassmen), at your last Spring Fling, and Senior Week. By the time you're ready to take your final stroll down Locust Walk in your cap and gown, you will have spent too much time in the library studying, too much time eating greasy food and drinking beer, and too many late nights doing Heaven knows what! But, if someone asks, you wouldn't hesitate for a second if you had to do it all again.

Groups

Extracurricular activities are a necessity among Penn students. Varsity and intramural athletics, singing and theater groups, and student government are among the most popular activities; however, no matter what it is that you're interested in, a group with many active members probably already exists and if it doesn't, you could start it yourself. Penn welcomes student initiative in exploring new areas.

Safety Program

As with any major city, Philadelphia has its fair share of problems. In recent years, there has been a safety issue mainly for students who reside off campus. Last year, the student government, along with the administration, introduced a new safety program that includes a larger Penn police force with nighttime foot and car patrol officers, an increased amount of blue light emergency telephones, and a new police station on 40th Street between Spruce and Walnut Streets. The off campus area surrounding the heart of Penn's campus, which houses a majority of the upperclassmen, has become much safer with the implementation of this program. The administration made safety its top priority on and off campus. There are also several resources that are available to students, such as escort services between the hours of 10:00 P.M. and 3:00 A.M. and Penn escort vans. After 3:00 A.M., students are encouraged to call Penn police escorts if they feel it necessary.

I spent three of my four years at Penn as president of my class. It was a phenomenal experience in terms of meeting thousands of people, spending time working with the administration on important issues, and making an effort to integrate a class of 2,300 students. Throwing Screamers at bars and planning events such as Homecoming and Hey Day were fun, but the most rewarding aspect of my position came about when safety became a major issue. Three other student leaders and I assisted the administration by providing student feedback and writing proposals for feasible safety programs. The final proposal was a joint collaboration between the administration and the students that would create a safer Penn than ever before.

The bottom line is that the boundless energy of Penn students allows them to find a balance between everything that they want to accomplish by the end of their four years at college. The more activities you get involved with or the more time you spend doing one activity at Penn, the more people you will have the chance to meet and the smaller Penn will become. College is a stepping-stone in life and Penn students create their own microcosm within the larger world of Penn.

FINANCIAL AID

As with all Ivy League schools, Penn has need-blind admissions, which guarantees that aid packages will be provided to those who require help. A financial aid award, also known as a "package," typically includes a federal work-study job, a federal student loan, and, in most cases, a grant. Penn participates in all federal assistance and state programs to provide students with a comprehensive financial aid program. Also as you'll find with all Ivy League schools, Penn is extremely expensive. Sixty percent of all students receive some form of financial aid, and most people graduate with loans to repay, but the loans are manageable, and few would say that their education wasn't worth the price.

PROMINENT GRADS

- P. Roy Vagelos, '50
- Leonard Lauder, '54, Entrepreneur
- Steve Winn, '63
- Ronald Lauder, '65, Entrepreneur
- Candice Bergen, '67, Actress
- Donald Trump, '68, Entrepreneur

GRADUATES

Sometimes it seems as though everyone at Penn is looking for a job in business. The annual senior job search is marked by the appearance of hundreds of business suit-clad students eager to spend 100-hour weeks working on Wall Street. Hundreds of interviewers from banks, consulting firms, and other businesses come to campus to recruit students from Wharton and the College of Arts and Sciences, as well as from the School of Engineering and Applied Science. An overwhelming number take jobs in business and industry following graduation.

It's a myth that only if you're in Wharton will you be able to get a job in business or industry. While it's true that most of the companies that target Penn students as prospective candidates are attracted to Wharton, students with other solid backgrounds are also rewarded with job offers. It's true that the interviewing process is more challenging when you're competing against "Whartonites," but it is possible.

A substantial number of students (more than thirty percent) go immediately to graduate school—law and medicine are the most popular. The rest of the class uses Career Planning's resources and their own research to find jobs in other areas or to apply to master's or doctoral programs. Many of Penn graduates enroll in a graduate program.

The Career Planning and Placement Center (CPPS) is very helpful and takes a proactive role in a student's placement before and after graduation. During the interviewing process, it is mandatory for students to meet with a class placement advisor to review their résumé as well as to tape a mock interview. The center has additional resources and information available to students on various companies and almost every graduate program in the country. You'll find yourself at CPPS almost every day during the first semester of senior year, but if you take advantage of the resources available to you, the whole process won't be too overwhelming and will be rewarding.

SUMMING UP

There is so much to say about the University of Pennsylvania, but it's almost better to let you get there and find out for yourself and that's what makes Penn so great. Every student has the chance to find his or her own direction and make Penn what he or she wants it to be. There are so many opportunities available at Penn that you are bound to satisfy any interest that you have, whether it be academic, extracurricular, or social. Students are generally so pleased with their Penn experience that they often find their way back to Penn as graduate students and most certainly as interested and involved alumni. Penn (or any school) can be used as a stepping-stone in life. Use that stepping-stone to help you reach the next level, whatever it may be—and if you don't know what that next level is, let Penn help you to discover it.

❏ *Neil Sheth, B.S.E.*

UNIVERSITY OF VIRGINIA

Photo by Dan Grogan

University of Virginia
Charlottesville, VA 22906

(804) 982-3200
Fax: (804) 924-3587

E-mail: undergrad_admission@virginia.edu
Web site: http:\\www.virginia.edu

Enrollment

Full-time ❏ women: 6,535
❏ men: 5,702

Part-time ❏ women: 39
❏ men: 20

INTRODUCING UVA

In the fall, Thomas Jefferson's village stretches out before you. The tops of the maple and ash trees lining the evergreen lawn burn with the reds, oranges, and yellows of the East Coast fall. The graceful lines of their trunks are echoed in the rows of white colonnades that frame the lawn and announce the historic pavilions and rooms, still living quarters for popular faculty and honored students. Everywhere, the vast expanse of grass is dotted with picnickers, students studying, mini football games, and picture-snapping tourists. Yet your gaze is drawn past all of this to the north end of the lawn, to the building commanding the entire scene, the world-famous Rotunda. Based on the Roman Pantheon, the sparkling marble of its flowing staircase and regal columns and the elegant arc of its majestic dome ensure that the Rotunda is not only a historical landmark, but one of the most beautiful structures ever to grace a college campus.

As I walk to my dreaded test, I smile as I remember that by the time I get out of class, the sun will have set and warm yellow light will be glowing within the many windows surrounding the lawn. I know that on my walk home, I'll feel more like a lucky tourist after closing time than an undergraduate headed to the dining hall.

Amazing aesthetics, however, is not the reason why UVa has long been known as the "Public Ivy," and why it attracts so many exceptional students and professors. Founded by Thomas Jefferson in 1819, UVa remains one of the highest ranked state-funded institutions in the nation. Offering undergraduate programs in architecture, arts and sciences, commerce, education, engineering and applied science, and nursing, the university continues to operate on its founder's belief in the importance of a solid liberal arts education. Of its 18,000 enrolled students, two-thirds are undergraduates, and while offering the opportunities and diversity of a medium size school, UVa still has a fairly concentrated main campus area, creating a smaller community feel. In other words, it will be virtually impossible to walk to class without recognizing at least a few faces. On its 1,094 acres, the university has 557 buildings, including 17 libraries. Many students and professors also take advantage of the extraordinary Special Collections Department of Alderman Library, which houses numerous rare historical books and items and also boasts one of the most extensive collections of Thomas Jefferson's effects and documents in the world. Although steeped in history and tradition, UVa remains on the cutting edge of technology, offering computerized library services, Internet access, and a variety of resources, including mainframes, minicomputers, PCs, and a network of printers, which are available to students at the many computer labs around grounds. Courses that use e-mail discussion groups or Internet news group subscriptions to enhance class communication are quite common. Special learning facilities at UVa include a learning resource center, an art gallery, radio and TV stations, and an art museum.

Attending UVa is more than just going through the motions of four years of tests, papers, and parties. It is an experience that will completely consume you. You will be a first-year instead of a freshman, you will live on grounds instead of on campus, you will be able to write the honor pledge in your sleep, you will learn "The Good Ole Song," and you will come to recognize Thomas Jefferson as some sort of deity. At the end of it all, you will be welcomed into one of the most close-knit, active, and supportive alumni networks in the country. But most important, you will have interacted with top-notch professors and students, will have been a part of Jefferson's still thriving vision of public education, and you will have done it all without you or your parents having to face the increasingly terrifying price tag of a private institution.

ADMISSIONS REQUIREMENTS

You've got the grades and the extracurricular activities. You've taken the toughest courses your high school offers, squared away your recommendations, and conquered the SAT. But in front of you lies one of the most comprehensive college applications in the country. There are several short essays as well as one long, open-ended and intimidating question. Since you've set your heart on UVa, you've done some research and discovered that sweating over these questions is indeed important. The Admissions Committee will be examining each of your responses in detail, giving your whole application the kind of attention it would typically only receive at a small, private school.

Each year, the qualifications of students applying to UVa are more impressive. Ninety-four percent of the current first-year class were in the top fifth of their high school class and ninety-eight percent of them were in the top two fifths. Their scores on the SAT I were as follows: Verbal—five percent below 500; twenty percent between 500 and 599; forty-eight percent between 600 and 700; twenty-seven percent above 700; Math—three percent below 500; sixteen percent between 500 and 599; forty-eight percent between 600 and 700; and thirty-two percent above 700.

All applicants must take the SAT I or the ACT, as well as the SAT II: Subject tests in Writing, Mathematics I or II, and a choice of Foreign Language, History, or Science. Although the GED is accepted, most successful candidates have graduated from accredited high schools and have completed sixteen academic courses including four courses of English, four of mathematics beginning with Algebra I, two of physics, biology, or chemistry (three if they are applying to engineering), and two years of a foreign language. AP credits are accepted. Recently about one out of every three applicants was accepted to UVa. You will generally have a slightly better chance if you are from Virginia, or if you fall into the legacy category by being the child of alumni. In any case, if you are seriously considering UVa, then you are probably an excellent student with impressive extracurricular activities, outstanding recommendations, and an eye-catching application essay.

ACADEMIC LIFE

For more than a year, I have worked one on one with a professor who was an expert in my area of interest. I exhausted every resource in the libraries and university archives. I read, researched, wrote, edited, and rewrote, and though I missed some parties and lost some sleep, I gained something else—the realization that UVa honors thesis is an experience I may never want to relive, but it's also one of which I will always be proud.

The distinguished majors program is just one example of the outstanding academic opportunities available at UVa. You can take part in internships, study abroad and accelerated degree programs, B.A.-B.S. degrees in chemistry and physics, dual majors in most arts and sciences programs, student-designed majors and an interdisciplinary major, as well as non-degree study and pass/fail options. A first-year on-grounds honors program and two national honor societies, including Phi Beta Kappa, are available, as are the departmental honors programs. If you take the time to explore the options and pursue your interests, the university is a once-in-a-lifetime shot at an amazing collection of knowledge, talent, and possibility. Ninety-two percent of the faculty hold Ph.D.s or terminal degrees and many are the recipients of such honors as the Pulitzer Prize, the National Book Award, the Humbolt Award, and Fullbright Fellowships. Graduate students do teach thirty-six percent of the introductory courses, with an average size of fifty-two students for an entry-level lecture and ninety for a laboratory. Yet the student faculty ratio remains thirteen to one, and the College of Arts and Sciences specializes in small, discussion-oriented seminars led by full professors. These courses often involve a significant work load, but they also usually cover the professor's favorite subject, from such topics as Native American poetry to cult studies or Civil War culture, and can be extremely informative, interesting, and entertaining.

Course Requirements

Depending on your major, your flexibility to choose electives and select courses will vary. For example, an English major will always have more decisions to make during registration than a premed biochemistry major. However, because UVa focuses on instilling a broad liberal arts background in all of its students, the distribution requirements insure that everyone gets a chance to sample the wide variety of course material offered. All undergraduates must complete twelve hours of mathematics and science, six hours each of humanities, composition, and social sciences, four semesters of foreign languages, three hours of historical studies, and three hours of non-Western perspectives. In total, by graduation, students must complete 120 credit hours, including 18 to 42 hours in their major, with a minimum GPA of 2.0.

Majors

English, history, and biology are the strongest majors academically, while commerce, biology, and psychology have the largest enrollments. UVa confers B.A., B.S., B.A.R.H., B.C.P., B.S.C., and B.S.N. degrees in addition to master's and doctoral degrees.

Echols Scholars Program

An example of academic opportunity at UVa, the Echols program offers talented students the means to make the most of their scholastic experience. Founded in 1960 by university faculty, the program continues to operate under the guidance of tenured or tenure-track professors who act as special advisors and mentors to the scholars. As an Echols scholar, your only requirement at UVa is to graduate with 120 approved credit hours. A scholar is free from the distribution requirements and even from declaring a major at all. Many scholars use this freedom to focus on "concentrations" in several of their areas of interest, to double major, or to truly invest themselves in a distinguished majors program. Echols scholars also enjoy priority in choosing courses from ISIS, UVa's computerized registration process, and a scholar will usually never have trouble adding into a restricted or full class. The Echols program also encourages richness in more than just the educational areas of college life. First-year scholars live together in adjacent dormitories and special group activities, both academic and social, are offered for scholars of all years. Participation in the Echols Scholars Program is usually based on an invitation process. Every UVa applicant is considered, and approximately ten percent of each entering class is chosen.

Honor Code

> *On my honor as a student, I have neither given nor received aid on this exam.*

You will sign and date this statement hundreds of times if you attend UVa, but what exactly does it mean, and why is it so important? Established in 1842 in order to ease tensions between faculty and students, the Honor System was soon adopted and maintained by the students. Although it has changed to reflect the ideals of the ever-shifting student body, the system remains an integral part of the UVa mind-set. The simple principles of honor establish a network of trust rarely found in a college setting, including unproctored tests, take-home exams, and even check-writing privileges throughout the local community. However, violating such significant trust also means significant consequences. If a student commits a willful, serious act of lying, cheating, or stealing, and is found guilty by a jury of peers, the only possible sanction is a permanent dismissal from the university. Since the system is entirely student-run, you may participate in many different facets, perhaps as a randomly selected juror, an honor committee member, or an honor advisor, counsel, or educator. Regardless of whether you seek it out, rest assured that the Honor System, its benefits and responsibilities, will be an important part of your daily student life.

Pressure and Competition

In general, the students at UVa were serious about academics when they were in high school and by the time they reach Charlottesville, they're even more determined to make the most of their college experience. At the same time though, there is rarely an overwhelming sense of academic pressure and competition. UVa students can usually excel in the classroom without losing their perspective on the larger picture. As one wide-eyed first-year student found out, a sense of humor is often involved in keeping stress under control.

It was 2:00 A.M. in the middle of finals week. I had been buried in my books since early that morning. Despite all my preparation, I was debating not even showing up for my test the next day, I was so sure I was going to fail. Just as I was about to close my book and give up completely, a group of students who had been studying together for hours right next to me suddenly jumped up on top of their table and began an impromptu striptease in the middle of Clemons Library. Pretty soon they had the entire room either participating or cheering them on. When it was over, everyone settled right back down and continued studying. It reminded me that life was not solely about finals. I suddenly realized that I would survive the week. After that, I didn't even mind reopening my books.

SOCIAL LIFE AND ACTIVITIES

At UVa football games, fans of all ages, sporting Cavalier paraphernalia, throng together at the back of the vehicles, imbibing homemade fried chicken, sandwiches, barbecue, beer, and all sorts of other goodies they don't serve at the dining halls. Luckily, my roommate was a legacy student with an entire family of enthusiastic, generous alumni, and I would find myself munching and mingling with the entire clan. A steady stream of students, many showing traditional spirit with their khakis and skirts, others waving banners and various body parts smeared with orange and blue paint, moves through the gates to descend on the bleachers.

Student Body

With their virtually universal appeal, football games are an example of a UVa social event that draws together all different sections of the student body and the local community, both of which have interesting dynamics. Each year, UVa seems to welcome a more diverse entering class. Of the 12,000 present undergraduate students, sixty-five percent are from Virginia, with the rest coming from forty-nine states and eighty-eight foreign countries, including Canada. Seventy-five percent of the students are white, eleven percent are African American, and ten percent Asian American. Forty-seven percent are Protestant, twenty-three percent are Catholic, and twenty percent claim no religious affiliation.

The Town

Charlottesville itself offers a unique mix of long-time residents and ever-present tourists. Although the city and surrounding Albemarle County have a population of 115,000 people, Charlottesville maintains a small friendly town feeling. At UVa, you are nestled just east of the Blue Ridge Mountains, only minutes from the homes of Thomas Jefferson, James Madison, and James Monroe, as well as the stunning sights of Shenandoah National Park and Skyline Drive. In short, there's never a problem finding activities when the relatives come to visit. As a student, you'll probably spend a significant amount of social time on "the corner," a group of shops, bookstores, restaurants, and bars within walking distance of grounds, or on the historic downtown pedestrian mall, which has movie theaters, local boutiques, plenty of coffee houses, and even a new ice skating rink.

Clubs and Organizations

While major school activities such as football games, the famous annual Virginia Film Festival, and the traditional FoxField Races bring everyone together, most students find an outlet for their social lives through one or more of the numerous activities offered on grounds. With more than 300 clubs and organizations to choose from, UVa students tend to be as active outside as they are inside the classroom. One of the more popular social opportunities is the Greek system. An example of deeply rooted tradition at the university, there are over sixty social and service fraternities and sororities in which twenty-eight percent of men and thirty percent of women are involved. Many more make treks to Rugby Road (the site of many of the fraternity and sorority houses) on Thursday, Friday, and Saturday nights, where there is never a shortage of parties.

For those who tire of the Greek scene, there is no shortage of alternative extracurricular pursuits. Aside from academic societies and professional clubs (including the oldest debating society for undergraduates in the nation) there are groups related to art, band, cheerleading, chess, choir, chorale, chorus, computers, dance, drama, culture, film, gay interests, honors, international concerns, photography, and politics. There are religious associations and special interest groups, including UVA-NOW and ROTC. UVa also has a daily newspaper, a weekly news journal, and plenty of student-run special-interest magazines, as well as three radio stations that broadcast on grounds. Another immensely popular organization is Madison House, through which students participate in a variety of community services.

Sports

Finally, activities that require more coordination, such as intramural sports, are also a favorite way to socialize. More than eighty-five percent of students participate in the thirty different sports available. For the more serious and talented athletes, UVa has twelve intercollegiate sports for men and twelve for women. The university is also a Division I member of the NCAA and competes in the Atlantic Coast Conference. From the 44,000-seat Scott Stadium, slated for a major expansion by the year 2000, and a 9,000-seat gymnasium to four recreation centers (including a new aquatic fitness facility), UVa offers students every opportunity to enhance their bodies as well as their minds.

Basically, on those rare occasions when you don't actually have to be studying something (and those more frequent times when you choose not to study something), you'll find plenty of other agendas you want to pursue. The key is to choose which activities are most important to you and to make sure you allot some of your precious nonacademic time to truly enjoying them.

FINANCIAL AID

Work-study is one of the most common financial aid programs offered at UVa. Twenty-five percent of undergraduates are involved in this part-time employment contract and the average earnings from college work for the school year are $1,200. Approximately forty-six percent of all undergraduates receive some form of financial aid, including Parents PLUS loans. Aside from Athletic Grants-in-Aid, non-need-based loan programs, and special scholarships, all undergraduate financial aid is based on financial need. To qualify for financial aid, entering students must complete and submit a Free Application for Federal Student Aid (FAFSA) and a Financial Aid Statement (FAS) by March 1.

GRADUATES

Under a massive oak behind the Rotunda, I, along with the close friends I have made over the last four years, lean together, a blur of caps, gowns, and tassels. The camera snaps one last time before I take my first steps in the procession that marks the end of our undergraduate education. As the May morning stretches lazily towards a steamy afternoon, I descend the steps of the Rotunda and gaze out over the lawn, now overflowing with a colorful mass of proud parents, camera-wielding grandparents, and wide-eyed siblings. Later, at my major ceremony, I hold out my hand and receive the long roll of paper that justifies and attests to all of the cramming, sleepless nights, three-hour finals, and fifteen-page papers of the last few years. Stepping off the stage, no longer a student, I realize that the diploma I clutch is not only a consummation of the past, but what will now also be a powerful key to my future.

PROMINENT GRADS

Since its foundation by one of the most famous presidents in American history, UVa has attracted and schooled many of the nation's notable political leaders, including President Woodrow Wilson; Senators Robert and Edward Kennedy, John Warner, Charles Robb, and Christopher "Kit" Bond; Congressman L.F. Payne; and Governors George Allen, Gerald Baliles, B. Evan Bayh III, James Gilmore, Angus King, and Lowell Weicker. Others include:

- **Lewis Allen, Broadway Producer**
- **Hanan Ashrawi, Palestinian Spokeswoman**
- **Katie Couric, Television Personality**
- **Mark Johnson, Movie Producer**
- **Edgar Allan Poe, Writer/Poet**
- **Walter Reed, Medical Pioneer**
- **Tom Shadyac, Hollywood Producer**

In a typical year, UVa awards nearly 3,000 bachelor's degrees. Among those graduates, the most popular majors are commerce, English, psychology, and biology. More than 500 companies recruited on grounds last year.

SUMMING UP

So ask yourself, why would you want to attend UVa? Because of its high rankings, its rigorous standards, and its feasible tuition? Obviously. Because you would have the chance to take a poetry seminar with former U.S. poet laureate Rita Dove, or a class on race relations from civil rights activist Julian Bond, or a political science lecture with renowned political analyst Larry Sabato? Of course. Because of the academic opportunities, including honors programs, student-run newspapers, magazines, and radio stations? Absolutely. Or even because of its outstanding Office of Career Planning and Placement, which offers internships, externships, résumé and job search guidance, and even arranges interviews with major companions on Grounds? Positively. Maybe because of the richness of UVa's history and tradition, from its creation by one of the most important men in America's past to its unique continuation of distinguished customs such as the student-run honor system or the benevolent and mysterious secret societies? Definitely. Is it because the school is located in the heart of a charming city from which you can drive for ten minutes and be in some of the most beautiful, rural scenery in the country? Certainly. Aside from all of this, you realize that you want to attend UVa because of all the little things, from painting Beta bridge, or attending the Restoration Ball, to working for Madison House, or living in La Maison Française, which make any student who attends this university a member of a community and a part of an experience that stretches far beyond a four-year education.

❑ *Larisa Barry, B.A.*

VASSAR COLLEGE

Vassar College
Poughkeepsie, NY 12601

(914) 437-7300, (800) 827-7270
Fax: (914) 437-7063

E-mail: admissions@vassar.edu
Web site: http://www.vassar.edu

Enrollment

Full-time ❑ women: 1,412
❑ men: 873

Part-time ❑ women: 51
❑ men: 25

INTRODUCING VASSAR

Matthew Vassar knew something about the school of life. So does Meryl Streep.

When the upstate New York brewer/philanthropist opened Vassar College's Main Building in 1865 as one of the country's first women's colleges, he set the cornerstone for an institution that thrives on a philosophy of education in the broadest sense of the word. When the award-winning actress, who graduated from Vassar in 1971, returns to speak or to teach on campus, she talks to students—about discovering that celebrity can't compare to the feeling of holding her firstborn child or about holding on to her college relationships.

What these two impressive figures say about the school that they both directly or indirectly represent is that a Vassar education, if you let it, can bring you on an enlightening journey through the lecture halls of academia. It can also lead you through the classroom to finding a place in the community. You can discover amazing possibilities in a place so academically strong. And you can taste the value of coming home after a harrowing exam to fall onto the shoulders of your housemate, who you know will bring you coffee again the next time you begin to edge dangerously toward preexam sleep.

In opening minds to the real possibility of women's higher education at a time when universities existed as bastions of learning for men only, Vassar began a tradition that still flows through the campus: a tradition of strengthening individual minds toward higher collective goals, while cultivating an ability to appreciate the importance of relationships. Today, 132 years later, and twenty-eight years after the admission of men, there is still a vibrant current of individualism that splashes the scenic Hudson Valley campus like the multimedia student projects that dot the tree-lined paths and the people-crammed College Center. Within the Vassar experience, it is possible to savor single moments forged by people coming together, while pursuing your dream to write the great American novel, to direct an Academy Award-winning film, to make the All-American team, to discover the cure.

The Campus

The good-intentioned brewer probably had no idea that his women's college would grow into a place where students might find the freedom to discover new ways to look at their ideas of self. Yet the founder's sense of innovation is celebrated to this day throughout the now 1,000-acre arboretum. The stunning campus he built in the heart of the Hudson Valley houses ninety-eight percent of the student body within its nine residence halls, town houses, and terrace apartments. Vassar boasts three theaters among the classroom buildings and residence halls, a collection of more than 14,000 paintings, sculptures, prints, drawings, and photographs in the Francis Lehman Loeb Art Gallery, and a brand new observatory overlooking Sunset Lake.

The founder and his profession as brewer are the namesakes for the sports teams (The Brewers) and for the legendary on-campus dance club known as Matthew's Mug (commonly referred to as simply The Mug). Annually, the college honors Matthew's birthday with Founder's Day, a wildly anticipated, campus-wide outdoor festival of music, food, dancing, games, rides, films, and fireworks. These celebrations are also prime examples of the way that Vassar students welcome challenge and demand high academic performance of themselves, while remaining equally dedicated to the motto of "all work and no play make Vassar a dull place."

Academics

Vassar's individually focused academic curriculum can be concentrated on a single discipline, an interdepartmental or multidisciplinary program, or an independent program. The academics can be rigorous, but Vassar students know the importance of making time to savor a night or two at the Dutch Cabin, the off-campus bar that is frequented by Vassar kids and town residents alike.

Traditions

Vassar celebrations are as varied as its eclectic student body, as the mood of individuality might suggest. You may find yourself walking home from dinner at a professor's house, swirling with thesis ideas from the conversation and breathing in the many stars you can view above the lush residential campus. (Vassar's setting, three miles from Poughkeepsie's city center, makes for great night skies.) There is a celebration of larger traditions, such as Serenading, an early fall competition during which underclass students either revere or disrespect the senior class through originally composed songs. Traditions live long at Vassar: from the familiar mealtime clinking of glasses that accompanies announcements of upcoming lectures, concerts, shows and games, to the annual Kente Cloth ceremony, during which seniors of color receive a traditional cloth while speaking about their Vassar experience.

Though Vassar continues to recognize traditions that weave a brilliant rose and gray fabric through campus life, the attitude on the Po'town campus is not one of rigidity. (The rose and gray school colors were chosen to represent the dawning of women's education through the gray of exclusion.) Change has always been welcome throughout Vassar's hallowed halls, even to the extent that national historic landmarks are remodeled. Main Building, a landmark modeled after the Tuileries in Paris, recently underwent renovations of mixed review. Some students refer to the main lobby as Taco Bell, in reference to the fast-food decor ceiling that appeared two summers ago. The same Main Building, which currently houses a residence hall and the College Center, is host to several rumors that Jane Fonda once rode a motorcycle through its wide hallways during her Vassar days.

Unquestionably, the tolerant attitude that emerges from the Vassar classroom steeps the cafe, the All Campus Dining Center (affectionately known as ACDC) and the dorms with the spirit that tells incoming students and seniors alike that they have found a place that will give them the freedom to teach themselves. In the classes they choose and in the relationships that they forge with community members, with fellow students, or with the immensely accessible faculty (eighty percent live on or within a two-mile radius of campus), all 2,250 Vassar students can discover a community that wasn't afraid to say, way back in 1865, that women were allowed.

Coeducation

Based on that tradition of independence, Vassar declined Yale's invitation to merge, instituting its own coed policy in 1969. So where does all this hype about Vassar's women-centered history leave the coeducational scene of today? How does the current ratio of forty percent male to sixty percent female serve to define the Vassar Man and the Vassar Woman? Some make the "quality not quantity argument" when discussing the somewhat unequal ratio of males to females. Most refuse to define, because labels don't set well with Vassar students. With the small size of the school, the social scene can feel slightly claustrophobic sometimes. Yet no matter what you are seeking, chances are you'll find someone at Vassar who is willing to listen and accept.

Overall, the coed, private liberal arts college that emerges today demands an attitude that cultures must respect each other, sexual preferences will be celebrated, and financial backgrounds will not dictate privilege here. The student body profile for the class of 2001 is composed of twenty-four percent students of color, sixty percent from public high schools, forty percent from private and parochial schools, twenty-eight percent from New York State, sixty-seven percent from out of state, and five percent from out of the country.

For many of the recipients of the approximately 620 B.A.s and B.S.s handed over each year, Vassar remains a place to find skills for the sharpest of minds and the most creative of spirits. It's also a place to feel unafraid to be yourself. Whether you are a drama-rama, a campus patroller, an athlete, a bio-chem major, a writer for the weekly *Miscellany News,* (and most likely, if you go to Vassar, you are several of the above), Vassar's tolerant attitude, challenging curriculum, hands-on faculty, and inexhaustible resources give you the tools to flex all the muscles of yourself, to develop ones you may have never known you had, and to exercise them in order to create your own Vassar experience.

ADMISSIONS REQUIREMENTS

It's difficult to define excellence here because we don't define it based on sameness. We define it on what makes someone stand out, what makes someone uniquely different enough to thrive at Vassar.

The current Vassar Student Association president offered this statement in response to a visiting alum's question about how Vassar defines excellence. Indeed, the variety of students on a campus are the best measure of a school's success. Vassar's accomplished merger of talented students from all over the globe comes not only from a search for academic excellence, but from a commitment to finding students who each hold something unique and exciting beneath their grades and test scores.

The Application

The application for admission, which requires a $60 fee, speaks to this effort to find the whole person who is applying to Vassar. In addition to the usual essay, test scores, and high school transcripts, Vassar asks students to fill out an optional section entitled "Your Space." Admissions officers have received responses as varied as scores to applicant-composed operas and sketches of original artwork. One notorious "Your Space" story tells of a brave incoming freshman who taped a pack of gum to his application and wrote, "Here is a refreshing snack for you to enjoy while you read my application." Throughout the first few ice-breaking weeks, witty and irreverent Vassar first-year students often swap stories of how they filled their "Space." The college store sold blank white T-shirts for several years that featured only an arrow pointing to the wearer and the words "Your Space" printed across the back. The "Your Space" idea, from one's first encounter with the Vassar's application, exemplifies the way in which Vassar truly becomes your space if you have something unique with which to fill it.

Of course, academic performance is essential for admission to Vassar. Of the 4,765 applicants to the class of 2001, forty-two percent were accepted. Eighty-six percent represent the top twenty percent of their high school class. The College Board middle fifty percent score range in this new Vassar class was 1240–1440 for composite SAT I scores and 28–32 for ACT.

Vassar does not prescribe a specific secondary school program, but applicants are expected to have elected the most demanding available courses. The candidate should report four years of English, including both literature and continuous practice in writing. Other required high school courses include four years of mathematics, at least three years of laboratory science, and two years of social science with a minimum of one year of history. Vassar also looks for three years of one ancient or modern foreign language or two years of one language and two of a second.

Candidates for the freshman class must take the SAT I and any three SAT II: Subject tests. Alternatively, candidates may take the ACT. All tests should be completed no later than December of the senior year of secondary school.

Applications and all supporting materials must be submitted by January 1. Applicants are notified in early April, and candidates to whom admission is offered must respond by May 1. For those candidates who have concluded that Vassar is a clear first choice, Vassar has two Early Decision deadlines: November 15 and January 1.

Transfer Students

Transfer students from two- and four-year institutions are typically admitted as transfers into the sophomore or junior class for matriculation each fall. The college also enrolls a few midyear transfer students.

Interviews

For incoming freshmen and transfer students alike, interviews are not required but may be helpful to applicants seeking more information about the college. On-campus interviews are only available for children and grandchildren of alumnae/i, but any applicant can request a local interview with an alumnae/i admission representative.

Web Site

The college has an extensive web site devoted to admission (www.vassar.edu). A campus visit, including an Admissions Office information session and campus tour, can provide a hands-on Vassar profile. One student spoke of her campus visit as the turning point in her decision-making process:

I had my heart set on another place—a big university in a big city—when I visited a friend who was a freshman at Vassar. I'd been admitted to Vassar, but I had also been accepted to the school that I thought I'd wanted to attend all of my life. I visited Vassar just to check things out and to visit my friend.

I fell completely in love with the people, the academic flexibility, the professors who spoke with me about my interests, and the breathtaking campus. I thought, "This library is so beautiful. This is where I want to study for my exams for the next four years!" I went home and changed my "yes" on the reply card for the other university to a "no," and changed the "no" on my Vassar reply card to a "yes." I had to Fed Ex my replies in order to meet the May 1 deadline. My family thought I'd never done anything so impulsive! I've never regretted it for a minute.

ACADEMIC LIFE

Circling the town houses, a group of Vassar-owned houses for juniors and seniors located on the edge of the campus, a recent Vassar graduate reflected on her comparative academic experiences. Fall had begun to settle across Poughkeepsie, dressing Vassar's campus in vibrant fall hues, as this visiting graduate shared, "Now that I'm in grad school, I realize that my work after Vassar isn't so difficult. Graduate school seems all right compared to what I did here."

Challenging and stimulating, yes. Unbearable, no. The Vassar faculty is unbelievably supportive and accessible, encouraging the kind of one-on-one, individually cultivated study that is unique to a school of Vassar's small size and large resource pool. Working with a faculty advisor, each student creates a personal study program. Opportunities for exploration and discovery are available through more than 1,000 courses, twenty-seven departmental majors, sixteen interdepartmental or multidisciplinary programs, and the option to design an independent program. The curriculum is somewhat like one of those "Choose Your Own Adventure" books, with several paths from which to choose.

Course Requirements

While Vassar does not demand a core curriculum, students are required to take 134 units for the bachelor of arts degree. Each student must fulfill the freshman course requirement, the quantitative course requirement, and the foreign language requirement.

Students are required to take one course emphasizing oral and written expression. Known as the freshman course requirement, this writing-intensive course can be selected across disciplines. As an introduction to the Vassar experience, these courses are limited to nineteen first-year students per class, a size typical of the Vassar classroom. Engaging topics such as Perspectives on the Global Village and Civilization in Question are offered to satisfy this broad-based requirement.

All students must complete a quantitative analysis requirement by the end of the sophomore year. To complete this course requirement, students have a choice of classes across the curriculum, including mathematics, economics, computer science, laboratory science, and psychology.

Finally, all students must demonstrate foreign language proficiency. A wide range of language and area studies programs, from Greek to Swahili, build a base for the 150-plus Vassar students who take part in global education through the Study Away Program. Many choose study abroad programs sponsored by other American colleges, which are approved for Vassar credit. Some participate in one of seven Vassar-sponsored programs (in Spain, England, Ireland, Germany, France, Italy, and Morocco). The opportunity to "Study Away" is so popular that in recent years, Metcalf, the college counseling service, has provided a support group for returning students who are readjusting to school after such life-changing experiences. Vassar also sponsors exchange programs with other American colleges and universities, including Amherst, Bowdoin, Dartmouth, Howard, Smith, Spelman, Wellesley, and others.

Declaring a Major

By the end of the sophomore year, most Vassar students declare a major. Four options are available for the pursuit of the degree: concentration in a single department such as English; interdepartmental programs such as biopsychology; multidisciplinary programs such as urban studies; or individually authored courses in the independent program. Within the major, requirements range from ten to eighteen courses. In a recent graduation, the most popular majors were English, psychology, film, art, political science, sociology, biology, history, economics, and drama.

In addition to a major concentration, a student can embark upon an optional correlate sequence, somewhat like choosing and completing a minor. Consisting of six courses, the correlate sequence provides the chance to organize classes outside of one's major, progressing toward advanced work under an additional advisor.

Advisors

The correlate advisor, the major advisor, and the pre-major advisor (assigned until a student decides on an area of concentration) are key to Vassar's advising system. The advice network is enhanced by deans, class advisors, individual faculty members, preprofessional advisors (for students pursuing careers in health professions and law), and house fellows. One or two faculty members, known as house fellows, and their families live in each of the residence halls. These professors are often found munching a Nilda's Cookie (a famous contributor to the extra pounds affectionately known as the "freshman fifteen") in the Retreat, an on-campus snack bar that is popular for meals. The ten-to-one ratio of students to professors and the average class size of seventeen allows for wonderful relationships with the impressive 200-member faculty. It's not uncommon to knock on a house fellow's door in the evening, just as you would visit a hallmate, or to find your history professor in your dorm parlor for an engaging discussion of Russian literature.

Facilities

This human network set up for academic and personal support is enhanced by the resources of the libraries and academic computing and information services. Vassar's main library, standing regally on campus, is often cited as inspirational. The gothic stone structure is bejeweled by stained glass windows (one of which depicts a scene of the first female student to ever receive her doctorate). The sun setting behind its towers, fanning out across the sprawling lawn, is the envy of all college view book cover photos.

One English major claimed that the library setting actually encouraged him academically:

> *I had a class with my favorite professor in the tower room of the library. It was called Rewriting the Text, and we read Austen and Ovid and Homer among shelves covered with seemingly ancient books. The leather-bound books in the room and the gargoyles outside of the stained glass window, combined with Professor Weedin's passion for his subject, really inspired me. Professor Weedin is the kind of professor who clutches the* Aeneid *to his heart when he talks about it.*

Nearly one million volumes strong, the library is experiencing an ambitious extension now and in the years to come. Primary materials, manuscripts, rare books, and archives are partnered with extensive service of CD-ROMs, electronic database searches, and access to millions of articles, bibliographies, and college library catalogs via national and international networks.

Computers

Electronic resources bind the entire campus—from the library to the dorm rooms—with extraordinary access. Those who do not bring computers to campus, where they can access e-mail and complete research from their rooms via Ethernet, have twenty-four-hour access in every residence hall via clusters of Macintosh and PowerMac computers in public areas. Clusters are also conveniently located in the College Center, the library, and in academic buildings. Overall, the campus computer center supports more than five hundred Macintoshes, PCs and Unix workstations throughout the campus. Every student has access to a free e-mail account.

An elated senior who completed his thesis offered:

I wrote all eighty-nine pages of my undergraduate thesis in the computer center. There was a Mac in the corner where I practically set up a living space every day. I think people just sensed that they should leave me to my thesis computer in the academic computer center if they saw me coming. It was like, "Move. Senior writing thesis coming into lab!" I think it's so great that I could successfully complete four years, actively computing and gaining computer literacy (at all hours of the day and night), without ever leaving the campus and without the expectation to buy a computer of my own.

Eighty nine pages, one million volumes, 2,250 students from fifty states and thirty countries—it all boils down to a campus, a student body, and an academic program that can satisfy your needs and offer many opportunities for explorations with others.

SOCIAL LIFE AND ACTIVITIES

A student tour guide popped out of her chair to meet a prospective student's parent and exuded more energy and enthusiasm than seemed humanly possible for a college student so early in the morning. After explaining that she'd been awake for some time working on a paper for her education class, rehearsing a student-produced play, and volunteering at a literacy program at a local prison, she was asked by the parent when she finds time to sleep. "Sleep?" she echoed, as if the concept were foreign to her. "I'll have the rest of my life to sleep. There's just too much to do while I'm here."

Residences

Beyond the myriad activities that make up Vassar's culture, students do sleep, and they catch their zzz's in places that are central to their social lives. Nearly all students choose to live on campus for all four years in nine residence halls that are home to almost eighty percent of students from all classes. Each house is self-governed and self-defined. Speaking generally, Josscelyn House is home to many a party; Jewett is known for its artsy crowd; Lathrop and Davidson tend to house a lot of student leaders and studious studiers; Strong is all women and appropriately named; Noyes's inhabitants are similar to its architecture—quirky students who can be found with science fiction in their hands; Ferry House is a student-run cooperative residence largely inhabited by vegetarians, vegans, and student activists. Another twenty percent—all upperclassmen and women—live in town houses and terrace apartments in groups of four or five students. These houses are unique living spaces, where juniors and seniors have the chance to live closely with their friends.

Also in the residence halls are peer advisors known as student fellows. Like resident advisors, they live nearby, but their responsibility is to provide nonjudgmental support for first-year and transfer students who are dealing with issues from academics to homesickness to forging new relationships. One new student explained:

> *My student fellow was there when I ran to his room at two in the morning frantic about a paper that was due the next day. He came to the Computer Cluster and brought me some coffee as well as moral support. He was there when I was struggling with an eating disorder. He came to my first performance with my* a cappella *group. That kind of instant support when you arrive as a new student is invaluable. And it provides friendships that sustain you throughout your time here.*

Clubs and Organizations

The student fellows often work on de-stressing such busy students, because there is so much to fill their space at Vassar. The college's more than eighty clubs and organizations are student-created and sustained via the Vassar Student Association (VSA), a government of elected students. The list of organizations focused on the performing arts (some of which include Philaletheis, Ebony Theater Ensemble, jazz ensemble, six *a cappella* groups), publications (*The Miscellany News*, *the Vassar Daily*), cultural/religious groups (BiGALA, Black Student Union, Jewish Union, Poder Latino, Asian Students Association), and service/political action groups (Hunger Action Committee, AIDS Education Committee, and Amnesty International, to name a few) is never complete because students are always forming new groups. Though it is nearly impossible to define one typical Vassar student, if there is one standard across the board, the Vassar student is involved—and busy. Friends are always flying by one another on the path to a practice, rehearsal, meeting, or event. They could be on their way to a lecture given by speakers like First Lady Hillary Rodham Clinton (who visited the campus in 1997) or to a game played by one of the twenty-two varsity teams, or one of the many intercollegiate club teams or intramural teams.

Sports

At the varsity level, Vassar competes in NCAA Division III against Amherst, New York University, Wesleyan, and others. Club teams like cycling, equestrian, and rugby fare as well as the varsity teams with respective All-Americans and national championships. Intramural sports offer involvement with the Brewers at all levels of competition. Each team takes advantage of Walker Field House, currently 42,250 square feet of uninterrupted playing space, weight rooms, and a six-lane swimming pool. Dance studios, squash courts, fourteen tennis courts, playing fields, and a nine-hole golf course grace the campus. The space is soon to expand; ground will be broken for an extension to Walker Field House in June 1998.

Campus Life

So much of campus life is contained on the campus—with ample athletic facilities, an on-campus pub/dance club, a cafe, a kiosk where students can charge Starbucks coffee to their meal plan, two dining options, drama department and student produced plays, a nightly film series, a Speaker's Series that has included Tom Wolfe and Joceleyn Elders, and a campus entertainment organization that brings big names like Ani Difranco, Billy Joel, and A Tribe Called Quest to the Vassar stage. Some Mug rats (as those who are regulars at the campus pub are lovingly called) manage to spend every weekend on campus. In fact, most Vassar students spend every weekend on campus.

The Mug, it should be mentioned, is a phenomenon in itself. All students have the freedom to dance and socialize there, but only students of legal age (with two forms of ID) can be braceleted to take advantage of the bar. The line can be a killer after midnight on weekends, as house music pumps from the steamy little basement pub. The Mug is open all week long for jazz nights and happy hours. By senior year, it becomes a place where friends meet at darkened corner tables with amaretto sours (only $2.50 for the kind of mixed drink that hurts your throat) and beer to commiserate about their theses. For underclass men and women, a lot of scheming and who-is-going-home-with-who-ing occurs among young girls in tank tops.

Off-Campus Life

Poughkeepsie's night life is not particularly exciting, but there are a host of restaurants, a few choice bars, and a wonderful cafe just outside of the college gates. (Stacey's scones at Cobbablu Bakery Cafe on College Avenue are out of this world!) The Hudson Valley also provides amazing opportunities for Vassar's Outing Club and for individual hikers, bikers, swimmers, and outdoor enthusiasts. Culture, shopping, and movies are not far at the Bardavon Opera House and the Poughkeepsie Galleria Mall, but students must be aware that Poughkeepsie buses stop running around 6 P.M. and cabs can be expensive, so it's nice to befriend someone who has a car. All students have the option of keeping a car on campus.

The proximity to New York City allows for a best-of-both worlds feel to Vassar. At the end of the Metro North commuter rail line, Poughkeepsie has the collegiate feel of an upstate campus, where academics and campus life can be a student's focus. When Broadway shows, East Village piercings, West Village shopping, Central Park rollerblading, and Upper East Side museum browsing call you away, the train takes about an hour and forty-five minutes to get you there and it's a $19 round-trip. Many departments use the city as a resource as well. The art history department sends students to the Metropolitan Museum of Art and the urban studies department takes trips to Sunnyside.

City lover, nature buff, cultural diva—it's there for you. Just catch a passing glimpse of the rainbow of flyers waving at you as you run to class. And running students is what you'll see after sleeping through your alarm recovering from a Thursday night (when the weekend begins at Vassar) at the Mug.

FINANCIAL AID

Vassar devotes a tremendous share of its institutional resources to financial aid—over $17 million in college funds in a recent year. Financial aid is only need-based and sixty percent of students receive it, with over fifty percent of first-year students receiving scholarship funds directly from Vassar. For many years, Vassar adhered to a need-blind admissions approach. Students who demonstrated an academic and extracurricular performance worthy of admission to Vassar were admitted without consideration of their financial need. In 1997, due to increasing financial challenges, Vassar officially adopted a need-sensitive approach, one that would allow for need-blind admission for most of the class, with ability to pay a consideration for only a small portion of the class, if any. Speakouts were staged in the College Center. A group of students protested to the Board of Trustees when the board visited campus. The class of '97 made scholarships and financial aid a main focus of their class gift to the college. For many Vassar students, generous aid packages are the reason that a Vassar education has been a part of their lives.

When the class of 2001 was admitted as the first class to be accepted under the new need-sensitive plan, Vassar fortunately did not have to drastically reduce the number of aid recipients.

It remains Vassar's policy to meet one hundred percent of the financial need for as many students as possible. The mood around campus since the change to need-sensitive has been one of caution. Yet the experience of the recently admitted class seems to allay some of the fears among upperclass men and women who experienced Vassar's official shift away from completely need-blind admissions. The Admissions Office stands by the claim ". . . more often than not, the college is able to assist all admitted students who meet the application deadline."

Financial aid remains a commitment on campus, for faculty and students alike. It's not easy for families or for the college to finance an education at Vassar. But it's heartening to know that students—aid recipients or not—will raise their voices and shout that they believe in the quality of a Vassar education for all students.

GRADUATES

We are leaving our home behind us, and it is no less difficult than it was four years ago. Today is not just the happiest day of our lives; it is the happiest sad day of our lives.

A recent class president gave these words at his commencement, touching a rain-soaked crowd of graduates and their families with a truth that holds for many who leave the serenity of Vassar to embark on their next journey. Equipped with the tools of a Vassar education, seventy-five percent of most classes enter the work force or pursue the Peace Corps, internships, and travel; twenty-five percent begin graduate study immediately.

Within five years of graduation, about eighty percent of Vassar grads continue toward advanced study, accepted regularly at America's most prestigious schools of law, medicine, business, and education. More than seventy percent of Vassar medical school applicants are regularly accepted to schools like Columbia, Harvard, Penn, Stanford, and Yale. A recent study ranks Vassar eighth among the nation's four-year independent colleges in the number of Ph.D.s earned by graduates, particularly in scientific fields.

Vassar assists many graduate pursuits by providing over $100,000 each year in fellowships to qualified graduates. Many grads also receive Marshall, Fulbright, Watston, Goldwater, and Beinecke scholarships.

PROMINENT GRADS

- **Edna St. Vincent Millay, '17, Poet**
- **Elizabeth Bishop, '34, Poet**
- **Jacqueline Kennedy Onassis, (attended), Former First Lady**
- **Jane Fonda, (attended), Actress, Political Activist**
- **Mary Richardson, '65, Former Commissioner, Internal Revenue Service**
- **Geraldine Laybourne, '69, President, Disney/ABC Cable Networks**
- **Jane Smiley, '71, Author**
- **Meryl Streep, '71 Actress**
- **Steven Korn, '75, Executive, CNN News**
- **Drew Zingg, '76, Musician**

SUMMING UP

The morning I left campus after graduation, my best friend and I were saying good-bye after a sleepless night of packing up our TA. Before climbing into her cab, she hugged me and said, "Thank you for Vassar." Between tears, I realized that this is what made this place mine: the relationships that strengthened us through years of crazy exams and fat papers, through nights of fried food at the Acropolis Diner, through professors who inspired us and professors who made us feel like pulling out all of our hair, through nights at the Mug and parties in the dorms and speakers like Meryl Streep, who told us to go out there and get the world.

I miss my best friend like crazy now that we don't share an apartment on our beautiful campus. But I think we're both listening to Meryl—and we both carry a little Vassar with us everywhere we go.

Vassar is a school that has always been unafraid to take a chance—opening its doors to women only, refusing to merge with its brother school, admitting men, attracting students who stand out but refuse to sit down when they have something to say. It's not a perfect place, and changes, bad and good, are happening at Vassar.

Walking around campus a few years ago, you might have seen more purple hair than you will today. Some lament an admissions trend that seems to be accepting a more "William's-type student." (Homogeneity will hopefully never be a code at Vassar. It is one thing that doesn't belong there.)

The social politics of Vassar boast words like safe space and tolerance, but issues crop up all over the aware campus. The HomoHop, an annual dance party sponsored by the campus Bisexual, Lesbian and Gay Association was canceled once in the past few years due to conflicting politics about the purpose of the party as an educational tool for all sexual orientations. The Inter Cultural Center (the ICC) is beautiful space where black, Caribbean, Latino, Asian, and all students of color can go to relax, study, meet in groups, etc. All students enjoy the events of the ICC, especially during multicultural week, and multicultural lifestyles are rightfully celebrated and revered. Yet Vassar students still live in the world, and in the world, tensions and conflicts around race and ethnicity will rear their ugly heads. Fortunately, at Vassar, spaces are always created for open, liberal discussion.

Vassar women may complain that Vassar men are not the most romantic. Indeed, dating isn't as common as it may be at some other schools. Maybe because of the ratio, Vassar men can adopt a certain arrogance. But Vassar men and women alike come to this school aware of its herstory and its history. And there are some couples—of different orientations—who find happiness beneath those gorgeous sunsets.

All students, regardless of their love life (or lack thereof) will agree that student and academic life certainly won't leave you wanting. What makes Vassar unique, and so difficult for some to leave at the end of four years, is the way it lets you fill your space to truly make it a place of your own.

❑ *Rachel Weimerskirch, B.A.*

WAKE FOREST UNIVERSITY

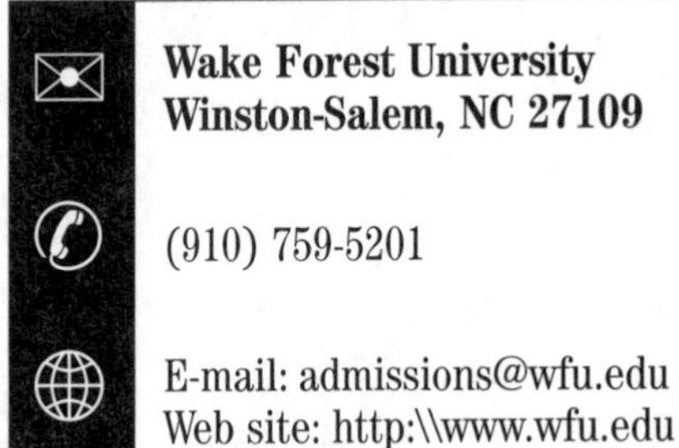

Wake Forest University
Winston-Salem, NC 27109

(910) 759-5201

E-mail: admissions@wfu.edu
Web site: http:\\www.wfu.edu

Enrollment

Full-time ❑ women: 1,808
❑ men: 1,778

Part-time ❑ women: 64
❑ men: 121

INTRODUCING WAKE FOREST

During orientation week at Wake Forest, one night is reserved for faculty to invite their first-year advisees to dinner. For most Wake students, this is only the first of dozens of opportunities they will have to spend time with their professors outside of class. During my freshman year, two of my classes were held at the homes of professors, located on the edges of campus. As part of another class, the professors took us all to see Twelfth Night. *I was surprised that during that first year, several of my professors invited the class into their homes. I remember in particular the evening my Italian teacher invited our class over for dinner. She and her husband had built their house to resemble the Italian homes they loved. The architecture blended with the authentic recipes and the sounds of the language to create the impression that we might actually be in Italy for the evening. In my mind, the truly remarkable thing about Wake Forest is that these kinds of occasions are quite common. Part of what it means to be a Wake student is to have the opportunity to have frequent contact with your professors. At graduation, I found myself looking forward to the departmental receptions, where I could introduce my family to the professors who had become my friends.*

At Wake Forest University, members of the faculty are beloved by students for their deep commitment to teaching and mentoring undergraduates. This emphasis on teaching, combined with Wake Forest's liberal arts curriculum requirements, small size, and beautiful self-contained campus, may make Wake Forest seem like a liberal arts college at first glance. But a closer look reveals that Wake is undeniably a university, with a university's wealth of resources, including state-of-the-art facilities and equipment, impressive library holdings, graduate and professional schools, and Division I sports.

Many Wake Forest alumni will tell you that this mix of small school liberal arts philosophy and big school resources creates the setting for an ideal undergraduate experience. With a 12-to-1 student-to-faculty ratio, more than 100 well-funded extracurriculars, and fewer than 4,000 undergraduates, it's easy for a Wake student to get involved with any field of study or extracurricular activity. And when a student does get involved, the immense resources of the university open many doors. For example, a student might do independent research with a physics professor in the laser lab, or go with an art professor on a university-sponsored trip to New York to buy art for the Wake Forest collection. Wake is a place where both personalized instruction and the tools for exploring any intellectual interest are readily available.

Wake Forest is located just outside of Winston-Salem, North Carolina, on a suburban campus characterized by expanses of green lawn, Georgian architecture, and flowering trees. The campus is strikingly beautiful, and students come to look forward to its seasonal changes: the spring daffodils lining the edge of the woods, the autumn leaves, the magnolias in full bloom, the rare snowfall. Wait Chapel, with its clock tower and its ivory-colored pillars, presides over the main quad, a reminder that Wake Forest was a Baptist-governed institution until 1986. Today, the university is a far more outward-looking and diverse place than the old Wake Forest, with students hailing from all over the United States and from more than thirty foreign countries. But the old sense of small-town friendliness and the focus on community linger. The campus is easily covered on foot in twenty minutes, and since the vast majority of students choose to live on campus for all four years, Wake Forest has the feeling of a very close-knit community. Social life also centers on the campus, whether in dorm rooms, the student center, or the fraternity and sorority lounges on the main quad.

Wake Forest is not so small that everybody knows everybody, but it is small enough that most students feel the urge to get away at intervals. The meadows and woodlands of Reynolda Gardens, adjacent to the main campus, provide the perfect place for picnics, jogging, rollerblading, and playing guitar on a sunny day. Winston-Salem, a city of 170,000 residents, offers several good restaurants, cafés, and parks, along with a few popular bars where students go to hear bands. The city also has far better cultural offerings than one would expect from a city of its size, thanks largely to the presence of the North Carolina School of the Arts, the South's premier arts conservatory. All students can have cars, and many do bring a car to campus at some point during their four years, the better to reach North Carolina's famous mountains and beaches, which are close enough for a weekend getaway.

People often think of Wake Forest as a southern school, and many of the region's distinctive traits, including sweet tea and southern accents, are to be found in abundance on campus. Fifty-eight percent of undergraduates come from Southern states (with about half of those coming from North Carolina), but the rest of the student body—and many of the faculty—bring their traits from other regions, making Wake Forest a fairly diverse place. Those who hail from other parts of the nation and other countries seem to enjoy some of the charms of living in the South, like year-round sunshine and unabashed friendliness, during their four year stay. But if the pace of southern living is relaxed, the academics are not. Students at Wake have a heavy work load, and they take their coursework seriously. Every student is required to spend the first two years satisfying divisional requirements in the natural and social sciences, the arts and humanities, and foreign language. The high quality of Wake's academic program has garnered national attention, and Wake Forest is increasingly mentioned as one of the very best places in the nation to get an undergraduate education.

Wake Forest's growing national reputation, in combination with several generous scholarship programs, is attracting some of the most talented students anywhere. Incoming students are bright, hard-working, and eager to join extracurricular activities. The required curriculum, with its emphasis on the pursuit of learning for its own sake, is designed to prod students to explore new fields of study, try out new hobbies, and consider a broad range of careers during their first two years. In the end, a significant number of Wake Forest's grads go on to careers in business, law, or medicine. Others build careers in such areas as the arts, scientific research, social work, academia, and government.

One way to get a sense of the Wake student body is to think about the variety of the places where students live. You've got the freshmen living on campus, in freshman dorms and freshman halls. Freshman hallways have this great feeling of all the kinds of people who come to Wake mixing and mingling, everybody from your preprofessional majors in Dockers to your black-clad Wake Radio disc jockeys. A lot of the freshmen live in substance-free housing, and the scene on those halls tends to be really creative and fun. Upperclassmen usually try to "block" with their friends, either in a section of a dorm affiliated with their fraternity or sorority or in an independent section. The Greek blocks tend to be near a lounge and some offices for that particular Greek organization, where members hang out quite a bit. The independent blocks often have their own little lounge areas, or share a big common area in a dorm, and people congregate there, too. A lot of relaxed hanging out takes place in rooms—guitar jams, watching your favorite shows, talking, listening to music. Then there's theme housing, either dorms or small houses where students come together based on shared interest in a language, or fine arts, or women's studies, etc. There are always new theme houses forming. The theme houses tend to have a more alternative atmosphere than the campus as a whole. Finally, you've got a small group of people, mostly seniors, who live off campus in nearby apartment complexes, who want a little more distance from Wake Forest. The thing is, as a Wake student, I went in almost every dorm and theme house on campus during my four years, and I think that's typical. Sure, you tend to hang out most with the people you live with, but the social scene is very fluid. You have to think of Wake as a place where there are a thousand small but distinctive groups—the painting students who hang out in the studio and the coffee shops downtown, the crowd of biology majors who like to go to the Outer Banks and do Habitat for Humanity, and so on. A single person tends to belong to several of these groups, which keeps things interesting, and makes it tough to generalize about Wake students.

Students choose Wake Forest for many reasons. Almost all are attracted by the beautiful campus and the genuine friendliness of the Wake Forest community. Most are impressed by Wake Forest's unique combination of the best aspects of both the small liberal arts college (access to professors, emphasis on teaching, liberal arts curriculum) and the large research university (tremendous facilities, state-of-the-art equipment, big-time sports). For students who like the feeling of a smaller school, but don't want to sacrifice the opportunities of a large university, Wake Forest is the ideal place to go to college.

ADMISSIONS REQUIREMENTS

Over the past decade, news of Wake Forest's outstanding academic program has been spreading beyond the South. *U.S. News and World Report* ranked Wake Forest one of America's top twenty-five national universities in 1997, and it is favorably evaluated in several other college guides. In recent years Wake's applicant pool has been growing, and competition for the 950 slots in the freshman class is keen. Slightly more than forty percent of applicants are accepted, and approximately thirty-five percent of those accepted decide to enroll. Early Decision is a commonly chosen option; recently, more than a fourth of the freshman class was made up of students accepted through Early Decision.

Admissions counselors at Wake Forest emphasize that they are more concerned about a student's high school record than about standardized test performance, although accepted students tend to be strong in both areas. Eighty-eight percent of recent incoming freshmen were ranked in the top fifth of their high school class. Most incoming freshmen performed very well on standardized tests, with eighty percent of the freshmen scoring over 600 on SAT I: Math, and seventy-nine percent scoring over 600 on SAT I: Verbal. But admissions staff place a great deal of emphasis on things other than test scores and grades. Leadership, extracurricular activities, and special talents are prized, and students with exceptional talents and achievements may be awarded one of Wake's extraordinarily generous merit scholarships (some of which require special applications).

Many on campus feel strongly that Wake Forest must do more to recruit students from diverse backgrounds. The administration has made a commitment to increasing the diversity of the student body, and Wake Forest's efforts are beginning to pay off. Recently, minority students made up eleven percent of the student body, and Wake is working actively to increase this proportion every year.

ACADEMIC LIFE

As a rule, classes at Wake Forest are small enough to allow you to get to know each person in the class. A few intro science courses have more than 100 students, but the vast majority of classes have less than thirty-five students, and even smaller courses are very common. In fact, you will sometimes find yourself in a class of a dozen people. On the whole, the faculty tends to encourage student participation in class discussions, and many professors reserve a portion of class time for student presentations, especially in the upper-level courses. The work load ranges from medium to heavy, and there are very few easy courses. Most weeknights are reserved for studying, and few students can afford to take the whole weekend off. The rigor pays off, though; Wake students go on to the nation's top graduate schools and find jobs with some of the most selective employers in the country.

Academic life at Wake Forest is divided into two halves: the first two years, when you spend all of your time becoming well-rounded, and the last two years, when you focus on your major and take electives. Not surprisingly, most students prefer the junior and senior years. On the other hand, many students find the first two years an invaluable opportunity to try out new fields and see what they really like. Students have flexibility within the long list of requirements for the first two years. Everybody has to take one course in fine arts, history, religion, and philosophy. In addition, three courses are required from each of the following categories: literature and the arts, the natural sciences and mathematics, and the social and behavioral sciences. The good news is that intro courses at Wake are typically very good. Because Wake professors genuinely love teaching, many of the best faculty members insist on teaching intro courses. And on the whole, faculty members devote as much time and attention to preparation of intro courses as they do to preparing their upper-level courses.

Study Abroad

Students must also take one foreign language through the literature level. The Romance languages are offered, along with German, Chinese, Japanese, and Russian. Although the language requirement proves to be one of the more difficult requirements, many students ease the pain by combining the requirement with study abroad. Wake Forest strongly encourages study abroad. The university owns residential centers in the Hampstead section of London and the Grand Canal in Venice, and offers programs in Dijon, France; Salamanca, Spain; and Tokai, Japan. Study opportunities are available in several other countries as well. To encourage a larger number of students to study overseas, Wake has recently committed additional funds to its study abroad scholarship program.

The requirements of the first two years are extensive, but Wake Forest does offer some flexible ways of meeting them. Advanced placement credit is accepted in lieu of many requirements, and interdisciplinary honors courses may sometimes be substituted for other required courses. In addition, a special program called the Open Curriculum admits a small number of very capable students each year. Open Curriculum students may substitute upper-level courses for intro courses in fulfilling their requirements.

Majors

B.A. and B.S. degrees are offered in thirty-three majors, including biology, business, communication, the arts, computer science, education, and the social sciences. At the end of the sophomore year, students declare a major, although many students change their mind again before graduation. In general, the more "practical" or preprofessional majors tend to enroll the most students. The most popular majors vary from year to year, but business, biology, and psychology tend to be among them. Students tend to be spread out pretty evenly across the departments, and every department has its fans. Because of the dispersion of the student body across majors, upperclassmen tend to be well-known to the faculty in their department, which allows them to arrange special independent projects. Some departments have special libraries or study areas where the majors like to congregate.

Faculty

All courses, with the exception of science and language laboratory sessions, are taught by full members of the faculty, ninety percent of whom hold doctorates. The faculty is diverse in terms of its politics, teaching philosophies, classroom styles, and grading schemes. Professors are similar in the way they facilitate open inquiry, the way they appreciate student initiative and curiosity, and their desire to continually improve as teachers and scholars. As a group, they are extraordinarily willing to meet with students outside of class and to write recommendations. Many of them also take on extra responsibilities, working one-on-one with students in independent research, or serving as advisors of student organizations.

Perhaps most importantly, faculty members serve as mentors and advisors to individual students. All students are assigned a student advisor and two faculty advisors during their time at Wake Forest. Advisors take their jobs seriously, and they are always available to help students find their way through the maze of requirements and schedules—or to talk about majors and minors, career paths, and grad school applications. Special advising is available for premed and prelaw majors. In addition, some staff members specialize in helping students to arrange independent studies in subjects not offered by departments, others in arranging internships and study abroad. Students who opt to seek a degree "with honors" in their discipline are assigned a special honors thesis advisor, with whom they work closely during their senior year.

Seminars

Wake Forest's focus on undergraduate teaching comes out in many features of its academic program. The freshman seminar program, begun last year, places every incoming student in a seminar of fifteen students, which is taught by a regular member of the faculty. Seminars focus on a single theme, such as medical ethics, film and culture, or the Internet and society. Through cyberspace, one seminar links Wake Forest students with scholars at the restored Globe Theatre in London. Another seminar program, the Interdisciplinary Honors Program, allows students the chance to participate in small seminars that examine important figures from different historical periods and different disciplines.

On-Campus Intellectual Events

The intellectual atmosphere of the campus is enhanced by the many university-wide events each year that bring outstanding lecturers and performers to campus. The Secrest Artist Series—free to students—brings top performers from music, dance, and drama to campus several times a year. Recent guests have included Itzhak Perlman, Wynton Marsalis, and The Netherlands Chamber Choir. A recent Year of the Arts celebration brought members of the Alvin Ailey Dance Company and actors James Earl Jones and Alec Baldwin to campus to teach master classes. The university's own Maya Angelou is frequently at the lectern or in the classroom. In addition, outstanding figures in academia and government frequently come to campus; in the past five years, two U.S. Supreme Court justices, a former president, and one vice presidential candidate have spoken at Wake Forest. At the popular culture end of the spectrum, Wake has welcomed director Jonathan Demme, comedian Chris Rock, and novelist Tom Clancy in recent years.

Facilities

Academic life is supported by top-notch facilities. The Z. Smith Reynolds Library has 1.3 million volumes, all-night study rooms, and countless comfortable chairs, tucked away in nooks all over the building. Soales Fine Arts Center contains music practice rooms with pianos, two theaters, a recital hall, a dance studio, a painting studio, a fine arts gallery, and facilities for printmaking, sculpture, and drawing. Several departments have special computing labs to assist students with advanced design or computation projects. All of the science buildings were recently renovated, and recent construction has expanded the classroom, study lounge, and office space for arts and humanities departments.

The Laptop Computer Program

In 1995 the university's trustees adopted the highly publicized "Undergraduate Plan," which provides even more resources for educating undergraduates. The plan provides additional funding for reducing class size, hiring more faculty, and increasing the amount of financial aid grants. As part of the plan, the university also introduced the freshman seminars, additional study-abroad scholarships, and the much-discussed laptop computer program. Through the laptop computer program, all incoming students receive an IBM laptop computer, the cost of which is covered by tuition. The residence halls and library are now outfitted with Ethernet connections, and most of the traditional computer labs are being phased out. For the most parts, students are pleased with the laptops and with the user support provided by the university, which includes technical RAs in the dorms, access via Ethernet connections, on-campus hardware experts, and a help desk hotline. The plan was somewhat controversial at the time of its adoption, and many students and faculty expressed concern that the emphasis on technology and the tuition increase would change Wake Forest fundamentally. But two years into the program virtually everyone on campus agrees that the plan has focused even more resources and attention on the university's primary mission of teaching undergraduates.

SOCIAL LIFE AND ACTIVITIES

Social life at Wake Forest centers on the campus. Fraternities and sororities, theme houses, residence hall councils, and various independent groups sponsor parties around campus every weekend night. And with two film series, a classical concert series, art openings, student plays, the Secrest Artist events, Demon Deacon sporting events, dance performances, and a Saturday Night Live- style comedy troupe, there's always something going on besides a party. Students enjoy going to "The Pit," the campus cafeteria, or Shorty's, a campus coffeehouse and gathering place. Also popular is the Benson University Center, the five-level student center opened in 1990 that houses everything from Pizza Hut and Taco Bell to a fitness center and student government offices. For students who want to get away, there are a handful of places in town that offer good alternative bands, both local and national, or the downtown scene: coffee shops and North Carolina School of the Arts performances.

New gatehouses that control access to campus operate from 10:00 P.M. to 6:00 A.M. Late-night visitors driving onto campus will find gates at two of the university's entrances. Wake Forest community members display stickers on their vehicles. Visitors must stop at the gate to identify themselves and their reason for being on campus. On the peaceful Wake campus, many students and faculty felt that the gates were unnecessary and created town/gown division; others felt that the gates would ensure the safety of the campus. At any rate, everyone seems to have adjusted to life with the gatehouses, and the campus remains an extremely safe one.

Athletics and Performing

Extracurriculars are a big part of life for most students. Thousands of students turn out for AGC basketball and football games, wearing gold and black and cheering, "Go Deacs!" Wake Forest is the second smallest school competing in Division I sports, but manages to be competitive. Victories are celebrated by "rolling the quad," a tradition of blanketing the campus with toilet paper. Wake Forest's men's basketball team claimed the AGC championship two years in a row, and several teams (including cross-country, golf, and tennis) have been nationally ranked.

Intramurals are extremely popular; they run pretty much year-round, in every sport imaginable, and leagues are created for different ability levels, so players of all kinds can enjoy the competition. Many students have their own show on the student radio station or TV station. The theater scene is remarkably active, with students directing and performing in one-acts and mainstage productions, and working on crews for both. Several student bands perform frequently, both on and off campus, while the classical musicians have plenty of options: three choral groups, orchestra, band, chamber groups, and a whole schedule of student recitals. Students of ballet and modern dance choreograph and perform their own work several times a year, and frequently work with guest choreographers. The debate team, consistently one of the top teams in the country, won the national tournament in 1996–97.

PARTIAL LISTING OF SPECIAL EVENTS, ONE WEEK AT WAKE FOREST, FALL 1997

- Fall Convocation: Bill Moyers, Journalist, Guest Speaker
- WFU Theater, *Much Ado About Nothing*
- Collegium Musicum, Renaissance Music Concert
- Student Comedy Troupe, Fall Show
- Museum of Anthropology Exhibit: "The Good Earth: Folk Art and Artifacts from the Chinese Countryside"
- Secrest Artist Series: Netherlands Chamber Choir
- University Jazz Ensemble Concert
- Art Exhibit: Famous Stage Designs
- Campus-Wide Card Tournament
- Philosophy Symposium: Jeremy Waldron, Columbia University, John Finnis, Oxford University
- Films showing on campus: *Ulee's Gold, The Preacher's Wife, Shine*
- Men's basketball, WFU vs. Georgetown
- Football, WFU vs. Florida State
- Women's Soccer, WFU vs. Chapel Hill
- Men's Soccer, WFU vs. Clemson

Clubs and Organizations

Students also belong to a wide variety of clubs and organizations, including service organizations, religious organizations, academic honor societies, political organizations, and special-interest clubs. Student government, Habitat for Humanity, the Black Student Association, the Volunteer Service Corps, and Intervarsity Christian Fellowship are among the most popular and active groups. Reflecting the school's motto, *Pro Humanitate,* hundreds of students volunteer regularly in the local community and some are engaged in international service projects as far away as Calcutta and Honduras. Also, each fall, the Volunteer Service Corps hosts Project Pumpkin, a Halloween festival that brings more than 1,000 children from community agencies to campus. Devoted groups of students spend long hours producing the award-winning campus newspaper, the *Old Gold and Black*, the yearbook, a literary magazine, and a journal of essays. Two literary/humanities clubs present informal lectures, poetry readings, a series of art/independent films, and other events linking academic life to life outside of class. It's easy to become involved with any student group, and many students start new clubs, with the help of student government funds set aside for organizations' expenses.

FINANCIAL AID

Wake Forest is committed to its need-blind admissions policy, and the university meets the demonstrated need of each student. Need is typically met through a combination of grants, loans, and work-study. About a quarter of all undergraduates work part-time, many of them in on-campus jobs with built-in study time.

There is no denying that Wake Forest is more expensive than it was a decade ago. Recent tuition hikes, most notably the large increase that accompanied the introduction of the laptop computer program, have driven costs up considerably. Where Wake was once priced within range of some state schools, it has now definitively joined the ranks of the higher-priced private schools. However, the university administration has worked actively to raise financial aid funds to keep pace with increases in tuition, reinforcing its commitment to admit students regardless of their ability to pay. And a Wake Forest education is still a good deal. Roughly one-third of Wake Forest students receive need-based aid. With an endowment greater than $600 million, Wake Forest is a financially secure institution and its students benefit from that security.

GRADUATES

During my senior year, I was invited to a meeting of the Half Century Club, a group of Wake alums who graduated at least fifty years ago. I couldn't believe how many people came back to Wake for the meeting. The alumni were so excited to be back at Wake Forest, and they took a genuine interest in me and in the other students who attended. The thing that I remember so clearly is how they had such fondness for Wake Forest, for the time they had spent there, and for their professors. Whenever you go to any alumni gathering, you get the strong feeling that by going to Wake, you have joined a close-knit community. It's a little like growing up together in the same small town. For all kinds of reasons, it's great to be an alumnus of a school that is so beloved by its graduates.

As private education costs climb, many students are increasingly concerned about life after college. The administration and faculty take that concern to heart; in fact, a large part of the impetus for the laptop computer program came from administrators' concerns about preparing Wake students to take twenty-first-century jobs. Wake's career services staff works diligently with individual students to plan summer internships and create job search strategies. Each year, more than 300 companies and organizations recruit on campus, and career information sessions are also held in other major cities. About half of each year's graduating seniors take their first jobs in business, banking, accountancy, or consulting, in places as close as Raleigh and as distant as the West Coast.

PROMINENT GRADS

- A.R. Ammons, Poet
- Wayne Calloway, Former Chairman and CEO, Pepsico
- Evelyn "Pat" Foote, Retired Brigadier General, U.S. Army
- Harold Hayes, Former Editor-In-Chief, *Esquire* magazine
- Al Hunt, Executive Washington Editor, *The Wall Street Journal*
- Penelope Niven, Biographer
- Arnold Palmer, Professional Golfer

About a third of each graduating class goes directly on to more school, whether graduate school or professional schools. The Wake Forest faculty is famous for their generosity in helping students to apply to graduate schools. Professors spend hours talking to students about how to choose the schools they will apply to, what kinds of research experiences might be helpful, and how to find funding. They also provide the essential recommendations. Wake graduates have a strong record of graduate and professional school acceptance (they are accepted to medical school at nearly twice the national average), and have competed successfully for even the most coveted postgraduate fellowships. Among the graduates of recent classes, Wake counts six Rhodes Scholars, two Mellon Fellows, and several National Science Foundation Fellows, Truman Scholars, and Rotary Scholars.

Although many Wake Forest students go on to careers in business, academia, medicine, government, social service, education, and law, countless others pursue less traditional routes. For example, recent issues of the alumni magazine have highlighted Wake graduates who work in the arts. Hundreds of graduates, spread throughout the United States and even abroad, now work full-time in creative professions—as authors, producers, artists, jewelry designers, musicians, and actors, among others. The rich variety of occupations that Wake graduates choose testifies to the lasting benefit of the liberal arts education, and the initiative and tenacity of the kind of person who chooses Wake Forest.

SUMMING UP

For students who want the kind of close-knit community afforded by a small school, but don't want to give up the advantages of university life, Wake Forest provides an opportunity to combine the two. The friendly, caring atmosphere of the campus-centered community allows students to feel connected to one another, to their professors, and ultimately to the school and its alumni. Wake Forest is large enough that you will never come close to meeting every student, but small enough for you to know most of the majors in your department by name. It's also small enough for you to have the experience of meeting someone interesting in the photography lab, then running into them in the cafeteria line and cementing the friendship. Wake is small enough for a single student to be able to dabble in any extracurricular, or register for any class. Classes are small enough that professors take a genuine interest in every student. The small classes also allow professors to do all the teaching, grading, and advising of the students in their courses, and enable professors to offer students almost unlimited access to their offices.

On the other hand, Wake Forest is large enough to have incredible facilities, excellent researchers and research opportunities, and Division I sports teams. Wake Forest is able to offer the full spectrum of courses, from Chinese Revolutionary Literature to Mime. It's large enough to have two radio stations, two theaters, more than two dozen pianos, a soccer stadium, a golf course, and almost every other facility you could want to support extracurriculars and sports. Wake's large library meets all but the most specialized research needs, and its extensive support staff can provide everything from personal counseling to computer repairs.

Of course, Wake Forest is not for everyone. Most students come to love the sense of community that Wake provides, but some students may find the small-school feeling stifling, or crave the kind of independence that is available only at a bigger school. Wake students enjoy the best elements of Southern friendliness and informality that continue to set the tone on campus, but this Southern character may be a turn-off to students looking for a different regional flavor, or a school with no distinct regional traits. Although Wake's rules governing parties, alcohol consumption, and other aspects of social life are determined in part by students and rarely interfere with social life, some students may seek a school where parties are not regulated and off-campus housing is more the norm. Finally, students who want a big city experience as part of their college education will not find it in Winston-Salem. While Winston-Salem is much bigger than many of the two-stoplight towns that other top schools call home, it is no New York City.

If, however, you are looking for a smaller, close-knit setting, a learning community, in which to spend the next four years, consider paying Wake Forest a visit. If you decide to pursue learning at Wake, you will have everything at your disposal: caring professors who love to teach and mentor, all the necessary resources, and a relaxed, friendly social scene to go back to after the homework is done. If you are looking for a school that brings together the best attributes of big and small schools in an incredibly beautiful environment, Wake Forest may be the place for you.

❑ *Joy Goodwin, B.A.*

WASHINGTON AND LEE UNIVERSITY

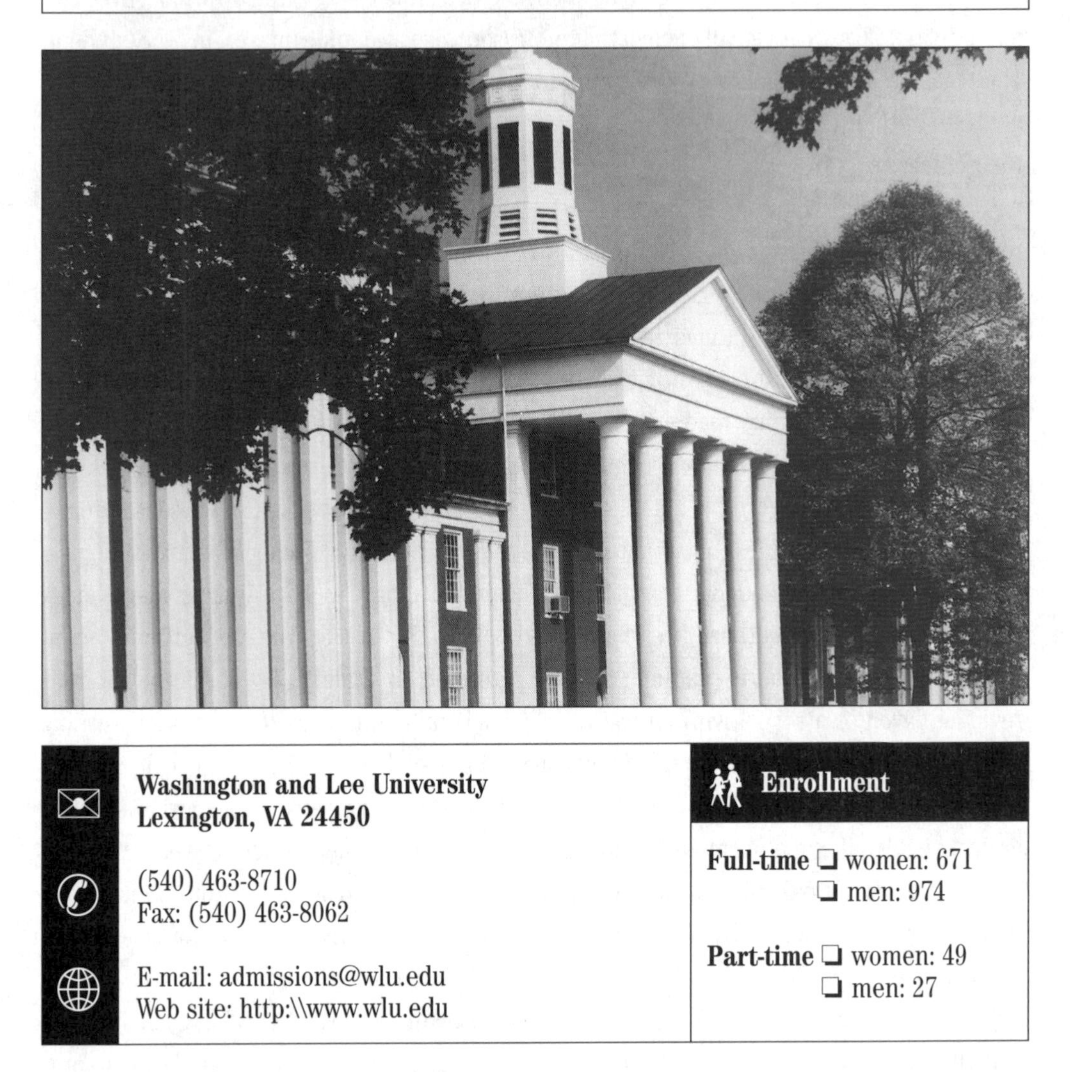

Washington and Lee University
Lexington, VA 24450

(540) 463-8710
Fax: (540) 463-8062

E-mail: admissions@wlu.edu
Web site: http:\\www.wlu.edu

Enrollment

Full-time ❑ women: 671
❑ men: 974

Part-time ❑ women: 49
❑ men: 27

INTRODUCING WASHINGTON AND LEE

On a crisp fall afternoon in Virginia, students walk up the grassy slope to Washington and Lee's colonnade, rows of white columns that define the face of the campus's red brick buildings. The students walk in the shadows of the columns and climb the worn steps of Payne Hall. Just inside their classroom is a bronze plaque commemorating the space where General Robert E. Lee took his oath of office as president of the school in 1865. The open windows frame more students passing along the back campus. Some enter Leyburn Library, a wide complex of concrete and brick. Others open the doors to the Great Hall of the new Science Center; vaulted, sky-lit ceilings expose balconies for each of the floors above, where more students move to and from completely modern classrooms and laboratories.

As these students cross Washington and Lee University's picturesque campus, they see its balance of the old and the new—traditions and changes. Founded in 1749, the university boasts a long and rich history. The school won critical support in 1796 when George Washington donated $20,000 to its endowment. (Washington's gift was the largest ever made to a private American school at the time, and the sum continues to pay a portion of every student's tuition.) The school was known as Washington College at the end of the Civil War, when Robert E. Lee assumed its presidency. Lee lead the college through far-reaching changes until his death in 1870. Today, students revere General Lee's memory with a love bordering on fanaticism. Visitors may mistake these students' adoration for a dead Confederate general as some bizarre wish to rekindle the Old South or the Civil War. In reality, Washington and Lee students cherish General Lee for his educational reforms: joining the college with a local law school, instituting classes in business and economics, creating the first college-level journalism program, and establishing the seeds of the student-governed Honor System. Those century-old innovations are now traditions that make Washington and Lee the fine liberal arts institution it is today. The university maintains these traditions and follows Lee's example, always initiating change. The last decade has witnessed additions to the curriculum, complete revitalization of the fraternity system, and construction of new facilities for the fine arts, athletics, and the sciences.

Students at Washington and Lee call their school "W&L," and their love for W&L is as loyal as their love for General Lee. One junior admits:

I called home crying a few times during my freshman year because I was so grateful to my parents for giving me the opportunity to come to W&L.

National surveys routinely rank W&L students among the happiest in the country. When naming what makes them happy, every student generation names the same strong traditions: a small student body of 1,600 that is truly a community, intimate classes averaging ten to twelve students, a faculty dedicated to students and to teaching, and an Honor System that creates a society of trust where no student will lie, cheat, or steal.

The small town of Lexington, Virginia forms the backdrop for all of this student bliss.

Although only 4,600 residents live in Lexington year-round, students from Washington and Lee and its neighbor, the Virginia Military Institute, add substantially to the town's true population. (The two schools add much to the town through their cultural and athletic programs as well.) One politics major notes:

> *The scenic, safe surroundings have allowed me to make W&L a home away from home, to enjoy the college experience without the worries and distractions of a big school or a big city.*

W&L students become active citizens of Lexington as "big brothers" or "big sisters" to local youths, as coaches for Little League teams, as members of church congregations, and as participants in outreach groups such as Habitat for Humanity.

Although all W&L students call Lexington "home," they journey from all corners of the United States to get there. Only twelve percent of undergraduates hail from Virginia. Other well-represented states include Florida, Georgia, New Jersey, Maryland, Pennsylvania, New York, and Texas. It surprises many to learn that the student body includes nearly as many Californians as North or South Carolinians. W&L truly has a national student body to match its national reputation. With students from more than twenty foreign countries, W&L obviously attracts international attention as well.

ADMISSIONS REQUIREMENTS

Word is out—magazines rank W&L one of the nation's premiere liberal arts institutions year after year. Its academic reputation, small size, and pure beauty attract an increasing number of applicants with increasingly stronger credentials. Because space in Washington and Lee's student body is limited, gaining admittance to the university has become increasingly difficult.

A glance at Washington and Lee's admissions statistics confirms just how selective the school has become. Of the 3,460 students who applied for admission into a recent class, only 1,087 were admitted, yielding a freshman class of 456 (241 men, 215 women). These enrolling students achieved remarkable scores on their standardized tests. The middle fifty percent range of their SAT scores spanned 1280–1400; the average ACT score was 29. These freshmen earned an average rank-in-class above ninety-two percent of their high school classmates.

Fifty-seven were valedictorians or salutatorians; thirty-one were National Merit Scholars or Finalists.

These facts certainly portray W&L's selectivity, but they do not illustrate the great care that its Admissions Office takes in reviewing all applications. Washington and Lee believes that the high school record is the surest sign of a student's admissibility. Admissions officers read every student's transcript, weighing grades against the difficulty of the curriculum. Successful applicants typically have strong grades in rigorous college-preparatory or Advanced Placement classes. Standardized tests are used as a uniform measurement in comparing students who often come from schools with drastically different curricula and grading scales. W&L also strives to evaluate each student's character and personality through essays and recommendations. In hopes of finding future members of the school's athletic teams, cultural groups, and student committees, W&L's Admissions Office further judges applicants by their extracurricular pursuits.

Interviews

Proof of Washington and Lee's genuine interest in getting to know applicants lies in the fact that it continues to offer personal interviews. Interviews and student-guided tours may be scheduled by calling the Admissions Office. For students who cannot travel to Lexington for a meeting with an admissions officer, interviews with alumni admissions program representatives are available in every major city in the United States.

Requirements

W&L's admissions requirements are clear and straightforward. Students must submit either SAT I or ACT scores. In addition, they must also submit results from three SAT II: Subject tests, one of which must be the SAT II: Writing test. Applicants complete Part I of the application for admission; this preliminary application asks for biographical information. After receiving Part I from applicants, W&L then sends Part II of the application. It includes transcript forms, two teacher recommendation forms, and guidelines for the submission of supplemental information (including an essay). The regular decision deadline for submission of applications is January 15. Students can expect replies from Washington and Lee in early April.

Early Decision

For students who want to attend Washington and Lee above all other schools, there is a binding Early Decision option. Early Decision applicants must send a letter to the W&L Admissions Office stating that Washington and Lee is their first choice and that they will attend if admitted. Early Decision applications are due by December 1; W&L delivers quick notice after December 20. Admitted students happily claim a coveted place in the freshman class. No one is denied admission; W&L defers consideration of those who are not admitted until the regular admissions process.

A third admissions deadline remains for applicants who want to vie for the university's many generous Honor Scholarships. These students complete an additional essay and submit their applications by December 15. W&L invites finalists to visit the campus during the late winter; the Admissions Office notifies scholarship recipients in early April.

ACADEMIC LIFE

Nothing shapes life at Washington and Lee more than its Honor System. The Honor System dates back to General Lee's simple demand that all of his students act honorably. Today, a committee of elected students (known as the Executive Committee) commands complete control of the Honor System, informing freshmen of its guidelines and enforcing its principles. The system is built upon trust; it holds that students who lie, cheat, or steal are not trustworthy and, therefore, not welcome in the Washington and Lee community. For that reason, there is only one sanction for any student found guilty of an honor violation: permanent removal from the student body.

Because the Honor System works so well, Washington and Lee students enjoy freedoms that would be impossible at other universities. All academic buildings on the W&L campus, including the library, remain open twenty-four hours a day. Since professors trust that cheating will not occur, students take unproctored tests and exams. Students even schedule their own exams during week-long exam periods. It is possible that every student in an English class could take the same exam in a different place at a different time; students are trusted to not discuss the content of their exams with their classmates. These freedoms extend beyond the classroom as well.

I constantly leave money in my backpack right in the middle of campus without giving a moment's thought to its security.

Classes

If there is one thing that defines all colleges, it must be the classroom. Today, many college classrooms are cavernous, badly lit lecture halls. A professor or, more likely, a teaching assistant speaks through a microphone to hundreds of students seated in row after row of identical chairs. W&L defines the classroom differently. Its students enjoy small, intimate classes that are never taught by a graduate student or a teaching assistant. A large class at W&L might contain thirty-five students. Average classes number ten to twelve. Many upperclassmen take seminar classes with fewer than ten other students. They all might sit around a single table with their professor, creating the kind of personal, in-depth interaction that is a W&L hallmark.

Professors

Small classes allow students to get to know their professors as people, and vice versa.

> *Teachers here seem to relish the opportunity to get to know the students, even if they realize that that particular student will only be taking that one class from them. Within your major, every professor knows you and begs you to take their classes. It's rather flattering.*

An alumnus remembers similar experiences:

> *I never lost my awe of my professors, but I really came to rely on many of them as friends. Of course, that made the stakes higher. I always felt that I had to do my best work because I didn't want to disappoint them.*

Professors keep long office hours so that they can meet with students outside of class. Most professors do not have strict attendance guidelines, but, because classes are so small, every student learns that an absence gets noticed. Although it may be unheard of at other universities, W&L students typically enjoy eating dinner at professors' homes.

Curriculum

Despite Washington and Lee's small size, the university offers a startlingly varied curriculum that a Washington Post article described as "the envy of many larger institutions." Committed to the ideal of a liberal arts education, W&L requires all students to meet general education requirements in composition; literature; a foreign language; the fine arts, history, philosophy, and religion; science and mathematics; the social sciences; and physical education. Most students meet these requirements by the end of their sophomore year. They spend their junior and senior years fulfilling a major course of study and dabbling in elective classes.

Students divide their time between the university's College of Arts and Sciences (which includes the School of Journalism or "J-School") and the Ernest Williams II School of Commerce, Economics, and Politics (or "C-School"). Students may earn Bachelor of Arts or Bachelor of Science degrees, in addition to Bachelor of Science degrees with Special Attainments in Chemistry and Bachelor of Science degrees with Special Attainments in Commerce. The Shepherd Program for the Interdisciplinary Study of Poverty as well as the Society and the Professions Studies in Applied Ethics are among W&L's unique, crosscurricular courses of study.

Study Areas

W&L students spread all over the campus to study. Carrels in Leyburn Library may be reserved on the first day of classes. Confident in the Honor System, students leave texts and notebooks in their carrels for the entire school year. Other students study in the libraries located in the Science Center, Journalism School, or Commerce School. Because academic buildings stay open twenty-four hours a day, an occasional student may "pull an all-nighter" while working in a classroom. Students compose their papers on computers in computer labs located in most academic buildings. Every dormitory room has access to electronic mail and the World Wide Web through direct modem connections to the university server.

W&L classes typically demand considerable reading and writing. Students quickly learn that no skill proves more valuable than the ability to write clearly and concisely; professors expect nothing less. Classes and workloads may be tough, but the academic mood at Washington and Lee never becomes cutthroat.

W&L may have competitive admissions, but students here enjoy learning more through cooperation and collaboration with peers.

This mood may be due, in part, to the Honor System. Students trust one another. They do not compete against one another; they compete against themselves.

The Academic Year

W&L has a unique academic year consisting of a twelve-week fall term, a twelve-week winter term, and a six-week spring term. Most students take four classes in the fall, four classes in the winter, and two classes in the spring. The spring term allows for a kind of academic flexibility that is truly uncommon. In years past, students in English classes spent the term studying five of Faulkner's novels in great detail. Those in botany classes traveled to the American West to examine its indigenous fauna. Members of economics classes journeyed to the financial centers of Europe to learn about the European Economic Community, while politics majors interned in Washington, D.C. Because the spring term closes the school year, students who study abroad or serve in internships for the term may continue to do so throughout the summer. Students who stay at W&L enjoy compressed classes, along with beautiful weather for reading outdoors or tubing down the Maury River.

SOCIAL LIFE AND ACTIVITIES

Phil Flickinger, a 1997 graduate of Washington and Lee, has published a collection of his cartoons that appeared in W&L's student newspapers. Entitled *Invasion of the Bug-Eyed Preppies,* the book captures many of the quirks of social life at W&L. Flickinger's most revealing cartoon juxtaposes two groups—"Generation X" and "Generation Lex." "Generation X" is a frowning, shaggy group of tattooed and pierced slackers. "Generation Lex" is a group of Lexington, Virginia's W&L students—straitlaced and smartly dressed. One W&L male in the cartoon asks, "Has anyone seen my Duckheads?"

Like most humor, this cartoon evokes a great deal of truth by use of stereotypes. Of course, every member of Generation X does not have a skateboard and a navel ring. Likewise, every student at W&L does not fit the cartoon's notion of a preppy. For every rule or stereotype, there are exceptions. It may be true that most W&L students are more conservative than their peers at other schools. Nevertheless, W&L's student body contains a strong mix of "ambitious, on-the-ball" individuals who pursue differing interests with differing attitudes. Somehow, they all seem bound by a single thread.

> *I still maintain that in no other school can one find such a classy group of well brought-up individuals. Everyone respects one another to an amazing degree.*

Residences

All W&L freshmen live in one of four freshman dormitories and take their meals in a dining hall that could double as a ballroom. Sophomores live on campus, too, in upper-class dorms and apartments, fraternity houses, and separate houses for groups such as the Outing Club. Juniors and seniors may live on campus, though many choose to live off campus. Apartments above downtown stores provide many options for students, as do legendary student homes with colorful names like Fishbait, Munster, Windfall, the Batcave, Aqua Velva, and Amityville. All students enjoy the majestic beauty of the surrounding Shenandoah Valley and Blue Ridge Mountains, which provide every imaginable outdoor activity.

The Greeks

Eighty percent of W&L men are in one of fifteen fraternities; sixty-five percent of W&L women are in one of five sororities. Much of Washington and Lee's social life evolves from fraternity parties, where all students are welcome—Greeks and non-Greeks alike. A student explains that "the W&L method of partying (heartily and often) is made safe by our concern for each other's well-being and made convenient by most parties being located right downtown."

Other Organizations

Greek organizations do not define the lives of W&L students, however. For a small school, Washington and Lee supports an impressive array of civic, cultural, and athletic organizations to meet every student's interests. The Society for the Arts, for example, sponsors dramatic performances and readings of student poetry and fiction. The Student Activities Board brings bands and comedians to campus. W&L's many journalism majors contribute to two rival student newspapers, the traditional *Ring-Tum Phi* and the more winsome *Trident*. The Contact Committee presents debates and lectures. Through club and intramural sports, choral groups, an orchestra, College Democrats, College Republicans, religious organizations, and service groups, any W&L student finds fulfilling diversions outside of class.

MEN'S VARSITY SPORTS

- ❍ Cross Country
- ❍ Football
- ❍ Soccer
- ❍ Basketball
- ❍ Swimming
- ❍ Indoor Track
- ❍ Wrestling
- ❍ Baseball
- ❍ Golf
- ❍ Lacrosse
- ❍ Tennis
- ❍ Track and Field

Sports

Many Washington and Lee students also chose to participate in varsity sports. W&L's Generals compete in Division III sports through the Old Dominion Athletic Conference, maintaining sterling academic and athletic records. Recently, 109 of W&L's 399 varsity athletes achieved GPAs of 3.5 or better. The Generals have had seven conference championship teams, nine All-American athletes, six conference players of the year, and sixty-seven first-team all-conference players. For three consecutive years, W&L teams won the ODAC Commissioner's Cup for the best all-around athletic program. Football and lacrosse remain the perennial favorites of spectators at W&L, attracting large and vocal crowds.

WOMEN'S VARSITY SPORTS

- ❍ Cross Country
- ❍ Soccer
- ❍ Tennis
- ❍ Volleyball
- ❍ Basketball
- ❍ Swimming
- ❍ Indoor Track
- ❍ Lacrosse
- ❍ Tennis
- ❍ Track and Field

Popular Events

Among W&L's most popular events are two campus-wide bonanzas: the Fancy Dress Ball and Mock Convention. A black-tie ball attended by students, alumni, and faculty, Fancy Dress (or "FD") is a yearly affair whose budget tops $80,000. A student committee sponsors a concert on a Thursday evening, followed by the ball on a Friday night. Festivities typically spill into the weekend, making for a marathon that only the most excited students can complete. Mock Convention (or "Mock Con") occurs with equal flair every four years. Organized to predict the presidential candidate for the political party out of office, Mock

Con approximates an actual political convention more closely than any other exercise. Students form state delegations and spend countless hours in research. They succeed in predicting candidates at an uncanny rate. The 1992 Mock Democratic Convention accurately selected Bill Clinton as its nominee. The 1996 Mock Republican Convention garnered live coverage on C-SPAN. House Speaker Newt Gingrich addressed the crowd of Washington and Lee students, and Bob Dole spoke to the assembly via cell phone when he accepted the convention's nomination.

FINANCIAL AID

Washington and Lee uses student tuition dollars as efficiently and fairly as any university in the country. At other schools, students and their families pay inflated tuitions; one full-paying student's cost of attending school also includes a portion of the fees necessary to educate another student who receives financial aid. In other words, students subsidize other students' tuitions. This never happens at W&L, where all financial aid dollars are drawn from grants and endowment, never from tuition revenues. Because a W&L student pays only for his or her own tuition, the cost of attending W&L is dramatically lower than the cost of attending other highly selective colleges.

Compare Washington and Lee's recent tuition fees ($16,040) to those of other competitive schools and you will see that other schools charge as much as $6,000 more per year. For a small school offering a world-class education, W&L is clearly a tremendous value. W&L students and their families find that the university possesses an intimate academic setting that rivals any other—at a considerably lower cost.

No one will claim that $16,040 is small change, however. The cost of any college education exceeds the budgets and imaginations of many American families. Washington and Lee strives to make tuition costs affordable by offering generous financial aid packages to students whenever possible.

W&L's admissions process is need-blind, so a student's ability to pay tuition is never a part of the admissions decision. W&L's Financial Aid Office, upon learning of a student's admission, works to ensure that a student's financial needs can be met.

In order to reach its goal of meeting a student's financial need, W&L's Financial Aid Office requires that a student's family fill out a few necessary forms. Completion of the Free Application for Federal Student Aid and the College Scholarship Service Financial Aid Profile is required. Both the FAFSA and registration forms for the CSS Profile may be found in most high school guidance offices. The Financial Aid Office strongly recommends submission of the FAFSA forms as well as registration through the College Scholarship Service by mid-January. Doing so will ensure receipt of all student information by mid-February. Additionally, W&L's Financial Aid Office requires a student's family to provide tax returns from the previous fiscal year.

Students applying through W&L's Early Decision program may obtain a financial aid estimate by registering with the College Scholarship Service in October and submitting forms through CSS in mid-November.

Because any college financial aid process may prove frustrating and confusing, W&L's Admissions Office recommends early, careful planning for any student's family. The Financial Aid Office takes great care in addressing each family's personal and individual needs.

Apart from its need-based aid programs, Washington and Lee also awards numerous merit-based scholarships every year. Ranging from partial tuition awards to scholarships that cover full tuition, room, and board, W&L's Honor Scholarships reward students who possess great academic and personal promise. Therefore, finalists must meet and exceed the university's admissions standards in addition to demonstrating potential campus leadership. Recipients carry their scholarships throughout their four-year tenure at Washington and Lee, provided they establish a minimum 3.0 grade-point average and maintain a personal record fitting an Honor Scholar. Students who wish to apply for these awards must submit their applications along with an additional Honor Scholarship essay by December 15.

Washington and Lee also sponsors Finalists in the National Merit Scholarship Competition. National Merit Finalists who are admitted to the university and designate Washington and Lee as their first choice of colleges with the National Merit Finalist Scholarship Corporation will receive at least $750 yearly.

GRADUATES

The percentage of freshmen who return to Washington and Lee for their sophomore years stands as a sure, impressive sign of student contentment: ninety-four to ninety-five percent of freshmen return to W&L as sophomores. A more impressive sign is the number of W&L students who enter as freshmen and graduate four years later. Of the Class of 1996, for example, eighty-nine percent of the original freshman class who arrived in

PROMINENT GRADS

- **Lloyd Dobyns, News Commentator**
- **Joseph Goldstein, Nobel Prize Winner**
- **Bill Johnson, President of the New York Stock Exchange**
- **David Low, Astronaut**
- **Roger Mudd, Journalist**
- **Lewis Powell, Supreme Court Justice**
- **Cy Twombly, Artist**
- **Tom Wolfe, Author**

Lexington in September of 1992 took their degrees at commencement in June of 1996. Clearly, Washington and Lee students stay at the university, and they stay happy. In an age when most college students need five years in order to earn a degree, the vast majority of W&L students find both adequate advisement and access to the classes they need in order to graduate in four years. A five-year stay at other schools may be commonplace; at W&L, a five-year stay is often scandalous.

Traditionally, W&L produces a high percentage of history, biology, and economics majors. That so many students should favor history at W&L, given the university's own long history, should be no surprise. The university's numerous biology majors include many who regularly establish a stellar record in gaining admittance to medical schools. Economics majors typically carry their expert training from W&L's Commerce School into the business world.

All Washington and Lee students receive excellent advice from the Career Development and Placement Office. The Career Development Office provides mock interview and résumé-review services. Students use the office's complete resources to research potential employers. The Placement Office welcomes over 100 companies to interview W&L students for jobs and summer internships every year. It further organizes off-campus interviews and enlists students in job fairs through the Selective Liberal Arts Consortium. These job fairs enable W&L students to meet employers in major American cities.

The Career Development and Placement Office also tracks W&L students as they leave W&L for employment and graduate school. Its report for the Class of 1996 shows seventy percent of graduates in employment, along with twenty-seven percent seeking postbaccalaureate degrees. A slim 2.6 percent either were seeking employment or were content taking time off after graduation. The report reveals that large numbers of working graduates found positions in business, banking and finance, or education. Companies that typically hire a high number of W&L graduates include Arthur Andersen, The May Company, First Union Bank, Crédit Suisse First Boston and the Cable News Network (CNN). Of the 1996 graduates who decided to pursue advanced degrees, thirty-three percent entered general graduate schools, twenty-nine percent entered law school, and nineteen percent entered medical school. Other students began studies in dental, veterinary, and business schools.

Because students come from all parts of the country to attend Washington and Lee, they also disperse themselves across the map after graduation. Recent trends show increasing numbers of W&L graduates moving to New York City, Washington, Charlotte, and Atlanta for work. In every city, existing alumni association chapters support and welcome new graduates.

Washington and Lee alumni share a unique experience that creates "an immediate bond" between them. They treasure their undergraduate memories and remain fiercely loyal to their alma mater. One graduate describes a revelation about the nature of Washington and Lee alumni this way:

I have a W&L trident decal on the back of my car, and I was at the gas station one day when a stranger asked me what it was. I explained that it was the symbol for my school, Washington and Lee University. The stranger said, "Oh, I thought maybe it was a sign for some kind of cult." I laughed, and then, the more I thought about it, the more I realized the stranger wasn't necessarily wrong. W&L is a kind of cult—but in a good way. We all believe very strongly in the same ideals and we all have a strong sense of belonging to a very special place.

SUMMING UP

Washington and Lee's four freshman dormitories form a cluster on the edge of campus. Baker, Davis, and Gilliam dorms face one another, creating a horseshoe; students gather in its "quad" every day. Just across the street, Graham-Lees—the oldest of the four dorms—overlooks the Baker-Davis-Gilliam quad. An arched breezeway passes through the building; on the left, a marble step between two columns is clearly worn more than the rest. Superstition holds that freshmen must walk up this step, between the columns, or risk failing their first test. Millions of feet have kept the tradition.

Just next door to Graham-Lees dormitory is the Lee House. General Lee built this home when he was the president of the school, and presidents of Washington and Lee have lived there ever since. Freshman voices can be heard in the Lee House as they echo from the dormitories. A past president joked that, although he preferred classical music, he could not help becoming familiar with the musical tastes of each freshman class.

That the president of the university lives so close to the freshman class demonstrates something wonderful about Washington and Lee: The person who runs the school shares the same block with those who are just learning the school's nuances. There is a continuity from the top of the administration to the bottom of the student body, and this continuity permeates the entire university.

There is almost a sense of family here. Everyone looks out for each other, professors and students can relate outside the classroom, and there is a sense of familiarity and camaraderie.

Washington and Lee students cherish this camaraderie and guard it closely long after they leave the quaint streets of Lexington.

❑ *Cameron Howell, B.A.*

WEBB INSTITUTE

Webb Institute
Glen Cove, NY 11542-1398

(516) 671-2213
Fax: (516) 674-9838

E-mail: admissions@webb-institute.edu
Web site: http:\\www.webb-institute.edu

Enrollment

Full-time ❑ women: 12
❑ men: 73

INTRODUCING WEBB INSTITUTE

Welcome to Webb Institute, one of the most unusual colleges in the world, but also one of the best. Let's set some things straight from the start:

- Webb Institute was founded in 1889 by millionaire William H. Webb, one of the preeminent shipbuilders of the mid-nineteenth century, the era of the clipper ships.
- The purpose of the school is to advance the art and science of shipbuilding in the United States by training promising young people for careers in that field; thus, Webb confers only

one undergraduate degree: a Bachelors of Science in Naval Architecture and Marine Engineering.

- The Webb program is a full, four-year, intense engineering education.
- All students receive a full-tuition scholarship for all four years. (Yes, it's an almost-free education, the only costs are room, board, and books.)
- The Webb campus is a mansion on Long Island Sound.
- Only about eighty students attend in total, with a maximum of twenty-five in a class.
- All Webb students have two months of practical work experience every winter, for a total of at least eight months experience upon graduation.
- All Webb sophomores sail on ships for their winter work term, some even overseas to the Caribbean, Europe, and Asia.
- Webb graduates are highly regarded in the maritime industry and eagerly recruited.
- Webb's placement rate is one-hundred percent.
- Graduates are regularly accepted into master's programs at schools with prestigious graduate programs such as MIT and Stanford.
- Webb is not a military school; it is a completely private institution, focusing primarily on the needs of the commercial shipbuilding market; therefore, students have no obligations to the school upon graduation.
- The Webb degree is readily transferable to a wide range of other engineering disciplines, not only shipbuilding.
- Webb is fully accredited.

To sum up, Webb Institute is one of the best (if not the best) engineering schools in the country, it's basically free, and it happens to focus on ships. If you have never heard of Webb, don't worry—many of the students presently attending didn't know about it either until their senior year in high school, when they received an introductory brochure in the mail! But don't let Webb's small size and apparent obscurity fool you: Webb may be one of the best-kept secrets in academia, but certainly not in the maritime industry. If you are interested in getting a great job right out of college, with little debt, and you are smart and willing to work hard to learn about engineering in shipbuilding, then read on.

ADMISSIONS REQUIREMENTS

The admissions form asks basic questions, such as, "Who are you? Where do you live? What do you like to do?" Other paperwork includes a doctor's evaluation, which is necessary mainly because of the physically taxing nature of the sophomore winter work term at sea; however, interested people with poor health or physical disabilities should not be discouraged from applying, because Webb will be glad to make other arrangements, if necessary. A teacher evaluation is also required. That's about it. Many students say the Webb application was the easiest one they filled out.

What kind of student does Webb want? The school was founded to entice the brightest and best young people in the United States to pursue careers in shipbuilding, mainly by offering them a great education at no cost; therefore, Webb has set very high standards for prospective freshmen. Applicants must be in the top twenty percent of their high school class and have a minimum GPA of 3.2. They must also take both the SAT I and the SAT II: Subject tests in Writing, Mathematics Level I or II, and Physics or Chemistry. A minimum score of 500 Verbal and 660 Math on the SAT I is required. Applicants must be United States citizens, either native-born or naturalized.

Webb also wants people who will do well in the Webb environment, with particular regard to the smallness of the school and the academic emphasis on ships and engineering. This means that people who are well-rounded and have at least some social skills are preferable to those who just sit in a corner and stare at the wall. Also, prospective freshmen must show dedication at least to engineering, if not to shipbuilding, specifically. These qualities show through in the extracurricular activities that an applicant lists on the form and through the required personal interview with the president of the school.

A couple of side notes are in order here. First, Webb accepts incoming students only as freshmen; in other words, there is no transferring from another school into the upper classes of Webb. Second, Webb does not give any Advanced Placement credit. So, in short, everyone starts out equally at Webb. However, this fact should not discourage Webb wannabees from taking AP classes in high school, particularly calculus, because it may give them a slight edge in admissions (as well as make Professor Stephan's first-semester race through integrals a little easier).

So what are an applicant's chances of acceptance? They are better than they might first appear, considering that only twenty-five freshmen are admitted each year. Bill Murray, the Executive Director of Student and Administrative Services, describes the admissions process from his perspective in this way: First, the qualified students are separated from the unqualified students, based upon their application forms and SAT scores. This first cut typically narrows down the applicant pool to about seventy. Next, Bill starts inviting the top prospects to the school for interviews; as they accept, the marginally qualified students are dropped from the bottom of the list. Over thirty of the seventy are invited for interviews, because sometimes after the interview, the school realizes that the prospective student is not right for it or the prospective student realizes Webb is not right for him or her. Bill said the really tough decisions are about the students in the "forty-to-fifty" range. These students are qualified, but ultimately some are not pursued, because of the high yield among the top thirty applicants. In summary, then, if an applicant meets Webb's academic standards, he or she stands greater than a fifty/fifty chance of acceptance. Then if that applicant is invited to interview and really wants to go to Webb, he or she is in.

There's one last item about admissions: It is Webb's policy not to discriminate on the basis of race, creed, gender, or physical handicap. This fact is important to keep in mind, especially when visiting the campus, because one quickly realizes that the vast majority of students are white males. However, female and minority students historically have not had any major problems with the students or the school. Webb's mission is to educate the best people, period. Basically, if you're a minority and you don't mind being in the minority, Webb is still a fine school for you to consider attending.

ACADEMIC LIFE

Webb doesn't teach you how to be smart. You're already smart when you come here. Webb teaches you how to work.

Webb is a hard school. There is no doubt about it. Nobody flies through Webb; everybody suffers alike. But that's what makes it good, and the 147 credits required to graduate (that's more than eighteen credits per semester) is only the tip of the iceberg. Add multiple field trips, highly respected faculty both in engineering and humanities classes, two months of practical work experience each year, and projects that few other schools dare to attempt—such as the senior thesis and the hand-drawing of ship's lines—and you begin to get the bigger picture. The incredible amount of learning and work that Webb crams into four years is what makes the school dear to alumni, and the alumni dear to employers.

Courses

Webb Institute confers only one undergraduate degree—the Bachelor of Science in Naval Architecture and Marine Engineering. Everyone takes the same technical classes over the course of four years. There are about six classes per semester, on average, with one being a humanities class. Freshman year, the courses are mostly basic scientific courses, such as calculus, physics, and chemistry, as are found in any good engineering school. Sophomore year, more fundamental engineering courses are presented, such as fluid dynamics, strength of materials, and thermodynamics. Then in the junior year, study tends toward more field-related work, beginning with ship resistance and propulsion and including ship structural analysis, ship auxiliary and steam systems, electrical engineering, and ship maneuverability. Finally, in the senior year, the courses are almost all marine-related and involve huge projects such as ship design (of a containership or tanker), ship's lines, machinery arrangement, propeller design, and a senior thesis of the student's choosing. Despite the above trends, one of the many unique aspects of Webb is that naval architecture and marine engineering courses are presented throughout the four-year program, as early as first-semester freshman year. This tactic helps to keep students interested and to prepare them (especially freshmen and sophomores) for their winter work jobs.

There tend to be two kinds of students at Webb: those who are interested in small, pleasure and utility craft and those who prefer to deal with large, ocean-going commercial and military vessels. The Webb curriculum distinctly favors the latter; however, the engineering and marine fundamentals learned often can be transferred to the design of smaller boats. The small craft design course in the junior year helps this transition, and discussion of small craft technologies, such as fiberglass hulls, is included in other classes.

Disciplines

Another good point about the Webb curriculum is that it is quite streamlined, yet still broadbased. This apparent dichotomy is possible because of the nature of naval architecture and marine engineering. Consider all the disciplines involved in designing a ship. First, there is the hull moving through the water; the study of this action involves knowledge of hydrodynamics (and even aerodynamics—a modern rudder is a type of wing). Next, there is the hull itself; the design of adequate structural integrity requires a good understanding of the principles of civil engineering. Then there are the guts of the ship—all the machinery and electrical equipment. The design of these systems requires, for example, knowledge of combustion and heat transfer (chemical engineering), engines and other auxiliary machinery (mechanical engineering), and ship electrical power distribution and electronic control systems (electrical engineering). All these various disciplines must be learned, but in only one, four-year degree program. Therefore, to accelerate the learning process, only the highlights of each discipline are discussed. The fundamental engineering principles are taught first, followed by those aspects pertaining to shipbuilding (for example, the use of steel and fiberglass). Irrelevant aspects (such as concrete) are reserved for independent study. This somewhat narrow approach can be maddening to people with purely scientific interests, but is great for those with an engineering inclination, who "just want to use it."

Humanities

When students grow sick of ships, they can take a break and work on their humanities classes.

There is one humanities class each semester. Standard topics range from technical communications to U.S. foreign policy to ethics. Occasionally, students are able to have some choice in what humanities courses they take, such as during the first semester of sophomore year, when, through an academic arrangement, students are able to take classes at nearby Hofstra University, a prestigious private institution. Professor Richard Harris, the sole full-time humanities professor currently at Webb, teaches several of the Webb courses, and the rest are taught by adjuncts, many of whom are fairly well-known in their fields. Through all these classes, Webb students can broaden their horizons and hone their communication skills, as much as is possible from a highly technical program. As alumni attest, many employers are impressed with the excellent writing and speaking abilities of Webb graduates.

Classrooms and Faculty

One of the big benefits of Webb is how conducive the environment is to learning. Each class (such as the sophomores) has its own classroom, with a desk or drafting table in it for each student. Almost all the classes are held in these four classrooms; the students stay put and the professors are the ones who have to run to their next class! Classes begin at 9:00 A.M. and go to noon; after an hour of lunch, they continue until three. On Tuesday mornings, there is a special one-hour lecture by a guest speaker from industry. Although these arrangements may be reminiscent of third grade with Mrs. Hoag, there is nothing elementary about the faculty or the lectures. The student-to-faculty ratio is around seven to one. All the Webb professors have their master's degrees, and several have their doctorates. The small class size and common coursework enable the professors to gage how much the students know and how much remains to be covered. Students often interrupt the lectures with questions, which the professors welcome, as this promotes understanding and allows the professors to move swiftly over the simple stuff and dwell more on the difficult material. After classes, the professors are readily available to answer further questions and to help students with problems.

Library, Computers, and Labs

After classes are done for the day, many students work together in the classroom, or in the Livingston Library, which is open twenty-four hours a day (like the rest of the campus) and contains one of the best collections on naval architecture and marine engineering in the country. When computers are needed to do homework (which happens often), students can use the couple of computers that are in each classroom or the approximately two dozen Pentiums that are networked in the computer room and have Internet access. High-quality printers and a high-speed plotter are available, as well as a photocopier—all for free. The student-run bookstore provides everything else necessary, from notebook paper to rulers to coffee mugs. Laboratory equipment is not always the state-of-the-art, but it is adequate. There are chemistry and physics laboratories in the basement of the main building, and marine engineering, fluids, and electrical engineering laboratories in the Haeberle Laboratory building. Special equipment in the Haeberle Laboratory includes a complete boiler/turbine steam system, two diesel engines with dynamometer, and a flow channel.

The Basin

The pride of Webb is the Robinson Model Basin. This basin is a long tank of water in which scale models of ships' hulls are towed and their resistances measured. Significant recent research in the basin includes testing of the navy's arsenal ship hull form as well as the establishment of a series of trimaran resistance predictions.

Work Load

It is appropriate at this point to emphasize the intense work load at Webb. Four hours per night tends to be the typical amount of time spent on homework, but it can often be much higher than that. Pulling all-nighters for major projects and even regular homework assignments is all too common. Most of the work is not overly difficult; it's just that there's so much of it that it takes forever to do. How to handle all that pressure is one of the major lessons that students learn at Webb. The other one is how to work together to have a shot at getting all the work done.

What do you call the guy who graduates last in the class? A naval architect!

Winter Work Program

Last but certainly not least is the winter work program. To understand this program, you must first understand Webb's unusual calendar year, which runs as follows: Fall semester starts at the end of August and goes until Christmas break; spring semester starts at the beginning of March and goes until late June. This arrangement leaves two two-month breaks in the year: January through February and July through August. The summer break is just that—time off that's free of scholastic obligations. For the winter break, however, all students are required to work at jobs that are related to the maritime industry, sort of like co-op jobs or internships. The school finds jobs with shipyards for freshmen who work hands-on as apprentices doing welding, fitting, etc. For sophomores, the school arranges berths on merchant ships, where the students work as cadets in the engine rooms, doing routine maintenance. Of course, one of the perks is that students get to travel, sometimes even overseas to the Caribbean, Europe, or Asia, depending on the particular ship. Junior and senior year, however, students are on their own and must find maritime, engineering-related jobs. Most students get jobs in shipyard engineering departments or separate design or consulting offices, though a wide range of opportunities exists because Webb is fairly broad on what it considers marine-related work. Thus, by the time a student graduates from Webb, he or she has first-hand experience of how a ship is designed and engineered, how it is physically constructed, and how it is operated at sea. This knowledge is invaluable to employers, especially when some competing graduates from other naval architecture schools have never even set foot on a deck!

SOCIAL LIFE AND ACTIVITIES

Most Webbies laugh sarcastically when someone mentions social life at Webb.

It is most unfortunate: a stellar social life is one of those things that students generally have to give up when they come to Webb for their college education. There is just no way that a school averaging around eighty undergraduates can offer the same amount of social diversity and opportunity that, say, a state school with 20,000 students can offer. This hard fact, coupled with the intense technical work load that Webb requires and (for many male students, at least) the realization that, in some years, you can count the female students on two hands and a foot, tends to make life at Webb seem almost monastic at times.

The above view is overly pessimistic, however. On those rare moments when you're through with your work and you finally have time to look around you, Webb is actually a great place to live. From the campus, to sports, to the student organization, to the City of Glen Cove, to nearby New York City, Webb has many positive attractions to enjoy.

The Campus

For starters, life at Webb is about as comfortable as a middle-class undergrad could hope for. The Webb campus is the former estate of Herbert L. Pratt, who is irrelevant to our story here except for the fact that he owned a really nice house on a really nice piece of property in a really nice area, and now it's Webb's. More specifically, Webb's mansion is located on twenty-six acres of prime waterfront property on beautiful Long Island Sound, in an area nicknamed the "Gold Coast" because of all the rich people who built their lavish estates here back in the Roaring Twenties.

Think The Great Gatsby, *and you'll have a pretty good idea of the look of the place. Or, if you haven't read that book, you can watch the movie* Batman Forever *and look for Webb as the exterior of Wayne Manor; the outdoor shots were filmed here in 1994!*

The main building is the mansion, of course. It houses all the important things in its three floors, including all four classrooms in the wings, undergraduate male residence, dining room, library, lecture hall, laundry room, computer room, faculty offices, and administrative offices. What this means is that a male student can stay completely indoors for whole weeks at a time (though this is not recommended). The female undergraduate students, on the other hand, have their dorm rooms on the second floor of the nearby Robinson Model Basin, so they are forced to get fresh air every day as they stroll a few yards over to the main building for classes and meals. Both male and female rooms are relatively spacious and are adequately furnished, with two students per room being typical. Phone jacks are in each room. All in all, it's a nice place to live.

Conveniences

What are really nice are all the conveniences that Webb offers. The food service provides three meals a day during the week and brunch and dinner on weekends, and the chefs do an excellent job (honestly, this is the best college food in the universe). Little things like free soap, a linen service, fifty-cent washers and dryers, free laundry detergent and bleach, and ample parking for all students (including freshmen) make life just that much easier. Also, the Student Organization (S.O.) services are particularly helpful. The S.O. treasury allows students to cash checks and make deposits and withdrawals. The S.O. kitchen allows students to refrigerate and microwave their own food. The S.O. bookstore has just about every academic tool necessary for classes. Other facilities include the S.O. garage, wood shop, and machine shop. All these services are accessible twenty-four hours a day. Almost anything a person needs to live and work comfortably can be found on campus, which is a big plus for students without cars.

The S.O.

The Student Organization merits further explanation. Basically, students govern themselves, and to a degree not found at most other schools. All students are members of the S.O. and agree to abide by the S.O. Handbook and the Honor Code. The handbook lays out all the chairmanships and rules, and the Honor Code forbids stealing, cheating, etc. Such documents are not peculiar to Webb; many schools have them. What is different about Webb is that students actually abide by these rules, for the most part. Thus, a tour of Webb will reveal unusual practices, such as dorm rooms with locks operated only from the inside, attic storage of students' belongings, books and calculators left on classroom desks and library tables, and the aforementioned twenty-four-hour-a-day access to almost every public room and building on campus. This freedom does not mean that Webb is unsafe, however. During the day, everyone is everywhere on campus, and with only eighty-some students, everybody knows everybody who should be there. A student Officer of the Day is also on duty to greet guests. At night, hired security patrols the campus. In short, Webb has not had any serious crimes in a long, long while, and any minor offenses are usually dealt with by the S.O. Honor Council and the school administration. Thus, students at Webb don't have to worry like students at other schools do about the safety of themselves and their belongings.

Sports

There are many sports and activities at Webb to help students eat up all their free time. For athletics, Webb belongs to the Hudson Valley Men's Athletic Conference, a sports league of small schools in the area. (Although it says Men's Athletic Conference, women are welcome to and often do play on the teams—it's really more like coed sports.) Popular conference sports include basketball and volleyball (played in the gymnasium), soccer (on Thorpe Field), and tennis (on the two courts on campus). Other sports include sailing, disc, and cross-country. For sailing, Webb owns several JY's for competition on the Sound, in addition to Lasers and a motorboat—all for qualified students to use. For personal fitness, Webb has some weight equipment in the gym; also, students can use the Glen Cove YMCA for free, with its complete weight room, pool, and gym. Actually, since Webb athletics are run primarily by the students, if students want to start a sport not currently offered, they can form a team, call up other schools in the area that have the sport, and, Presto! there's competition.

Look, Ma, I'm playing college basketball!

The above description may make talented athletes and sports enthusiasts cringe when they read it. Admittedly, you'll never see Webb in the NCAA basketball final four or in the Rose Bowl. However, the general informality of Webb athletics does not mean that athletes do not play hard or that competition is not fierce and fun. All of the Webb teams have won several games in their recent seasons. The sailing team is particularly good and regularly places highly in regattas, beating schools like Cornell and the U.S. Naval Academy. And this success is all achieved with ordinary students, not elite athletes. Many students who would not otherwise ever play intercollegiate sports can show up for practices and then proceed to beat the tar out of teams from schools ten times larger. Or, if that's not your style, you can play on an intermural team and just beat the tar out of your roommate.

Social Events

Webb has several social events throughout the year, both large and small, formal and informal. A small event may be an evening of eating, drinking, and shooting pool and the breeze in the student pub while a local guy plucks out some songs on his guitar. Big events include Homecoming, Parents Weekend, the Beach, Halloween and Christmas parties, and the biggest one of all—Webbstock. Webbstock is held on a Saturday in June, just before the school year is out, and entails six or seven bands (some of them famous), free drinks and food, and all sorts of sports, games, and activities out on the terraces under the hot sun in front of the blue Sound. It's quite an experience.

Off Campus

Finally, some reports indicate that there is life outside of Webb. Glen Cove is a quiet suburban town, with a movie theater, various stores, several different churches and houses of worship, public beaches and parks, and the all-important Taco Bell (it stays open the latest). Students with musical talent are welcome to join the North Shore Symphony Orchestra. In addition, students can hop on the Long Island Rail Road and be at Pennsylvania Station in downtown Manhattan in under an hour and a half. Of course, if you have a car, all of Long Island and New York City is within a couple of hours driving time, at most. So, in summary, there are a lot of fun things to do at Webb, both on and off campus, if you have the time...*if you have the time.*

FINANCIAL AID

Financial aid can be very simple at Webb. First of all, Webb provides a full-tuition scholarship to all students; this is possible because of a huge endowment created by the generous donations made by William Webb and others. Thus, the only major expenses are about $6,000 a year for room and board (living in a mansion is not cheap!) and about $300 to $500 per semester for books (though for the first semester of freshman year it's more like $900 for books). However, Webb Institute is dedicated to providing whatever financial aid is necessary to allow all students to attend, because that was one of William Webb's original stipulations when he founded the school and donated his millions to it. First of all, Webb participates in the Pell Grant program and the Family Federal Educational Loan program, which includes Plus and Stafford loans. Any further needs are met with Webb's own Brockett grants and Lance scholarships. The bottom line is that graduates from Webb don't have the tens of thousands of dollars worth of debt to pay off that many graduates from other top-notch schools do, and any debt that Webbies do incur is small and easily paid off with the high starting salaries that Webb graduates procure.

GRADUATES

After four excruciating years, it's nice to know that you can get into just about any graduate school in the country or go straight into industry with a high-paying job and a promising future. Webb's record is one-hundred-percent placement, even in an industry that has been shrinking in the United States for the past couple of decades. That kind of security is really hard to beat in an era of corporate downsizing.

First of all, let's reiterate: Webb is NOT a military school. There are no obligations whatsoever upon graduation, not even to stay in the maritime industry. You're free to do as you please with your life.

The next question, of course, is, "What do you do with a degree in naval architecture and marine engineering?" It's a good question, with a multitude of answers. Webbies always seem to be in demand at shipyards across the country, where they do engineering work as they design the ships of the future. Independent design and consulting offices offer attractive jobs with many different kinds of technical work. Just about any shore-based maritime work is open for graduates, since the Webb degree covers many different areas of learning. Outside of the maritime industry, there are many engineering jobs for which Webb graduates are qualified, especially if they obtain a master's degree in the particular field. Actually, Webb graduates are not even limited to engineering; business, managerial, and finance positions seem to be popular destinations among the alumni. Basically, the rule of thumb seems to be that as long as there is a maritime industry in the United States, Webb graduates will always have jobs.

To be completely honest, the demand for Webb grads does not rest solely on the quality of the Webb education, no matter how good it is. In reality, the way many Webb students get jobs for winter work and after graduation is by calling up Webb alumni who work at the particular companies of interest. Many of the key people in the maritime industry are Webb alumni, and they are usually more than willing to help a fellow Webbie get a job. This reality may sound slightly like a "good-ol'-boy" network, but many times even graduates from other schools express that they think Webbies are the best.

If graduates don't want to go into the maritime industry, or if they know they want to be in research or management, graduate school becomes an attractive option. Almost every year one or more graduates go to MIT to pursue either technical degrees in areas such as hydrodynamics, or a maritime business degree in Ocean Systems Management. Many graduates obtain an MBA within five to ten years after graduation. Almost any field is open for Webb graduates to study; however, some graduate studies may require the completion of a few prerequisite courses.

One last point about graduating from Webb: The maritime industry is an international field. What this means is that if you would like to work overseas, there are many opportunities, even for winter work. For example, during the winter of 1998, two students worked in Germany, and one worked in London. The possibilities are endless!

SUMMING UP

Webb Institute is a rare school; and like many rare things, it is invaluable, if you can recognize and appreciate it. Admittedly, Webb is not for everybody. It is a hard, taxing, and focused school. It's like being in the Marine Corps for the mind. But, the status and opportunity that come with a degree from Webb certainly make it all worthwhile. A Webb education is a top-notch education, certainly better for engineering than any Ivy League or technical school—and the price just can't be beat. So, if you have the interest in ships, the smarts, and the stamina necessary to make it through Webb, by all means, DO IT! It may very well be the most accelerating four years your career will ever see.

❑ *Alan Boline, B.S.*

WELLESLEY COLLEGE

Wellesley College
106 Central Street
Wellesley, MA 02181

(781) 283-1000
Fax: 781-283-3678

E-mail: admission@wellesley.edu
Web site: http://www.wellesley.edu

Enrollment

Full-time ❑ women: 2,176
❑ men: 0

Part-time ❑ women: 143
❑ men: 0

INTRODUCING WELLESLEY

Wellesley's unofficial motto is to "educate women who will make a difference in the world." And if there's one thing a Wellesley education will give you, it's a sense of empowerment that you have the skills, confidence, and know-how to succeed at anything you choose.

Consistently ranked among the top five liberal arts colleges in the nation, Wellesley offers its students a serious intellectual environment combined with a fun, all-women atmosphere. It's not uncommon to find friends gossiping until early morning, baking cookies together while cramming for an exam, or crowded around the dorm television on Thursday nights for a study break.

Wellesley is a college where the emphasis is on you. You'll never be a number at Wellesley; all of your professors will know you by your name and the quality of your work. Student opinions not only count but are actively solicited, from determining which professors receive tenure, to selecting your commencement speaker, to campus and dorm governance issues.

My first year at Wellesley, several students were chosen to help select the next president of the college. And our input didn't stop there! The new president asked us to call her by her first name, Diana, and always said hello when we saw her walking across campus or jogging around the lake. She also came to many of the college's activities, from attending school plays, soccer games, and student body meetings, to greeting trick-or-treaters at her home on Halloween. She gave us the feeling she really cared, and she did.

Part of Wellesley's charm also comes from its surroundings. Nestled in the suburb of Wellesley, Massachusetts, twelve miles outside of Boston, the college is located on a 500-acre campus that boasts one of the most spectacular settings in New England. Students often spend their weekends canoeing on Lake Waban, reading on Green Beach, or "traying" down Severance Green in the snow.

But during the week, students focus almost exclusively on their work. Wellesley is a teaching college rather than a research university, so students receive plenty of individual attention. Professors hold extensive office hours and some will even bake brownies for class or have students over to their homes. Every professor assigns and grades papers and exams; no graduate students compete for your attention or evaluate your work.

Political science, English, and psychology are among the most popular majors, although students dabble in everything from economics of Third World countries to sports medicine to Greek art. Many students choose to double-major, while others will select a minor, often a foreign language. Students can take only fourteen of their thirty-two credits in their major, so they are forced to broaden their education beyond a few departments.

Outside of the classroom, students spend much of their time participating in sports, music groups, dee-jaying at the college radio station, and exploring Boston. While Wellesley is not a party school, social opportunities abound if you're determined and aggressive. On campus, very few students choose not to participate in an extracurricular activity. And if your favorite activity on campus doesn't exist, simply propose it to college government—chances are, it will be approved.

An open mind is one of the crucial elements of being a Wellesley student, and the colleges stresses racial, ethnic, and religious diversity among its students. While most women call the mid-Atlantic home, students come from all fifty states and hail from sixty-nine countries. Although everyone is required to take a course from the multicultural curriculum, students often learn best about other cultures and customs from spending time with one another in the dorms.

I went to the Divali, or "festival of lights," dinner with one of my friends sophomore year. She was dressed in a beautiful Indian robe and took part in a traditional dance like I had never seen before. Afterwards, we had home-cooked dishes from Indian recipes that were both exotic and delicious. It was a wonderful, eye-opening experience.

The staff at Wellesley also pampers you, with elaborate exam "teas" and bedtime stories on Sunday nights in one hall. The dorms each have their own distinct character and it's easy to get to know both older and younger students, since dorms are not separated by class.

All in all, you'll work hard at Wellesley, but you'll never regret it. Wellesley will push you to your intellectual and physical limits, but you'll finish college with excellent preparation for whatever next step you choose to take. Wellesley may drive you crazy as a student, but as an alumna, you'll realize it was the best decision you've ever made.

ADMISSIONS REQUIREMENTS

As Wellesley's profile has risen in recent years, the number of students admitted has declined from fifty percent to about forty percent. But if you have a strong academic record, are motivated and enthusiastic, and know you want to attend a top school, Wellesley should be an easy choice.

Since the college believes a diverse student body is important, Wellesley seeks to bring together a group of individuals who enrich the school by their different races, ethnicities, religions, geographic backgrounds, and interests. Approximately half the student body is white, twenty-five percent is Asian, and the other twenty-five percent is African American, Latino, and Native American. While seventy percent have attended public high schools, the other thirty percent have gone to private schools.

Decision Plans

The college offers three decision plans for prospective students, each with different deadlines and each geared toward a different kind of applicant. All, though, require the standard application fee of $50.

- *Early Decision* is designed for women who are sure they want to attend Wellesley; about one-fifth of incoming students are accepted under this plan. If you think you might fall into this category, it's best to visit the college early, attend a few classes, meet some professors, and arrange an overnight stay with a student in her dorm room. The Early Decision deadline falls on November 1, so you must take the SATs or ACTs by October. The advantage of this plan is that you'll know by the winter holidays whether you've been admitted or deferred to the regular application pool. The only disadvantage is that the decision is binding, so if accepted, you must withdraw your applications from all other schools.
- For students who are strongly considering Wellesley but aren't sure they want to commit to the Early Decision program, the *Early Evaluation* plan has a deadline of January 1. You'll receive a letter by the end of February that indicates your chances of acceptance, but the final decision is not sent out until April. Early Evaluation is a smart plan for people who want to know how realistic their chances of admission are without having to pledge to one school.
- Finally, Wellesley offers a *Traditional Regular Decision* plan. Applications are due January 15, so you can take standardized tests through December of your senior year. Again, the Board of Admissions will notify you of its decision in April. Students placed on the wait list will also be notified at this time.

After you've chosen which plan is right for you, it's time to think about assembling your application package.

Application Requirements

Wellesley requires its applicants to take either the ACT or SAT I and three SAT II exams, including Writing and any other two subjects. In a recent incoming class, first-year students typically scored between 600 and 700 on the Math section and between 600 and 800 on the Verbal section.

Of course, standardized tests are only one part of your Wellesley application. High school grades are equally, if not more, important. Ninety-four percent of incoming students were in the top fifth of their class; all ranked in the top two-fifths. You'll also need three letters of recommendation, including one from an English teacher. It's best to choose faculty members who know you well from the classroom and extracurricular activities, and who can easily talk about your abilities, development as a student, personality, and potential as a Wellesley woman.

Along with the regular admissions paperwork, Wellesley requires a personal essay. The essay is one of the most crucial parts of the application, because it tells the admission board who you are, what you think, and why you would make a good candidate for Wellesley. It's also a chance for you to stand out from everybody else and tout your achievements. Remember, students, professors, and admissions officers are reading your essay, so your chances are best if you gear it toward a general audience.

Finally, Wellesley recommends, but does not require, an admissions interview. Try to have the interview on campus, so you can get a flavor for the school. Remember, the interview is not just a chance for the admissions officers to learn more about you, but for you to learn more about Wellesley. If you can't make it up to Boston, you can meet with an alumna in your area.

> *Applying to college seemed like a daunting process, but the Wellesley students and professors I met were so encouraging I felt as though they really wanted me there. The admissions office also went out of its way. When my parents and I arrived late for the campus tour, a student took us individually to our tour group and showed us sights along the way. The experience was actually symbolic of my years at Wellesley—everyone makes an extra effort to help each other out and is always supportive.*

A few other points: AP credits are accepted, provided you score a four or five on most tests. Interviews are required of transfer students, as are high school and college transcripts, and SAT I scores. Students applying from abroad must take the college boards and submit scores from their native countries' college entrance exams. Furthermore, a TOEFL exam is required for students whose native language is not English.

ACADEMIC LIFE

One of the best things about a Wellesley education is the opportunity to study a broad array of topics. Wellesley's curriculum offers up a plate of anything and everything, but leaves the choice to you.

The college provides major and minor programs of study in more than twenty-five departments and programs. The most popular majors include psychology, English, and art history.

When I was a first-year student at Wellesley, my parents told me they had a few requirements of their own, that I should take art history, economics, history, and a course in Shakespeare while in college. I put them off until junior and senior years—what a mistake! I regretted not minoring in history. And now when I go to art museums, I understand so much more: the time period, the artist's purposes, and color schemes.

Courses

Before students can graduate, they must meet some basic requirements. All students must complete thirty-two units of credits (usually one credit per course), at least eight of which are in your major. You also must maintain a 2.0, or C, average. In addition, all students must pass three courses in each of three subject groupings, namely humanities, social science, and natural sciences and math; a multicultural class; an expository writing course; one year of physical education; and demonstrated proficiency in a foreign language. Students must also complete four 300-level, or the most specialized, courses, at least two of which are in your major, to ensure you have in-depth knowledge in several subjects. If this all sounds daunting, it's not. Remember, you have eight semesters to spread these classes out. Most professors would advise, however, that you complete these courses during your first two years at Wellesley, so you can concentrate on completing your major and travel abroad during your junior and senior years.

Beyond the requirements, though, you can break your own academic path at Wellesley, including devising your own major and the courses needed to complete it. It's wise to experiment with a wide variety of offerings; many students find they have strong interests in subjects as different as English and physics, and love spending hours poring over books in the Reserve Room, but also relish nights spent stargazing at the Observatory. The college offers many courses without prerequisites, so you don't have to be a whiz at something before you walk into the classroom.

A SAMPLING OF COURSES AT WELLESLEY

- ❍ The Victorian Novel
- ❍ Women of Russia: A Portrait Gallery
- ❍ Comparative Physiology and Anatomy of Vertebrates with Laboratory
- ❍ Islamic Society in Historical Perspective
- ❍ Race and Ethnicity in American Literature
- ❍ Vergil's *Aeneid*
- ❍ Conservatism and Liberalism in Contemporary American Politics
- ❍ Government Policy: Its Effect on the Marketplace
- ❍ Christianity and the Third World
- ❍ Sociology of the Family
- ❍ Paris: City of Light
- ❍ Techniques of Acting
- ❍ Psychology of Language
- ❍ Paleontology with Laboratory
- ❍ Presidential-Congressional Relations
- ❍ African American Feminism
- ❍ Renaissance Art in Venice and in Northern Italy
- ❍ New Literatures: Lesbian and Gay Writing in America

Faculty

The strongest aspect of Wellesley's academic life is its professors. The faculty's 320 members are about evenly split between men and women, all of whom hold degrees in their fields from the top schools. And with a faculty-student ratio of ten to one, you'll not only know but most likely become friends with your professors.

Although research is considered a vital part of any professor's résumé, Wellesley professors are at the college principally because they want to teach, not because they want to do research. This means they'll know you by name and grade your work, and that you'll have valuable personal contacts when it comes time to ask for career advice and graduate school recommendations. They'll also take an interest in your life outside the classroom: how the soccer team did, if your family is visiting for Parents' Weekend, and when your theater production will be appearing on campus. At Wellesley, the average course size ranges from fifteen to twenty-five students, depending on the type of class.

My parents recently visited Wellesley and had lunch with one of my professors. Even though I graduated several years ago, he jumped at the chance to meet them again and spent an hour and a half reminiscing with them about my years as a student and sharing personal stories. It was a great experience that I doubt would have happened at any other school.

Another advantage of such an intimate class setting is that you'll have a unique chance to engage in truly intellectual debates that will often last more than the regular seventy minutes of class time. Professors also go out of their way to bring some of the brightest minds in their field to campus to meet with students in group settings, answer your questions, and spur your curiosity.

Course Load

The course load at Wellesley is not easy, but it is manageable. You can expect to stay up late reading Chaucer, spend your Sunday afternoons in the laboratory running chemistry experiments, and devote your mornings to practicing French in the language lab. But you'll be surprised at how much you come to enjoy each of these experiences, and you'll still have plenty of time left to participate in extracurricular activities and enjoy a healthy social life.

Wellesley students are allowed to elect up to five courses a semester; they can also audit classes and take courses pass/fail. The college's Honor Code allows students to schedule their own exams at the end of the semester. While this option allows you to take finals at your own pace, self-discipline in studying is a must.

Honors Program

For those who want to earn extra kudos in the classroom, the college offers an honors program for seniors. Provided students meet a high GPA in their major and choose an appropriate topic for study, they can work with several professors to complete a year-long thesis, thus qualifying for departmental honors. Students can also qualify for Latin Honors, which are recognized at graduation.

Exchange Program

If you have an interest that takes you beyond campus borders, you can participate in the Twelve College Exchange Program, a fully-accredited semester or year away from any of the following schools: Amherst, Bowdoin, Connecticut College, Dartmouth, Mount Holyoke, Smith, Trinity, Vassar, Wesleyan, Wheaton, and Williams. Most students travel off campus junior year. Other programs that the college sponsors include exchanges at Spelman College in Georgia, Mills College in California, and programs in France, Germany, Spain, Japan, Italy, and England. Students who want to study elsewhere must obtain permission from the college.

SOCIAL LIFE AND ACTIVITIES

Clubs

From the ice hockey team to the Texas Club to the more traditional activities such as the campus newspaper and student government, it's all yours for the taking at Wellesley.

Wellesley prides itself on offering just about any activity its students could want. If you're a dancer or singer, a literary lover, or a philosophy guru, there's a club for you. In all, Wellesley offers about 150 student groups and most have no membership requirements or dues—those are included in your annual student activity fee.

While these clubs will take as much of your time as you let them, they will also comprise some of your fondest college memories. You'll share the experience of running an organization together, from top to bottom, and learn both management and organizational skills far superior to those you'd get out of most internships. Few Wellesley students participate in no clubs at all; on average, students play major roles in at least one or two groups each year.

As a resident advisor my sophomore year, I was both the leader on my floor and part of a management team that arranged activities for my fellow dorm-mates. When the resident advisors met each Wednesday night, we'd talk about our individual problems and successes, and the direction we wanted to help take the dorm in. It was a wonderful chance to be a team player, see the impact our decisions had on our peers, and learn from their feedback.

PROMINENT RELIGIOUS GROUPS AT WELLESLEY

- Newman Catholic Ministry
- Al-Muslimat
- Hillel
- The Buddhist community
- Protestant
- Bahai
- Hindu
- Unitarian Universalist
- Native American religions

Wellesley encourages first-year students to participate in all activities. Most clubs thrive on the energy and enthusiasm new students bring; they're also a great way to meet Wellesley women of all ages. A student activities' night is held at the beginning of each school year, so you can check out clubs that sound interesting. The Schneider Student Center is the base of extracurricular life, although most activities take students everywhere from campus to the entire northeast corridor.

Sports

Wellesley also offers a variety of sports teams that compete with other Seven Sisters and regional schools, including soccer, basketball, volleyball, swimming, lacrosse, cross-country, and tennis. The college prides itself on graduating well-rounded individuals, so students are encouraged to take part in sports, whether on a varsity or intramural level. And with the Nannerl O. Keohane Sports Center on campus, that's not hard to do. The Keohane Sports Center, named after Wellesley's eleventh president, includes a huge indoor track, pool, sauna, basketball and tennis courts, and weight room. In the fall and spring, students also canoe on Lake Waban and row on the Charles River in Boston.

I took golf during my junior year at Wellesley and loved it! We played on the college's beautiful course across the street from campus and learned all about the strokes and various clubs. The best part, though, was that we were able to laugh together about our mistakes as beginners but also able to actually play nine holes when the semester ended!

Dorms

While clubs and sports are a great way to meet other students, dorms provide the most natural setting for getting to know your Wellesley sisters. Almost all students live in the dorms, and on-campus housing for four years is guaranteed, with most juniors and seniors guaranteed single rooms. Some students also live in co-ops, cooking their own food and living in a relaxed residential system. In most dorms, though, heads of house, house presidents, first-year coordinators, and resident advisors plan activities, from showing videos to having leaf-jumping parties, to holding study breaks complete with café lattes and Milano cookies. The favorite activity of the year is Holiday Dinner, where seniors dress in their gowns, students gather to sing holiday songs, and the dining halls prepare a fabulous feast, complete with the college's own peppermint stick pie and cheesecake bar.

Wellesley does not have a Greek system, but students with interests in art, music, and Shakespeare can join one of the four society houses on campus. The groups arrange campus-wide lectures and events, as well as provide another social outlet for members.

Parties

Keep in mind that Wellesley is not a party school. The opportunities are there, if you want to attend Harvard and MIT parties each weekend, go clubbing, or be a sister at a fraternity house. While many first-year students do all of the above, older students often spend weekends on campus, listening to comedians and musicians at Molly's, the campus pub; taking advantage of the college theater; seeing classic 1980s movies at the Film Society; and just enjoying each other's company. As with most other things at Wellesley, you create the path you want to take.

FINANCIAL AID

College these days is expensive, but one of Wellesley's most important priorities is maintaining its need-blind admissions policy. More than half of Wellesley students receive some form of financial aid.

A Wellesley education costs about $26,000 per year, including tuition, room, board, and the student activity and facilities fees. Students may also elect to enroll in the college's health insurance program for an additional charge.

While a financial aid award depends on a student's need, the college provides aid for about fifty-three percent of first-year students and fifty-five percent of continuing students.

Payment Plans

Wellesley offers three payment plans to help students pay for their education:

- The semester payment plan allows students and their families to pay tuition and other expenses twice each year; this program is generally recommended for parents who are using savings to pay for college or have loans guaranteed at very favorable rates.
- The ten-month payment plan assists families who are using current earnings to pay for tuition in five installments.
- The prepaid tuition stabilization plan allows families to pay the entire cost of a Wellesley education upon entrance to the school. This program sets the cost of tuition at the first-year rate and will not reflect any subsequent increases during the course of the student's education.

Students who are interested in obtaining financial aid must submit their most recent income tax returns, along with the FAFSA, or Wellesley's own financial statement. The deadline for financial aid applications is February 1.

Working on Campus

To raise money for their education, most students work on campus in activities ranging from being a guard in the college's new Davis Museum and Cultural Center, to working as an assistant in one of the departments, to helping serve and prepare food in a dining hall. The average annual intake from these jobs is about $1,250. It's also a great way to meet fellow students, work alongside your professors, and spend time enjoying the campus.

Loans and Grants

Wellesley also offers four types of loans to incoming students: the federal Stafford Loan, the federal Perkins Loan, the Wellesley College Student's Aid Society Loan, and the Wellesley College Loan program.

The federal Stafford and Perkins loans are repayable starting six months after graduation. While the Stafford Loan has a variable interest rate that is set each summer for the upcoming year, the Perkins Loan has a set interest rate of five percent and is available to students who demonstrate high financial need.

The Wellesley College Student's Aid Society Loan carries a five percent interest rate and must be repaid within five years and nine months of graduation. The Wellesley College Loan program, which is geared toward international students, has a nine percent interest rate and requires payments twice a year following graduation.

Wellesley also offers grants from the college's funds and from the Federal Supplemental Opportunity Grant Program. In addition, students who think they may be eligible for state grants and the Federal Pell Grant should contact the financial aid office, which verifies students' enrollment and eligibility.

Finally, financial awards from outside organizations are calculated into the work-loan-grant program administered by the college. The college also operates a professional clothing store for students receiving aid. And to raise some extra spending cash, Wellesley keeps a roster of people and organizations in the area who are looking for paid interns, house sitters, and baby-sitters.

GRADUATES

Chances are you've heard of some of Wellesley's most famous graduates: First Lady Hillary Rodham Clinton, Secretary of State Madeleine Korbel Albright, and screenwriter/director Nora Ephron (of *When Harry Met Sally* and *Sleepless in Seattle* fame), to name just a few. But in truth, whether they're famous or not, most Wellesley alumnae are very successful at (and very happy with) what they do.

Wellesley graduates about 580 to 620 students each year, with about half of them choosing to go on to graduate school and about half going into the working world. Eighty-seven percent of students graduate within six years of enrollment. Although political science, psychology, and English are among the most popular majors at Wellesley, many students choose a career in business, very often starting out as a management consultant at a high-powered Manhattan or Boston firm. Other popular careers include law, journalism, and medicine.

More than 100 companies, ranging from Microsoft to Smith Barney, recruit on campus each year. Students find that the recruiting process is a great way to learn more about these companies, practice their interviewing skills, and, of course, land that all-important first job. Because Wellesley graduates are so successful, most companies return year after year.

The college also offers a well-staffed Center for Work and Service to talk with students about postgraduation plans. From advice on polishing up your résumé to helping you apply for fellowship programs, the center's employees are knowledgeable and accessible. The center also pairs up students and mentors for a day-long "shadow" program in January, and keeps a database with names of alumnae all over the world who have offered to share their professional insights.

OTHER PROMINENT GRADS

- Eleanor Dean Acheson, Assistant Attorney General
- Katharine Lee Bates, Professor, Author, *America the Beautiful*
- Marjory Stoneman Douglas, Environmentalist
- Wendy Lee Gramm, Former Chair, Commodities Futures Trading Commission
- Mildred McAfee Horton, Founder of WAVES
- Madame Chiang Kai-Shek, Nationalist Chinese Leader
- Nannerl O. Keohane, Political Scientist, President of Duke University
- Ali McGraw, Actress
- Cokie Roberts, Journalist
- Diane Sawyer, Journalist
- Leticia Ramos Shahani, Philippine Senator
- Rose Styron, Author, Activist

The alumnae association provides several programs for juniors and seniors, too, including a mentoring night, where students share dinner and conversation with alumnae in the Boston area who have similar career interests. In addition, the association sponsors workshops on buying a car, renting an apartment, finding a job, and generally making it on your own without Mom and Dad's financial help.

I went to the mentoring night my senior year, and sat around an alumna's living room chatting about our common interest in journalism. One alum, Jean Dietz, had been a correspondent for The Boston Globe. *Another, Callie Crossley, was a producer with the ABC newsmagazine,* 20/20. *It was great to hear about their experiences as successful women in journalism, and they were genuinely interested in helping me start my career.*

Many Wellesley alumnae have been pathbreakers in their careers and all of them want to see you succeed; you'll find that this support network of more than 35,000 women worldwide will follow you wherever you go and is always ready to lend a hand. Wellesley graduates are in every field imaginable, and take with them the skills and curiosity they learned as students, along with the college's mission, "not to be served, but to serve."

Once you leave Wellesley, you'll find that all your networks of career support are still available to help you, and that local alumnae clubs throughout the world sponsor events, from happy hours, hayrides, and Sunday afternoon tea to lectures by professors who are visiting the area and pizza nights with prospective students. Graduates also serve on the Board of Trustees, as advisors to various groups, and as admissions representatives. But the best part of being a graduate may be taking part in the reunion parades, where graduates dress in their class colors, take part in Stepsinging—a favorite college tradition—have a chance to revisit the campus in the spring, and catch up with their friends.

SUMMING UP

Although Wellesley women are diverse in their interests, backgrounds, and personalities, all of them share the experience of having attended the top women's college in the country. Wellesley offers its students the opportunity to expand their minds, challenge their limits, and learn to be meaningful leaders in a changing world.

Wellesley women share more than an education, though. From Flower Sunday in September, when sophomores give their "little sisters," or first-year students, a daisy as a sign of welcome and friendship, to commencement, when seniors pop champagne corks together, Wellesley develops in its students a sense of sisterhood, a camaraderie that can only be shared at a women's college. While students may complain about a lack of social life during their four years there, they will also revel in the chance to study without distraction and to be completely in the company of a group of outstanding women. As the favorite campus saying goes, "Not a girls' school without men, but a women's college without boys."

The campus is also a sanctuary, a safe and well-policed atmosphere, where you will find yourself enveloped by the beautiful Massachusetts environment. The college's staff also pampers your needs, providing special events such as a Food Festival at the beginning of the year, with fresh lobsters, steak, and even cotton candy, to emotional support at the Stone Center and the Office of Religious Life.

Professors are there to offer a hand as well; many of them have been known to spend an hour or more with each student answering questions during office hours. As a student, you'll not only learn facts and figures, but how to analyze and apply that information to other problems. Your professors will challenge you to become active thinkers and participants in and out of the classroom, by sharing your enthusiasm and success, offering advice, and also becoming lifelong friends.

Wellesley is a college where you will be known by your first name, whether you're the college president, a professor, or a student. You can also choose whether to be the student body president, or just a member of the student body. You become empowered because you make the decisions and you shape your future.

If you have a preconceived notion of a women's college, chances are it's not true at Wellesley—the college is not a bastion of lesbianism, nor a stronghold of left-wing, radical feminism. It's also not a place for meek-mannered women who don't know how to hold their own with men. What Wellesley is, is a supportive environment that gives its students a sense of self-esteem, accomplishment, and the ability to apply that knowledge and confidence elsewhere. What Wellesley does is to successfully educate women who do, time and time again, make a difference in the world.

❑ *Mary Lynn F. Jones, B.A.*

WESLEYAN UNIVERSITY

Photo by Nancy Wolz

Wesleyan University
Middletown, CT 06457

(860) 685-3000
Fax: (860) 685-3001

E-mail: admissions@wesleyan.edu
Web site: http://www.admiss.wesleyan.edu

Enrollment

Full-time ❑ women: 1,400
❑ men: 1,300

Part-time ❑ women: 15
❑ men: 10

INTRODUCING WESLEYAN

Wesleyan students feel a unique bond with one another that goes beyond school spirit. When you meet someone who went to Wes you feel like you know them already, in the sense that you've both shared in the discovery of some wonderful secret.

For years, Wesleyan has been one of America's best-kept educational secrets, but it seems that the word is getting out. Increasing numbers of applicants are realizing that Wesleyan's unparalleled academics and unique student body make for a college experience unsurpassed elsewhere. Its top-notch faculty includes some of the best in the country in both research and teaching, and the students are driven by the inner desire to work hard and to have fun. To add to this, Wesleyan is a college on the edge of the future, with an administration and a president, Douglas J. Bennet, committed to leading Wesleyan with vision, demonstrating the value of a liberal arts education to the world.

Three things set Wesleyan apart from the rest: size, academic intensity, and its student body. Wesleyan is a small-to-medium liberal arts college (2,700 undergraduates) set on a beautiful and spacious New England campus, comparable to schools like Amherst and Williams. But as a thriving research university, with a small population of 150 graduates, the productivity and distinction of Wesleyan faculty in research rival that of faculty at much larger institutions. Because of its unique size, undergraduate students make use of graduate resources and enjoy small seminar-sized classes and opportunities to personally get to know professors.

Many students choose Wes over the Ivy League for its intellectual environment, which differs from other competitive schools in one key quality: While students at other universities are often encouraged to compete against others, Wesleyan students only compete to do better than they did last week. Wes students feel comfortable helping each other with work, and talking about intellectual ideas even (gasp!) outside the classroom.

Wesleyan fosters independence—its approach to liberal arts education encourages undergraduates to invest deeply in their courses of study, without mandating a set of core courses that every student must slog through. What students do have in common is *passion*—they are passionate about their studies, passionate about their artistic endeavors, and passionate about their politics. "The greatest thing that Wesleyan did for me was help me define my own education," said one graduating senior. This might seem daunting to some, but Wesleyan students rise to the occasion.

You're in a place where no one tells you how to live, how to dress, or (heaven forbid) what to think—academically or otherwise. I tend to see it as a challenge.

The university's president, Douglas Bennet, is the perfect leader for Wesleyan because he embodies all of the qualities that every Wes graduate hopes to leave with—initiative, creativity, and, above all, a sense of humor. As former assistant secretary of state to President Clinton, and as CEO and president of National Public Radio, it is no surprise that he also graduated from Wesleyan in 1959. As was the case with President Bennet, Wesleyan students today are fed a healthy ration of responsibility and independence, and it is with these qualities that they will leave Wes, enter the world, and contribute to society. "Wesleyan prepared me for the real world more than any other experience I can imagine," says a recent graduate. "I didn't go to Wesleyan specifically to get this training—I went to learn. The preparation happened along the way."

ADMISSIONS REQUIREMENTS

There is no question that Wesleyan is one of America's "hot" schools. The Office of Admissions has seen a twenty-two percent increase in applications over the last five years—less than one out of three of those who applied in a recent year were admitted.

What students should apply? Make no mistake: Wesleyan is academically rigorous; in general, applicants have performed extraordinarily well in high school. Of a recent class, sixty-nine percent ranked in the top ten percent of their high school classes; thirty-two percent were class president, team captain, or editor-in-chief. As with many colleges, the high school transcript is considered the most important element of the application, but Wesleyan prides itself on taking the time to get to know each applicant as a person and not as a series of numbers, weighing heavily the personal essay, recommendations, and interview. Average SAT I scores are: Verbal—680, Math—670. (The SAT I or ACT is required, as are the SAT II: Subject tests in Writing and two other subjects.)

Students at Wesleyan are stellar beyond SAT scores, grades, and lists of activities. They are intellectually curious, take initiative, and have proved that they will contribute to the Wesleyan community. A recent freshman class included a student who was the first female member of her high school football team, an award-winning playwright, a nationally ranked chess player, and a student who started a midnight basketball program in his hometown. Every year, there are many students who excel as starting players on varsity sports teams, leaders of high school student bodies, and active volunteers in their communities. Applicants to Wes must prove that they have made use of the resources and options available in high school, and plan to continue to be active and engaged in college.

For the student who is serious about Wesleyan, applying Early Decision provides a slight edge in the application process. It is a popular option, but encouraged only for those who have selected Wes as the top choice. Admittance to Wesleyan ED is binding.

ACADEMIC LIFE

It took me a while to get used to the demanding academic schedule at Wesleyan. But when I did, I really came to realize what makes it so special. As well as one-on-one attention from my professors, I really benefited from their scholarship. I began to learn with my professors, rather than from them.

Wesleyan has earned a reputation as one of the finest schools in the country for good reason: its professors are top scholars and teachers, and its students take initiative and have a passion for learning. Wesleyan differs from other top-ranked institutions, however, in the depth of its commitment to fostering the pursuit of individual intellectual interests.

Course Offerings

The breadth of offerings at Wesleyan is outstanding. Typical liberal arts disciplines such as history, English, and physics, exist side by side with such departments as molecular biology and biochemistry (MB & B), East Asian studies, and film studies.

I was amazed when, in my senior year of high school, I found the Wesleyan course catalog in our guidance center. I thought I might have to go to a huge state university to take the range of courses I was interested in, but Wesleyan had it all—from Oceanography to Linguistics, Archaeology to Film—I felt that I'd finally found a school that would keep pace with my interests.

Wesleyan's unique academic course offerings include Myth and Ideology at the Movies, Nabokov and Cultural Synthesis, and Biology and the Politics of Reproduction. Another of Wesleyan's major strengths is its arts curriculum; introductory courses are open to all and most graduating seniors, regardless of their majors, have taken at least one dance, studio art, or music course. Popular choices include Introduction to Drawing, West African Dance, and Worlds of Music.

The free and open aspect of the Wesleyan curriculum goes beyond the arts. Because there are very few classes reserved only for majors, students can follow many interests and not feel blocked out of classes. So how does a student decide which four or five classes a semester to take from over 900 courses in 38 departments and programs and 46 major fields of study? Upon arrival on the campus, each student is assigned a faculty advisor. The FA works with the student to define an academic mission and choose classes, all via Wesleyan's high-tech and student-friendly on-line course registration system.

FYI Classes

From the very first semester, academic exploration at Wesleyan is encouraged. Freshmen are prioritized for admittance to a host of small, intellectually rigorous seminars known as First-Year Initiatives, or FYI classes. The first two years at Wesleyan are generally reserved for exploration of the wide-ranging curriculum. To fulfill Wesleyan's General Education Expectations (GenEds), students must take at least three courses (from at least two different departments) in each of three categories: humanities and arts, social and behavioral sciences, and natural sciences and mathematics. The vast majority of Wesleyan students fulfill these expectations without ever trying, though it is possible to opt out of the Expectations with a valid academic reason.

Majors

A student's final two years at Wesleyan are when he or she can truly delve into a chosen course of study. Majors are declared at the end of the sophomore year. The most-declared majors at Wes are English, history, and biology, but double-majoring is common, and more students triple-major than one might imagine. Interdepartmental majors such as psychology-sociology, African American studies, medieval studies, and East Asian studies are popular, and the American studies department at Wes is considered to be one of the finest undergraduate programs in the country—soon to be housed in the Center for the Americas with Latin American studies. Students may also, with faculty approval, create a university major, joining two or more areas of study not already conjoined under the auspices of an interdepartmental major. Wesleyan also features two special interdisciplinary majors that must be declared during freshman year, the College of Letters (COL), which combines literature, history, philosophy, and foreign languages, and the College of Social Studies (CSS), combining history, government, philosophy, and economics (sometimes called the "College of Suicidal Sophomores," in reference to its demanding sophomore year schedule of a ten-page paper a week).

Study Abroad

Many students choose to augment their on-campus experience at Wesleyan by taking one or two semesters abroad or away from campus. With the assistance of the Office of International Studies, students can study abroad in Wesleyan programs in Paris, Jerusalem, Madrid, or Regensburg. Wesleyan also has consortial relations with programs in China, Japan, and Italy, and students can go on any of the other 100 programs approved by the Office of International Studies. Wesleyan is also part of the twelve-college exchange, a group of prestigious New England colleges that offers exchanges for the semester or year.

The Thesis

The grand finale of a student's academic life at Wesleyan is often the completion of a thesis. Though it is only through the optional thesis process that a student can earn university honors (there is a separate Phi Beta Kappa selection process), many students choose to do a thesis simply to fulfill personal intellectual goals. The most common theses at Wesleyan are year-long research projects, producing papers that range in length from 30 to 45 pages in the sciences to 100 to 160 pages in English or history. Dance, theater, and music majors perform their theses for the Wesleyan community, while studio arts majors participate in a three-week gallery exhibition and the thesis films constitute a special slate of screenings at the end of the semester.

Faculty

Wesleyan faculty is outstanding and engaging. In recent studies, Wesleyan professors have tipped the scales in scholarship—science faculty placed second in the number of publications compared to seventy-four colleges, and the economics department is renowned as one of the best in the country. Unlike many larger institutions, however, the most productive scholars at Wesleyan are often highly regarded as the best teachers. All faculty members (260 full-time) teach undergraduates. Professors frequently structure classes around their current interests and research, allowing for timely, engaging classroom discussion. Students frequently become involved in helping professors with research, and in the sciences students have been known to copublish papers with their professors. Professors are generally accessible, and it is not unheard of to have a class meet in a professor's living room, or for professors to join students for dinner. The faculty includes

Pulitzer-Prize-winning writer Annie Dillard, jazz musician and MacArthur Genius Grant Award winner Anthony Braxton, film authority Jeanine Basinger, international terrorism expert Martha Crenshaw, *Art Bulletin* editor John Paoletti, award-winning American Studies scholar Richard Slotkin, experimental music composer Alvin Lucier, prominent DNA researcher David Beveridge, writer and biographer Phyllis Rose, and noted historian of China Vera Schwarcz. A recent study also rated four Wes economists as among the best in their fields.

Despite the depth and breadth of the curriculum, students may find they wish to explore a subject not covered by any class offered. In that event, they may, in consultation with a faculty member, design a tutorial to study the subject they are interested in. Recent student-organized tutorials have included topics in Native American studies, literature seminars focusing on Don DeLillo and Anne Rice, and a survey of "Complexity Theory."

Facilities

It is nearly impossible for any single student to exhaust Wesleyan's academic resources, but it may be even more difficult to exhaust its physical resources. Wesleyan's modern, technologically adaptable classroom space is enhanced by several fine computer labs, e-mail and Internet connections in each dorm room, and more lab space in the Science Center per student than any other science research institution in the country. Olin Library, the university's largest library, has one million volumes including a music library and a rare book collection (including a Shakespeare First Folio). The Smith room on the first floor is a popular place to meet friends in the evening, and the small, quiet study rooms on the second and third floors are for those who prefer dead silence (many seniors who write honors theses get their own thesis carrels, small private rooms, many with window views). Across the street from Olin, the Science Library houses science-oriented materials along with the Cutter Collection, an eclectic collection of one family's turn-of-the-century books, and a small natural history museum. Across campus in the Center for the Arts (CFA), the Davison Art Center is a national landmark that houses the art library and 10,000 prints by old masters and modern artists.

SOCIAL LIFE AND ACTIVITIES

The variety of Wesleyan's academic life is equaled, if not exceeded, by the variety of its social life. There is a popular theory at Wesleyan that if you get any students into conversation, you will find that they do something fascinating—from leading the Ultimate Frisbee team to directing a short film. It is a place teeming with students who are interested in living in a charged environment. Each week, the student body hosts a wide variety of activities ranging from dance performances to sports games to live music, and it is not uncommon to attend several of such different events in one day.

Although Middletown is located thirty minutes from New Haven, thirty minutes from Hartford, and two hours from New York City and Boston, Wesleyan students often don't feel the need to venture very far to have fun, and the focus of the social life is located on campus. Middletown has a variety of restaurants popular with students (it can be difficult to get a table at O'Rourke's Diner on a Sunday morning, where students have entertained Clint Eastwood and Allen Ginsberg), but for nightlife Wesleyan sticks close to home. Walk the streets of campus on a weekend night and you will hear bands performing in the WestCo Cafe, plays in the '92 Theater, movies at the cinema, and hip-hop shows in MoConoughy Dining Hall.

Parties

There are as many different kinds of parties as there are kinds of people—gatherings ranging from house parties to all-campus parties to dorm parties to parties sponsored by student groups. Often parties have themes: a costume party in LoRise, an eighties dance at Psi Upsilon fraternity, or a swing ball to celebrate the Senior Film Festival. Parties range from small and intimate to large and loud, but they are never exclusive, and never focused exclusively around drinking. Often a group such as the Black and Latino Brotherhood or the women's rugby team will sponsor a campus event that attracts a broad cross section of students. Each year, two large musical events—Fall Ball and Spring Fling—attract big-name bands to campus. Recently featured were Parliament-Funkadelic, De La Soul, Phish, and Spin Doctors. Eclectic, a smaller concert space, frequently brings in bands like Morphine, Superchunk, Velocity Girl, and Ani Defranco.

The first year at Wes is the only year social activities are arranged; after orientation, students plan their own social calendars. In general, the more adventurous students are, the more events they will attend and the more people they will meet. Friendships grow out of social events, residential life, classes, clubs, and sports teams. While Wesleyan students don't go on traditional "dates," a couple might meet at Klekolo, a local cafe, or drive to the always-open Athenian Diner.

I try to go to as many things I can and meet as many people I can, but there's always more—I'm always reluctant to go away for the weekend, because I'm afraid I'll miss something.

Dining on Campus

Dining on campus can be an adventure. At any other school something as pedestrian as a freshman dining hall wouldn't arouse the same kind of passion and creativity that those at Wesleyan have shown toward MoCon. Described alternatively as "a church in the style of the Jetsons," or a building "waiting to be reunited with the mother ship," MoCon boasts one of the longest salad bars in Connecticut (yes, people measure these things), as well as one of the most popular weekend brunches in town. Monthly theme meals include everything from a Texas-style barbeque to a romantic candle-lit meal for Valentine's Day. During the period before exams—known to Wes students as Reading Week—MoCon sponsors a free midnight pancake breakfast. And no Wesleyan experience is complete until one has made an announcement from the landing (or pulpit) at the top of MoCon's semicircular staircase. (Much to the delight of the diners, many visiting parents have embarrassed themselves by pausing too long on the landing to enjoy the view.) MoCon is also a social center, host to a multitude of events, ranging from Doug Bennet's inaugural dinner to frequent and popular video dance parties.

Although upperclass students sometimes eat in MoCon, eating at the dining hall is the primary social focus of first year. First-year students may also eat at Summerfields, which offers primarily vegetarian and vegan choices, or the Havurah, which offers kosher meals. After first year, students can eat at any of these places but can also use ID cards to eat at the Campus Center, Summerfields, Wes Wings, or in one of the eating clubs located in the fraternity houses. Always handy is Weshop, the campus "grocery store," which stocks more like a 7-11 (primarily junk food) but does allow students to buy food on the ID point-system.

Housing

Wesleyan is one of the only schools I know of where freshmen can live in a single if they want to; in fact, it's one of the reasons I chose to go there. I value that students are allowed that independence even from day one.

Wesleyan housing is prime real estate compared to some other schools. On-campus housing is guaranteed all four years, and can range from traditional freshman dorms to small New England houses on tree-lined streets. Ninety-eight percent of students live on campus. First-year students can live in dorms with single rooms, double rooms, suites, quads, two-room doubles, or special-interests. Upperclassmen either select to stay in the dorms or live in apartments, townhouses, New England clapboard houses, fraternities, or special-interest houses. Special-interest houses include everything from Spanish House to Womanist House to Outhouse (home to the Outing Club). These houses sponsor educational and social events for the whole campus.

Fraternities and Sororities

Fraternities are an option for housing and also for social life: fifteen percent of students are involved in the seven fraternities (some coed) and two sororities on campus. The Mystical Seven and The Skull and Serpent, secret societies both located on Wyllys Avenue at the gateway to the Center for the Arts, date from the early 1900s and are shrouded in mystery, but no one lives here. (We think.)

Organizations

Wesleyan students like to get involved. They serve on every university committee, organize orientation and graduation, and independently allocate funds to the 200 student organizations, which include groups devoted to politics, athletics, and artistic and cultural interests. Fifteen student publications are sent to press at least once a semester, ranging from the school newspaper, the *Argus*, to magazines of fiction, humor, women's issues, activism, and poetry. Students are also responsible for the wide variety of lectures and artists who visit campus. WESU-FM, the campus radio station, is a something to be proud of, not just because it is the oldest continuously operating college radio station in the country, but because it plays cool music and anyone can become a DJ.

Athletics

Although many people do not know it until they visit campus, Wesleyan's Freeman Athletic Center (affectionately nicknamed The Palace) is one of the finest college athletic centers in New England. Completed in 1991 at the cost of $22 million, it has a 3,000-seat gymnasium, a 50-meter Olympic pool, a 400-meter outdoor track, a 200-meter indoor track, a hockey arena, and a strength and fitness center. Athletics at Wesleyan are top-notch and interest top athletes: fourteen men's varsity and fourteen women's varsity athletic teams compete at the Division III level. About sixty percent of students are involved in some sort of organized athletics. Some of the "winningest" teams at Wes are the men's soccer, women's rugby, the track and cross-country teams, and the crew teams. Football and women's ice hockey have been on the upswing in recent years, and many other teams have successful programs. The campus is also home to a 5,000-seat stadium, sixteen tennis courts, fourteen squash courts, four soccer fields, two football practice fields, two rugby pitches, and fields for field hockey, Ultimate Frisbee, baseball, and softball. The new Macomber Boathouse is home to Wesleyan's nationally ranked crew team, set on a beautiful spot on the historic Connecticut River.

One fascinating thing about social and extracurricular life at Wesleyan is that it doesn't happen exclusive of faculty and the administration. Professors often attend cultural events, and President Bennet is not above showing up at campus parties. One student invited President Bennet to a birthday party, and although travel plans obliged Doug and his wife Midge to send their regrets, before leaving Midge baked a pound cake for the student, wrapped in red and black ribbon. Attached to the cake was a note from Midge: "Sorry we missed your party." On the back of the card Doug wrote: "She really baked it."

FINANCIAL AID

If you are applying to colleges and are also in need of financial aid, keep this in mind: Wesleyan is the one of the last colleges in the country to hold firm to need-blind admissions, meaning that Wesleyan admits students without knowledge of their financial need. Recently, when several schools around the country gave up their need-blind programs, Wesleyan students led the country's college students in protest of this change in policy. Students had rallied their cause to *The New York Times* in 1992.

Wesleyan awards aid to all admitted students to the full extent of demonstrated need. Wesleyan is generous with financial aid; most students receiving aid from Wesleyan get a package that includes a grant, student loans, parent loans, government-supported loans, and work-study jobs.

Tuition at Wesleyan is not cheap. To pay the full amount required—not to mention the other costs in room, board, and personal expenses—about half of the student body receives financial aid, the average package being $15,000.

GRADUATES

Education at Wesleyan is more about learning to live your life than memorizing the vagaries of some obscure academic discipline. Wesleyan is the definitive liberal arts college—

here, students learn how to think critically, write clearly, and make informed decisions. Graduates can succeed in any situation; they are flexible, creative, and roll with the punches. It is not uncommon for English majors to become computer programmers, psychology majors to go to law school, economics majors to go to film school, and music majors to become math teachers.

There is no single field of endeavor pursued by the majority of Wesleyan grads. Of a recent class, thirty-five percent of students are in business, thirteen percent are in law school or law-related fields, twelve percent are in education, thirteen percent are in grad school, thirteen percent in medicine or health, and twelve percent in the arts. While Wesleyan had the country's second highest number of seniors applying to the Peace Corps, the top employer hiring students from the class of 1997 was Lehman Brothers—a Wall Street investment bank.

PROMINENT GRADS

- **Gerald Baliles, Former Virginia Governor**
- **David Britt, President and CEO, Children's Television Workshop**
- **Robin Cook, Author**
- **Robert Hunter, NATO Ambassador**
- **Herb Kelleher, CEO of Southwest Airlines**
- **Jay Levy, AIDS Researcher**
- **Robert Ludlum, Author**
- **Randall Pinkston, CBS Reporter**
- **Ted Shaw, Chief Counsel, NAACP Legal Defense and Educational Fund**
- **David Skaggs, Congressman**
- **Jon Turteltaub, Film Director**
- **Walter Wriston, Former Chairman of Citicorp**

As for continuing education after Wesleyan, about fifteen percent of students go to graduate school immediately after graduation. Five years after graduation, about seventy-five percent will have gone to some kind of graduate school, and acceptance rates to professional schools remain close to ninety percent. In addition to formal schooling, Wesleyan graduates have also won more Watson Fellowships for self-designed student projects than any other school in the country. This year, graduates are pursuing such topics as "Beyond the Conquistadors: Urban Growth in Former Spanish Colonies," and "Interface of Knowledge: Biotechnology and Local Practice."

Wesleyan students spend plenty of time visiting the excellent library and friendly staff of the Career Resource Center (CRC), which helps students plan ahead for leaving campus, even in the first year of college. With help from the CRC, many students opt for internships over January break and in the summer, often with Wesleyan alumni or parents in their field of interest. Wesleyan has a tight network of alumni and parents in the field who can also help in the latter years at Wesleyan by providing informational interviews and even offering jobs.

SUMMING UP

So, picture this: It's fall in New England, the air is crisp, your ears are red from the slight bite of the cold, and the leaves of the trees are slowly turning the bright color of fire. You walk from the Campus Center to the steps of Olin Library, one of the oldest buildings on campus, where students have gathered in the afternoon sun to chat and read. You enter the building and follow the hall leading to the front face of the building, the north side of massive arched windows overlooking the football field, and take a seat in one of its funky pink easy chairs.

From here, one has the best view of what Wesleyan has to offer. Across the football field is the old gym, where generations of Wesleyan alumni have thrown a few hoops. Beyond that (and beyond the new Office of Admission, which has to be seen to be believed), is the Center for the Arts, where generations of students have also learned to play the Javanese Gamalon, an instrument so large it takes twenty people to play. To the west is Foss Hill, a definite social center of campus, and to the east is the scenic and historic college row, where it all began.

Here you can get a vision for Wesleyan's future. The room you are in, the north room of Olin Library, built in 1985, encompasses the original face of the historic building, designed by Henry Bacon in 1831. The addition is more than an architectural element; it is a symbol of the past and future of Wesleyan. Founded as a small Methodist college for men in the early nineteenth century on the principles of community and the value of a liberal arts education, Wesleyan has held fast to these values, at the same time that it has built on, renovated, and transformed the school into a modern small university. It has seen coeducation, racial tension, peace rallies, and firebombings—few American schools have seen as much change. But at the same time, Wesleyan has still remained consistent—just as the old bricks of Olin Library have always faced the football field, the school has always been leading the pack—a place where high-quality students and top-notch faculty gather to learn and explore.

Wesleyan is unique because it attracts vibrant, open-minded, creative students, and because it rewards these students for pursuing intellectual interests and outside pursuits with rigor. At the same time that they engage students in the classroom, Wesleyan's faculty contribute high-level scholarship and is made up of dedicated and caring teachers. Wesleyan is a small-college atmosphere, yet it is a place where students are challenged to make new discoveries about themselves and others. Because of this, it will always be the special place, the undiscovered secret, the definitive liberal arts education of the twenty-first century. Take a moment to discover it for yourself.

❑ *Stacy Theberge, B.A.*

WILLIAMS COLLEGE

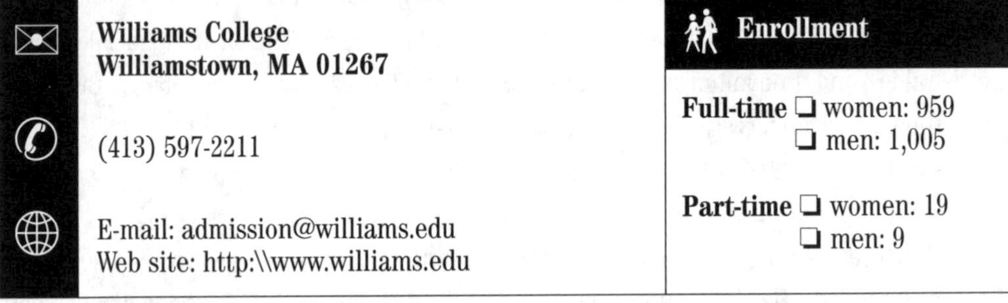

Williams College
Williamstown, MA 01267

(413) 597-2211

E-mail: admission@williams.edu
Web site: http:\\www.williams.edu

Enrollment

Full-time ❑ women: 959
❑ men: 1,005

Part-time ❑ women: 19
❑ men: 9

INTRODUCING WILLIAMS

Williams College is a small liberal arts college located in the idyllic Berkshire Mountains of northwestern Massachusetts. At Williams students receive an education that, in its breadth, stands in stark contrast to the school's small size and remote location. After having been surrounded by nationally renowned professors, world class art, spectacular scenery, and most importantly, some of the brightest and most active students in the country for four years, it is no surprise that a graduate with a Williams degree is looked upon with a great deal of respect by both employers and graduate schools.

Notwithstanding its splendid facilities and superb teachers, it is the student body itself that makes Williams a special place to attend college. Few schools of any size can claim as well-rounded a student body as Williams. Chances are that your first year suitemates could be a concert violinist, a professional magician, and a soccer star. The geographic and cultural base from which these students are drawn is just as impressive as their backgrounds. Students come to Williams from all fifty states (eighty-nine percent are from outside Massachusetts), and over forty different countries. The split between public and private school students is about even, roughly one quarter are minorities, and over forty percent of all students receive some sort of financial aid. With almost all students living on campus, eating in the same dining halls, and gathering together in small classes for four years, every day spent at Williams is one in which you are confronted with new and intriguing ideas.

Classes at Williams very rarely consist of a professor lecturing at you for an hour. More likely it is a lively debate involving the students and the professor. These debates rarely stop at the end of class. Countless times I stayed up to all hours of the night with my suitemates discussing anything from the success of soft-authoritarian regimes in Southeast Asia to the sculpture of Bernini. These discussions consistently bombarded me with new ideas and made me reflect on my opinions and honed my thought processes.

The constant challenges to their ideas lead Williams students to continuously examine the institutions of Williams itself. Despite a strong sense of tradition that stretches back to the college's founding in 1793, the Williams community is always searching for ways to make the school a better place. In the sixties and seventies the school made a pair of decisions that at the time were a great shock to the system: abolishing fraternities and admitting the first female students. Today it would be hard to find more than a handful of alumni or students who would say that these changes have been anything but a complete success.

Recent changes have not been so drastic but have still served to make the school a better place. The residential system was reformed several years ago to make housing more equitable and allow for more freedom of movement from year to year. A yearlong survey of all aspects of student life was recently completed and one of the main results was a renewed commitment by the administration to create more common space on campus in which students can gather to hold meetings, study, or simply relax and enjoy themselves. A new studio art building was built in 1996 and a state-of-the-art science complex is planned to open early in the next millennium. The college has also kept up with the changing technology of the information age—all of the dorm rooms on campus are connected to the college's computer network, and the student run Web site (http://wso.williams.edu) has won national acclaim. The college has essentially modeled itself after the type of graduate it likes to produce—a solid foundation that is constantly open to new ideas and challenging itself to be even better.

ADMISSIONS REQUIREMENTS

As indicated by its inclusion in this book, Williams is one of the most selective colleges in the nation. In one recent class, just 1,154, or twenty-five percent, of the over 4,500 applicants were accepted. Of those who were accepted, 545 eventually enrolled. Many prospective applicants believe that they need some sort of special talent or a gimmick for their application that will make them stand out. Certainly, being a star athlete, scoring 1600 on SATs or being a concert flautist will help your chances to get in; however, most of the students at Williams don't have one such talent that sets them apart. Obviously, virtually all of them measure up to the college's high academic standards—of those admitted into a recent class ninety-five percent graduated in the top quintile of their high school class. Important to the Admissions Department is your eagerness to seek out academic challenges—good grades are even more impressive when they come in the highest level or most demanding classes your school has to offer. Williams would prefer students who have shown initiative and a willingness to challenge themselves to those who have padded their grades by taking easy classes. Williams requires prospective applicants to take either SAT I or the ACT as well as three SAT II: Subject tests. In considering your application, the Admissions Department will look at your best score in each of the Verbal and Math sections of SAT I, your best composite score on the ACT and your best score on each of the SAT II: Subject tests. The test scores for incoming classes are just as impressive as their grades: fifty-four percent scored better than 700 on SAT Verbal and forty-five percent scored better than 700 on the Math section. As a result of the constantly improving statistics of each successive freshman class, it is a running joke at Williams that the senior class is the dumbest class on campus.

Although academics are important, the Admissions Department rejects plenty of students that measure up to the standards mentioned above. The students who end up receiving good news in the spring are the ones who can show that they are more than just bookworms. The bulk of the Williams experience is found outside the classroom, so it is important that applicants show that they will appreciate that aspect of the school. A telling statistic from a recent freshman class was that sixty percent had held top leadership positions in more than one high school activity. Quite simply, the college's goal is to create a class that, in the words of the Admissions Department, "brings a breadth of skills, experiences, and passions to campus."

I hadn't even heard of Williams until I started looking at colleges the spring before my senior year. Reading about the high standards of the school made me somewhat nervous, as did the fact that no one in recent memory from my high school had gone to Williams. But when I arrived at the school for a tour and interview, all of my fears were set aside. Everyone I met, including the Director of Admissions, was completely down to earth and put me at ease. It was such a relaxed and friendly atmosphere that even though I was visiting on a bleak day in the middle of January, the people I met at Williams immediately made it the school I wanted to attend.

The best way to get the flavor of a school, especially one with as unique an atmosphere as Williams, is to visit the campus. The Admissions Department is constantly running tours and information sessions. They are also more than happy to arrange an overnight visit where you can attend classes, participate in campus activities, and experience the social atmosphere of Williams students. A visit to the campus is also an excellent chance to have an interview with a representative of the Admissions Office. If you can't make it to the college, it is often possible to have an interview with a representative of the school in your area. Although an interview is not a requirement of the admissions process at Williams, it certainly can't hurt your chances. Williams interviews are very relaxed and informal and allow the Admissions Office to put a face and a personality to an application. More importantly, it is a chance for you to ask any lingering questions that you may have; after all, not everything you want to know can be found in a guidebook or brochure.

ACADEMIC LIFE

The academic calendar is in the 4-1-4 format. Each student takes four courses in each of the fall and spring semesters and one class during the month of January in what is known as Winter Study. To graduate students must have completed thirty-two semester credits with a C- average, plus fulfilled the requirements of their major. Students decide their majors at the end of the sophomore year, but are free to change their minds as long as they are able to fulfill the requirements of their new major. Because students have so much freedom in choosing their classes, it is very common for students to spend their first couple of years sampling classes and departments, finding the subjects that are right for them. There are very few students who come to Williams with their minds set on one particular course of study.

Divisional Requirements

As a liberal arts college the academic goal of Williams is to produce graduates with an education in a wide range of topics. This goal is the basis for Williams' divisional requirements. Students must take at least three courses in each of three divisions: Division I consists of English, foreign languages, and the arts; the social sciences such as history, economics, and political sciences make up Division II; Division III is math and the sciences. The one other requirement for all students is to take a class fulfilling the peoples and cultures requirement. These are classes determined by the college to be beyond the North American and European perspective. Classes in this category are plentiful and can be found in almost every major. Even within a major, students are encouraged, if not required, to get a broadbased education; for instance, a history major whose primary interest may be in the study of colonial America, may need to take ancient Chinese history and modern Latin American history to meet the requirements for the major. Students must also complete eight quarters (four semesters) of phys ed. There is an incredible variety of classes for phys ed including golf lessons, fly fishing, and independent running. Playing for a club or varsity athletic team can also qualify toward your eight quarters.

Courses

Despite divisional and major requirements, students still have a wide range of choices. A typical major has a requirement of only nine classes, and if you need seven more classes to meet your divisional requirements, that still leaves you half of your thirty-two classes all to yourself. If this is still not enough to sample all of the classes you want, you are able to take one additional class each semester on a pass/fail basis, which, during the semester, can be changed to a regular graded course. Students are also free, with the professor's permission, to audit courses.

It is nice to have so much freedom because there is such a wide range of courses offered at Williams. These vary from the stock college courses like Psych and Econ 101, to a student-designed and -run course in community work. Consistently popular classes are Crime in The Streets, a sociology class, and the feature film class offered by the English department.

The class that I am the most thankful I took at Williams was one that before I got to Williams I never would have imagined myself taking. The class, a survey course in art history, opened up a world that was completely foreign to me. The atmosphere at Williams encourages student to try new things and go out on a limb. Art history had nothing to do with my major and certainly didn't do anything to help my GPA, but it made me a much more rounded person. To me that is what a liberal arts education is all about.

The art history department is one of two departments, economics being the other, that has a graduate department attached to it. Senior-level students in these majors have the advantage of taking graduate-level courses. Classes taken with the students from the Center for Development Economics, which brings in masters-level students from developing countries around the world, can offer a very interesting perspective on views on development from those with an active stake in the process. Because there are only two graduate schools affiliated with Williams, students at Williams escape what can be a drawback at larger schools—that is, classes being taught by graduate students.

Faculty

Almost every class at Williams is taught by a member of the faculty (the only exception being student-designed and -run courses). Professors at Williams view students as the reason they are there, not as a nuisance that must be tolerated so they can continue their research. Professors are incredibly accessible, encouraging students to seek them out outside of class. Many are often seen meeting with students in the snack bar or local coffee shops to discuss the class; others regularly invite students to their homes for dinner to prepare for final exams or to celebrate the end of the semester. Despite their commitment to teaching, professors are still often on the cutting edge of research in their fields. Do not be surprised to find yourself in class using a text or reading journal articles written by your professor. Their commitment to their students extends into their research as well. Every summer a couple of hundred students can be found on campus working on research projects with professors from a wide variety of disciplines.

WINTER STUDY

Winters in Williamstown can be somewhat bleak, so for the month of January students get something of a break. During what is known as Winter Study, students take just one class and it is graded pass/fail. The classes are often on an irreverent topic and generally fall outside of the general scope of a department's curriculum. Professors can use this time to teach something of special interest to them, away from their main field of study, for instance, a Latin American history professor teaching a course on baseball and popular culture or a math professor teaching a course on the game of chess. Students also use this time to get experiences that are not available in the classroom—premed students can spend the month learning at the side of a local doctor, and many prospective teachers participate in a program that has them helping teach at schools in Harlem and the Bronx. Having just one class leaves students plenty of time to go skiing at one of the nearby mountains or spend more time on their extracurricular activities. Winter Study culminates with the Winter Carnival, a festival including snow sculpture contests, ski events, and a number of semiformal parties. All in all, it is a much appreciated break in the grind of the academic year.

Study Abroad

The chance to study abroad opens up a whole world of academic opportunities. A large number of students choose to take all or part of their junior year studying away from Williams. Students can choose almost any location they want with popular destinations being France, Australia, and Scotland. There is always a great deal of competition to secure a spot in the Williams-Oxford program in which Williams students spend their junior year studying at Oxford University in England. The destinations are not always foreign ones. Some students chose to spend time at other universities in the United States or spend a semester at Williams' maritime studies program at Mystic, Connecticut.

SOCIAL LIFE AND ACTIVITIES

Let's face it, you're going to be in class only ten hours a week, and you can only spend so much time in the library before you go crazy—you need something else to keep you sane. You may be wondering what there possibly can be to do in a tiny town in the middle of the mountains of Massachusetts. Well, when you have 2,000 students crammed into that small town, a certain critical mass is achieved and it seems like there is a club for almost every possible type of interest a student could have. If you're interested in politics, chances are that the campus Republicans or Democrats are helping out a local candidate for State Assembly. If you're interested in theater, you'll have the chance to write the play, or be in the play, or write about the play, or just watch the play. And, if you're interested is simply kicking back, having a beer, and playing Sega, you'll have no trouble finding someone to join you at that too.

Not much of what one typically refers to as dating goes on at Williams. When people get together socially, whether going to a party, dinner, or a movie, it tends to be in larger groups rather than in the traditional one-on-one date. Lots of students still have very serious boyfriends or girlfriends, but for the most part they still socialize with their other friends in larger groups.

Off Campus

The natural geography of the Berkshires has its advantages as well. In the winter there are ski hills fifteen minutes away and hiking and camping in the nearby mountains is a frequent weekend distraction for many. The college even has one of the top-rated college golf courses in the country on campus, something many don't truly appreciate until they've graduated.

Campus Parties

Most Ephs (as Williams students are called) unwind at the regular Saturday night keg parties around campus. In the last few years the college has imposed tighter restrictions on campus parties involving alcohol and there are limits on the amount of alcohol that can be served at campus parties based on the number of people expected and the length of the party. Also, those who wish to host parties must go through a special training session with campus security and health counselors. Despite these restrictions, students are still having as much fun as always at these parties. There are no fraternities at Williams so dorms, sports teams, or clubs organize the parties on campus. Parties that are always greatly anticipated are those that fall on the big weekends (Homecoming, Winter Carnival, Spring Fling) and those sponsored by the International Club and the college paper, *The Record*.

On Campus

If keg parties are not your scene, there is still lots to do on campus. For the movie buff the campus film group is usually showing something on Friday and Saturday nights. There is also a one-screen theater in town that shows an excellent selection of a wide range of films that appeal to the college crowd. There are regular student theater performances. The college generally brings in at least one big name band or musical performer each year—Natalie Merchant, Blues Traveler, Dave Matthews, A Tribe Called Quest, and De La Soul have all performed in recent years. There are also lesser-known bands performing on a more regular basis; legend has it R.E.M. came in the early 1980s and no one came to listen. The college is also constantly sponsoring lectures in a wide range of topics. If all else fails, there are always buses that make the three-hour trip to Boston or New York.

Athletics

About half of the student body participates on one of the varsity or club athletic teams, and even more participate in the wide-ranging intramural sports program. Sports are taken very seriously at Williams—there are few big parties on Friday nights because so many students have athletic commitments the next day. Williams' academic success is matched by its athletic success—the college has won the Sears Director's Cup for the top athletic program in Division III every year it has been awarded. Since Williams began participating in NCAA championships in the fall of 1993, the school has won national championships in men's cross-country and soccer and in several of the recent years every single team on campus finished with winning records. There are few things that will get an Eph as excited as sitting in a packed Chandler Gymnasium for a basketball game against arch-rival Amherst.

Among the highlights of my four years at Williams were the two Division III soccer Final Fours the college hosted. My sophomore year we experienced the pain of seeing our team lose in the finals, but that only made it sweeter two years later when it won the whole thing. The championship came on a cold and windy November day but that didn't dampen the spirits of the thousand plus students who were there to rush onto the field to mob the team when the game ended. Although they're not playing on national TV or playing in domed stadiums, sports teams are probably more important at a place like Williams than at a big Division I school. Here you actually know the athletes—they eat in the same dining halls, go to the same classes, and live in the same dorms. This makes it all the more special when they succeed; you're not just cheering for some anonymous basketball player who happens to have your school logo on his chest, you're cheering for your friends.

Residences

In their first year at Williams students live in what are referred to as entries. These generally consist of twenty first-year students, both male and female, and two junior advisors, juniors who spend the year helping freshmen make the adjustment to Williams. There is a rigorous, student-run selection process for junior advisors and, even though it is an unpaid position, applicants outnumber JAs four to one. The entry is the social focus point of the freshman year and for the first month or two most freshmen can be seen traveling in packs to the dining hall, parties, or *a capella* concerts. From sophomore year on, housing is determined by a lottery system in which students are assigned a number individually or as a group. The seniors, who get first pick, generally live in large singles in old fraternity houses that line the road running through the center of campus. Juniors and sophomores generally end up in smaller singles in some of the more recently built buildings, or in the doubles in the old fraternity houses.

FINANCIAL AID

For many applicants, getting into Williams is not as hard as coming up with a way to pay for it. A Williams education is expensive. The ability of a student to pay for the Williams education is never a factor in the admissions process. Admissions at Williams are need-blind; you are admitted solely based on your merits as a potential student.

Once accepted, students receive aid from the college solely based on need; there is no merit-based assistance at Williams. Since everyone is bringing something unique to the school, it seems only fair that the money go to those who need it the most. Financial awards are based on many factors including the size of the family and its income and assets. The assistance comes in the form of scholarships or grants, loans, and campus jobs. Students are also expected to contribute some summer earnings toward paying for college. This money will make up the difference between what the college judges the family can pay and the cost of the student's education. Families are also encouraged to seek outside scholarships or grants.

Nearly fifty percent of all freshmen and forty percent of continuing students receive some sort of student aid and the average award for incoming students is approximately $20,000, including work at a campus job. The average indebtedness of one recent graduating class was approximately $15,000.

The cost of the Williams education should not scare you off from the admissions process. If you are someone the school wants to have, it will do everything in its power to make it possible for you to attend.

GRADUATES

A college's ultimate goal is to prepare its students to face the world beyond its gates. Judging by the success of its graduates, Williams is fulfilling its mission. Fitting for a liberal arts college, students from Williams go on to any number of fields. Most potential employers know that a great deal of the specific knowledge needed for any position is learned on the job. Their goal is to find students who know how to learn and who have intangible qualities such as the ability to communicate effectively and manage their time. Employers know that Williams instills qualities such as these in its graduates.

Careers

Jobs in management consulting and investment banking are probably the two fields most sought after by graduating seniors. But not everyone who graduates Williams joins the business world and wears a suit every day. Classmates of mine have gone off to be politicians, teachers, journalists, chefs, actors, baseball scouts, and professional athletes. Others have decided to further their education at medical school, law school, dental school, or by pursuing a master's or a Ph.D. Others still have yet to settle on anything and are simply traveling until they find their true calling. The common advantage that all Williams graduates have in any field they choose is that they find their Williams education has prepared them well to handle whatever challenges they face. They also know that they have an incredible support network of other Williams graduates waiting to help them get ahead in whatever field they choose.

Most Williams students find their first job with the help of the school's Office of Career Counseling. Over 100 companies and organizations recruit on campus at Williams, as high a number as you'll find anywhere in the country. The staff at the OCC will help you fine-tune your résumé or letters to prospective employers; it also gives workshops in how to prepare for and perform well in job interviews. Most importantly, it is able to put you in touch with other recent graduates who have entered into the field you want to pursue. Advice from recent graduates—someone who has gone through the process that you will be going through—is far more valuable than anything you will read in a book or a corporate brochure.

Alums

The enthusiasm that alumni show for Williams is a sure sign that they viewed their experience at Williams as a positive one. The Williams Society of Alumni, founded in 1821, is the oldest such society in the world, showing that even back in the 1800s Williams graduates were proud of their school and the education they received there. Currently, over sixty percent of graduates contribute actively to the college. These donations help the school to constantly improve itself through the construction of new facilities such as the recently completed art building and the new science facilities currently under construction.

PROMINENT GRADS

- **William Bennett, Former Secretary of Education**
- **Arne Carlson, Minnesota Governor**
- **Dominick Dunne, Writer**
- **John Frankenheimer, Movie and TV Director**
- **James Garfield, President of the United States**
- **Richard M. Helms, Former CIA Director and Ambassador to Iran**
- **Elia Kazan, Director and Writer**
- **Thomas Krens, Guggenheim Museum Director**
- **Arthur Levitt, SEC Chairman**
- **Stephen Sondheim, Composer**

When it comes to pride in the school, more illustrative than the money donated is to see how graduates' eyes light up when they talk of their time spent at Williams. The recounting of athletic feats, memories of late night study sessions, and especially the mention of old friends—these are the things that bring smiles to the faces of Williams grads. The bonds that are formed at Williams are stronger than any that you will ever build with future coworkers. There is something very special about spending four years tucked in a mountain valley with someone. It is that special bond that keeps pulling Ephs back to that valley for homecoming and reunions, and why one of the happiest days for so many Williams graduates is the day their son or daughter goes off to Williams for their first year, so they too can build those types of friendships.

SUMMING UP

There are certainly reasons why people would not want to go to Williams. Those who feel they need a big city experience may feel that Williamstown is too isolated for them. Those who want to attend a college where they can fade into the background probably will not like the individual attention lavished on students by professors and the college's close-knit community. Those who want an education narrow in focus probably wouldn't like the divisional requirements that promote a broad-based education. Those who want to spend their college years with students just like themselves probably wouldn't benefit from meeting students from around the country and from a variety of social and economic backgrounds. Williams is a place for those who appreciate an atmosphere where you are able to sample from a wide range of ideas and activities. It is a place for those who want to spend their college years in an active and challenging environment.

Students at Williams thrive off of one another. Being with the best mathematicians, best writers, and best athletes only serves to make one a better mathematician, writer, and athlete. The intellectual challenges one experiences in the classroom come not just from your professors, but your classmates as well. Any competition between students is not for grades but to add something to the discussion or to ask a question no one else had thought to pose.

Life at Williams is not easy, but it is rewarding. Many times students have wondered how they will be able to find the time to finish their history paper, study for their biology exam, go to practice, and broadcast their show on the campus radio station. Somehow they always find a way, even after lingering for an hour over their Philly Cheese Steak in the dining hall. Students are able to handle it all because that's what everyone else does—no one does nothing at Williams; everyone is active in something, and your friends and classmates serve as your inspiration. When you do get to relax at Williams, the satisfaction from having completed everything makes that time even better.

High academic standards, a tradition of athletic excellence, an active student body, beautiful location, and a faculty enthusiastic about teaching—it would seem that Williams has everything. However, many would feel stifled in the small town atmosphere and the small size of the school, while others believe that spending four years in a mountain valley with 2,000 other students is heaven on earth. Back in 1844 Thoreau, after visiting Williams, said, "It would be no small advantage if every college were thus located at the base of a mountain." For most of those who attend Williams those words still ring true today.

❑ *Graeme Scandrett, B.A.*

YALE UNIVERSITY

Photo by Michael Marsland

Yale University
Office of Undergraduate Admission
P.O. Box 208234
New Haven, CT 06520-8234

(203) 432-9300
Fax: (203) 432-9392

E-mail: undergraduate.admissions@yale.edu
Web site: http://www.yale.edu

Enrollment

Full-time ❑ women: 2,553
❑ men: 2,683

Part-time ❑ women: 49
❑ men: 41

INTRODUCING YALE

If you've decided to attend Yale, "Where are you going to school?" can be a complicated question. If you're like most Yale students, you're so excited about coming to the school that you'll want to jump out and say "Yale!" loud and clear, eyes and cheeks aglow. But answering the question so directly provokes many different reactions, based on Yale's reputation as one of the finest universities in the world. So students and even alumni practice several indirect responses, including "New Haven" (there are a handful of other colleges and universities here;

just read the exit sign for "Yale Univ." and "Albertus Magnus"); "Connecticut" (a state with MANY colleges), and the even more vague "Back East."

Like many of the questions that hold great import before you begin college, this one soon fades into oblivion. A freshman will quickly observe and follow the pattern set by the undergraduate body: Everyone is too busy taking maximum advantage of the university's vast resources to boast or even think about Yale's reputation. The 1998 yearbook is titled *Unlimited Capacity*. Indeed, students are in overdrive most of the time. Yale's unwavering commitment to undergraduate education, the residential college system, and the breadth of academic and extracurricular opportunities are central tenets of the Yale experience. These are the reasons why Yalies have chosen Yale, not for its reputation, and not for its location in the small New England city (though it seems more of a town) of New Haven, Connecticut.

Yalies joke about the question "Where do you go to school?" because Yale is not simply where people go to school. It is a community, and the happiest members of that community are those who actively participate in it. Many students remember being hit with the Yale fever almost immediately upon arriving on campus—that's how tangible the sense of community is.

On my first walk around the campus, I just knew that this was where I wanted to go to college. Students were rushing to get to class, while I was struggling to read my campus map that was torn and wrinkled by a strong wind (which I've now come to recognize as a robust sea breeze from the nearby Long Island Sound). Then a student stopped and asked me if I needed directions. I wound up going to his English class, where he introduced me to his professor. Then he took me to Durfee's Sweet Shop, and directed me to other buildings he thought I'd want to see. All his enthusiasm and helpfulness got me hooked. Now I look out for maps blowing in the wind, and am always glad for the chance to talk to prospective students—even after almost four years here, a couple of labor strikes, and a housing crunch.

ADMISSIONS REQUIREMENTS

Ask students what they know about admissions and you're likely to hear that the hardest thing about Yale is getting in. Look past that casual statement, however, to recognize a deeper truth: There's no set formula for admission to a place that seeks to maintain a diverse student body. As the Admissions Committee says on its web page (http://www.yale.edu/admit/), the two basic questions it brings to the process are "Who is likely to make the most of Yale's resources?" and "Who will contribute significantly to the Yale community?" It's a complex approach, one designed to select a class of motivated, energetic achievers with broad interests and skills, all of whom are enticed by the opportunities Yale offers both in and out of the classroom.

Beyond that stated mission, applicants should be aware of several general facts:

- First, admission is extremely competitive, as the committee aims for a class of approximately 1,300 from over 12,000 applicants.
- Second, while there are no official score cut-offs and applicants' test results vary widely, medians on the Verbal and Mathematical parts of the SAT generally fall in the low 700s, and ACT composites in the low 30s.
- Third, the great majority of Yalies placed in the top tenth of their high school class; a distinguished record in a demanding college preparatory program may compensate for modest standardized test scores, but the reverse is usually not true.
- Fourth, the committee is searching for students with some less tangible qualities suggested by the various documents in their applications. Some successful candidates are well rounded, while others have specialized talents, some have displayed leadership capabilities in extracurricular activities while others have shown dedication to an after-school job, but all, hopefully, show a capacity for involvement, commitment, and personal growth.
- Finally, Yale has a need-blind admissions policy, meaning that an applicant's financial circumstances will not be given any weight during the admission process. (It is only a factor among international applicants because the funds for foreign student financial aid are limited.) You won't be rejected because you apply for financial aid, as Yale is strongly committed to the idea of equality of opportunity, seeking to shape a class of students from all parts of the country and all segments of society.

The admissions process produces a class that reflects Yale's interest in diversity, not only in academic and extracurricular interests but also in ethnicity and geographical distribution. Today, minorities comprise more than thirty percent of the student body, and Yalies hail from all fifty states and over fifty countries. Be prepared to meet people of all cultural, social, and financial backgrounds, and also be prepared to meet people who have worn Yale blue since birth—"legacies" make up around ten percent of each class.

Early Decision

Applicants who are certain that Yale is their first choice may want to consider taking advantage of the Early Decision program (recently adopted by the university in place of its nonbinding Early Action option). As with Early Decision programs elsewhere, an Early Decision application is considered a binding commitment from the student, who must submit a complete application by November 1. In mid-December the committee will respond with an acceptance or denial of admission, or a deferral, which postpones the final decision until April, when all applicants are notified. The deferral releases the applicant from the Early Decision commitment, and guarantees a decision of admission or denial (rather than placement on a waiting list) after consideration of the total applicant pool in the spring. (The final application deadline is December 31).

Being admitted to Yale signals the Admission Committee's faith in the applicant's ability to be a successful Yale student. Does that mean that admission is, in fact, the hardest part of Yale? Well, all students have to face that question on their own. Yalies tend to make life hard on themselves by pursuing their academics and activities so intensely—clearly they have proven their stamina by the time they graduate.

ACADEMIC LIFE

I've found that the amount of work at Yale varies from student to student, from course to course, from semester to semester, and even from night to night. My two roommates major in the sciences, and have a pretty consistent work load: a bunch of problem sets and lab reports each week. I'm a history major, which means that I've always got a lot of reading to try to keep up with, but my busy periods are more sporadic—basically the few times a semester I have papers due, when my life can get totally crazy. It seems that whether they put in the effort seven days a week, or just seven times a semester, all Yale students develop an ability to instantaneously calculate when they'll have to go to sleep to get that recommended eight hours.

In 1701 ten Connecticut clergymen met in the town of Branford, each with a gift of books to contribute for the founding of the college that would become Yale. From those forty folios, the university's holdings have grown to include over ten million volumes; the extensive library system is the seventh largest research library in the world. A library is the heart of any learning institution, and the prominence of Yale's collections (not to mention the imposing sight of Sterling Memorial Library's Gothic tower looming over the central campus) reminds students that while they may spend countless hours dashing around to eagerly explore extracurricular interests, their intellectual development is paramount.

To foster that development, Yale has always remained committed to the idea of a liberal arts education. According to one faculty report, "Our object is not to teach that which is peculiar to any one of the professions, but to lay the foundation which is common to them all..." Those words were written in 1828, and they still characterize the Yale philosophy today. Simply put, Yale wants to teach you how to think. The university doesn't have career-oriented fields of study—if you want to major in communications or marketing, for example, look elsewhere—but, instead, aims to provide students with the tools to succeed in any field.

Majors and Work Load

What you *can* major in is any of almost seventy disciplines, from astronomy to film studies to Russian. Yale also allows you to double major and, if you can convince a faculty committee that it's necessary and that you're up to the challenge, to design your own major. In a recent year, the most popular fields of study were history, biology, economics, and political science.

Yale has no required courses, but employs a framework of distributional requirements to make sure that students explore a sufficient diversity of subjects. Each course is placed in one of four distributional groups—languages and literature; the humanities (including history, art, music, philosophy, and other disciplines); the social sciences; and mathematics, science, and engineering. Each student must take at least twelve classes from outside the distributional group that includes the major and at least three in each of the remaining distributional groups. Students must also demonstrate proficiency in a foreign language, a requirement that can be satisfied either by AP scores, a proficiency test, or completing the intermediate level foreign language course at Yale. While most colleges require a normal four-year course load of thirty-two credits, a Yale degree requires thirty-six, meaning students spend some semesters trying to manage five courses simultaneously.

It's a lot to grasp at first, and it's no surprise that the structure of a Yale education means things can get pretty hectic and intense at times. However, the system makes perfect sense from a liberal arts perspective, giving students the freedom and responsibility to shape their academic careers, while guaranteeing a certain amount of breadth of study in addition to the depth one experiences in a major. As an added incentive to explore, some courses can be taken Credit/D/Fail, which means that a grade of C or above will show up as a "CR" on one's transcript. Many Yalies grumble about the various distributional requirements (complaints about the work load are a favorite pastime), but if you press them, most will admit they're glad they took that English or geology course that initially seemed so unconnected to their interests, because it exposed them to different people and different ways of thinking.

"Shopping" for Classes

These notions of academic exploration, freedom, and responsibility, are embodied in Yale's unique shopping period, the first two weeks of each semester in which students shop for classes. Most colleges require students to preregister for classes, but Yale allows its students to attend almost any course offered at the start of the semester, filling out their schedules only after hearing the professors and perusing the syllabi. Shopping period is a great opportunity to shape an interesting schedule while trying to balance the various times, demands (tests, papers, problem sets), and sizes (seminars, small and large lectures) of the classes. For some, shopping period can literally be a life-changing experience—one student dropped in on an introductory architecture lecture sophomore year, found himself enthralled by the professor, and spent the next two years immersed in blueprints and models. Many professors dislike shopping period, since they start off the semester with no idea of how many students will eventually take their classes, but students will tell you it's one of the best things about the Yale experience.

Reading Week

The end of term equivalent to shopping period is reading week, a week between the end of classes and the start of finals that makes Yale students the envy of their peers at most other institutions. Ideally a time to pause, reflect, and study in preparation for finals, it's more often a time of late-night paper writing and catching up on reading not completed on time. Studying, of course, includes study breaks, and reading week is also a time of catching up with friends before winter break and summer vacation.

Faculty

Yale's graduate schools are well respected, but the college remains the physical, intellectual, and even emotional center of Yale. Graduate students lead the smaller discussion sections and teach a number of seminars each year (their status as both students and employees has been publicly debated in recent years), but students at Yale still have the opportunity to study with the nation's top professors. As a leading research institution attracting scholars of international renown in every field, Yale expects its faculty to put time and energy into teaching undergraduates. Faculty members welcome the opportunity to share their enthusiasm with students, and many of Yale's most distinguished senior professors teach introductory courses. Some have attained cult status and attract hundreds of students.

Yale is not merely a place for academic excellence. In fact, many students won't even cite the academic environment as the most important aspect of their college years. It is academic excellence, however, that makes the Yale experience and reputation so distinctive and attracts so many applicants each year.

SOCIAL LIFE AND ACTIVITIES

Freshman Orientation

The first few days of freshman year lay the groundwork for a rich and intricate life outside of the classroom.They may begin with a seven-day hiking trip in the wilderness or a two-day retreat at a nearby summer camp. About a third of the class takes part in these programs, known as FOOT (Freshman Outdoor Orientation Trip) and Freshperson Conference. Even though their duration is brief, and students scatter in all directions once classes begin, many alumni of these orientation programs have reunions throughout college. The FOOT program has recently started an electronic listserve for alumni to share their most recent hiking adventures.

The day these programs end, Camp Yale—the official freshman orientation—begins. Wearing navy T-shirts that announce, "Ask me for help," freshman counselors—seniors who have gone through a rigorous training program to serve as peer advisors to the freshman class, and who live with them—stand outside of the entryways on the old campus to meet their new charges. At convocation, the president addresses the freshman class. This is followed by a reception at his house. Finally, the upperclassmen get their chance to meet and greet, during a bazaar of undergraduate activities. Before classes have even begun, organization leaders line the sidewalks of the old campus to recruit freshmen. The freshman counselors also hold meetings with their counselees where they go over the course selection process and review many of the resources available to students, from a twenty-four-hour shuttle bus to free condoms to professional counseling.

This flurry of activity during the first few days exemplifies Yale's commitment to its undergraduates. As soon as students arrive, they are part of the community, and are asked to become active in it. There are many different levels of support and orientation; students manage their way through the array of decisions and opportunities differently. Some will visit their freshman counselor every day, while others will turn to upperclassmen or to their faculty advisor. Freedom and choice prevail; Yale expects and relies on students to act responsibly.

Residential Colleges

The primary way to identify new students at Yale is by the residential college. A couple of months before school starts, every incoming student is randomly assigned to one of twelve residential colleges, an affiliation that lasts throughout one's four years at Yale, and beyond. The college system breaks down each class of approximately 1,300 students into much smaller and more intimate units of approximately 120 students who live and eat together. Ideally, during the time students live there, this place feels like home, and has many of the amenities one could wish for: television rooms, libraries, music practice rooms, computer rooms, even performance spaces and printing presses.

Each college has a master, a faculty member who lives with his or her family in the master's house. In addition to their professorial duties of teaching and research, the master oversees the social life of the college—intramural teams, dances, tailgates, and arts festivals, for instance. The master eats regularly in the dining hall and invites students frequently into his home, sometimes for the relaxed social interchange of a study break or the chance to meet an author, politician, or other dignitary during a Master's Tea. The residential college deans also live in the college and oversee the freshman counselors and the academic lives of students. A dean must approve a student's schedule, and is the only person authorized to grant a student a "dean's excuse" for not meeting academic deadlines.

While most freshmen live on the old campus together, and are encouraged to bond as a class, they also participate fully in residential college life. At the beginning of their sophomore year, students move into their colleges. There they room with classmates, but live in an entryway or on a hallway with juniors and seniors. In randomly assigning students to residential colleges, Yale's aim is to create twelve microcosms of the larger undergraduate community. Students with different interests and backgrounds—and, outside of the residential college, entirely different lives—live and learn side by side. This structured integration draws criticism from some students, who feel forced into being part of a community they had no say in selecting.

I'm just thankful I got a single this year. I feel isolated, since my closest friends are not in my college.

About fifteen percent of students decide to live off campus, though Yale recently instituted a new policy that requires undergraduates to live on campus for two years.

The residential college system could be described as part of Yale's infrastructure. It's open to criticism, and indeed it has been under fire since the residential colleges were first built in the 1920s. During commencement, all students graduate in a ceremony on the old campus, but return to their residential colleges to receive their diplomas. Most "class notes" in the monthly *Yale Alumni Magazine*, which all graduates of the college automatically receive, identify people by their college. It is an extremely efficient way to give students the best of both worlds at Yale—the resources of a large research university, with the attention, support, and sense of community of a small liberal arts college.

Athletics

The residential colleges also create an infrastructure for students to participate in athletics. Intramurals are recreational and everyone in the college, regardless of previous experience, is encouraged to participate. Competitions between the colleges usually take place in the afternoon or evening, and results are tallied on a weekly basis as residential colleges strive for the Tyng Cup, awarded at the end of the year to the college with the most wins. Less publicly fought for but nonetheless a source of college pride is the Gimbel Cup, awarded annually to the residential college with the highest grade point average. Lastly, there's the Tang Cup, awarded to college teams in a one-day competition organized in association with the fraternities. Because of the residential college system, fraternities and sororities are not a major social force at Yale, but they do exist, and provide community service and social outlets for the students who participate.

SEVEN THINGS YOU CAN DO AT YALE

- ❍ **Climb the steps to the top of Harkness Tower**
- ❍ **Take a walk through Grove Street Cemetery**
- ❍ **Take a trip to the Whitlock Book Barn**
- ❍ **Go apple-picking at Bishop's Orchard**
- ❍ **Picnic on the top of East Rock**
- ❍ **Spend an afternoon reading on the Divinity School lawn**
- ❍ **Compete in intramural coed inner tube water polo**

Clubs and Organizations

Of course, many other communities and affiliations abound at Yale—the ones students create and choose for themselves. There are twelve possible responses to the question, "What college are you in?" There are hundreds of possible responses to the next-important question, "What do you do?" On any given weeknight during dinner, a group of students is planning their next singing jam, magazine deadline, political debate, student rally, chamber orchestra recital, juggling demonstration, Habitat for Humanity project, or play auditions. There's a club for chess players, engineers, anglophiles and polar bears (those who dare to swim in the Long Island Sound during the winter). There's scripted comedy, improv comedy, and published comedy, not to mention many student-produced comic strips. There's opera, klezmer, and black spiritual music, available live and on CD. It's exhausting to even think of how many options are available—and even more exhausting to recognize that students spend large portions of their time sustaining these organizations. Over 300 groups register with the Yale College Dean's Office, including fourteen *a cappella* groups (from the tuxedoed Whiffenpoofs to the Dylan-inspired Tangled Up In Blue), thirty undergraduate publications (including the oldest college daily), and two dozen cultural groups.

You will never lack for something to do on the Yale campus, and if you ever did find yourself in that position, you would do as many have done before you: start your own group for your own hobby. If you're not copyediting final pages into the wee hours of the morning, you're trying to figure out how to see your friends in their three separate productions. Most likely, you'll see the productions back to back and then do your copyediting. One cannot measure a student's devotion, nor can one imagine a limit to a student's energy. The majority of students aren't merely involved in a group, they're leading one. Only during reading period, the week before final exams start, does the campus start to settle down. The kiosks all over campus, usually plastered with posters advertising events, begin to look bare as the libraries swell with students for the first time all semester.

Sometimes I wish I could take a semester off from classes, given my other commitments. Filofaxes are for professionals, but many people at Yale have them just to keep track of the meetings and dinners they take part in. I try to take my classes on Tuesdays and Thursdays so I have three full free days to work my campus job, do my activities, and study. I feel wired all of the time, but everyone does. There's this frenetic energy or buzz on campus that's very difficult to escape. If I'm not doing something, I feel like a slacker. It's difficult to find time just to hang out, though luckily, I see my friends regularly, since most of them are involved in the same groups. During vacations, I sleep. A lot.

New Haven

New Haven, a moderate-sized port city, is about two hours away from New York. That's far enough away to make Yale part of New England, and not a New York offshoot, but a city with urban problems of its very own. To call it a port city is perhaps misleading, since its days as a prosperous center of shipping and industry are long past. New Haven would be much worse off without Yale, and while town-gown relations have sometimes been strained in Yale's history, today their interaction is characterized by collaboration and cooperation. Yale is the city's biggest employer, and the university has joined forces with the city to build a new economic base—the latest goal is to utilize Yale's academic resources to develop a profit-minded biotechnology center.

The campus is a few miles from Long Island Sound, and refreshing sea breezes can still be felt, even if you have to climb one of the towers on campus to see the water. Beach towns along the Connecticut coast, though difficult to visit if you don't have a car, offer antique shops, fresh seafood, and farms for hayrides and apple picking. Sleeping Giant State Park is a twenty-minute bike ride away. In short, though the campus is enveloped by a ring of low-income housing, and the homeless quickly become a familiar presence, many of the pastoral diversions completely absent from a big city campus are quite accessible to Yale students. Far from hiding in their dorm rooms in the walled-in courtyards of green lawns and shady trees, students are aware and caring of their surroundings. Over half of the students pursue community service projects in New Haven. The locked gates and visibility of both Yale and New Haven police patrols don't seem to bother students, but do serve to keep students safe.

Some students say that Yale would be perfect were it not in New Haven. While the Elm City may not be as nationally recognized as cities that host other Ivy League schools, its charms grow on students, who often decide to stay in New Haven during the summers or attend graduate school at Yale. The small portion of students who do stick to campus life exclusively miss out on a modest but eclectic music and arts scene, and treasures like the best hamburger (Louis' Lunch), the best greasy spoon (The Yankee Doodle), and, of course, the best pizza (Sally's and Pepes, located in Wooster Square—about a twenty-minute walk from campus). The chance to get involved and be useful to the city fosters a civic identity that graduates carry with them. Last year, more than 100 seniors took jobs with Teach for America and The Peace Corps.

FINANCIAL AID

In its admissions process Yale may be need-blind, but no one should be blind to the financial realities connected with attendance. The actual cost of attending college varies from student to student. There are the following usual expenses: tuition and fees, room and board, books, and personal expenses, and a yearly hospitalization coverage fee and other optional and incidental expenses.

The basis of all financial aid awards at Yale is the student's "demonstrated financial need," the difference between the estimated cost of attendance and the expected family contribution. For a recent academic year, more than fifty-seven percent of all undergraduates qualified to receive financial assistance in the form of scholarships, grants, low-interest educational loans, and work-study from all sources. Yale does not offer academic or athletic scholarships or any other type of special scholarship that is not based on demonstrated need. More than $45 million in university-controlled need-based aid was offered to forty-one percent of the undergraduate student body.

The expected contribution is determined by the Financial Aid Office, which analyzes the FAFSA, CSS Financial Aid Profile, and other forms submitted by the family, and measures the family's ability to contribute toward Yale's costs.

Packages

After consideration of these factors, the university offers financial aid in the form of a package with two basic components: "self-help" (a combination of term-time employment and educational loans) and "gift aid," which covers any need beyond that covered by self-help. While other types of loans are available, the primary source of long-term, low-interest loans is the federal Stafford Loan Program, for which citizens or permanent residents of the United States are eligible. Students who apply for financial aid will automatically be considered for all types of "gift aid," which consists of scholarships from the university, as well as Yale alumni clubs, and from endowed and federal funds, including federal Supplemental Educational Opportunity Grants, administered by the university. Additionally, Yale participates in a number of financing options that can assist families in paying for college, whether or not the family is determined to have demonstrated financial need.

Jobs

> *It helped me pay for college, but my job (in a campus office that doesn't interact much with students) also became something I really enjoyed. The truth is, when you spend your whole day surrounded by eighteen- to twenty-two-year-olds, sometimes it's nice to be around people who aren't students or professors, people who drive into New Haven for the day. It was basic office work, but it was good to have an enforced break from academics and the intensity of the Yale experience.*

On-campus jobs (available also to students not on financial aid, though aid recipients have priority) offer a wide variety of opportunities. Students fill positions as dining hall workers, library clerks, laboratory assistants, research assistants, and aides to residential college masters. Jobs also abound in various campus offices. Recently, wage rates for university jobs ranged from $6.40 for entry-level positions to over $8 per hour for dining hall workers. A large number of Yale students balance school and employment.

For more in-depth information on financing a Yale education, including an example of a financial aid award, check out http://www.yale.edu/admit/financing.html.

GRADUATES

It's difficult enough to describe the intense experience of four years at Yale. Once they enter the world at large, Yalies go off to do a multitude of impressive things. Part of Yale's mission is to train leaders, and Yale's alumni do lead, as presidents, CEOs, academics, journalists, lawyers, advocates. Living in New Haven, a city where volunteerism can make such a difference, is a life-shaping experience for students, many of whom later gravitate to public service in government or nonprofit organizations. The diversity of Yale's student body, and the breadth of its academic offerings, prepares graduates for diverse careers. A sampling of recent graduates should give you an idea: investment banker, peace corp volunteer, reporter in Indonesia, computer programmer, book publicist, teacher. When alumni reach out to one another, they continue to learn from their classmates' endeavors.

PROMINENT GRADS

- William F. Buckley, Jr., Writer
- George Bush, President of the United States
- Jodie Foster, Actress/Director
- Maya Lin, Architect
- David McCullough, Historian
- Paul Rudnick, Screenwriter
- Gene Siskel, Movie Critic
- Calvin Trillin, Columnist
- Garry Trudeau, "Doonesbury" creator

And also:

- Four Signers of the Declaration of Independence
- Three Members of the Constitutional Convention of 1787
- Inventors of the Telegraph and the Cotton Gin
- Founder of Federal Express

The Association of Yale Alumni oversees a network of more than 100 local Yale Clubs and associations that have a mission to connect and reconnect the alumni to the university. These groups also involve alumni volunteers in the admissions process, as they are charged with interviewing students in their area and filling out evaluation forms. Many local groups host receptions for admitted students. Fund-raising is carried out by the Alumni Fund, a separate organization that can boast one of the highest participation rates of the Ivy League. The university recently completed a successful $1.7 billion capital campaign, largely fueled by the generosity of its alumni. That alumni are devoted and loyal is a good sign of the quality of the experience they had during their time here.

Yalies enjoy coming back to campus. Twice yearly, over 200 alumni, elected as delegates by their local associations, convene in New Haven to address the latest news and developments at Yale and discuss alumni affairs. Some fly in from as far away as Switzerland and Hong Kong. Reunions bring thousands more back to campus in the spring, for a weekend of dancing, dining, and catching up. Many current students work during reunions, and have the extra treat of meeting alums who lived in their residential college or perhaps took a class with the same instructor. Recently, the university has embarked on "A Day with Yale" program, which puts administrators and faculty members on the road to share their knowledge and talents with the alumni population.

An alumni gathering would not be complete without the spirited singing of the alma mater, "Bright College Years." The lyrics sum up the immense loyalty and nostalgia shared by Yale graduates.

Bright College years, with pleasure rife,
The shortest, gladdest years of life;
How swiftly are ye gliding by!
Oh, why doth time so quickly fly?

Oh, let us strive that ever we
May let these words our watch-cry be,
Where'er upon life's sea we sail:
"For God, for Country, and for Yale!"

SUMMING UP

Go to the "front door" of the Yale World Wide Web site (http://www.yale.edu/) and you'll see an image of six leather-bound, aged volumes. The image, based on a portion of Elihu Yale's library, evokes the university's origins, even as it represents a commitment toward the technological future. As Yale approaches its tercentenary in 2001, the same mingling of past and future is palpable on the campus. For example, students' increasing use of e-mail occurs in the computer center located in the basement of Connecticut Hall, the university's oldest building. While the university remains committed to perpetuating its traditional strengths, it also allows its energetic and intellectually enthusiastic student body to lead it toward a new future.

❑ *Amanda Gordon, B.A.*
❑ *Seth Oltman, B.A.*

STRATEGIES

by
Rachel Weimerskirch

APPLICATION STRATEGIES

1. Use the application as a chance to best present yourself on paper.
2. Make your essay shine.
3. Give yourself time to meet your deadlines.
4. Remember all the housekeeping details.
5. Apply to schools that feel right for you.

1. USE THE APPLICATION AS A CHANCE TO BEST PRESENT YOURSELF ON PAPER

- CONSIDER THE COMPETITION: If you're an admissions officer, a typical day might look something like this: over your mug of morning coffee, you're peering at a stack of hundreds—maybe thousands—of applications from all over the world. SATs, GPAs, and other acronyms are standards to consider in determining the strongest candidates. After the numbers are crunched, who will catch your eye and hold your interest? Sometimes even the straight A student/captain of the hockey team/organizer of a program at a homeless shelter won't make the cut—unless, of course, he or she knows how to paint his or her own self-portrait in the most flattering light.
- APPROACH THE APPLICATION AS AN OPPORTUNITY: For the applicant, the application doesn't have to be daunting—or a chore. Think of it as one of life's rare opportunities to design your own image. Applying to college can really stress you out, or applying to college can be an opportunity to recreate yourself for an audience of admissions officers who are looking for someone original, creative, and stellar. They are looking for that edge, that extra something beyond the mainstream that tells them you are right for their school and that their school is a match for you.
- IT'S ALL ABOUT YOU: It's sometimes hard to flaunt your good qualities, throwing modesty to the wind, but this time, piece together all of your valuable high school accomplishments and brag about them—loud! Be specific about all of your leadership roles, your significant contributions to an area of interest. Were you president of a student body? Editor-in-chief of a newspaper? A rated athlete? Have you been recognized as an All-State or an MVP? Did you organize others in support of a cause? Write about and emphasize the activities that inspire you. They'll serve as vibrant colors for your self-portrait.
- TO SUPPLEMENT OR NOT TO SUPPLEMENT: If you've been visited by the muse, some colleges welcome supplementary material. Sending original poetry, music, or art may help to introduce a fuller picture of you as a person. If something means a lot to you, send it, but be brutal in your selections—pick only the best of your best.

  Other schools clearly request only materials that adhere to application requirements. Read carefully to determine whether or not supplementary materials will be accepted and considered. Don't provide an original score of your aspiring Broadway musical if the school isn't going to consider it a factor in your acceptance.

2. MAKE YOUR ESSAY SHINE

- SEE IT AS YOUR SPACE: A memorable essay is one of the best ways to reveal the true you. What is not on the application that you would like the college or university to know? If the stack of applications you face seems to reduce you to a list of activities, grades, and courses, use the freedom that the essay gives you to choose your topic and to use your voice.
- THE WRITING IMPULSE: Write about your passions; they will speak for you and allow your voice to shout through the paper. Use the essay questions to let the college get to know you as a person.

3. GIVE YOURSELF TIME TO MEET YOUR DEADLINES

- PROCRASTINATION WILL ALWAYS GET YOU DOWN: In the line-up of college application tasks, pacing is one of the most important strategies. Give yourself a realistic timeline when devising a schedule for yourself. You don't want to run out of energy before you reach the finish line.
- CREATE A PLAN OF ATTACK: Maybe you want to dive head first into the application that has the earliest deadline, devoting all of your after-school hours until you polish it off. Or perhaps you will begin with the application to your first-choice school so that you can dedicate your freshest enthusiasms to number one on your wish list. Whatever way you begin, be sure that you remain on top of the required dates of submission—not just for the application proper, but for the test scores, letters of recommendation, and so on. (Remember that colleges might have different dates for specific tests; some require more SAT IIs than others, for example.) A college application is a many-layered process. Sometimes each layer contains a different date to consider.
- INVEST IN A CALENDAR: It doesn't hurt to write down on a calendar all of the important dates for each school. You can color code according to school or according to layers (for example, dates for letters of recommendation can be sea green while dates for the registration of appropriate tests can be periwinkle). Make the application process a priority.

4. REMEMBER ALL THE HOUSEKEEPING DETAILS

- PROOFREAD... If you take your time, you'll make sure that details are not overlooked. (Did I sign the application? Did I send the University of Chicago a check made payable to

Colgate?) Go beyond Spell Check and really proofread your work carefully until you are sure it's in its best form.

- ...AND PROOFREAD AGAIN WITH SOMEONE ELSE'S EYES: After you have read and reread your essay and application, you may feel too close to it to catch any missing commas. Show it to some objective observers who will see it with fresh eyes—counselors, Mom, Dad, teachers, those who know you well. They will see it for the first time, just as an admissions officer will. If the application is striking, they may even discover something about you that they didn't know before.
- TYPE, DON'T WRITE: Maybe your third-grade teacher worked your fingers to the bone practicing your penmanship, but your perfect script will not make it for the reader who is looking at countless other applications. Your essay should be computer-generated. For the application, taking the extra time to line up those little lines and boxes to a typewriter or word processor is worth the effort.

5. APPLY TO SCHOOLS THAT FEEL RIGHT FOR YOU

- CHOOSE THE SCHOOL TO WHICH YOU'RE GUARANTEED TO BE ACCEPTED WITH THE SAME CARE SPENT SELECTING YOUR DREAM SCHOOL: While you read on and on about the selectivity of schools and about the importance of really impressing those to which you have chosen to apply, don't forget that you are, in a sense, interviewing the schools almost as much as they are interviewing you. An application is a hefty investment of yourself. Each school you choose should be one that you can see yourself attending, whether it's choice number one or choice number five. Each application should be tailored to the school where it will end its journey. Keep your schools in mind as you complete their applications. The application—and the school—should bring out your best points—carefully, thoughtfully, honestly, and creatively.

ESSAY-WRITING STRATEGIES

1. What does the college want in your essay? That is the question.
2. Start rough. Then refine.
3. Pen to paper (or fingers to keyboard): The write stuff about you.
4. Organize.
5. Trust the power of the written word. Trust yourself.

When you write, you lay out a line of words. The line of words is a miner's pick, a wood-carver's gouge, a surgeon's probe. You wield it, and it digs a path you follow. Soon you find yourself deep in new territory. Is it a dead end, or have you located the real subject? You will know tomorrow, or this time next year.

❑ *Annie Dillard*
From The Writing Life. *Harper and Row, 1989.*

What you write now in your personal statements and essays *will* determine tomorrow. Don't stop short of inspiring work. It could help open the door to your dream school.

1. WHAT DOES THE COLLEGE WANT IN YOUR ESSAY? THAT IS THE QUESTION

- ASSESS YOUR OPTIONS FOR THE ESSAY QUESTION: Some colleges and universities provide specific questions to direct your essay writing. You may be asked to offer your views on a particular topic or issue. ("If you could change anything in the world, what would you change and how?" or "Describe an experience that changed you.") Others leave the essay topic relatively open-ended and personal, allowing you the somewhat daunting task: "Tell us about *you*."

  Whether you decide to comment on the state of the Union or to recount an inspirational volunteer job, you often have a few essay questions from which to choose. Study the question that feels most comfortable to you and pick it apart to plan your approach.
- GET TO THE HEART OF THE QUESTION: You are anxious to write your college essay about that one life-changing moment. How do you fit that experience into an answer to the college's question? It's a good idea to look into what is being asked, address the question directly, and elaborate on your answer to their query with some interesting experiences of your own. The questions offered on the application are meant for you to choose in order to let the college get to know you better, so mold the question to you personally. If you discuss the topics that are asked in the question of your choice and describe personal experiences, you can't go wrong.

2. START ROUGH. THEN REFINE

- CREATE AN OUTLINE/ROUGH DRAFT: First, organize your thoughts around your topic and outline some important points that you plan to stress. Start with a draft that captures your feelings and images, then return to it again and again to make it lucid and refined.
- DO NOT BE AFRAID OF CHANGE: Elizabeth Bishop worked through multiple drafts for each of her poems, and her revisions filled pages at times. The most inspiring of poets, bards, novelists, and essayists are unafraid to "kill a few of their babies," as they say in the literary world. All well-written material reaches fluidity through revision and change. Don't let the raw emotion of your personal statement be the only strength that makes it impressive. Editing for content, making changes, and reorganizing your thoughts will enhance the quality of your writing. Admissions officers will be unimpressed by writing that is anything less than careful and thoughtful.

3. PEN TO PAPER (OR FINGERS TO KEYBOARD): THE WRITE STUFF ABOUT YOU

- HAVE FUN WITH IT (BUT DON'T BUY INTO GIMMICKS): You are looking for that edge in your essay that will attract the attention of admission officers who have read more essays than they can count. Something about you is unique and outstanding. Enjoy the chance to use your voice creatively, without simply boasting about your good qualities. Let the admissions officers know you by telling a well-written story and completely selling yourself.

  One admissions officer at a top college claims that it is the essay that makes or breaks an application in her mind, and if a student has the ability to take over a creative written space with an essay that sticks with her, she's sold. An applicant who writes succinctly, well, and with a twist impresses her. A student who wrote about his track career and sent his old track shoes attached to the essay did not.
- HONESTY IS THE BEST POLICY: The old adage is true: write what you know. Don't be afraid to be honest and to be yourself.

4. ORGANIZE

- KEEP THE SCHOOL IN MIND WHEN WRITING ABOUT YOURSELF: The essay can be a further exploration of why you are right for that particular school and why that school is right for you. In reflecting on who you are right now, you will also be able to look forward to what you wish to become through your experiences at your future school.

- REDUCE, REUSE, RECYCLE: If something has inspired you to create a piece that really speaks about you, adapt it to fit into various college applications. It's okay to use one essay for more than one school. After all, the admissions officers at Yale rarely compare specifics with the admissions officers at Berkeley. Some essay topics and questions are flexible enough so that you can tailor your essay to more than one school. You are attracted to these schools for reasons that are personal and specific. The essay is your chance to let them know the things about you that fit with the things you like about them. You are not cheating if you say the same thing about yourself to more than one admissions office.
- DON'T FORGET THE FINISHING TOUCHES: Type the essay. Check the spelling. Correct margins and punctuation. Have several readers look it over for you. Sounds like a drill, but neatness and care can't hurt.

5. TRUST THE POWER OF THE WRITTEN WORD. TRUST YOURSELF

- LET YOUR ESSAY SPEAK FOR YOU: Writing is a powerful tool. Unlike speaking in an interview or filling in boxes on an application, writing a personal statement or answering an essay question allows you to think, plan, and revise an interesting, articulate presentation of yourself. Be as complete as possible and don't be afraid to take risks by telling your own story. Discussing a personal experience takes strength—the chance to use your voice is a gift; wrap it in language and give it to the college of your choice. They'll open it carefully and, if they remember it, it is a gift that will bring many happy returns.

FINANCING STRATEGIES

1. Know what is expected of you.
2. Set a timetable and get an early start.
3. Explore every possible source of funding.
4. Lean on you.
5. College is worth the investment!

Regardless of your family's income, college is no small feat. The cost of tuition, room and board, books, travel, and related expenses continues to rise in an intimidating, discouraging way. Applying for financial aid is the first step in scaling that monetary hurdle. In all cases, no matter what your income bracket, applying for financial aid is definitely the first sign of a smart, bright, college-bound student.

1. KNOW WHAT IS EXPECTED OF YOU

- GET THE FACTS: Don't just stare at that pile of tax returns and financial information. As with all things, the best place to begin is at the beginning. Sharpen your number two pencils, but before you start, make sure you remember these guidelines:

  Males must be registered for the draft when applying for aid.
  Don't leave blanks on any financial aid form, whether it is for the school, the agency, or a loan.
  Sign and keep copies of all forms. Send only originals.
  Include the correct processing fees.

- DEFINE YOUR TERMS: You'll need to know the language before you travel through the process of financial aid. There is a dizzying amount of terms and acronyms (the financial aid world loves acronyms). Consider this your official dictionary of Financial Aid Jargon (FAJ).

  Acknowledgment Report: Notification to the student after the need form has been received by a processing agency.

  College Scholarship Service (CSS): Service that analyzes family need and contribution.

  Expected Family Contribution (EFC): Amount determined by the federal government that your family should have accessible to help pay for school; used in determining your eligibility for grants and loans.

  Free Application for Federal Student Aid (FAFSA): Free federal application that must be filed to determine eligibility for federal student loans.

  Financial Aid Forms (FAF): Forms processed by the College Scholarship Service of the College Board to determine your family's financial need and contribution; results are sent by the CSS to colleges and universities.

  Information Request Form: Form that the federal government may send to ask for further or corrected information before granting a federal Pell Grant.

Payment Voucher: Part Three of the Student Aid Report; submitted to the school financial aid officer to determine the Pell Grant amount.

Student Aid Report (SAR): Official notification of federal Pell Grant eligibility, usually received by the student and the school four to six weeks after submission of the application.

Verification: Process of checking financial aid applications for accuracy.

2. SET A TIMETABLE AND GET AN EARLY START

- JANUARY: Gather all of the necessary financial aid forms from your schools and from processing agencies. Collect the documents and information that you will need to complete these required forms (such as tax returns, bank statements, and so on). Send your completed forms to the processors soon after January 1.
- FEBRUARY: Three to six weeks after submitting your application, its receipt will be confirmed via mail. A report will follow that will outline your family's expected contribution and eligibility for aid. Look for the SAR, which you will submit to the school you ultimately choose to attend. Discuss the results with your family and direct any questions you have to your financial aid officer.
- MARCH–JULY: Colleges and universities make financial aid decisions at this time, so be sure that your application is complete. The financial aid award letter from your school indicates the amount of aid you will receive for the year, including all federal grants and loans, outside awards, and state aid. Sign and return a copy of the letter if you accept the school's package. If you need more assistance or have questions about the offer, contact the school's aid officer now. Don't wait!

3. EXPLORE EVERY POSSIBLE SOURCE OF FUNDING

- PARENTS: Figure out ahead of time what role your family will play in helping to finance your education.
- THE FEDS: Despite cuts and obstacles, the government still provides most of the aid that is awarded to college students.
- THE STATE: Many states offer need- and merit-based aid. Inquire into your home base resources for the college-bound.
- COLLEGES AND UNIVERSITIES: Check the philosophy of the schools to which you are applying. Need-blind? (The school does not consider financial need in admissions.) Need-

sensitive? (The school considers financial need only when deliberating over candidates after subsidiary funds have been allocated.) How is aid distributed? Will your freshman year aid package be guaranteed for four years? Don't be afraid to pose the tough questions to the financial aid director or advisor. Paying for college is one of the most important investments you will make. You have the right to be an educated consumer.

- PRIVATE ORGANIZATIONS AND FOUNDATIONS: If you have particular talents or aspirations, examine organizations that award merit-based aid. Many organizations offer assistance to students heading towards a certain major or grant help to high school seniors from a specific area. Investigate all your options at your local library.

4. LEAN ON YOU

- WORK IT...BORROW IT: Students have the responsibility of thinking about saving a bit in high school, finding summer jobs, taking out loans, and working during college. Many financial aid packages include on-campus jobs. Both on- and off-campus work is not only lucrative for spending money and tuition money, it can provide valuable experiences that contribute to more than just your payment plan.

5. COLLEGE IS WORTH THE INVESTMENT!

- DON'T FEAR THE NUMBERS: It more than adds up. What you get for your money is often priceless. The degree equals the architecture of a life and a future. The major yields connections and expertise in a field that excites you. The experience gained in obtaining that slip of paper written in Latin can be so rich and full and once-in-a-lifetime, it almost doesn't hurt to make the loan payments afterwards. Almost. Because, in a perfect world, the fine-tuning of our minds wouldn't cost a penny. Until we reach that glorious place, it pays to plan a way to make the refinement of our mental sensibilities as affordable as possible.

STUDY STRATEGIES

1. Time management: the key to staying on top.
2. Establish blocks of time for each commitment.
3. Learn to love your classes.
4. Plan ahead.
5. Prioritize!

It is two o'clock in the morning. You have just stumbled back to your dorm room after a late rehearsal for a production headed by a very serious senior director. Your legs are still sore from rugby tryouts earlier in the week. That psychology assignment is due tomorrow afternoon, but you have to finish it in the twenty-four-hour computer lab tonight because you have to work at the café in the morning. Your roommate is still awake, waiting to hear your advice on this great-new-somebody he or she just met.

Now what are you going to do to make sure that all of the high school preparation, careful application work, diligent essay-writing, hard-won financial aid, and lofty aspirations will play out successfully on the stage of this collegiate experience?

1. TIME MANAGEMENT: THE KEY TO STAYING ON TOP

- FINDING THE BALANCE: College is a nonstop mélange of experiences. Juggling studies with social life, extracurricular activities, jobs, and friends can be harrowing. The idea is to enjoy each facet of your life to the fullest, without losing sight of important priorities.

  You know yourself. Try not to take on too much if you are the kind of student who needs as little distraction as possible. Try not to take on too little if you thrive on a tight schedule to keep yourself motivated and challenged. Above all, develop a schedule that will focus on your classes, with occasional varied, diverse, and interesting demands on your time.
- THE FILOFAX SYNDROME: Electronic planners and little black books are no longer accessories to be found only in the boardrooms of corporate America. They can be spotted peeking out of many a backpack, tucked away among Henry James novels in dorm rooms, and present on the desks at student government meetings. College students aren't kidding about "penciling you in." It's often wise to keep track of your commitments in writing. You'd be surprised how much easier deadlines, meetings, and social events fall in beside each other when you can see them written in front of you.

2. ESTABLISH BLOCKS OF TIME FOR EACH COMMITMENT

- BREAK UP THE DAYS OF THE WEEK: Set aside chunks of time that you regularly spend dedicating yourself to your classes. Just as you would make a work schedule at any job, you should have an academic work schedule that you attempt to follow. You are your own boss, so punch in for physics on Monday evenings after dinner, English lit on Tuesday mornings before practice, and so on.

You won't have to set your academic plan in stone. In fact, you'll need plenty of flexibility (for the weeks when you have an English paper due, but no physics lab because you finished it early). The point is to promise yourself that you have blocks of time solely for the subjects you are studying each semester.

- USE THE IN-BETWEEN HOURS: Maybe on Thursdays you have two hours in mid-afternoon between your seminar and your art class. You could fill those two hours with errands that you've been meaning to take care of. You could score two extra hours in the library researching a project. You could finish a problem set or run to the gym to work out. It's important to steal the hours in your day that are sandwiched between other commitments. That precious time can be easily lost in the Bermuda Triangle where time runs when you are busy and thirsty for more hours in the day. Instead, grab it and put it to good use before it gets away. Making each moment count is the key. (That doesn't mean you can't use those hours to meet a friend for coffee. A little R and R is definitely a priority, too.)

3. LEARN TO LOVE YOUR CLASSES

- ELECT PASSIONS: Not every class of your college career will change your life, but you will definitely move from high school chem labs and single-sex phys ed to more engaging academic pursuits. You'll find flexibility, even within the requirements. Your major will allow you to focus on something that you feel strongly about, while still dabbling in areas that are new and challenging.
- EXPERIMENT. PUSH YOURSELF. TRY NEW THINGS: If you have no idea what a cognitive science course called "Time" could possibly cover, but the idea of meeting to discuss such a broad subject fascinates you, take it! If you love the humanities, make sure you take a science as well. And if you admire art with the eye of a true aesthete, but you can't draw to save your life, make sure you sign up for basic life drawing at some point in your college career. Studying something that falls outside of your main line of interest is an excellent way to spice up your classwork.
- THIS IS A RICH, RARE TIME: Even when the work load brings you down and your calendar is filled with deadlines for papers, exams, presentations, and projects, try not to forget how lucky you are to have this time in your life. You are being asked to study, to work, to grow, to expand your mind, and to look through frames of reference and windows that you have never experienced before now. College is a precious opportunity. Covet your right to acquire so much knowledge in such an individual way.

4. PLAN AHEAD

- LOOK AT THE SYLLABUS: Early in the term, your professors will provide careful plans of what they will cover throughout the semester. Most professors let you know right away the important dates to remember, required readings, and class topics for the duration of the course. The class syllabus can jump-start your timeline for the final paper, or allow you to stay on top of things for the midterm project. Check the syllabus in the beginning of the course for all of your classes. You can coordinate the crunch times (such as those times before breaks when every professor assigns work as if his or hers is your only class!). Knowing ahead of time allows you to be prepared for the avalanches. When you are prepared and you have stocked your research and your resources, it becomes easier to successfully weather any academic storm.
- MEET THE PROFESSOR AND/OR THE TA: Know the professor's office hours and take advantage of them. Find out if professors or assistants are accessible via e-mail or phone and contact them frequently to talk about your work, your ideas, your progress.

5. PRIORITIZE!

- MAKE CLASSES NUMBER ONE: Want to do well in college? Then make college classes your first, most important priority and look out for number one. You will be making room in your life for lots of things: jobs, volunteerism, sports, clubs and activities, friends, dating…the list goes on and on. Believe it or not, there are enough hours in the day to get to everything. Although it is impossible to accomplish all that you think you might want to try between freshman and senior year, it is feasible to try everything and still succeed academically. Just make sure that the library becomes an important part of your week (and yes, sometimes your weekend, too!) and get your priorities in order.

A MOST COMPETITIVE COMPARISON

SCHOOL	NUMBER OF APPLICATIONS	ACCEPTED	ENROLLED	M/F RATIO	SAT I SCORES VERBAL	MATH	COMB.	COSTS
Amherst College	5,210	1,039	434	53/47	706	700	1,406	$29,064
Bates College	3,636	1,241	459	47/53	n/av	n/av	n/av	$28,650
Boston College	16,455	6,455	2,168	47/53	n/av	n/av	n/av	$28,062
Bowdoin College	3,974	1,355	473	50/50	670	660	1,330	$29,020
Brown University	14,900	2,670	1,411	47/53	700	700	1,400	$30,063
California Institute of Technology	2,389	540	217	73/27	725	768	1,493	$24,516
Carnegie Mellon University	13,115	5,650	1,270	66/34	650	710	1,360	$26,600
Claremont McKenna College	2,733	882	262	57/43	670	690	1,360	$25,740
Colby College	4,203	1,422	504	47/53	650	650	1,300	$29,190
Colgate University	5,852	2,448	716	49/51	634	643	1,277	$28,875
College of the Holy Cross	4,183	1,978	728	47/53	620	620	1,240	$27,980
College of William and Mary	6,596	3,032	1,334	n/av	650	640	1,290	$9,618
Columbia University/ Barnard College	3,554	1,421	563	all women	n/av	n/av	n/av	$29,712
Columbia University/ Columbia College	11,192	1,958	967	50/50	n/av	n/av	n/av	$29,994
Columbia University/ School of Engineering and Applied Science (SEAS)	1,902	724	320	74/26	n/av	n/av	n/av	$29,994

SCHOOL	NUMBER OF APPLICATIONS	ACCEPTED	ENROLLED	M/F RATIO	SAT I SCORES VERBAL	MATH	COMB.	COSTS
Cornell University	19,854	6,715	2,944	52/48	660	680	1,340	$29,024
Dartmouth University	10,647	2,311	1,106	52/48	710	720	1,430	$29,565
Davidson College	3,183	1,150	472	51/49	660	665	1,325	$26,513
Duke University	13,365	4,063	1,623	51/49	690	710	1,400	$29,026
Georgetown University	13,712	2,928	1,397	47/53	n/av	n/av	n/av	$29,496
Georgia Institute of Technology	7,676	n/av	1,848	72/28	632	673	1,305	$7,464 (in state) / $14,184 (out of state)
Harvard University/ Harvard College	16,598	2,143	1,652	55/45	n/av	n/av	n/av	$30,080
Harvard University/ Radcliffe College	n/av	n/av	n/av	all women	n/av	n/av	n/av	$30,080
Harvey Mudd College	1,426	613	183	76/24	710	760	1,470	$27,850
Haverford College	2,769	946	298	49/51	n/av	n/av	n/av	$28,810
Johns Hopkins University	8,543	3,448	945	60/40	670	690	1,360	$29,055
Massachusetts Institute of Technology	7,836	1,938	1,064	60/40	699	748	1,447	$30,286
Middlebury College	4,741	1,471	567	49/51	710	690	1,400	$29,340
New College, University of South Florida	487	340	145	43/57	700	640	1,340	$6,404 (in state) / $13,504 (out of state)
Northwestern University	16,674	4,909	1,891	48/52	670	690	1,360	$25,525
Pomona College	3,892	1,228	393	52/48	710	710	1,420	$28,860
Princeton University	13,400	1,723	1,131	53/47	n/av	n/av	n/av	$29,435
Rice University	6,375	1,748	706	53/47	n/av	n/av	n/av	$20,500
Stanford University	16,359	2,634	1,614	50/50	n/av	n/av	n/av	$27,830
Swarthmore College	4,270	994	373	47/53	720	710	1,430	$29,500
Tufts University	12,291	3,899	1,273	48/52	660	670	1,330	$29,615

SCHOOL	NUMBER OF APPLICATIONS	ACCEPTED	ENROLLED	M/F RATIO	SAT I SCORES VERBAL	MATH	COMB.	COSTS
United States Air Force Academy	9,802	1,485	1,118	84/16	630	660	1,290	$0
United States Coast Guard Academy	2,378	441	288	72/28	610	640	1,250	$0
United States Military Academy	12,745	1,597	1,131	86/14	620	644	1,264	$0
United States Naval Academy	10,119	1,447	1,175	86/14	634	659	1,293	$0
University of Chicago	5,361	3,311	1,000	53/47	680	680	1,360	$30,275
University of Notre Dame	9,071	3,664	1,906	56/44	647	667	1,314	$24,860
University of Pennsylvania	15,464	4,828	2,349	51/49	670	700	1,370	$29,530
University of Virginia	16,189	5,755	2,908	47/53	650	660	1,310	$9,065 (in state) / $19,309 (out of state)
Vassar College	4,765	2,025	650	38/62	666	641	1,307	$28,560
Wake Forest University	6,536	2,848	965	50/50	644	651	1,295	$24,829
Washington and Lee University	3,460	1,087	454	57/43	n/av	n/av	n/av	$21,291
Webb Institute	67	31	24	83/17	690	690	1,380	(room & board) $6,050 (no tuition)
Wellesley College	3,174	1,390	597	all women	672	656	1,328	$28,330
Wesleyan University	5,853	1,944	701	48/52	680	670	1,350	$29,190
Williams College	4,537	1,159	545	52/48	n/av	n/av	n/av	$29,360
Yale University	12,046	2,144	1,307	51/49	720	720	1,440	$29,950

COLLEGE SUMMARIES

❑ COLLEGE SUMMARIES ❑

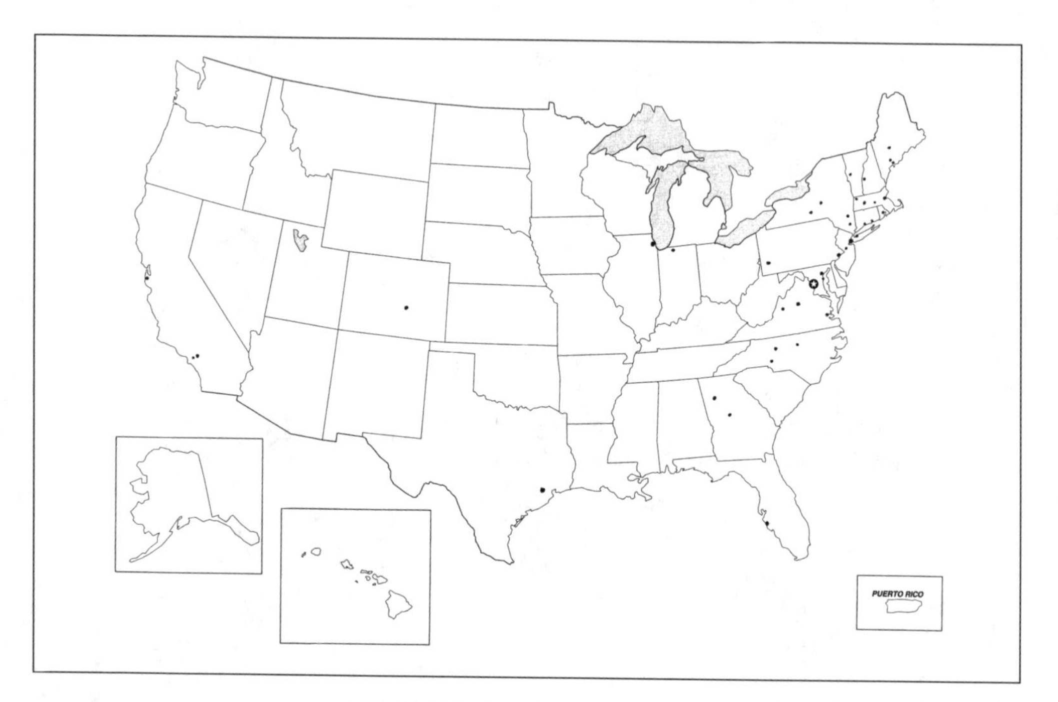

COLLEGE SUMMARY INDEX

❑ **Amherst College**, at first glance, is a picturesque New England liberal arts college. But beyond the red brick and fall foliage are the people who make the college what it is—the top-notch faculty, the accessible administration, the successful alumni, and most importantly, the energetic and expressive students. Collectively, those who make Amherst what it is give to the school its character, effort, and intellect, and receive in turn, the character, effort, and intellect of their fellow colleagues and students, making Amherst more than an academic institution, but a community.

❑ **Bates College** is small, friendly, yet academically excellent. Bates does not require standardized test scores for admission. It is strongly committed to a program of broad education including the humanities and the sciences. The student body and faculty are unusually supportive and inclusive. One example is the absence of fraternities and sororities. Bates continues to be committed to providing an environment in which students can excel. A Bates education extends beyond the walls of academic buildings, and is formed in the integration of academics, athletics, and activities. Located midway between the Atlantic coastline and the mountains, the school offers a broad choice of sports and outdoor activities.

❑ **Boston College** is a Jesuit university that was founded in 1863 to provide students with an education that fosters both intellectual and personal development. Students at BC participate in a rigorous academic program and are also encouraged to become involved in community service projects. The setting of Boston College is also unique. Located in a suburban neighborhood, it is only six miles west of Boston, an extremely advantageous characteristic. Students have easy access to a major city but also enjoy the beauty and safety of a suburban town.

❑ **Bowdoin College** is a nationally recognized prestigious liberal arts college situated on the coast of Maine just north of Portland. The 203-year-old school offers a wide spectrum of courses, from biology and neuroscience to English and art history, which prepare students to be leaders in their fields. Well known for its athletic prowess and distinguished alumni, Bowdoin is catapulting into the twenty-first century with newly constructed dormitories, state-of-the-art science facilities, and the Smith Union, which is the hub of social life. Bowdoin graduates professionals who are well versed not only in academics and athletics, but also the arts, world cultures, and volunteerism.

❑ **Brown University** is an Ivy League school located in Providence, Rhode Island. The school is known for its liberal curriculum, the emphasis its administration places upon individual choice in the learning process, and the generally easygoing student body. Brown encourages its students to determine their own academic and social paths and provides them with the opportunity to follow their interests. It also possesses a faculty that is eager to help undergraduates flourish in this atmosphere. Brown is a perfect university for self-motivated and confident students who desire a top-flight education on their own terms. This freedom allows students to produce high-quality work and helps many Brown graduates to either continue their studies at top graduate and professional schools or take positions in industry.

❑ At the **California Institute of Technology**, better known as Caltech, some of the best students and faculty in the world are gathered together with one mission: to create the science of tomorrow. Caltech has been and will continue to be a powerhouse of breakthrough scientific research, with twenty-six Nobel prizes won by Caltech faculty and alumni during its 100-year history. Located on a beautiful campus in Pasadena, California, Caltech is a small but very focused institution with only 900 undergraduate students and 1,000 faculty members. Yet Caltech's outstanding resources and facilites, including the Jet Propulsion Laboratory (JPL), make it the ideal place for students with a passion for science and engineering. Academic excellence, dedication to the pursuit of knowledge, a strong sense of personal integrity, and a quirky sense of humor are the hallmarks of the Caltech student.

❑ **Carnegie Mellon** is a highly competitive university offering degrees in everything from art to engineering. Known particularly for its computer science and engineering programs, as well as programs in the arts, Carnegie Mellon educates a wide range of students from all over the world. The six colleges of Carnegie Mellon offer degrees in a wide range of programs and specialties.

❑ **Claremont McKenna College** is a small liberal arts institution located in Claremont, California. The surrounding Norman Rockwellesque community has the appearance of an eastern seaboard town, and is conveniently located just thirty-five miles east of downtown Los Angeles. CMC's academic program focuses on the development of strong leadership and communication skills. Boasting a student-to-faculty ratio of nine to one, CMC ensures a high-quality, individualized learning environment for all students.

❑ **Colby College** is a small liberal arts institution located in Waterville, Maine. The size of the student body allows strong and personalized interaction with Colby's award-winning faculty and customized academic paths for motivated students. Athletics, along with social and cultural activities, provide students with pleasurable experiences outside the classroom. And if campus activities don't offer enough variety, Colby's proximity to Maine's rich coast, ski resorts, and beautiful national parks, as well as Portland's and Boston's metropolitan atmosphere, creates an ideally well-rounded environment.

❑ Tucked away in rural Hamilton, New York, **Colgate** is a small university that offers its talented students great academics along with a stunning campus setting that together meet the ideal of a great liberal arts school. Small classes and an outstanding faculty distinguish a Colgate education, but an active, engaging student body, along with atheletic and academic opportunities usually found only at much larger schools, make Colgate an exciting experience inside and outside the classroom.

❑ **College of the Holy Cross** is highly respected for its superior undergraduate academic programs, excellent faculty, and the intelligence, imagination, and achievements of its students. It is also well known for its strong, well-supported, and enthusiastic commitment to the principle of educating men and women for others, in a community that generates a strong feeling of belonging and a vital sense of loyalty. Holy Cross is a place to learn how to learn, and not a place to seek job training. The fundamental purpose of the college is not to train students for specific occupations but to inform the mind and to foster clear thought and expression through the balanced study of the arts and the sciences.

❑ The **College of William and Mary** is a small public university with a primary focus on developing a strong undergraduate education and experience for its students. The college, the second oldest college in the country, is steeped in history. Its beautifully laid-out campus sits adjacent to Colonial Williamsburg and fits in with the rest of picturesque Williamsburg. William and Mary emphasizes the development of responsibility and motivation in its students by providing personalized support in every capacity but also allowing students the freedom to control their own living, learning, and social environments. Students at the college work hard but also find time to relax and enjoy time with friends. William and Mary challenges its students to be the best they can be at everything they are involved in while at the college. This type of well-rounded training proves to be essential to students upon graduating and entering the work world.

❑ **Columbia University/Barnard College** is an independent college for women affliated with Columbia University and located in New York City. The 2,300 undergraduates pursue a broad variety of liberal arts majors. Graduation requirements are flexibly structured so students can fashion a course of study to meet their needs. Those interested in professional or graduate schools in law, business, medicine, or other areas are advised on appropriate courses. Over 2,500 internships are available to students through the Career Development Office, which also sponsors on-campus recruitment and workshops. Eighty or so student organizations are complemented by those at Columbia University, offering a wealth of activity and opportunity for leadership and involvement; varsity athletes compete in Division I.

Barnard's unique combination of strengths—a commited faculty of teacher-scholars, full access to the resources of a great university, and the abundant offerings of New York City—make it an excellent choice for young women interested in an urban setting and an excellent, well-rounded education.

❑ **Columbia University/Columbia College**, one of four undergraduate schools at Columbia University, distinguishes itself academically with its core curriculum—a series of required classes concentrating on the great Western contributions in art, philosophy, music, and literature to the modern world. With the core, students learn how to merge information in the classroom with knowledge from New York City, where Columbia is located. Visits to museums, musical performances, and art galleries become standard learning fare with the core. The Columbia student's four-year experience is also constantly enhanced by the exciting world of New York; Broadway, Museum Mile, Central Park, Greenwich Village, and Wall Street are all just a subway ride away. The college also boasts a diverse student population, outstanding faculty who are leaders in their fields, and sixty-four different majors and concentrations in forty-nine academic departments.

❏ Attending **Columbia University/SEAS** means being in the presence of knowledge-seeking people. Of course, Columbia offers an excellent academic experience, but it also draws its students to learning, and to sharing the educationally diverse life experiences of a metropolitan environment. It is virtually impossible to describe Columbia and do justice to its reputation. Not only is acceptance to Columbia testimony of hard work prior to college, but it is also evidence that you are eager to be challenged in all aspects of life while being supported by a strong community.

❏ **Cornell University** is made up of undergraduates colleges, one graduate school, three professional schools, 18,000 students, and 457 buildings It sits on 745 acres in the Finger Lakes region of New York State. In these breathtaking surroundings, students observe Cornell's founding philosophy, "where anyone can find instruction in any study." Cornell is a big school where students are constantly challenged, whether they like it or not, and where achieving great things is the rule, not the exception. There are hundreds of extracurricular activities to get involved in, and the athletes work as hard as anyone else. Cornell provides a challenging academic life and amazing out-of-classroom experiences.

❏ **Dartmouth College**, smallest of the eight Ivy League schools, is distinguished by its northern location, year-round calendar, and focus on the undergraduate experience. Known for its top-notch academics, Dartmouth offers small classes, close faculty-student relationships, and a host of research opportunities. Dartmouth students take three classes per ten-week term, are required to spend their sophomore summer on campus, and have the opportunity to take part in more than forty study abroad programs. With its diverse but intimate atmosphere, Dartmouth breeds some of the highest student satisfaction rates in the country.

❑ Dedicated to undergraduate teaching and learning, **Davidson College** is a place where ideas flourish, honor matters, and character counts. Davidson's liberal arts curriculum challenges students to explore their interests and discover new strengths. With a student-faculty ratio of 12:1 and small classes, students and faculty develop close relationships and engage in a constant discourse that encourages a lifelong appreciation of learning. Located in a small town, yet just twenty minutes from Charlotte, North Carolina, one of the fastest-growing cities in the United States, Davidson students enjoy the benefits of both of these worlds. At Davidson, students meet the challenges of demanding professors, a variety of diverse and interesting community activities, and an Honor Code that forms a community based on mutual trust and respect.

❑ The momentum and pulse of energy that run through **Duke University** mirror the explosive growth of North Carolina's Triangle—Raleigh, Chapel Hill, and Durham, Duke's home—and the famous Research Triangle Park it helped to create. A residential campus, Duke's rise in national preeminence is a result of its diverse, inquisitive student body working with renowned scholars and Duke's world-class program and medical center. Independent studies and out-of-class learning experiences complement a demanding liberal arts curriculum. Duke's continuing push for excellence is coupled with an intimate feeling of community that encourages collaboration and student development. Constant club activities, top-notch athletics, and community service top off the opportunities for student involvement. Active students, engaged faculty, and the most spectacular campus environment in the country make for an idyllic setting to learn and grow during the undergraduate years.

❑ **Georgetown University** excels in providing its diverse student body with a solid liberal arts education, while instilling in its students a strong social consciousness. Georgetown was founded in 1789 and is located in Washington, D.C. Politicians, business leaders, and humanitarians alike have called Hilltop home.

❑ **The Georgia Institute of Technology,** located in the heart of downtown Atlanta, offers its 13,000 students the opportunity to graduate on the leading edge of technology. This atmosphere of excellence is enhanced by Georgia Tech's support structure of faculty, business, industry, and alumni. Georgia Tech consistently ranks among the best buys in higher education, making it a logical choice for a student interested in any technological field.

❑ Founded in 1636, **Harvard University/Harvard College** is the oldest college in the United States. Harvard is home to the world's largest university library system, a world-renowned faculty, and a student body of many talents and interests. Located in Cambridge, Massachusetts, Harvard offers its undergraduates a broad liberal arts education and the exciting urban atmosphere of Boston, one of America's great college towns.

❑ As part of **Harvard University, Radcliffe College** offers undergraduate programs, research and policy institutes, and a network of alumnae that enrich the undergraduate experience for women at Harvard. While male students graduate with only a Harvard College degree, women graduate from both Harvard and Radcliffe Colleges, benefiting from the vast resources of Harvard; the unique leadership, research, and mentoring programs at Radcliffe; and the intellectual and social communities the two provide both during college and beyond.

❑ Located in Claremont, California, **Harvey Mudd College** is a small school of 650 students with a rigorous curriculum and a narrow academic focus on math, science, and engineering. The curriculum consists of six majors (engineering, math, computer science, biology, chemistry, and physics). The college has a broad academic approach with an emphasis on the humanities and social sciences as well as core science, math, and engineering principals. The residential campus is vibrant with a student body that is widely talented, dynamic, and eccentric, in addition to being academically gifted. HMC is bolstered by its participation in the Claremont Colleges consortium, which gives Mudd students access to academic resources, course offerings, athletics, and other opportunities that could not otherwise be supported by a small technical college. The student-run Honor Code demands integrity and honesty from every student. Students at Mudd would be able to more fully enjoy the beaches, mountains, and nightlife of Southern California if they were not so caught up in getting a fine education and having a great time without ever leaving the campus.

❑ **Haverford College** has emerged as one of the top private colleges in the country. Drawing on a distinguished faculty, small classroom environment, and the resources of a tri-college partnership, Haverford is an excellent educational experience. An effective and comprehensive Honor Code provides a background of trust and respect that students take seriously and carry with them after graduation. Ten miles outside of Philadelphia, Haverford has a small, but thriving social life, a wealth of extracurricular activities, and an education that will last a lifetime.

❑ The Krieger School of Arts and Sciences and the Whiting School of Engineering are the heart of **Johns Hopkins University**, the first American research university. Enrolling only 3,400 full-time undergraduates, Hopkins has many of the qualities of a small liberal arts school with strong programs across all disciplines, small classes, and accessible faculty who actually teach the class. On the other hand, Hopkins also has all the resources of a major research university, offering leading scholars and scientists incredible resources and unparalleled research opportunities.

❑ It's tough to get accepted at **Massachusetts Institute of Technology**—and the academic life is even more challenging. It's expensive—but financial aid is reliable. With a reputation for science and engineering, MIT surprises some with its highly rated economics, philosophy, and music departments (among others). Whether you go on to graduate or professional school, or confront the job market, a degree from MIT will serve you very well.

❑ **Middlebury College** is one of the nation's best small liberal arts colleges, but with the additional features of an international university. Middlebury Schools Abroad operate in Madrid, Mainz, Paris, and Russia, and the faculty and facilities on its scenic Vermont campus are world class. As Middlebury celebrates its bicentennial in the year 2000, it intends to be "the college of the future, the college of choice" for students who wish to compete in the global economy of the twenty-first century. Vermont's Green Mountains provide extensive recreational opportunities, and a metaphor for the college's strengths. The college community is very close-knit. Friendships and a sense of family endure well beyond graduation. Extracurricular activities abound. Middlebury prepares students not just for their first job, but for a well-balanced life overall.

❑ **New College of the University of South Florida** is the honors college of the State University System of Florida. New College possesses a unique academic environment that involves written evaluations in lieu of letter grades, extensive original research, and a substantial thesis required for graduation. Located in sunny Sarasota, Florida, ten minutes from to the sugar-white beaches, New College has a free-flowing social life, embracing uniqueness and individuality.

❑ The six undergraduate schools of **Northwestern University** practice a combination of liberal arts learning with real-world experience. Located in the first suburb north of Chicago, this university utilizes the city for its many learning and entertainment opportunities. Students are extremely motivated, which creates an intense academic environment but translates into successful graduate school acceptance and employment rates.

❑ **Pomona College** is a small, academically rigorous liberal arts college located thirty-five miles from Los Angeles. It is the largest of The Claremont Colleges, a consortium of six undergraduate colleges and a graduate university that share some facilities and work together to provide their students with classroom and extracurricular opportunities. Graduates can rely on their perception, analysis, and communication skills to go anywhere they want and do whatever they dream.

❑ **Princeton University's** commitment to undergraduate education sets it apart from other universities of comparable stature. Because the world-class faculty concentrates on undergraduates, students have a high degree of flexibility in designing academic programs and remarkable access to professors for precepts and independent study. In fact, the culmination of the Princeton undergraduate career, the senior thesis, gives every student a chance to work one-on-one with an advising professor on a level that is often not achieved in graduate school programs. In addition to the extraordinary academic experience, Princeton also provides social and extracurricular activities that create a rich and rewarding experience for gifted students of diverse backgrounds and interests.

❑ **Rice University** may be the best-kept secret in higher education. In addition to offering intense academics, a renowned Honor Code, small classes, a top-notch research program, a residential college system, a beautiful campus, the resources of Houston, strong intramural sports, Division I athletics, a student alcohol policy, Gulf Coast weather, a school of music, an institute for public policy, a center for nanoscale science and technology, a student-to-faculty ratio of nine to one, a student-run orientation week, great computing facilities, thousands of trees, some of the best students in the country, and a tuition half that at competing universities, Rice also has a really neat mascot and a cool-sounding name.

❑ Far removed from the cold winters and deep-rooted tradition of the Ivy League, **Stanford University**, just over 100 years old, is a young institution still in the process of creating its identity and traditions. Things move quickly at Stanford, due to both the quarter system and the academic changes that are made as the school continues to develop. With a stellar faculty and constantly expanding academic offerings, Stanford is an exciting arena for undergraduate studies. Students at Stanford involve themselves in every facet of the school, from research to involvement in the direction that the university takes academically and socially through organizations and protests. Student organizations and events abound, making for a dynamic environment both in and out of the classroom. Add to that a nationally renowned athletic program and a beautiful California setting, and you have a package that is hard to beat.

❑ A small liberal arts and engineering school renowned for its immoderately long reading lists and breakneck pace, **Swarthmore College** is situated within a serene, green, 330-acre campus outside Philadelphia. Its students are of remarkable intellect, imagination, diversity, and commitment to social change. Classes are quite small—most with fifteen students or fewer—and focused heavily on writing, reading, and lab work. Juniors and seniors may choose to be part of its unique External Examination program, taking even smaller, double-credit seminars for two years, and eventually being evaluated by a panel of professors from other universities. When they finally come out of the libraries, Swarthmore students are part of a small, almost familial social scene, characterized by on-campus parties and lots of dorm bonding.

❑ **Tufts University** combines all the benefits of a large city university with a small, suburban liberal arts college. The Tufts administration and faculty are dedicated to opening students' minds through educational and social diversity through small classroom settings, special events, and extracurricular activities. Located just a few short miles from Boston and Cambridge, Tufts offers students the opportunity to explore the biggest college town in the country while earning a top education.

❑ **The U.S. Air Force Academy**, established in 1954, is the youngest of the three service academies. It is nestled in the side of the Rocky Mountains in beautiful Colorado Springs, Colorado. The 4,000-strong cadet wing comes from all fifty states and forty foreign countries. The academy offers twenty-nine accredited majors, an excellent teaching staff, access to the Internet and local area network, and extensive reference and media support from the library. Extracurricular activites are in abundance as USAFA supports twenty-seven varsity teams and eighty-seven different competitive, noncompetitive clubs and religious groups. Most importantly, USAFA strives to develop professional Air Force officers through the four-year challenging program by training them in the core values of "Integrity First, Service Before Self, and Excellence in All We Do."

❑ **The U.S. Coast Guard Academy** is the best-kept secret of the Armed Forces service academies. Located on the Thames River in New London, Connecticut, the academy is home to 850 Coast Guard cadets who toil relentlessly through an exacting academic and military program. Paid for with a five-year service obligation, a cadet can earn a highly respected academic degree, an officer's commission in the U.S. Coast Guard, and an exciting, demanding career. The academy strives to produce young men and women with "sound bodies, stout hearts, and alert minds," future officers with courage, stamina, and integrity.

❑ **The U.S. Military Academy** at West Point, the nation's oldest service academy, is a four-year, federally funded program, aimed at developing commissioned leaders of character for our army and our nation. The West Point experience is one that is unforgettable. It "stretches your intellect, develops your self-confidence and overall potential, and prepares you for an important leadership role while serving the nation." The academy challenges cadets intellectually, physically, and militarily. The program is tough, the rewards are many, and the opportunities are endless. At West Point "much of the history we teach was made by people we taught."

❑ **The U.S. Naval Academy** is the navy's four-year undergraduate educational institution. Established in 1845, it prepares young men and women for careers as officers in both the navy and marine corps. Graduates earn a bachelor of science degree in one of eighteen majors in engineering, mathematics, applied sciences, social sciences, and the humanities. Tuition, room, and board are paid for by the federal government. As repayment, all graduates incur a five-year service obligation as either naval or marine corps officers after graduation.

❑ **The University of Chicago** relishes intellectual intensity, expressed both through hard work and through sincere conversation. The ideal student is, like a Renaissance man or a Ciceronian rhetorician, a complete person, with a well-rounded education, a wide-ranging curiosity, and a deep-driving commitment to civic life. Social life tends to be low-key and friendly, without emphasis on drinking, large parties, or status. All students must complete the common core, a unique curriculum developed and taught by leading professors, but complemented by a specialized concentration, sometimes in a tradition discipline, sometimes designed by the student. Athletics and student activities, particularly community involvement, help students to flourish and to practice the ethical ideals and social theories articulated by the great books of the common core.

❑ **The University of Notre Dame** is a liberal arts university located in South Bend, Indiana. One of the most prestigious Roman Catholic universities in the country, Notre Dame is known for its family-like environment and loyal alumni network. Students are active participants in community service projects, athletics, and dorm-based activities. Notre Dame is deeply rooted in tradition and heritage that extends beyond the football season.

❑ **The University of Pennsylvania** occupies its own little corner of West Philadelphia, Pennsylvania. With an undergraduate population of nearly 10,000 students and an equivalent number of graduate students, Penn ranks as one of the largest Ivy League institutions. Housing four separate undergraduate colleges—the College of Arts and Sciences, The Wharton School, The School of Engineering and Applied Science, and the Nursing School—Penn offers a wide variety of opportunities for students. Graduate students are able to choose from twelve different schools, with most ranking among the top schools in the country.

The general atmosphere is laid back and students foster a "work-hard, play-hard" attitude. With hundreds of extracurricular activities to choose from, Penn students seldom find themselves with nothing to do. Old traditions add to Penn's character and allow for unique experiences. Each student has the opportunity to shape his or her own experience and no two Penn experiences are the same. Because Penn provides each individual with the opportunity to develop both intellectually and personally, students leave the university feeling extremely pleased with their experience and often find themselves returning to campus for events such as Homecoming, commencement, and Alumni Weekend.

❑ **The University of Virginia** is an institution famous for the rigor and quality of its academics, the richness of its history, and the beauty of its architecture and setting. With a total of 18,000 enrolled students, UVa maintains its status as the public ivy by offering an outstanding liberal arts education, and attracting superior faculty as well as students.

Wahoos become part of Thomas Jefferson's legacy as they pursue their studies in an intimate academic community and maintain that community through the student-run Honor System and government. UVa is nestled amidst rolling farmland just minutes from the Blue Ridge mountains in the friendly, bustling city of Charlottesville, Virginia.

❑ **Vassar College** is a small liberal arts school quietly tucked into New York's lush and beautiful Hudson Valley. The college has distinguished itself for its intense and challenging academic program, but perhaps its greatest treasures are the immensely accessible faculty and the open-minded attitudes. With small classes and constant support, students and professors develop close relationships through which students are given guidance to freely tailor their courses of study. Outside of classes, Vassar students enjoy a panoply of events, clubs, teams, productions, and lectures. It's almost tempting to never leave the arboreal campus, where the starry nighttime sky can leave one breathless. But the playground of New York City is a brief train ride away and it cuts a cosmopolitan edge into the Vassar scene. Remaining committedly unafraid to take risks, Vassar offers the best of both worlds in an ivy-covered bastion of excellence that has never been stifled by the ivy.

❑ **Wake Forest University** is located in Winston-Salem, North Carolina on a beautiful, expansive campus. Wake Forest is known as a top liberal arts school where undergraduates have incredible access to the outstanding faculty. Wake students complete a large number of academic requirements, and courses are rigorous. Nevertheless, a relaxed, friendly atmosphere pervades the campus, and the school has the feeling of a warm community. Wake's roots are southern, but today the school is increasingly diverse, enrolling students from all over the nation. Wake enrolls less than 6,000 students (counting graduate and professional schools), but has the resources of a much larger university, allowing its students to reap the benefits of both small school academic life and big school facilities and opportunities.

❑ Located in the heart of Virginia's beautiful Shenandoah Valley, **Washington and Lee University** takes its name from two great American generals who shaped the school in its early history. In 1796 George Washington made his era's largest donation to a private American institution when he awarded $20,000 to the fledgling college. Robert E. Lee served as the school's president after the Civil War. Today, Washington and Lee University exemplifies the value of a liberal arts education. Its student body of 1,600 undergraduates comes from all parts of the United States to enjoy small classes, personal interaction with an excellent faculty, a varied and challenging curriculum, and an Honor System that creates an environment of trust. The university continues to sustain traditions while remaining modern as it prepares for its 250th anniversary.

❑ **Webb Institute** is the oldest school devoted to naval architecture and marine engineering (shipbuilding) in the United States. Founded and endowed in 1889 by millionaire and shipbuilder William H. Webb, the school is located in Glen Cove, New York, on Long Island Sound. Its rigorous, four-year engineering program focuses on the fundamentals of commercial ship design. Each of the approximately eighty students receives a full-tuition scholarship for all four years, regardless of need; students pay only for room, board, and books. Financial aid for these costs is available. Each winter, students gain two months of practical work experience in a shipyard, on board a ship, or in a design firm. Finally, Webb's placement rate is one-hundred percent, with graduates either attending graduate school or entering the maritime or other industries.

❑ **Wellesley College** educates women who will be smart, successful, and concerned leaders of their communities. Wellesley provides valuable hands-on experiences, from allowing students to run organizations to engaging their professors and peers in intellectual debates both in and out of the classroom. Nestled just outside of Boston in the town of Wellesley, Massachusetts, the college offers both on-campus activities and easy access to a large city. The ten-to-one faculty-student ratio means students receive individual attention, while the all-women's environment produces a strong sense of sisterhood in a supportive atmosphere. But the best part of the Wellesley experience is the deep friendships students form as the college pushes them to excel and develop to their potential.

SUMMARIES

❑ **Wesleyan University** is a small liberal arts college in Connecticut that attracts vibrant, open-minded, and creative students. Its nationally recognized professors are tops in their fields, and within a small-college atmosphere, they reward students for pursuing intellectual interests with rigor. Students tend to keep busy; they work hard at their studies, have fun, and explore outside the classroom. Wesleyan is a great place for students to grow and learn in a comfortable, open atmosphere.

❑ The liberal arts education provided by **Williams College** recognizes that, even though its professors are some of the finest teachers in the nation, much of what the student takes from college comes from outside the classroom. Students learn valuable lessons on the athletic field, hiking in the surrounding mountains with the Outing Club, or participating in one of Williams' many organizations. Most important, small classes and a close-knit campus create the perfect opportunity to learn from the college's most valuable resource—its students.

❑ **Yale University's** superior academic program, together with a unique residential college system and energetic extracurricular atmosphere, offer students a place to expand their minds, explore their interests, and have fun juggling it all. The atmosphere is intense, but in diverse ways; Yalies work and play hard. While they enjoy the resources of a great research university, they enjoy even more the focus on undergraduate education that exists at Yale. The vision and excellence of the students provide an education in itself, creating hundreds of tight-knit communities within the larger social structure. Yale is a place to be dazzled by peers and professors, a place that graduates continue to remember with fondness long after they have graduated.

AUTHOR BIOGRAPHIES

❑ AUTHOR BIOGRAPHIES ❑

INDEX

GEORGIA INSTITUTE OF TECHNOLOGY ❑ **Brian Alexander** received a Bachelor's of Mechanical Engineering in 1995. Since then he has been an applications sales engineer at Blake and Pendleton, Inc., Norcross, Georgia.

❑ **Brenda Alexander** received a Bachelor's of Science in history, technology, and society in 1995. She then attended graduate school at Georgia Tech while working at the Georgia Tech Alumni Association. She has since worked for customer service, Delta Air Lines and as a field operations consultant for Volvo Cars of North America.

COLBY COLLEGE ❑ **Jeff Baron** graduated from Colby College in 1993 with a B.A. in government. Outside the classroom, Jeff was president of his class and worked as the college's Student Sports Information Director for four years. Following school, he worked with a small software company in Cambridge, Massachusetts, in sales and account development. He is currently working toward his M.B.A. at Cornell University's Johnson Graduate School of Management.

CORNELL UNIVERSITY ❑ **Laura Barrantes** graduated from the College of Arts and Sciences in 1997 as a government major. While at Cornell, she was cochair of the Orientation Steering Committee, a member of the Senior Honor Society of the Quill and Dagger, a Cornell Tradition Fellow, a member of Alpha Phi Omega National Service Fraternity, and a Cornell National Scholar. She serves as one of the reunion chairs for the class and currently works in Washington, D.C., with the American Political Science Association.

UNIVERSITY OF VIRGINIA ❑ **Larisa Barry** graduated with a B.A. from UVa with a distinguished major in English and a minor in French in 1997. She is now an assistant editor with an environmental consulting firm in Arlington, Virginia.

UNIVERSITY OF CHICAGO ❑ **Jonathan Beere** graduated from the University of Chicago in 1995 with a concentration in history, philosophy, and social studies of science and medicine. He studied classics at Oxford University as a Rhodes Scholar. He is currently pursuing a Ph.D. in philosophy at Princeton.

WEBB INSTITUTE ❑ **Alan Bolind** holds a Bachelor of Science in naval architecture and marine engineering. While at Webb he played soccer during his freshman year and was later on the yearbook staff. His plans for the future include Webb graduate school.

NEW COLLEGE OF THE UNIVERSITY OF SOUTH FLORIDA ❑ **Ann Burget** graduated in 1991 with a B.A. in economics. Since graduating, she has worked at the White House Office of Management and Budget in Washington, D.C., and most recently at the Corporation for Public Broadcasting. She is now specializing in strategic planning around the introduction of digital television and other advanced technology for public broadcasting.

BATES COLLEGE ❑ **Christopher Byrne** graduated from Bates in 1997 with a Bachelor of Science degree majoring in biology. Chris was a four-year member of the varsity lacrosse team. He is currently conducting research on leukemia at the Dana Farber Cancer Institute, and is expecting to go on to medical school.

POMONA COLLEGE ❑ **Christina Caldwell** graduated from Pomona College in 1994 with an international relations degree, then moved to northern Virginia to help defeat Oliver North's bid for the U.S. Senate. She now works in Boston, Massachusetts, for the U.S. Department of Education, helping colleges, universities, and trade schools around New England to implement the William D. Ford Federal Direct Student Loan program. She plans to begin graduate business school in the fall of 1998.

MIDDLEBURY COLLEGE ❑ **Robert Carolla** graduated from Middlebury College in 1978 and Boston University Law School in 1982. He was legislative assistant to former U.S. Senate Majority Leader George Mitchell (D-ME) from 1985 to 1994, and currently serves as communications director for Americans for Democratic Action (ADA). A history major at Middlebury and editor of the student newspaper, *The Campus*, he studied on the Washington Semester program and interned for ADA during the fall 1976 presidential campaign. During winter term 1977 he conducted an independent creative writing project in South America that received an award from the Vermont Academy of Arts and Sciences. He wrote his senior thesis on *Crisis of Liberalism: The Presidential Election of 1968*.

NORTHWESTERN UNIVERSITY ❑ **Jennifer Caruso** will graduate from Northwestern University in 1999 with bachelor's degrees in journalism and political science. One of the two undergraduate contributors to this book, she has worked for *The Chagrin Valley Times* (Cleveland, Ohio) and The American Enterprise Institute, a think tank in Washington, D.C., and has participated in the Washington Semester program at American University. Jennifer has held several editorial positions including Editor-in-Chief for Northwestern's yearbook, the *Syllabus*, and has helped to produce the J.L. Kellogg Graduate School of Management's newspaper (Evanston, Illinois). She has also been a member of several Northwestern organizations, including the Student Admission Council, the Student Alumni Advisory Board, InterVarsity Christian Fellowship, and Kappa Delta sorority.

JOHNS HOPKINS UNIVERSITY ❑ **Judy Chung** graduated from Johns Hopkins University in 1995 with a B.A. in psychology. Following graduation, she worked as the regional admissions counselor for the Johns Hopkins Undergraduate Admission Office in the New England region. She currently works for the Johns Hopkins Office of Alumni Relations.

U.S. AIR FORCE ACADEMY ❑ **Lt. Melissa S. (Davidson) Cunningham** graduated from the U.S. Air Force Academy on May 29, 1996. While at the academy, she was a member of Cadet Squadron 37 all four years. Military jobs she held while at the academy were first sergeant, group athletic officer, squadron operations officer, and group operations officer. She was a political science major with a concentrated interest in international affairs, minored in Arabic, and finished as a Distinguished Graduate from the academy. Lt. Cunningham and her husband, Fred, a C-5 pilot from the class of 1994, are stationed at Travis Air Force Base, California. She is a communications-computer officer working for the 615th Air Mobility Operations Squadron, which supports worldwide contingencies with a twelve-hour response.

BIOGRAPHIES

CARNEGIE MELLON UNIVERSITY ❑ **Jessica Demers**, from Granville, Vermont, is one of two undergraduate contributors. She majored in professional writing. She also works as a Sleeping Bag Weekend student coordinator through the Office of Admission.

U.S. COAST GUARD ACADEMY ❑ **Lt. Jared Dillian** graduated from the U.S. Coast Guard Academy in 1996 with a bachelor's degree in math/computer science, and was subsequently assigned to the U.S. Coast Guard Cutter *Active* in Port Angeles, Washington, where he has served as weapons officer and first lieutenant.

HARVARD UNIVERSITY/HARVARD COLLEGE ❑ **Brooke Earley** received an A.B. in history *magna cum laude* from Harvard and Radcliffe Colleges in 1994 and an M.Ed. from Harvard University in 1998. She is currently an admissions officer and freshman advisor at Harvard and Radcliffe.

BOSTON COLLEGE ❑ **Christen English** graduated from Boston College *summa cum laude* in 1996 with a Bachelor of Arts degree. While at B.C. she majored in communication, was a four-year member of the varsity swim team, and was a teaching assistant for a core course in communication. Currently, she is a second-year law student at the Catholic University of America, Columbus School of Law.

WAKE FOREST UNIVERSITY ❑ **Joy Goodwin** received a B.A. in English in 1995. While at Wake Forest, she served as editor of a campus journal of essays and as president of Philomathesian Society, a campus humanities society. She received her M.A. in public policy from Harvard in 1997 and currently works as a social policy analyst at RAND, a think tank in Santa Monica, California.

YALE UNIVERSITY ❑ **Amanda Gordon** is an assistant editor at *Glamour Magazine* and currently plans activities and edits a newsletter for New York-area Yale alumni. She graduated in 1994 with a B.A. in English. At Yale she worked in the Admissions Office, the Dean's Office, and the Master's Office of Ezra Stiles College.

❑ **Seth Oltman** graduated from Yale in 1997 with a B.A. in history. At Yale he edited the *Yale Record* (a humor magazine) and *Urim v'Tumim* (a Jewish journal), tutored at a local elementary school, and worked for four years at the Yale University Press. He is an editorial assistant at *Chief Executive Magazine.*

U.S. NAVAL ACADEMY ❑ **Ens. Anthony Holds**, USNR, is a surface warfare officer in the U.S. Navy. After his graduation from the U.S. Naval Academy in May of 1997, he worked as the music department coordinator at the academy for seven months. He then completed a stint in Newport, Rhode Island, at the navy's Surface Warfare Officer School. Upon graduation from that training program, he entered the operational fleet as a division officer onboard a navy ship. Ensign Holds' long-term ambitions are in the professional theater, and he plans to relocate to New York City upon completion of his service commitment to pursue a career as an actor/singer.

WASHINGTON AND LEE UNIVERSITY ❑ **Cameron Howell** was born and raised in Columbia, South Carolina. He graduated from Washington and Lee University in 1994 and now resides in Charlottesville, Virginia.

WELLESLEY COLLEGE ❑ **Mary Lynn Jones** served as editor-in-chief of *The Wellesley News* and graduated from Wellesley College in 1996 with departmental honors in political science. She received her M.S.J. from the Columbia University Graduate School of Journalism in 1997. Mary Lynn is currently a staff writer at *The Hill* newspaper in Washington, D.C., where she covers the Senate and lobbying.

COLLEGE OF THE HOLY CROSS ❑ **Tim Keller** graduated with an A.B. in economics and served a year in the Jesuit Volunteer Corps where he taught an entrepreneurial business class to "at-risk" youth in Southern California. A native of the Midwest, he recently moved to Chicago, where he now works as a financial analyst for Bank of America.

BIOGRAPHIES

UNIVERSITY OF NOTRE DAME ❑ **Meghan Kelley**, '95, was a history and American studies major at the University of Notre Dame and resided in Walsh Hall for three years. While in school, Meghan was active with the Center for Social Concerns, and intramural sports, and studied in London her junior year. After graduation, Meghan volunteered with Boys Hope/Girls Hope and currently works in public relations in Chicago.

STANFORD UNIVERSITY ❑ **Libusha Kelly** graduated from Stanford with a B.A. in human biology in 1997. She is currently the webmaster and a technical writer for the Stanford Human Genome Center, and an undergraduate advisor at Stanford.

DAVIDSON COLLEGE ❑ **Kristi Kessler** graduated from Davidson in 1991 with a major in religion. While on campus she served as the vice president of the student body, sang with the Concert Choir, and was involved in the Reach Out community service organization. After graduating, she worked for one year with Duke Power Company as a marketing associate and for four years in the Davidson Office of Admission and Financial Aid. In 1996, she returned to school to pursue a law degree at the University of North Carolina at Chapel Hill.

RICE UNIVERSITY ❑ **Bruce Knuteson** graduated with honors from Rice in 1997 with a B.A. in physics and mathematics. While at Rice, Bruce was heavily involved in Orientation Week, physics instruction, and a variety of sports. He is currently at the University of California at Berkeley pursuing a Ph.D. in high energy experimental physics.

COLUMBIA UNIVERSITY/SEAS ❑ **Kelly Lenz** received her B.S. in biomedical engineering from Columbia University's Fu Foundation's School of Engineering and Applied Science. Presently, she is the project coordinator of the New York City Multidisciplinary Child Fatality Review, a project funded by New York State, managed by Medical and Health Research for New York City, Inc. (MHRA), and cosponsored by the New York City Office of the Chief Medical Examiner. In addition to having a strong background in the sciences, Kelly is also an alumna of Fiorello H. La Guardia High School of Music and Art and the Performing Arts, with a major in vocal performance.

DARTMOUTH COLLEGE ❑ **Suzanne Leonard** graduated from Dartmouth in 1996 with a double major in English and psychology. While at school, she studied abroad in Madrid and London, had an internship with *Psychology Today*, and was involved with the *Dartmouth Alumni Magazine*. After graduating, she attended the Radcliffe publishing course in Cambridge, Massachusetts. Currently she is working as an editorial assistant at *Fitness* magazine, living in Brooklyn, and contemplating a move to graduate school in England.

AMHERST COLLEGE ❑ **Molly Lyons,** class of '97, is currently an editorial assistant at *Elle Decor Magazine*.

HAVERFORD COLLEGE ❑ **Steve Manning** graduated in 1996 from Haverford, where he majored in history and played baseball and basketball. Since graduation he has worked at the college in the publications office, writing the alumni magazine and maintaining the Haverford home page.

MASSACHUSETTS INSTITUTE OF TECHNOLOGY ❑ **Stacy McGeever,** SB '93, majored in mathematics and computer science at MIT.

COLLEGE OF WILLIAM AND MARY ❑ **Kathleen McKeon** graduated from William and Mary in the spring of 1997 with a B.A. in sociology. She is currently employed at the Society of the Alumni of the College of William and Mary as an assistant director of alumni affairs.

TUFTS UNIVERSITY ❑ **David Meyers** graduated from Tufts in 1996 with a bachelor's degree in English and political science. While at Tufts, he was editor-in-chief of *The Tufts Daily*, a member of the student/faculty committee on the university budget and priorities, and a member of the Media Advisory Board. Since graduation, he has worked at *Roll Call*, a Washington, D.C., newspaper covering Congress, where he is currently the copy editor. He has stayed active in the Tufts community as a fund-raiser and a member of the Washington Tufts Alliance Steering Committee.

BOWDOIN COLLEGE ❑ **Nathaniel Bride** was awarded an A.B. in 1993 with a double major in government and history. Since November of 1993, he has been employed at Brown Brothers Harriman and Co. in Boston as an administrative officer, and is considering going to business school. He is also a volunteer for Bowdoin and is organizing his fifth year reunion.

❑ **Holly Pompeo** was awarded an A.B. in 1992 with a double major in government and Spanish. Over the past four years she has worked as a fund-raiser at two New England colleges, and is presently the assistant director of the Tufts University Medical, Dental, and Nutrition Annual Funds. She is also an admissions and fund-raising volunteer for Bowdoin.

COLUMBIA UNIVERSITY/COLUMBIA COLLEGE ❑ **Anna Lisa Raya** graduated from Columbia College in 1995 with a bachelor's degree in English. One year later, she earned her master's in journalism from Columbia's Graduate School of Journalism, where she also received the Richard T. Baker award for magazine writing. While a CC student, she became active in many Latino student organizations, dabbled in photography, and worked on a student-run magazine for fashion enthusiasts. Currently, she's a deputy news editor at *People* magazine in New York City.

HARVEY MUDD COLLEGE ❑ **Erik Ring** majored in engineering and graduated from Harvey Mudd in 1996. He currently lives and works in Irvine, California, and has a job that keeps him in front of a computer most of the time. Running, backpacking, tennis, and his pet turtle Curly keep him busy the rest of the time.

WILLIAMS COLLEGE ❑ **Graeme Scandrett** is originally from Toronto, Canada. He graduated from Williams in 1996 with a B.A. in economics. While at Williams he served as managing editor of the newspaper and covered football and basketball for the paper and Williams' Sports Information Department. Currently, he lives in New York City and works for an economic consulting firm.

U.S. MILITARY ACADEMY ❑ **Lt. Megan Scanlon** received her B.S. in 1997 from the U.S. Military Academy at West Point. While at West Point, she studied law and systems engineering, and also played on the women's lacrosse team. Megan is stationed at Fort Eustis, Virginia, training as an army transportation corps officer.

UNIVERSITY OF PENNSYLVANIA ❑ **Neil Sheth** received a Bachelor of Science in engineering-bioengineering with a minor in mathematics. While at Penn he was president of the class of 1997 in his sophomore, junior, and senior years. He was tapped for Pipe & Stein Junior Honor Society and also received the highest men's senior honor award, the Spoon Award. Neil is currently a financial analyst in Salomon Smith Barney's Health Care Investment Banking Group in New York City.

GEORGETOWN UNIVERSITY ❑ **John Sikking** graduated from Georgetown in 1993 with a B.A. in history and a minor in psychology. While attending Georgetown, he played on the varsity football team in his freshman year, participated in student government in his junior year, and worked at the campus computer center for all four years. He currently works for Georgetown University administering the School of Business's e-mail system and coordinating all video teleconferencing projects. He is currently an M.B.A. applicant, and he hopes to continue his education in Georgetown's M.B.A. program.

PRINCETON UNIVERSITY ❑ **M. Kathryn Taylor** majored in English at Princeton and graduated in 1974. After receiving her M.A. from the University of Pennsylvania, she left the academic world for a career in banking. In 1987 she returned to teaching and for several years was chairman of the English department at the Baldwin School in Bryn Mawr, Pennsylvania. For the past five years she has combined part-time teaching with freelance writing. Her clients include corporations, banks, law firms, nonprofit arts organizations, and schools, including Princeton, where she has done writing assignments for the Alumni Council, the Office of Communications and Publications, and the *Princeton Alumni Weekly*. Her essays have also appeared in the *Philadelphia Inquirer Sunday Magazine*.

WESLEYAN UNIVERSITY ❑ **Stacy Theberge**, '95, majored in English at Wesleyan, and spent many hours researching an out-of-print novel and rollerblading down Wyllys Avenue. She currently lives in Los Angeles, and would like to thank Morgan Fahey, '95, Henry Myers, '95, and Sadia Shepard, '97 for contributing to this article.

DUKE UNIVERSITY ❑ **John Tolsma**, '95, served as student body president during the 1994–1995 academic year. After working as an executive aide for Lamar Alexander's 1996 presidential bid, he is in the J.D./M.B.A. program at Harvard Law and Business Schools.

CALIFORNIA INSTITUTE OF TECHNOLOGY ❑ After studying biology at Caltech for two years, **Debi Tuttle** changed options and became one of Caltech's few literature majors, graduating with honors in 1993. She then spent two years living and working in rural Japan as an English teacher. After a brief stint as a web site designer, Debi is now a graduate student at the California State University, Long Beach, where she is working on a master's degree in counseling and student development in higher education.

CLAREMONT MCKENNA COLLEGE ❑ **Holly Vicente,** CMC class of 1995, B.A. in literature/government, was involved in College Republicans, Women's Forum, Volunteer Student Admission Committee, *Forum* (CMC newspaper), and *Collage* (newspaper of the Claremont Colleges). She served as a dormitory president, on class council, and as a representative to the Social Affairs Committee. She is currently employed as a fashion/lifestyles reporter for the *Inland Valley Daily Bulletin*, Ontario, California.

BROWN UNIVERSITY ❑ **Edward Watts** is a 1997 graduate of Brown who completed a concentration in classics (with honors) in addition to one in ancient and medieval culture. He also was a four-year member of the track and field team. Presently he is a Mellon Fellow and is enrolled as a Ph.D. candidate in the department of history at Yale University.

COLUMBIA UNIVERSITY/BARNARD COLLEGE ❑ **Catherine Webster** is an assistant dean at Barnard. She has served Barnard as first-year class dean, associate director of the Pre-College Program, and director of the First-Year Focus Program. She holds M.A. degrees from New York University (in French literature) and Columbia's Teachers College (in College Student Personnel Administration) and a B.A. from Columbia College, where she was a member of the first coeducational class.

SWARTHMORE COLLEGE ❑ **Sylvia Weedman** graduated from Swarthmore with high honors in 1997. A history major and a political science minor, she was the codirector of the Writing Associate program and wrote for the campus newspaper, *The Phoenix*, and the humor magazine, *Spike*. She is now an assistant editor at *The American Prospect* magazine in Cambridge, Massachusetts.

VASSAR COLLEGE ❑ **Rachel Weimerskirch** was a Mug Rat and English major who once co-planned Founder's Day, wrote for the *Miscellany News*, acted in Philaletheis productions, and worked with the Vassar Volunteers. She has joined a very different student body of kindergartners through sixth graders as a teacher at Family Academy in Harlem, New York.

COLGATE UNIVERSITY ❑ **Scott Worden,** '96, was a political science major at Colgate and editor of the weekly campus newspaper, the *Colgate Maroon-News*. After graduation he completed a fellowship at the Carnegie Endowment for International Peace in Washington and has completed his first year at Harvard Law School.

HARVARD UNIVERSITY/RADCLIFFE COLLEGE ❑ **Lauren Young** received an A.B. in economics *magna cum laude* from Harvard-Radcliffe in 1996. She is currently a research analyst at Mercer Management Consulting in New York City. Her e-mail address is Lauren_Young@MercerMC.com.

❑ INDEX BY STATE ❑

CALIFORNIA

COLORADO

CONNECTICUT

DISTRICT OF COLUMBIA

FLORIDA

GEORGIA

ILLINOIS

INDIANA

MAINE

MARYLAND

MASSACHUSETTS

NEW HAMPSHIRE

NEW JERSEY

NEW YORK

NORTH CAROLINA

PENNSYLVANIA

RHODE ISLAND

TEXAS

VERMONT

VIRGINIA